# TRANSFORMING ENVIRONMENTS AND REHABILITATION

How can environments play a role in assisting and sustaining personal change in individuals incarcerated within the criminal justice system? Can a failure to address contextual issues reduce or undermine the effectiveness of clinical intervention? Bringing together a range of leading forensic psychologists, this book explores and illustrates inter-relationships between interventions and the environment in which they take place.

This book examines how the environment can be better utilised to contribute to processes of change and how therapeutic principles and practices can be more strongly embedded through being applied in supportive, facilitative environments. In addition, it expands on emerging conceptualisations of how psychological functioning and environmental context are inextricably linked and offers an alternative to prevailing intrapsychic or 'essentialist' views of areas such as personality and cognition.

Providing new and challenging insights and perspectives on issues of central relevance to forensic psychology and related disciplines, this book contributes to the development of innovative and unifying directions for research, practice and theory. This book will be an essential resource for those who work with or intend to work with offenders, particularly practitioners, researchers and students in the fields of psychology, criminology, psychiatry, psychotherapy and social work.

**Geraldine Akerman** is a chartered and HCPC registered Forensic Psychologist and Associate Fellow of the British Psychological Society and Europsych. She currently works as a Therapy Manager at HMP Grendon and is a Visiting Lecturer at the University of Birmingham and Cardiff Metropolitan University.

**Adrian Needs** is a Forensic Psychologist by background, qualified as a practitioner with experience including 14 years in HM Prison Service. He runs the MSc Forensic Psychology course at the University of Portsmouth and through the BPS played a prominent role in steering the formulation of national standards for postgraduate training in this field. His current research interests include transition and offending in former members of the armed forces.

**Claire Bainbridge** is a chartered and HCPC registered Forensic Psychologist and Associate Fellow of the British Psychological Society. She has over twenty years' experience of working with offenders in a variety of settings, including prison, health, police and probation services and is currently a Consultant Forensic Psychologist within the Offender Health and Forensic Community Service at Tees, Esk and Wear Valleys NHS Foundation Trust.

# Issues in Forensic Psychology
Edited by Richard Shuker, HMP Grendon
and Geraldine Akerman, HMP Grendon

*Issues in Forensic Psychology* is a book series which aims to promote forensic psychology to a broad range of forensic practitioners. It aims to provide analysis and debate on current issues and to publish and promote the work of forensic psychologists and other associated professionals.

The views expressed by the authors/editors may not necessarily be those held by the Series Editor or NOMS.

# TRANSFORMING ENVIRONMENTS AND REHABILITATION

A Guide for Practitioners in Forensic Settings and Criminal Justice

*Edited by Geraldine Akerman, Adrian Needs and Claire Bainbridge*

Routledge
Taylor & Francis Group

LONDON AND NEW YORK

First published 2018
by Routledge
2 Park Square, Milton Park, Abingdon, Oxon OX14 4RN

and by Routledge
711 Third Avenue, New York, NY 10017

*Routledge is an imprint of the Taylor & Francis Group, an informa business*

*British Library Cataloguing-in-Publication Data*
A catalogue record for this book is available from the British Library

*Library of Congress Cataloging-in-Publication Data*
Names: Akerman, Geraldine, editor. | Needs, Adrian, editor. | Bainbridge, Claire, editor.
Title: Transforming environments and rehabilitation : a guide for practitioners in forensic settings and criminal justice / edited by Geraldine Akerman, Adrian Needs and Claire Bainbridge.
Description: Abingdon, Oxon; New York, NY : Routledge, 2018. | Series: Issues in forensic psychology; 7 |
Includes bibliographical references and index.
Identifiers: LCCN 2017017918| ISBN 9781138959118 (hardback) | ISBN 9781138959125 (pbk.) | ISBN 9781315660813 (ebook)
Subjects: LCSH: Forensic psychology. | Environmental psychology.
Classification: LCC RA1148 .T73 2018 | DDC 614/.15—dc23
LC record available at https://lccn.loc.gov/2017017918

ISBN: 978-1-138-95911-8 (hbk)
ISBN: 978-1-138-95912-5 (pbk)
ISBN: 978-1-315-66081-3 (ebk)

Typeset in Bembo
by diacriTech, Chennai

# CONTENTS

# ILLUSTRATIONS

## Figures

## Table

## Boxes

# CONTRIBUTORS

**Geraldine Akerman** is a chartered and HCPC registered Forensic Psychologist and Associate Fellow of the British Psychological Society and Europsych. She has worked for the prison service since 1999, assessing risk and providing treatment to men convicted of violent and sexual offences with personality disorders. She has been on the research committees of the Division of Forensic Psychology and National Organisation for the Treatment of Abusers, and a member of ATSA and the International Association of Forensic Psychotherapists. Geraldine was the co-editor of *Forensic Update* and is currently a reviewer for this journal. She has published book chapters and articles in peer-reviewed journals on the subjects of offence-paralleling behaviour, managing deviant sexual fantasies, sexual interests, sexual offending and ex-service personnel in prison. Geraldine is a Visiting Lecturer at the University of Birmingham and Cardiff Metropolitan University. She currently works as a Therapy Manager at HMP Grendon and completed her PhD at the University of Birmingham.

**Alethea Adair-Stantiall** is a Clinical Psychologist working in the Pan Dorset singPathfinder team, a service providing intensive input for high-risk personality disordered offenders across inpatient and community settings. Prior to this she worked across low and medium secure services within Hampshire after completing a Doctorate in Clinical Psychology at the University of Southampton. She has also developed specialist knowledge in neuropsychology whilst working at Queen Alexandra Hospital, Portsmouth for the last three years. Her areas of interest include schema therapy, trauma, personality disorder, neuropsychological assessment and staff training. Alethea is currently in the final year of the MSc Forensic Psychology at the University of Portsmouth.

**Claire Bainbridge** is a Principal Forensic Psychologist with twenty years' experience of working with offenders in a variety of settings, including prison, health, police and probation services. She is currently the Lead Psychologist for two services within the Offender PD Pathway in County Durham and Teesside. Claire's main clinical interests are in the areas of stalking and harassment, malingering of mental illness and women offenders. She also sits on the British Psychological Society's Division of Forensic Psychology Executive Committee, with the specific role of organising the Annual Conference.

**Nick Benefield** has recently retired as Department of Health Lead for Personality Disorder and as Joint Head of the NHS/NOMS Offender Personality Disorder Team. He remains an advisor to the OPD Programme. He trained in social work and as a Jungian analyst. Nick has a background in the therapeutic treatment of young offenders, inner-city community social group work and community mental health services. He has worked as a clinician, trainer, manager, commissioner and policy maker and has an ongoing interest in the development of psycho social environments in the criminal justice and wider social and educational settings.

**Alice L. Bennett** is a Forensic Psychologist in Training at the Westgate Personality Disorder Treatment Service, HMP Frankland. Her role involves assessment, treatment and research with this specific population. She completed her BSc. (Hons) Forensic Psychology degree at the University of Central Lancashire and MRes Psychology at Northumbria University. Her research interests include self-harm, assessment and treatment of personality disordered prisoners.

**Lucinda Bolger** is a Consultant Forensic Clinical Psychologist and PIPE Design Lead. She is Consultant to the Personality Disorder Strategy Implementation Team. She is also a Clinical Lead for military veterans.

**Michael Brookes** OBE is currently the MSc Forensic Psychology Programme Director at Birmingham City University and a Consultant Chartered and Registered Forensic Psychologist. Formerly he was Director of Therapeutic Communities at HMP Grendon. Professor Brookes acts as an expert advisor to the Counselling in Prison Network and is a member of the Royal College of Psychiatrists Therapeutic Community Accreditation Panel. He has held a number of senior HMPS establishment and headquarters posts where he has developed the provision of psychological and psychologically informed services. His recent publications have concentrated on demonstrating the positive impact of therapeutic communities on the lives of prisoners and the organisational dynamics of managing prison therapeutic communities. He has presented at national and international conferences on the contribution of democratic therapeutic communities to reducing re-offending and improving the psychological health of prisoners with complex needs.

**Andrew Day** is a Fellow of the Australian Psychological Society and Professor and Head of Indigenous Research in the Australian Aboriginal and Torres Strait Islander Centre at James Cook University in Queensland, Australia. Before joining academia he was employed as a clinical psychologist in South Australia and the UK, having gained his Doctorate in Clinical Psychology from the University of Birmingham and his Masters in Applied Criminological Psychology from the University of London. He is widely published in many areas of forensic psychology, with a focus on the development of effective and evidence based approaches to offender rehabilitation.

**Andrew Frost** has been involved in the human services field some 25 years, working and researching in offender rehabilitation since 1993. At Kia Marama, a prison-based programme for sexual offenders with the New Zealand Department of Corrections, he was involved in the provision and supervision of group therapy, and the establishment of a forensic therapeutic community. These areas remain central to his research interests. Andrew is currently senior lecturer in Human Services and Social Work at the University of Canterbury, where he is the director of the Te Awatea Violence Research Centre. Along with his teaching and research, he remains involved in supervision, training, credentialing and consultation.

**Emma Guthrie** is a serving Prison Officer with fifteen years' experience of working with female and juvenile offenders. She currently works on one of the first PIPE Units to be commissioned in the Prison Service and is a trainer for the Enabling Environments Award. Emma has delivered many presentations regarding her experience of working on PIPE and with personality disordered offenders and has spoken at National Conferences.

**Dana J. Hubbard** is an Associate Professor at Cleveland State University in the Criminology, Anthropology, and Sociology department. She is also a Research Associate in the Criminology Research Center at Cleveland State. Her research interests include women and crime, race and crime, and corrections and the intersection of all of these areas. She has published in journal such as Justice Quarterly, Crime and Delinquency, and the Prison Journal. She has also been the recipient of numerous grants associated with evaluation research.

**Lawrence Jones** is a Clinical and Forensic Psychologist working at Rampton Hospital where he is Head of Psychology. He has an interest in and has published on therapeutic communities, offence paralleling behaviour, motivation and engagement assessment and interventions and trauma and trauma-informed care in forensic settings.

**Kevin Leggett** is the Governor of HMP YOI Aylesbury.

**Sarah Lewis** is a Senior Lecturer in Criminal Psychology at the Institute of Criminal Justice Studies, University of Portsmouth. Up until 2012, Sarah worked for Hampshire Probation Trust for six years, starting her career in prison and moving into the community as a programme facilitator, delivering cognitive behavioural programmes to probationers. She has experience in developing programmes for short-term prisoners and females who are domestically abusive and has research experience in both the community and in prison. Her academic interests include desistance, contextual factors linked to offender rehabilitation, prison and probation and therapeutic relationships. She carried out her doctoral studies examining therapeutic relationships within a rehabilitative setting, considering the mechanisms that underpin therapeutic relationships and relational ruptures. In 2015 she engaged in researching, through participatory means, prison relationships and penal climate in a prison in Norway.

**Patrick Mandikate** is the former Head of Psychotherapy at HMP Grendon and former Director of The Institute of Group Analysis.

**Betsy Matthews** earned her PhD in Criminal Justice from the University of Cincinnati in 2004 and is currently an Associate Professor in the School of Justice Studies at Eastern Kentucky University. She has worked as a child care worker in a residential treatment facility for behaviorally disordered adolescent girls, an adult probation officer position in Greene County, Ohio, and a research associate with the American Probation and Parole Association. Her primary specialty areas are community corrections and correctional rehabilitation and she has published several articles and book chapters on these issues. Her most recent publications focus on working effectively with girls in the juvenile justice system and the importance of the helping alliance between correctional staff and the people they serve. Dr Matthews has served as a consultant providing training and technical assistance to state and federal agencies on risk assessment and other evidence-based practices.

**Annette McKeown** is a chartered and registered forensic psychologist with ten years' experience working in forensic settings. For the last eight years, she has worked in the Primrose Service for female personality disordered offenders. She is the treatment lead of the Life Minus Violence-Enhanced (LMV-E) intervention and Firesetting Intervention Programme for Mentally Disordered Offenders (FIP-MO) within the service. Annette has a specialist interest in the areas of violence, psychopathy, risk assessment, domestic violence and firesetting. She is a member of the *Forensic Update* editorial team and is a visiting lecturer at a number of universities. Annette has a number of publications, particularly in the area of risk assessment and violence.

**Adrian Needs** is a chartered and HCPC registered forensic psychologist. He worked in the HM Prison Service for 14 years. Work ranged from assessment and treatment of lifers and sex offenders to the management of individuals with personality disorders, from the facilitation of staff teams to the design and delivery of training for specialised units. Non-routine activities included providing a negotiation lead in hostage and firearms incidents and post-incident counselling to prison staff. He runs the MSc Forensic Psychology course at the University of Portsmouth and through the BPS has played a prominent role in steering the formulation of national standards for postgraduate training in this field. In an academic setting he has maintained an involvement in consultancy and contributed to national working groups on disasters, homicide and mental illness. His research interests include the operation of negative life events as precursors to violent offending, processes involved in personal change and transition and trauma in the lives of former military personnel.

**Rachel O'Rourke** is a chartered and HCPC registered forensic psychologist and Associate Fellow of the British Psychological Society. She has worked for the Prison Service for 15 years, assessing risk and providing treatment to juveniles, adults and young adults convicted of violent and sexual offences. She was one of the first graduates from the MSc in 'Working with Personality Disorder' and led on the development of a new Pathways Service for young men at HMP YOI Aylesbury with emerging complex needs. Rachel currently works as a Cluster Lead Psychologist for South Central Psychological Services, HM Prison Service, and is based at HMP YOI Aylesbury.

**Sarah Paget** is a Programme Manager for a quality network for therapeutic communities and the Enabling Environments Award at the Royal College of Psychiatrists' Centre for Quality Improvement (spaget@rcpsych.ac.uk). Sarah has a background in nursing and social psychology and has been involved in therapeutic communities and Enabling Environments for the past 30 years. She is a member of the *International Journal of Therapeutic Communities'* Editorial Advisory Board and has presented and published widely. She is currently developing a psychosocial approach to organisations and works across all sectors and client populations to support the development of healthy organisational culture.

**Dominic A.S. Pearson** is a chartered and registered forensic psychologist with a background of working as a practitioner psychologist for the UK probation services. As senior lecturer at the University of Portsmouth, he contributes to the MSc in Forensic Psychology. His published research is in the areas of forensic risk assessment and the evaluation and development of programmes to reduce re-offending.

**Jo Shingler** is a chartered psychologist and registered forensic psychologist with over 20 years' experience in the assessment and treatment of sexual offenders. She has worked in a variety of contexts, including in prisons, in the community, for HM Prison Service, the Probation Service and the National Health Service, and latterly in private practice. She was a member of the Parole Board of England and Wales between 2004 and 2007. In addition to continuing to work as a Consultant Forensic Psychologist, Jo is currently studying for a PhD at the University of Portsmouth, focusing on the process of psychological risk assessment.

**Richard Shuker** is a chartered forensic psychologist and Head of Clinical Services at HMP Grendon, a therapeutic community prison for personality disordered offenders. He has managed cognitive behavioural treatment programmes within adult and young offender prisons and is currently lead clinician on the assessment unit at Grendon. His special interests include the assessment and treatment of offenders with personality disorders and other complex needs. He is Series Editor for the book series 'Issues in Forensic Psychology'. He has published in areas including risk assessment, treatment readiness, therapeutic outcome and clinical intervention. He has recently co-edited a book on Grendon's work, research and outcomes.

**Laura Smillie** is a Primrose Prison Officer with 15 years' experience working with female prisoners. She has been a prison officer on the Primrose Service for female personality disordered offenders for the last four years. Laura has a leading role in the Chromis Motivation and Engagement intervention within the service. She is also the deputy treatment manager of the Life Minus Violence-Enhanced (LMV-E) intervention within the service. Laura has delivered numerous awareness and training packages on working with personality disordered offenders. She has also spoken at national conferences on the topic.

**Annie Taylor** currently works for the National Psychology Service, HM Prison and Probation Service and has a responsibility for accredited interventions. She has a background in mental health, offending behaviour treatment programmes and prison service senior management and is currently completing her forensic psychologist chartership.

**Jon Taylor** is a consultant forensic psychologist and psychotherapist with a particular interest in the treatment of offenders with intellectual disability and personality disorder. Jon was instrumental in the development of a treatment programme for offenders with intellectual disability and severe personality disorder at the national ID high secure service at Rampton Hospital and has led on the development of a similar programme within a medium secure service at St. Andrews Healthcare in Nottinghamshire. He has also lead on the implementation of a treatment programme for prisoners with intellectual disability and personality disorder across three English prisons and has developed a Structured Professional Judgement Assessment tool to support the identification of treatment needs for this particular population.

**Jenny Tew** is a registered psychologist with the UK's Health Professions Council, a chartered forensic psychologist with the British Psychological Society and Associate Fellow of the British Psychological Society. Jenny works for the National Offender Management Service in the UK as a Quality and Evidence specialist within Interventions Services. She has worked in both custody and community forensic settings in the UK including HMP Grendon therapeutic community prison. Jenny is currently undertaking a PhD with the Centre for Forensic and Criminological

Psychology at the University of Birmingham. She has published papers relating to the assessment and treatment of offenders with high levels of psychopathic traits.

**Kirk Turner** is the NOMS PIPE Project Lead and Senior Co-Commissioning Manager for the Personality Disorder Team.

**Helen Tyrer** has been a Senior Clinical Research Fellow at Imperial College since 1995. She has worked as a general practitioner and hospital physician in genitourinary medicine, and is especially interested in psychological treatments for complex problems at the interface of mental and physical disorders. She has written *Tackling Health Anxiety: a CBT Handbook* and acted as a trainer for practitioners wishing to develop this treatment. She has been a nidotherapy practitioner since 2005.

**Peter Tyrer** is Emeritus Professor of Community Psychiatry in the Centre for Psychiatry in the Department of Medicine at Imperial College, London, having previously been head of department and a professor at Imperial College since 1991. He was editor of the British Journal of Psychiatry from 2003 to 2013. He has chaired NICE guideline groups for borderline personality disorder, substance misuse and psychosis, and management of imminent aggression for the Department of Health in England, has written over 500 original articles mainly about anxiety, depression, personality disorder and their treatment. He developed nidotherapy in 1990 as a response to continuing failure of standard treatments for many mental disorders.

**James Vess** is the Mental Health Administrator for Training and Field Operations in the California Department of Corrections and Rehabilitation. Prior to his current position, he held academic positions at Victoria University of Wellington in New Zealand and Deakin University in Australia. He has also held a range of clinical, supervisory and administrative positions at Atascadero State Hospital, California's secure forensic inpatient facility for male offenders. He obtained his doctoral degree in clinical psychology from the Ohio State University. His primary research and clinical interests are in the areas of risk assessment, offender rehabilitation, and public policy for managing violent and sexual offenders.

**Jayson Ware** is currently the Group Director, Offender Services & Programs, Corrective Services New South Wales, Australia. He has researched or worked with sexual offenders for the past twenty years and has authored 35 journal articles or book chapters primarily relating to the treatment of sexual offenders. He is currently working toward a Doctorate in Psychology at University of New South Wales, Australia.

**Roland Woodward** is the Enabling Environments Lead at the Centre for Quality Improvement with the Royal College of Psychiatry. He is a Consultant Chartered Psychologist and former Director of the Retreat in York. He was Director of Forensic and Personality Disorder Services and Director of the Therapeutic Community at HMP Dovegate.

# FOREWORD

Therapeutic environments have almost certainly existed since time immemorial, but it is a struggle to recognise their importance in a modern world where individualistic enumeration of all our activities has become paramount. In his grand sweep of anthropology and history, Harari persuasively argues that our forebears, as hunter-gatherers, and even Neanderthals, were more socially cooperative and community-minded than we are.[1] Perhaps we have lost something that we need to rediscover – or reinvent – in order to improve our lives today.

The earliest documented accounts of a deliberately constructed therapeutic community, or enabling environment, is usually given as the village of Geel in thirteenth-century Flanders – where those with 'mental afflictions' came as pilgrims to worship at the holy shrine of St Dymphna. Most of the pilgrims would probably be diagnosed with learning disability or epilepsy nowadays. When they arrived in Geel, they were taken into the care of the villagers, who were all engaged in working on the land. The success of their care was measured by an annual weighing ceremony, where those who had gained the most weight were the ones thought to be doing the best. An environment was constructed in which people with severe disabilities could be treated as human, and have their basic physical and social needs met.

Other notable events in history show the same interest in the 'psychosocial environment' – such as the implementation of 'moral treatment' by the Quakers in York at the end of the eighteenth century, progressive education and democratic schooling for troubled children since the end of the nineteenth century, the rehabilitation of battle-shocked soldiers at Northfield and Mill Hill in the Second World War, and R.D. Laing's rather chaotic experiments with 'unlabelled living' in the sixties. Perhaps one day historians will add the current reform of penal institutions, with the realisation that attention to the same factors can make twenty-first century prisons more effective and humane.

The British criminal justice sector has been important at several points in devising the structure for 'Enabling Environments', on which most of this work is based. In 1998, the 'Kennard and Lees Audit Checklist' (KLAC) was produced in order to be able to audit the prison therapeutic communities (TCs) as part of the Offending Behaviour Programmes Unit. The prison TCs were at that time seen as the only area for therapeutic communities which seemed to have a positive future, as all other sectors seemed to be closing them down or reducing their size. The KLAC formed one of the most important documents in setting the standards for all therapeutic communities when the 'Community of Communities' quality network was started at the Royal College of Psychiatrists in 2002. After the network had gathered much data over five or six years, the 'core values' were extracted and used to define the requirements for the 'Enabling Environments' (EE) Award. With this, the essential relational qualities of therapeutic communities could be used in any setting, without needing the whole apparatus of particular groups, specific staffing and suitable buildings – or the need to formally consider oneself as a 'therapeutic community'. Therapeutic communities remained the specialist and 'pure' implementation of a highly structured psychosocial therapeutic programme, but the 'quality of relationships' upon which they were built could now be replicated elsewhere.

This facilitated the development of 'Psychologically Informed Planned Environments' (PIPEs) – which had a particular structure, defined by the National Offender Management Service – as part of the response to the Bradley Report on the management of Mentally Disordered Offenders. By this time the concept of 'relational security' was also becoming well known in high secure NHS settings. At the core of the PIPEs was a process which trained and supported staff to establish their prison wings or other units as Enabling Environments, and to work towards achieving the Royal College of Psychiatrists award to recognise that.

A parallel process, started in the government's Department for Communities and Local Government, but without the continuing support or funding, established 'Psychologically Informed Environments' (PIEs) for the homelessness sector. PIEs are more loosely defined than PIPEs, and do not require participating services to meet EE standards, but they have a clearly articulated structure which is based on the same relational values.

Once non-participating prison units saw the value of PIPEs, many of them decided to apply to become Enabling Environments, independently of the PIPEs programme. This has raised wider awareness of healthy psychosocial environments throughout the criminal justice sector, and at the time of writing two whole prison establishments are working towards becoming 'whole prison EEs', rather than just specific wings and units. At a conference in early 2016, the head of the National Offender Management Service affirmed the priority which is now being given to this work.

However, it is not easy. As well as the institutional inertia and the staff's personal feelings of resistance to change and loss, there are major structural obstacles. The task for us in penal settings is to accommodate the very exacting and precise demands of policies and procedures, which allow no flexibility and very little individual discretion, alongside the recognition that basic humanity in relationships is required in order to stop prisons from having persistent negative effects on prisoners.

This book offers hope that it is possible to do both: to recognise the profound importance of the social matrix and milieu, while measuring, regulating and risk-managing all the necessary aspects of participants' behaviour. Prisons and forensic settings are amongst the most socially controlled settings, where operational details of security must always trump therapeutic principles – and all the work must demonstrate metrics of outcome such as reduced probability of future offending. Yet this collection of chapters shows that it is possible to find space for humanity, in the way people relate to each other, in these difficult settings. If there is hope here, maybe there is hope for us all!

**Rex Haigh**
**Enabling Environments Lead, Royal College of Psychiatrists**
**Honorary Professor of Therapeutic Environments and Relational Health,**
**Nottingham University**
**March 2017**

## Note

1 Yuval Noah Harari (2014) *Sapiens: A Brief History of Humankind.* New York, NY: Harper Collins.

# ACKNOWLEDGEMENTS

We are grateful to those in the Routledge series 'Issues in Forensic Psychology' and in particular Richard Shuker for support in bringing this project to fruition. Thanks to Hannah Catterall at Routledge for all her support and guidance and extreme tolerance with this project. Thanks to all the authors for their hard work and attention to detail and of course to all the service users to whom this book is dedicated.

GA: Firstly, thanks to Michael Brookes for the inspiration for this volume, and to all those who have guided me through the process of editing. Thanks to the authors for their patience and responsiveness to feedback; to Hannah Catterall for her advice and support and to Routledge for making it possible. Mainly, thanks to my family, Rob, Dan, Carly, Kirsty and Shelley who are so tolerant and supportive of me while I work.

AN: I should like to thank my mother Joan (a few months ago we celebrated her ninetieth birthday), my wife Lisa, son Tom and daughter Alice for their support and encouragement.

I should also like to present a dedication from my MSc students to the memory of Roxana Negru (1992–2017): "In recognition of all the people you helped and would have helped. Your voice will carry through the heavens as you sing with the angels. You will always be our beacon of light." These words have a particular resonance for those who knew Roxy (for example, she really did have an outstanding singing voice). In keeping with a major theme of this book, she provided a vivid example of how connectedness and concern for each other can inspire and sustain us.

CB: Thank you to my family, especially Carl, Molly and Archie who have been extremely patient and allowed me the space to undertake this piece of work. My appreciation to my colleagues at Tees, Esk and Wear Valleys NHS Foundation

Trust, especially Ruby Bell and Lisa Taylor, for their support and encouragement. Thanks to all who have contributed to this volume for their insight and inspiration and continued dedication to providing therapeutic environments to those who have committed crimes. Finally, thank you to all who read this, I hope you are encouraged to make a difference to the lives of service users, regardless of which setting they may reside.

# INTRODUCTION

## Geraldine Akerman, Adrian Needs and Claire Bainbridge

"No man is an island, entire of itself". Although it has been used before, it was difficult to resist starting this Introduction with John Donne's famous line. Yet perhaps it is a little too famous (and 'man' may offend modern sensibilities). When quotations are overly familiar it is easy to move on without exploring any deeper resonance or implications. As befits the work of a poet writing in the meditative tradition the words are certainly worth reflecting upon and few could deny their relevance to some of the major themes of this book. So we issue an invitation to the reader to reflect on Donne's words as the rest of the book is encountered. This parallels recommendations in the opening chapter concerning developments in science that are particularly concerned with interaction and connectedness. For the moment we will move in some different directions.

For example, less than four decades after the appearance in 1624 of Donne's Meditation XVII from 'Devotions upon Emergent[1] Occasions', the Royal Society started its regular meetings. It shifted its focus from a metaphysical heritage not dissimilar to Donne's to an overriding concern with empirical research and demonstration. (There may have been more than one reason why an innovative and affiliated sailing vessel was named *The Experiment*.) Much had happened in those four intervening decades including civil war, a republic, and then restoration of the monarchy. This might be taken as an illustration of how contexts can influence science. However it could be argued that science has not always returned the favour, taking insufficient account of the influence of contexts on its objects of study. Jonathan Swift's satirical portrayal, with more than a sidelong glance at the Royal Society, of scientists seeking to extract sunbeams from cucumbers is perhaps directed in part towards a perceived tendency to 'take things out of context' in rather rarefied research; it also parodies the often related kind of viewpoint where processes are turned too readily into a kind of object.

Nonetheless, the achievements of the empirical approach represented by the Royal Society and others have been impressive. Just short of two hundred years after its founding, one of its fellows, Charles Darwin, published a rather influential theory, informed largely by observation and taking as a starting point the adaptation of species to island habitats. Its descendants include the study of ecosystems in biology. Similarly, the ancestry of current understanding of astronomy and the universe includes the observational and mathematical work of members (and presidents) of the Royal Society concerning phenomena such as planetary orbits and gravity. However, what the study of ecosystems and the wider universe have in common, rather obviously, is a willingness to explore the operation of context and related systemic processes. Indeed the 'context principle' now characterises understanding in areas such as the role of epigenetic factors in gene expression in genetics, the reactivity of functional groups of organic molecules or compounds in chemistry and the relativity of time and space in physics (Barrett, Mesquita & Smith, 2010).

The present volume is concerned with increasing awareness of the potential influences of past and present contexts on the behaviour and rehabilitation of individuals in custodial environments. To hijack a familiar cliché, can daily life in residential settings be made 'part of the solution rather than part of the problem'? At present, in conventional regimes, outcomes seem far from optimal or all too often even at an acceptable minimum. The prevailing 'Risk–Need–Responsivity' approach has made valuable contributions to the field of interventions although its own proponents have on occasion acknowledged that insufficient attention has been given to contextual and environmental factors (Andrews, 2011). In addition, neither its focus on the identification of group differences on a limited range of simplified and deficit-orientated variables in research, nor its emphasis on didactic methods of intervention do much to advance our understanding of processes involved in adaptation and change (Polaschek, 2012). Even long-awaited studies on outcomes associated with the strengths-based 'Good Lives Model' give few grounds for complacency (Netto, Carter & Bonell, 2014; Quill, 2015) although we note its compatibility with attempts to make custodial environments more supportive of rehabilitation and associated values (Fortune, Ward & Polaschek, 2014). A major source of impetus for the present volume, reflected in several chapters, is the 'Enabling Environments' initiative. As some of the chapters demonstrate, there may well be scope for integration of aspects of these approaches.

There is also scope for integration of frameworks concerned precisely with the development, functioning and interaction of systems (including individuals as inherently social beings) and the nature of transitions. This might also provide a new vocabulary for understanding crime itself and provide a perspective for understanding what might be effective in helping new pathways of development through primarily interpersonal means. It is not being claimed here that the processes that connect us to other people, that shape us and to a large extent constitute us, are invariably positive. Aberrant variations and compensations can contribute to debased forms such as gang violence, atrocities in wartime or the cruelties of distorted religious extremism (Dutton, 2012). A case can be built that other, more individual forms of offending are also influenced by processes that ultimately relate to what an individual has developed to function in a world of other people and associated dynamics. To put it simply, we are social beings and when things go wrong in related areas there is scope for them to go very wrong indeed. No man is an island, but many individuals in secure settings may experience themselves as such even if the words are unfamiliar. To confuse the metaphor slightly, there may even be a sense of being marooned, of being a castaway. Conditions that foster a sense of connectedness may be necessary both for openness to change and ultimately for reintegration. Social processes can go wrong but they also offer the most powerful means of instigating and supporting positive development. This also has implications for staff in the criminal justice system in areas such as resilience. Here, for example, we might draw upon the example of survival on an island provided by Cacioppo, Reis and Zautra (2011).

So for people who are held within the criminal justice system, the environment in which they reside can play a significant part in their recovery and rehabilitation. Consideration of the support and structure for people as they transition from the community to custody and from stages of incarceration is imperative if interactions with the environment are to be a vehicle by which change can be facilitated. In combination and synergy with other opportunities, considerate interactions that build supportive relationships can ultimately contribute to a renewed sense of identity and belonging.

This volume developed out of practitioners and researchers acknowledging the importance of treatment and rehabilitation programmes being conducted in an environment which supports their effectiveness. The variety of authors helps enrich the content and provides examples of innovative practice in a range of settings. Rex Haigh sets the scene with a sketch of the growth in awareness of the importance of social context for us as social beings. The opening chapter by Alethea Adair-Stantiall and Adrian Needs considers how psychology has tended to sideline the influence of context in favour of an 'essentialist' view, in which most aspects of psychological functioning are attributed to internal causes. It outlines approaches that have adopted a more holistic and systemic perspective and suggests that progress will require a willingness to explore new ways of thinking about science. This theme is taken up by the same authors in the second chapter, where it is proposed that social context and personal development are inextricably related. It suggests that facets that affect and are affected by transitions in life (such as identity) can be seen in systemic terms and may be related to offending. It also offers an integrating perspective on conditions associated with therapeutic change and argues that maintenance of progress is unlikely to occur if relevant social processes are neglected. The third chapter, by Adrian Needs, extends analysis of relationships between social context and personal transition to the area of trauma. It cautions against uncritical embracing of familiar assumptions whilst recognising recent developments in the field and encouraging exploring of a greater range of potential continuities and parallels with processes (such as intersubjectivity) that have become well established in research in other areas. As such it provides an example of how approaching an area in terms of processes related to social context and personal transition can reframe understanding and implications for intervention and support.

Taken together, these three (slightly longer and more heavily referenced than the rest) chapters suggest that taking seriously the environmental context of rehabilitation may involve engaging with ways of understanding (such as non-linear dynamic systems, extended mind and dialogicality) that are suited to such an endeavour in ways that essentialism is not. The reader is encouraged also to think in terms of developing research into areas that have been rather under-developed in forensic psychology (such as life events in relation to risk or the role of rejection as an instigator to aggression) despite the provenance of these concepts in other fields. As is stated above and in the first chapter, the reader is invited to ponder any resonance between these chapters and those that follow.

In terms of clinical issues Lawrence Jones continues on the theme of trauma informed care when working with those who have experienced adverse experiences, and considers the need for practice which helps rather than exacerbates their progress in the light of this. While considering aspects of the climate which can have a major impact, Sarah Lewis discusses the importance of the therapeutic relationship within various treatment settings. In a similar vein, Andrew Day and James Vess highlight the importance of personal safety when working in a forensic setting using a case example to illustrate their points.

The volume continues with a chapter by Michael Brookes, who expands on the points raised previously, relates them to the setting of forensic therapeutic communities (TCs) and explains how a TC holds the quality of the environment at its heart. Geraldine Akerman and Patrick Mandikate go on to describe some of the perils and pitfalls of starting a TC from scratch and comment on what can be learned from their experience. The importance of continuing to support residents as they progress is described by Nick Benefield, Kirk Turner, Lucinda Bolger and Claire Bainbridge through the use of psychologically informed planned environments. Considering the diversity of residents in treatment interventions, Jon Taylor discusses the challenges of working with clients who have learning difficulties and how important a supportive environment is for them. Richard Shuker provides the service-user perspective and how they contribute to the enabling environment. Emma Guthrie, Laura Smillie, Annette McKeown and Claire Bainbridge discuss the challenges faced by those working in a therapeutic setting.

As we continue, Sarah Paget and Roland Woodward introduce the Enabling Environments award and how its relatively recent introduction has helped to formalise the pathway to improving each environment. Continuing on this theme, Alice Bennett and Jenny Tew describe the work put into developing an enabling environment for those in custody who are deemed to be at high risk of reoffending and have complex needs. As we consider the diverse needs of those in custodial settings the team from Aylesbury Young Offender Institution describe how they developed their Enabling Environments award. Continuing with this theme, Andrew Frost and Jason Ware discuss the heart and soul of a transforming environment while working with those who have committed sexual offences. Dana Hubbard and Betsy Matthews comment on the importance of the treatment environment in working with females.

In terms of enriching the treatment environment, Jo Shingler and Adrian Needs discuss how important it is to develop a rapport with those whom practitioners are assessing in order to gain the most informed (and unbiased in terms of extraneous processes) assessment of risk. Dominic Pearson discusses the 'real world' outside of custody and the need for ongoing maintenance of the progress made in more secure settings and how these can be applied practically. Peter Tyrer describes his principles of nidotherapy, and how each interaction with another impacts on the relationship and efficacy of treatment.

A pervasive theme in these chapters is the importance of establishing and nurturing a supportive and healthy psychosocial environment for those whose lives are absorbed into the criminal justice system. A lack of attention to such processes increases the risks of treatment failure, continued offending and a range of problems in institutional settings. Conversely, providing a sense of normality, positive psychosocial interactions and opportunities for new development are imperative if people are to lead law-abiding lives, both in custody and when in the community. This in turn requires new ways of understanding that bring social context and processes of change into the foreground. Seen from perspectives such as attachment, extended mind, intersubjectivity and non-linear dynamics no man (or woman) *is* an island.

We hope you find the book informative and thought-provoking and are able to translate these thoughts into the areas where you work.

## Note

1  This is a word for complexity theorists to get excited about!

## References

Andrews, D. A. (2011). The impact of nonprogrammatic factors on criminal-justice interventions. *Legal and Criminological Psychology*, 16, 1–23.

Barrett, L. F., Mesquita, B. & Smith, E. R. (2010). The context principle. In B. Mesquita, L. F. Barrett & E. R. Smith (Eds.) *The Mind in Context*. New York, NY: Guilford Press.

Cacioppo, J. T., Reis, H. T. & Zautra, A. J. (2011). Social resilience. The value of social fitness with an application to the military. *American Psychologist*, 66(1), 43–51.

Dutton, D. (2012). Transitional processes culminating in extreme violence. *Aggression, Conflict and Peace Research*, 4(1), 45–53.

Fortune, C.-A., Ward, T. & Polaschek, D. L. L. (2014). The Good Lives Model and therapeutic environments in forensic settings. *Therapeutic Communities: The International Journal of Therapeutic Communities*, 35(3), 95–104.

Netto, N. R., Carter, J. M. & Bonell, C. (2014). A systematic review of interventions that adopt the 'Good Lives' approach to offender rehabilitation. *Journal of Offender Rehabilitation*, 53(6), 403–432.

Polaschek, D.L.L. (2012). An appraisal of the risk–need–responsivity (RNR) model of offender rehabilitation and its application in correctional treatment. *Legal and Criminological Psychology*, 17(1), 1–17.

Quill, E. (2015). Developing a scale for assessing the forensic experience of recovery: The SAFER questionnaire and clinical research portfolio. D Clin Psy thesis, University of Glasgow. Retrieved from http://theses.gla.ac.uk/6675/.

# 1

# STEPS TO AN ECOLOGY OF HUMAN FUNCTIONING FOR FORENSIC PSYCHOLOGY

*Alethea Adair-Stantiall and Adrian Needs*

## Introduction

> *[A] very large part of the fundamental structure of nineteenth-century science was inappropriate or irrelevant to the problems and phenomena which confronted the biological and behavioural scientist.*
>
> — Bateson, 1972, p. 27

Since its inception in the late 19th century, the discipline of psychology has been aligned with the physical sciences. Conceptualisations of people and human behaviour have historically been reduced to constituent 'parts' in much the same way a scientist might analyse chemical compounds to get to an underlying structure. Through embracing the notion that psychological knowledge is akin to the subject matter of chemistry, physics or biology, we have come to 'essentialise' what we study, searching for the 'true' nature of the person and the significant enduring features of their functioning. Against this backdrop and the prevailing Western view of the individualised self, explanations centred upon factors and mechanisms 'within' the person have flourished and continue to dominate our thinking today at the expense of considering the role of context. Mesquita, Barrett, and Smith (2010) refer to this as the 'essentialism error' in psychology. They highlight the way in which experimental methodology, imported from the natural sciences, has contributed to a fragmented representation of the mind which views psychological phenomena such as personality traits, emotions and attitudes as separate from each other. Moreover, they argue that such methods have encouraged contextual influences to be thought of as potential sources of interference or 'measurement error' as opposed to the central aspect within which psychological processes are embedded and constituted (Barrett, Mesquita & Smith, 2010). Mesquita et al. (2010) present an impressive array of evidence for what they term "the context principle", the idea that human behaviours and their associated thoughts, feelings and psychological states occur as a result of "multiple transactive processes", which emerge from "moment-by-moment interaction with the environment" (Barrett et al., 2010, p. 5).

Context is inescapable (in the words of the Goon Show "everyone has to be somewhere") but this very ubiquity may contribute to it being overlooked. This tendency has supported the continued construction and use of frameworks for understanding and changing behavior that are incomplete at best, even in settings (such as prisons) where the context is rather distinctive. Another reason for this neglect is that it leads to ways of thinking that are likely to be unfamiliar to many practitioners and researchers. After considering the complexities inherent in defining and conceptualising context, this chapter considers a range of reasons for our tendency to 'decontextualise' human behaviour and notes something of the history of alternatives to this. It then argues that dominant approaches to working with what used to be termed 'offenders' are themselves largely the result of research and evaluations that gave relatively little attention to contextual aspects or related issues such as process. The field of evaluation, meanwhile, has been developing an increasingly sophisticated awareness of the importance of context, process and the wider 'systems' in which these occur. It draws towards a close with a brief outline of concepts that have become established in the study of complex systems. These have in many cases eclipsed or replaced traditional approaches in the sciences that psychology has sought to emulate.

Some readers will recognise the respectful nod in the title of this chapter to Gregory Bateson's (1972) collection of essays 'Steps to an Ecology of Mind'. At this point we will invite the reader to consider Bateson's question of where we may most usefully locate the boundary of a blind person's mind. Does mind end with the skull or with the fingers that hold the white stick, or does it extend into the world through the stick? Similar questions from earlier authors might be asked (see Palmer, 2004): at what point does ingested food become part of an organism rather than part of its environment (Bentley, 1927), or in the case of a person with an artificial arm trying to repair an engine, is the arm part of the person or part of the machinery (Ashby, 1960)? Although these might sound like questions introduced into a conversation in a pub, their implications are far from trivial. The study of context, of relationships between person and environment, demands that we reflect carefully upon some of our most long held assumptions.

## Defining context – stating the obvious?

Whilst everyday language (e.g. "let me put it in context") and dictionary definitions of the word suggest that knowing 'the context' is important to understanding communication, there is a general consensus amongst researchers that precise definitions of the term remain elusive (Cohen & Siegel, 1991), if not impossible (Goodwin & Duranti, 1992). As Cohen and Siegel (1991) point out, accurately defining context is "like having a note taped to your back, you know it's there, but it remains out of sight when you turn to view it" (p. 3). In their 2005 paper, 'Understanding context before using it', Bazire and Brezillon (2005) systematically examined 66 definitions of context across a number of academic disciplines. They highlight the confusion arising from the multiplicity of terms used synonymously to refer to context, such as 'field', 'situation', 'environment', 'setting' and 'background'. Secondly, they note how difficulties arise due to the fact that defining context (somewhat ironically) depends on the context in which it is being used, both in terms of the discipline applying it and the goal of its use. The reported definitions are diverse and the range encompasses, for example, reference to surrounding environment, a shared goal, interaction between people, interrelated conditions in which something exists or occurs, parts [preceding and following] of discourse that fix meaning, knowledge and beliefs, culture, ecology and community.

All these facets are relevant to a consideration of context. However, this multi-faceted reality of what Siegel and Cohen (1991) refer to as "fuzzy boundaries" leaves us struggling to articulate an unambiguous description of contexts even though intuitively, we know what they are (p. 313). They argue that this latter point (contexts as intuitive knowledge) is central to understanding the dilemma of context definition. They draw on the work of White (1983) to discuss two broad classifications of knowledge that humans have about the world: 'grandmother knowledge' and 'scientific knowledge'. The former comprises implicit information, or laypersons' understanding about how the world works, akin to the kind of knowledge required to raise a child. It is gained through processes such as imitation and is passed down generations through informal education. In contrast, 'scientific knowledge' deals with tangible facts about the world. It can be rationally explained and is communicated through formal education (Siegel & Cohen, 1991). Our understanding of context, they argue, is an example of 'grandmother knowledge'; intuitively we 'get it', but attempts to identify clear cut descriptions leave us struggling to articulate what we mean.

Nevertheless, this lack of a formal and complete definition, although unsettling, is perhaps as Goodwin and Duranti (1992) suggest, "not a situation that necessarily requires a remedy" (p. 2). That said, it is important to provide some clarity in our descriptions of concepts to avoid the risk of them becoming meaningless. With these points in mind, we will proceed by discussing some general principles relevant to a consideration of context.

## Towards an understanding of context

The word 'context' originates from the Latin 'contextus', meaning to weave together (Oxford English Dictionary, OED; 2015). To weave also means to intertwine, suggesting that context refers to an intricate, mutually bound relationship between two or more entities (Goodwin & Duranti, 1992). Similarly, Houts (1991) states that "context is concerned with ... part–whole relations, and with how structures composed of elements affect isolated parts of the structure" (p. 27). A contextual approach to understanding human behaviour is therefore inherently ecological, the underlying assumption being that we must attend to interactions between people and their environments. However, rather than proceeding with a "science as usual" approach that treats the individual and environment as separate 'parts' that influence each other, there is a need to appreciate the constant dynamic reciprocal interplay between person–context transactions which constitute situations and which themselves usefully comprise the unit of focus (Cohen & Siegel, 1991; Moen, Elder Jr, & Luscher, 1995). This approach is consistent with Kurt Lewin's (1935) notion that behaviour results from an interaction between the person and their context at that moment in time (known famously through the equation $B = f(PE)$).

In addition to the above is the recognition highlighted previously that attending to context improves our understanding of the topic at hand. Indeed, the OED refers to context as the circumstances surrounding an event which contribute to it being fully understood and the parts of language or text which clarify its meaning. What is striking about this is the implication that in the absence of considering context, the phenomena under scrutiny (for our purposes, human behaviour), not only cannot be fully understood, but is stripped of meaning. As Schegloff (1993) suggests, by placing something in context, it is "accordingly … treated as transforming and correcting our understanding" (p. 193). In this sense, context is akin to Goffman's (1974) notion of a discursive frame; it constitutes the components surrounding an idea or event that equips us to interpret 'what is going on'.

These two principles of context, that it comprises mutually constitutive relationships between elements of 'the whole' and increases our ability to interpret information meaningfully, are relatively easy to grasp. However, the picture becomes more complicated when we consider, in relation to an analysis of human behaviour, the elements of context to be included and how to characterise the relationships between them.

### The individual in context

The position adopted by Cohen and Siegel (1991) argues for the transactional, inseparable relationship between the person and context in accounting for human behaviour. In their discussion of the individual in context, Cohen and Siegel highlight the work of Rogoff (1982) who refers to this as the 'contextual event perspective', where person–context transactions are placed centre stage in our analyses, implicit within which is "a flavour of the whole being greater than the sum of its parts" (p. 10). Perhaps the notion of 'an individual in context' is conceptually misleading, invoking images of the person operating as a discrete entity 'within' but yet independent of a set of external influences collectively entitled 'context'. It is possibly for this reason that Cohen and Siegel call attention to an integrated approach in contextually rich explanations of human behaviour. Individuals are not simply 'influenced' by context. Their development and behaviour is mutually constituted by the context in a continuously evolving dynamic 'co-production'. Individuals and their associated 'intra' processes are pivotal, but they do not and cannot exist independently of the contexts in which that person has lived, continues to operate, selects or helps create (Kihlstrom, 2012). Even supposedly stable indices of variation such as neuroticism are susceptible to alteration as a result of exposure to life events (Jeronimus, Riese, Sanderman & Ormel, 2014).

## Context as social system(s)

Cohen and Siegel (1991) provide a helpful framework for considering context in terms of social systems by drawing upon Urie Bronfenbrenner's (1986, 1988) developmental theory. This highlights the importance of considering the impact of both proximal and distal social features in understanding behaviour. Although Bronfenbrenner's work was originally developed to account for children's development, his ideas have applicability across psychological disciplines and are relevant for considering context across the lifespan (Cassidy, 2013; Clausen, 1995). At the heart of his theory is the idea of a set of nested systems, which serve as an explanatory basis for how various proximal and distal social relationships might operate interdependently in both a direct and indirect way to influence a person's experience and behaviour (Cassidy, 2013; Cohen & Siegel, 1991). His Ecological Systems Theory was later updated and entitled the Bioecological Model to account for the influence of biology on behaviour (Bronfenbrenner, 1995). A snapshot of the key concepts within the model is illustrated in Box 1.1.

Bronfenbrenner's model represents an example of a systemic perspective in that it is concerned with the interconnection between the person and the various systems in which they are embedded and the communication between them. It is inherently relational and interactive, encouraging us to consider the person and their experience not just in their own right, but in terms of what they are a part of. Clarke and Crossland (1985) made a similar point, arguing that neglect of context in favour of the more familiar 'taking apart' of functioning can render action largely unintelligible. Whilst it is possible 'objectively' to measure the physical actions involved in a handshake with great precision and detail, this does little to clarify why the handshake was performed (for example as a greeting or parting, or to seal a bargain). Attempting to study part of a system without consideration of the system constrains understanding and can alter the character of both, as in removing a heart (Clarke & Crossland, 1985; also see Palmer, 2004). In his ecological approach to visual perception, Gibson (1979) coined the term 'affordance', referring to the notion that the external environment provides the opportunity (or 'affords') particular types of action. Crucially, this potential for action was not regarded as a property of either the person or the environment alone. In this regard, Van Geert (2003) pointed out that to someone who has learned to read, a book is more than just a physical object.

It is entirely consistent with such a view to consider the physical environment, or as it is often named, the 'behaviour setting', when accounting for context. Consideration of how one might behave in settings as diverse as a tube station, a football stadium, a prison, the post office queue and our own homes highlights how our immediate environment provides us with contextual information about

**Box 1.1** *Bronfenbrenner's ecological systems theory*

**Microsystem:** Consists of relationships and associated roles with those closest to the individual (e.g. family, peers).

**Mesosystem:** Those interactions and connections between microsystems. Implicit is the idea that aspects of the individuals' microsystem do not operate individually but assert influence on one another.

**Exosystem:** The individual is not an active participant in the exosystem, but is affected indirectly by actions occurring within it. Examples include the impact on a child of a parent losing their job and changes in the law or education system.

**Macrosystem:** The cultural context a person lives in, along with associated ideologies, norms and values which exert an influence on the whole system.

(adapted from Bronfenbrenner, 1992)

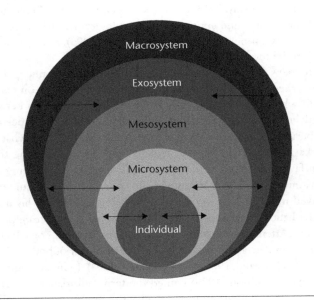

the role(s) to adopt and the variations in behaviour that are possible or acceptable (Argyle, Furnham, & Graham, 1981; Cassidy, 2013). This latter point highlights the way that physical environments and their impact on behaviour cannot be separated from the social features of any situation, including the presence of implicit social norms. Ecological psychologist Roger Barker was a key figure in promoting a focus on an understanding of human behaviour in the environment (Barker, 1968, 1978). Although his work has been criticised for neglecting the person (Graesser & Magliano, 1991), Barker and colleagues have accumulated an impressive array of evidence demonstrating the power of behaviour settings in shaping behaviour (Schoggen, 1991).

## Context as evolving over time

Cohen and Siegel's (1991) facets are derived from developmental psychology and so consideration of change over time as an enduring feature of context is unsurprising. Nevertheless, it is argued that paying attention to all human behaviour within a temporal framework is important for two reasons. Firstly, it encourages a focus on process and the dynamic aspects of people's lives. People change over time. Whilst there may be a sense of some enduring characteristics that remain stable in our perception of ourselves, it is unlikely that we would describe our lives in similar ways at the age of 15, 21, 35, 50 and so on. The research literature delineates factors such as life stage (Clausen, 1995; Elder & Rockwell, 1979) and life events (O'Connor, Robert, Perodeau & Seguin, 2015; Park, 2010) as central to making sense of our experience and behaviour at any point in time. At the other end of the temporal scale, even cognition within a single episode usually involves active exploration, responsive engagement and emergent sense-making even when (perhaps especially when) apparently automatic (Bargh & Chartrand, 1999; Ormerod, Barrett & Taylor, 2008; Radley, 1977); the constraints of laboratory-based methods have often failed to capture these embodied and temporally-based aspects (Glenberg, Witt & Metcalfe, 2013; Neisser, 1976).

Appreciating the role of processes helps us move away from 'within-person' explanations that essentialise human functioning towards an understanding of the person operating within an 'ecological niche' (Bronfenbrenner, 1995; Reis, Collins & Berscheid, 2000). As researchers such as Moen et al. (1995) have highlighted, not only is such a move likely to require increased innovation in our research methodology, it will also necessitate greater integration of academic disciplines (points we will return to later). Arguably, it also requires us to understand why the tendency to engage in the 'essentialism error' (or what Merlo in his 2011 paper from the field of health referred to as the 'psychologistic fallacy') to date has been so enticing.

## The draw to decontextualise

> [W]hy do we – and here we mean to include even those who do our work in this area – need to constantly remind ourselves of the central role context plays?
>
> (Dunham & Banaji, 2010, p. 204)

Despite increasing awareness in the last ten years of the importance of a contextual approach in psychology (Mesquita et al., 2010; Shoda, Cervone & Downey, 2007), there is still a propensity among both lay and scientific communities to adopt simplified, categorical ways of conceptualising psychological processes alongside a tendency to perpetuate what Semin and Smith (2002) refer to as "the illusion of inner causes of behaviour" (p. 5). As highlighted in the Introduction, the 'psychology as natural science' metaphor has played a key part here and the idea of viewing psychological processes through a reductionist scientific lens as problematic is far from new. Discussions of this kind are of course part of broader epistemological and ontological debates which have characterised social science disciplines for years and space permits only limited coverage of these here. Our position is most closely aligned to that of Ann Hartman who, in her article 'Many Ways of Knowing' (1990), highlights how the vastness and complexity of our subject matter necessitates using multiple approaches because each brings with it the possibility to add to our knowledge and develop understanding.

One of the challenges in integrating psychological perspectives is the temptation to categorise in a fashion that is preemptive and restrictive (Barrett et al., 2010; Kelly, 1955). This is reflected in, for example, how psychology journals have been organised in ways that separate interrelated 'parts' of the whole person such as cognition, motivation, emotion, identity and personality (Bronfenbrenner, 1995). Added to this, it has long been recognised that categories tend to be defined by contrasts (for example an appreciation of goodness is brought into sharper focus by an awareness of badness) or, as Kelly asserted, constructs are bipolar. A problem is that such contrasting can leave behind any relative, provisional perspective. Adams and Marshall (1996) refer to this in their description of the development of identity in context. Using the examples of individuality/relatedness, agency/communion and self/other to illustrate how such concepts are set apart from one another even though they are inextricably linked and mutually formed, they draw on Damon's (1995) work to label this 'false oppositions'.

Evidence of our use of polarised concepts abounds not just within academia but in society generally. In addition, whilst the longevity of the 'nature–nurture' debate attests to the persistent need for categorising complexity into neat binary concepts and a corresponding unfamiliarity with more realistic, process-oriented 'transactional' formulations (Rutter, 1975) it may, with an ironic twist, have origins in which both nurture and nature make a contribution. In the words of Bloom (2005, p. 12), "dualistic thinking comes naturally to us". As a cultural influence, the notion of dualism can be dated back to the Greek philosopher Plato (429–327 BC), through Gnosticism in early Christianity and subsequently to Rene Descartes, the French philosopher who set apart the workings of the body and soul (or mind). For Descartes, our bodies (*res extensa*) and our minds (*res cogitans*) functioned independently of one another. The underlying philosophy that these two aspects of being human are not 'one' paved the way for what is known as the Cartesian mind–body dichotomy. In terms of 'nature', Bloom (2005) presents compelling evidence from developmental psychology and neuroscience to argue that humans have evolved to see the world and make sense of events in dualistic terms. Similarly, Dunham and Banaji (2010) advocate that infants appear to enter life with a propensity to attribute causal explanations of behaviour into different 'types'; evolution has provided us with efficient ways of seeing the world, but the 'payoff' for this is an inherent difficulty in attributing more sophisticated causal explanations for behaviour that account for context.

In addition to the argument regarding our innate tendency for dualism, categorisation "gives promise of relieving the pains of cognitive uncertainty ... (and) makes us all vulnerable" (Koch, Finkelman & Kessel, 1999, pp. 408–409). The alternative to a sense of certainty can be "deep epistemological panic" (Bateson & Bateson, 1987, p. 15); attempts to avoid or mitigate this can encompass the constrictions of involvements and sense-making, resistance to other potential perspectives (including those of others) and attempts to impose or extort validational evidence in order to avoid testing or revision of one's own that are characteristic of both mental disorder and poor science (Kelly, 1955; Walker & Winter, 2005). In support of this, other research suggests, for example, that intolerance of uncertainty is associated with lack of openness to experience (Fergus & Rowatt, 2014) and uncertainty can lead to a defensive stance with regard to one's views of the world (Stillman & Baumeister, 2009). It is perhaps related to the need to maintain meaningfulness through a sense of purpose, efficacy, value and self-worth proposed by the latter authors that under some circumstances individuals favour dispositional views of others whilst allowing understanding of their own behavior to be informed by context – the 'fundamental attribution error' (Ross, 1989). It also appears that contextual effects can operate outside of our conscious awareness. The latter argument has been put forward by Dunham and Banaji (2010), who cite examples from social psychological studies employing implicit association techniques to demonstrate that we often employ "naïve psychological explanations" (p. 208) which do not accurately account for what is really going on. The collective tendency to underestimate contextual influences is referred to by Dunham and Banaji as 'Platonic Blindness' after Plato's belief in the possibility of describing an objective external reality devoid of context. Processes such as these are compounded by the role of language.

One enduring feature of our language is the way we speak of people and objects possessing characteristics: 'he has such a temper', 'that chair is comfortable', 'her kindness knows no bounds'. We need a way of making sense of and communicating ideas about the world around us. As Bateson (2002) suggests, "That is how our language is made" (p. 56). He also highlights that "this way of talking is not good enough in science" (p. 57). Bateson goes on to argue for an approach to description that is synonymous with adhering to the context principle, that the 'thing' under scrutiny must be understood in terms of its internal properties, its relationship with other things and with the person doing the describing (Bateson, 2002).

By emphasising interaction, Bateson argued the need to move away from the use of nouns to explain behavioural phenomena. Barsalou et al. (2010) elaborate on Bateson's argument by describing the issues faced in psychology when we nominalise our subject matter. Nominalising refers to the act of using nouns to describe phenomena that are not nouns. It is akin to transforming a process into an entity. Barsalou et al. use the example of 'cognition'. As they point out, there are likely to be multiple cognitive processes that occur during our day-to-day experience, which are dynamically influenced by a host of proximal and distal factors and which change over time. However, the word 'cognition' invites us to infer that it is a stable, discrete entity which can be thought of as relatively context-free. Barsalou et al. go on to describe the consequences of "coercing processes into object concepts" (p. 340). For example, it leads us to simplify complexity and essentialise our subject matter (cognition is one example, but also consider words such as emotion, affect, identity and self). This, they argue, leads to erroneous assumptions that we can easily manipulate, control and infer causal relationships between such phenomena. Whilst Barsalou et al. also highlight the advantages of nominalising, such as the ease with which we can represent concepts, hold and retrieve them in memory and communicate, they also acknowledge that nominalising is less common in non-Western countries where relational concepts are emphasised and associated verb categories used more frequently.

There are other likely influences on this tendency to neglect context that are particularly relevant to forensic psychology. As suggested below, an important source has been the tendency to base research and practice primarily on studies of group differences. The 'managerialist' approach in which much practice is embedded also invites thinking in terms of boxes to tick rather than processes to be encouraged and supported (Bryans, 2000; Needs, 2016). As with other training-centred interventions, there can be neglect of contextual factors such as contingencies that can compromise transfer and durability of taught content and failure to consider other forms of intervention (Rummler & Brache, 1995; also see Pearson, this volume). This bias in work with forensic clients has been legitimised by an approach (see below) that has been compared to the 'medical model' in the field of mental health (McNeill, 2002). This certainly appears more tangible and circumscribed than attempting to address complex societal problems that contribute to offending (Thomas-Peter, 2006). There may also be a moral imperative to distance ourselves from 'offenders' by seeing them as inherently different to ourselves (Howells, 1980).

## Beyond the individual

> [W]hen biased by the psychologistic fallacy we disregard the context, and assume that individual level outcomes are only explained by individual level characteristics
>
> (Merlo, 2011, p. 110)

The explanations above go some way to explaining why a dualistic approach to psychological thinking has endured for so long, despite attention to the issue being raised over 100 years ago by John Dewey (1896) in his concept of the 'reflex arc'. In contrast to the idea of a bi-directional 'stimulus-response' explanation of behaviour, which encouraged the view of people as comprised of "a patchwork of disjointed parts", Dewey argued that sensations and responses were mutually constituted, with one providing the context for the next. He described the arc as "a fundamental psychical unity" comprising "functioning factors, within the single concrete whole"

(p. 358). An organism is in a constant state of transaction, conceived not so much as living within an environment but by means of an environment (Dewey & Bentley, 1949). In this sense, Dewey's ideas represent one of the first examples of Mesquita et al.'s (2010) 'context principle' (Barrett et al., 2010).

Moving throughout the 20th century, it is possible to see how other researchers have emphasised the role of context. In 1941, Angyal wrote about the 'biosphere' which comprised the social, biological and psychological aspects of experience. These elements, she argued, interacted to create "aspects of a single reality" (p. 100) in which "the organism is entirely permeated by the environment" whilst it also "penetrates into its environment" (p. 97). Further, Vygotsky's (1978) Sociocultural Theory placed context as central to children's social and cognitive development, whilst Gibson's (1979) ecological approach and the concept of 'affordance' described how features of both the person and environment contributed to possibilities for action in any given situation. Bronfenbrenner's (1979) ecological model high-lighted how human development is comprised of experiences traced throughout numerous 'nested' systems that impact at both a direct and indirect level. Around the same time, Walter Mischel (1968, 1973) revolutionised the field of personality psychology when he called into question the usefulness and accuracy of traditional trait theories of personality in favour of more contextually embedded explanations of behaviour (Cervone, Shoda & Downey, 2007; Mischel & Shoda, 1995).

There is an additional perspective that takes the challenge to essentialist epis-temology to a new level. Researchers from a broad spectrum of disciplines have argued that thoughts, feelings and action exist as interactions within the wider con-text of biological, social, physical environment and cultural systems (Clancey, 2009; Clark, 1998, 2007, 2008; Menary, 2007; Robbins & Aydede, 2009; Wilson & Clark, 2009). The collection of principles advocated within this approach is wide-ranging; however, they are commonly referred to as 'situated cognition' (Smith & Collins, 2010). Parallel terms have included 'distributed cognition' and 'extended mind theory', which as the words suggest, refer to the notion that processes previously considered internal to the person are in fact derived through reciprocal interactions with the external world (Robbins & Aydede, 2009). Referred to as 'embodiment', this has been allied with a renewed emphasis on the biological body and the inter-active nature of sensorimotor action and perception with the environment (Smith & Collins, 2010). One of the assumptions at the heart of embodiment, and situated cognition more generally, is that human beings are designed for adaptive action and consequently our cognitive processes (such as problem solving, decision-making, memory, perception) exist not as static discrete entities, but are mobilised as part of a dynamic process with the external environment in order to achieve particular motives and goals (Semin & Smith, 2002; Semin, 2007; Smith & Conrey, 2009). Clark (2007) refers to this when he speaks of humans as 'ecological controllers', arguing that implicit in this idea is that people have greater cognitive plasticity than previously thought, which enables them to function and adapt according to the specific environment. In this sense, the environment acts as a kind of 'cognitive scaffolding' (Clark, 2008). For example, a pilot interacts with external components within the cockpit (such as dials, lights, penciled marks on the indicator panel) to adequately perform their role (Hutchins, 1995). Approaches to rehabilitation in acquired brain injury such as functional task analysis that rely heavily on environmental cues to support the actions of the individual also highlight the way in which cognition 'extends' out into the world in the completion of daily tasks (Giles & Clark-Wilson, 2013).

As Clark and Chalmers (1998) argue, this way of conceptualising thinking and action as contingent on environmental processes alters our perception of cognition as something that exists in people's heads to one where cognitive action occurs as part of a wider system that incorporates the person and their immediate setting (Smith & Collins, 2010). Extended mind theory and an emphasis on situated and embodied cognition gained momentum in the early to mid-1990s; however, it was not until some years later that researchers turned their attention to the contribution of social psychology to this field (Semin & Smith, 2002; Smith & Semin, 2004, 2007; Smith & Conrey, 2009), with researchers subsequently emphasising a 'socially extended mind thesis' to address the aspects of the social context including implicit cultural norms, the need to belong, roles, power and group processes play in shaping cognition (Pickett, Gardner & Knowles, 2004; Smith & Collins, 2010). Smith and Semin (2004) point out that "the relevant situation in which cognition takes place, is almost always a *social* situation" (emphasis from original authors, p. 151). Social contexts and processes are considered more comprehensively in the second chapter.

Perhaps the most direct application of ideas from situated cognition in forensic psychology is Tony Ward's application of 'extended mind' theory to individuals with a history of sexually harmful behaviour (Ward, 2009; Ward & Casey, 2010). In particular, Ward provides a detailed application of extended mind principles to how we conceptualise cognitive distortions. Drawing on themes such as Clark's (2007) notion of cognition and the environment constituting a cognitive system, he argues for the need to re-conceptualise cognitive distortions as contextually embedded, dynamic experiences. Consequently, to understand their role in offending behaviour we must consider the wider social, physical and cultural context in which an offender resides. As Ward highlights, relevant contextual features include therapist relationships, group dynamics in treatment and wider social supports as well as more practical components in the environment relevant to risk such as internet pornography and chat rooms. Ward's ideas are consistent with those advocated by Vivian-Byrne (2002, 2004) who calls into question the usefulness of dominant treatment approaches based on the premise that changing people's minds will alter their behaviour without consideration of the broader context of their offending. Rather than restructuring an offender's apparent thinking errors in a manner akin to "a simple engineering job" where the person is "passively in receipt of the technique" (p. 185), Vivian-Byrne points toward alternative more contextually sensitive approaches. In much the same way as Ward and Casey (2010) refer to the need to account for "mind/body/world loops" (p. 57) in understanding individuals' sense of self, Vivian-Byrne (2004) argues that understanding offending behaviour requires us to understand that human functioning is "a continuous feedback process to and from the world out there" which "shapes our actions and beliefs about ourselves and others" (p. 190).

## Does context really matter to forensic psychology?

*[T]he focus of attention should be on the processes or mechanisms, rather than on variables*

(Rutter, 1987, p. 320)

For over a quarter of a century, the twin mantras of "evidence-based practice" and "What works?" have dominated work with forensic clients. This has been seen by many as part of a narrative of the discipline coming of age that has allowed inconsistencies, sometimes disappointing outcomes and pessimism to be left behind (Ogloff, 2002). As suggested earlier, the new pragmatism, based on large scale empirical and procedural regularities mobilised around the aim of reducing risk, dovetailed with a governmental ethos that privileged efficiency and accountability for resources. In terms of scale, standardisation of delivery and understanding, the development of infrastructures and gradual refinement of associated research and practice the achievements appear impressive.

"What works?", the question at the core of the prevailing Risk–Need–Responsivity approach (RNR) (Andrews, Bonta & Hoge, 1990; Andrews & Bonta, 2010), could be paraphrased as "What makes a difference?". Group-based cognitive-behavioural programmes targeting factors identified as associated with offending were shown to be superior to both other interventions and to no treatment in the difference they made to re-offending rates. Similarly, configurations of certain variables associated with re-offending provided a focus for the assessment of future risk that improved upon the accuracy of predictions based on less empirically-derived approaches or what would have been expected by chance. Reported effect sizes and similar statistical measures calculated from evaluations of procedures compare favourably with those adduced in medical research (Douglas, Cox & Webster, 1999). "What makes a difference?" has become the principal driving force behind conceptualisations of what must be done to reduce and assess risk of re-offending. However, reported effect sizes are typically less than what would be desired, sometimes substantially so, whilst group differences without regard for context or processes tell us little about why effects vary and how they might be improved. This problem has been recognised more widely within the field of evaluation.

### Evaluation

In fields such as public health, social policy and education there has been a shift away from reliance on large evaluative studies concerned with measures of central tendency and preserving uniformity. With an increasing awareness of the ways in which contexts impact upon both implementation and outcomes of an intervention, measurement of contextual features and responsiveness to local needs have become priorities (Fitzpatrick, 2012; Ling, 2012; Rog, 2012). Many readers will be familiar with the idea of 'programme integrity' in relation to programmes intended to modify offending behaviour (see Hollin, 1995) and the principle ('responsivity') denoted by the second 'R' in 'RNR'. Andrews (2011) acknowledged that responsivity, centred on adapting delivery of programme content according to local aspects such as the nature of the client group, was the least developed of the core principles. This may have been one of the reasons why early evaluations of cognitive skills programmes in England and Wales found the site of delivery to be a major source of variation in outcome (Falshaw, Friendship, Travers & Nugent, 2003). Such a pattern appears to have persisted for several years at least, with Hough (2010) commenting on a tendency towards attenuation of treatment gains from programmes as differences mount up between new settings and those where a programme was developed. It should be emphasised that this is not confined to offending behaviour programmes. In other initiatives in relation to crime or criminal justice inconsistency and unpredictability in a series of findings appears to be the norm (Gill & Turbin, 1999; Pycroft, 2014; Tilley, 2000). Neither is this pattern confined to the criminal justice system. In a range of settings, including education and even medicine (see Daniel & Poole, 2009) the most appropriate answer the question of whether or not an intervention works is "It depends" (Ling, 2012).

"Does it work?" provides a limited basis for advancing understanding and practice (Byrne, 2013; Rog, 2012). Knowledge of differences can be very useful. It was, for example, several centuries before the positively mistaken medical practice of 'bleeding' (that resulted in additional blood loss to already wounded victims of the battlefield) was ended after it was found that patients who had not been subjected to this procedure tended to fare rather better than those to whom it had been applied. On the other hand, even when apparently successful interventions share discernible characteristics identified through meta-analysis, other questions come into view. It is helpful to know more about what aspects of an intervention work for whom, why and in which circumstances (Rycroft-Malone, Fontenla, Bick & Seers, 2010). These issues focus attention on variations between individuals in outcomes and upon patterns of change, mediators and moderating influences (including context) and processes (Rog, 2012). The study of differences, whether between before and after an intervention, between different interventions or between other groups (such as recidivists compared to non-recidivists) can make a useful contribution at a pragmatic, provisional level. However, it has little to say about issues such as process and how this knowledge might guide the minutiae of practice; these points were recognised by the American Psychological Association's task force on evaluating therapies (see Pachankis & Goldfried, 2007).

Partly as a response to the limitations of quasi-experimental methods, there has been a growth of interest in more theory-centred approaches. These share an emphasis on mechanisms of change and the influence of contextual aspects on outcomes (Blamey & Mackenzie, 2007; Marchal, van Belle, van Olmen, Hoeree & Kegels, 2012). Prominent amongst these is 'realistic evaluation' (sometimes referred to as 'realist evaluation'). First described in detail by Pawson and Tilley in 1997, a central feature is the construction of 'Context–Mechanism–Outcome' configurations. It is proposed that measures will vary in their impact depending of the conditions in which they are introduced. In other words, under what conditions will an intervention produce its impacts? For example, gunpowder only explodes if there is enough and it is sufficiently dry and compacted: the conditions have to be right (Tilley, 2000). 'Context' refers to the conditions needed for a measure to trigger the mechanisms necessary to produce particular outcome patterns. 'Mechanism' attempts to explain why a measure may have a particular outcome pattern in a given context. 'Outcome' patterns refer to the practical effects produced by causal mechanisms being triggered in a given context. The empirical part of an evaluation comprises a test of CMO 'theories' (see Tilley, 2000, for an example of how the approach was used to clarify the circumstances under which closed-circuit television is likely to be either successful or unsuccessful in reducing crime in car parks).

In practice, differentiating mechanisms and contexts and tracing clear threads can be challenging as well as time-consuming (Blamey & Mackenzie, 2007; Marchal et al., 2012; Rycroft-Malone et al., 2010). Part of the problem is that the foundation of relevant research to build on is relatively small. Many evaluators at local level may be more comfortable with group comparisons using statistics such as t-tests on questionnaire data even when these obscure individual patterns, ignore standard errors of measures and fail to consider clinical significance (Friendship & Falshaw, 2003). This may in itself be part of a more fundamental unfamiliarity with conceptualising and operationalising contexts, processes and how they might be entwined. Perhaps especially when applied within evaluation context is "complex, dynamic and difficult to get right" (Conner, Fitzpatrick & Rog, 2012, p. 93). Certainly, in the field of evaluation research the term has been used in a variety of ways, all of which may be important (Greene, 2005). Greene drew attention to the potential role of demographics, material and economic features, institutional or organisational climate, patterns of relating and political interests, issues and dynamics. Such domains are indicative of potentially key 'systems' in which clients, staff and crucially, interventions must operate (Ling, 2012). These systems form part of the context of many evaluations in public sector organisations (Connolly, Reid, & Mooney, 2014) and it has been suggested that their influence may make even the supposed gold standard of randomised control trials "effectively useless" (Byrne, 2013).

Systems such as these tend to impact rather heavily upon both the implementation and outcomes of an intervention or other procedure (Rog, 2012). Nonstad and Webster (2011) present a humorous but pointed account of how to derail the implementation of a risk assessment scheme ("or any other new procedure") by ignoring the realities of the organisational context. Hackley et al. (2013) detail a compelling analysis of how the interpersonal context of binge drinking can render government initiatives to promote responsible drinking largely ineffective amongst those whom it most seeks to target. Programmes in prison often have to operate in the face of a climate of distrust and discouragement generated by prisoners and staff alike (Ross, Polaschek & Ward, 2008) as well as other considerations at the personal and environmental levels (Burrowes & Needs, 2009). This resonates with an early study by Kirchner, Kennedy and Draguns (1979) that suggested that prisoners may reject assertiveness as an alternative to aggressiveness as it is seen as 'soft'. Whilst reflecting the realities of subcultural dynamics in a prison setting, this is also a reminder that a person may usefully be construed as a 'person–context system' (Van Geert & Fischer, 2009). To continue the example of aggression in prisons, it appears that the exercise of violence is related to institutional features such as staff morale and training (Cooke, Wozniak & Johnstone, 2008) and the interpersonal context of attachment, identity and associated patterns (Butler, 2009). Similarly, analyses of bullying in prisons "emphasise the role of the prison environment in promoting and maintaining bullying, providing evidence against a focus on approaches attending solely to individual psychopathology" (Ireland, 2006 p. 114).

Advances in the understanding of systems that have arisen in fields of study such as biological ecosystems, the production of chemical compounds, embryology, weather systems, health policy in developing countries and economics have begun to be applied to psychology (Guastello, Koopman & Pincus, 2009), criminology and social work (Pycroft & Bartollas, 2014) and human development (Van Geert, 2003; Van Geert & Fischer, 2009) and it is to these works (and short introductions by, for example, Kernick, 2006 and Rickles, Hawe & Shiell, 2007) that the reader is referred. Although not a single approach, such advances are usually brought together under the titles of 'complexity theory' or 'non-linear dynamic' (or 'dynamical') systems.

## Complexity and non-linear dynamics

A system is constituted by interconnected parts. Its complexity increases with the interactions between parts and it is dynamic in that these interactions change the parts over time, often moment by moment. As in Bronfenbrenner's ecological approach mentioned earlier, systems typically are nested within and interact with other systems. The organisation or internal order of complex systems increases with openness to information from the surrounding environment; in contrast to 'closed' systems, they adapt. In addition, their own outputs become part of the context for other interactions within the system, also influencing environmental conditions that in a feedback loop become new inputs to the open system. These processes lead to 'emergent' properties that are not reducible to the parts of the system in isolation; what the system does is indeed greater than the sum of its parts.

Such developments are not haphazard, however. Dynamic systems tend to evolve (moment by moment as well as in the longer term) towards an end state or 'attractor' where equilibrium is attained. ('Chaos', in the sense of chaos theory, from the mathematics of which complexity theory developed, is something of a misnomer.) There is more than one form of equilibrium, including those represented by the momentary resting point of a pendulum, or by planetary orbits to 'fractal' patterns nested within other patterns. Nonetheless, with changes in surrounding conditions, alterations in the system can occur. Recognised changes include bifurcation, where a system attains greater complexity as alternative states arise and a switch to a new state occurs, often preceded by fluctuations as the system begins to reorganise. Systems displaced from equilibrium tend to 'self-organise' in order to achieve greater economy in the utilisation of energy or information, famously referred to by Kauffman (1993) as "order for free". This capacity for self-organisation "at the edge of chaos" is necessary for continued evolution and adaptation. Its occurrence is influenced by previous development of the system, including the strength and effective range (or 'basin') of existing attractors and conditions that affect being able to operate far from equilibrium. Resembling Vygotsky's idea of the 'zone of proximal development', the edge of chaos occurs in the region between preserving the familiar and predictable and exposure to inputs that, taken to extremes, would be overwhelming and disruptive.

Under some circumstances small changes in one area of a system can result in major changes across the system as a whole. Conversely, major inputs can sometimes result in minimal change. These are examples of non-linearity. In the more familiar notion of linearity, small inputs invariably produce small effects and large inputs produce large effects. Non-linear relationships are characteristic of complex as distinct from simple (or merely complicated) systems, arising from the operation of feedback loops as elements of a system interact. Negative feedback dampens and tends towards stability of the system whilst positive feedback amplifies effects, moving the system towards instability. The latter is necessary for growth but can also result in, for example, interventions having unforeseen and unintended consequences. Complex systems can be extremely sensitive to initial starting configurations, as suggested by the question posed in the title of Edward Lorenz's 1972 paper of whether the flap of a butterfly's wings in Brazil might set off a tornado in Texas.

## Looking ahead

Returning to evaluation, all this is rather different to a view of the world based on group differences. We may consider the following words of Kernick (2006): "Prevailing statistical models which by their nature are aggregative and assume independence of system elements may have limited utility in the analysis of complex systems" (p. 388). Such are the origins of the currently dominant approaches to interventions and assessing risk. It should be emphasised that we are not advocating abandonment of these or denigrating their achievements (although we would, unsurprisingly, suggest seeing them in context in every sense of the phrase). Our stance is one of identifying limitations so these can be understood, addressed or compensated for more consistently as part of the ongoing development of the field. Notable amongst these is a tendency to give insufficient attention to issues relating to context and process.

The present volume provides examples of several areas of relevant and emerging practice, arising from a variety of theoretical backgrounds, which suggest that context may be as necessary to providing coherence to rehabilitation as it is to written or spoken words referred to by dictionary definitions. Some limitations, like the arguable use of crude measurement, insensitive statistical techniques and simplistic conceptualisation of variables (Case & Haines, 2009, 2014; Polaschek, 2012) or the intrinsic problems of extrapolating from the general to the particular case (Cooke & Michie, 2010) are not unique to the RNR and allied approaches. Neither is a complexity-based approach free from criticism. At the present state of application and development it may indeed be regarded best as complementary to more conventional approaches (Kernick, 2006).

This is not to say that complex and contextually-sensitive approaches are synonymous, although there are many areas of compatibility that are worth exploring in depth (van Geert & Fischer, 2009). Throughout the chapters that follow, the reader is invited to consider any resonance with the cursory introduction presented above or indeed with the other arguments presented in this chapter. This might raise issues such as whether there are optimal or even necessary surrounding conditions for encouraging and supporting individual development, what can be done in relation to other complex systems that have the potential to undermine this, how certain views of the world might be reflected in and perpetuated by institutional subcultures, the extent of non-linear processes in change (and offences and relapse), the openness of the individual as an 'open system' and the circumstances under which connectedness might be experienced as such and whether this matters. The reader should not lose sight of the premise that mind should be regarded as extending beyond the individual into a world that includes the minds of other people. This might lead to pondering further how the apprehension of other subjectivities might have a crucial role in facilitating or impeding psychological change. One of the most compelling reasons for closer examination of context as it relates to working with offenders is offered by Cohen and Siegel (1991, p. 4), who assert that the concept of change is "at the very core of a contextual perspective". Some ways in which this might be so are picked up in the following chapter.

## References

Adams, G.R. & Marshall, S.K. (1996). A developmental social psychology of identity: Understanding the person-in-context. *Journal of Adolescence*, 19, 429–442.

Andrews, D.A. (2011). The impact of nonprogrammatic factors on criminal-justice interventions. *Legal and Criminological Psychology*, 16, 1–23.

Andrews, D.A. & Bonta, J. (2010). *The Psychology of Criminal Conduct*. New Providence, NJ: Routledge.

Andrews, D.A., Bonta, J. & Hoge, R.D. (1990). Classification for effective rehabilitation: Rediscovering psychology. *Criminal Justice and Behavior*, 17, 19–52.

Angyal, A. (1941). *Foundations for a Science of Personality*. New York, NY: The Commonwealth Fund.

Argyle, M., Furnham, A. & Graham, J.A. (1981). *Social Situations*. Cambridge: Cambridge University Press.

Ashby, W.R. (1960). *Design for a Brain*. New York, NY: Wiley.

Bargh, J.A. & Chartrand, T.L. (1999). The unbearable automaticity of being. *American Psychologist*, 54(7), 462–479.

Barker, R. (1968). *Ecological Psychology: Concepts and Methods for Studying the Environment of Human Behavior.* Stanford, CA: Stanford University Press.

Barker, R. (1978). *Habits, Environments, and Human Behavior.* San Francisco, CA: Jossey-Bass Incorporated.

Barrett, L.F., Mesquita, B. & Smith, E.R. (2010). The context principle. In B. Mesquita, L. F. Barrett & E. Smith (Eds.), *The Mind in Context* (pp. 1–24). London: Guildford Press.

Barsalou, L.W., Wilson, C.D., Hasenkamp, W., Mesquita, B., Feldman Barrett, L. & Smith, E. (2010). On the vices of nominalization and the virtues of contextualizing. In B. Mesquita, L.F. Barrett & E. Smith (Eds.), *The Mind in Context* (pp. 334–360). London: Guildford Press.

Bateson, G. (1972). *Steps to an Ecology of Mind: Collected Essays in Anthropology, Psychiatry, Evolution, and Epistemology.* Chicago, IL: University of Chicago Press.

Bateson, G. (2002). *Mind and Nature: A Necessary Unity.* Cresskill, NJ: Hampton Press.

Bateson, G. & Bateson, M.C. (1987). *Angels Fear: Towards an Epistemology of the Sacred.* New York, NY: Macmillan.

Bazire, M., & Brezillon, P. (2005). Understanding context before using it. In A. Dey, B. Kokinov, D. Leake & R. Turner (Eds), *Modelling and Using Context* (pp. 29–40). Berlin, Heidelberg: Springer.

Bentley, M. (1927). Environment and context. *The American Journal of Psychology*, 39(1/4), 54–61.

Blamey, A. & Mackenzie, M. (2007). Theories of change and realistic evaluation: Peas in a pod or apples and oranges? *Evaluation*, 13, 439–455.

Bloom, P. (2005). *Descartes' Baby: How the Science of Child Development Explains What Makes Us Human.* New York, NY: Basic Books.

Bronfenbrenner, U. (1979). The Ecology of Human Development: Experiements by Nature and Design. Massachusetts: Harvard University Press.

Bronfenbrenner, U. (1986). Ecology of the family as a context for human development: Research perspectives. *Developmental Psychology*, 22, 723–742.

Bronfenbrenner, U. (1988). Interacting systems in human development: Research paradigms, present and future. In N. Bolger, A. Caspi & G.M.M. Downey (Eds.), *Persons in Context: Developmental Processes* (pp. 25–49). New York, NY: Cambridge University Press.

Bronfenbrenner, U. (1992). *Ecological Systems Theory.* London: Jessica Kingsley Publishers.

Bronfenbrenner, U. (1995). Developmental ecology through space and time: A future perspective. In P. Moen, G.H. Elder Jr & K. Luscher (Eds.), *Examining Lives in Context: Perspectives on the Ecology of Human Development* (pp. 619–647). Washington, DC: American Psychological Association.

Bryans, S. (2000). The managerialisation of prisons: Efficiency without a purpose? *Criminal Justice Matters*, 40, 7–9.

Burrowes, N. & Needs, A. (2009). Time to contemplate change? A framework for assessing readiness to change with offenders. *Aggression and Violent Behavior*, 14(1), 39–49.

Butler, U.M. (2009). Freedom, revolt and citizenship: Three pillars of identity for youngsters living on the streets of Rio de Janeiro. *Childhood*, 16(1), 11–29.

Byrne, D. (2013). Evaluating complex interventions in a complex world. *Evaluation*, 19, 217–228.

Case, S. & Haines, K. (2009). *Understanding Youth Offending: Risk Factor Research: Policy and Practice.* Cullompton: Willan Publishing.

Case, S. & Haines, K. (2014). Youth justice: From linear risk paradigm to complexity. In A. Pycroft & C. Bartollas (Eds.), *Applying Complexity Theory: Whole Systems Approaches to Criminal Justice and Social Work.* Bristol: Policy Press.

Cassidy, T. (2013). *Environmental Psychology: Behaviour and Experience in Context.* Hove, East Sussex: Psychology Press.

Cervone, D., Shoda, Y. & Downey, G. (2007). Construing persons in context: On building a science of the individual. In Y. Shoda, D. Cervone & G. Downey (Eds.), *Persons in Context: Building a Science of the Individual* (pp. 3–18). New York, NY: Guilford Press.

Clancey, W.J. (2009). Scientific antecedents of situated cognition. In P. Robbins & M. Aydede (Eds.), *Cambridge Handbook of Situated Cognition* (pp. 11–34). Cambridge, MA: Cambridge University Press.

Clark, A. (1998). *Being There: Putting Brain, Body, and World Together Again.* Cambridge, MA: MIT Press.

Clark, A. (2007). Soft selves and ecological control. In D. Spurrett, D. Ross, M. Kincaid & L. Stephens (Eds.), *Distributed Cognition and the Will: Individual Volition and Social Context* (pp. 101–122). Cambridge, MA: MIT Press.

Clark, A. (2008). *Supersizing the Mind: Embodiment, Action, and Cognitive Extension.* Oxford: Oxford University Press.

Clark, A. & Chalmers, D. (1998). The extended mind. *Analysis*, 58, 10–23.

Clarke, D.D. & Crossland, J. (1985). *Action Systems: An Introduction to the Analysis of Complex Behaviour.* London: Methuen Publishing.

Clausen, J.A. (1995). *American Lives: Looking Back at the Children of the Great Depression.* Berkeley, CA: University of California Press.

Cohen, R. & Siegel, A.W. (1991). A context for context: Toward an analysis of context and development. In R. Cohen & A.W. Siegel (Eds.), *Context and Development* (pp. 3–23). London: Lawrence Erlbaum Associates.

Conner, R.F., Fitzpatrick, J.L., & Rog, D.J. (2012). A first step forward: Context assessment. In Rog, D.J., Fitzpatrick, J.L., Conner, R.F. *Context: A Framework for Its Influence on Evaluation Practice* (pp. 89–105). Hoboken, NJ: Wiley.

Connolly, J., Reid, G. & Mooney, A. (2014). Facilitating the evaluation of complexity in the public sector: Learning from the NHS in Scotland. *Teaching Public Administration*, 33, 74–92.

Cooke, D.J. & Michie, C. (2010). Limitations of diagnostic precision and predictive utility in the individual case: A challenge for forensic practice. *Law and Human Behavior*, 34(4), 259–274.

Cooke, D.J., Wozniak, E. & Johnstone, L. (2008). Casting light on prison violence in Scotland: Evaluating the impact of situational risk factors. Criminal Justice and Behavior, 35(8), 1065–1078.

Damon, W. (1995). *Greater Expectations: Overcoming the Culture of Indulgence in America's Homes and Schools.* Old Tappen, NJ: The Free Press.

Daniel, D.B. & Poole, D.A. (2009). Learning for life: An ecological approach to pedagogical research. *Perspectives on Psychological Science*, 4, 91–96.

Dewey, J. (1896). The reflex arc concept in psychology. *Psychological Review*, 3, 357–370.

Dewey, A.F. & Bentley, A. (1949). Knowing and the known. In J.A. Boydston (Ed.), *John Dewy: The Later Works* (Vol. 16). Carbondale, IL: Southern Illinois University Press.

Douglas, K.S., Cox, D.N. & Webster, C.D. (1999). Violence risk assessment: Science and practice. *Legal and Criminological Psychology*, 4, 149–184.

Dunham, Y. & Banaji, M.R. (2010). Platonic blindness and the challenge of understanding context. In B. Mesquita, L.F. Barrett, & E.R. Smith (Eds.), *Mind in Context* (pp. 201–213). New York, NY: The Guilford Press.

Elder, G.H. & Rockwell, R.C. (1979). The life-course and human development: An ecological perspective. *International Journal of Behavioral Development*, 2, 1–21.

Falshaw, L., Friendship, C., Travers, R. & Nugent, F. (2003). *Searching for 'What Works': An Evaluation of Cognitive Skills Programmes*. London: Home Office. Research, Development and Statistics Directorate.

Fergus, T.A. & Rowatt, W.C. (2014). Intolerance of uncertainty and personality: Experiential permeability is associated with difficulties tolerating uncertainty. *Personality and Individual Differences*, 58, 128–131.

Fitzpatrick, J.L. (2012). An introduction to context and its role in evaluation practice. *New Directions for Evaluation*, 135, 7–24.

Friendship, C. & Falshaw, L. (2003). Evaluating groupwork in prisons. In G. Towl (Ed.), *Psychology in Prisons*. Oxford: BPS Blackwell.

Gibson, J.J. (1979). *The Ecological Approach to Visual Perception*. Boston, MA: Houghton Mifflin.

Giles, G.M., & Clark-Wilson, J. (2013). *Brain Injury Rehabilitation: A Neurofunctional Approach*. New York, NY: Springer.

Gill, M. & Turbin, V. (1999). Evaluating realistic evaluation: Evidence from a study of CCTV. *Crime Prevention Studies*, 10, 179–199.

Glenberg, A.M., Witt, J.K., & Metcalfe, J. (2013). From the revolution to embodiment 25 years of cognitive psychology. *Perspectives on Psychological Science*, 8(5), 573–585.

Goffman, E. (1974). *Frame Analysis: An Essay on the Organization of Experience*. Cambridge, MA: Harvard University Press.

Goodwin, C. & Duranti, A. (1992). *Rethinking Context: Language as an Interactive Phenomenon*. Cambridge, UK: Cambridge University Press.

Graesser, A.C. & Magliano, J.P. (1991). Context and cognition. In R. Cohen & A.W. Siegel (Eds.), *Context and Development* (pp. 57–76). London: Lawrence Erlbaum Associates.

Greene, J.C. (2005). Context. In S. Mathison (Ed.), *Encyclopedia of Evaluation* (pp. 82–84). Thousand Oaks, CA: Sage.

Guastello, S.J., Koopmans, M. & Pincus, D. (2009). *Chaos and Complexity in Psychology*. Cambridge, UK: Cambridge University Press.

Hackley, C., Bengry-Howell, A., Griffin, C., Mistral, W., Szmigin, I. & Tiwsakul, R.A.H.N. (2013). Young adults and 'binge' drinking: A Bakhtinian analysis. *Journal of Marketing Management*, 29(7–8), 933–949.

Hartman, A. (1990). Many ways of knowing. *Social Work*, 35, 3–4.

Hollin, C.R. (1995). The meaning and implications of "programme integrity". In J. McGuire (Ed.), (pp. 195–208). Chichester: John Wiley & Sons.

Hough, M. (2010). Gold standard or fools gold? The pursuit of certainty in experimental criminology. *Criminology and Criminal Justice*, 10, 11–22.

Houts, A.C. (1991). The contextualist turn in empirical social science: Epistemological issues, methodological implications, and adjusted expectations. In R. Cohen & A.W. Siegel (Eds.), *Context and Development* (pp. 25–54). London: Lawrence Erlbaum Associates.

Howells, K. (1980). Social reactions to sexual deviance. In D.J. West (Ed.), *Sex Offenders in the Criminal Justice System*. Cambridge: University of Cambridge Institute of Criminology.

Hutchins, E. (1995). How a cockpit remembers its speeds. *Cognitive Science*, 19, 265–288.

Ireland, J.L. (2006). The effective management of bullying in prisons: Working towards an evidence-based approach. In G. Towl (Ed.), *Psychological Research in Prisons* (pp. 95–115). Oxford: Blackwell Publishing.

Jeronimus, B.F., Riese, H., Sanderman, R. & Ormel, J. (2014). Mutual reinforcement between neuroticism and life experiences: A five-wave, 16-year study to test reciprocal causation. *Journal of Personality and Social Psychology*, 107(4), 751–764.

Kauffman, S.A. (1993). *The Origins of Order: Self Organization and Selection in Evolution.* New York, NY: Oxford University Press.

Kelly, G.A. (1955). *The Psychology of Personal Constructs.* London: Routledge.

Kernick, D. (2006). Wanted – new methodologies for health service research. Is complexity theory the answer? *Family Practice,* 23(3), 385–390.

Kihlstrom, A. (2012). Luhmann's system theory in social work: Criticism and reflections. *Journal of Social Work,* 12, 287–299.

Kirchner, E.P., Kennedy, R.E. & Draguns, J. G. (1979). Assertion and aggression in adult offenders. *Behavior Therapy,* 10(4), 452–471.

Koch, S., Finkelman, D. & Kessel, F. (1999). *Psychology in Human Context: Essays in Dissidence and Reconstruction.* Chicago, IL: University of Chicago Press.

Lewin, K. (1935). *A Dynamic Theory of Personality: Selected Papers.* New York, NY: McGraw-Hill.

Ling, T. (2012). Evaluating complex and unfolding interventions in real time. *Evaluation,* 18(1), 79–91.

Lorenz, E.N. (1972, December). Predictability: Does the Flap of a Butterfly's Wings in Brazil Set Off a Tornado in Texas? Presented at the 139th Annual Meeting of the American Association for the Advancement of Science. Cambridge, Massachusetts.

Marchal, B., van Belle, S., van Olmen, J., Hoeree, T., & Kegels, G. (2012). Is realist evaluation keeping its promise? A review of published empirical studies in the field of health systems research. *Evaluation,* 18, 192–212.

McNeill, F. (2002). *Beyond 'What Works': How and Why Do People Stop Offending?.* Edinburgh: Criminal Justice and Social Work Development Centre for Scotland. Retrieved from http://strathprints.strath.ac.uk/39655/

Menary, R. (2007). *Cognitive Integration: Mind and Cognition Unbounded.* Basingstoke: Palgrave Macmillan.

Merlo, J. (2011). Contextual influences on the individual life course: Building a research framework for social epidemiology. *Psychosocial Intervention,* 20(1), 109–118.

Mesquita, B., Barrett, L.F. & Smith, E.R. (2010). *The Mind in Context.* New York, NY: Guilford Press.

Mischel, W. (1968). *Personality and Assessment.* New York, NY: Wiley.

Mischel, W. (1973). Toward a cognitive social learning reconceptualization of personality. *Psychological Review,* 80, 252–283.

Mischel, W. & Shoda, Y. (1995). A cognitive-affective system theory of personality: Reconceptualizing situations, dispositions, dynamics, and invariance in personality structure. *Psychological Review,* 102, 246–268.

Moen, P.E., Elder Jr, G.H. & Luscher, K.E. (1995). *Examining Lives in Context: Perspectives on the Ecology of Human Development.* Washington, DC: American Psychological Association.

Needs, A. (2016). Rehabilitation: Writing a new story. *The Psychologist,* 29(3), 192–195.

Neisser, U. (1976). *Cognition and Reality: Principles and Implications of Cognitive Psychology.* New York, NY: WH Freeman/Times Books/Henry Holt & Company.

Nonstad, K. & Webster, C.D. (2011). How to fail in the implementation of a risk assessment scheme or any other new procedure in your organization. *American Journal of Orthopsychiatry,* 81(1), 94–99.

O'Connor, K., Robert, M., Pérodeau, G. & Séguin, M. (2015). Trajectory-based methods in clinical psychology: A person centred narrative approach. *New Ideas in Psychology,* 39, 12–22.

Ogloff, J.R. (2002). Offender rehabilitation: From nothing works to what next? *Australian Psychologist,* 37, 245–252.

Ormerod, T., Barrett, E. & Taylor, P.J. (2008). Investigative sense-making in criminal contexts. In J.M. Schraggen, L.G. Miltello, T. Ormerod & R. Lipshitz (Eds.), *Naturalistic Decision Making and Macrocognition* (pp. 81–102). Aldershot: Ashgate.

Pachankis, J.E., & Goldfried, M.R. (2007). On the next generation of process research. *Clinical Psychology Review*, 27(6), 760–768.

Palmer, D.K. (2004). On the organism-environment distinction in psychology. *Behavior and Philosophy*, 32, 317–347.

Park, C.L. (2010). Making sense of the meaning literature: An integrative review of meaning making and its effects on adjustment to stressful life events. *Psychological Bulletin*, 136(2), 257.

Pawson, R. & Tilley, N. (1997). *Realistic Evaluation*. London: Sage.

Pickett, C.L., Gardner, W.L. & Knowles, M. (2004). Getting a cue: The need to belong and enhanced sensitivity to social cues. *Personality and Social Psychology Bulletin*, 30, 1095–1107.

Polaschek, D. L. (2012). An appraisal of the risk-need-responsivity (RNR) model of offender rehabilitation and its application in correctional treatment. *Legal and Criminological Psychology*, 17, 1–17.

Pycroft, A. (2014). Probation practice and creativity in England and Wales: A complex systems analysis. In A. Pycroft & C. Bartollas (Eds.), *Applying Complexity Theory: Whole Systems Approaches to Criminal Justice and Social Work* (pp. 199–220). Bristol: Policy Press.

Pycroft, A. & Bartollas, C. (2014). *Applying Complexity Theory: Whole Systems Approaches to Criminal Justice and Social Work*. Bristol: Policy Press.

Radley, A. (1977). Living on the horizon. In D. Bannister (Ed.), *New Perspectives in Personal Construct Psychology* (pp. 221–249). London: Academic Press.

Reis, H.T., Collins, W.A. & Berscheid, E. (2000). The relationship context of human behavior and development. *Psychological Bulletin*, 126, 844–872.

Rickles, D., Hawe, P. & Shiell, A. (2007). A simple guide to chaos and complexity. *Journal of Epidemiology and Community Health*, 61(11), 933–937.

Robbins, P. & Aydede, M. (2009). A short primer on situated cognition. In P. Robbins & M. Aydede (Eds.), *Cambridge Handbook of Situated Cognition* (pp. 3–10). Cambridge, MA: Cambridge University Press.

Rog, D.J. (2012). When background becomes foreground: Toward context-sensitive evaluation practice. *New Directions in Evaluation*, 135, 25–40.

Rogoff, B. (1982). Integrating context and cognitive development. In M.E. Lamb & A.L. Brown (Eds.), *Advances in Developmental Psychology* (Vol. 2, pp. 125–170). Hillsdale, NJ: Lawrence Erlbaum Associates.

Ross, E.C., Polaschek, D.L. & Ward, T. (2008). The therapeutic alliance: A theoretical revision for offender rehabilitation. *Aggression and Violent Behavior*, 13(6), 462–480.

Ross, M. (1989). Relation of implicit theories to the construction of personal histories. *Psychological Review*, 96(2), 341.

Rummler, G.A. & Brache, A.P. (1995). *Improving Performance: How to Manage the White Space on the Organization Chart* (2nd edn.). San Francisco, CA: Jossey-Bass.

Rutter, M. (1975). *Helping Troubled Children*. Harmondsworth: Penguin.

Rutter, M. (1987). Psychosocial resilience and protective mechanisms. *American Journal of Orthopsychiatry*, 57, 316–331.

Rycroft-Malone, J., Fontenla, M., Bick, D. & Seers, K. (2010). A realistic evaluation: The case of protocol-based care. *Implementation Science*, 5, 38.

Schegloff, E.A. (1993). Reflections on quantification in the study of conversation. *Research on Language and Social Interaction*, 26, 99–128.

Schoggen, P. (1991). Ecological psychology: One approach to development in context. In R. Cohen & A.W. Siegel (Eds.), *Context and Development* (pp. 281–304). London: Lawrence Erlbaum Associates.

Semin, G.R. (2007). Grounding communication: Synchrony. In A. Kruglaski & E.T. Higgins (Eds.), *Social Psychology: Handbook of Basic Principles* (2nd edn., pp. 630–644). New York, NY: Guilford Publications.

Semin, G.R. & Smith, E.R. (2002). Interfaces of social psychology with situated and embodied cognition. *Cognitive Systems Research*, 3, 385–396.

Shoda, Y., Cervone, D., & Downey, G. (2007). *Persons in Context: Building a Science of the Individual*. New York, NY: Guilford Press.

Siegel, A.W. & Cohen, R. (1991). Why a house is not a home? Constructing contexts for development. In R. Cohen & A.W. Siegel (Eds.), *Context and Development* (pp. 305–316). London: Lawrence Erlbaum Associates.

Smith, E.R. & Collins, E.C. (2010). Situated cognition. In B. Mesquita, L.F. Barrett & E.R. Smith (Eds.), *Mind in Context* (pp. 126–145). New York, NY: The Guilford Press.

Smith, E.R. & Conrey, F.R. (2009). The social context of cognition. In P. Robbins & M. Aydede (Eds.), *Cambridge Handbook of Situated Cognition* (pp. 454–466). Cambridge: Cambridge University Press.

Stillman, T.F. & Baumeister, R.F. (2009). Uncertainty, belongingness, and four needs for meaning. *Psychological Inquiry*, 20(4), 249–251.

Thomas-Peter, B.A. (2006). The needs of offenders and the process of changing them. In G. Towl (Ed.), *Psychological Research in Prisons* (pp. 40–53). Oxford: BPS Blackwell.

Tilley, N. (2000). *Realistic Evaluation: An Overview*. Paper presented at the Founding Conference of the Danish Evaluation Society. Retrieved from http://evidence-basedmanagement.com/wp-content/uploads/2011/11/nick_tilley.pdf.

Van Geert, P. (2003). Dynamic systems approaches and modeling of developmental processes. In J. Valsiner & K.J. Conolly (Eds.), *Handbook of Developmental Psychology* (pp. 640–672). London: Sage.

Van Geert, P. & Fischer, K.W. (2009). Dynamic systems and the quest for individual-based models of change and development. In J.P. Spencer, M.S. Thomas & J.L. McClelland (Eds.), *Toward a New Grand Theory of Development* (pp. 313–336). Oxford: Oxford University Press.

Vivian-Byrne, S. (2004). Changing people's minds. *Journal of Sexual Aggression*, 10, 181–192.

Vivian-Byrne, S.E. (2002). Using context and difference in sex offender treatment: An integrated systemic approach. *Journal of Sexual Aggression*, 8, 59–73.

Vygotsky, L.S. (1978). *Mind in Society: The Development of Higher Mental Process*. Cambridge, MA: Harvard University Press.

Walker, B.M. & Winter, D.A. (2005). Psychological disorder and reconstruction. In D.A. Winter & L.L. Viney (Eds.) *Personal Construct Psychotherapy: Advances in Theory, Practice and Research* (pp. 21–33). London: Whurr Publishers.

Ward, T. (2009). The extended mind theory of cognitive distortions in sex offenders. *Journal of Sexual Aggression*, 15, 247–259.

Ward, T. & Casey, A. (2010). Extending the mind into the world: A new theory of cognitive distortions in sex offenders. *Aggression and Violent Behavior*, 15, 49–58.

White, S.H. (1983). Developmental psychology, bewildered and paranoid: A reply to Kaplan. In R.M. Lerner (Ed.), *Developmental Psychology: Historical and Philosophical Perspectives* (pp. 233–239). Hillsdale, NJ: Lawrence Erlbaum Associates.

Wilson, R.A. & Clark, A. (2009). How to situate cognition: Letting nature take its course. In P. Robbins & M. Aydede (Eds.), *Cambridge Handbook of Situated Cognition* (pp. 55–77). Cambridge: Cambridge University Press.

# 2

# THE SOCIAL CONTEXT OF TRANSITION AND REHABILITATION

*Adrian Needs and Alethea Adair-Stantiall*

## The development and constriction of social agency

The capacity for adaptive change is an essential characteristic of biological and social systems (Bateson, 1972). The boundaried network of mutually generating and sustaining processes that comprise a system ensures its continued self-generation and self-organisation; interactions with other systems are necessary for its growth, learning and survival and to form more complex and adaptive systems (De Jaegher & Froese, 2009). Organisms live not just within, but by means of their environments and it is through embodied engagement and interaction with the world that mind emerges (Palmer, 2004; Shani, 2013). For human beings that world is principally one of other human beings. Those able to operate in such a world ('social agents') are both constitutive of and constituted *by* social interaction and mind is inherently relational in its functioning. This is evident even when people are not in the company of others. For example we can talk to ourselves, be guided by social norms or imagine what other people might think (De Jaegher & Froese, 2009). The present chapter argues that negative variants of the same processes that enable social agency and growth can constrict constructive engagement in life's transitions and adversities. Such engagement often requires implicit (and explicit) renegotiation and reconciliation in core areas that, for convenience (after Ashforth, 2001) can be referred to as identity, meaning, control and belonging. A framework based on these areas permits integration of bodies of research and theory that are often neglected in forensic psychology. They can also be seen as the necessary characteristics of a system capable of adaptive change and social agency, negative variants of which may heighten the risk of engaging in behaviour that is harmful to others whilst also limiting the capacity for adaptive change. Custodial environments often reflect and perpetuate these patterns, currently negating a substantial amount of the effort and resources that are put into rehabilitation. There is sufficient consistency in the literature on conditions that facilitate therapeutic change to suggest that it is possible to facilitate more adaptive forms of engagement and reconciliation with life's unfolding, although such efforts must become established more consistently in the daily life of mainstream custodial environments. This has less to do with 'being nice to' prisoners and patients than with effectiveness and bringing to bear ways of understanding that would come as little surprise to scientists in fields such as physics and biology.

Consider this extract from an important paper by Karlen Lyons-Ruth concerning a teenage single mother who is "doing very well" with her nine-month-old infant:

> She is engaging her preverbal baby in a constant dialogue of affectively inflected sounds and gestures, she is following his focus of attention, she is responding sensitively to his cues, and she is assisting in the elaboration of his initiative. He responds by entering enthusiastically into the positive rhythms of the relationship, and we see little distress.
>
> (Lyons-Ruth, 2007, p. 601)

In this account the caregiver is certainly being attentive and caring but her responsiveness goes considerably beyond this. There is a moment-by-moment coordination with the baby's actions and experiencing that might be expected to contribute to a context of reciprocity, mutual acknowledgement and a sense of connectedness. An orientation towards 'contingent responsiveness' appears to be present in newborns and an interest in sharing in the intentions of the other through engagement in joint activities is evident even before the appearance of language (Trevarthen, 2002). These processes demonstrate intersubjectivity, the propensity to apprehend, participate in and coordinate with the subjectivities (intentions, perspectives and emotional states) of others.

Intersubjective processes are intrinsic to social interaction and to social development. Embodied mind emerges through active, reciprocal engagement in the world and increasingly, intersubjectivity has been seen as the 'psychological system' or 'space between persons' in which development takes place, including development of the self (Marks-Tarlow, 1999) and moral experience (Parish, 2014). Some actions are only possible or have significance in interaction with other people, whilst the meanings of the world to others and the meanings of other's actions are experienced through communication and collaboration in relation to joint experience (De Jaegher & Froese, 2009; Trevarthen, 2002). People as social agents typically engage with other people as *subjects* rather than as *objects*, can make sense *with* them rather than just *of* them and what emerges is not reducible to the behaviour of either in isolation (De Jaegher, Di Paolo & Gallagher, 2010). Seen in these terms, the past emphasis in much of attachment theory on overt behaviours indicative of seeking proximity to the caregiver or the activation of a specialised motivational system at times of loss or separation may provide an account that is incomplete (Lyons-Ruth, 2007). The sequence described above by Lyons-Ruth highlights instead a moment-by-moment exchange of affective cues that requires continued sensitivity to the cues of the infant. It is this kind of process that plays a dominant role in the regulation of stress responses and maintains affectively positive states of reciprocal engagement that encourage elaboration and connection. Evidence suggests that emerging intersubjectivity can to a very substantial degree override temperamental differences, genetic predispositions and biological motives (Lyons-Ruth, 2007).

Such a process might be regarded as prototypical of secure attachment. It has parallels with, and implications for, the creation of a 'secure base' of the sort that has been advocated in contexts such as forensic mental health nursing (Aiyegbusi, 2004); this will be returned to later in this chapter. Secure attachment provides conditions necessary for the developing individual to explore the world free from negative arousal and a sense of threat. It enables the person to resolve confusion, to "broaden and build", and "opens a person's mind to new possibilities and perspectives" (Mikulincer & Shaver, 2007, p. 142). Openness facilitates the integration of one's own perspectives with those of others (Kyselo, 2016), thus harnessing more fully the operation of intersubjectivity in ongoing development. It is heavily influenced by trust (Gillespie, 2011), usually defined in terms of a willingness to accept vulnerability and uncertainty in relation to the intentions of others (Rousseau, Sitkin, Burt & Camerer, 1998). In the language of complexity theory it stimulates development 'at the edge of chaos', where there is sufficient stability in a system to allow it to confront and accommodate the unfamiliar without being overwhelmed.

Of course the relational context of development can be far from optimal. Erratic and unpredictable responsiveness from caregivers of the sort associated with anxious attachment appears to amplify negative arousal and preoccupations with availability and responsiveness; a more consistent lack of responsiveness is associated with avoidant attachment where availability and responsiveness come to be ignored or dismissed (Mikulincer & Shaver, 2007). Life may seem less painful that way and certainly less ambiguous. In disorganised attachment, the fluctuating needs of the parent take precedence over the states of the young child until the child learns to reverse roles and assume the initiative (Lyons-Ruth, 2007). The likelihood of a child experiencing abuse in such an environment may be elevated and in inverse proportion to processes such as social support that promote resilience and recovery, but the potential long-term impact of less dramatic failures of contingent responsiveness should not be underestimated (Needs, this volume). It is equally important that attachment 'styles' should not be assumed to be immutable and mutually exclusive, like blood groups (Ansbro, 2008). Changes in contexts and recent experiences in the interpersonal domain can have modifying effects (Baldwin et al., 1996). The influence of contingently responsive, intersubjective exchanges remains pervasive (Gillespie & Cornish, 2010), although some developmental consequences and patterns of engagement with the environment may work against adaptive change.

The latter can be understood in terms of the interaction of processes within the wider functional system of organism and environment (Palmer, 2004) generating and sustaining a form of stasis or equilibrium to which functioning tends to return. To take a simple physical analogy, a ping-pong ball in a basin will tend to return to the same resting point. This therefore has the characteristics of an 'attractor' and the system is no longer truly 'open' (to behaving differently and in a more complex manner) as long as its self-organisation and the conditions acting upon this remain stable. The capacity for continuous adaptive development, involving an increase in complexity and the creation of novel forms (Van Geert & Fischer, 2009), becomes constricted. The system is no longer growing at the edge of chaos and is, in effect, constrained to repeat familiar patterns. In human terms this can have profoundly deleterious effects on ongoing development and therefore mental health and well-being. Problems in this domain have, for example, been characterised in existentialist formulations by Heidegger and others as involving a state of closedness to the world (Cooper, Chak, Cornish & Gillespie, 2013), in personal construct theory as a failure to revise one's anticipations and causal models in a way that respects those of others (Walker & Winter, 2007) and, in the early venture into a transdiagnostic approach of 'personal illness', as egocentricity (Foulds, 1965). Other approaches have drawn attention to features that indicate and perpetuate constriction and closedness, such as repeated enactment of rigid sequences of behaviour, cognition and emotional preoccupations (Hayes & Yasinski, 2015), low dimensionality of meaning systems and self-definitions (Button, 1983; Marks-Tarlow, 1999; Stein & Markus, 1996), poor perspective-taking (Needs, Salmann & Kiddle, 2011) and reductions in exploratory social behaviour (Puchalska-Wasyl, Chmielnicka-Kuter & Oleś, 2008). These might be seen as the human equivalent of the ping-pong ball going in ever- decreasing circles before coming to rest.

A key part of this is the relationship over time between person and environment, including the often reciprocal influence of individuals on environments and events. An important process is that individuals often have a major role in what happens to them, increasing their exposure to certain kinds of events and circumstances which may tighten the screw of adversity on already strained or inadequate personal, social and material resources. Thus, for example, the preoccupations and poor self-regulation associated with borderline personality disorder can lead to a preponderance of difficulties with relationships, health or the law (Pagano et al., 2004; Shevlin, Dorahy, Adamson & Murphy, 2007), socially obnoxious behaviour can result in ostracism (Hales, Kassner, Williams & Graziano, 2016) and being troubled or troublesome can reduce opportunities that might have helped life develop in a different direction (Dobash et al., 2007). The actual quality of what is afforded by an individual's environment should not be overlooked: some people are or have been impoverished, marginalised or in relationships with intractable people (Weaver & McNeill, 2015) although the literature on resilience suggests that effects are far from uniformly detrimental (Ungar, 2013). Equally, sometimes the advent of other processes (such as finding the 'right' person or occupation) can set in motion a more benign trajectory, but this may require an active willingness to engage in a process of 'intentional self-change' (Paternoster et al., 2016).

These processes are consonant with the transactional model of development described by Rutter (1975) using the analogy of a river. In this "the constituents of the river become altered and modified by the minerals in the river bed over which it flows, the pollution it encounters at various points and the additional impetus provided by the multiple tiny streams which join it on its way to the sea" and "each new encounter is influenced by the last" (p. 115). In human life there are also recurring patterns in engagement with the environment that shape and reflect what might be regarded as most distinctive of a given individual. A degree of stability is normal (see Kihlstrom, 2012, for an account of relevant processes) and necessary for the system to develop at the edge of chaos without being overwhelmed. However problems arise when the system is not open to new possibilities and perspectives. Aspects of individual functioning that exist to serve action may come primarily to serve their own preservation (c.f. Becker, 1964). This failure of the corrective and constitutive influence of intersubjectivity may occur when the subjectivity of others is experienced as a real or potential threat to the sustainability and viability of one's own perspectives and intentions. Attempts at preservation of subjectivity in the face of 'existential threat' may become increasingly extreme in an escalating 'criminal spin' (Elisha, Idrisis & Ronel, 2013). An individual who has become locked in such a cycle may also be likely to have difficulty in changing in other contexts, such as rehabilitation. The term that is central to the exploration of adaptive change and its difficulties is *transition*.

## A framework for transition: processes and pitfalls

A perspective based on the idea of transition highlights the interconnectedness of factors internal and external to the individual and suggests that awareness of the situation of the person in transition should be regarded as a core therapeutic skill (Serin & Lloyd, 2009; Serin, Lloyd & Hanby, 2010). Even what might appear to be relatively straightforward role transitions in the course of a work career can be seen as requiring successful reconciliation within several important areas of psychological need or motive (Ashforth, 2001). Ashforth's framework is based on four overlapping needs or motives: *identity* (a sense of personal coherence and continuity), *meaning* (a sense of purpose, values and goals), *control* (a sense of agency and self-efficacy) and *belonging* (a sense of membership, affiliation, support, openness, mutuality and connectedness). Its applicability beyond the occupational field is helped by the congruence of Ashforth's framework with, for example, the fundamental human needs postulated in areas including personal recovery in mental health (Leamy et al., 2011). The four interconnected areas can also be seen as having their origins in mechanisms of self-organisation intrinsic to an autonomous sense-making system that has the potential for social agency. The first author has found the framework to have considerable utility in integrating factors relevant to the problems of former members of the armed forces (Needs, 2014), the role of life events and situational processes in relation to violent crime (Needs, 2015) and the dynamics of trauma (Needs, this volume). It can cast new light on facets such as identity and narrative that figure prominently in the literature on desistance from offending (e.g. Healy, 2014; Maruna, 2001) and on some aspects that have figured less prominently.

## *Identity*

'Identity' and the related concept of 'self' have been defined and differentiated in several ways and a number of processes seen as involved in their generation (Oyserman, Elmore & Smith, 2012; Rocque, Posick & Paternoster, 2016; Schwartz et al., 2011); here, space permits only a rather crude and conflated sketch for heuristic purposes. Mind may not be brainbound but it is embodied, providing both an autonomous locus of experience and the means of action (De Jaegher & Di Paolo, 2007; Kyselo, 2016). From an evolutionary standpoint, such a first-person perspective is integral to the capacity to form and act on intentions that is intrinsic to agency (Ward, 2017). What William James (1890) referred to as the 'I' or 'self as knower' is crucial in adaptation and learning, constituting "an active, self-maintaining knowledge structure – that is, a schema" (Pratkanis & Greenwald, 1985, p. 323) or "self-organizing dynamical system" (Vallacher, Read & Nowack, 2002, p. 271), which "organises and interprets experience" (Fonagy & Target, 1997). Such facets also make the sense of self a unique and ever-present reference point, "probably the major single anchorage point to which new stimuli are related" (Rosenberg, 1965, p. 323). Yet a sense of separateness and uniqueness does not operate in isolation from the other fundamental biological 'given' of connectedness and belonging (Sander, 2008) and, according to Baumeister and Leary (1995) belonging is a basic human need of pivotal evolutionary significance. A major prerequisite for the emergence of a coherent sense of self is that the person has a sense of distinctness, "a sense of coherence through time, which involves experiencing oneself as a responsible and unique unity"; another prerequisite, particularly necessary for social agency, is a sense of participation in the world of other people – "a sense of connectedness, openness or belonging to others" (Kyselo, 2016, p. 604). The reconciliation of these potential sources of tension has been seen as crucial to identity and the self-determination that emerges from 'autonomy within connectedness' (see Lichtwarck-Aschoff, Van Geert, Bosma & Kunnen, 2008).

A continuous need to reconcile these processes results in the experience of self being "inherently fragile" Kyselo (2016, p. 610) and a substantial body of research and theory supports the idea that the self as an autonomous sense-making system has a concern with its own viability and continuity. As Wright (1984) suggested, because of its "ubiquity as a reference point for his experiences, both good and bad, the behaving person develops a concern for the well-being and worth of the entity that he or she defines as self" (p. 118). However, such a sense of well-being and worth is largely dependent on relations with other people (Leary, 2007). In the words of Athay and Darley (1981, p. 290), "all actors, powerful and weak, depend on each other for confirmation of their perspectives, affirmation of their performances, and other psychological commodities". The promise and provision of validation has been seen as central to compatibility and commitment in dyadic or group relationships (Duck, 1980; Iversen et al., 2008). The negative side of this is that a sense of personal viability and coherence can be undermined when validation is not forthcoming, such as might occur with the dissolution of an intimate relationship (Cruwys et al., 2014; Duck & Lea, 1983), major role transitions (Sadeh & Karniol, 2012), social isolation (Stein & Tuval-Mashiach, 2015), or where an individual's needs have long been subordinated to those of another (Linehan, 1993; Lyons-Ruth, 2007).

A variety of strategies are available to the individual who wishes to defend, restore or enhance understanding of self (Luke & Stopa, 2009). Problematic behaviour and experience may be especially likely at the interface between distinctness and connectedness when the sense of self is precarious and social integration (and validation) is limited. So, for example, whilst the centrality of immediate threats to self-esteem in anger and aggression has been noted by a numerous researchers (e.g. Baumeister, Smart & Boden, 1996), sensitivity to such threats is especially likely when self-esteem is unstable (Kernis & Goldman, 2003; Kernis, Granneman & Barclay, 1989). Unstable self-esteem is also associated with, for example, heightened reactivity to daily stressors that have implications for self-evaluation (Greenier et al., 1999) and with paranoid thinking where the intentions of other people are a major preoccupation (Thewissen et al., 2007, 2008). Elevated reactivity to external feedback is characteristic of a wider lack of clarity, coherence and continuity of the self-concept (Campbell, Assanand & Di Paula, 2003; Ritchie et al., 2011; Zeigler-Hill & Showers, 2007). Self-concept clarity, with origins in conditions similar to those described in relation to attachment, has been shown to influence and be influenced by the commitments that are an integral part of identity and to underpin both trait self-esteem and momentary self-evaluations (Schwartz et al., 2011; Wong, Vallacher & Nowack, 2014).

A related construct that has been explored increasingly in relation to any association between aggression and the sense of self is shame (Tangney, Stuewig & Hafez, 2011; Velotti, Elison & Garofalo, 2014). It has also been linked to substance misuse (Dearing, Stuewig & Tangney, 2005) and recidivism in young offenders (Hosser, Windzio & Greve, 2008). Shame has been characterised in terms of a pervasive sense of unacceptability and derogation (Gilbert & Procter, 2006; Maercker & Horn, 2013). Thus located in the world of others, the way is open to feelings of inferiority, a desire to conceal deficiencies and an enduring sense of vulnerability (Tangney, Stuewig & Mashek, 2007). Apprehension of the expressed, implicit or imaginary perspectives of others may be coloured by a preoccupation with events that instigate or threaten shame such as perceived insults, infidelity or betrayal (Lawrence & Taft, 2013). These preoccupations influence how individuals cope with difficulties in relationships and contribute to a climate that increases the likelihood of conflict and 'negative reciprocity' (Buss & Duntley, 2011; Covert, Tangney, Maddux & Heleno, 2003; Salazar, 2015). Many episodes of intimate partner violence may involve such dynamics (Hundt & Holahan, 2012) especially when individuals lack other means of restoring threatened self-esteem and attempts to elude the implications of such events extend to rigid, constricted, short-term thinking akin to an 'escape from self' (Baumeister, 1990). To accept perceived violations of one's personal rights and freedom can itself be construed as shameful, a pattern characteristic of 'cultures of honour' (Altheimer, 2013) although the enactment of antisocial behaviours can be confined to situations seen as relevant to a particular social identity (Strocka, 2008, cited in Boduszek & Hyland, 2011). An indication of the intensity of feeling that can be evoked by threats to identity is provided by Felson and Steadman's (1983) contention that many lethal altercations involve the escalation of 'identity assaults'.

## Meaning

According to Kyselo (2016), in addition to a person as a self-organising system producing "a perspective on the world from which she can act as the centre and by which she separates herself from the rest of the world", sense-making (or meaning) "emerges because a person evaluates and predicts the environment with regard to what matters to the continuation of her existence as a whole" (p. 604). As we saw earlier, at a fundamental level identity can be construed as an embodied system with a sense of its own functioning and concern for its own validity and viability, geared for action and channelled by anticipation. As such it abstracts information relevant to its own purposes, including goals and most fundamentally of all, its own continuity. It was noted above that a sense of unacceptability can be accompanied by a sense of vulnerability and an unstable, unclear sense of self heightens sensitivity to external feedback; in Kernis and Goldman's (2003) phrase the self is "continually on the line". A lack of validation of self, perspectives and intentions (including the attainability of goals) in a person's life may elevate a preoccupation with guarding against invalidation. This requires vigilance regarding the perspectives and intentions of others towards the self. Additional defences include 'semantic barriers', analogous to the operation of the body's immune system, that help neutralise threats to the person's perspectives and intentions by means that can include denigrating those of others (Gillespie, 2011). This mistrustful orientation may predispose to a sense of affront and provocation when value, validity or viability of the self is called into question and is discernible in, for example, the sensitivities of chronically lonely individuals (Check, Perlman & Malamuth, 1985; Hawkley & Cacioppo, 2010), including those that work against change (Winter, 1992). Past and present experiences of relationships may leave a sense of vulnerability that demands vigilance and punishment of transgressors (Batchelor, 2005).

Pronounced concerns with betrayal by others and the impossibility of exercising self-control resemble prominent themes identified in the implicit beliefs of violence-prone individuals such as intimate partner violence perpetrators (Gilchrist, 2009; Pornari, Dixon & Humphreys, 2013), rapists (Murphy & Winder, 2016; Polaschek & Gannon, 2004) and sexual murderers (Beech, Fisher & Ward, 2005). Something similar is represented in questionnaire-based or clinical studies of personality disorder (Beck et al., 2001; Bhar, Brown & Beck, 2008; Livesley, 2007). They may be given greater coherence by being embedded in a wider narrative of the person in relation to others (Presser, 2009) although events can challenge this and new reconciliations occur over time (Ferrito, Needs & Adshead, 2017). Like the self for which they furnish a context, they can be seen in cognitive terms as "information-processing structures" (Ward & Maruna, 2007, p. 85) and they provide a platform for, for example, 'scripts', 'biases' and moral justifications that have been identified in perpetrators of violence (Gannon, 2009; Niebieszczanski, Harkins, Judson, Smith & Dixon, 2015). Following the work of McAdams (e.g. 2008) the idea that a personal narrative, "personal myth" (Ward & Maruna, 2007, p. 85) or "unfolding personal story" (Canter & Youngs, 2009, 2013) may related to an offending trajectory has become widely recognised if not always accepted (Ward, 2012).

In addition to constructing "an agent with thoughts, feelings and goals in an event" (Graci & Fivush, 2016, p. 8) and embodying 'positions' (as narrator or central protagonist), narratives also imply audiences that are real, historical, generalised or imagined (Kögler, 2012; Meichenbaum, 2006). Like other stories, to achieve coherence narratives demand expression, an intersubjective process (Nolan & Walsh, 2012) even if degraded by the narrator's engagement with a limited or distorted view of the subjectivity of others. This may occur due to developmental impairment of the capacity for reflective functioning (Fonagy & Target, 1997; Lyons-Ruth, 2007; Ryan, 2005), isolation from the regulatory and normative influences of social interaction (Rierdan, 1980) or seeing the world through an 'affective lens' of negative emotionality (Ward, 2017). Yet there is more than one way of expressing a narrative and the identity that a narrative implies may be unfettered by respect for other people's subjectivity. Characterising oneself in terms such as 'victim' or 'revenger' may do more than imply casting others, including victims, into complementary roles; they may then be treated as 'objects' to be used, 'vehicles' to vent feelings on or as a participant in a pseudo-relationship (Canter & Youngs, 2009, 2013). Thus an individual who molests children sexually may adopt a role such as 'master' or 'teacher' that requires a child to complete this (see Goffman, 1974) by acting as a 'slave' or 'student' (Navathe, Ward & Rose, 2013). This is unlikely to require accurate perspective-taking (see Hermans, 2001). To consider other possible variations, some violent or criminal acts can bring greater clarity of identity and purpose by setting the individual apart from significant others and society (Howells, 1978) whilst some may be perpetrated in part because the experience itself promises greater elaboration, coherence or insight (Needs, 1992a; Winter, 2003). In other cases attempts to maintain inflexible meaning systems may collapse under the weight of invalidation (Howells, 1981; Ruotolo, 1968).

## Control

It has been suggested that intersubjectivity is a central process in both engagement with others and psychological development as a social and moral agent. To engage with another person as a subject (i.e. capable of subjectivity) rather than object involves apprehension of the existence of intentions, perspectives and feelings that are external to one's own and the origins of this capacity appear to lie in repeated early experiences of contingency, responsiveness and mutuality in the exchange of affective cues in coordinated, shared activity. It enables people to participate in or take the perspectives of others, providing vantage points for reflecting upon and changing personal perspectives or positions. Whilst it has been argued that this is a central process in the construction of a coherent identity (Berman, Schwartz, Kurtines & Berman, 2001), moving between positions – a psychological distancing from immersion in a single perspective – has also been seen as the basis of agency that allows action to reach beyond an immediate situation (Gillespie, 2012; Kögler, 2012). It is possible mentally to travel in time between interpretations of the present, memories of the past and imaginings of the future, to span perspectives associated with personal pronouns from 'I' through to 'they', or move between different positions of the I inspired by culture, media and social affiliations (Boucher & Scoboria, 2015; Hermans, 2008; Zittoun & Gillespie, 2014). Drawing attention to movement between positions allows lack of self- control (including impulsivity) to be re-framed as a lack of agency, a failure to respond to one's perspectives and intentions from other standpoints or extricate oneself from a developing situation (Gillespie, 2012).This may be especially likely under conditions of social exclusion (see below).

A 'dialogue' between positions is facilitated greatly if there is openness between them (Cooper et al., 2013) and a range of semantic barriers, including rigid and polarised views can preserve one's positions from transformation by contact with other positions. Amongst the most persistent and effective impediments to openness is mistrust (Gillespie, 2011; Gillespie & Richardson, 2011). As we have seen, mistrust is well-represented in investigations of the beliefs of violent or disordered individuals. Just as attachment security "opens a person's mind to new possibilities and perspectives" (Mikulincer & Shaver, 2007, p. 142), a pervasive sense of vulnerability to the intentions and perspectives of others may result in unwillingness to engage in social interaction as the negotiation of "an intersubjectively open process" (Shani, 2013).This may help to prevent the self and sense-making "unraveling through contact with other information sources" (Marks-Tarlow, 1999, p. 337) but closed- mindedness typically incurs costs. Flexible exploration is likely to be limited further by lack of sharing in mutual encounters (Lyons-Ruth, 2007), limited perspective-taking (Schwartz et al., 2011) anger and associated attributions (Gerace, Day, Casey & Mohr, 2013). Living in a precarious world requires a readiness to mobilise barriers at the expense of more complex sense-making (Marks-Tarlow, 1999) and low dimensionality of the cognitive system is associated with limited apprehension of other perspectives (e.g. Olson & Partington, 1977).This may also be a source of premature judgement ('seizing') and rigid adherence to conclusions and solutions ('freezing': see Acar-Burkay, Fennis & Warlop, 2014; Roets,Van Hiel & Cornelis, 2006) and may contribute to a reliance upon restricted involvements and styles of engagement that may limit scope for the wider exercise of anticipation and resilience (Côté & Reker, 1979; Fransella, 1972; Stein & Markus, 1996; Ward, 2017). It is possible to keep threatened invalidation at bay through the attempted operation of a 'false self', but barriers confine as well as protect (Laing, 1960). A lack of openness constrains authentic channelling into 'possible selves' (Markus & Nurius, 1986) that may provide a foothold for change, whilst closing off the individual from the acknowledgement by others that may validate these positions (Kögler, 2012).

Through closed-mindedness agency is diminished and apparently self-defeating and perplexing behaviour may be maintained because the individual, in effect, has no better ways of posing life's 'questions' (Kelly, 1970; Needs, 1992a). One dysfunctional form of this is what Kelly (1955) referred to as 'hostility' (see Needs & Jones, 2017). In this an individual takes the initiative by attempting to impose his or her subjectivity on others. Behaviour may take the form of "destructive self-confirmatory actions, which function to preserve his mistaken expectations and flawed causal models" and "may result in actions designed to prove the model correct or lead to the rationalization of any subsequent discourse" (Ward, 2017, p. 26). This kind of process, consistent with, for example, Toch's (1969) notion of the violent 'self-image promoter', may also be one of the mechanisms by which ongoing development is impeded and an individual comes to move in ever-decreasing circles. In contrast to unreflective rigidity or impulsivity based on immersion in a single perspective, autonomous behaviour "has a quality of openness and flexibility" (Ryan, 2005, p. 989) and this, as noted above, tends to accompany secure attachment (Mikulincer & Arad, 1999).

## *Belonging*

Human beings have evolved to make connections with other people (Blackhart, Baumeister & Twenge, 2006). It has been argued that survival of the individual depended largely on acceptance (and avoiding exclusion) by the group just as survival of the group depended on the commitment and coordination of its constituent members (Baumeister & Leary, 1995; Leary & Cottrell, 2013). Furthermore, the generation of culture and socially distributed learning, enabling people to integrate and build upon the knowledge of others, has been seen as a major catalyst to human evolution (Lyons-Ruth, 2007). Human capacities such as self-regulation and participation in shared systems of meaning emerged in such an innately social context (Stillman & Baumeister, 2013) and, whilst navigating the physical environment may have nurtured a propensity to construct predictive causal models (Ward, 2017), exploring the human environment through coordinated social activity is likely to have been an inextricable part of this (Lyons-Ruth, 2007).

Some of these processes are paralleled within the development of the individual. As systems, individuals organise and are sustained through relatedness and interaction with other systems. Social interaction is a "co-regulated, self-sustaining pattern of joint activity" (De Jaegher et al., 2010, p. 443) in which people participate in each other's sense-making through coordination. It is a process that is enabled by, but also enables individual minds (De Jaegher & Froese, 2009). This builds on differentiation and reconciliation of separateness and connectedness and experiences of responsiveness and reciprocity in early exchanges with those to whom the individual is oriented for safety (Kyselo, 2016; Mikulincer & Shaver, 2013). The dynamics of intersubjective exchanges continue to shape the system and create patterns that are not reducible to individuals in isolation (Shoda, Tiernan & Mischel, 2002). Mutual and reciprocal relating to others fosters a sense of connectedness (Weaver & McNeill, 2015). By the same token, social exclusion (or rejection or ostracism), where connectedness is diminished and issues may be raised concerning an individual's acceptability as well as acceptance, can have major consequences. These include (with echoes of Ashforth's framework) undermining of self-esteem, sense of meaningful existence, control and belonging (Knowles, 2013; Williams, 2001, 2007). Social exclusion takes a variety of forms, its behavioural consequences are affected by a range of contextual factors and major influences on individual differences in response have been identified; however effects can be profound (De Wall & Twenge, 2013; Richman & Leary, 2009; Twenge et al., 2001).

Experiences of rejection contrived in experimental work typically lead to emotional numbing rather than emotional distress (Blackhart, Nelson, Knowles & Baumeister, 2009). Often accompanied by a decrease in positive and an increase in negative behaviour towards others even when this is self-defeating, this may indicate a relinquishing of self-regulation when engagement with others (the primary purpose they exist to serve) is compromised (Stillman & Baumeister, 2013); the means for regulation of social interaction are also the means for self-regulation (De Jaegher, Peräkylä & Stevanovic, 2016). Self-regulation may be resumed if it is believed to lead to acceptance (Blackhart et al., 2006) but in the absence of this an individual may shift into a mode of 'cognitive deconstruction' characterised by decreased awareness of self, emotions, values or consequences of actions (De Wall, Baumeister, Stillman & Gailliot, 2007; Twenge, Catanese & Baumeister, 2002, 2003). Self-esteem may become unstable. Amongst the contextual factors affecting the nature of an individual's response to rejection are persistence and chronicity, likelihood of repair and construal of instigating events (Richman & Leary, 2009). Anger often accompanies perceived rejection but appears to be less an intrinsic response to social exclusion than a reaction to experiencing instigating circumstances as involving unfairness, injustice or other violations (Leary & Leder, 2009; Richman & Leary, 2009). This highlights the pivotal role in social engagement of apprehension of the intentions and perspectives of the other in relation to personal concerns and how these are often evaluated in 'moral' terms (Needs, this volume; Parish, 2014). Aggressive behaviour can then function as a means to punish, deter, or restore control over a situation (Leary, Twenge & Quinlivan, 2006) and the neutralising of threatened self- blame and the assertion of one's moral identity may facilitate this (e.g. Niebieszczcanski et al., 2015; Vecina & Marzana, 2016); reorganising of self may be evaded through attempted regulation, not of self but of the subjectivity of another.

This process may be especially relevant to some instances of intimate partner violence (Lila, Gracia & Murgui, 2013), including relationships where a preoccupation with rejection may come to be a self-fulfilling prophecy (Downey, Freitas, Michelis & Khouri, 1998). The victim is not necessarily the source of perceived rejection and sometimes the instigating events appear in themselves quite trivial (Pedersen, Gonzales & Miller, 2000). Many examples of intimate partner violence can be seen as involving anxiously attached people who have an elevated sensitivity to rejection along with related 'hyperactivation' strategies such as vigilance regarding the relational intentions of others towards self. This tends to be tempered with doubt, pessimism and ready intensification of negative affect (Dutton & White,

2012; Mikulincer & Shaver, 2013). The 'deactivating' strategies associated with attachment avoidance of limited empathy, self-awareness or use of interpersonal support also do little to promote successful relationships and are likely to contribute to situations of conflict. Meta-analysis indicates that insecure attachment heightens the risk of all types of criminality even in the absence of psychopathology (Ogilvie, Newman, Todd & Peck, 2014). The period after dissolution of a formerly intimate relationship (see Duck & Lea, 1983) can be one of increased risk for homicide (Silverman & Mukherjee, 1987) or sexual offences (Marshall, 1989), perhaps aggravated by the effects of heavy drinking in the wake of the separation (Day, Howells, Heseltine, & Casey, 2003).

Few events highlight an association between violence and rejection as conspicuously as school shootings in the United States (Leary, Kowalski, Smith & Phillips, 2003), but in a generally comparable age group a sense of exclusion or marginalising that extends beyond peers has been seen as contributing to affiliation in gangs; here individuals join with others in a similar situation to themselves, united also by norms which are a reversal of those of the wider community and by lifestyles that proclaim that rejection is mutual (Boduszek & Hyland, 2011). Belonging and meaning are often closely related (Jetten et al., 2014; Lambert et al., 2013; Stavrova & Luhmann, 2016). As intimate partner violence illustrates, however, many examples of an association between rejection and violence concern individuals with an ostensibly more conventional lifestyle. Some instances are likely to involve narcissistic individuals with high but fragile (unstable) self-esteem who tend to settle for nothing less than admiration (Twenge & Campbell, 2003). Further research is needed to explore possible links between the sorts of degrading of cognitive functioning following social exclusion found by Baumeister and colleagues and the thinking 'skills' targeted by cognitive skills programmes. This should also take into account apparent similarities between the latter and the problems in reflective functioning associated with insecure attachment and flawed intersubjectivity reported by Fonagy and Target (1997). It might also include consideration of how such ways of engaging the world may be perpetuated by resonance between early experiences and a custodial environment where both safety and responsiveness of care are likely to be less than optimal.

## Custodial environments

Prisons and other secure environments and the individuals within them are far from homogeneous (Gadon, Johnstone & Cooke, 2006; Ross & Pfafflin, 2007). Nonetheless, the following sketch includes examples of processes that may be applicable fairly widely. These might be expected to complicate further the possibility of reconciliation within the areas outlined above.

Following incarceration, views of self may become unstable with removal from previous interaction partners and restricted opportunities for interactions, roles and relationships (Asencio & Burke, 2011) whilst reminders of defectiveness and exclusion from society are never far away (Ross, Polaschek & Ward, 2008). The pre-prison self may appear to have reduced relevance and may be a source of vulnerability, whilst needing to be protected in order to maintain a degree of continuity with past and future (Schmid & Jones, 1991). 'Front management', often involving the presentation of a tough, masculine persona, can seem necessary to prevent exploitation and bullying while maintaining a sense of autonomy and social legitimacy. This typically entails a willingness to embrace challenges to identity such as confrontation (Bandyopadhay, 2006; Butler, 2008; De Viggiani, 2006, 2007, 2012). The alternative can be the acceptance of 'alienative modes' such as withdrawal or servility (King & Elliott, 1977; Sykes, 1958). A false front may come to merge with an individual's pre-prison identity but, combined with awareness that others are doing the same, can stifle opportunities for relationships based on openness and trust (Schmid & Jones, 1991). Authentic intersubjectivity is constricted and without openness, individuals may come to rely instead on schematic processing and hostile group norms (Perry & Sibley, 2013).

As in gang membership, such norms may involve the repudiation of those of outside society (Peat & Winfree, 1992). An adversarial, 'dog eat dog', 'look after Number One' view of the world may be reflected and perpetuated by existing and emergent concerns in the restricted environment and taken up more widely. (A similar effect may be found in relation to the volatile relationships in women's prisons with a high prevalence of 'borderline' characteristics amongst the prisoners; as Farquharson (2004) noted, there may also be parallels with the dynamics of certain 'reality TV' shows.) This survival-oriented stance may be exacerbated by aspects of the experience of prison such as bullying, lack of safety, opportunity and poor facilities (Day & Doyle, 2010; Fortune, Ward & Polaschek, 2014; Ireland, 2002). Conditions may be seen as discrepant with standards of decency and morality (Liebling, 2004) and the legitimate (fair, respectful and ethical) use of authority. Many rules can be seen as arbitrary and petty (King & McDermott, 1990) and some prisoners adopt a position towards staff and society of 'condemning the condemners' (Sykes & Matza, 1957). Narratives of injustice (Schinkel, 2015) are no more a basis for personal growth than those of condemnation (Maruna, 2001) and it is in the area of opportunities for personal development that a perceived lack of legitimacy may be felt most acutely (Brown & Toyoki, 2013).

Facets such as idleness, apathy, boredom and limited access to goods occur alongside a loss of responsibilities as a citizen and lack of control over external events to erode autonomy (De Viggiani, 2003). A qualitative study of forensic patients by Mason and Adler (2012) reported that limited opportunities for choice and decision-making were regarded as especially pernicious. Lowering expectations can make a strategy of limiting horizons and 'getting your head down' appear the best option, but whilst this reduced openness may assist self-preservation during incarceration it does little to promote successful adaptation on release (Schinkel, 2015). Loss of autonomy has a marked association with impaired mental health (De Viggiani, 2006, 2007), especially in prisoners with pre-existing mental health problems (Birmingham, 2003). Gaining social support, found in other contexts to reduce the likelihood of symptoms and promote recovery (Blackhart et al., 2006), is likely to be particularly problematic.

In many prison environments opportunities for positive, validating contacts with others are likely to be depleted. Aspects of prison life such as being locked up for long periods can instil a sense of isolation (Goomany & Dickinson, 2015), disconnection from family is difficult to bear (Nurse, Woodcock & Ormsby, 2003) and emotional (lack of closeness) and social (lack of belonging) loneliness have been found to have detrimental effects on mental well-being (Ireland & Qualter, 2008). On the other hand, negative, superficial or constraining contacts and "the effects of living in a tense, tight, personally invasive social world with other offenders, where there is constant pressure to conform and become socially accepted" cannot be avoided (De Viggiani, 2006, p. 72). As De Viggiani noted, the social environment of prisoners is characterised by rapid turnover, limited topics of conversation, competitiveness, exaggeration, banter, prejudice and suppression of emotions with individuals whose attitudes, values and habits may be distasteful. In relation to staff and prisoners alike all too often there can be a climate of mistrust, confrontation and discouragement that is fundamentally incompatible with therapeutic engagement and change (Ross et al., 2008).

## Facilitating personal change

### Therapeutic alliance

It appears then, that there is much in custodial environments to stabilise adaptations of identity, meaning, control and belonging in ways that work against the transition to desistance. The arguments of the Boston Change Process Study Group (2002) that therapy should include destabilising of existing 'attractors' may be especially relevant in such contexts. Effective therapy "moves individuals from disabling rigid patterns to more flexible and adaptive ones" (Hayes & Yasinski, 2015, p. 1). Otherwise individuals may return to familiar patterns even if transiently dislodged by therapeutic engagement. With parallels with Lewin's (1951) force field analysis, it is first necessary to establish conditions that help set change in motion. A key area in relation to 'treatment readiness' is the therapeutic alliance (Kozar, 2010). Criticising Bordin's (1979) influential descriptive framework as lacking in explanatory depth, Ross et al. (2008) characterised the therapeutic alliance in highly systemic terms as "both a process and an entity … implying that complex and often reciprocal interactions exist between variables" (p. 476). Using similarly systemic language, however, Safran & Muran (2006) had earlier criticised the very notion of a therapeutic alliance, recasting it in terms of emergent properties of interaction such as trust and intersubjective processes centred upon negotiation. It has been suggested that the process of negotiating goals may be as relevant to a therapeutic process as the goals that are agreed (Hardy, Cahill & Barkham, 2007), providing direct experience of what may be new ways of interacting with others (Lyons-Ruth, 2007) and elaborating new perspectives and intentions through shared experience within an 'intersubjective field' (Boston Change Process Study Group, 2002, 2013). Therapeutic progress is often characterised by repetition, relatively small incremental changes and frequent lapses (Marks–Tarlow, 1999) in which the repair of virtually inevitable ruptures as therapeutic collaboration progresses often assumes substantial significance (Hardy et al., 2007). Above all, dislodgement from previous positions and openness to renewed exploration requires a sense of safety (Boston Change Process Study Group, 2002).

The growing use of an attachment-based approach in understanding a range of problems (e.g. Meyer & Pilkonis, 2005; Timmerman & Emmelkamp, 2006) has been followed by increasing advocacy of the importance for therapeutic success of establishing a 'secure base' for exploration and development away from the legacies of attachment insecurity (Mikulincer & Arad, 1999; Mikulincer & Shaver, 2007; Willmot & McMurran, 2016). One implication of this is that conveying a sense of safety, with at least the possibility of trust should begin at an early stage of contact. Such a perspective is consistent with the widely recommended therapist style centred upon warmth, empathy and genuineness (Hardy et al., 2007; Marshall & Burton, 2010). Provisionally accepting a degree of vulnerability to the perspectives and intentions of another is necessary for openness in exploring where coordinated engagement might lead. Largely unfamiliar experiences of feeling accepted, valued and understood (Willmot & McMurran, 2013, 2016; Lambert & Barley, 2001) tend to encourage deeper engagement and the enactment of new perspectives and possibilities (Mikulincer & Shaver, 2007). The relationship also "provides the context in which specific techniques exert their influence" (Lambert & Barley, 2001, p. 359). Whilst the therapeutic relationship has been found to have a 'modest' or 'moderate' association with therapeutic outcome that nonetheless usually far exceeds the variance accounted for by specific techniques (Assay & Lambert, 1999; Marshall & Burton, 2010; Norcross & Lambert 2011), the relationship is not of course an end in itself. A therapist who failed to achieve an appropriate balance between "being personable and being purposeful" (Kozar & Day, 2012, p. 483) would be unlikely to maintain direction or be seen as a legitimate reference point. Similarly, a lack of professionalism and associated boundaries would do little to sustain credibility (Levitt, Butler & Hill, 2006; Hardy et al., 2007). Indeed proper boundaries are intrinsic to the sense of safety and containment of distress that is necessary for a secure base (Adshead, 2004; Haigh, 2013).

## Group cohesiveness

Kozar and Day (2012) point out that most research into therapeutic relationships has taken place in dyads, whereas most current practice in custodial environments centres upon groups. There do, however, appear to be certain parallels. For example, quality of relationships as indicated by group cohesiveness has a positive association with therapeutic outcomes that also appears to surpass that of particular techniques (Beech & Hamilton-Giachritis, 2005). In groups based in therapeutic communities, the negotiation of relationships, exploration of differences and development of an autonomous identity take place in a 'transitional space'; interdependence (and therefore responsibility) emerges through intersubjectivity (Haigh, 2013). In groups in other settings, too, negotiation has been regarded as a therapeutic influence and in a group setting this can be applied in learning to help others (Burlinghame, Fuhriman & Johnson, 2001) and repairing ruptures. Again, individual differences require different strategies and particular processes are likely to be relevant at particular stages of involvement (Harkins, Beech & Thornton, 2013; Kozar & Day, 2012). Where successful, group cohesiveness fosters a sense of being accepted, valued and understood (even when being challenged) that can be accompanied by a sense of belonging and commitment (Burlinghame et al., 2001). As with individual therapy these potential benefits are not inevitable. Issues such as the frequent contradiction between what goes on in programmes and the daily life of residential areas (Howells, Watt, Hall & Baldwin, 1997) apart, practice within the Risk–Needs–Responsivity (RNR) model has been criticised for a focus on manuals and procedures at the expense of sensitivity to process (Marshall & Serran, 2004; McNeill, 2012). A manual can no more ensure or replace therapeutic skill than an academic curriculum can guarantee or substitute for good teaching (Day, Kozar & Davey, 2013). Even a major proponent of the RNR approach has expressed regret at its relatively limited development of 'responsivity' (Andrews, 2011).

## Social climate

It has also been recognised that neglect of 'non-programmatic' factors such as staff attitudes, knowledge and behaviour can diminish the effectiveness of techniques and programme content (Dowden & Andrews, 2004; Hough, 2010; Marshall & Burton, 2010). Andrews (2011, p. 16) went so far as to warn that such neglect "virtually guarantees" failure. Relationships outside of therapy have the potential to encourage and support therapeutic change (Willmot & McMurran, 2016). As noted, they can also do the opposite (Ross et al., 2008) but many staff are committed and routinely show high levels of discretion and interpersonal skill (Hay & Sparks, 1991; Liebling & Tait, 2006). Non-professional relationships can also have a major influence (Burrowes & Needs, 2009; Weaver & McNeill, 2015). Overall, the moment-by-moment conversation and shared activity of ordinary social interaction often have an influence on mental health that is at least as important as 'social support' in relation to distress (Lakey, Vander Molen, Fies & Andrews, 2015). Naturally occurring events such as chance conversations in corridors or disagreements in residential facilities can have or be utilised to have therapeutic value (Whiteley & Collis, 1987; Haigh, 2013) especially in (but not only in) the 'living–learning' environment of a therapeutic community (Cullen, 1994). More generally, encouraging a sense of community in a custodial environment presents opportunities for residents to experience a more coherent, worthwhile and competent identity (Smith & Smith, 2005) and the availability of roles for supporting others can enhance a sense of purpose, meaning and social integration (Perrin & Blagden, 2014).

Patterns and practices in relation to areas such as the above are part of the 'social climate' of an institutional setting, its own distinct 'personality' by which it can be distinguished from other settings (Timko & Moos, 2004). The attempt to conceptualise the distinctive character of organisations and the consequences of relevant aspects for those within them has a long history (Griffin, 2001) and Rudolph Moos' hope that understanding of this area should be as familiar to psychologists as personality theories (Moos, 1973) has not been realised. In custodial environments there have been promising findings in relation to areas such as institutional behaviour (including violence and suicide) and creating a climate for therapeutic change (Casey, Day & Reynolds, 2016; Eltink, Van der Helm, Wissink & Stams, 2015; Harding, 2014; Timko & Moos, 2004). Interestingly in view of the latter, Van der Helm et al. (2012) found a negative association between perspective taking and a repressive prison climate. However the area remains in need of further development, especially in terms of theoretical frameworks to accompany refinements in measurement (Griffin, 2001; Tonkin, 2016; Woessner & Schwedler, 2014). It is suggested here that development of the field requires willingness to explore issues of context and process by incorporating frameworks (such as intersubjectivity, attachment and non-linear dynamical systems) that are uniquely suited to this. Thus, for example, it may be noted that interpersonal support, availability where appropriate of autonomy and the provision of order without excessive control are associated with therapeutic change (Timko & Moos, 2004). In several ways this configuration parallels the secure base advocated by Adshead (2004), Aiyegbusi (2004), Barber et al. (2006), Mikulincer and Arad (1999) and others that is likely to foster renewed exploration and openness to transition. It also steers us full circle to the essential features of the interaction described in the second paragraph.

## Conclusions and prospects

The importance of the "continuous exposure to corrective social encounters, enabling them to develop trust and confidence in others" for even the most socially disadvantaged prisoners (Elisha, Idisis & Ronel, 2013, p. 75) cannot be overstated. Person–context interactions are iterative, with outcomes of interactions becoming the starting points for new interactions (Lichtwarck-Aschoff et al., 2008); thus subtle changes occur over time. Within the sense of safety and openness encouraged by a secure base, experience of benign intersubjectivity may have benefits in areas such as new commitments of identity and compassion towards the self (Lichtwarck-Aschoff et al., 2008; Morley, 2015), meaning based on connectedness (Ferrito, Needs & Adshead, 2017; Stavrova & Luhmann, 2016) and perspective-taking necessary to exploration and agency (Schwartz et al., 2011). We can draw upon existing literature on styles associated with positive therapeutic outcomes to get an idea of how interpersonal and goal-oriented activities might allow emergence of a social climate that encourages and supports rather than contradicts and undermines rehabilitative activities and personal change. There are precedents to utilise in initiatives such as prosocial modelling (Cherry, 2005), motivational interviewing (Miller & Rollnick, 2012), a focus on prosocial, personal goals and strengths (e.g. Ward & Brown, 2004) the targeted use of everyday opportunities for interaction (Miles, 2016; Needs, 1992b) and the support, supervision and training of staff (see Campling, Davies & Farquharson, 2004). There is certainly scope for combining the insights of intersubjectivity with mentalisation-based interventions (Liljenfors & Lundh, 2015). Understanding the process of transition from propensities that give rise to offending to new reconciliations of identity, meaning, control and belonging sustained at new points of equilibrium may benefit further from integration of compatible themes in the criminological literature centred on areas such as identity, narratives, agency and relational contexts (e.g. Giordano, Cernkovich & Rudolph, 2002; Maruna & LeBel, 2009; McNeill, 2012; Paternoster et al., 2016; Vaughan, 2007; Weaver, 2012). A recent prospective quantitative study, for example, gave strong support to earlier, largely qualitatively-based arguments that changes in identity precede decreased involvement in crime and may need to precede related changes (Rocque et al., 2016). Throughout, it will be crucial to move from a focus on variables in isolation and attempt to "capture the synergistic reciprocity essential to trajectories" (Gerace et al., 2013, p. 12).

The initiatives and advances in understanding described in the present volume illustrate how positive contextual influences might be cultivated to encourage and support transition to improved functioning and desistance from crime. In the present chapter examples have been given of how problematic development in the key areas of identity, meaning, control and belonging can impede or distort capacities to meet life's demands and increase the likelihood of actions that are often profoundly against the interests of others. Offending offends precisely because it violates principles of reciprocity, mutuality and connectedness (Weaver & McNeill, 2015). Ostensible attempts to reintegrate individuals into society through ways which themselves violate these principles are unlikely to be effective. The present volume shows that it might be possible instead to harness them.

## References

Acar-Burkay, S., Fennis, B.M. & Warlop, L. (2014). Trusting others: The polarisation effect of need for closure. *Journal of Personality and Social Psychology*, 107(4), 719–735.

Adshead, G. (2004). Three degrees of security: Attachment and forensic institutions. In F. Pfäfflin & G. Adshead (Eds.) *A Matter of Security: The Application of Attachment Theory to Forensic Psychiatry and Psychotherapy*. London, UK: Jessica Kingsley.

Aiyegbusi, A. (2004). Forensic mental health nursing: Care with security in mind. In F. Pfäfflin & G. Adshead (Eds.) *A Matter of Security: The Application of Attachment Theory to Forensic Psychiatry and Psychotherapy*. London, UK: Jessica Kingsley.

Altheimer, I. (2013). Cultural processes and homicide across nations. *International Journal of Offender Therapy and Comparative Criminology*, 57, 842–863.

Andrews, D.A. (2011). The impact of nonprogrammatic factors on criminal-justice interventions. *Legal and Criminological Psychology*, 16, 1–23.

Ansbro, M. (2008). Using attachment theory with offenders. *Probation Journal*, 55(3), 231–244.

Asencio, E.K. & Burke, P.J. (2011). Does incarceration change the criminal identity? A synthesis of labelling and identity theory perspectives on identity change. *Sociological Perspectives*, 54(2), 163–182.

Ashforth, B.E. (2001). *Role Transitions in Organizational Life: An Identity-Based Perspective*. New Jersey, NJ: Lawrence Erlbaum Associates.

Assay, T.P. & Lambert, M.J. (1999). The empirical case for the common factors in therapy: Quantitative findings. In B.L. Duncan, M.A. Hubble, & S.D. Miller (Eds.) *The Heart and Soul of Change.* Washington, DC: American Psychological Association.

Athay, M. & Darley, J.M. (1981). Toward an interaction-cented theory of personality. In J.T. Tedeschi (Ed.) *Impression Management Theory and Social Psychological Research.* New York, NY: Academic Press.

Baldwin, M.W., Keelan, J.P.R., Fehr, B., Enns, V. & Koh-Rangarajoo, E. (1996). Social cognitive conceptualization of attachment styles: Availability and accessibility effects. *Journal of Personality and Social Psychology,* 71, 94–109.

Bandyopadhay, M. (2006). Competing masculinities in a prison. *Men and Masculinities,* 9, 186–203.

Barber, M., Short, J., Clarke-Moore, J., Lougher, M., Huckle, P. & Amos, T. (2006). A secure attachment model of care: Meeting the needs of people with mental health problems and antisocial behaviour. *Criminal Behaviour and Mental Health,* 16, 3–10.

Batchelor, S. (2005). 'Prove me the bam!': Victimization and agency in the lives of young women who commit violent offences. *Probation Journal,* 52 (4), 358–375.

Bateson, G. (1972). *Steps to an Ecology of Mind.* St Albans, UK: Paladin Frogmore.

Baumeister, R.F. (1990). Suicide as escape from self. *Psychological Review,* 97, 90–113.

Baumeister, R.F. & Leary, M.R. (1995). The need to belong: Desire for interpersonal attachments as a fundamental human motivation. *Psychological Bulletin,* 117(3), 497–529.

Baumeister, R.F., Smart, L. & Boden, J.M. (1996). Relation of threatened egotism to violence and aggression: The dark side of high self- esteem. *Psychological Review,* 103(1), 5–33.

Beck, A.T., Butler, A.C., Brown, G.K., Dahlsgard, K.K., Newman, C.F. & Beck, J.S. (2001). Dysfunctional beliefs discriminate personality disorders. *Behaviour Research and Therapy,* 39(10), 1213–1225.

Becker, E. (1964). *Revolution in Psychiatry: The New Understanding of Man.* New York, NY: Free Press, Macmillan.

Beech, A.R., Fisher, D. & Ward, T. (2005). Sexual murderers' implicit theories. *Journal of Interpersonal Violence,* 20 (11), 1366–1389.

Beech, A.R. & Hamilton-Giachritis, C.E. (2005). Relationship between therapeutic climate and treatment outcome on group- based sexual offender treatment programs. *Sexual Abuse: A Journal of Research and Treatment,* 17, 127–140.

Berman, A. M., Schwartz, S. J., Kurtines, W. M. & Berman, S.L. (2001). The process of exploration in identity formation: The role of style and competence. *Journal of Adolescence,* 24, 513–528.

Bhar, S.S., Brown, G.K. & Beck, A.T. (2008). Dysfunctional beliefs and psychopathology in borderline personality disorder. *Journal of Personality Disorders,* 22(2), 165–177.

Birmingham, L. (2003). The mental health of prisoners. *Journal of Continuing Professional Development,* 9, 191–199.

Blackhart, G.C., Baumeister, R.F. & Twenge, J.M. (2006). Rejection's impact on self-defeating, prosocial, antisocial, and self- regulatory behaviours. In K.D. Vohs & E.J. Finkel (Eds.) *Self and Relationships: Connecting Intrapersonal and Interpersonal Processes.* New York, NY: Guilford Press.

Blackhart, G.C., Nelson, B.C., Knowles, M.L. & Baumeister, R.F. (2009). Rejection elicits emotional reactions but neither causes immediate distress nor lowers self-esteem: A meta-analytic review of 192 studies on social exclusion. *Personality and Social Psychology Review,* 11, 167–203.

Boduszek, D. & Hyland, P. (2011). The theoretical model of criminal social identity: Psychosocial perspective. *International Journal of Criminology and Sociological Theory,* 4(1), 604–615.

Bordin, E.S. (1979). The generalizability of the therapeutic concept of the working alliance: New directions. In O. Horvath & L.S. Greenberg (Eds.) *The Working Alliance*. New York, NY: Wiley.

Boston Change Process Study Group (2002). Explicating the implicit: The local level and the microprocess of change in the analytic situation. *International Journal of Psychoanalysis*, 83, 1051–1062.

Boston Change Process Study Group (2013). Enactment and the emergence of new relational organization. *Journal of the American Psychoanalytic Association*, 61(4), 727–749.

Boucher, C.M. & Scoboria, A. (2015). Reappraising past and future transitional events: The effects of mental focus on present perceptions of personal impact and self-relevance. *Journal of Personality*, 83(4), 361–375.

Brown, A.D. & Toyoki, S. (2013). Identity work and legitimacy. *Organization Studies*, 34 (7), 875–896.

Burlinghame, G.M., Fuhriman, A. & Johnson, J.J. (2001). Cohesion in group psychotherapy. *Psychotherapy*, 38(4), 373–379.

Burrowes, N. & Needs, A. (2009). Time to contemplate change? A framework for assessing readiness to change in offenders. *Aggression and Violent Behavior*, 14, 39–49.

Buss, D.M. & Duntley, J.D. (2011). The evolution of intimate partner violence. *Aggression and Violent Behavior*, 16, 411–419.

Butler, M. (2008). What are you looking at? Prisoner confrontations and the search for respect. *British Journal of Criminology*, 48, 856–873.

Button, E.J. (1983). Personal construct theory and psychological well-being. *British Journal of Medical Psychology*, 56, 313–321.

Campbell, J.D., Assanand, S. & Di Paula, A. (2003). The structure of the self- concept and its relation to psychological adjustment. *Journal of Personality*, 71(1), 116–140.

Campling, P., Davies, S. & Farquharson, G. (2004). *From Toxic Institutions to Therapeutic Environments: Residential Settings in Mental Health Services*. London, UK: Gaskell/Royal College of Psychiatrists.

Canter, D. & Youngs, D. (2009). *Investigative Psychology: Offender Profiling and the Analysis of Criminal Action*. Chichester, UK: Wiley.

Canter, D. & Youngs, D. (2013). Sexual and violent offenders' victim role assignments: A general model of offending style. *The Journal of Forensic Psychiatry & Psychology*, 23(3), 297–326.

Casey, S., Day, A. & Reynolds, J. (2016). The influence of incarceration length and protection status on perceptions of prison social climate. *Criminal Justice and Behavior*, 43(2), 285–296.

Check, J.V.P., Perlman, D. & Malamuth, N.M. (1985). Loneliness and aggressive behaviour. *Journal of Social and Personal Relationships*, 2, 243–252.

Cherry, S. (2005). *Transforming Behaviour: Pro-social Modelling in Practice*. Cullompton, Devon, UK: Willan.

Cooper, M., Chak, A., Cornish, F. & Gillespie, A. (2013). Dialogue: Bridging personal, community and social transformation. *Journal of Humanistic Psychology*, 53(1), 70–93.

Côté, J.E. & Reker, G.T. (1979). Cognitive complexity and ego identity formation: A synthesis of cognitive and ego psychology. *Social Behavior and Personality*, 7, 107–112.

Covert M.V., Tangney, J.P., Maddux, J.E. & Heleno, N.M. (2003). Shame-proneness, guilt-proneness, and interpersonal problem solving: A social cognitive analysis. *Journal of Social and Clinical Psychology*, 22, 1–12.

Cruwys, T., Haslam, S.A., Dingle, G.A., Haslam, C. & Jetten, J. (2014). Depression and social identity: An integrative review. Personality and Social Psychology Review, 18(3), 215–238.

Cullen, E. (1994). Grendon: The therapeutic community that works. *Therapeutic Communities*, 15, 301–311.

Day, A. & Doyle, P. (2010). Violent offender rehabilitation and the therapeutic community model of treatment: Towards integrated service provision. *Aggression and Violent Behavior*, 15, 380–386.

Day, A., Howells, K., Heseltine, K. & Casey, S. (2003). Alcohol use and negative affect in the offence cycle. *Criminal Behaviour and Mental Health*, 13, 45–58.

Day, A., Kozar, C. & Davey, L. (2013). Treatment approaches and offending behaviour programs. *Aggression and Violent Behavior*, 18, 630–635.

Dearing, R.L., Stuewig, J. & Tangney, J.P. (2005). On the importance of distinguishing shame from guilt: Relations to problematic alcohol and drug use. *Addictive Behaviors*, 30, 1392–1404.

De Jaegher, H. & Di Paolo, E. (2007). Participatory sense-making: An enactive approach to social cognition. *Phenomenology and the Cognitive Sciences*, 6(4), 485–507.

De Jaegher H., Di Paolo, E. & Gallagher, S. (2010). Can social interaction constitute social cognition? *Trends in Cognitive Sciences*, 14(10), 441–447.

De Jaegher, H. & Froese, T. (2009). On the role of social interaction in individual agency. *Adaptive Behavior*, 17 (5), 444–460.

De Jaegher, H., Peräkylä, A.M. & Stevanovic. (2016). The co-creation of meaningful action: Bridging enaction and interactional sociology. *Philosophical Transactions of the Royal Society B: Biological Sciences*, 371(1693). DOI: 10.1098/ rstb.2015.0378.

De Viggiani, N. (2006). Surviving prison: Exploring prison social life as a determinant of health. *International Journal of Prisoner Health*, 2(2), 71–89.

De Viggiani, N. (2007). Unhealthy prisons: Exploring structural determinants of prison health. *Sociology of Health and Illness*, 29(1), 115–135.

De Wall, C.N., Baumeister, R.F., Stillman, T.F. & Gailliot, M.T. (2007). Violence restrained: Effects of self-regulation and its depletion on aggression. *Journal of Experimental Social Psychology*, 43, 62–76.

De Wall, C.N. & Twenge, J.M. (2013). Rejection and aggression: Explaining the paradox. In C.N. De Wall (Ed.) *The Oxford Handbook of Social Exclusion*. New York, NY: Oxford University Press.

Dobash, R.P., Dobash, R.E., Cavanagh, K., Smith, D. & Medina-Ariza, J. (2007). Onset of offending and life-course among men convicted of murder. *Homicide Studies*, 11(4), 243–271.

Dowden, C. & Andrews, D.A. (2004). The importance of staff practice in delivering effective correctional treatment: A meta-analytic review of core correctional practice. *International Journal of Offender Therapy and Comparative Criminology*, 48(2), 203–2014.

Downey, G., Freitas, A., Michaelis, B. & Khouri, H. (1998). The self-fulfilling prophecy in close relationships: Rejection sensitivity and rejection by romantic partners. *Journal of Personality and Social Psychology*, 75, 545–560.

Duck, S.W. (1980). The personal context: Intimate relationships. In P. Feldman & J. Orford (Eds.) *Psychological Problems: The Social Context*. Chichester, UK: Wiley.

Duck, S.W. & Lea, M. (1983). Breakdown of personal relationships and the threat to personal identity. In G. Breakwell (Ed.) *Threatened Identities*. Chichester, UK: Wiley.

Dutton, D.G. & White, K.R. (2012). Attachment security and intimate partner violence. *Aggression and Violent Behavior*, 17, 475–481.

Elisha, E., Idisis, Y. & Ronel, N. (2013). Positive criminology and imprisoned sex offenders: Demonstration of a way out from a criminal spin through acceptance relationships. *Journal of Sexual Aggression*, 19(1), 66–80.

Eltink, M.A., Van der Helm, P., Wissink, I.B. & Stams, G.J.J.M. (2015). The relationship between living group climate and reactions to social problem situations in detained adolescents:"I stabbed him because he looked mean at me". *International Journal of Forensic Mental Health*, 14(2), 101–109.

Farquharson, G. (2004). How good staff become bad. In P. Campling, S. Davies & G. Farquharson (Eds.) *From Toxic Institutions to Therapeutic Environments: Residential Settings in Mental Health Services*. London, UK: Gaskell/The Royal College of Psychiatrists.

Felson, R.B. & Steadman, H.J. (1983). Situational factors in disputes leading to criminal violence. *Criminology*, 21, 59–74.

Ferrito, M., Needs, A. & Adshead, G. (2017). Unveiling the shadows of meaning: Meaning-making for perpetrators of homicide. *Aggression and Violent Behavior*, 34, 263–272.

Fonagy, P. & Target, M. (1997). Attachment and reflective function: Their role in self-organization. *Development and Psychopathology*, 9, 679–700.

Fortune, C.A., Ward, T. & Polaschek, D.L.L. (2014). The Good Lives Model and therapeutic environments in forensic settings. *Therapeutic Communities: The International Journal of Therapeutic Communities*, 35(3), 95–104.

Foulds, G.A. (1967). *Personality and Personal Illness*. London, UK: Tavistock.

Fransella, F. (1972). *Personal Change and Reconstruction*. London, UK: Academic Press.

Gadon, L., Johnstone, L. & Cooke, D. (2006). Situational variables and institutional violence: A systematic view of the literature. *Clinical Psychology Review*, 26, 515–536.

Gannon, T.A. (2009). Social cognition in violent and sexual offending: An overview. *Psychology, Crime & Law*, 15(2), 97–118.

Gerace, A., Day, A., Casey, S. & Mohr, P. (2013). An exploratory investigation of the process of perspective taking in interpersonal situations. *Journal of Relationships Research*, 4, (6), 1–12.

Gilbert, P. & Procter, S. (2006). Compassionate mind training for people with high shame and self-criticism: Overview and pilot study of a group therapy approach. *Clinical Psychology and Psychotherapy*, 13, 353–379.

Gilchrist, E. (2009). Implicit thinking about implicit theories in intimate partner violence. *Psychology, Crime and Law*, 15, 131–145.

Gillespie, A. (2011). Contact without transformation: The context, process and content of distrust. In I. Marková & A. Gillespie (Eds.) *Trust and Conflict: Representation, Culture and Dialogue*. London, UK: Routledge.

Gillespie, A. (2012). Position exchange: The social development of agency. *New Ideas in Psychology*, 30, 32–46.

Gillespie, A. & Richardson, B. (2011). Exchanging social positions: Enhancing perspective taking within a cooperative problem solving task. *European Journal of Social Psychology*, 41, 608–616.

Giordano, P.C., Cernkovich, S.A. & Rudolph, J.L. (2002). Gender, crime and desistance: Toward a theory of cognitive transformation. *American Journal of Sociology*, 107, 990–1064.

Goffman, E. (1974). *Frame Analysis: An Essay on the Organisation of Experience*. New York, NY: Harper and Row.

Goomany, A. & Dickinson, T. (2015). The influence of prison climate on the mental health of adult prisoners: A literature review. *Journal of Psychiatric and Mental Health Nursing*, 22, 413–422.

Graci, M.E. & Fivush, R. (2016). Narrative meaning making, attachment, and psychological growth and stress. *Journal of Social and Personal Relationships*, 34 (4)1–24.

Greenier, K.G., Kernis, M.H., Whisehunt, C.R., Waschull, S.B., Berry, A.J., Herlocker, C.E. & Asbend, T. (1999). Examining individual differences in reactivity to daily events: examining the roles of stability and level of self- esteem. *Journal of Personality*, 67, 185–208.

Griffin, M.L. (2001). *The Use of Force by Detention Officers*. New York, NY: LFB Scholarly Publishing LLC.

Haigh, R. (2013). The quintessence of a therapeutic environment. *Therapeutic Communities: The International Journal of Therapeutic Communities*, 34(1), 6–15.

Hales, A.H., Kassner, M.P., Williams, K.D. & Graziano, W.G. (2016). Disagreeableness as a cause and consequence of ostracism. *Personality and Social Psychological Bulletin*, 42(6), 782–797.

Harding, R. (2014). Rehabilitation and prison social climate: Do 'what works' rehabilitation programs work better in prisons that have a positive social climate? *Australian & New Zealand Journal of Criminology*, 47(2), 163–175.

Hardy, G., Cahill, J. & Barkham, M. (2007). Active ingredients of the therapeutic relationship that promote client change. A research perspective. In P. Gilbert & R.L. Leahy (Eds.) *The Therapeutic Relationship in the Cognitive Behavioural Therapies*. London, UK: Routledge.

Harkins, L., Beech, A.R. & Thornton, D. (2013). The influence of risk and psychopathy on the therapeutic climate in sex offender treatment. *Sexual Abuse: A Journal of Research and Treatment*, 25(2), 103–122.

Hawkley, L.C. & Cacioppo, J.T. (2010). Loneliness matters: A theoretical and empirical review of consequences and mechanisms. *Annals of Behavioral Medicine*, 40(2), 218–227.

Hay, W. & Sparks, R. (1991). What is a prison officer? *Prison Service Journal*, 83, 2–7.

Hayes, A.M. & Yasinski, C. (2015). Pattern destabilization and emotional processing in cognitive therapy for personality disorders. *Frontiers in Psychology*, 6(107), 1–13.

Healy, D. (2014). Becoming a desister: Exploring the role of agency, coping and imagination in the construction of a new self. *British Journal of Criminology*, 54(5), 873–891.

Hermans, H.J.M. (2001). The dialogical self: Towards a theory of personal and cultural positioning. *Culture & Psychology*, 7, 243–281.

Hermans, H.J.M. (2008). How to perform research on the basis of dialogical self theory? Introduction to the special issue. *Journal of Constructivist Psychology*, 21, 185–199.

Hosser, D., Windzio, M. & Greve, W. (2008). Guilt and shame as predictors of recidivism: A longitudinal study with young prisoners. *Criminal Justice and Behavior*, 35(1), 138–152.

Hough, M. (2010). Gold standard or fool's gold? The pursuit of certainty in experimental criminology. *Criminology and Criminal Justice*, 10(1), 11–22.

Howells, K. (1978). The meaning of poisoning to a person diagnosed as a psychopath. *Medicine, Science & the Law*, 8, 179–184.

Howells, K. (1981). Social construing and violent behaviour in mentally disordered offenders. In J. Hinton (Ed.) *Dangerousness: Problems of Assessment and Prediction*. London, UK: Allen & Unwin.

Howells, K., Watt, B., Hall, G. & Baldwin, S. (1997). Developing programmes for violent offenders. *Legal and Criminological Psychology*, 2, 117–128.

Hundt, N.E. & Holohan, D.R. (2012). The role of shame in distinguishing perpetrators of intimate partner violence in U.S. veterans. Journal of Traumatic Stress, 25(2), 191–197.

Ireland, J.L. (2002). Bullying among prisoners: Evidence, research and intervention strategies. Hove, UK: Brunner-Routledge.

Ireland, J.L. & Qualter, P. (2008). Bullying and social and emotional loneliness in a sample of adult male prisoners. *International Journal of Law and Psychiatry*, 31, 19–29.

Iversen, A., Fear, N.T., Ehlers, A., Hacker Hughes, J., Hull, L., Earnshaw, M. et al. (2008). Risk factors for post-traumatic stress disorder among UK Armed Forces personnel. *Psychological Medicine*, 38(4), 511–522.

James, W. (1890). *The Principles of Psychology*. New York, NY: Dover Publications.

Jetten, J., Haslam, C., Haslam, S.A., Dingle, G. & Jones, J.M. (2014). How groups affect our health and well-being: The path from theory to policy. *Social Issues and Policy Review*, 8(1), 103–130.

Kelly, G.A. (1955). *The Psychology of Personal Constructs.* New York, NY: Norton.

Kelly, G.A. (1970). Behaviour is an experiment. In D. Bannister (Ed.) *Perspectives in Personal Construct Theory.* London, UK: Academic Press.

Kernis, M.H. & Goldman, B.M. (2003). Stability and variability in self-concept and self-esteem. In M. Leary & J.P. Tangney (Eds.) *Handbook of Self and Identity.* New York, NY: Guilford.

Kernis, M.H., Granneman, B.D. & Barclay, L.C. (1989). Stability and level of self- esteem as predictors of anger arousal and hostility. *Journal of Personality and Social Psychology*, 56(6), 1013–1022.

Kihlstrom, J.F. (2012). The person-situation interaction. In D. Carlston, (Ed.) *The Oxford Handbook of Social Cognition.* New York, NY: Oxford University Press.

King, R.D. & Elliott, K.W. (1977). *Albany: Birth of a Prison – End of an Era.* London, UK: Routledge & Kegan Paul.

King, R.D. & McDermott, K. (1990). 'My geranium is subversive': Some notes on the management of trouble in prisons. *The British Journal of Sociology*, 41(4), 445–471.

Knowles, M.L. (2013). Behavioral regulation through the use of (para) social surrogates. In C.N. De Wall (Ed.) *The Oxford Handbook of Social Exclusion.* New York, NY: Oxford University Press.

Kögler, H.H. (2012). Agency and the other: On the intersubjective roots of self-identity. *New Ideas in Psychology*, 30, 47–64.

Kozar, C. (2010). Treatment readiness and the therapeutic alliance. In A. Day, S. Casey, T. Ward, K. Howells & J. Vess (Eds.) *Transitions to Better Lives: Offender Readiness and Rehabilitation.* Cullompton, Devon, UK: Willan.

Kozar, C.J. & Day, A. (2012). The therapeutic alliance in offending behaviour programs: A necessary and sufficient condition for change? *Aggression and Violent Behavior*, 17, 482–487.

Kyselo, M. (2016). The enactive approach and disorders of the self – the case of schizophrenia. *Phenomenology and the Cognitive Sciences*, 15, 591–616.

Laing, R.D. (1960). *The Divided Self: An Existential Study in Sanity and Madness.* Harmondsworth, UK: Penguin.

Lakey, B., Vander Molen, R.J., Fies, E. & Andrews, J. (2015). Ordinary social interaction and the main effect between perceived support and affect. *Journal of Personality*, 84(5), 671–684.

Lambert, M.J. & Barley, D.E. (2001). Research summary on the therapeutic relationship and psychotherapy outcome. *Psychotherapy*, 38(4), 357–361.

Lambert, N.M., Stillman, T.F., Hicks, J.A., Kamble, S., Baumeister, R.F. & Fincham, F.D. (2013). To belong is to matter: Sense of belonging enhances meaning in life. *Personality and Social Psychology Bulletin, 39,* 1418–1427.

Lawrence, A.E. & Taft, C.T. (2013). Shame, posttraumatic stress disorder, and intimate partner violence perpetration. *Aggression and Violent Behavior*, 18(2), 191–194.

Leamy, M., Bird, V., Le Boutillier, C., Williams, J. & Slade, M. (2011). Conceptual framework for personal recovery in mental health: Systematic review and narrative synthesis. *British Journal of Psychiatry*, 199, 445–452.

Leary, M.R. (2007). Motivational and emotional aspects of the self. *Annual Review of Psychology*, 58, 317–344.

Leary, M.R. & Cottrell, C.A. (2013). Evolutionary perspectives on interpersonal acceptance and rejection. In C.N. De Wall (Ed.) *The Oxford Handbook of Social Exclusion.* New York, NY: Oxford University Press.

Leary, M.R., Kowalski, R.M., Smith, L. & Phillips, S. (2003). Teasing, rejection and violence: Case studies of the school shootings. *Aggressive Behavior*, 29, 202–214.

Leary, M.R. & Leder, S. (2009). The nature of hurt feelings: Emotional experience and cognitive appraisals. In A. Vangelisti (Ed.) *Feeling Hurt in Close Relationships.* New York, NY: Cambridge University Press.

Leary, M.R., Twenge, J.M. & Quinlivan, E. (2006). Interpersonal rejection as a determinant of anger and aggression. *Personality and Social Psychology Review,* 10 (2), 111–132.

Levitt, H., Butler, M. & Hill, T. (2006). What clients find helpful in psychotherapy: Developing principles for facilitating moment-to-moment change. *Journal of Counseling Psychology,* 53(3), 314–324.

Lewin, K. (1951). *Field Theory in Social Science.* New York, NY: Harper and Row.

Lichtwarck-Aschoff, A., Van Geert, P., Bosma, H. & Kunnen, S. (2008). Time and identity: A framework for research and theory formation. *Developmental Review,* 28, 370–400.

Liebling, A. (2004). *Prisons and their Moral Performance: A Study of Values, Quality and Prison Life.* Oxford, UK: Oxford University Press.

Liebling, A. & Tait, S. (2006). Improving staff-prisoner relationships. In G.E. Dear (Ed.) *Preventing Suicide and Other Self-Harm in Prison.* Basingstoke, UK: Palgrave Macmillan.

Lila, M., Gracia, E. & Murgui, S. (2013). Psychological adjustment and victim-blaming among intimate partner violence offenders: The role of social support and stressful life events. *The European Journal of Psychology Applied to Legal Contexts,* 5(2), 147–153.

Liljenfors, R. & Lundh, L.G. (2015). Mentalization and intersubjectivity: Towards a theorectical integration. *Psychoanalytic Psychology,* 32(1), 36–60.

Linehan, M.M. (1993). *Cognitive Behavioural Therapy for Borderline Personality Disorder.* New York, NY: Guilford.

Livesley, W.J. (2007). An integrated approach to the study of personality disorder. *Journal of Mental Health,* 16, 131–148.

Luke, M. & Stopa, L. (2009). Psychological theories of the self and their application to clinical disorders. In L. Stopa (Ed.) *Imagery and the Threatened Self: Perspectives on Mental Imagery and the Self in Cognitive Therapy.* Hove, UK: Routledge.

Lyons-Ruth, K. (2007). Interfacing attachment and intersubjectivity: Perspective from the longitudinal study of disorganised attachment. *Psychoanalytic Inquiry,* 26(4), 595–616.

Maercker, A. & Horn, A.B. (2013). A socio-interpersonal perspective on PTSD: The case for environments and interpersonal processes. *Clinical Psychology and Psychotherapy,* 20(6), 465–481.

Marks-Tarlow, T. (1999). The self as a dynamical system. *Nonlinear Dynamics, Psychology, and Life Sciences,* 3(4), 311–345.

Marshall, W.L. (1989). Intimacy, loneliness and sexual offenders. *Behavior, Research and Therapy,* 27, 491–503.

Marshall, W.L. & Burton, D.L. (2010). The importance of group processes in offender treatment. *Aggression and Violent Behavior,* 15, 141–149.

Marshall, W.L. & Serran, G.A. (2004). The role of the therapist in offender treatment. *Psychology, Crime and Law,* 10(3), 309–320.

Maruna, S. (2001). *Making Good: How Ex Convicts Reform and Rebuild Their Lives.* Washington, DC: American Psychological Association.

Maruna, S. & LeBel, T.P. (2009). Strengths-based approaches to re-entry: Extra mileage toward reintegration and destigmatization. *Japanese Journal of Sociological Criminology,* 34, 59–80.

Mason, K. & Adler, J.R. (2012). Group-work therapeutic engagement in a high secure hospital: Male service user perspectives. *The British Journal of Forensic Practice,* 14(2), 92–103.

McAdams, D.P. (2008). Personal narratives and the life story. In O.P. John, R.W. Robins & L.A. Pervin (Eds.) *Handbook of Personality: Theory and Research*. New York, NY: Guilford Press.

McNeill, F. (2012). Four forms of 'offender' rehabilitation: Towards an interdisciplinary perspective. *Legal and Criminological Psychology*, 17, 1–19.

Meichenbaum, D. (2006). Resilience and post-traumatic growth: A constructive narrative perspective. In G.C. Calhoun & R.G. Tedeschi (Eds.) *Handbook of Posttraumatic Growth*. New Jersey, NJ: Lawrence Erlbaum.

Meyer, B. & Pilkonis, P.A. (2005). An attachment model of personality disorders. In M.F. Lenzenweger & J.F. Clarkin (Eds.) *Major Theories of Personality Disorder*. New York, NY: Guildford.

Mikulincer, M. & Arad, D. (1999). Attachment working models and cognitive openness in close relationships: A test of chronic and temporary accessibility effects. *Journal of Personality and Social Psychology*, 77, 710–725.

Mikulincer, M. & Shaver, P.R. (2007). Boosting attachment security to promote mental health, prosocial values, and inter- group tolerance. *Psychological Inquiry*, 18(3), 139–156.

Mikulincer, M. & Shaver, P.R. (2013). Attachment orientations and meaning in life. In J.A. Hicks & C. Routledge (Eds.) *The Experience of Meaning in Life: Classical Perspectives, Emerging Themes, and Controversies*. New York, NY: Springer.

Miles, C. (2016). Five minute intervention: FMI. Paper presented at the Conference of the Division of Forensic Psychology, Brighton.

Miller, W.R. & Rollnick, S. (2012). *Motivational Interviewing: Preparing People for Change* (3rd edn.). New York, NY: Guilford Press.

Moos, R.H. (1973). Conceptualisations of human environments. *American Psychologist, 28*, 652–665.

Morley, R.H. (2015). Violent criminality and self-compassion. *Aggression & Violent Behavior*, 24, 226–240.

Murphy, R. & Winder, B. (2016). 'If you'd had my life, you'd have done it too': Exploring the experiences of adult males who rape elderly females. *Psychology, Crime & Law*, 22(8), 798–816.

Navathe, S., Ward, T. & Rose, C. (2013). The development of the sex offender relationship frames model. *Psychiatry, Psychology and Law*, 20(1), 60–72.

Needs, A. (1992a). Some issues raised by the application of personal construct theory to the sexual abuse of children. In P. Maitland & D. Brennan (Eds.) *Personal Construct Theory, Deviancy and Social Work* (2nd edn.). London, UK: Inner London Probation Service/ Centre for Personal Construct Psychology.

Needs, A. (1992b). *Working with Personality Disorders: Some Points for Special Unit Staff*. Unpub. training manual, H.M. Prison Service.

Needs, A. (2014). A framework for understanding the transition process in veterans. *Wessex Branch, BPS 3rd Military Psychology Conference: Veterans in Transition*, Defence Academy, Shrivenham.

Needs, A. (2015). Outrageous fortune: Transitions and related concerns in the genesis of violence. Paper presented at the *Conference of the International Academy for Law and Mental Health, Vienna*.

Needs, A. & Jones, L. (2017). Personal construct psychotherapy. In J. Davies & C. Miles (Eds.) *Individual Psychotherapy with Clients in Forensic Settings*. Chichester, UK: Wiley.

Needs, A., Salmann, L. & Kiddle, R. (2011). Personality characteristics, change and attitudes to bullying in a therapeutic community. Paper presented at the *Conference of the Division of Forensic Psychology*, Portsmouth.

Niebieszczanski, R., Harkins, L., Judson, S., Smith, K. & Dixon, L. (2015). The role of moral disengagement in street gang offending. *Psychology, Crime & Law*, 21(6), 589–605.

Norcross, J.C. & Lambert, M.J. (2011). Psychotherapy relationships that work II. *Psychotherapy*, 48(1), 4–8.

Nurse, J., Woodcock, P. & Ormsby, J. (2003). Influence of environmental factors on mental health within prisons: Focus group study. *British Medical Journal*, 327, 480–485.

Ogilvie, C. A., Newman, E., Todd, L. & Peck, D. (2014). Attachment & violent offending: A meta-analysis. *Aggression and Violent Behavior*, 19, 322–339.

Olson, J.M. & Partington, J.T. (1977). An integrative analysis of two cognitive models of interpersonal effectiveness. *British Journal of Social and Clinical Psychology*, 16, 13–14.

Oyserman, D., Elmore, K. & Smith, G. (2012). Self, Self-Concept, and Identity. In M.R. Leary & J.P. Tangney (Eds.) *Handbook of Self and Identity* (2nd edn.) New York, NY: Guilford Press.

Pagano, M.E., Skodol, A.E., Stout, R.L., Shea, M.T., Yen, S., Grilo, C.M. et al. (2004). Stressful life events as predictors of functioning: Findings from the collaborative longitudinal personality disorders study. *Acta Psychiatrica Scandinavica*, 110, 421–429.

Palmer, D.K. (2004). On the organism-environment distinction in psychology. *Behavior and Philosophy*, 32, 317–347.

Parish, S.M. (2014). Between persons: How concepts of the person make moral experience possible. *Ethos*, 42, 31–50.

Paternoster, R., Bachman, R., Kerrison, E., O'Connell, D. & Smith, L. (2016). Desistance from crime and identity. An empirical test with survival time. *Criminal Justice and Behavior*, 43(9), 1204–1224.

Peat, B.J. & Winfree, L.T. Jr., (1992). Reducing the intra-institutional effects of "prisonization": A study of a therapeutic community for drug-using inmates. *Criminal Justice and Behavior*, 19, 206–225.

Pedersen, W.C., Gonzales, C. & Miller, N. (2000). The moderating effect of trivial triggering provocation on displaced aggression. *Journal of Personality and Social Psychology*, 78, 913–927.

Perrin, C. & Blagden, N. (2014). Accumulating meaning, purpose and opportunities to change 'drip by drip': The impact of being a listener in prison. *Psychology, Crime & Law*, 20(9), 902–920.

Perry, R. & Sibley, C.G. (2013). Seize and freeze: Openness to experience shapes judgments of societal threat. *Journal of Research in Personality*, 47, 677–686.

Polaschek, D.L. & Gannon, T.A. (2004). The implicit theories of rapists: What convicted offenders tell us. *Sexual abuse: A journal of Research and Treatment*, 16(4), 299–314.

Pornari, C.D., Dixon, L. & Humphreys, G.W. (2013). Systematically identifying implicit theories in male and female intimate partner violence perpetrators. *Aggression and Violent Behavior*, 18, 496–505.

Pratkanis, A.R. & Greenwald, A.G. (1985). How shall the self be conceived? *Journal for the Theory of Social Behaviour*, 15, 311–328.

Presser, L. (2009). The narratives of offenders. *Theoretical Criminology*, 13(2), 177–200.

Puchalska-Wasyl, M., Chmielnicka-Kuter, E. & Oleś, P. (2008). From internal interlocutors to psychological functions of dialogical activity. *Journal of Constructivist Psychology*, 21(3), 239–269.

Richman, L. & Leary, M.R. (2009). Reactions to discrimination, stigmatization, ostracism, and other forms of interpersonal rejection: A multimotive model. *Psychological Review*, 116(2), 365–383.

Rierdan, J. (1980). Word associations of socially isolated adolescents. *Journal of Abnormal Psychology*, 89, 98–100.

Ritchie, T.D., Sedikides, C., Wildschut, T., Arndt, J. & Gidron, Y. (2011). Self-concept clarity mediates the relation between stress and subjective well- being. *Self and Identity*, 10, 493–508.

Rocque, M., Posick, C. & Paternoster, R. (2016). Identities through time: An exploration of identity change as a cause of desistance. *Justice Quarterly*, 33(1), 45–72.

Roets, A., Van Hiel, A. & Cornelis, I. (2006). The dimensional structure of the need for cognitive closure scale: Relationships with "seizing" and "freezing" processes. *Social Cognition*, 24(1), 22–45.

Rosenberg, M. (1965). *Society and the Adolescent Self-Image*. Princeton, NJ: Princeton University Press.

Ross, E.C., Polaschek, D.L.L. & Ward, T. (2008). The therapeutic alliance: A theoretical revision for offender rehabilitation. *Aggression and Violent Behavior*, 14, 462–480.

Ross, T. & Pfäfflin, F. (2007). Attachment and interpersonal problems in a prison environment. *The Journal of Forensic Psychiatry & Psychology*, 18(1), 90–98.

Rousseau, D.M., Sitkin, S.B., Burt, R.S. & Camerer, C. (1998). Not so different at all: A cross-discipline view of trust. *Academy of Management Review*, 23, 393–404.

Ruotolo, A.K. (1968). Dynamics of sudden murder. *American Journal of Psychoanalysis*, 28, 162–176.

Rutter, M. (1975). *Helping Troubled Children*. Harmondsworth, UK: Penguin.

Ryan, R.M. (2005). The developmental line of autonomy in the etiology, dynamics, and treatment of borderline personality disorders. *Development and Psychopathology*, 17, 987–1006.

Sadeh, N. & Karniol, R. (2012). The sense of self-continuity as a resource in adaptive coping with job loss. *Journal of Vocational Behavior*, 80, 93–99.

Safran, J.D. & Muran, J.C. (2006). Has the concept of the therapeutic alliance outlived its usefulness? *Psychotherapy: Theory, Research, Practice, Training*, 43(3), 286–291.

Salazar, L.R. (2015). The negative reciprocity process in marital relationships: A literature review. *Aggression and Violent Behavior*, 24, 113–119.

Sander, L. (2008). *Living Systems, Evolving Consciousness, and the Emerging Person: A Selection of Papers from the Life Work of Louis Sander*. New York, NY: Analytic Press.

Schinkel, M. (2015). Adaptation, the meaning of imprisonment and outcomes after release: The impact of the prison regime. *Prison Service Journal*, 219, 24–29.

Schmid, T.J. & Jones, R.S. (1991). Suspended identity: Identity transformation in a maximum security prison. *Symbolic Interaction*, 14, 415–432.

Schwartz, S.J., Klimstra, T.A., Luyckx, K., Hale, W.W., Frijns, T., Oosterwegel, A., Van Lier, P.A.C., Koot, H.M. & Meus, W.H.J. (2011). Daily dynamics of personal identity and self-concept clarity. *European Journal of Personality*, 25, 373–385.

Serin, R.C. & Lloyd, C.D. (2009). Examining the process of offender change: The transition to crime desistance. *Psychology, Crime & Law*, 15 (4), 347–364.

Serin, R.C., Lloyd, C.D. & Hanby, L.J. (2010). Enhancing offender re-entry. An integrated model for enhancing offender re-entry. *European Journal of Probation*, 2(2), 53–75.

Shani, I. (2013). Making it mental: In search of the golden mean of the extended cognition controversy. *Phenomenology and the Cognitive Sciences*, 12(1), 1–26.

Shevlin, M., Dorahy, M., Adamson, G. & Murphy, J. (2007). Subtypes of borderline personality disorder, associated clinical disorders and stressful life-events: A latent class analysis based on the British Psychiatric Morbidity Survey. *British Journal of Clinical Psychology*, 46, 273–281.

Shoda, Y., Tiernan, S.L. & Mischel, W. (2002). Personality as a dynamical system: Emergence of stability and distinctiveness from intra- and interpersonal interactions. *Personality and Social Psychology Review*, 6(4), 316–325.

Silverman, R.A. & Mukherjee, S.K. (1987). Intimate homicide: An analysis of violent social relationships. *Behavioural Sciences and the Law*, 5(1), 37–47.

Smith, P. & Smith, W.A. (2005). Experiencing community through the eyes of young female offenders. *Journal of Contemporary Criminal Justice*, 21(4), 364–385.

Stavrova, O. & Luhmann, M. (2016). Social connectedness as a source and consequence of meaning in life. *The Journal of Positive Psychology*, 11(5), 470–479.

Stein, J. & Tuval-Mashiach, R. (2015). The social construction of loneliness: An integrative conceptualization. *Journal of Constructivist Psychology*, 28(3), 210–227.

Stein, K.F. & Markus, H.R. (1996). The role of the self in behavioral change. *Journal of Psychotherapy Integration*, 6(4), 349–384.

Stillman, T.F. & Baumeister, R.F. (2013). Social rejection reduces intelligent thought and self-regulation. In C.N. De Wall (Ed.) *The Oxford Handbook of Social Exclusion*. New York, NY: Oxford University Press.

Sykes, D. (1958). *The Society of Captives: A Study of a Maximum Security Prison*. New Jersey, NJ: Princeton University Press.

Sykes, G.M. & Matza, D. (1957). Techniques of neutralization: A theory of delinquency. *American Sociological Review*, 22, 664–670.

Tangney, J.P., Stuewig, J. & Hafez, L. (2011). Shame, guilt and remorse: Implications for offender populations. *Journal of Forensic Psychiatry & Psychology*, 22, 706–723.

Tangney, J.P., Stuewig, J. & Mashek, D. (2007). Moral emotions and moral behaviour. *Annual Review of Psychology*, 58, 345–372.

Thewissen, V., Bentall, R.P., Lecomte, T., van Os, J. & Myin-Germeys, I. (2008). Fluctuations in self-esteem and paranoia in the context of daily life. *Journal of Abnormal Psychology*, 117(1), 143–153.

Thewissen, V., Myin-Germeys, I., Bentall, R.P., de Graaf, R., Vollebergh, W. & van Os, J. (2007). Instability of self-esteem and paranoia in a general population sample. *Social Psychiatry and Psychiatric Epidemiology*, 42, 1–5.

Timko, C. & Moos, R.H. (2004). Measuring the therapeutic environment. In P. Campling, S. Davies & G. Farquharson (Eds.) *From Toxic Institutions to Therapeutic Environments: Residential Settings in Mental Health Services*. London, UK: Gaskell/The Royal College of Psychiatrists.

Timmerman, I.G.H. & Emmelkamp, P.M.G. (2006). The relationship between attachment styles and cluster B personality disorders in prisoners and forensic inpatients. *International Journal of Law and Psychiatry*, 29, 48–56.

Toch, H. (1969). *Violent Men*. Chicago, IL: Aldine.

Tonkin, M. (2016). A review of questionnaire measures for assessing the social climate in prisons and forensic psychiatric hospitals. *International Journal of Offender Therapy and Comparative Criminology*, 60(12), 1376–1405.

Trevarthen, C. (2002). Making sense of infants making sense. *Intellectica*, 34, 164–188.

Twenge, J.M., Baumeister, R.F., Tice, D.M. & Stucke, T.S. (2001). If you can't join them, beat them: Effects of social exclusion on aggressive behavior. *Journal of Personality and Social Psychology*, 81(6), 1058–1069.

Twenge, J.M. & Campbell, W.K. (2003). 'Isn't it fun to get the respect that we're going to deserve?' Narcissism, social rejection and aggression. *Personality and Social Psychology Bulletin*, 29, 261–272.

Twenge, J.M., Catanese, K.R. & Baumeister, R.F. (2002). Social exclusion causes self-defeating behavior. *Journal of Personality and Social Psychology*, 83(3), 606–615.

Twenge, J.M., Catanese, K.R. & Baumeister, R.F. (2003). Social exclusion and the deconstructed state: Time perception, meaninglessness, lethargy, lack of emotion, and self-awareness. *Journal of Personality and Social Psychology*, 85, 409–423.

Ungar, M. (2013). Resilience, trauma, context, and culture. *Trauma, Violence and Abuse*, 14(3), 255–266.

Vallacher, R.R., Read, S.J. & Nowack, A. (2002). The dynamical perspective in personality and social psychology. *Personality and Social Psychology Review*, 6(4), 264–273.

Van der Helm, G.H.P., Stams, G.J.J.M. & Van der Laans, P.H. (2011). Measuring group climate in a forensic setting. *The Prison Journal*, 91, 158–177.

Van der Helm, G.H.P., Stams, G.J.J.M., van der Stel, J.C., van Langen, M.A.M. & van der Laan, P.H. (2012). Group climate and empathy in a sample of incarcerated boys. *International Journal of Offender Therapy and Comparative Criminology*, 56, 1149–1160.

Van Geert, P.L.C. & Fischer, K.W. (2009). Dynamic systems and the quest for individual-based models of change and development. In J.P. Spencer, M.S.C. Thomas, & J. McClelland (Eds.) *Toward a New Grand Theory of Development? Connectionism and Dynamic Systems Theory Reconsidered*. Oxford, UK: Oxford University Press.

Vaughan, B. (2007). The internal narrative of desistance. *British Journal of Criminology*, 47, 390–404.

Vecina, M.L. & Marzan, D. (2016). Always looking for a moral identity: The moral licensing effect in men convicted of domestic violence. *New Ideas in Psychology*, 41, 33–38.

Velotti, P., Elison, J. & Garafalo, C. (2014). Shame and aggression: Different trajectories and implications. *Aggression and Violent Behavior*, 19, 454–461.

Ward, T. (2012). Narrative identity and forensic psychology: A commentary on Youngs and Canter. *Legal and Criminological Psychology*, 17, 250–261.

Ward, T. (2017). Prediction and agency: The role of protective factors in correctional rehabilitation and desistance. *Aggression and Violent Behaviour*, 32, 19–28.

Ward, T. & Brown, M. (2004). The Good Lives Model and conceptual issues in offender rehabilitation. *Psychology, Crime & Law*, 10, 243–257.

Ward, T. & Maruna, S. (2007). *Rehabilitation: Beyond the Risk Paradigm*. London, UK: Routledge.

Waters, T.E.A. & Fivush, R. (2015). Relations between narrative coherence, identity, and psychological well-being in emerging adulthood. *Journal of Personality*, 83(4), 441–451.

Weaver, B. (2012). The relational context of desistance: Some implications and opportunities for social policy. *Social Policy and Administration*, 46(4), 395–412.

Weaver, B. & McNeill, F. (2015). Lifelines: Desistance, social relations, and reciprocity. *Criminal Justice & Behavior*, 42(1), 95–107.

Whiteley, J.S. & Collis, M. (1987). The therapeutic factors in group psychotherapy applied to the therapeutic community. *International Journal of Therapeutic Communities*, 8, 21–32.

Winter, D.A. (1992). A personal construct theory view of social skills training. In P. Maitland & D. Brennan (Eds.) *Personal Construct Theory, Deviancy and Social Work* (2nd edn.). London, UK: Inner London Probation Service/Centre for Personal Construct Psychology.

Winter, D.A. (2003). A credulous approach to violence and homicide. In J. Horley (Ed.) *Personal Construct Perspectives on Forensic Psychology*. Hove, UK: Brunner-Routledge.

Williams, K. (2001). *Ostracism: The Power of Silence*. New York, NY: Guilford Press.

Williams, K. (2007). Ostracism. *Annual Review of Psychology*, 58, 425–452.

Willmot, P. & McMurran, M. (2013). The views of male forensic inpatients on how treatment for personality disorder works. *The Journal of Forensic Psychiatry and Psychology*, 24, 594–609.

Willmot, P. & McMurran, M. (2016). An attachment-based model of therapeutic change processes in the treatment of personality disorder among male forensic inpatients. *Legal and Criminological Psychology*, 21, 390–406.

Woessner, G. & Schwedler, A. (2014). Correctional treatment of sexual and violent offenders: Therapeutic change, prison climate and recidivism. *Criminal Justice and Behavior*, 41(7), 862–879.

Wong, A.E., Vallacher, R.R. & Nowack, A. (2014). Fractal dynamics in self-evaluation reveal self-concept clarity. *Non-Linear Dynamics, Psychology and Life Sciences*, 18(4), 349–369.

Wright, P.H. (1984). Self-referent motivation and the intrinsic quality of friendship. *Journal of Social and Personal Relationships*, 1, 115–130.

Zeigler-Hill, V. & Showers, C.J. (2007). Self-structure and self-esteem stability: The hidden vulnerability of compartmentalization. *Personality and Social Psychology Bulletin*, 33(2), 143–159.

Zittoun, T. & Gillespie, A. (2014). Integrating experiences: Body and mind moving between contexts. The Annual Niels Bohr Lecture in Cultural Psychology. In B. Wagoner, Chaudhary, N. & P. Hviid (Ed.) *Integrating Experiences: Body and Mind Moving between Contexts*. Charlotte, NC: Information Age Publishing.

# 3

# ONLY CONNECT

## Implications of social processes and contexts for understanding trauma

*Adrian Needs*

## Introduction

Some experiences disrupt experiencing and impair related capacities, intruding upon engagement with life and influencing subsequent development. The concept of trauma can appear to offer the key to unlocking and resolving experiences that seem to account for areas of disturbance that perplex and distress both the sufferer and other people. Many would agree that there is an urgent need for recognition and greater understanding in custodial settings of what is an inherently poignant area. In these settings the effects of trauma often go unrecognised and profoundly troubled individuals can be regarded merely as troublesome (Jones, this volume). It does not detract from any of this to suggest that the area is more multifaceted and fraught with controversy than is sometimes assumed.

The realigning of custodial environments advocated in the present volume requires a willingness to recognise the operation of contexts and processes in the past and ongoing development of those held within them. An emphasis on what goes on 'within' rather than between people, an example of what Merlo (2011) termed the 'psychologistic fallacy', has limited consideration of contextual influences on rehabilitation and personal change more generally. Failure to explore beyond this bias at a time of increasing recognition of the role of severe adversity in the lives of many within custodial environments may result in certain conceptual knots pulling ever tighter.

The present chapter sketches some areas of contention in the wider field and considers the developmental consequences of early adversity, referring especially to problems in attachment and patterns of interaction. It then offers an integrative framework for understanding interpersonal processes, contexts and consequences of profoundly adverse events more generally. From examining the effects of developmental trauma and more recent responses to profound adversity there is much to support the view that "risk and recovery are highly dependent on social phenomena" (Charuvastra & Cloitre, 2008 p. 302). This has major implications for how we think about contextual influences and processes in rehabilitative environments. There is perhaps a need to consider this even before we concentrate on specific vulnerabilities and the provision of trauma-informed care, areas elaborated admirably in the present volume in the chapter by Lawrence Jones.

## Some controversies

Competing and emerging perspectives should be expected during the growth of any field of study and the concepts of trauma and post-traumatic stress disorder (PTSD) have undoubtedly been major catalysts for research and the development of clinical practice. Yet in prisons and other custodial environments, oversimplified formulations and interventions in relation to trauma run the risk of causing additional harm or prompting disengagement (Rogers & Law, 2010). Clients in other settings have been known to resist what they see as a 'medicalising' (as opposed to 'normalising') approach to their experiences (Straits-Troster et al., 2011). There have also been numerous reported instances of well-intentioned therapists in a variety of settings unwittingly cultivating in their clients false 'memories' of abuse (Nash & Ost, 2017; Wright, Ost & French, 2006). This cautions against falling into circular reasoning in which trauma is assumed from the patterns of behaving, thinking and feeling that the concept is invoked to explain. It is perhaps also a reminder of the dangers of losing sight of the emergent properties of social interaction, especially in the co-construction of narratives that are influenced by 'idioms of distress' (De Jaegher & Di Paolo, 2007; Hinton & Lewis-Fernandez, 2010).

The origins of oversimplification arguably include a "mostly exclusive focus on the inner world" of the individual (Maercker & Horn, 2013 p. 467). Largely separated from social context, much research and theorising in relation to PTSD has centred on the idea of impaired or incomplete information processing of traumatic events at the individual level (Regel & Joseph, 2010). However, widespread beliefs derived from such a focus have received considerably less empirical support than might be supposed. A review by Rosen and Lilienfeld (2008) suggested that many influential core assumptions concerning, for example, fragmentation or inaccessibility of traumatic memories are based on inconsistent or methodologically flawed empirical findings. Similar claims have been advanced concerning over-inclusive or uncritical assertions in relation to the apparent alterations of consciousness referred to as dissociation (Lynn et al., 2014).

Even the assumption that PTSD is best viewed in terms of a single underlying condition or 'latent variable' has been challenged (McNally et al., 2015). Contending rather memorably that this approach "collapses under the weight of its own implausibility" (p. 839) the latter authors propose an alternative focus on interactions between symptoms as constituting rather than reflecting disorder. For example, rather than both being manifestations of a deeper condition, difficulty in concentrating might be due to sleep loss. It is also consistent with such a view to suggest that the symptoms that come to prominence will vary according to aspects such as the population studied and the nature of the stressful occurrence. As McNally et al. recognise, the centrality of hypervigilance for threat identified in their 'network analysis' of symptoms will not necessarily be found in every study beyond their research with Chinese earthquake survivors. Equally, however, we should be cautious of assumptions of homogeneity even in relation to ostensibly similar episodes. Research with members of the armed forces supports the view that individual appraisals predict PTSD more accurately than the 'objective' severity of stressors (Halligan, Michael, Clark & Ehlers, 2003; Iversen et al., 2008; Weiss et al, 2010). Striking a balance between comprehensiveness and parsimony has been a persistent challenge in attempts to define instigating events (McNally, 2010; Carlson, Smith & Dalenberg, 2013).

There is also substantial variation across (and within) individuals. It should not be overlooked that many people exposed to potentially traumatic events do not suffer major long-term problems. Although some suffer from subsets of symptoms associated with PTSD, perhaps at a 'sub-diagnostic' level which nonetheless results in significant distress and impairment (Sharp, Fonagy & Allen, 2012; Litz, Steenkamp & Nash, 2014), many more suffer from other problems such as depression, anxiety or alcohol misuse, some suffer periodically or after an apparent delay whilst others are relatively unaffected (Egeressy, Butler & Hunter, 2009; Fear et al., 2010; O'Brien, 1998). The attempt to explain heterogeneity in outcomes has contributed to a movement towards a 'trajectory' perspective that takes into account the interactions between a range of prior vulnerabilities and contextual influences surrounding and following exposure to potentially traumatic events (Freeman & Freeman, 2009). We should be alert to the possibility of multiple interacting pathways (Litz et al., 2014).

One of the reasons why agreement has been elusive in the past is that exposure to discrete events often studied as prototypical of trauma (such as motor vehicle accidents or adult rape) may not reflect adequately the impact of exposure to multiple events within what are already challenging circumstances. The latter is likely to be more representative of what can be encountered within contexts such as combat roles in the military (Artra, 2014; Hunt, 2010), being a refugee or civilian survivor of torture (Ebert & Dyck, 2004; Johnson & Thompson, 2008) and dysfunctional families (Wilson, Droždek & Turkovic, 2006). Recognition that this kind of pattern tends to be associated with more complex presentations has prompted developments in theory and practice. It is likely (Greenberg, Brookes & Dunn, 2015) that ICD 11 will include 'complex PTSD' (Courtois & Ford, 2013; Herman, 1992) as a formal diagnosis. Complex PTSD is regarded as a response to multiple or sustained forms of interpersonal trauma, often where escape is not possible. Related terms include 'disorders of extreme stress not otherwise specified' (DESNOS: e.g. Van der Kolk et al., 1996) and areas where it is proposed that functioning is likely to be altered include self-perception, meaning systems, affect regulation and relationships (Pelcovitz et al., 1994). Rogers and Law (2010) argue that this perspective is especially relevant to clients in the criminal justice system, for whom repeated traumatic experiences often tended to be experienced "in the context of disrupted early attachments, neglect, social and emotional deprivation and family breakdown" (p. 156). As in other settings, those most affected are often not recognised by mental health services and treatment, where given, tends to be confined to amelioration of a limited range of symptoms (Corrigan & Hull, 2015).

It is clear that the field of 'trauma' is a varied one, covering a range of presentations, instigating events, surrounding conditions and outcomes. Amongst researchers and clinicians who come from different starting points there is less agreement than might be assumed from popular but overgeneralised or erroneous ideas (for example, that certain experiences almost invariably lead to a single condition referred to as PTSD). As in other fields, understanding can be enhanced by a focus on potentially integrating processes that in turn are likely to be dependent on context (Pawson & Tilley, 1997). Any explanatory account must accommodate well-established findings that both vulnerability and outcomes are heavily influenced by the availability and quality of social support (Brewin, Andrews & Valentine, 2000; Ozer, Best, Lipsey & Weiss, 2003). With added impetus from studies of the influence of early attachment, there is a growing view that many relevant processes and contextual influences in this field are inherently interpersonal and social in nature (Charuvastra & Cloitre, 2008; Maercker & Horn, 2013; Sharp et al., 2012). This view can be applied to understanding developmental trajectories as much as reactions to more discrete or recent events.

In both these areas, questions might be raised concerning the extent to which processes which constitute or influence what is usually referred to as 'trauma' can be understood independently of the interpersonal contexts in which they occur. Neglect of such questions may have encouraged a tendency, indicated below, to focus on episodes of clear-cut abuse in childhood at the expense of the less dramatic but cumulative and pernicious effects of more ordinary negative or limited interactions. In the study of stress more generally, it is widely accepted that how an event or situation is experienced (and whether or not it evokes a 'stress response') is determined largely by how it is appraised in relation to an individual's capacities and resources (Lazarus & Folkman, 1984). Where trauma is concerned, the intrinsically social nature of many stressors has implications for facets that include an individual's social identity, normative beliefs or sense of connectedness. Capacities such as self-regulation or self-esteem develop and are largely sustained through social interaction and integration (see Chapter 2). Pivotal resources include social support (encompassing functions ranging from practical support and guidance to affirmation of identity) but also meanings. Meanings, too, are largely socially determined and thus reach beyond the individual. Relevant aspects are reframed and discussed in more detail below.

It will be apparent that there is a high degree of interdependence between the elements just referred to. This is not necessarily best seen in terms of separate, building-block type variables 'within' the person operating in a linear fashion where an increase or decrease in an 'independent' variable has predictable, incremental effects on a variable that is 'dependent'. As discussed elsewhere in this book (e.g. Chapter 1), 'mind' is part of a system that includes the environment. Extending this to seeing mind and environment in terms of a complex dynamic system highlights, for example, that later states build on earlier ones, that some elements are more loosely coupled that others (elements that are slow to change in the presence of another are still important) and that it is possible for the system to transition abruptly (i.e. discontinuously) from a previous to a new state (e.g. Van Geert, 2003). Several interacting elements will be involved in how or whether the threshold for this is reached (Freeman & Freeman, 2009). In addition, how the environment is apprehended at a given point depends upon the individual's engagement within the environment including intentions and the perspectives of other people (De Jaegher, Di Paolo & Gallagher, 2010; McGann, 2014). It is suggested below that the concept of intersubjectivity develops further the social and interpersonal orientation to understanding trauma and related areas and has important implications for intervention and support.

## Forms and developmental consequences of early 'trauma'

Childhood maltreatment is associated with a range of behavioural and emotional problems likely to contribute to offending (Ardino, 2012; Fagan, 2005; Feiring, Miller-Johnson & Cleland, 2007; Kim, Tajima, Herrenkobl & Huang, 2009; Topitzes, Mersky & Reynolds, 2012). It should be emphasised that these developmental consequences are not necessarily reducible to the impact of discrete episodes of abuse. For example neglect, seemingly the most common form of maltreatment of children, contributes to the prediction of aggression and delinquency in adolescents (especially boys) even after controlling for other forms of maltreatment (Logan-Greene & Jones, 2015). Similarly, the forms of adversity encountered in a "disadvantaged and disadvantaging environment" (Sadeh & McNiel, 2015, p. 575) can lead to negative outcomes in adult life independently of experiences of abuse (Sameroff, 2009). It is apparent that the consequences of maltreatment in childhood for functioning in adulthood do not follow a single pathway (Kendall-Tackett, 2002).

Of course in reality abuse in its different forms and neglect often co-exist (Agaibi & Wilson, 2005) and there is considerable overlap in their effects (Mullen, Martin, Anderson & Herbison, 1996). It has also been reported that exposure to a greater range of forms of early adversity predisposes to later clinical complexity and a wider range of symptoms (Putnam, Harris & Putnam, 2013). It may, however, be useful to attempt to differentiate processes that might be involved. Physical and sexual forms of abuse in childhood refer to events, whilst emotional abuse and neglect are characteristics of a relationship (Glaser, 2000). A child may be placed at risk of abusive events by the nature of a relationship, but the relationship is likely to have very substantial effects on the child's development of its own. As discussed below, dysfunctional interaction patterns in childhood may play a greater part than previously realised in the development of tendencies that are often attributed to abusive events. An additional caveat should be raised. Glaser cautions against regarding abuse and trauma as synonymous, recognising that childhood sexual abuse can be associated with a range of outcomes, arguing, along with other authors (e.g. Kendall-Tackett, Williams & Finkelhor, 1993; Luthar & Zigler, 1991) that it does not invariably give rise to major and enduring problems. This may seem startlingly insensitive but in this it would be no different to other forms of potentially traumatic event, despite issues such as abuse of power and a child's developmental disadvantages. In fact this lack of uniformity in consequences is true of maltreatment in childhood more generally (McGloin & Widom, 2001; Zielinski & Bradshaw, 2006). Some of this variation might be attributed to differences in exposure to abusive events in terms of severity, frequency and chronicity and their occurrence as well as responses to them can be influenced by aspects such as age, gender and temperament (Glaser, 2000; Tyler, 2002). Much also depends on the nature of the physical and social environment. For example, a high level of support following disclosure of sexual abuse has been found to guard against the development of post-traumatic symptoms and a positive relationship with parents reduces the likelihood of subsequent adjustment problems (Bal, De Bourdenhuij, Crombez & Van Oost, 2003; Hyman, Gold & Cott, 2003; Piquero, Farrington & Blumstein, 2003). Conversely, an important predictor of non-resilience in sexually abused girls is heavy drinking by the mother (Chandy, Blum & Resnick, 1996).

## Attachment and parenting

Findings such as the above are a reminder of the developmental consequences of attachment relationships and early interactions. The focus here is on the relationship between a child and his or her primary caregiver (usually the mother) in early childhood, often characterised in terms of quality of interactions in relation to the child's distress, discomfort and proximity seeking (Mikulincer & Shaver, 2007). Others have shifted the emphasis to repeated interactions more generally, seeing these as essential to the child's evolving ability to engage with the actions and perspectives of other people (Lyons-Ruth, 2007). It has been argued that this is a major influence on the child's responses to adversity later in life as well as his or her approaches to social interaction (Charuvastra & Cloitre, 2008; Sharp et al., 2012).

Styles of attachment and their sequelae are described elsewhere in this volume (e.g. Chapter 2). Of particular relevance to conceptualisations of trauma is disorganised attachment. Disorganised attachment can develop in children who have been abused or neglected (Carlson, Cicchetti, Barnett & Braunwald, 1989; Sroufe, Egeland, Carlson & Collins, 2005). It can be seen as involving a tendency to vacillate between elements associated with avoidant and anxious styles (MacBeth, Schwannauer & Gumley, 2008); alternations between avoidance and approach may occur unexpectedly, as if under stress the individual lacked a coherent attachment strategy (Fonagy & Target, 1997; Obsuth, Brumariu, Henninghausen & Lyons-Ruth, 2013). This lack of coherence may have its origins in a caregiver being simultaneously a source of comfort and alarm (Main & Hesse, 1990), but the reality may be both more complex and more mundane (Lyons-Ruth, 2007).

Here too, there is a need to 'disentangle' effects of specific incidents of abuse from more sustained disturbances in the daily interactions between parent and child; the latter may be more pervasive in extent and consequences (Dutra, Bureau, Holmes, Lyubchik, & Lyons-Ruth, 2009; Lyons-Ruth, Melnick, Patrick & Hobson, 2006). It has been pointed out by Karlen Lyons-Ruth that a very young child has a limited capacity for gauging *actual* threat to survival; threat is evaluated primarily in terms of proximity of the caregiver and the latter's responses to the child's distress, discomfort and communication of needs and desires (Lyons-Ruth et al., 2006; Schuder & Lyons-Ruth, 2004). These authors also suggest that repeated failure of the caregiver to help regulate the young child's distress can itself be seen as a 'hidden trauma'. Without help in regulation, distress is likely to escalate to excessive proportions as part of a cycle that is never far away. Within this cycle there can be little room for a sense of safety and trust in others (Stone, Becker, Huber & Catalano, 2012) or even coherent understanding one's own experience.

An exclusive focus on overt episodes of abuse at the expense of more ordinary but pervasive patterns may therefore be misplaced. In support of this, the best predictor of 'borderline' features in early adulthood has been found in longitudinal work to be maternal withdrawal at the age of 18 months (Lyons-Ruth et al., 2013). Even the development of detached forms of experiencing referred to as 'dissociation' may owe more to distorted communication (in which the child is discouraged from treating his or her own intermittent distress as a legitimate object of attention) than to more overtly abusive events (Dutra et al., 2009; Ogawa et al., 1997; Putnam, 1997). Interactional styles with potentially profound effects upon a child's development have been described, including distinctive profiles characterised as 'hostile/self-referential' and 'helpless/fearful' (Goldberg, Benoit, Blokland & Madigan, 2003; Lyons-Ruth et al., 2006). Apparently related to the mothers' own experiences of sub-optimal parenting or other mental health problems, these have been associated with the emergence of what might be regarded as a role reversal. In this the child attempts to take the initiative in gaining the caregiver's involvement through controlling behaviour such as being punitive or solicitous (Lyons-Ruth et al., 2006). Such a pattern tends to result in confusion over boundaries in relationships and in the exceeding of developmental capacities (Macfie, Brumariu & Lyons-Ruth, 2015). Strategies that develop in these circumstances appear to contribute to the development of, for example, impulsive or depressive tendencies that persist into adolescence and possibly beyond (Obsuth et al., 2013). However, few would regard these styles as PTSD-like reactions to discrete events.

Problems of parents (such as substance misuse, depression, poverty or their own attachment difficulties) that contribute to them maltreating their children often play a part in "exacerbating deleterious outcomes" in other ways (Zielinski & Bradshaw, 2006 p. 54). As Zielinski and Bradshaw note, these include failure to provide adequate supervision, social support or structure. Research in the field of developmental psychopathology suggests that parental styles that perpetuate confusion may develop into especially pernicious forms. Where attempts at sense-making are ignored, dismissed, intruded upon or tainted with blame and coercion by adults the environment can be regarded as 'invalidating' (Linehan, 1993). The developing individual may repeatedly be subjected to the "experience of being punished precisely for being right in one's own view of the context ... (an individual's) messages ... are received as if they were in some way different from that which he thought he intended" (Bateson, 1972, pp. 206–207). Relentless criticism has been identified in meta-analysis as a key predictor of relapse in later psychological problems such as psychosis, mood and eating disorders (Butzlaff & Hooley, 1998). In childhood and adolescence similar sequences do little to foster a sense of agency, autonomy or a sense of one's positions and perspectives as coherent and viable (Liotti, 1992; Ryan, 2005).

## Consequences and influences beyond the family

Outside of the family, children with a history of maltreatment have been described as showing rigid interpersonal behaviour with situationally inappropriate affective displays, limited emotional self-awareness and poor recovery from distress (Shields & Cicchetti, 1997, 1998). Their attention is frequently directed towards cues of anger and hostility at the expense of positive cues or those that indicate situational contingencies such as the availability of reward (Pollak, 2015). What maltreated children have often learned from their early interactions include a propensity for distrust, seeing the world as a dangerous place, experiencing a reduced sense of personal control over circumstances, with difficulties in relationships and in accessing social support (Kendall-Tackett, 2002). Negative or unrewarding interpersonal styles heighten the risk of rejection by peers. This in turn can contribute to social withdrawal, restricting opportunities for affiliation with prosocial peers and the exercise of ordinary social skills (Tyler, 2002). In such ways individuals can have an active role in shaping future contexts and influencing their own developmental trajectories.[1]

A child disadvantaged in his or her development is likely to be aware of the consequences rather than the process, even when the child has learned to internalise blame and presume responsibility for abuse or for abandonment or rejection in the case of family breakdown. It should be noted at this point that many individuals in custodial settings have backgrounds in institutional or other forms of 'out of home' care: Williams, Papadopoulou and Booth (2012) reported an estimate of around a quarter in England and Wales, although their sample was restricted to prisoners serving four years or under. Moving into care often follows exposure to a variety of forms of maltreatment, although in line with other research emotional abuse and neglect appear most common (Kay & Green, 2016). Attachment problems may occur in institutions even where (as recent scandals concerning historical abuse in children's homes indicate has not always been the case) provision and protection are adequate in other ways (Oliveira et al., 2015). Foster care can improve developmental outcomes for maltreated children but multiple placements, especially, are often experienced as disruptive (Heller, Larrieu, D'Imperio & Boris, 1999).

It is possible for negative trajectories to be set on a different course by positive involvements with other adults such as grandparents or teachers or by involvement with prosocial peers (Zielinski & Bradshaw, 2006), but a child who has learned to expect the worst is not always receptive. Later in life, at least, the availability and utilising of social support can be compromised if an individual responds to difficulties with anger, aggression or social withdrawal (Sharp et al, 2012; Sippel et al., 2015). Nonetheless, the belief that even one person cares about them can make a substantial difference to a maltreated child's self-esteem and resilience (Zielinski &

Bradshaw, 2006). Developmental trajectories are also altered by changes in parental circumstances including life stress, social support and mental health (Sroufe, Egeland, Carlson & Collins, 2005). All too often, however, there is a continuing spiral of negative behaviour, outcomes and outlook. It is worth reflecting that the possibility of increased exposure to adversity amongst those who are least able to cope with it (Needs, 2016) may have parallels with the idea of 'hidden trauma' mentioned earlier.

## Healthy development

A crucial process associated with healthy psychological development is that the child's experience must be acknowledged in ways that are understood by the child (Lyons-Ruth et al., 2006; Whitmer, 2001). For very young children this typically involves exaggerated mirroring of the child's emotions (Fonagy, Gergely, Junst & Target, 2004) and a dialogue of movement patterns between caregiver and child (Stone & De Koeyer-Laros, 2012). In these ways the child comes to 'know' and explore his or her own embodied intentions and anticipations in relation to those of the caregiver and wider meanings of the external world (Borelli, 2007; Target, 2007; Trevarthen, 1979, 2002). A social rather than a cognitive process (Reddy, 2008), this provides the beginnings of dialogical 'positions' (Lyons-Ruth, 2007; Stone & De Koeyer-Laros, 2012) and what Fonagy and Target (1997) termed reflective function. From this process also arises a sense of connectedness to others and this remains a foundation of meaningfulness throughout the life course (Cruwys, Haslam, Dingle, Haslam & Jetten, 2014; Lambert et al., 2013). The mutual awareness of perspectives that constitutes intersubjectivity comes to replace physical proximity as a developmentally appropriate means of attaining connectedness (Borelli, 2006; Lyons-Ruth, 2006).

Supported by experiences beyond the parent–child dyad such as exploration of roles and perspectives in play (Gillespie & Cornish, 2010), the child learns in interactions to be "truthful and sensitive to the states of mind of both parties" (Lyons-Ruth, 2007, p. 604). This provides vital experience of understanding 'with' other people (De Jaegher et al., 2010). From its origins in early interactions with the caregiver, intersubjectivity moves to an awareness of groups (such as families, peers, occupations, cultures and movements in society) and their normative beliefs, patterns and values. Burgeoning group affiliations help the individual to reduce subjective uncertainty, impose order on a potentially confusing world of other subjectivities and derive meaning from the appropriation of norms and routines; they also foster the pursuit of collective goals and confer a sense of stability, shared social identity and feeling of being part of something that transcends the boundaries of self (Lambert et al., 2013).

## Development and trauma in perspective

It has been seen how early social experience involving attachment and maltreatment can limit or skew such development. This can lead to, for example, the emergence of negative and limiting preoccupations, strategies and vulnerabilities in interpersonal encounters (Baker & Beech, 2004; Beck et al., 2001; Bernstein, Arntz & de Vos, 2007; Platts, Tyson & Mason, 2002) that predispose to later negative outcomes. The sequelae of complex trauma can be difficult to separate from personality disorder (Greenberg et al., 2015), but a developmental perspective suggests that the array of problems typically encountered in prisoners with mental health problems cannot be reduced to a narrow focus on even multiple traumatic events (Rogers & Law, 2010). Observations in maltreated children of heightened attention to threat cues and tendencies to rumination might be presumed to mirror symptoms associated with PTSD, but an emphasis on the processes by which these arise (Pollak, 2015) is more consistent with the focus on symptoms proposed by McNally et al. (2015) than the 'latent variable' approach which these authors criticise. A developmental approach is also necessary to place attachment in perspective. It should not be reduced to an immutable style, rather like a blood group (Ansbro, 2008). Meta-analysis suggests that attachment is associated with delinquency, but the mean effect size is small to moderate (Hoeve et al., 2009). This does not mean it is relatively unimportant. It is what would be expected when later interactions involving developmental processes and contextual factors are also relevant and relationships are non-linear.

## Processes in relation to traumatic events and problematic life changes

The developmental consequences of early adversity extend to increasing the risk of exposure to further potentially traumatic events in a variety of domains, including relationships. New events may occur as a result of, for example, risk-taking, substance misuse, emotional volatility or sensitivity to rejection (Carlson, Egeland & Sroufe, 2009; Pagano et al., 2004). In addition, childhood adversity appears to confer a heightened vulnerability to the effects of stressful events later in life (McLaughlin, Conron, Koenen & Gilman, 2010), with both early trauma and other forms of adversity predisposing to a later diagnosis of PTSD (Kessler, Chiu, Demelers & Walters, 2005; Yehuda et al., 1995). In view of this it is unsurprising that disruptive events experienced by those within the prison population are far from confined to childhood. Events of more recent origin, including incarceration, the index offence, even activities during gang membership can also have major effects (Adshead, Ferrito & Bose, 2015; Kerig, Chaplo, Bennett & Modrowski, 2016a; also see Jones, this volume).

The nature and implications of recent events and circumstances can resonate with earlier (not necessarily childhood) events and circumstances to the point that poorly reconciled implications, memories and somatic and other emotional aspects are activated. This appears especially likely when contextual factors such as depleted social support have eroded an individual's resilience. This has been proposed, for example, in relation to the emergence of distressing preoccupations following the transition from military to civilian life (Needs, 2015a). The following discussion draws upon limited research relevant to this area, also raising briefly the role of life changes and contextual factors in the background to offences to which some of these aspects may be relevant (Needs, 2015b). Also highlighted is the possibility that, even in the absence of significant childhood adversity the necessarily social basis of participating in a world of other human beings carries vulnerabilities which are often exposed when an individual is wounded by events.

Much less research has addressed in detail the impact of recent events and contextual influences on offending than has been conducted on establishing long-term associations between childhood adversity, crime and delinquency. This is despite the arguable relevance of proximal events, their meanings and possible recurrence for analysing past violence and future risk (Needs & Towl, 1997; Silver & Teasdale, 2005). Such neglect also contrasts with the attention given to the role of positive outcomes such as employment and supportive relationships in the desistance literature (e.g. Laub & Sampson, 2003). Turning this on its head would prompt us to consider the potentially destabilising implications of profound disruption in these or similar areas *prior* to offending (Needs, 2015b). Furthermore, it has been suggested that individual differences in an "increased sensitivity to fear, threat and worry" heighten the risk of PTSD in prisoners and that this propensity is primarily biologically based (Egeressy et al., 2009, p. 219). Yet recent research suggests that similar characteristics ('neuroticism') can be increased by a preponderance of major negative life events (Jeronimus, Riese, Sanderman & Ormel, 2014). Similarly resilience, the capacity to adjust successfully to current adversity (Agaibi & Wilson, 2005), is heavily influenced by current social networks and social support (Sippel et al., 2015).

It is suggested below that many events and attendant circumstances associated with symptoms of trauma derive some of their impact from severely challenging implications for an individual's senses of identity, meaning, control and belonging. These can be seen as necessary and interdependent elements of a system capable of social agency (see Chapter 2). Reconciling previous adaptations in these areas with new circumstances is a central process in life's transitions (Ashforth, 2001) but some changes in life are abrupt, intense, threatening, undermining and entirely involuntary. Loss of previous adaptation in one element can make adaptation in another unsustainable. Thus feeling betrayed by members of a group that was identified with can disrupt the identity and meaning that were predicated on belonging to the group. Disruption may spiral and intensify through iterative cycles of interaction between elements, where outputs of processes such as rumination or conflict become part of the context of the next iteration. This may continue until reconciliation begins to be achieved. Thus, for example, a 'criminal spin' can sometimes be ended through conditional acceptance by others (Elisha, Idisis & Ronel, 2013).

These areas of identity, meaning, control and belonging are also relevant to understanding the impact of major negative life events and adverse circumstances that often precede severe violent or sexual offending (Needs, 2015b). Originally proposed in the field of role transitions during careers (Ashforth, 2001) and resembling areas typically affected by social exclusion (Williams, 2001, 2007), these largely interdependent areas have been described in terms of their possible wider relevance in more detail elsewhere (see Chapter 2). The following section outlines how the framework can be used to integrate important aspects of trauma beyond a narrow focus on 'symptoms'.

## Identity

Reconciling a sense of distinctness and connectedness is at the heart of the development of the self (Kyselo, 2016), self-determination (Deci & Ryan, 2000) and moral experience (Parish, 2014); autonomy and interdependence exist in a relationship of 'mutual irreducibility' (Tsekeris, 2015). Traumatic experiences tend to dominate autobiographical memory as much as they permeate feelings towards other people with a sense of alienation. Any previous view of self as capable and acceptable (and thus able to achieve important life goals) is profoundly challenged and this can maintain a sense of threat as potently as external stressors (Ehlers & Clark, 2000; Jobson, 2009).

Whilst social alignments entail shared norms, goals and aspirations that are an integral part of structuring and navigating the social world, they also provide a basis for shared perspectives, including how an individual believes he or she may be seen by others (Cruwys et al., 2014; Jetten, Haslam, Haslam, Dingle & Jones, 2014). The latter is a major source of evaluations of the self, encompassing, for example, the perceptions of worth and competence that constitute self-esteem (Leary, 2007) and the discrepancy between standards that connect to others and the acts, or failures to act, associated with guilt (Tangney, Stuewig & Mashek, 2007).

Guilt and shame have both been considered as major influences on the experience of trauma (Lee, Scragg & Turner, 2001; Taylor, 2015; Wilson et al., 2006). Shame has been seen as the more pervasive and painful 'moral emotion', referring to the individual's seemingly core self (rather than specific behaviours) and often involving a sense of shrinking, smallness and exposure (Tangney et al., 2007). It has also been seen as "the quintessential social emotion underlying social threat" (Budden, 2009, p. 1033). In Budden's formulation, shame and threat to the 'social self' are central to both the development and course of PTSD. Feelings of being devalued, blameworthy or excluded from socially defined roles may be especially persistent when stigma is involved (Murphy & Bussutil, 2014) or when previous social integration is lost (Hatch et al., 2013).

The kind of disruption often associated with major negative life changes (and potentially traumatic events) typically gives rise to a sense of 'self-discontinuity', a "sense of disjointedness between one's past and present self" (Sedikides, Wildschut, Routledge & Arndt, 2015, p. 52). When the viability of past and present self is denied a desired and coherent future self may seem obscure or unattainable, although a feared possible self may seem distressingly close (Stein & Markus, 1996; Paternoster & Bushway, 2009).

## Meaning

Events and circumstances may also disrupt the 'narrative' or life story that embeds the first-person perspective, supporting and integrating the sense of identity (Meichenbaum, 2007; Neimeyer, 2006). Sustaining assumptions concerning the safety, justice or the benevolence of the world in which it unfolds may be undermined

(Janoff-Bulman, 1992). Events that are discrepant with existing meaning can trigger cycles of rumination and avoidance that persist until the growth of new meaning occurs; this is often experienced in terms of reconciliation, coherence and purpose (Joseph & Linley, 2011; Park, 2010). Alternatively, rumination and avoidance can be accompanied by the increasing domination of negative themes and interpretations that are congruent with the instigating events and circumstances (Berntsen & Rubin, 2006; Park, 2010).

Given the role in the appropriation and construction of meaning of social phenomena such as norms and identity it is unsurprising that social exclusion (including ostracism, rejection and stigma) has been found to reduce a sense of meaning in life (Stillman et al., 2009; Williams, 2001, 2007). In addition many traumatic events, by their nature as well as their consequences, are ones that set the individual apart from other people. Consistent with this idea in recent years there has been a growth of interest in the "moral injury" of "events that challenge one's basic sense of humanity" (Currier, Holland & Malott, 2015, p. 230). Originating in work with former members of the armed forces (Drescher et al., 2011; Litz et al., 2009), this has also been applied to distress in occupational settings such as nursing (Musto, Rodney & Vanderheide, 2015).

Morality is closely linked to a sense of connectedness to others. If people adhere to positive norms, values and roles this makes the world a safer and more reliable place; violation of these by people tends to have the opposite effect (Parish, 2014). This is why the occurrences most often associated with severe psychological consequences are those seen as due to 'human intent' (Charuvastra & Cloitre, 2008). In military samples, especially problematic events that violate basic norms of human conduct include encountering atrocities or those that potentiate recognition of common humanity with enemy combatants (Farnsworth, Drescher, Nieuwstra & Walser, 2014; King, Foy & Gudanowski, 1996). Reconciling the subjectivity (including intentions and perspectives) of others with one's own through intersubjectivity is fundamental to communication, even in very young children (Trevarthen, 1979, 2002). Understanding 'with' is also an important way in which we co-construct and receive validation of our understanding (De Jaegher et al., 2010). Conversely, events perceived in terms of betrayal, callousness and indifference to basic standards – or to one's own subjectivity – are especially difficult to reconcile and are linked to severity of symptoms associated with PTSD (Dunsmore, Clark & Ehlers, 2001; Kelley, Weathers, Mason & Pruneau, 2012). These attributes might be seen as the antithesis of trust, social support and certainty and may, as suggested below, deprive the individual of the benefits of intersubjectivity in becoming reconciled with events.

## Control

Events that appear to strip an individual of dignity, violate norms and expectations, trap, render powerless or involve domination or subjugation by others often damage the individual's sense of personal control, integrity and agency (Budden, 2009). This might be aggravated by the intensity of a range of emotions and an overwhelming of capacities for coping and self-regulation (Glaser, 2000; Holmes, Grey & Young, 2005). However, Brewin, Andrews and Rose (2000) noted that some individuals appear not to have experienced intense emotions during the event itself. Reasons for the latter range from the sense of unreality and numbing associated with peri-traumatic disso-ciation to the more purposive 'getting on with the job' inculcated in the military by training, culture and commitment to one's comrades (Keegan, 1976; Scurfield, 2009). However, the subjective context of many instigating events suggests that an enduring sense of threat, foreboding and uncertainty (Ehlers & Clark, 2000) associated with PTSD may be due to more than a simple process akin to classical conditioning of emotions to environmental stimuli and this seems to be especially true of individuals in prison (Rogers & Law, 2010). Emotional numbing appears to play an important role in the offending of detained young people (Kerig et al., 2016b).

In addition, research in other areas supports differentiation of factors related to onset from those associated with persistence. The experience of lack of control over events (particularly those entailing one or more forms of loss) is a major precipi-tant of episodes of anxiety and depression, with persistence tending to be associ-ated with a continued sense of vulnerability (Kendler, Hettema, Butera, Gardner & Prescott, 2003). Exposure to sudden, uncontrollable events that threaten or trigger the emotional pain of loss (such as abandonment) can be associated with symptoms of trauma as strongly as more familiar stressors such as those that evoke fear (Carlson et.al., 2013). Conversely, positive outcomes in a range of disorders are strongly linked to an individual's sense of self-efficacy (Benight & Bandura, 2004), although the capacity for related constructs such as self-determination and autonomy can be impaired by both current and past interpersonal and self-regulatory influences (Ellemers, Gilder & Haslam, 2004; Ryan, 2005). This is consistent with arguments that human agency involves being able to act independently of the immediate sit-uation through an intersubjective process of reflecting upon, identifying with and participating in other perspectives and concerns (Gillespie, 2012). Certainly, social resources appear to have a major bearing on resilience (Ungar, 2013), with depleted social resources in the form of low social support showing an association with the use of avoidant coping (Silva et al., 2000). Avoidant coping, including patterns such as substance misuse that typically create additional problems in a person's life, has been found to be a consistent predictor of poor outcomes in trauma victims (Charuvastra & Cloitre, 2008). Agency and resilience appear largely to depend on the availability and use of social resources.

## Belonging

It is no small irony that the withdrawn or angry patterns of interpersonal behaviour of many people suffering the effects of severe adversity and trauma can drive away the very support that might have helped them (Kaniasty & Norris, 2008; Ozer, Best, Lipsey & Weiss, 2008). As with depression (Cruwys et al., 2014), withdrawal can exacerbate as well as be prompted by an impaired sense of con-nectedness with others. The sense of belonging and more widely, connectedness appears to be a fundamental concern in human existence (Baumeister & Leary, 1995). What connectedness encompasses includes subscription to shared norms, values and beliefs and participation in joint activities. In a manner that could be seen as consistent with the operation of extended mind (Chapter 1) "the social context is not only a resource for meaning but the very source of meaning itself" (Brinn & Auerbach, 2015 p. 82). Crucially (and rather obviously, were it not for the common tendency to conceptualise process in terms of what Cruwys et al. referred to as 'individual-level deficits'), connectedness also involves intersubjectivity (Borelli, 2006). This may be especially important in the context of trauma. It was noted above that traumatic events and their aftermath often involve isolation from others and that this can take a variety of forms (including physically, morally and socially).

In this regard military research is particularly evocative, given the traditional emphasis in this context on social integration against a background of risk of physical harm and extreme experiences (Hatch et al., 2013). Thus social support has been described as a "substantial component" of unit cohesion (Jones et al., 2012, p. 56). Here social support refers to resources (such as confirmation of social identity), connections between members (such as commitment to the unit and its values) and consequences (such as perceived control and confidence; see Iversen et al., 2008). As with other teams and of particular interest in relation to intersubjectivity, making sense of situations can usefully be seen as taking place between team or unit members rather than at the level of isolated individuals (Pedersen & Cooke, 2006). The narratives or 'stories' generated and shared within a group are important determinants of outcomes following exposure to potential trauma (Meichenbaum, 2006; 2014). As Meichenbaum notes, the construction of narratives (like resilience) is an inherently social rather than a purely individual process. Storytelling has an established place in military culture, especially in units exposed to high levels of risk and demand (Thornborrow & Brown, 2009). This exchange and negotiation of perspectives in an intersubjective process aids meaning-making, a sense of validation, coherence and reconciliation of the implications of challenging events (Burnell, Coleman & Hunt, 2006; Hunt, 2010). Again in the words of Brinn and Auerbach (2015, p. 82), "models of meaning-making and social support have begun to overlap".

In other settings, too, shared views of reality are more likely to be trusted and enhance a sense of connectedness and validation (Echterhoff, Higgins & Levine, 2009). The continued importance of the interpersonal context is highlighted, however, by the observation that problems as a result of experiences in military service are most likely to surface when the social integration (including shared perspectives and intersubjectivity) that was a sustaining influence in the military is impaired or no longer available following the transition to civilian life (Needs, 2015a). Just as more generally, perceived social acknowledgement was found by Maercker and Muller (2004) to correlate negatively with the severity of PTSD symptoms, the isolation and sense of difference to others felt by troubled Israeli veterans was characterised by Stein and Tuval-Mashiach (2015) as 'failed intersubjectivity'.

## Creating conditions for connectedness: a context for intervention

Ways in which processes related to social exclusion and a sense of rejection might contribute to offending are discussed elsewhere in this volume (see Chapter 2). It has been noted in the present chapter that in the context of adversity issues relevant to connectedness, morality and safety appear to be intimately and reciprocally related. Even to a young child, other people are likely to be the principal threat to safety and experienced safety is as much a matter of connectedness to others as the absence of fear (Lyons–Ruth, 2007). In the words of Parish (2014, p. 47), "the world we experienced as moral and safe (safe because moral) can come to seem dangerously not moral, not safe". As Parish also notes, perceptions of morality are closely entwined with the experience of emotions such as shame, guilt, contempt, anger or vengefulness and these can be as much a part of trauma as fear (Budden, 2009). They also involve judgements concerning the viewpoints of others (Maercker & Horn, 2013). Like shame (and with echoes of the interpersonal styles of maltreated children) they may result in rigid, constricted and short-term thinking that has been characterised as an 'escape from self' (Baumeister, 1990). Such a process also makes the possibility of connection with others (and the benefits of intersubjectivity described by Gillespie, 2012) ever more remote.

As a result, some individuals may find it difficult to sustain or identify with conventional 'moral' behaviour. Along with reduced prosocial agency and increased disillusionment they may inhabit a less safe world in which threat is more readily perceived. There is growing evidence that responses to social and physical threat and pain share much of the same neural circuitry (e.g. Eisenberger, 2013; Eisenberger & Lieberman, 2004), perhaps related to an evolutionary past when survival of the individual could be crucially dependent on being a member of a group (Baumeister & Leary, 1995). An individual in this situation of perceived vulnerability and uncertainty might be more sensitive to the perceived intentions (including indifference to one's own perspectives) and moral transgressions of others. It is possible that this is one source of prisoners' preoccupation with issues of 'legitimacy' in custodial environments (Liebling, 2004). There can also be much within custodial environments that is intrinsically unsafe (Butler, 2008; Day, this volume).

Both acknowledgement (Maercker & Müller, 2004) and the negotiation of intentions are intrinsic aspects of an intersubjective process that results in a working, shared understanding and apprehension of other perspectives and possibilities (see Chapter 2). This bringing together of one's own subjectivity with the subjectivities of other people provides a resource, an additional perspective that helps in making sense of events just as it is a crucial aspect of agency (Gillespie, 2012). 'Processing' might best be seen (and accomplished) as an intersubjective rather than as an intrapsychic activity, aided by being able to bring to bear other dialogical positions (c.f. Kogler, 2012) in understanding and a sense that one is affirmed, valued and not alone. Intersubjectivity may be a source of enhancement if not an essential ingredient of exposure-based therapies, but it is noteworthy that Bleiberg and Markowitz (2005) found that improving social bonds results in improvement of PTSD symptoms even in the absence of exposure-based work (see also Markowitz et al., 2015). It is intrinsic to an effective therapeutic alliance and helps explain the significant protective and ameliorative effects of social support. It is perfectly consistent with such a view, however, to recognise that social support can only be effective when it is sensitive to context and genuinely responsive to the individual's perspective (Robitaille, Orpana & McIntosh, 2012).

Establishing trust is paramount as a condition for intersubjectivity and therefore adaptive change (Gillespie, 2011). This includes creating a sense of safety (Mikulincer & Shaver, 2007; Pearlman & Courtois, 2005). It is especially necessary when denial, undermining or challenging of one's own subjectivity or the alien, threatening implications of the perspectives and intentions of other people were intrinsic to the experience and consequences of exposure to potentially traumatic events. Ultimately, it counters a sense of threat and the legacies of moral injury and reduced connectedness. A troubled individual needs to benefit from understanding 'with' other human beings, but also needs to know that this is possible. It would, however, be naive to expect every individual whose development has been predicated to a large degree on negative and limiting experiences readily to relinquish long-standing strategies for self-preservation in the face of expectations of threat, especially when self-regulatory and other capacities are fragile at best. Many will resort, understandably, to a variety of tactics for testing would-be helpers, even denigrating them and their efforts in order to maintain familiar understanding. Aside from therapeutic (largely intersubjective) skill, patience and perseverance, movement is best achieved within a 'secure base' that goes beyond a single therapeutic relationship to the current interpersonal environment itself (see Chapter 2). Even then, attrition within therapeutic communities underlines that progress at a given point in time is not guaranteed (Haigh, 2013). We should be neither surprised nor too disheartened by this; research in the field of psychotherapy more generally indicates that change often follows a discontinuous, non-linear course (Hayes et al., 2007; Laurenceau, Hayes, & Feldman, 2007). What we can be certain of is that custodial environments that are experienced as threatening, unresponsive or lacking in legitimacy increase the chances that an individual will remain guarded or even antagonistic in ways that preclude openness to other perspectives (see Chapter 2).

Such an understanding may help to explain the essentially moral dimension to the narratives of redemption and condemnation identified by Maruna (2001). A sense of redemption may arise from connectedness beyond the confines of either the individual's past or the prison subculture, enabling a social identity that permits openness to other perspectives and adherence to wider norms, beliefs and values. This provides a new context for making sense of troubling experiences. The process is essentially one of reconciliation (Ferrito, Needs & Adshead, 2017; Hunt, 2010) and helps enlist the possibilities of post-traumatic growth in working towards desistance from offending (Mapham & Hefferon, 2012).

## Conclusion

The role of severe adversity in the lives of many residents of custodial institutions has often been overlooked. Yet attempts to address the consequences of adversity have led to the embracing of assumptions that can obscure the origins of difficulties. Although forms of maltreatment tend to co-occur, the influence and implications of unresponsive, non-reciprocal social interactions with caregivers can be neglected in favour of more overt forms of abuse. This is not to deny either the existence or the potential impact of the latter. However, the quality of repeated interactions is related to resilience and lack of contingent responsiveness tends to cause problems in its own right. These may be wrongly attributed to discrete episodes of more dramatic forms of abuse; failure to regulate a child's escalating and overwhelming distress, for example, has been seen as a form of unacknowledged trauma. The consequences of developmental disadvantages also include limited and precarious ways of navigating and negotiating life's subsequent exigencies in a variety of domains. These are often reflected in offending and difficulties in engaging constructively in necessary transitions, including desistance from offending (see Chapter 2). Vulnerability to extreme reactions to negative life events (even if the individual may have contributed to their occurrence) may produce echoes of the unacknowledged, unregulated distress of childhood trauma in the experience of states such as anguish, confusion and subjective isolation and in the seemingly unexceptional nature of some of the events concerned. However exposure to profoundly destabilising events, sometimes in what are already challenging or undermining circumstances, can occur for a variety of reasons and come to affect even the most resilient of individuals. Responses are heavily dependent upon the perceived nature of the event(s) and, crucially, by contextual factors such as social support.

The present chapter suggests that there may be parallels or even continuities between developmental and later trauma. It draws upon a framework originally designed to help understand processes involved in transitions (i.e. in adjustments to major changes) during the life course. Some experiences defy ready reconciliation with existing or hoped for adaptations that can be represented heuristically as identity, meaning, control and belonging. Crises in areas such as self-continuity, coherence and worth, sense-making and purpose, agency and self-regulation, affiliation and connectedness may be acute, chronic or delayed, often depending on the availability of resources that aid reconciliation. Until reconciliation occurs interactions between elements of the person as an autonomous sense-making system (De Jaegher & Froese, 2009) are likely to instigate physiological effects that have a volition of their own (e.g. Van der Kolk, 2014).

The world in general may appear a profoundly altered place as a result of severe adversity, but key aspects are often centred on our connections with other people. Traumatic events often involve attributions of human intent that in some cases may be difficult to avoid and can challenge a sense of connectedness at a fundamental level (Charuvastra & Cloitre, 2008; Heine, Proulx & Vohs, 2006). This might then deny the individual the benefits of intersubjectivity, the understanding 'with' other people (De Jaegher et al., 2010) that may be crucial to what is usually referred to as processing and which may be a major active ingredient in several forms of therapy. This may also, for example, help sustain resilience during military service but at the cost of conferring a degree of vulnerability following the altered contexts of the transition to civilian life. Perhaps above all, or at least as a starting point, people need a sense of acknowledgement (Maercker & Horn, 2013); indeed perceived deficiencies in this regard in avowedly therapeutic relationships in the criminal justice system can be experienced as quite damaging (Goldhill, 2015).

Negative experiences within custodial institutions can aggravate the legacies of trauma (see Jones, this volume) and fall short of providing opportunities for new reconciliations of needs for identity, meaning, control and belonging. All too often, such settings do too little to revise apprehensions of the intentions of others or enable the exercise of genuine intersubjectivity, within a secure base, that is necessary to fostering and sustaining new development (Chapter 2). Several chapters in the present volume indicate that it is possible to go further in the direction of organising provision around positive relationships and opportunities for growth. This may be essential if rehabilitative approaches are to become more consistently effective. To use an analogy from medicine, in the present mainstream it is as if advances in surgery had been unmatched by improvements in hygiene.

A focus on ameliorating (and avoiding aggravating) symptoms, promoting reconciliation of experiences and supporting transition is undeniably important. Nonetheless, it is worth considering seriously the conclusion of Ungar (2013), on the basis of a sizable and varied amount of empirical research on resilience in community settings, that "Far more individuals will adapt positively after traumatic events when we make environments benign than if we try and change individuals" (p. 263).

## Notes

1  It is also entirely consistent with such a perspective to highlight the possibility that from birth a caregiver's behaviour may have been influenced by the child's innate emotional reactivity, emotional modulation and sociability (Linehan, 1993; Lyons-Ruth, 2006). Conditions such as foetal alcohol syndrome (Popova, Lange, Bekmuradov, Mihic & Rehm, 2011) are a reminder that prior to this, biological propensities may have been influenced by the prenatal environment provided by the mother (Trevarthen & Aitken, 2001).

## References

Adshead, G., Ferrito, M. & Bose, S. (2015). Recovery after homicide: Narrative shifts in therapy with homicide perpetrators. *Criminal Justice and Behavior*, 42(1), 70–81.

Agaibi, C.E. & Wilson, J.P. (2005). Trauma, PTSD, and resilience: A review of the literature. *Trauma, Violence and Abuse*, 6, 195–216.

Ansbro, M. (2008). Using attachment theory with offenders. *Probation Journal*, 55, 231–244.

Ardino, V. (2012). Offending behaviour: The role of trauma and PTSD. *European Journal of Psychotraumatology*, 3, 10.3402/ejpt.v3i0.18968.

Artra, I.P. (2014). Transparent assessment: Discovering authentic meanings made by combat veterans. *Journal of Constructivist Psychology*, 27(3), 211–235.

Ashforth, B.A. (2001). *Role Transitions in Organisational Life: An Identity-Based Perspective.* Mahwah, NJ: Lawrence Erlbaum Associates.

Baker, E. & Beech, A.R. (2004). Dissociation and variability of adult attachment dimensions and early maladaptive schemas in sexual and violent offenders. *Journal of Interpersonal Violence*, 19, 1119–1136.

Bal, S., Crombez, G., Van Oost, P. & Debourdeaudhuij I. (2003). The role of social support in well-being and coping with self-reported stressful events in adolescents. *Child Abuse and Neglect*, 27, 1377–1395.

Bateson, G. (1972). *Steps to an Ecology of Mind.* Frogmore, UK: Paladin.

Baumeister, R.F. (1990). Suicide as escape from self. *Psychological Review*, 97, 90–113.

Baumeister, R.F. & Leary, M.R. (1995). The need to belong: Desire for attachment as a fundamental human motivation. *Psychological Bulletin*, 117, 497–539.

Beck, A.T., Butler, A.C., Brown, G.K., Dahlsgard, K.K., Newman, C.F., & Beck, J.S. (2001). Dysfunctional beliefs discriminate personality disorders. *Behavior Research & Therapy*, 39(10), 1213–1225.

Benight, C.C. & Bandura, A. (2004). Social cognitive theory of posttraumatic recovery: The role of perceived self-efficacy. *Behaviour Research and Therapy*, 42, 1129–1148.

Bernstein, D.P., Arntz, A. & de Vos, N. (2007). Schema focused therapy in forensic settings: Theoretical model and recommendations for best clinical practice. *International Journal of Forensic Mental Health*, 6, 169–183.

Berntsen, D. & Rubin, D.C. (2006). The centrality of event scale: A measure of integrating a trauma into one's identity and its relation to post-traumatic stress disorder symptoms. *Behaviour Research and Therapy*, 44, 219–231.

Bleiberg, K.L. & Markowitz, J.C. (2005). A pilot study of interpersonal psychotherapy for posttraumatic stress disorder. *American Journal of Psychiatry*, 162, 181–183.

Borelli J.L. (2007). The importance of emotion regulation in understanding attachment and intersubjectivity: A comment on Lyons-Ruth. *Psychoanalytic Inquiry*, 26(4), 622–630.

Brewin, C.R., Andrews, B. & Rose, S. (2000). Fear, helplessness, and horror in posttraumatic stress disorder: Investigating DSM-IV criterion A2 in victims of violent crime. *Journal of Traumatic Stress*, 13, 499–509. doi:10.1023/A:1007741526169.

Brewin, C., Andrews, B. & Valentine, J.D. (2000). Meta-analysis of risk factors for posttraumatic stress disorder in trauma-exposed adults. *Journal of Consulting and Clinical Psychology*, 68, 748–766.

Brinn, A.J. & Auerbach, C.F. (2015). The warrior's journey: Sociocontextual meaning-making in military transitions. *Traumatology*, 21(2), 82–89.

Budden, A. (2009). The role of shame in posttraumatic stress disorder: A proposal for a socio-emotional model for DSM-V. *Social Science & Medicine*, 69(7), 1032–1039.

Burnell, K.J., Coleman, P.G., & Hunt, N. (2006). Falklands War veteran's perceptions of social support and the reconciliation of traumatic memories. *Aging & Mental Health*, 10, 282–289.

Butler, M. (2008). What are you looking at? Prisoner confrontations and the search for respect. *British Journal of Criminology*, 48, 856–873.

Butzlaff, R.L. & Hooley, J.M. (1998). Expressed emotion and psychiatric relapse: A meta-analysis. *Archive of General Psychiatry*, 55, 547–552.

Carlson, V., Cicchetti, D., Barnett, D. & Braunwald, K. (1989). Disorganized/disoriented attachment relationships in maltreated infants. *Developmental Psychology*, 25, 525–531.

Carlson, E.A., Egeland, B. & Sroufe, L.A. (2009). A prospective investigation of the development of borderline personality symptoms. *Development and Psychopathology*, 21, 1311–1334.

Carlson, E.B., Smith, S.R. & Dalenberg, C.J. (2013). Can sudden, severe emotional loss be a traumatic stressor? *Journal of Trauma Dissociation*, 14, 519–528.

Chandy, J.M., Blum, R.W. & Resnick, M.D. (1996). Gender-specific outcomes for sexually abused adolescents. *Child Abuse and Neglect*, 20, 1219–1231.

Charuvastra, A. & Cloitre, M. (2008). Social bonds and posttraumatic stress disorder. *Annual Review of Psychology*, 59, 301–328.

Corrigan, F.M. & Hull, A.M. (2015). Neglect of the complex: Why psychotherapy for post-traumatic clinical presentations is often ineffective. *British Journal of Psychiatry Bulletin*, 39, 86–89.

Courtois, C.A. & Ford, J.D. (Eds.) (2013). *Treating Complex Traumatic Stress Disorders (Adults) Scientific Foundations and Therapeutic Models*. New York: Guildford Press.

Cruwys, T., Haslam, A., Dingle, G.A., Haslam, C. & Jetten, J. (2014). Depression and social identity: An integrative review. *Personality and Social Psychology Review*, 18(3), 215–238.

Currier, J.M., Holland, J.M. & Malott, J. (2015). Moral injury, meaning making, and mental health in returning veterans. *Journal of Clinical Psychology*, 71, 229–240.

Deci, E.L. & Ryan, R.M. (2000). The "what" and "why" of goal pursuits: Human needs and the self-determination of behavior. *Psychological Inquiry*, 11(4), 227–268.

De Jaegher, H. & Di Paolo, E. (2007). Participatory sense-making: An enactive approach to social cognition. *Phenomenology and the Cognitive Sciences*, 6(4), 485–507.

De Jaegher H., Di Paolo, E. & Gallagher, S. (2010). Can social interaction constitute social cognition? *Trends in Cognitive Sciences*, 14(10), 441–447.

De Jaegher, H. & Froese, T. (2009). On the role of social interaction in individual agency. *Adaptive Behavior*, 17(5), 444–460.

Drescher, K. D., Foy, D. W., Kelly, C., Leshner, A., Schutz, K. & Litz, B. (2011). An exploration of the viability and usefulness of the construct of moral injury in war veterans. *Traumatology*, 17, 8–13.

Dunsmore, E., Clark, D.M. & Ehlers, A. (2001). A prospective investigation of the role of cognitive factors in persistent posttraumatic stress disorder (PTSD) after physical or sexual assault. *Behaviour Research and Therapy*, 39, 1063–1084.

Dutra, L., Bureau, J.F., Holmes, B., Lyubchik, A. & Lyons-Ruth, K. (2009). Quality of early care and childhood trauma: A prospective study of developmental pathways to dissociation. *The Journal of Nervous and Mental Disease*, 197, 383–390.

Ebert, A. & Dyck, M.J. (2004). The experience of mental death: The core feature of complex posttraumatic stress disorder. *Clinical Psychology Review*, 24, 617–635.

Echterhoff, G., Higgins, E.T. & Levine, J.M. (2009). Shared reality: Experiencing commonality with others' inner states about the world. *Perspectives on Psychological Science*, 4, 496–521.

Egeressy, A., Butler, T. & Hunter, M. (2009). 'Traumatisers or traumatised': Trauma experiences and personality characteristics of Australian prisoners. *International Journal of Prisoner Health*, 5(4), 212–222.

Ehlers, A. & Clark, D.M. (2000). A cognitive model of posttraumatic stress disorder. *Behaviour Research and Therapy*, 38, 319–345.

Eisenberger, N.I. (2013). Why rejection hurts: The neuroscience of social pain. In C.N. De Wall (Ed.), *The Oxford Handbook of Social Exclusion*. New York, NY: Oxford University Press.

Eisenberger, N.I., & Lieberman, M.D. (2004). Why rejection hurts: A common neural alarm system for physical and social pain. *Trends in Cognitive Science*, 8, 294–300.

Elisha, E., Idisis, Y. & Ronel, N. (2013). Positive criminology and imprisoned sex offenders: Demonstration of a way out from a criminal spin through acceptance relationships. *Journal of Sexual Aggression*, 19(1), 66–80.

Ellemers, N., De Gilder, D. & Haslam, S. A. (2004). Motivating individuals and groups at work: A social identity perspective on leadership and group performance. *Academy of Management Review*, 29, 459–478.

Fagan, A.A. (2005). The relationship between adolescent physical abuse and criminal offending: Support for an enduring and generalized cycle of violence. *Journal of Family Violence*, 20(5), 279–290.

Farnsworth, J.K., Drescher, D., Nieuwsma, J.A. & Walser, R.A. (2014). The role of moral emotions in military trauma: Implications for the study and treatment of moral injury. *Review of General Psychology in the Public Domain*, 18, 249–262.

Fear, N.T., Jones, M., Murphy, D., Hull, L., Iversen, A.C., Coker, B., … Wessely, S. (2010). What are the consequences of deployment to Iraq and Afghanistan on the mental health of the UK armed forces? A cohort study. *Lancet*, 22, 1783–1797.

Feiring, C., Miller-Johnson, S. & Cleland, C.M. (2007). Potential pathways from stigmatization and internalizing symptoms to delinquency in sexually abused youth. *Child Maltreatment*, 12, 220–232.

Ferrito, M., Needs, A., & Adshead, G. (2017). Unveiling the shadows of meaning: Meaning-making for perpetrators of homicide. *Aggression and Violent Behavior*, 34, 263–272.

Fonagy, P., Gergely, G., Jurist, E.L. & Targe, M. (2004). *Affect Regulation, Mentalization, and the Development of the Self*. New York, NY: Other Press.

Fonagy, P. & Target, M. (1997). Attachment and reflective function: Their role in self-organization. *Development and Psychopathology*, 9, 697–700.

Freeman, A. & Freeman, S.M. (2009). Vulnerability factors: Raising and lowering the threshold for response. In S.M. Freeman, B.A. Moore & A. Freeman (Eds.), *Living and Surviving in Harm's Way: A Psychological Treatment Handbook for Pre- and Post-Deployment of Military Personnel*. New York, NY: Routledge.

Gillespie, A. (2011). Contact without transformation: The context, process and content of distrust. In I. Marková & A. Gillespie (Eds.), *Trust and Conflict: Representation, Culture and Dialogue*. London, UK: Routledge.

Gillespie, A. (2012). Position exchange: The social development of agency. *New Ideas in Psychology*, 30, 32–46.

Gillespie, A. & Cornish, F. (2010). Intersubjectivity: Towards a dialogical analysis. *Journal for the Theory of Social Behaviour*, 40(1), 19–46.

Glaser, D. (2000). Child abuse and neglect and the brain: A review. *Journal of Child Psychology and Psychiatry*, 41, 97–116.

Greenberg, N., Brookes, S., & Dunn, R. (2015). Latest developments in post-traumatic stress disorder: diagnosis and treatment. *British Medical Bulletin*, 114, 147–155.

Goldberg, S., Benoit, D., Blokland, K. & Madigan, S. (2003). A typical maternal behavior, maternal representations, and infant disorganized attachment. *Development and Psychopathology*, 15, 239–257.

Goldhill, R. (2015). Reflections on working with vulnerable women: Connecting, cans of worms, closures and copingRachel Goldhill. *British Journal of Social Work*, 46(5), 1336–1353.

Haigh, R. (2013). The quintessence of a therapeutic environment. *Therapeutic Communities: The International Journal of Therapeutic Communities,* 34(1), 6–15.

Halligan, S.L., Michael, T., Clark, D.M. & Ehlers, A. (2003). Posttraumatic stress disorder following assault: The role of cognitive processing, trauma memory, and appraisals. *Journal of Consultant Clinical Psychology*, 71, 419–431.

Hatch, S.L., Harvey, S.B., Dandeker, C., Burdett, H., Greenberg, N., Fear, N.T. & Wessely, S. (2013). Life in and after the armed forces: Social networks and mental health in the UK military. *Sociology of Health & Illness*, 35(7), 1043–1064.

Hayes, A.M., Laurenceau, J.P., Feldman, G., Strauss, J.L. & Cardaciotto, L.A. (2007). Change is not always linear: The study of nonlinear and discontinuous patterns of change in psychotherapy. *Clinical Psychology Review*, 27, 715–723.

Heine, S.J., Proulx, T. & Vohs, K.D. (2006). The meaning maintenance model: On the coherence of social motivations. *Personality and Social Psychological Review*, 10(2), 88–111.

Heller, S.S., Larrieu, J.A., D'Imperio, R. & Boris, N.W. (1999). Research on resilience to child maltreatment: Empirical considerations. *Child Abuse & Neglect*, 23(4), 321–338.

Herman, J. (1992). *Trauma and Recovery*. New York, NY: Basic Books.

Hinton, D.E. & Lewis-Fernandez, R. (2010). Idioms of distress among trauma survivors: Subtypes and clinical utility. *Culture, Medicine & Psychiatry*, 34, 209–218.

Hoeve, M., Dubas, J.S., Eichelsheim, V.I., Van der Laan, P.H., Smeenk, W.H. & Gerris, J. R.M. (2009). The relationship between parenting and delinquency: A meta-analysis. *Journal of Abnormal Child Psychology*, 37, 749–775.

Holmes, E.A., Grey, N. & Young, K.A. (2005). Intrusive images and "hotspots" of trauma memories in posttraumatic stress disorder: An exploratory investigation of emotions and cognitive themes. *Journal of Behavior Therapy and Experimental Psychiatry*, 36, 3–17.

Hunt, N. (2010). *Memory, War and Trauma*. Cambridge, UK: Cambridge University Press.

Hyman, S.M., Gold, S.N. & Cott, M.A. (2003). Forms of social support that moderate PTSD in childhood sexual abuse survivors. *Journal of Family Violence*, 18, 295–300.

Iversen, A.C., Fear, N.T., Ehlers, A., Hacker Hughes, J., Hull, L., Earnshaw, M., … Hotopf M. (2008). Risk factors for post-traumatic stress disorder among UK armed forces personnel. *Psychological Medicine*, 38, 511–522.

Janoff-Bulman, R. (1992). *Shattered Assumptions: Towards a New Psychology of Trauma*. New York, NY: Free Press.

Jeronimus, B.F., Riese, H., Sanderman, R. & Ormel, J. (2014). Mutual reinforcement between neuroticism and life experiences: A five-wave, 16-year study to test reciprocal causation. *Journal of Personality and Social Psychology*, 107, 751–764.

Jetten, J., Haslam, C., Haslam, S.A., Dingle, G. & Jones, J.M. (2014). How groups affect our health and well-being: The path from theory to policy. *Social Issues and Policy Review*, 8(1), 103–130.

Jobson, L. (2009). Drawing current posttraumatic stress disorder models into the cultural sphere: The development of the 'threat to the conceptual self' model. *Clinical Psychology Review*, 29, 368–381.

Johnson, H. & Thompson, A. (2008). The development and maintenance of post-traumatic stress disorder (PTSD) in civilian adult survivors of war trauma and torture: A review. *Clinical Psychology Review*, 28, 36–47.

Jones, N., Sneddon, R., Fear, N. T., McAllister, P., Wessely, S. & Greenberg, N. (2012). Leadership, cohesion, morale and the mental health of UK Armed Forces in Afghanistan. *Psychiatry*, 75(1), 49–59.

Joseph, P.A. & Linley, S. (2011). Meaning in life and posttraumatic growth. *Journal of Loss and Trauma*, 16, 150–159.

Kaniasty, K. & Norris, F.H. (2008). Longitudinal linkages between perceived social support and posttraumatic stress symptoms: Sequential roles of social causation and social selection. *Journal of Traumatic Stress*, 21, 274–281. doi: 10.1002/jts.20334.

Kay, C.L. & Green, J.M. (2016). Social cognitive deficits and biases in maltreated adolescents in UK out-of-home care: Relation to disinhibited attachment disorder and psychopathology. *Development and Psychopathology*, 28, 73–83.

Keegan, J. (1976). *The Face of Battle: A Study of Agincourt, Waterloo, and the Somme*. London, UK: Penguin Books.

Kelley, L.P., Weathers, F.W., Mason, E.A. & Pruneau, G.M. (2012). Association of life threat and betrayal with posttraumatic stress disorder symptom severity. *Journal of Traumatic Stress*, 25, 408–415.

Kendall-Tackett, K. A. (2002). The health effects of childhood abuse: Four pathways by which abuse can influence health. *Child Abuse & Neglect*, 26, 715–729.

Kendall-Tackett, K.A., Williams, L.M. & Finkelhor, D. (1993). Impact of sexual abuse on children: A review and synthesis of recent empirical studies. *Psychological Bulletin*, 113, 164–180.

Kendler, K.S., Hettema, J.M., Butera, F., Gardner, C.O. & Prescott, C.A. (2003). Life event dimensions of loss, humiliation, entrapment, and danger in the prediction of onsets of major depression and generalized anxiety. *Archives of General Psychiatry*, 60, 789–796.

Kerig, P.K., Chaplo, S.D., Bennett, D.C. & Modrowski, C.A. (2016a). Gang membership, perpetration trauma and posttraumatic stress symptoms among youth in the juvenile justice system. *Criminal Justice and Behavior*, 43(5), 635–652.

Kerig, P.K., Chaplo, S.D., Bennett, D.C., Modrowski, C.A. & McGee, A.B. (2016b). Numbing of positive, negative and general emotions: Associations with trauma exposure, posttraumatic stress, and depressive symptoms among justice-involved youth. *Journal of Traumatic Stress*, 29, 111–119.

Kessler, R.C., Chiu, W. T., Demeler, O. & Walters, E. E. (2005). Prevalence, severity, and comorbidity of 12-month DSM-IV disorders in the National Comorbidity Survey Replication. *Archives of General Psychiatry*, 62, 617–627.

Kim, M.J., Tajima, E.A., Herrenkobl, T.I. & Huang, B. (2009). Early child maltreatment, runaway youths, and risk of delinquency and victimization in adolescence: A mediational model. *Social Work Research*, 33, 19–28.

King, D.W., King, L.A., Foy, D.W. & Gudanowski, D.M. (1996). Prewar factors in combatrelated posttraumatic stress disorder: Structural equation modeling with a national sample of female and male Vietnam veterans. *Journal of Consulting and Clinical Psychology*, 64, 520–531.

Kogler, H.H. (2012). Agency and the other: On the intersubjective roots of self-identity. *New Ideas in Psychology*, 30, 47–64.

Kyselo, M. (2016). The enactive approach and disorders of the self – the case of schizophrenia. *Phenomenology and the Cognitive Sciences*, 15, 591–616.

Lambert, N.M., Stillman, T.F., Hicks, J.A., Kamble, S., Baumeister, R.F. & Fincham, F.D. (2013). To belong is to matter: Sense of belonging enhances meaning in life. *Personality and Social Psychology Bulletin, 39,* 1418–1427.

Laub, J. & Sampson, R. (2003). *Shared Beginnings, Divergent Lives: Delinquent Boys to Age Seventy*. Cambridge, MA: Harvard University Press.

Laurenceau, J.P., Hayes, A.M. & Feldman, G.C. (2007). Some methodological and statistical issues in the study of change processes in psychotherapy, *Clinical Psychology Review*, 27, 682–695.

Lazarus, R.S. & Folkman, S. (1984). *Stress, Appraisal, And Coping*. New York, NY: Springer.

Leary, M.R. (2007). Motivational and emotional aspects of the self. *Annual Review of Psychology*, 58, 317–344.

Lee, D.A., Scragg, P. & Turner, S.W. (2001). The role of shame and guilt in reactions to traumatic events: A clinical formulation of shame-based and guilt-based PTSD. *British Journal of Medical Psychology, 74,* 451–466.

Liebling, A. (2004). *Prisons and their Moral Performance. A Study of Values, Quality and Prison Life*. Clarendon Studies in Criminology. Oxford, UK: Oxford University Press.

Linehan, M.M. (1993). *Cognitive Behavioral Therapy of Borderline Personality Disorder*. New York, NY: Guildford Press.

Liotti, G. (1992). Disorganized/disoriented attachment in the etiology of the dissociative disorders. *Dissociation*, 5, 196–204.

Litz, B.T., Steenkamp, M.M. & Nash, W.P. (2014). Resilience and recovery in the military. In N.C. Feeny & L. Zoellner (Eds.), *Facilitating Resilience and Recovery Following Traumatic Events*. New York, NY: Guilford.

Litz, B.T., Stein, N., Delaney, E., Lebowitz, L., Nash, W.P., Silva, C. & Maguen, S. (2009). Moral injury and moral repair in war veterans: A preliminary model and intervention strategy. *Clinical Psychology Review*, 29, 695–706.

Logan-Greene, P. & Jones, A.S. (2015). Chronic neglect and aggression/delinquency: A longitudinal examination. *Child Abuse and Neglect*, 45, 9–20.

Luthar, S.S. & Zigler, E. (1991). Vulnerability and competence: A review of research on resilience in childhood. *American Journal of Orthopsychiatry*, 61, 6–22.

Lyons-Ruth, K. (2006). Interfacing attachment and intersubjectivity: Perspective from the longitudinal study of disorganised attachment. *Psychoanalytic Inquiry*, 26(4), 595–616.

Lyons-Ruth, K., Melnick., S, Patrick, M. & Hobson, R.P. (2006). A controlled study of hostile-helpless states of mind among borderline and dysthymic women. *Attachment and Human Development*, 9, 1–16.

Lyons-Ruth, K., Bureau, J.F., Easterbrooks, M.A., Obsuth, I., Hennighausen, K. & Vulliez-Coady, L. (2013). Parsing the construct of maternal insensitivity: Distinct longitudinal pathways associated with early maternal withdrawal, *Attachment & Human Development*, 15(5–6), 562–582.

Lynn, S.J., Lilienfeld, S.O., Merckelbach, H., Giesbrecht, T., McNally, R.J., Loftus, E.F., ... Malaktaris, A. (2014). The trauma model of dissociation: Inconvenient truths and stubborn fictions. Comment on Dalenberg et al. (2012). *Psychological Bulletin*, 140(3), 896–910.

MacBeth, A., Schwannauer, M. & Gumley, A. (2008). The association between attachment style, social mentalities, and paranoid ideation: An analogue study. *Psychology and Psychotherapy: Theory, Research and Practice*, 81, 79–93.

Macfie, J., Brumariu, L.E. & Lyons-Ruth, K. (2015). Parent–child role-confusion: A critical review of an emerging concept. *Developmental Review*, 36, 24–57.

McGann, M. (2014). Enacting a social ecology: Radically embodied intersubjectivity. *Frontiers in Psychology*, 5, 1321.

Maercker, A. & Horn, A.B. (2013). A socio-interpersonal perspective on PTSD: The case for environments and interpersonal processes. *Clinical Psychology and Psychotherapy*, 20, 465–481. doi:http://dx.doi.org/10.1002/cpp.1805.

Maercker, A. & Müller, J. (2004). Social acknowledgment as a victim or survivor: A scale to measure a recovery factor of PTSD. *Journal of Traumatic Stress*, 17, 345–351.

Main, M. & Hesse, E. (1990). Parents' unresolved traumatic experiences are related to infant disorganized attachment status: Is frightened or frightening parental behavior the linking mechanism? In M. Greenberg, D. Cicchetti & E. M. Cummings (Eds.), *Attachment in the Preschool Years* (pp. 161–182). Chicago, IL: University of Chicago Press.

Mapham, A. & Hefferon, K. (2012). "I used to be an offender – now I'm a defender." Positive psychology approaches in the facilitation of posttraumatic growth in offenders. *Journal of Offender Rehabilitation*, 51(6), 389–413.

Markowitz, J.C., Petkova, E., Neria, Y., Van Meter, P.E., Zhao, Y., Hembree, E., ... Marshall, R.D. (2015). Is exposure necessary? A randomized clinical trial of interpersonal psychotherapy for PTSD. *American Journal of Psychiatry*, 172(5), 430–440.

Maruna, S. (2001). *Making Good: How Ex-Convicts Reform and Rebuild Their Lives*. Washington, DC: American Psychological Association.

McGloin, J.M. & Widom, C.S. (2001). Resilience among abused and neglected children grown up. *Development and Psychopathology*, 13, 1021–1038.

McLaughlin, K.A., Conron, K.J., Koenen, K.C. & Gilman, S. E. (2010). Childhood adversity, adult stressful life events, and risk of past-year psychiatric disorder: A test of the stress sensitization hypothesis in a population-based sample of adults. *Psychological Medicine*, 40, 1647–1658.

McNally, R.J. (2010). Can we salvage the concept of psychological trauma? *The Psychologist*, 23(5), 386–389.

McNally, R.J., Robinaugh, D.J., Wu, G.W.Y., Wang, L., Deserno, M. & Borsboom D. (2015). Mental disorders as causal systems: A network approach to posttraumatic stress disorder. *Clinical Psychological Science*, 3, 836–849.

Meichenbaum, D. (2006). Resilience and posttraumatic growth: A constructive narrative perspective. In L.G. Calhoun & R.G. Tedeschi (Eds.), *Handbook of Posttraumatic Growth: Research and Practice* (pp. 355–368). Mahwah, NJ: Lawrence Erlbaum Associates.

Meichenbaum, D. (2014). *Roadmap to Resilience: A Guide for Military, Trauma Victims and Their Families.* NC: Institute Press.

Merlo, J. (2011). Contextual influences on the individual life course: Building a research framework for social epidemiology. *Psychosocial Intervention*, 20(1), 109–118.

Mikulincer, M. & Shaver, P.R. (2007). Boosting attachment security to promote mental health, prosocial values, and inter-group tolerance. *Psychological Inquiry*, 18(3), 139–156.

Mullen, P.E., Martin, J.L., Anderson, J.E., & Herbison, G.P. (1996). The long-term impact of the physical, emotional, and sexual abuse of children: A community study. *Child Abuse & Neglect*, 20, 7–21.

Murphy, D. & Bussutil, W. (2014). PTSD, stigma and barriers to help-seeking within the UK armed forces. *Journal of the Royal Army Medical Corps*, 161, 322–326.

Musto, L.C., Rodney, P.A. & Vanderheide, R. (2015). Toward interventions to address moral distress: Navigating structure and agency. *Nursing Ethics*, 22(1), 91–102.

Needs, A. (2015a) The transition process, trauma and rebuilding resilience. Paper presented at the *Wessex Branch, BPS 4th Military Psychology Conference: Resilience through Change*, Basingstoke.

Needs, A. (2015b). Outrageous fortune: Transitions and related concerns in the genesis of violence. Paper presented at the *Conference of the International Academy for Law and Mental Health*, Vienna.

Needs, A. (2016). Psychological processes in life's transitions. Paper presented at the conference on *New Perspectives in Risk and Rehabilitation*, Portsmouth.

Needs, A. & Towl, G. (1997). Reflections on clinical risk assessments with lifers. *Prison Service Journal*, 113, 14–17.

Neimeyer, R.A. (2006). Bereavement and the quest for meaning: Rewriting stories of loss and grief. *Hellenic Journal of Psychology*, 3, 181–188.

Obsuth, I., Brumariu, L., Hennighausen, K. & Lyons-Ruth, K. (2013). Disorganized behavior in adolescent-parent interactions: Relations to attachment state of mind, partner abuse, and psychopathology. *Child Development*, 85, 370–387.

O'Brien, L.S. (1998). *Traumatic Events and Mental Health.* Cambridge, UK: Cambridge University Press.

Ogawa, J.R., Sroufe, L.A., Weinfield, N.S., Carlson, E.A. & Egeland, B. (1997). Development and the fragmented self: Longitudinal study of dissociative symptomatology in a nonclinical sample. *Development and Psychopathology*, 9, 855–879.

Oliveira, P.S., Pasco Fearon, R.M.P., Belsky, J., Fachada, I. & Soares, I. (2015). Quality of institutional care and early childhood development. *International Journal of Behavioral Development*, 39(2), 161–170.

Ozer, E.J., Best, S.R., Lipsey, T.L. & Weiss, D.S. (2003). Predictors of posttraumatic stress disorder and symptoms in adults: A meta-analysis. *Psychological Bulletin*, 129, 52–73.

Ozer E. J., Best, S. R., Lipsey, T. L. & Weiss, D.S. (2008). Predictors of posttraumatic stress disorder and symptoms in adult: A meta-analysis. *Psychological Trauma: Theory, Research, Practice, and Policy*, 1, 3–36. doi:10.1037/1942-9681.S.1.3.

Pagano, M.E., Skodol, A.E., Stout, R.L., Shea, M.T., Yen, S., Grilo, C.M. et al. (2004). Stressful life events as predictors of functioning: Findings from the collaborative longitudinal personality disorders study. *Acta Psychiatrica Scandinavica*, 110, 421–429.

Parish, S.M. (2014). Between persons: How concepts of the person make moral experience possible. *Ethos*, 42, 31–50.

Park, C.L. (2010). Making sense of the meaning literature: An integrative review of meaning making and its effects on adjustment to stressful life events. *Psychological Bulletin*, 136, 257–301.

Paternoster, R. & Bushway, S. (2009). Desistance and the feared self: Toward an identity theory of desistance. *Journal of Criminal Law and Criminology*, 99, 1103–1156.

Pawson, R. & Tilley, N. (1997). *Realistic Evaluation*. London, UK: Sage.

Pearlman, L.A. & Courtois, C.A. (2005). Clinical applications of the attachment framework: Relational treatment of complex trauma. *Journal of Traumatic Stress*, 18, 449–459.

Pedersen, H.K. & Cooke, N.J. (2006). From battle plans to football plays: Extending military team cognition to football. *International Journal of Sport and Exercise Psychology*, 4, 422–446.

Pelcovitz, D., Kaplan, S., Goldenberg, B., Mandel, F., Lehane, J. & Guarrera, J. (1994). Posttraumatic stress disorder in physically abused adolescents. *Journal of the American Academy of Child and Adolescent Psychiatry*, 33, 305–312.

Piquero, A.R., Farrington, D.P. & Blumstein, A. (2003). The criminal career paradigm. *Crime and Justice*, 30, 359–506.

Platts, H., Tyson, M. & Mason, O. (2002). Adult attachment style and core beliefs: Are they linked? *Clinical Psychology and Psychotherapy*, 9, 332–348.

Pollak, S.D. (2015). Multilevel developmental approaches to understanding the effects of child maltreatment: Recent advances and future challenges. *Development and Psychopathology*, 27, 1387–1397.

Popova, S., Lange, S., Bekmuradov, D., Mihic, A. & Rehm, J. (2011). Fetal alcohol spectrum disorder prevalence estimates in correctional systems: A systematic literature review. *Canadian Journal of Public Health*, 102(5), 336–340.

Putnam, F.W. (1997). *Dissociation in Children and Adolescents: A Developmental Perspective*. London, UK: Guildford Press.

Putnam, K.T., Harris, W.W. & Putnam, F.W. (2013). Synergistic childhood adversities and complex adult psychopathology. *Journal of Trauma Stress*, 26, 435–442. doi: 10.1002/jts.21833.

Reddy, V. (2008). How infants know minds. London: Harvard University Press.

Regel, S. & Joseph, S. (2010). *Post-Traumatic Stress: The Facts*. Cambridge, UK: Oxford University Press.

Robitaille, A., Orpana, H. & McIntosh, C.N. (2012). Reciprocal relationship between social support and psychological distress among a national sample of older adults: An autoregressive cross-lagged model. *Canadian Journal on Aging*, 31(1), 13–24.

Rogers, A. & Law, H. (2010). Working with trauma in a prison setting. In J. Harvey & K. Smedley (Eds.), *Psychological Therapy in Prisons and Other Secure Settings*. Abingdon, UK: Willan.

Rosen, G.M. & Lilienfeld, S.O. (2008). Posttraumatic stress disorder: An empirical evaluation of core assumptions. *Clinical Psychology Review*, 28, 837–868.

Ryan, R.M. (2005). The developmental line of autonomy in the etiology, dynamics and treatment of borderline personality disorders. *Development and Psychopathology*, 17, 987–1006.

Sadeh, N. & McNiel, D.E. (2015). Posttraumatic stress disorder increases risk of criminal recidivism among justice-involved persons with mental disorders. *Criminal Justice and Behavior*, 42, 573–586.

Sameroff, A. (2009). The transactional model. In A. Sameroff (Ed.), *The Transactional Model of Development: How Children and Contexts Shape Each Other*. Washington, DC: American Psychological Association.

Schuder, M. & Lyons-Ruth, K. (2004). "Hidden trauma" in infancy: Attachment, fearful arousal, and early dysfunction of the stress response system. In J. Osofsky (Ed.), *Trauma in Infancy and Early Childhood*. New York, NY: Guilford Press.

Scurfield, R.M. (2009). The nexus between the Iraq War and Katrina recovery. Clinical and policy issues. *Trauma, Violence and Abuse*, 10(2), 181–192.

Sedikides, C., Wildschut, T., Routledge, C. & Arndt, J. (2015). Nostalgia counteracts self-discontinuity and restores self-continuity, *European Journal of Social Psychology*, 45, 52–61.

Sharp, C., Fonagy, P. & Allen, J. G. (2012). Posttraumatic stress disorder: A social-cognitive perspective. *Clinical Psychology: Science and Practice*, 19, 229–240.

Shields, A. & Cicchetti, D. (1997). Emotion regulation among school-age children: The development and validation of a new criterion Q-sort scale. *Developmental Psychology*, 33, 906–916.

Shields, A. & Cicchetti, D. (1998). Reactive aggression among maltreated children: The contributions of attention and emotion dysregulation. *Journal of Clinical Child Psychology*, 27, 381–395.

Silva, R.R., Alpert, M., Munoz, D.M., Singh, S., Matzner, F. & Dummit, S. (2000). Stress and vulnerability to posttraumatic stress disorder in children and adolescents. *American Journal of Psychiatry*, 157(8), 1229–1235.

Silver, E. & Teasdale, B. (2005). Mental disorder and violence: An examination of stressful life events and impaired social support. *Social Problems*, 52(1), 62–78.

Sippel, L. M., Pietrzak, R. H., Charney, D. S., Mayes, L. C. & Southwick, S. M. (2015). How does social support enhance resilience in the trauma-exposed individual? *Ecology and Society*, 20, 1–10. http://dx.doi.org/10.5751/ES-07832-200410.

Sroufe, L.A., Egeland, B., Carlson, E.A. & Collins, W.A. (2005). *The Development of the Person: The Minnesota Study of Risk and Adaptation from Birth to Adulthood*. New York, NY: Guilford Press.

Stein, K.F. & Markus, H.R. (1996). The role of the self in behavioral change. *Journal of Psychotherapy Integration*, 6(4), 349–384.

Stein, J. & Tuval-Mashiach, R. (2015). The social construction of loneliness: An integrative conceptualization. *Journal of Constructivist Psychology*, 28(3), 210–227.

Stillman, T.F., Baumeister, R.F., Lambert, N.M., Crescioni, A.W., DeWall, C.N. & Fincham, F.D. (2009). Alone and without meaning: Life loses meaning following social exclusion. *Journal of Experimental Social Psychology*, 45, 686–694.

Stone, A.L., Becker, L.G., Huber, A.M. & Catalano, R.F. (2012). Review of risk and protective factors of substance use and problem use in emerging adulthood. *Addict Behavior*, 37, 747–775.

Stone, S.A. & DeKoeyer-Laros, I. (2012). Self and other dialogue in infancy: Normal versus compromised developmental pathways. *New Directions for Child and Adolescent Development*, 137, 23–38.

Straits-Troster, K., Gierisch, J.M., Calhoun, P.S., Strauss, J.L., Voils, C. & Kudler, H. (2011). Living in transition: Young veterans' health and the postdeployment shift to family life. In D.C. Kelly, S. Howe-Barksdale & D. Gitelson (Eds.), *Treating Young Veterans: Promoting Resilience through Practice and Advocacy*. New York, NY: Springer.

Tangney, J.P., Stuewig, J. & Mashek, D.J. (2007). Moral emotions and moral behavior. *Annual Review of Psychology*, 58, 345–372.

Target, M. (2007). The interface between attachment and intersubjectivity: Another contribution from Karlen Lyons-Ruth. *Psychoanalytic Inquiry*, 26(4), 617–621.

Taylor, T.F. (2015). The influence of shame on posttrauma disorders: Have we failed to see the obvious? *European Journal of Psychotraumatology*, 22:6:28847. doi: 10.3402/ejpt.v6.28847.

Thornborrow, T. & Brown, A.D. (2009). 'Being regimented': Aspiration, discipline and identity work in the British Parachute Regiment. *Organization Studies*, 30, 355–376.

Topitzes, J., Mersky, J.P. & Reynolds, A.J. (2012). From child maltreatment to violent offending: An examination of mixed-gender and gender-specific models. *Journal of Interpersonal Violence*, 27, 2322–2347.

Trevarthen, C. (1979). Communication and cooperation in early infancy: A description of primary intersubjectivity. In M. Bullowa (Ed.), *Before Speech*. Cambridge: Cambridge University Press.

Trevarthen, C. (2002). Making sense of infants making sense. *Intellectica*, 34, 164–188.

Trevarthen, C. & Aitken, K.J. (2001). Infant intersubjectivity: Research, theory, and clinical applications. *Journal of Child Psychology and Psychiatry*, 42(1), 3–48.

Tsekeris, C. (2015). Contextualising the self in contemporary social science. *Contemporary Social Science*, 10(1), 1–14.

Tyler, K. (2002). Social and emotional outcomes of childhood sexual abuse: A review of recent research. *Aggression and Violent Behavior*, 7, 567–589.

Ungar, M. (2013). Resilience, trauma, context and culture. *Trauma, Violence and Abuse*, 14(3), 255–266.

Van der Kolk, B.A. (2014). *The Body Keeps the Score: Mind, Brain and Body in the Transformation of Trauma*. London, UK: Allen Lane/Penguin.

Van der Kolk, B.A., Pelcovitz, D., Roth, S., Mandel, F., McFarlane, A. & Herman, J.L. (1996). Dissociation, somatization, and affect dysregulation: The complexity of adaptation to trauma. *American Journal of Psychiatry*, 153, 83–93.

Van Geert, P. (2003). Dynamic systems approaches and modeling of developmental processes. In J. Valsiner & K.J. Conolly (Eds.), *Handbook of Developmental Psychology* (pp. 640–672). London, UK: Sage.

Weiss, D.S., Brunet, A., Best, S.R., Metzler, T.J., Liberman, A., Pole, N., Fagan, J.A. & Marmar, C.R. (2010). Frequency and severity approaches to indexing exposure to trauma: The Critical Incident History Questionnaire for police officers. *Journal of Traumatic Stress*, 23(6), 734–743.

Whitmer, G. (2001). On the nature of dissociation. *The Psychoanalytic Quarterly*, 70(4), 807–837.

Williams, K. (2001). *Ostracism: The Power of Silence*. New York, NY: Guilford Press.

Williams, K. D. (2007). Ostracism. *Annual Review of Psychology*, 58, 425–452.

Williams, K., Papadopoulou, V. & Booth, N. (2012). Prisoners' childhood and family backgrounds Results from the Surveying Prisoner Crime Reduction (SPCR) longitudinal cohort study of prisoners. *Ministry of Justice Research Series 4/12* March 2012.

Wilson, J.P., Droždek, B. & Turkovic, S. (2006). Posttraumatic shame and guilt. *Trauma, Violence, & Abuse*, 7, 122–141.

Wright, D.B., Ost, J. & French, C.C. (2006). Ten years after: What we know now that we didn't know then about recovered and false memories. *The Psychologist*, 19, 352–355.

Yehuda, R., Keefe, R.S.E., Harvey, P.D., Levengood, R.A., Gerber, D.K., Geni, J. & Siever, L.J. (1995). Learning and memory in combat veterans with posttraumatic stress disorder. *American Journal of Psychiatry*, 152, 137–139.

Zielinski, D.S. & Bradshaw, C.P. (2006). Ecological influences on the sequelae of child maltreatment: A review of the literature. *Child Maltreatment*, 11, 49–63.

# 4

# TRAUMA-INFORMED CARE AND 'GOOD LIVES' IN CONFINEMENT

## Acknowledging and offsetting adverse impacts of chronic trauma and loss of liberty

*Lawrence Jones*

This chapter will highlight toxic reactions to confinement in people with trauma-related problems and how the effects of adverse experiences can be played out in custodial settings. It will also highlight the importance of working with the social milieu and staff responses to trauma-related presentations in order to offset cycles of misunderstanding, reactions and counter-reactions that render the setting unsafe and re-traumatising for residents.

In this chapter context is conceptualised as an interaction between two components: the internal psychological milieu – emerging out of the individual's developmental history – and the current social milieu (Shoda & Lee Tiernan, 2002). From this perspective, the internal component (what the situation/stimulus context means and how it is perceived by the individual) is critical to defining a situation. Context is thus not construed as one static definable setting but as a uniquely individual response emerging out of that individual's distinctive historically determined experiential repertoire.

A number of critical areas need to be addressed in milieu-based interventions designed to build new, less destructive and more fulfilling lifestyles. The range of adverse and propitious developmental experiences, apparent through their impact on the individual's current functioning and the regime features that serve to mitigate or exacerbate these need to be taken seriously. In addition, opportunities for rehearsing new ways of living custodial 'good lives' (Ward, Yates & Willis, 2012) and the impact of traumatised and traumatising inmates on staff and organisations should be central concerns.

It is useful to see the internal psychological milieu as the cumulative dialogical (e.g. Leiman 2004) response to an individual's history of exposure to different contexts in the course of development. It is particularly influenced by exposure across the lifespan to contexts that are distressing, aversive, destructive or harmful. Recent thinking about the kinds of early experiences that are behind different kinds of offending behaviour and psychological distress are increasingly highlighting the role of a range of often interrelated forms of trauma and adversity (see below).

Trauma as a concept is too broad (e.g. McNally, 2016). Recent emphasis on the critically social nature and impact of adverse experiences highlights the social interactional nature of these problems – for further exploration of this see Needs in this volume (Chapter 3). In this chapter some effort will be made to follow the suggestion of Brown (1992) of using types of adverse experience and responses to these to characterise people's problems – moving away from the medical model approach and concepts such as PTSD. In addition the literature on the mutual influence of trauma and the traumatising milieu will be explored in terms of the notion that staff and organisations can be adversely impacted by ill-understood traumatic experiences that are ubiquitous in these settings.

There is evidence that traumatic experiences are significant factors in the aetiology of male and female sexual offending, violent behaviour, different kinds of personality disorder and substance misuse (Jones, submitted). A similar story is emerging in the literature on psychosis (e.g. Read, Agar, Argyle & Aderhold, 2003; Bentall, 2006; Bentall et al., 2014; Moskowitz, Farrelly, Rudegeair & Williams, 2009).

There is also evidence that some offenders have been traumatised by their experiences of committing offences (Kruppa, Hickey & Hubbard, 1995; Gray et al., 2003; Pollock, 1999). Other work highlights the role of trauma in the development of hostile dominant traits (Podubinski, Hollander & Daffern, 2016) identified as common amongst offenders, and callous unemotional traits (Bennett & Kerig, 2014; Kerig & Becker, 2010). Theorists propose a number of different pathways linking trauma with offending. One common linking process is one in which people repeat in their own lives a version of what happened to them. Examining personality disorder, Cohen et al. (2014) propose that personality develops in a manner congruent with the abuse (e.g. anti-social personality disorder with violent abuse). Pfaus (2012) similarly proposes that early sexual experiences can have the effect of effectively imprinting the individual's later sexual interests. Another theme in the literature is the role of attachment in facilitating – in the case of poor attachment – or being a protective factor – in the case of good attachment – the role of trauma in the development of offending (Langton, Murad & Humbert, 2015; Craissati, McClurg & Brown, 2002). As indicated above, all traumatic experiences need to be thought of as being fundamentally relational; they are defined significantly by their impact on the capacity to relate.

The development of the concept of trauma-informed care, (e.g. Bloom & Farragher, 2013) has been growing in recent years in the delivery of mental health services and more recently in working with offenders. Trauma-informed custodial care (TICC) (Miller & Najavits, 2012) is increasingly being recognised as a helpful approach to milieu design. Others too have developed this concept; Ardino (2012) calls for a more systematic approach to researching and delivering TICC and Levenson (2013) makes the case for TICC with sex offenders. Jones (2015) argues that prison contexts can be retraumatising for inmates and explores ways in which aspects of the custodial milieu can resonate with earlier experiences of trauma.

Stein, Wilmot and Solomon (2016) make the point that the response to a setting where trauma is ongoing is different in that often the traumatic response focusses on fears in relation to the future that are at heart rational; the task of restoring a sense of safety is foregrounded by the ongoing threat experienced.

---

John was taken away from the family home at the age of nine when social services decided that his parents were not able to care for him, due to physical maltreatment and neglect. They moved him into care. He reported that that he had 'positive' memories about when he was moved to a children's home where several members of staff were sexually abusing children residing there. John was groomed by one of the carers and made to feel special and then was engaged in sexual activity. Another carer had been sadistic with him and would beat him with a cane before going on to rape him anally. He believed that the sexual experiences with the carers that groomed him were a normal expression of affection. He contrasted this with the violent sexual and physical abuse he had experienced that he was frequently having flashbacks about. As an adult he offended sexually against female children. He described this as showing his victims care. In custody he reported having flashbacks and nightmares about being raped. He described a history of self-harm and suicide attempts linked with these. He also reported a history of substance misuse that he indicated was aimed at coping with some of these experiences. He would often approach staff telling them that they were special and attempting to offer them food or sweets. He had also been reprimanded for giving sweets to inmates.

---

In this example John is replaying an aspect of one of his abusive experiences, involving grooming, in his offending and with people in the custodial setting. Another abusive experience was linked with his self-harm and may also have contributed to his offending. It is clear from this vignette that trauma-informed care can contribute significantly to both addressing mental health issues/risk to self and risk rehabilitation initiatives in custodial settings.

The experience of trauma is often, but not always, linked to a propensity to being triggered into altered states of consciousness (Lanius, Bluhm & Frewen, 2011). These altered states are linked with different ways of thinking, relating and behaving. Panksepp (e.g. 2006) identifies post-traumatic presentations as being linked with the fight or flight system that evolved in order to facilitate survival. Becoming sensitive to and reacting quickly, and unthinkingly, to situations that resemble the context in which a life-threatening experience had occurred is thought to have evolved on this basis. This may also be true for activation of the more explicitly social sexual, attachment and dominance systems, all of which are likely to be significantly impacted by early experiences of abuse. Moreover, intensely pleasurable experiences – love, sexual arousal, substance misuse – can also be associated with intrusive thoughts, altered states of consciousness – like dissociation – and impulsive behaviour (Jones, 2004). In an important sense many of these experiences are de-socialised; the person has to keep them a secret and make sense of them on their own because of taboos about talking about them and because there is no common language for talking about them. Much of the damage done by these experiences is underpinned by this aspect of their manifestation.

Different presentations of trauma will now be considered in relation to how they are triggered or influenced by aspects of custodial regimes.

## Traumatic flashbacks

Flashbacks are memories of the traumatic episode that intrude on the individual's consciousness. The content of the memories are aspects of what actually happened being replayed, sometimes to the extent that the individual feels as if they are re-experiencing the event. Often these experiences are not discussed and are relegated to a private secretive domain. They are experienced as distressing and subjected to a range of interpretations by the person experiencing them. Some see the memories as 'not them'. Voice hearing, for instance, can be hearing things that the person had heard whilst they were being abused, with persecutory voices being voices of past abusers. Memories can also become embedded in a process of rumination about revenge, or seen as ways in which the perpetrator is still being allowed to impact on the person; such memories can exacerbate any tendency to self-blame. Self-harm and assaults in custodial contexts can often be preceded by triggered traumatic flashbacks linked with some kind of panic response.

James had been sexually and violently abused by carers as a child. He would have flashbacks if he heard an item on the news about sexual abuse or if one of his peers talked to him about sexual experiences. He would often have flashbacks to a time when he was violently restrained and sexually abused and in the context of this abuse he had been sexually aroused. When he was having these flashbacks he would always feel dirty and disgusted, both with the perpetrators of the abuse and with himself for becoming sexually aroused in the abuse. He was also angry with himself for having the flashback. He didn't see the memory as something he had little choice over but rather he saw it as something that he had chosen to have and was disgusted with himself for 'choosing' to have his flashback. He thought that this meant that he was sexually interested in men and was angry about this. These experiences, and the interpretation of them that he had developed, led to him becoming homophobic and on occasion he had assaulted fellow inmates when he was acting on these beliefs.

In the fictional vignette of James it becomes clear why it is critical for staff to have a good understanding of trauma. Without this key component of the formulation staff will see this kind of behaviour as unpredictable and hard to comprehend. Under such circumstances it is tempting for staff to make dispositional attributions (Ross & Nisbett, 1991) and see this kind of behaviour being driven by folk psychological constructs such as 'nasty personality being evil'. This punitive stance that can ensue from taking the individual's behaviour 'out of context' will be a common theme in the responses highlighted here.

## Intrusive thoughts

Thoughts as well as memories can be experienced as intrusive. The thoughts are often about concerns linked with traumatic experience and the individual may for example, be preoccupied with safety and repeatedly make efforts to feel safer when objectively they are relatively safe. The individual may not recognise that their intrusive thoughts have traumatic origins and, as with flashbacks, the sense that the individual makes of their propensity to have intrusive thoughts is significant. These metacognitions (e.g. "I am having these thoughts because …"; "I enjoyed what happened to me even though it was wrong"; "I want to get revenge and I won't forget until I do get revenge"; "I want revenge on those who allowed me to be abused by not doing anything") are critical to recognising how the intrusive thoughts are impacting on the individual. It is difficult to see thoughts as not being something that has been chosen and engaged in willingly. The individual constructs narratives around the intrusions that explain them as thoughts that have been chosen for a reason and this then becomes part of their sense of self.

In the context of repeated abuse these narratives can become more pernicious and fixated. It isn't just one person that is now experienced as persecutory but often whole classes of people. The victim of abuse may come to identify with subcultural expressions of being an 'outsider' and focus upon a totemic issue that offers the prospect of some kind of collective revenge (such as opposition to women, parents of young children, people from a particular cultural or ethnic background, people in authority, gay people, foreign people, older people and so on).

This kind of belief system also plays out in the custodial context in the form of, for example, opposition to authority. If these attitudes and responses are not understood in the context of the traumatic backstories of violent and or sexual abuse then they may be responded to by staff in a way that feeds them rather than allowing them to move forwards. Whilst it is critical to maintaining safety in a prison setting for the staff to exert some forms of authority it is also important for them to be cognisant of the possible sources of these anti-authoritarian stances and to think about how different kinds of exertion of authority will be experienced in this context.

## Dissociation and derealisation

Dissociation is an experience of detachment from reality. In its everyday forms it involves aspects such as daydreaming and being 'distracted'; in its more problematic forms it can involve changes in states of consciousness involving memory (e.g. amnesia), the self (depersonalisation) or the phenomenal world (derealisation) (Frewen & Lanius, 2015). Dissociative states can be both aversive and pleasant or sought after. They can serve a function of avoiding or escaping from the intense distress associated with flashbacks and/or intrusive memories (Jones, submitted). They can allow a cutting off or numbness in relation to these other trauma-related experiences and are thus a form of coping. Like the other aspects of responding to trauma they are often not 'chosen', but emerge as part of a triggered trauma response. They can however be sought after and deliberately induced by, for instance, self-harming, being violent to others, sexual acting out or substance misuse – all of which can be associated with experiences of dissociation that can mitigate re-lived pain of trauma.

Kerig, Bennett, Thompson and Becker (2012) discuss the ways in which trauma can lead to 'acquired callousness' in people who have been abused who go on to offend. Dissociation and cutting off emotionally as a coping response can also have the effect of desensitising the individual to the effects of violence or offending on others. This can facilitate a pattern of repeatedly obtaining needs through coercive activity. Trauma can contribute to offending through people reacting pre-emptively to what they misconstrue as a threat to themselves or a background of exposure to violence, desensitisation to distress and associated dissociation can allow instrumental violence to flourish.

To equip staff with a basic understanding of what throws the individual into a more dissociated state is a critical task both in terms of risk management and in terms of a constructive response. Strategies to facilitate grounding and bringing people back into the here and now – e.g. mindfulness, using the therapeutic relationship – are very important in helping people to re-access capacities to relate to others in a more adaptive and humane manner. Not understanding dissociative altered states of consciousness may cause staff to underestimate the extent to which a person has changed in these capacities, perhaps seeing them as being deliberately distant and rejecting and responding by personalising this and, again, making negative attributions about insensitivity to others. This can be compounded by the fact that deceit and 'lying' are also associated with dissociation as a response to trauma (Putnam, 1991). These issues will be addressed in the section on staff.

## Freezing or becoming aggressive

Activation of the threat system can also involve becoming either paralysed with fear or aggressive and violent in a panicked and unregulated manner: the flight or fight response. Again, unlike instances where aggression is used in an instrumental manner, this kind of aggressive response has an urgent, defensive and impulsive quality. It is a response that has evolved to manage contexts where the individual is in danger. When a trauma trigger releases this response it is replayed in the absence of the original trauma and as such no longer has the same adaptive value. In a custodial context the individual may be exposed to a higher frequency of threatening episodes and these are likely to be triggers for trauma-based reactions such as becoming defensively violent or retreating into a state of withdrawal. Staff are not in a position to help the individual navigate their way out of these states if they are not familiar with where they are coming from. Trauma-driven violence might be misunderstood as instrumental violence or seen simply as 'mad' and unpredictable and irrational. This prevents the provision of a containing response and can precipitate overly restrictive and punitive responses that can parallel the responses that the individual experienced in the context of the original trauma. Staff may then be seen as being like those who have abused them (or apparently colluded with abuse) and are responded to as such. Again an iatrogenic spiral of misunderstanding can evolve, either rapidly within an incident or a slow-burning version over longer periods of time. The anti-social identity identified within the RNR model (Andrews & Bonta, 1998) is likely to be underpinned by this kind of systemic process being played out over long periods of relating in custodial or care settings not attuned to trauma.

## Generalising reactions to staff that remind them of perpetrators of abuse

This escalating process leading to the individual seeing all staff as potentially, even violently, abusive may gradually generalise to categories of staff such as all officers or nurses, police, social workers and psychologists or 'straight people' (i.e. people seen as being not involved in offending subcultures). For minority groups this can become an even more destructive process in which the individual retreats into a persecuted version of whatever cultural background they come from, identifying with collective victimhood that can then feed collective versions of vengeful justification for a range of different kinds of offending. Bentall's (Bentall & Fernyhough, 2008) exploration of the development of paranoid thinking in the context of minority or culturally alien (e.g. immigrant) status is a useful framework for formulating this kind of process. Offender subcultures – the RNR anti-social peer group – are often similarly marginalised and may be locked into anti-social action in part as a form of collective revenge for both early abuse and custodial or systemic abuse in custodial and care contexts. In its most paranoid forms there can be hypervigilance for both violence and sudden movements within the system that the individual is not informed about ('ghosting').

---

Peter was always expecting to be moved. In care he had been moved frequently from location to location without being told because he had reacted badly when he did know that he was going to be moved. When he went to bed each night he had an overbearing fear of being 'ghosted'. Expecting to be taken away in the night he would go to sleep dressed, with his shoes on, ready to jump up and respond if staff came in at night. This fear would become more intense as he formed a therapeutic relationship because the more he felt he cared the greater the anxiety about sudden unpredictable moves – deriving from an accumulated experience of such moves in the past.

## Consequences of neglect

Whilst neglect is often seen as being a form of trauma or abuse, it plays out very differently from other kinds of trauma. In childhood it leads to the individual not growing and developing in the same way as other children. Lack of parental supervision can lead to the individual being exposed to a wide range of abuse and trauma as it increases the opportunities for this to happen. Difficulties in taking initiative and agency are also a feature of experiencing neglect.

In custodial settings this process can be continued. Benn (2002) describes the process of 'skills atrophy' experienced by people spending long periods away from their original contexts and lifestyles. Key aspects of social development are not enabled to develop through the kinds of learning experiences that come out of having attentive and responsive care givers. Indeed Bateman and Fonagy (2010) highlight the way in which lack of adequate attachment experiences can lead to the individual not developing the capacity to think about and understand their own experiences and the experiences of others. Milieu need to be responsive and attentive to the feelings and needs of residents if they are going to learn how to be aware of and responsive to their own and other people's needs in the future.

## Trauma-related psychological processes linked with risk

A useful exploration of trauma-related risk mechanisms (Kerig & Becker, 2010, 2015) linking trauma and offending behaviour highlights a range of processes linking adverse early experiences and offending. In this section these will be examined with respect to the ways in which they are typically exercised in custodial settings. From this, contextual changes in the milieu that can potentially meet the unique trauma related needs presented by each individual case will be explored.

### Affect dysregulation

PTSD and chronic trauma is often associated with either rapid switching between unmanaged and often overwhelming emotional states or attempts to offset these states through over-control. This emotional dysregulation is generally not 'chosen' or intended by the person experiencing it and it is often linked to trauma reminders or triggers. The underlying processes occur within what Panksepp and Biven (2012) describe as the fear, panic, grief and anger systems – social emotional states and processes that have evolved to aid survival in traumatic situations. These are experienced by the individual as being out of their control and in some sense 'done to' them as opposed to 'lived' with an active sense of agency. The sense that the individual makes of the state is often an important aspect of how it plays out. If it is understood to be a process that is escalating and getting more and more out of control then the sense of foreboding can feed a further sense of panic. The duration of the episode can vary and can be associated with frantic efforts to manage the affect including avoidance, angry behaviour, self-harm or controlling attempts to solicit care. From an attachment perspective the individual may be experiencing a repetition of both the traumatic event from the past and the absence of a secure attachment context that can facilitate the re-establishment of emotional equilibrium. Conversely, Lee, James and Gilbert (2013) highlight the way in which the attachment system, when effectively activated, inhibits the panic/fear system. Bateman and Fonagy (2010) highlight the way that the capacity to be aware of one's own mind and that of others is also dependent on attachment system activation and reflecting on one's own and others' personal experiences.

In custodial contexts a number of developments can impact adversely on this process. Where, for example, narratives that the person is being 'manipulative' are used to explain the behaviour this can lead either to ignoring it or responding in an overbearing way by warning the individual that there will be negative consequences for them if they continue. In this sense the systemic response to the individual parallels what is happening internally. This can also parallel the ways in which the original attachment context was not attuned or containing of the emotional responses and in turn this can trigger angry reliving of feelings associated with thinking that caregivers are betraying them by not protecting them (Freyd, 1996). This kind of reaction can be part of a reciprocating climate of high levels of expressed emotion: hostile, critical, and emotionally over-involved patterns of relating have been shown both in families and in staff to be particularly associated with adverse outcomes such as relapse in mental health (Barrowclough et al., 2001; Butzlaff & Hooley, 1998; Hooley, 1986; Hooley & Hiller, 2000; Hooley & Hoffman, 1999). Staff levels of expressed emotion can have a significant impact on relapse in residential settings (Ball, Moore & Kuipers, 1992). Beliefs that change in behaviour is brought about through criticism can themselves contribute to relapse (Wendel, Miklowitz, Richards & George, 2000). This can also be a process that sets in motion trauma-linked offence paralleling and offending behaviour (Jones, 2004, 2010).

### Emotional numbing

Kerig and Becker (2010) also describe a delinquency-related process of acquisition of callousness, linked with trauma-related emotional numbing and learned detachment. In custodial settings with a punitive response to transgressions it is likely that rather than punishment acting as a deterrent it can serve to sustain emotional numbing. In addition custodial cultures can become increasingly violent and traumatising if they are made up of a significant number of individuals with these kinds of traits and where these are tacitly or explicitly supported.

Jones (1997) describes a process whereby custodial contexts can be implicitly managed by an unspoken agreement between the custodians – prison officers or nurses – and the most dominant members of the inmate community who are left alone in exchange for ensuring that good order is maintained. This uneasy agreement can however result in those at the top of the inmate hierarchy behaving in increasingly overbearing and callous ways to the point where they are removed and a new order evolves to take its place. This can evolve into a particularly traumatogenic culture if it gets out of hand and violence, sexual abuse and substance misuse takes hold. Those caught up in it are likely to become brutalised, increasingly learning to detach and become callous. The process of dehumanisation may be exacerbated by dissociation and emotional numbing as well as desensitisation through exposure and the influence of social learning on the adoption of aggressive 'scripts'. Callousness can become a survival strategy and a way of procuring 'goods' within the custodial setting (Ireland, 2002). Not to address this kind of trauma-facilitating aspect of prison culture is potentially to increase the risk of offending in the future.

## Experiential avoidance

In addition Kerig and Becker (2010) describe emotional, cognitive and behavioural efforts to distance oneself from a traumatic experience as trauma sequelae. These can feed into a range of disturbed behaviours in custodial contexts. This kind of response to trauma is especially pronounced in trauma involving betrayal in personal relationships (Freyd, 1996), where forgetting the abusive experience may be more common and driven partly by a desire to protect the abuser from anger linked with the trauma. Anecdotally tension-reduction behaviour such as self-harming, aggression, sexual acting-out and suicide threats may be increased by experiential avoidance whilst avoiding reminders of the trauma, particularly when triggered, can lead to people becoming increasingly withdrawn. The individual might avoid social contact or certain aspects of the regime if they feel it has features that are like the context in which they experienced abuse. Spending long periods of time alone in their cell or actively seeking out segregation to enable them to be away from the felt sense of risk when around other inmates may be two ways in which avoidance is evident.

Trauma reminders can be anything that was present at the time of the original incident, including sights, smells, behaviours, colours, tone of voice and anniversaries. Trauma-aware staff can recognise the possibility that avoidance is linked with trauma and help the individual work their way through difficult feelings and dissociative mental states associated with triggering whilst helping the individual to ground themselves and bring themselves back into the here and now. This prevents the avoidance either being covertly supported – and thereby perpetuated – or being punitively challenged as indolence or being anti-social and thereby evidencing a fundamental lack of empathy and understanding.

## Emotion recognition

Another feature is emotional recognition styles. Kerig and Becker (2010) describe a process whereby victims of violent abuse become primed to perceive ambiguous facial expressions as anger. As a survival strategy in an abusive context this makes sense. Scanning the environment for anger or hostility in a hypervigilant manner, being overly reactive to the smallest indications of anger in others and viewing the world as a hostile place are all features of this trauma response. Unfortunately in custodial contexts where violence is used pre-emptively these responses to trauma may remain adaptive and become more entrenched. Survival in such a culture also involves vigilance for manoeuvres perceived as humiliating and shaming from staff or peers which resonate with early experiences of insecure attachment and emotional and neglectful abuse.

### Cognitive and interpersonal processes

Kerig and Becker (2010) go on to argue that an abused or traumatised individual's perception of being 'damaged goods' (stigma) and the perception of personal inherent 'badness' can lead to feeling responsible for negative events (shame). The extent of this self-identification can be missed because it is often underpinned by the most difficult and shame-linked aspects of the traumatic experience. These can relate to experiences where the individual has, for example, apparently solicited the abuse because they misconstrued it as being 'loving' in what was a fundamentally loveless environment or where they have abused other children in the context of being abused themselves. These experiences of stigma and shame can then lead to a cascade of aggressive behaviour aimed at retaliating, avoiding shame and perhaps achieving status. Association with delinquent peers is consonant with the belief "I am bad" and identification with others with a similar background and self-perception.

Maruna (2001) describes the pervasiveness of condemnation narratives in repeat offenders. Perceiving the self as 'damaged goods' can feed into this narrative. Individuals who hold this kind of 'story' experience themselves as an outsider looking in, both in life outside custody and during custody or confinement. The perception of those who they construe as having a different trajectory in life may be tainted by a sense of injustice, envy and vengefulness. These become a backdrop to permission giving internal narratives supporting offending or disengagement from rehabilitation initiatives. Milieu-based interventions that are not sensitised to this dynamic can implicitly reinforce the condemnation narrative, with being discharged in less than satisfactory circumstances especially likely to compound an underlying belief of irredeemability. Careful management of this process by avoiding drop out if possible and working with those who have dropped out, taking care not to collude with 'damaged goods' narratives, is critical.

### Violence subcultures supported by abuse-linked perception of and valorisation of violence

An additional factor is valorisation of violence. Kerig and Becker (2010) cite work by Dodge, Pettit, Bates and Valente (1995) finding that children with a history of physical abuse were likely to misread social cues, to have positive evaluations of aggression, to misperceive others' intentions as hostile, and to readily access aggressive strategies in response to interpersonal problems. Recognising the often abusive origins of these hostile attribution biases is a critical task for custodial regimes.

The valorisation of violence and devaluing of affiliation in many prison cultures may be built in part on the collective experiences of violent abuse – both as children and in care and custodial settings – of the prison inmates. Hilburn-Cobb (2004) highlights the way in which children who cannot meet their needs for safety and intimacy through the attachment system switch to meeting them through the dominance system. Violence can be a way of keeping potential abusers, real or imagined, at arm's length. Working with these cultures through supplanting violence-based status systems (without undermining or ignoring the need for status, achieved in pro-social ways) and developing the capacity to meet needs through attachments and affiliation is central to a nurturing milieu. Such tasks need however to be built upon work addressing and unpicking the traumatic origins of these behaviours and beliefs.

## Moral disengagement

Kerig and Becker (2010) also elaborate on the work of Garbarino (1999), who found that trauma can influence the development of a moral outlook that justifies victimising others. The 'moral circle' – the group of people about whom the person feels a need to think in a moral way – becomes smaller, leaving more people outside the domain of those about whom one has moral feelings. Neglect can also lead to an absence of moral development through a range of pathways; for example lack of parental monitoring can lead to the thriving of bullying cultures that become linked with offence justification and beliefs supportive of this kind of behaviour. See also Needs in Chapter 3 in this volume on the concept of moral injury. Part of the walling off of emotions found in emotional numbing and avoidant (or 'dismissive') attachment can be a process of shutting off or shutting away the capacity for empathic responding (Batemen & Fonagy, 2004; Fonagy & Target, 1997). If staff are unaware of these processes then, as with other sequelae, they may misattribute their origins and blame the individual. The task for the milieu includes establishing moral engagement by trying to widen the group of people (Gabarino's moral circle) seen as warranting moral responses. More widely, the central movement must involve a sense of reconciliation if not forgiveness and redemption (e.g. Maruna, 2001).

Linked with the narrowing of the moral circle is a process described by Kerig and Becker (2010) as alienation involving feelings of powerlessness, self-estrangement, normlessness, isolation, meaninglessness and societal estrangement. This alienation extends to the self. This process can feed into the previously discussed identification with anti-social peers and subcultures and milieux can exacerbate this process by allowing people to fester in this state by, for example, locking them up for hours or providing a regime where people can get away with bullying with impunity. This amounts to a form of neglect that can parallel those experienced in the past. To offset this it is critical that a milieu has a framework for discussing and targeting this kind of process collectively and individually, working on each individual's experience of alienation and working to offer positive experiences. Ultimately, meaning, agency and a viable social and personal identity depend on a sense of belonging and social support (Needs & Adair-Stantiall, this volume). A possible complication is that through negative expectations, a sense of psychological threat and associated anger or withdrawal, traumatised individuals may do little to foster the latter. Amongst the consequences of this may be a continued preoccupation with rejection by others that may play a pivotal role in offending (Chapter 3, this volume).

Kerig and Becker (2010) cite work by Saigh (1992) indicating that children who have experienced abuse often do not believe that they will marry, have children of their own, or live a normal span of life. They term this 'futurelessness' and describe it as being associated with the belief that it is best to 'live for today' which is in turn linked with risk-taking, reckless behaviour, and disregard for consequences.

## Gender identity difficulties

Many survivors have trouble identifying as men/women, or do not like what they perceive men/women to be, because the abuser was a man/woman and because the abuse focused on their male/female body. They experience ambivalence about being a man/women because in their minds being a man/woman is associated with being a victim, and/or being sexualised. In addition people can be confused about their sexuality if they experience sexual arousal in the context of sexual abuse. They can either blame themselves for the abuse because they became aroused and mis-attribute this arousal as meaning that they wanted what had happened to happen, or they can shut down sexual feelings altogether and attempt to live an asexual lifestyle. This can then lead to self-disgust and/or confusion about sexual identity. In the prison context where coercive sexual activity is more common issues relating to these trauma sequelae are more likely to be triggered.

## Cultural insensitivity

Trauma-informed care is also about ensuring the cultural context − both internal and external past and present − is taken seriously. Culture here needs to include a broader definition of culture to include subcultures. An individual's loyalty or ambivalence − the range of types of relationship an individual has with their culture(s) is not unlike the types of attachment − towards their culture and how they work with more than one culture is critical to the task of making sense of their trauma experiences and the protective and criminogenic mental health impact they have. Friedman and Marsella (1996) emphasise the different ways trauma presents, is interpreted, is expressed, and is offered help in different cultural contexts. Culturally competent staff (Lopez, 1997) need to be supported and have reflective spaces facilitated so that during the inevitable times when cultural insensitivity or hostility emerges efforts are made to learn from this. Practitioners have begun to develop trauma-informed interventions for people with unique cultural needs (Day, Nakata & Howells, 2008; Delauney, 2013) and to some extent this has been extended to milieu-based interventions.

## Regression and state-dependant loss of commitment to self-regulation

Any experienced practitioner working in a setting in which people experience confinement will have observed the ways in which some individuals' presentations change when they are going through the crises associated with being either secluded or segregated following a serious incident. Very little has been written about the kinds of change in presentation linked with these events. Seclusion is often accompanied by an eruption of disturbed and distressed behaviour. Trauma-related responses can present with an initial burst of outrage and a cascading sequence of relinquishing commitment to self-regulation linked with a sense of betrayal and desire for revenge. This can lead to an escalation in verbal and physical hostility aimed at others and the self; in the absence of people this is targeted at property. This is linked both with whatever conflict episode – with staff or patient – led to the seclusion, the experience of being restrained and moved to the seclusion room and the experience of being locked in a room with little other than a bed and strong bedding. All of these experiences can be very strong trauma triggers (Figure 4.1).

If the person has had a history of violent abuse, violent sexual abuse or extreme neglect where caregivers have locked them up for long periods of time, for example, then the response to the process of being secluded will inevitably recapitulate and trigger past experiences. The actions of staff in the process of restraint and seclusion, in this context, take on a different significance. Staff are seen as abusers to varying extents – varying from having a flashback to an abuser who is experienced as actually being there in the room repeating the abuse to, at the other end of the scale, identifying the staff members as being like people from the past. Whether staff attributions and actions in response to such episodes are influenced by 'counter-transference', the prevailing staff culture or their own stress, morale and perceptions of support, there is scope for a vicious circle.

People often behave in ways that are difficult to understand when they are secluded. Some people become very frightened and try to hide, for example cowering in a

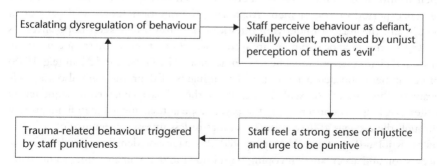

**FIGURE 4.1**  Escalating cycle of dysregulation driven by trauma being triggered by punitive reactions.

corner, whilst others become extremely angry and violently hit the walls and windows screaming abuse aimed at frightening staff, for example, "I know where you live, I will kill you and your children"; some become sexually disinhibited and masturbate in front of staff deliberately trying to humiliate and disturb them.

This process may extend beyond the immediate episode. Individuals who acquire a reputation as hostile and difficult are likely to be viewed with suspicion by staff even when they transfer to a new environment. Each party may be especially vigilant for any signs of challenge from the other and respond accordingly. Some, however, may feel that they are only safe in seclusion and this can create problems of its own whereby the individual repeatedly seeks out seclusion as a way of meeting safety needs.

## Adverse impact of imprisonment

Jones (2015), building on the work of Lambie and Randell (2013), identified a number of ways in which custodial contexts can adversely impact their residents.

Deprivation of opportunity to be exposed to 'normative experiences' promoting a sense of mastery and competence, providing experiences of prosocial relationships, or fostering a positive identity as well as repeated exposure to real or threatened violent and abusive behaviour at the hands of staff and other residents means that the coping responses of individuals need to be seen as a response to an ongoing experience of unsafety.

These processes of institutionalisation are best seen as a continuation of a process that often started with neglectful parenting or being caught up in a sometimes highly abusive care system.

## The impact of the loss of liberty

Custody is therefore a form of disabling environment and this aspect of the custodial experience is often damaging to those who experience it. Perhaps one of the most frequent subjects to be raised by people undergoing a custodial experience is their relationship with the loss of liberty and their perceptions of the end of their sentence/period of confinement. Answering the question "How do I get out of here?" and the related underlying questions of "How can I keep hope alive?" is central to the task of surviving in a custodial context. How these questions are answered changes over time. The notion developed by Gilbert and Allan (e.g. 1998) of entrapment and defeat being key determinants of depression are also very relevant to this process. As with bereavement there is a characteristic sequence of stages that helps to conceptualise the psychological tasks involved; individuals step through these stages as they come to a more or less uneasy acceptance of confinement. Kübler-Ross (e.g. 2005) proposed the stages of denial, anger, bargaining, depression and acceptance in coping with knowing that you are going to die (later used as a way of describing the stages of grief over somebody else dying). The milieu can be sensitive to and exacerbating of these responses in different ways.

The individual may deny the offence and seek to get out by appealing conviction. Hope is vested in the prospect of being set free through some legal process. Like the response to traumatic experiences generally this can result in significant avoidance of the realities of both the offence and the experiences of being in custody.

Anger at loss of liberty is very significant for some individuals, particularly at the beginning of their sentence. It can become an all-consuming preoccupation and is linked with strong feelings of injustice either at the fact of being imprisoned or as a consequence of not accepting that they have committed the offence in the first place. This is exacerbated by the sense of loss of dignity and agency linked with imprisonment. The anger has a vengeful quality in so far as the individual experiences imprisonment as an injustice and a form of abuse. They then invest energy in a vengeful stance in which they construe actions against the system as justifiable. When this same response is evident in other prisoners, often at an early stage of imprisonment, the vengeful stance can become a cultural flag around which a group of peers can gather.

Not responding to this anger sympathetically and normalising it can lead to it being triggered and exacerbated. If for example the anger is seen as evidence simply that the individual is 'still a risk' and responded to by becoming more and more restrictive in terms of the regime offered then a malevolent cycle can be established whereby the individual reacts more and more angrily to the regime becoming more and more restrictive and possibly punitive.

In some ways this angry response to incarceration can be important as it reflects a valuing of freedom that can be motivating and enables energy to be put into efforts to move towards rehabilitation. Passive acceptance of incarceration is potentially damaging insofar as it gets in the way of actively – as opposed to going through the motions – engaging with the change process.

Engagement with the system and requirements to participate in treatment can start with some initial steps whereby the individual begins to attend sessions with those delivering services and begins to participate in some aspects of the treatment programme – albeit sometimes not wholeheartedly (see Jones, 1997 for a typology of ways of responding to custody). This is perhaps equivalent to the bargaining stage of bereavement.

Over time the emotional recognition that something significant – in this case freedom – has been lost is associated often with a strong sense of grief and loss. Rumination about the life that has been lost and the life that could have been had they not been imprisoned becomes more intense and distressing. The more limited the person is in being able to have a healthy emotional or sexual life the more likely it is that they turn to fantasy to meet these needs.

Acceptance of custody comes about after the individual has recognised that they cannot change the fact of imprisonment and that the way forwards is to engage with the sentence and work towards release. Acceptance is however a double-edged sword; whilst it can facilitate engage with treatment initiatives, it can also lead to a kind of institutionalisation where the individual gradually accepts more and more the custodial context as a kind of home and becomes fearful – openly or tacitly – of moving on. The experience of imprisonment becomes an attachment experience and the prospect of liberty is experienced as a form of abandonment or rejection.

## Enactments as situational

A central construct in the literature on trauma is the idea of an enactment. This is some form of replaying or re-enactment of the original trauma often involving the victim playing some other role. Whilst enactments are often documented in the literature, it is not clear what it is that drives or underpins this kind of behaviour. In the analytic literature it is typically seen as a replaying of an early trauma but with somebody else taking the victim's role and this process is seen as a primitive form of communication – projective identification – in which the distress of the trauma is communicated directly to someone else. Other models for this could be based simply on social learning, that being exposed to certain kinds of abuse can lead to the person exposed to the experiences learning how to perpetrate the same offences on other people. This learning happens both at a behavioural level and at the level of acquiring beliefs about values and about what is permissible and what is not. The key idea behind this notion is, however, that the individual keeps returning to a situation in which these behaviours get replayed.

Recognition of this kind of process in custodial settings is critical for a milieu that is attuned to the way that trauma impacts on day-to-day living. The links between this kind of enactment and offending or offence paralleling behaviour (OPB) – behaviour that plays out patterns that parallel those that were around during the offence – need to be identified and explored in order to achieve this. It is important to recognise the extent to which this kind of enactment is about organisational problems and not to just locate them in the individual. Managers and senior practitioners need to maintain a systemic perspective in making sense of this kind of process.

## Trauma-informed care is about generating disparity and cognisant mentalising

Briere (2002) describes the experience of what he terms 'disparity', "i.e. the fact that reliving the memory means reliving danger and trauma, whereas, in reality, the current environment is not dangerous or traumatic" (p. 7), as being a critical task in bringing about change for those with trauma histories. Unfortunately, custodial contexts are often dangerous and traumatic. At minimum a custodial milieu has the ethical responsibility to prevent deterioration and, in particular, prevent iatrogenic outcomes. Ideally they should also work towards change. These goals are currently obstructed by the failure to assess and intervene, individually and systemically, with the impact of custody. Custodial experiences should offer an opportunity to develop a prefiguring trial 'good life' (Ward et al., 2012) that also implicitly and explicitly offers trauma 'disparity'. There is perhaps a political bias in the literature in that to research the harm done by imprisonment is, for many practitioners, to bite the hand that feeds you. These aims are further hampered by the lack of recognition of the way that organisations develop a parallel process (Bloom, 2006) when working with traumatised populations. Without an open strategy to recognise and address trauma, staff and custodial cultures can unthinkingly develop trauma-related qualities, such as acquired callousness, emotional avoidance and dehumanising selves and others in their relations with each other and with the inmates. Lack of recognition and intervention to pre-empt vicarious or secondary trauma in staff (e.g. Bride, 2007; Craig & Sprang, 2010; Dunkley & Whelan, 2006; Figley, 1995) can amplify systemic processes that lead to iatrogenic outcomes; trauma-informed care and careful supervision for all staff can help to prevent this process.

Levenson (2013) writes, "When in the therapeutic setting, however, clinicians should model respectful and collaborative communication lest they reproduce and reinforce the very types of disempowering relational patterns they seek to correct" (p. 7). TICC seeks to create a safe, trustworthy treatment setting in which choice, collaboration and empowerment are emphasised (Elliott, Bjelajac, Fallot, Markoff & Reed, 2005; Harris & Fallot, 2001). Above all, it ensures that the dynamics of abusive relationships are not unwittingly replicated in the helping relationship (Elliott et al., 2005; Harris & Fallot, 2001). This kind of approach also dovetails well with the recovery model (e.g. Drennan & Alred, 2012).

Briere (2002) highlights the problem of chronic avoidance as a major obstacle to change: "In the extreme case, very low affect regulation capacities in the face of especially painful childhood memories may result in chronic and extreme avoidance strategies (e.g. substance addiction, dissociative disorders) that, in fact, nullify the effects of intrusion and block recovery entirely" (p. 8). Serious offenders typically fall into this category and it is (a) an ethically difficult decision to decide whether to work on trauma or not in the light of the dangers of precipitating serious offending behaviour and (b) if it is decided to proceed it is ethically critical that not just the therapists are on board with the decision but the whole milieu. If the milieu is not ready for serious changes in behaviour, state and propensity to use offence-related self-regulation strategies linked with the trauma work then it is a strong possibility that the intervention will fail and result in an iatrogenic outcome.

## Conclusions

The ubiquitous presence of trauma of many different kinds in prison and hospital settings catering for people who have offended requires that services take a trauma-informed perspective. This means recognising the nature and pervasiveness of these issues and adapting routines, policies and practices to be responsive to these issues in the population. This means building a milieu that supports the development of positive non-stigmatised identities and which actively avoids re-traumatising and triggering trauma reactions. The concept of a 'good life' is, then, not something to be planned for in the future but something to be prefigured and rehearsed in the custodial context. The harmful impact of custody is something that there is a moral imperative to avoid. Reducing skills atrophy, responding to bereavement at the loss of liberty, and protecting people from the potentially traumatising impact of exposure to people who are actively engaging in abusive and harmful behaviour in custody are all central tasks to the task of facilitating the appropriation of a 'good life' and staying away from offending.

## References

Andrews, D.A. & Bonta, J. (1998). *The Psychology of Criminal Conduct*. 2nd Edition. Cincinnati, OH: Anderson Publishing.

Ardino, V. (2012). Offending behaviour: The role of trauma and PTSD. *European Journal of Psychotraumatology*, 3, 1–3.

Ball, A., Moore, E. & Kuipers, E. (1992). Expressed emotion in community care staff. *Social Psychiatry*, 27, 35–39.

Barrowclough, C., Haddock, G., Lowens, I., Connor, A., Pidliswyi, J. & Tracey, N. (2001). Staff expressed emotion and causal attributions for client problems on a low security unit: An exploratory study. *Schizophrenia Bulletin*, 27, 517–526.

Bateman, A.W. & Fonagy, P. (2004). Mentalization-based treatment of BPD. *Journal of Personality Disorders*, 18, 36–51.

Bateman, A. & Fonagy, P. (2010). Mentalization based treatment for borderline personality disorder. *World Psychiatry*, 9, 11–15.

Benn, A. (2002). Cognitive behaviour therapy for psychosis in conditions of high security: Cases 13 (Malcolm) and 14 (Colin). In D. Kingdon & D. Turgington (Eds.), *The Case Study Guide to Cognitive Behaviour Therapy of Psychosis* (pp. 159–182). Chichester, UK: Wiley.

Bennett, D. C. & Kerig, P. K. (2014). Investigating the construct of trauma-related acquired callousness among juvenile justice-involved youth: Differences in emotion processing. *Journal of Traumatic Stress*, 27, 414–422.

Bentall, R. (2006). The environment and psychosis: Rethinking the evidence. In W. Larkin and A. Morrison (Eds.), *Trauma and Psychosis: New Directions for Theory and Therapy* (pp. 7–22). London, UK: Routledge.

Bentall, R.P. & Fernyhough, C. (2008). Social predictors of psychotic experiences: Specificity and psychological mechanisms. *Schizophrenia Bulletin*, 34, 1012–1020.

Bentall, R.P., de Sousa, P., Varese, F., Wickham, S., Sitko, K., Haarmans, M. & Read, J. (2014). From adversity to psychosis: Pathways and mechanisms from specific adversities to specific symptoms. *Social Psychiatry Psychiatric Epidemiology*, 49, 1011–1022.

Bloom, S.L. (2006). *Organizational Stress as a Barrier to Trauma-Sensitive Change and System Transformation,* White Paper for the National Technical Assistance Center for State Mental Health Planning (NTAC), National Association of State Mental Health Program Directors. https://ncfy.acf.hhs.gov/sites/default/files/docs/21360-Organizational_Stress_as_a_Barrier_to_Trauma-Informed.pdf

Bloom, S. & Farragher, B. (2013). *Restoring Sanctuary: A New Operating System for Trauma-Informed Systems of Care*. New York, NY: Oxford University Press.

Bride, B.E. (2007). Prevalence of secondary traumatic stress among social workers. *Social Work*, 52, 63–70.

Briere, J. (2002). Treating adult survivors of severe childhood abuse and neglect: Further development of an integrative model. In J.E.B. Myers, L. Berliner, J. Briere, C.T. Hendrix, C. Jenny, et al. (Eds.), *The APSAC Handbook on Child Maltreatment* (2nd ed., pp. 175–203). Thousand Oaks, CA: Sage Publications.

Brown, L.S. (1992). A feminist critique of the personality disorders. In L.S. Brown & M. Ballou (Eds.), *Personality and Psychopathology: Feminist Reappraisals*. New York, NY: Guilford Publications.

Butzlaff, R.L. & Hooley, J.M. (1998). Expressed emotion and psychiatric relapse: A meta-analysis. *Archives of General Psychiatry*, 55, 547–552.

Cohen, L.J., Tanis, T., Bhattacharjee, R., Nesci, C., Halmi, W. & Galynker, I. (2014). Are there differential relationships between different types of childhood maltreatment and different types of adult personality pathology? *Psychiatry Research*, 215, 192–201.

Craig, C. & Sprang, G. (2010). Compassion satisfaction, compassion fatigue, and burnout in a national sample of trauma treatment therapists. *Anxiety, Stress, and Coping*, 23, 319–339.

Craissati, J., McClurg, G. & Browne, K. (2002). Characteristics of perpetrators of child sexual abuse who have been sexually victimized as children. *Sexual Abuse: A Journal of Research and Treatment*, 14, 225–239.

Day, A., Nakata, M. & Howells, K. (2008). *Anger and Indigenous Men: Understanding and Responding to Violent Behavior*. Leichardt, Australia: Federation Press.

Delauney, T. (2013). Fractured culture: Educare as a healing approach to indigenous trauma. *The International Journal of Science in Society*, 4, 53–62.

Dodge, K.A., Pettit, G.S., Bates, J.E. & Valente, E. (1995). Social information-processing patterns partially mediate the effect of early physical abuse on later conduct problems. *Journal of Abnormal Psychology*, 104, 632–643.

Drennan, G. & Alred, D. (2012). *Secure Recovery: Approaches to Recovery in Forensic Mental Health Settings*. London, UK: Routledge.

Dunkley, J. & Whelan, T. (2006). Vicarious traumatisation in telephone counsellors: Internal and external influences. *British Journal of Guidance and Counselling*, 4, 451–469.

Elliott, D.E., Bjelajac, P., Fallot, R.D., Markoff, L.S. & Reed, B. G. (2005). Trauma-informed or trauma-denied: Principles and implementation of trauma-informed services for women. *Journal of Community Psychology*, 33, 461–477.

Figley, C.R. (1995). Compassion fatigue as secondary traumatic stress disorder: An overview. In C.R. Figley (Ed.), *Compassion Fatigue: Coping with Secondary Traumatic Stress Disorder in Those Who Treat the Traumatised* (pp. 1–20). New York, NY: Brunner/Mazel Publishers.

Fonagy, P. & Target, M. (1997). Attachment and reflective function: Their role in self organization. *Development and Psychopathology*, 9, 679–700.

Frewen, P. & Lanius, R. (2015). *Healing the Traumatized Self: Consciousness, Neuroscience, Treatment*. New York, NY: WW Norton & Company.

Friedman, M. & Marsella, A. (1996). Posttraumatic Stress Disorder: An Overview of the Concept. In A. Marsella, M. Friedman, E. Gerrity & R. Scurfield (Eds), *Ethnocultural Aspects of Post-Traumatic Stress Disorder. Issues, Research, and Clinical Applications* (pp. 11–32). Washington, DC: American Psychological Association.

Freyd, J.J. (1996). *Betrayal Trauma: The Logic of Forgetting Abuse*. Cambridge, MA: Harvard University Press.

Garbarino, J. (1999). *Lost Boys: Why Our Sons Turn Violent and How We Can Save Them*. New York, NY: The Free Press.

Gilbert, P. & Allan, S. (1998). The role of defeat and entrapment (arrested flight) in depression: An exploration of an evolutionary view. *Psychological Medicine*, 28, 585–598.

Gray, N.S., Carman, N.G., Rogers, P., MacCulloch, M. J., Hayward, P. & Snowden, R.J. (2003). Post-traumatic stress disorder caused in mentally disordered offenders by the committing of a serious violent or sexual offence. *The Journal of Forensic Psychiatry & Psychology*, 14, 27–43.

Harris, M.E. & Fallot, R.D. (2001). *Using Trauma Theory to Design Service Systems*. San Francisco, CA: Jossey-Bass.

Hilburn-Cobb, C. (2004). Adolescent psychopathology in terms of multiple behavioral systems: The role of attachment and controlling strategies and frankly disorganized behaviour. In L. Atkinson & S. Goldberg (Eds.), *Attachment Issues in Psychopathology and Intervention* (pp. 95–136). Mahwah, NJ: Lawrence Erlbaum Associates.

Hooley, J.M. (1986). Expressed emotion and depression: Interactions between patients and high-versus low-expressed-emotion spouses. *Journal of Abnormal Psychology*, 93, 237–246.

Hooley, J.M. & Hiller, J. B. (2000). Personality and expressed emotion. *Journal of Abnormal Psychology*, 109, 40–44.

Hooley, J.M. & Hoffman, P. D. (1999). Expressed emotion and clinical outcome in borderline personality disorder. *American Journal of Psychiatry*, 156, 1557–1562.

Ireland, J.L. (2002). *Bullying among Prisoners: Evidence, Research and Intervention Strategies*. London, UK: Brunner-Routledge.

Jones, L. (1997). Developing models for managing treatment integrity and efficacy in a prison based TC: The Max Glatt Centre. In E. Cullen, L. Jones & R. Woodward (Eds.), *Therapeutic Communities for Offenders* (pp. 121–158). Chichester, UK: John Wiley & Sons.

Jones, L. (2004). Offence Paralleling Behaviour (OPB) as a framework for assessment and interventions with offenders. In A. Needs and G. Towl (Eds.), *Applying Psychology to Forensic Practice* (pp. 34–63). Oxford, UK: Blackwell.

Jones, L.F. (2010). History of the offence paralleling behavior construct and related concepts. In M. Daffern, L. Jones & J. Shine (Eds.), *Offence Paralleling Behaviour: A Case Formulation Approach to Offender Assessment and Intervention* (pp. 3–24). Chichester, UK: John Wiley & Sons Ltd.

Jones, L.F. (2015). The Peaks unit: From a pilot for 'untreatable' psychopaths to trauma informed milieu therapy. *Prison Service Journal*, 218, 17–23.

Jones, L.F. (Submitted). New developments in interventions for working with offending behaviour. In A. Ward and D. Polaschek, D. (Eds.), *The Wiley International Handbook of Correctional Psychology*. Malden, MA: Wiley.

Kerig, P.K. & Becker, S.P. (2010). From internalizing to externalizing: Theoretical models of the processes linking PTSD to juvenile delinquency. In S.J. Egan (Ed.), *Posttraumatic Stress Disorder (PTSD): Causes, Symptoms and Treatment* (pp. 33–78). Hauppauge, NY: Nova Science Publishers.

Kerig, P.K. & Becker, S.P. (2015). Early abuse and neglect as predictors of antisocial outcomes in adolescence and adulthood. In J. Morizot & L. Kazemian (Eds.), *The Development of Criminal and Antisocial Behavior: Theoretical Foundations and Practical Applications* (pp. 181–199). New York, NY: Springer.

Kerig, P.K., Bennett, D.C., Thompson, M. & Becker, S.P. (2012). "Nothing really matters": Emotional numbing as a link between trauma exposure and callousness in delinquent youth. *Journal of Traumatic Stress*, 25, 272–279.

Kruppa, I., Hickey, N. & Hubbard, C. (1995). The Prevalence of Post-traumatic Stress Disorder in a Special Hospital Population of Legal Psychopaths. *Psychology, Crime and Law*, 2, 131–141.

Kübler-Ross, E. (2005). *On Grief and Grieving: Finding the Meaning of Grief through the Five Stages of Loss*. New York, NY: Simon & Schuster Ltd.

Lambie, I. & Randell, I. (2013). The impact of incarceration on juvenile offenders. *Clinical Psychology Review*, 33, 448–459.

Langton, C.M., Murad, Z. & Humbert, B. (2015). Childhood sexual abuse, attachments in childhood and adulthood, and coercive sexual behaviors in community males: Main effects and a moderating function for attachment. *Sexual Abuse: A Journal of Research and Treatment*, 29(3), 207–238.

Lanius, R.A., Bluhm, R.L. & Frewen, P.A. (2011). How understanding the neurobiology of complex post-traumatic stress disorder can inform clinical practice: A social cognitive and affective neuroscience approach. *Acta Psychiatrica Scandinavica*, 124, 331–348.

Lee, D., James, S. & Gilbert, P. (2013). *The Compassionate-Mind Guide to Recovering from Trauma and PTSD: Using Compassion-Focused Therapy to Overcome Flashbacks, Shame, Guilt, and Fear*. Oakland, CA: New Harbinger Press.

Leiman, M. (2004). Dialogical sequence analysis. In H.J.M. Hermans & G. Dimaggio (Eds.), *The Dialogical Self in Psychotherapy* (pp. 255–270). London, UK: Brunner-Routledge.

Levenson, J. (2013). Incorporating trauma-informed care into evidence-based sex offender treatment. *Journal of Sexual Aggression*, 20(1), 1–14.

Lopez, S.R. (1997). Cultural competence in psychotherapy: A guide for clinicians and their supervisors. In C.E. Watkins, Jr., (Ed.), *Handbook of Psychotherapy Supervision*. New York, NY: Wiley.

Maruna, S. (2001). *Making Good: How Ex-Convicts Reform and Rebuild Their Lives*. Washington, DC: American Psychological Association.

McNally, R. (2016). The expanding empire of psychopathology: The case of PTSD. *Psychological Inquiry*, 27, 46–49.

Miller, N.A. & Najavits, L.M. (2012). Creating trauma-informed correctional care: A balance of goals and environment. *European Journal of Psychotraumatology*, 3, 1–8.

Moskowitz, A., Read, J., Farrelly, S., Rudegeair, T. & Williams, O. (2009). Are psychotic symptoms traumatic in origin and dissociative in kind? In P. Dell & J. O'Neill (Eds.), *Dissociation and the Dissociative Disorders: DSM-V and Beyond* (pp. 521–33). New York, NY: Routledge.

Panksepp, J. (2006). Emotional endophenotypes in evolutionary psychiatry. *Progress in Neuro-Psychopharmacology & Biological Psychiatry*, 30, 774–784.

Panksepp, J. & Biven, L. (2012). *Archaeology of Mind: The Neuroevolutionary Origins of Human Emotions*. New York, NY: Norton.

Pfaus, M. (2012). Who, what, where, when (and maybe even why)? How the experience of sexual reward connects sexual desire, preference, and performance. *Archives of Sexual Behavior*, 41, 31–62.

Podubinski, T., Lee, S., Hollander, Y. & Daffern, M. (2016). An examination of the stability of interpersonal hostile-dominance and its relationship with psychiatric symptomatology and post-discharge aggression. *Aggressive Behavior*, 42, 324–332.

Pollock, P.H. (1999). When the killer suffers: Post-traumatic stress reactions following homicide. *Legal and Criminological Psychology*, 4, 185–202.

Putnam, F.W. (1991). Dissociative disorders in children and adolescents: A developmental perspective. *Psychiatric Clinics of North America*, 14, 519–531.

Read, J., Agar, K., Argyle, N. & Aderhold, V. (2003). Sexual and physical abuse during childhood and adulthood as predictors of hallucinations, delusions and thought disorder. *Psychology and Psychotherapy: Research, Theory and Practice*, 76, 11–22.

Ross, L. & Nisbett, R.E. (1991). *The Person and the Situation: Perspectives of Social Psychology*. New York, NY: McGraw-Hill.

Saigh, P.A. (Ed.) (1992). *Post-Traumatic Stress Disorder: A Behavioral Approach to Assessment and Treatment*. New York, NY: Macmillan Publishing Company.

Shoda, Y. & Lee Tiernan, S. (2002). What remains invariant? Finding order within a person's thoughts, feelings, and behaviors across situations. In D. Cervone & W. Mischel (Eds.), *Advances in Personality Science* (pp. 241–270). New York, NY: Guilford Press.

Stein, J.Y, Wilmot, D.V. & Solomon, Z. (2016). Does one size fit all? Nosological, clinical and scientific implications of variations in PTSD Criterion A. *Journal of Anxiety Disorders*. 43, 106–117.

Ward, T., Yates, P.M. & Willis, G.M. (2012). The Good Lives Model and the Risk Need Responsivity Model: A critical response to Andrews, Bonta, and Wormith (2011). *Criminal Justice and Behavior*, 3, 94–110.

Wendel, J.S., Miklowitz, D.J., Richards, J.A. & George, E.L. (2000). Expressed emotion and attributions in the relatives of bipolar patients: An analysis of problem-solving interactions. *Journal of Abnormal Psychology*, 109, 792–796.

# 5

# A CAMPAIGN *FOR* CLIMATE CHANGE

## The role of therapeutic relationships within a climate of control

*Sarah Lewis*

With increased levels of prison violence, self-harm and suicide in England and Wales today (Inspectorate of Prisons, 2015), this chapter considers the current penal climate in England and Wales and turns to the academic literature to present an argument *for* climate change. Initially, it will address 'climate' itself as a socially constructed notion, highlighting the challenges of climate when viewed in isolation. It will then consider therapeutic correctional relationships and how they might operate differently under certain climates. This chapter aims to illuminate reasons why contextual factors require deeper consideration and how therapeutic climates provide a fertile ground for productive and valuable work. This is not a call to 'fix' prisons in order to substantiate and justify their existence. It is clear that alternatives to prison need to be recognised, pursued and actualised. As stated by Ryan and Ward (2015, p. 116): "The abolitionist dream is a combination of penal and social change that will be complete only when prisons are no longer required because other practices have replaced state punishment". However, as long as prisons are required, examination of contextual factors is paramount within which we pose the question: how can we construct a climate which supports rehabilitative aims and desistance from crime? Drawing on Garland's notion of a culture of control (Garland, 2001), it is concluded that if prisons in England and Wales choose to operate within a *climate* of control, meaningful work and opportunities for growth will be compromised. Conversely, under favourable conditions the connection and interaction between climate and the individual may provide transformative opportunities for personal growth. This chapter will present the need and benefits of looking beyond penal contexts by broadening the parameters of climate, to societal levels and beyond. By stirring new imaginations, positive and sustainable climates have the power to promote personal growth and desistance from crime.

Moran and Jewkes (2014) acknowledge that little attention has been paid to the emotional and affective geographies of prisons and how the people within them engage with such an environment. Much attention has been paid to the moral performance of prisons and the ways in which a prison can be perceived as 'healthy' (see Liebling, 2004). Research has also articulated the notion of prison culture and the extent to which it forms and plays out within a prison environment (see Ben Crewe's work). The focus on climate, however, not only considers the interaction between carceral environments and 'ways of being' within them; it also encapsulates the dynamic negotiation and changeable nature of climates within a penal context. This malleability also brings advantages and disadvantages from a relational perspective, heightening the opportunities for relational learning, which may nudge an individual towards desistance or conversely contribute to a counterproductive exclusion. This chapter argues (1) that prison climates need attention and transformation in order to support and sustain long-term change and (2) that de-carceration as a progression within contemporary penal practice requires attention to societal climates.

## The notion of climate

Prison climates – like environmental climates – are malleable, fluid and changeable (Lewis, 2016), due to the physical, psychological and social layers that form them. Climates are *felt* by those that exist within them, as one would experience humidity or aridness, though individuals differ with respect to their level of tolerance. This tolerance to climate may be based on, for example, prior expectations, coping strategies or the position of the individual during their life-course of criminality, including previous experiences of the criminal justice system. It may also move and shift due to local factors. For example, Liebling (2004) notes that prison climates may vary between different areas or zones of a prison and this may be dependent upon the functions or other characteristics which operate within these spaces. There is also a temporal dimension. As Nylander, Lindberg and Bruhn (2011) articulate, how a prisoner is addressed in the morning when the door is opened may influence the mood they feel for the rest of the day. The recent acknowledgement that 'every contact matters' (National Offender Management Service [NOMS], 2014) has been a positive development at policy level and holds great potential, if fully implemented. This highlights that small changes to the prison environment may contribute to change and extend to alleviating some experiences of vulnerability. This vulnerability may unsettle the day-to-day routine, create a tense or unnerving atmosphere or even increase the sense of vulnerability of the subjects that exist within the climate itself.

Climate is subjectively felt, dependent on the people that exist within it and the connections and meanings between them (Martin, Jefferson & Bandyopadhyay, 2014). It is the social environment rather than individuals and their dispositions that fully articulates climate (Schlosser, 2013). Indeed Ross, Diamond, Liebling and Saylor (2008) highlight the complexities of prison climate and refer to social, emotional, organisational and physical characteristics of the correctional institution perceived by prisoners and staff within a prison environment. This depiction of multiple sources of variation means that measuring climate becomes increasingly problematic and complex (Day, Casey, Vess & Huisy, 2011). Tools have been developed to establish what a 'healthy' prison may look like. For instance, Liebling's work (2004) has been instrumental in much of this development, illuminating how the moral performance of an institution can be understood, and identifying patterns of aspects such as relationships, regime and social structure in environments that are more conducive to personal growth, safety and stability. Rison and Wittenberg (1994) acknowledge that one of the key contributing factors to the stability or otherwise of a prison is its social climate, with Gadon, Johnstone and Cooke (2006) recognising behaviour does not exist in a vacuum and situational factors are important. To illustrate, Gadon et al. (2006) highlight that the risk of prison violence increases with prisoner mix, high traffic areas with low staff presence and relational connection between managers and staff. Such work points to the possibility that the quality of an environment can be measured and provide important information regarding how a prison may improve. Whilst Ross et al. (2008b) acknowledge the importance of reliably and comprehensively measuring prison climate, due to the above complexities some aspects of climate remain elusive and hard to articulate. This does not mean that capturing climate is a futile exploration; such an investigation can provide us with an understanding of what kind of climates may be most beneficial for those that reside (and work) within them.

## Therapeutic correctional relationships and micro-climates

How therapeutic relationships can live and breathe within a prison setting is of great interest. Like any relationship, those relationships within a prison setting shift and alter between different contexts and over time, as relationships deepen or degrade. This means that while a larger prison climate is being experienced by the prisoner (as they walk onto a landing or move through the prison), micro-climates are experienced between prisoner and practitioner, which are established and co-constructed through the correctional relationship itself. A correctional relationship can be defined as *any* relationship that exists within a correctional context, between a criminal justice practitioner and an individual who has offended (Lewis, 2016). This encapsulates negative, controlling and unhealthy aspects of relationships, as well as relationships which could be described as positive, mutual and healthy. Many have highlighted that a therapeutic correctional relationship is a relationship which nurtures positive change within a correctional context (Ward & Marshall, 2007; Neville, Miller & Fritzon, 2007; Lewis, 2016). Therefore, it is important to note that correctional relationships are ultimately defined by the context in which they are situated.

Lewis (2016) presents the notion that relationships ebb and flow within a therapeutic climate, depending upon the dyadic experience between the practitioner and those that have offended. From previous research on therapeutic correctional relationships within a community-based probation environment, Lewis (2016) outlines three micro-climates. First, practitioners and service users both described a space outside of the therapeutic climate. This position could be described as 'distance-far', as the two individuals are not receptive or motivated to relate to one another. This exclusionary position creates a shallow bond (which is played out through 'shallow-acting', Nylander et al., 2011) between the practitioner and service user, with low levels of trust, legitimacy or respect. In the event that both individuals move closer, with the intention to relate and bond, they enter into the therapeutic climate. This climate, in its purest sense, represents a positive place embodied with mutual respect, trust, legitimacy and acceptance. Whether a relationship is therapeutic depends upon the level of bond that exists between the practitioner and service user and the degree to which they agree and work together in addressing the individual's needs, goals and tasks (see Lewis, 2016). A final micro-climate was identified within the research, as both players draw *too* close to one another. With an over-focus on bond, knowledge about both players is clouded and this space may increase the likelihood of collusion and manipulation.

The key finding from this research suggested that relationships that were situated within the therapeutic climate hold transformative potential. Realistically, however, an event may temporarily cause either the practitioner or service user (or both) to move away from one another, altering the bond that exists between them and the psychological and social distance. This has been defined within the psychotherapeutic literature as a *rupture* (Safran & Muran, 2003). If a relationship maintains an *inclusive* position, through the principles of relational practice (see Lewis, 2016), and survives the inevitable occurrences of ruptures, then a greater understanding of the service user can emerge, as well as opportunities for personal growth. It is important to be aware not only of where the practitioner or service user is positioned within the correctional relationship, but the movement of the players which may contribute towards positive changes. Whilst it is accepted that the service user has relational agency and can move away from the practitioner at their will, it is also argued that creating a therapeutic climate which is filled with hope holds many transformative benefits (described further in Akerman and Mandikate, this volume and Brookes, this volume).

How practitioners encourage individuals who offend to enter into the therapeutic climate is therefore important and contingent on a number of variables including the openness to a relationship, the level of trust (held by both players) and the distance (or bond) between the practitioner and service user. Some may never experience this position for a number of reasons, which may be explained by their developed attachments on deeper and broader levels. Creating a climate of hope can also be very difficult, as experienced within a therapeutic correctional setting, especially when prisoners may feel that they are working against the odds. Creating enclaves of hope, within a punitive, exclusionary context could be the most meaningful aspect for a prisoner during their incarceration. Embedding relational practice within the fabric of penal practice creates greater transformative power and settling for less would compromise the potential influence of relationships in prison practice.

Relational ruptures have recently been explored within correctional practice (see Lewis, 2016) and this work has illuminated how events within practice can create a tear within a relationship and lead to withdrawal from the relationship and unavailability. This may be due to a confrontational moment or an act which is deemed unfair or illegitimate, or through relational games which are played. Lewis (2016) identified three rupture games, baiting, battling and blocking, from her work in the community. These games involve practitioners provoking the service user (baiting), verbally fighting (battling) or dismissing or excluding a service user (blocking). Such games were believed to increase the likelihood of a confrontational rupture (fighting back) or a withdrawal rupture (moving away). Through a critical analysis of these micro-processes of relationships within a correctional setting, it was concluded that when power was made visible by the practitioner through such actions, service users were more likely to withdraw from the therapeutic climate and instead, exist within a space which was distant and exclusionary. If both the players positioned themselves outside of the therapeutic climate, this consequently influenced the level of understanding they had of one another and therefore the rehabilitative efforts, risk management and the relationship itself.

Turning our attention to prison specifically, Crewe (2011a) proposes that it is challenging to sustain positive relationships in an environment that is punitive and controlling. Within this coercive environment, climate alters the flow of relationships and can impede their ability to thrive. Due to the fluid nature of both relationships and climate, it can be observed that even in the most punitive conditions, positive relationships can exist against all adversity. This would suggest that there are hollowed out relational spaces within an environment, which may temporarily alter the meaningful and usefulness of that space. Crewe (2011a) states that staff–prisoner relationships situated in a hostile climate can result in prisoners struggling to overcome feelings of mistrust. Crewe (2011a) also describes relationships which may be courteous, which are not congruent to a therapeutic correctional relationship, due to their shallow level of bond and lack of trust. This is where culture may play a role in constructing aspects of climate, as informal rules go against the ideas of fully trusting prison officers. The sometimes ambiguous role of the prison officer makes it difficult to convince prisoners that they can be trusted and this is exacerbated by an inmate culture which does little to promote trust (E. Ross, Polaschek & Ward, 2008a). Thus, the context many determine to some extent the prisoner's willingness to engage in a deep therapeutic correctional relationship, particularly if relational scripts are entrenched due to previous negative experiences of correctional relationships and living in an environment characterised by low levels of trust (Liebling, 2004).

Within a probation context, Lewis (2016) identified that ruptures were found to be an inevitable part of practice and even the most authentic and virtuous practitioners were not immune to the lure of relational power. It is not so much the aim that ruptures should be eliminated from practice, more that ruptures are acknowledged and *utilised* as practitioners become aware of their actions and the reasons behind them. Research within psychotherapy has found that resolving a tear or rupture within a relationship can lead to an opportunity for growth (see Safran & Muran, 2003). It is the process of *repairing* which can develop new relational experiences. Climate is introduced here as providing a place in which mending can take place. An environment which promotes those aspects linked to moral performance (such as decency, trust, fairness and respect) is instrumental during the mending process. The environment can therefore be utilised to create a space to repair and resolve ruptures.

## Relational power in carceral climates

Climate is constructed and multifaceted, but also subjective. Individuals perceive climates differently, and take significance and meaning from them in different ways. As stated previously, this may be one reason why it is so difficult to measure and conceptualise social climates (Day et al., 2011 and in this volume). There are also differences between culture and climate, as culture is founded upon the philosophies of an organisation, which then shape behaviour (Melnick, Ulaszek, Lin & Wexler, 2009) whilst climate is more suggestive of the perceptions of 'the way things are' (Taxman, Cropsey, Melnick & Perdoni, 2008). Whilst culture and climate influence and shape one another, how an individual sees and experiences a prison environment may be influenced by how they see the world more generally. On a relational level, the schemata (mental models) and attachment strategies an individual adopts may alter or filter out certain aspects of the climate, which are not congruent with their working models of life. The other distinction between culture and climate may align to the sensory experience. Culture may shape behaviour with the input of philosophies and rules that exist within prison, whereas a variety of climates exist within a prison environment. Some of these climates may be more stable than others. To illustrate, when entering Bastøy prison (a humane ecological island prison in Norway with a working farm) there is a real sense of ease and safety. During the author's research project in 2015, the prison was searched for drugs, and pockets of darkness were experienced, which caused worry and unease. On the day in which a horse went into labour on the farm, there was a breeze of excitement and nervousness in the air. Subsequently, when the horse delivered a stillborn foal, the clouds of climate became immediately heavy across the prison. Beneath these experiences, the culture stayed relatively stable as the philosophies of Bastøy remained intact. It was the *climate* which moved and changed the way in which these experiences were synthesised. It is therefore the power of climate which is of interest here. As a prisoner sits, immersed in a climate, how might it shape imagination, identity and self? How might it alter perspective or challenge past ways of being?

Certainly there can be differences depending upon where one stands within a prison and such differences may create discrepancies within a prison climate. To illustrate, although Moos' Correctional Institutions Environment Scale (1997) has suffered much criticism (see Schalast, Redies, Collins, Stacey & Howells, 2008) with respect to its validity and internal consistency, Moos (1997) found that practitioners were generally found to be more positive than prisoners when they shared their perceptions of climate. How a practitioner experiences 'safety' may differ to how a prisoner experiences 'safety'. Developing this further, a prisoner who has been convicted of a child sex offence may experience 'safety' very differently to a prisoner who has committed fraud. This perspective on climate may widen even further if a rupture has occurred within a prison environment, which may be connected to either an individual or group of individuals. It is therefore important to not only uncover those elements of climate which are relatively static, but also acknowledge and understand those elements which are dynamic, drawing on what Brunt and Rask (2005) refers to as the 'psychosocial atmosphere'.

The relevance of an important aspect of this, emotional climate, is illustrated by Ruiz's (2007) work in Latin America. Ruiz (2007) highlighted that aspects of organisational culture, stress and support are negatively correlated with post-traumatic stress disorder and avoidant coping while positively correlating with internal locus of control and subjective social support. Climate has an important function in fostering a positive emotional response and contributing to other important processes related to more nurturing atmospheres generally. For example, Tran (2010) found that when hope and joy are felt within a social climate, this triggers important mechanisms that allow positive climates to grow, be sustained and develop through innovation and creativity. Such aspects have major implications for psychological intervention (Bottoms, 2003). Bottoms (2003) recognised the importance of contextual factors when delivering interventions within a prison context and E. Ross et al. (2008a) acknowledged that prison climate can act as an enabler or disenabler to intervention success. E. Ross et al. (2008a) also proposed that constructing a healthy and therapeutic climate can influence problematic behaviour in prison (such as self-harm, violence and drug use) and reduce the risk of re-offending. The Bradley report (Department of Health, 2009) also suggests that prison environments can contribute to a deteriorating of mental health, an exacerbation of vulnerability and an increased risk of self-harm. This is further supported by Day et al. (2011), who warn that a negative social climate in prisons can be counter-therapeutic and hinder desistance; therefore, a lot may be at stake if climates are toxic.

Situating these findings within the desistance literature allows us to more fully appreciate the implications of positive climates. The desistance literature focuses upon how individuals move away from crime, rather than criminogenic aspects of an individual, focusing upon processes rather than outcomes. Gaining perceived control over one's life in order to re-configure and transform an individual's identity is an important aspect of desistance, alongside experiencing meaningful support and positive social bonds (Maruna, 2001). This suggests a shift in emphasis from measuring prison climates to determine whether they are 'good' or 'bad' to asking how knowledge of desistance can help shape the construction of climates.

This immediately raises the question of whether prison is the right place for desistance-focused practice, or whether alternatives to punishment may be more conducive to such proposals. Let us draw back to the work of Toch (1977) and Liebling (2004) and pose the question, what might the most appropriate place to support an individual to desist from crime be? This puts our society under the spotlight as much as our prisons. As previously argued (Lewis, 2014, p. 53):

> Within a prison environment ... the cocktail of top-down punitive prac-
> tice, exclusion and othering (or distancing) creates a difficult atmosphere for
> rights-based practice to exist.

With this in mind, do we need to persist in trying to shoehorn rehabilitation into a system whose foundations are retributive? It is not only climate change within prison which is questioned, but climate change on broader levels. In England we are fully immersed into a free market, neo-liberal economy which is characterised by competition, consumerism and instability. Services are temporary and fluid, focused on outcome, whilst positive, healthy, collaborative relationships are struggling to find ground to grow. Society could be described similarly to Crewe's (2011b) words specific to prison; both are deep with control and heavy with surveillance, although some populations are affected more than others. Within this climate of control and competition, it also seems harder for organisations to trust, collaborate and share new ideas. As in organisations more generally, policy and routine decisions within criminal justice often owe more to compromise between competing priorities and extraneous influences than to careful analysis of focal issues (Needs, 2010).

## Growing climates: a look at physical place

The possibility of variations in climate across different areas of prisons, linked inex-tricably to mobility and therefore time, was touched upon earlier. Such aspects are relevant to Merleau-Ponty's (2001) idea of 'being in the world' as a dynamic expe-rience that is fundamental to perceptual phenomena. The following discussion cen-tres upon the ramifications of place. Consider, for example, a prison library, where prisoners may be able to carve out spaces of autonomy, as they move around freely within a defined space. Prisoners may have more freedom, such as choosing where to sit, what to read and where to walk. Therefore, a library may serve the function of more than simply a place where one reads, but a place where one moves and has space to imagine, be stimulated and feel a sense of freedom.

When transposed into a criminal justice context the idea of therapeutic land-scapes holds real fascination. Jiang (2014) highlighted the long traditions of nature as a natural healer. Velarde, Fry and Tveit (2007) acknowledge the link between natural and historical features and the maintenance of well-being. Gesler (2003) went as far as proposing that 'place' can contribute to physical and spiritual healing. Links between ecological psychology, horticultural therapy and environmental psy-chology are beginning to create greater currency from a therapeutic perspective, though such discussions within a penal context are a rarity. And yet, therapeutic landscapes have been seen to be restorative, helping to relieve physical symptoms, illness, stress and trauma. Indeed, similar ideas were founded upon the establishment of mental health sanctuaries. Whilst Goffman (1968) highlighted that the rationale of total institutions was to separate the patient or prisoner from the outside, Kearns and Joseph (2000) expressed the argument that the removal of an individual from the stress of everyday activity can be calming and support individuals with their re-entry back into the community or during treatment. This is of course highly contingent upon the way in which environments are constructed and their therapeutic worth.

## Physical environments

Kearns and Joseph (2000) state that spaces of calmness and sanctuary, deemed as 'spaces of transition', can encourage a degree of connection between the community and institutional environment, creating a 'managed permeability'. Such spaces are not invariably images that are conjured up when we consider penal contexts and spaces; these are usually designed out, rather than designed into prison architecture. The architecture and the physical environment can be seen as onerous and oppressive, with little scope for mobility, due to the security and other institutional procedures which are in place, though high visibility is also for many prisoners a source of safety. Schweitzer, Gilpin and Frampton (2004) highlight that the design of a building can improve the flow of relationships and the importance of opportunities for social connectedness, whilst poor design can conversely restrict practice (for example with family access).

Drawing on Bastøy prison in Norway, this resonates heavily. This island prison holds 115 men in a low-security setting and has visiting rights, which take place at a visitors' centre. This features self-contained apartments for families to have space and time together. Outside the centre, there is a small play area and a beach, where families can have a barbecue, away from the prison officers' gaze. The feeling associated with this arrangement is greater ease and comfort, within the confines of the prison. The opportunity for meaningful connections was highlighted as a value of the prison and the interaction between the blue space of the sea and green space of the trees make it a place where relationships can flourish, immersed in a place of growth. Pierce (2015) recognises that visiting environments can affect the quality of contact and proposes that this can reduce the potential of recidivism. This highlights how spaces can be hollowed out, within a prison environment, to promote the social connections with family which may be so important for a prisoner.

The symbolic nature of carceral climates is important in terms of how they are viewed and what meaning they bring. It is not just about place and its symbolic construction, but imagined spaces and places (Andrews, 2004). This can be observed through the attachment of metaphorical thought to feelings (the sun rising as a new start) and making an environment stimulating. Andrews (2004) found that using visualisation and the imagination of non-physical places can enhance mental health and well-being and assist in coping. This presents the idea that it is not only physical 'place' that may be important, but also *how* space, relational practice and the connection of these can bring about a nurturing imagination. It may be beneficial therefore to expand the therapeutic landscape beyond physicality and focus on how the relational self and landscape interact and influence identity over time and space (Conradson, 2005). These benefits may not just be experienced and appreciated by the prisoners, but also the practitioner, assisting them in the preservation of hope, which is vital for quality relational work.

Therapeutic landscapes have recently been discussed within a carceral context (though institutions like therapeutic communities have a longer history). Moran and Jewkes (2014) present us with the concept of green prisons, with nurturing environments, though warn that these are only feasible in "decarcerative settings imbued with a rehabilitative, rather than retributive atmosphere" (p. 345), acknowledging how prison could heal rather than harm by constructing and nurturing therapeutic landscapes. The sense of place is noted as relational as it addresses all aspects of the individual and their interactions with others, providing a 'healthy' place which addresses physical, emotional, spiritual, societal and environmental needs (Moran, 2015) as well as opportunities to experience a healthy interaction, where an individual feels comfort and connection.

Whilst Gesler (1992) highlighted therapeutic landscapes and their healing properties, counter-therapeutic experiences have also been discussed (Andrews & Holmes, 2007). Andrews and Holmes (2007) acknowledge that negative or toxic environments are associated with risk, fear and exclusion. As Milligan (2007) points out, climates can move from restorative to risky. If climates become riskier, unsafe, fearful and exclusionary, as acknowledged in recent research by Liebling, Arnold and Straub (2011), uncertainty and mistrust can emerge and poison the therapeutic milieu. It is proposed that in toxic environments, where mistrust exudes through day-to-day living, relational ruptures are more likely and a lack of reciprocity make relationships difficult to reach. Being treated as 'the other' anchors down the prisoner in such a way that it excludes them from relational participation. They are undeserving of rehabilitation, respect or even the comfort or relatedness associated with relationships. They are the moral stranger. This exclusionary practice may operate both overtly (through segregation) or covertly (through rupture games associated with softer uses of power), but ultimately places prisoners in a space where moving forward with their rehabilitation becomes increasingly difficult.

Such social bonds on broader levels not only have advantages within society, but also permeate through the carceral walls. This has been observed in Norway, as prison staff often discussed how prisoners will one day be their neighbour and society plays a role in the reintegration of prisoners, once released. This may not be generalised throughout the Nordic penal system, but the values associated with belonging and sameness may influence the way in which cultures are constructed and climates are experienced. This value implies a broader reciprocity which is characteristic of a healthy and secure societal attachment. The institutional environment thus creates a particular way of acting and thinking, which ultimately extends into the community.

Halden prison in Norway represents some of the key values of the Norwegian society and was designed with rehabilitation in mind. Walking around this prison, you cannot help being impressed by its motivation to dull the pains of prison, through a consideration of place. The architectural design uses colour to create variety and nature, to ease the monotonous existence of those that reside there. It takes away traditional bars and dirty spaces. It is mindful of climate and its influence. As Hancock and Jewkes (2011) also describe, the exploitation of natural light, art and sculpture presents openness and recognition of humanistic values. Hancock and Jewkes (2011) state how this encourages a personal creativity and vividness of experience. As discussed, this may not only contribute to a sense of agency, but provide spaces where imaginations can grow and a re-imagining of identity may flourish. This is not limited to closed spaces either. Bastøy prison embraces a humane ecological principle, which promotes prisoner interaction and seeking meaning from the environment around them. This not only represents values of the broader society, but also engages aspects of desistance within a whole systems framework. This environment raises questions around identity more broadly than previously considered. It is not focused solely on the aspects of the 'criminogenic' self, but encapsulates the whole self and new articulations of it. Kuhn (2001) highlighted that uncovering aspects of being fully human, through the psychological relationship with our environment, holds great potential. It is not the case that those who have offended are separate from the wider environment, but part of it. This encourages prisoners to look inwards and outwards, and understand that there is something much bigger than them. Kuhn (2001) argued that expanding the ecological self in this way, through empathic relationships, may contribute to processes of self-actualisation through inter-relatedness. Similarly, Fox (1995) considered the expansion of identity with other humans, animals, plants and places. Additionally, Lutze (1998, p. 549) highlights that environment and institutional support can promote psychological and emotional change, stating, "such support provides social and emotional sustenance that empowers inmates to seek help from prison staff, programs, and other inmates". If applied to relational work, this would suggest that prison environments can provide greater opportunities for relational connection by nurturing supportive relationships to promote personal insight and growth. Broadening out relational practice from human relationships to other relational connections might magnify the power relationships hold within a carceral context.

## Macro-climates

Larger systemic climates may also influence the way in which regimes and atmospheres are constructed. As Wacquant (2012) professes, prison has become a place where problem populations reside and a culture of control is delivered, without much thought of the future implications both ethically and psychologically. This focus upon control rather than welfare has been observed within the changing discourse at policy level, which Feeley and Simon (1992) and Garland (2001) identify as the New Penology. As risk assessments thrive in a risk society, they identify that the emergent role of the criminal justice system is not to rehabilitate, but instead to control and manage 'them'. As prisons respond to this change, dual relationships become increasing problematic, as complexity increases. From a relational perspective, relationships take a backseat as uncertainty creates a distancing between those that offend and those that work within prison. This also has an impact upon rehabilitative goals. The ethical position of the practitioner has become increasing muddied, as the purpose of their efforts is no longer for the greater good of reha-bilitation, but managing people who are 'risky'. Day and Casey (2009) highlight the conflict between the needs of the public, the service user and the therapist and the subsequent danger of considering the process of rehabilitation as 'for the people', thus omitting the service user, who is responsible for most of the work. Where responsibility lies is likely to become increasingly blurred in organisations keen to reap the benefits under payment by results. In light of this duality in criminal justice, Day and Ward (2010) point out that a tension exists between the desire to be respectful and supportive whilst working within an environment which is ulti-mately punitive. And yet, as these tensions and contradictions exist, practice persists and positive change does occur against this punitive tide.

Garland (2001) proposes that economic and cultural changes during late modernity have led to a 'culture of control', in which governments have presented and implemented strategies that are based on repression and anxiety. Garland (2001) argues that anxiety and neurosis arise concerning 'dangerous offenders' and this assumes that socially constructed groupings of 'offenders' are homogeneous, whilst exclusionary practices distil fear and isolate those individuals that we under-stand little about. Pratt (2007) argued that the politicisation of criminal justice has increased in order that public sentiment rather than the expert drives policy as populism is propelled through the mass media. Wilkinson and Pickett (2010) acknowledge the social distancing between 'them and us' continues to widen and this widening not only impacts on the prison climate but also everyday life, as a 'criminology of the other' becomes embedded within the fabric of our commu-nities. It is therefore not only the carceral climate which may hold rehabilitative significance but broader relational climates, at a societal level. This may include the practising of 'othering' within the community through blocked opportunities, stigma and policy which targets those who are considered 'underserving'. This punitive push may be less the product of an increasingly retributive and unforgiv-ing society than of mass unawareness regarding what works to support desistance. It is necessary to encourage education regarding punishment to create a climate which embodies intelligent practice.

From this perspective, relational practice (that is, practice focused upon rela-tionships and meaningful connections) permeates all levels of society. Creating a greater alignment between inside and outside the carceral walls would hold many benefits, which some countries are experiencing already. Nordic countries have been recognised as having this quality (Pratt, 2008a,b) and whilst there is an active debate regarding the extent of penal exceptionalism within the Nordic countries, it is fair to say that there is a greater congruence between the inside and outside of prisons due to the principle of normalisation. The principle of normalisation states that prisoners are given the same rights as those in the community and this focus upon equality and sameness lessens the differences between the societal climate and prison climate. As Ross et al. state (2008b, p. 454):

> Prison climate occurs within a more prevailing climatic system affected by the winds of political opportunism, popular sentiment, emotion, criminology research, the media, human rights and legal issues, and economic considerations.

This is somewhat problematic due to the contradictory nature of these winds, some of which may drive punitive practice and some of which may counter against it. There are forces associated with the culture of control which promote punitive climates. In contrast, pushing against the punitive tide may include aspects of relational practice, desistance-focused approaches and rights-based efforts. If relationships can be nurtured in broader climates (through organisations such as Circles of Support and Accountability and St. Giles Trust[1]), it is proposed that this will create greater alignment between the inside and outside of the prison and increase the transformative power of relational work in the future.

What Garland (2001) presents as a 'culture of control' creates contradictions ideologically and tensions within penal practice when placed alongside more strength-based, rehabilitative approaches to punishment. With a campaign *for* climate change proposed, contextual factors within the penal arena need greater attention; such a perspective may create a more integrated awareness of processes and potential consequences. At its focus is the co-construction of rehabilitative climates that nurture authentic and meaningful relationships. It also highlights fluctuations of climate and *movement within* and *between* environments. Its timeliness is indicated by recent whispers (Crozier, 2015) of a culture of hope and empowerment.

## Conclusion

In conclusion, this chapter has presented a rationale for penal climate change. Penal climates are fluid and malleable and climates are not dichotomous. Instead, climates move and shift over time and space, with the possibility of micro-climates being carved out of environments, through therapeutic correctional relationships. During a time at which a culture of control permeates through all levels of society, creating pockets of growth within prison provides some opportunities for rehabilitation but this is not sustainable. Relational practice requires fertile soil to grow and develop in order to achieve its transformative potentiality. This chapter argues that greater relational congruence and consistency in penal practice could maximise the power of relationships and contribute to constructing favourable conditions for personal growth. While relational ruptures are inevitable within practice, more could be done to support practitioners in repairing ruptures to convert relational tears into opportunities for relational growth. This chapter has also spent some time exploring the climate which exists beyond the carceral walls. Climates are socially constructed on an interpersonal level though extend beyond human interaction and physical therapeutic spaces towards connections with the natural and spiritual world. Therefore, re-imagining how desistance and growth can be supported by extending the reach of relational practice into broader terrains is called for. This leads to an expansion of imagination and widening of relational practice, which may provide transformative power for personal growth.

To achieve this, this chapter calls for a whole systems approach, to fully actualise how climates operate at all levels of the criminal justice system. In order to do this, a fusion between academia and policy is paramount. It is not enough to think about climate. As part of the relational revolution, the author calls for *action* in the campaign for penal climate change.

## Note

1  Circles of Support and Accountability is a community-based project which supports the reintegration of sex offenders back into the community. See www.circles-uk.org.uk for more information. St. Giles Trust is a charity that supports prisoners when they are released from prison, promoting the work of mentoring, peer advisors and preventative work in the community. See http://site.stgilestrust.org.uk for more information.

## References

Andrews, G. (2004). (Re)thinking the dynamics between healthcare and place: Therapeutic geographies in treatment and care practices. *Area*, 36, 307–318.

Andrews, G. & Holmes, D. (2007). Gay bathhouses: The transgression of health in therapeutic places. In A. Williams (Ed.), *Therapeutic Landscapes: The Dynamic between Place and Wellness* (pp. 221–233). Lanham, MD: University Press of America.

Bottoms, A. (2003). Theoretical reflections on the evaluation of a penal policy initiative. In L. Zedner and A. Ashworth (Eds.), *The Criminological Foundation of Penal Policy: Essays in Honor of Roger Hood* (pp. 107–194). Oxford, UK: Oxford University Press.

Brunt, D. & Rask, M. (2005). Patient and staff perceptions of the ward atmosphere in a Swedish maximum-security forensic psychiatric hospital. *The Journal of Forensic Psychiatry and Psychology*, 16, 263–276.

Conradson, D. (2005). Landscape, care and the relational self: Therapeutic encounters in rural England, *Health and Place*, 11, 337–348.

Crewe, B. (2011a). Soft power in prison: Implications for staff-prisoner relationships, liberty and legitimacy. *European Journal of Criminology*, 8, 455–468.

Crewe, B. (2011b). Depth, width, tightness: Revisiting the pains of imprisonment. *Punishment and Society*, 13, 509–529.

Crozier, S. (October, 2015). *Probation in Prisons Update*. National Offender Management Service.

Day, A. & Casey, S. (2009). Values in forensic and correctional psychology. *Aggression and Violent Behaviour*, 14, 232–238.

Day, A., Casey, S., Vess, J. & Huisy, G. (2011). Assessing the social climate of Australian prisons. Trends and issues in crime and criminal justice. *Australian Institute of Criminology*, 427, 1–6.

Day, A. & Ward, T. (2010). Offender rehabilitation as a value-laden process. *International Journal of Offender Therapy and Comparative Criminology*, 54, 289–306.

Department of Health (2009). *The Bradley Report: Lord Bradley's Review of People with Mental Health Problems or Learning Disabilities in the Criminal Justice System*. London: Department of Health. Retrieved from: www.centreformentalhealth.org.uk/pdfs/Bradley_report_2009.pdf.

Feeley, M. & Simon, J. (1992). The new penology: Notes on the emerging strategy of corrections and its application. *Criminology*, 30, 449–470.

Fox, W. (1995). *Toward a Transpersonal Ecology*. Albany, NY: State University of New York Press.

Gadon, L., Johnston, L. & Cooke, D. (2006). Situational variables and institutional violence: A systematic review of the literature. *Clinical Psychology Review*, 26, 515–534.

Garland, D. (2001). *A Culture of Control: Crime and Social Order in Contemporary Society*. Oxford, UK: Oxford University Press.

Gesler, W. (1992). Therapeutic landscapes: Medical issues in light of the new cultural geography. *Social Science and Medicine*, 34, 735–746.

Gesler, W. (2003). *Healing Places*. Maryland, MD: Rowman and Littlefield.

Goffman, E. (1968). *Asylums: Essays on the Social Situation of Mental Patients and Other Inmates*. Harmondsworth, UK: Penguin.

Hancock, P. & Jewkes, Y. (2011). Architectures of incarceration: The spatial pains of imprisonment. *Punishment and Society*, 13, 611–629.

HM Inspectorate of Prisons (2015). *Annual Report 2014–2015*. Retrieved from: www.justiceinspectorates.gov.uk/hmiprisons/wp-content/uploads/sites/4/2015/07/HMIP-AR_2014-15_TSO_Final1.pdf.

Jiang, S. (2014). Therapeutic landscapes and healing gardens: A review of Chinese literature in relation to the studies in western countries. *Frontiers in Architectural Research*, 3, 141–153.

Kearns, R. & Joseph, A. (2000). Contracting opportunities: Interpreting post-asylum geographies of mental health care in Auckland New Zealand. *Health and Place*, 6, 159–169.

Kuhn, J. (2001). Toward an ecological humanistic psychology. *Journal of Humanistic Psychology*, 41, 9–24.

Lewis, S. (2014). Responding to domestic abuse: Multi agented systems, probation programmes and emergent outcomes. In A. Pycroft & C. Bartollas (Eds.), *Applying Complexity Theory: Whole Systems Approaches in Criminal Justice and Social Work* (pp. 221–246). Bristol, UK: Policy Press.

Lewis, S. (2016). *Therapeutic Correctional Relationships: Theory, Research and Practice*. London: Routledge.

Liebling, A. (2004) *Prisons and Their Moral Performance: A Study of Values, Quality and Prison Life*. Oxford, UK: Oxford University Press.

Liebling, A., Arnold, H. & Straub, C. (2011). *An Exploration of Staff-Prisoner Relationships at HMP Whitemoor: 12 Years On*. Cambridge Institute of Criminology: Prison Research Centre. Retrieved from: www.gov.uk/government/uploads/system/uploads/attachment_data/file/217381/staff-prisoner-relations-whitemoor.pdf.

Lutze, F. (1998). Are shock incarceration programs more rehabilitative than traditional prisons? A survey of inmates. *Justice Quarterly*, 15, 547–563.

Martin, T., Jefferson, A. & Bandyopadhyay, M. (2014). Sensing prison climate: Governance, survival and transition. *Focaal*, 68, 3–17.

Maruna, S. (2001). *Making Good: How Ex-Convicts Reform and Rebuild Their Lives*. Washington, DC: American Psychological Association.

Melnick, G., Ulaszek, W., Lin, H-J. & Wezler, H. (2009). When goals diverge: Staff consensus and the organisational climate. *Drug and Alcohol Dependence*, 103, S17–S22.

Merleau-Ponty, M (2001). *Phenomenology of Perception* (2nd ed.). London: Routledge.

Milligan, C. (2007). Restoration or risk? Exploring the place of the common place. In Williams, A. (Ed.), *Therapeutic Landscapes: The Dynamic Between Place and Wellness* (pp. 255–273). Lanham, MD: University Press of America.

Moos, R. (1997). *Evaluating Treatment Environments. The Quality of Psychiatric and Substance Abuse Programs*. New Brunswick, NJ: Transaction.

Moran, D. (2015). *Carceral Geography: Spaces and Practices of Incarceration*. Farnham, UK: Ashgate.

Moran D. & Jewkes, Y. (2014). "Green" prisons: Rethinking the "sustainability" of the carceral estate. *Geographica Helvetica, 69*, 345–353.

Needs, A. (2010). Systemic failure and human error. In C. Ireland & M. Fisher (Eds.), *Consultancy and Advising in Forensic Practice: Empirical and Practical Guidelines* (pp. 203–219). Chichester, UK: Wiley-Blackwell.

Neville, L., Miller, S. & Fritzon, K. (2007). Understanding change in a therapeutic community: An action systems approach. *Journal of Forensic Psychiatry & Psychology, 18*, 181–203.

NOMS (2014). *National Offender Management Business Plan 2014–2015*. London: Ministry of Justice.

Nylander, P.-Å., Lindberg, O. & Bruhn, A. (2011). Emotional labour and emotional strain among Swedish prison officers. *European Journal of Criminology, 8*, 469–483.

Pierce, M. (2015). Male inmate perceptions of the visitation experience. *Prison Journal, 95*, 370–396.

Pratt, J. (2007). *Penal Populism: Key Ideas in Criminology*. New York: Routledge.

Pratt, J. (2008a). Scandinavian exceptionalism in an era of penal excess: Part 1: The nature and roots of Scandinavian exceptionalism. *British Journal of Criminology, 48*, 119–137.

Pratt, J. (2008b). Scandinavian exceptionalism in an era of penal excess: Part 2: Does Scandinavian exceptionalism have a future? *British Journal of Criminology, 48*, 275–292.

Rison, R. & Wittenberg, P. (1994). Disaster theory: Avoiding crisis in a prison environment. *Federal Probation, 58*, 45–50.

Ross, E.C., Polaschek, D.L.L. & Ward, T. (2008a). The therapeutic alliance: A theoretical revision for offender rehabilitation. *Aggression and Violent Behavior, 13*, 462–480.

Ross, M., Diamond, P., Liebling, A. & Saylor, W. (2008b). Measurement of prison social climate: A comparison of an inmate measure in England and the USA. *Punishment and Society, 10*, 447–474.

Ruiz, J. (2007). Emotional climate in organisations: Application in Latin American prisons. *Journal of Social Issues, 63*, 289–306.

Ryan, M. & Ward, T. (2015). Prison abolition in the UK: They dare not speak its name? *Social Justice, 41*, 107–199.

Safran, J. & Muran, J. (2003). *Negotiating the Therapeutic Alliance: A Relational Treatment Guide*. New York: Guildford Press.

Schalast, N., Redies, M., Collins, M., Stacey, J. & Howells, K. (2008). EssenCES: A short questionnaire for assessing the social climate of forensic psychiatric wards. *Criminal Behaviour and Mental Heath, 18*, 49–58.

Schlosser, J. (2013). Bourdieu & Foucault: A conceptual integration towards an empirical sociology of prison. *Critical Criminology, 21*, 31–46.

Schweitzer, M., Gilpin, L. & Frampton, S. (2004). Healing spaces: Elements of environmental design that make an impact on health. *The Journal of Alternative and Complementary Medicine, 10*, 71–83.

Taxman, F., Cropsey, K., Melnick, G. & Perdoni, M. (2008). COD services in community correctional settings: An examination of organisational factors that affect service delivery. *Behavioural Sciences and the Law, 26*, 435–455.

Toch, H. (1977). *Living in Prison: The Ecology of Survival*. New York: Free Press.

Tran, V. (2010). The role of emotional climates of joy and fear in team creativity and innovation. *CEB Working Paper N° 10/054*. Brussels: School of Economics and Management Centre Emile Bernheim.

Velarde, M., Fry, G. & Tveit, M. (2007). Health effects of viewing landscapes – landscape types in environmental psychology. *Urban Green*, 6, 199–212.

Wacquant, L. (2012). The prison is an outlaw institution, *The Howard Journal*, 51, 1–15.

Ward, T. & Marshall, B. (2007). Narrative identity and offender rehabilitation. *International Journal of Offender Therapy & Comparative Criminology*, 51, 279–297.

Wilkinson, R. & Pickett, K. (2010). *The Spirit Level: Why Equality Is Better for Everyone*. London: Penguin.

# 6

# THE IMPORTANCE OF PERSONAL SAFETY TO THERAPEUTIC OUTCOME IN THE PRISON SETTING

*Andrew Day and James Vess*

## Introduction

It is well accepted that certain aspects of the prison environment will inevitably act in ways that mitigate against therapeutic progress (Davies, 2004). As Gordon and Wong (2002) have noted, for example, prison environments that fail to support pro-social attitudes and behaviour and are unable to substitute positive peer group pressure for negative peer group pressure are unlikely to be particularly success-ful in rehabilitating offenders (see also Harding, 2014). Our focus in this chapter, however, is on understanding one particular aspect of the institutional environment which we suspect will often have a profound impact on rehabilitation programme outcomes – threats to personal safety. At the most basic level, some prisoners will decline to participate in treatment if they believe that this will place them at risk, whilst others will pursue accommodation changes (to different units or different prisons) when they are afraid, thereby disrupting treatment. Even more powerful perhaps is the impact of threats to personal safety on the behaviour of those who actually attend treatment, especially if this inhibits their ability to engage in the rehabilitative process. The following (hypothetical) case example has been devel-oped to illustrate just how some of these threats can arise in prison settings and profoundly interfere with rehabilitation.

## The nature of threat

The case of Mr. Jones provides an illustration of what we believe are some unique features of the prison environments that have the potential to hinder therapeutic change. These are, however, by no means unique to this particular offender; inves-tigations into the experiences of prisoners have typically shown that many have significant concerns about personal safety (see Liebling, Crewe & Hulley, 2011;

## CASE EXAMPLE: MR. JONES

Mr. Jones is a 27-year-old Caucasian inmate who is serving a seven-year prison sentence for burglary, receiving stolen property, and possession of methamphetamine. This is his second prison term. He has a long criminal history, beginning in adolescence, mainly for various forms of theft and drug possession, although most of his previous convictions have resulted in non-custodial sentences.

Mr. Jones is the youngest of three siblings, with an older brother and sister. His father left the family home when Mr. Jones was three years old and has had no contact with them for many years. His mother raised the children as a single parent, and struggled with the financial burden of providing for her family. This was compounded by periods of her own substance abuse. She had a variety of short-term relationships with men, several of whom were verbally abusive toward the children; two of them physically abused Mr. Jones. He began using a variety of substances in early adolescence, including marijuana, methamphetamines and alcohol. He began stealing from neighbourhood cars and houses to support his drug use at age 14, and dropped out of high school at age 16. He has no known history of participating in gang activities and denies any gang involvement.

Shortly after his arrival in prison Mr. Jones was approached by other Caucasian inmates and warned to "stay with his own kind", meaning that he should not associate with other races. After he was noticed speaking with a black inmate in the prison yard, he was warned that it would "lead to trouble" if he did not conform to the expectations of racial separation. It was clearly implied that he would become the target of assault from other white inmates. It was also made clear that he would be vulnerable to attack by prisoners from other races and, unless he was 'in' with the white inmates, no one would come to his assistance.

These threats caused him to feel increasing anxiety, especially when he was outside of his cell in the presence of other prisoners. He began to isolate himself and refuse to leave his cell for meals or trips to the exercise yard. He also began to show signs of depression; he lost weight and did not sleep well. He became less and less responsive to the custody officers and other prison staff. This brought him to the attention of the prison's mental health services. He was seen by a prison psychologist, who began brief weekly sessions of Cognitive Behaviour Therapy. He was also evaluated by a psychiatrist, who prescribed medication for his anxiety and depression. However, these mental health services brought him additional unwanted attention from his fellow prisoners. Two prisoners from adjacent cells became aware of his treatment by the psychiatrist, and began to pressure him to obtain medications that he

(continued)

(*continued*)

was to turn over to them for sale in the prison yard. They coached him on the symptoms he should describe, and the specific medications he should ask for. They made it clear that it would be dangerous for him to refuse and when he resisted, he was assaulted by one of the prisoners, who struck him in the face, causing bruising. When questioned by the custody officers on his unit, he stated that he had fallen in his cell; he was fearful that if he informed on his attackers, he would face escalating reprisals. He did not trust that the custody staff would adequately protect him, nor could he safely disclose to the mental health clinicians what was happening. To reveal this information would be to snitch on other inmates, and he had been clearly warned, "snitches get stitches".

These experiences re-activated Mr. Jones' childhood experiences of abandonment and abuse. He became increasingly depressed and anxious, and sank into a pervasive sense of helplessness and despair. He felt trapped, and believed that no one could help him, no one could protect him. As his condition worsened, he began to have thoughts of ending his life as the only way to escape his suffering. Yet he would not reveal his concerns or his suicidal thoughts to any member of staff. One night after lights out, he fashioned a noose from his bed sheet and wrapped it around his neck. He tied the sheet off on the ventilation grate over his bed, and lowered his weight against the noose. He had lost consciousness and stopped breathing when a custody officer doing his rounds discovered him. A quick response by the unit staff saved Mr. Jones from dying.

The suicide attempt caused the prison staff to assign Mr. Jones to a unit designated for inmates receiving more intensive mental health services. He was seen individually by a psychologist and enrolled in several treatment groups, including groups targeting depression management, coping skills and substance abuse prevention. Yet his fears of revealing himself remained.

One aspect he found particularly troubling was that the therapists who conducted the groups appeared to be afraid of violence from some of the prisoners who participated. Mr. Jones noticed that whenever strong emotions were expressed by someone in the group, especially anger, the therapists seemed very uncomfortable, and quickly steered the focus toward safer subjects. This prevented the group from dealing with important issues that were occurring in the here and now, which seemed to present the greatest opportunities for real therapeutic change. It also left Mr. Jones with the impression that the staff could not effectively handle potentially threatening topics or situations.

Fortunately for Mr. Jones, he had an experienced and skillful therapist for his individual sessions. This psychologist was able to develop an effective clinical case formulation in terms of the predisposing, perpetuating, precipitating and protective factors that shaped his responses to the current prison environment. The psychologist saw that Mr. Jones' early developmental experiences left him with several maladaptive but enduring schemas. Because of his father's abandonment and his mother's neglect, Mr. Jones had internalised the beliefs that he was unworthy of love, respect or compassion from others. He could not trust that others would not abandon or abuse him. The world was not a safe place, and he was often helpless to protect himself.

Whereas earlier in his life been he had able to self-medicate through substance abuse in order to fend off his negative emotions and bolster his poor self-regard, this option was no longer readily available to him. Although drugs were common in the prison, the drug trade was almost entirely controlled by various gangs, and he was far too afraid to have any dealings with gang members. His one consistent source of support over the years had been his sister. But he was now imprisoned far from where she lived, and her own work and family responsibilities diminished the contact she had with him. However, this relationship had provided him with some experience of a positive and trusting attachment, and offered hope that he might be able to establish a viable therapeutic alliance.

With this understanding, his therapist began to work explicitly with Mr. Jones' issues about trust and self-regard. He patiently explored Mr. Jones' developmental history, including his early traumatic experiences, and began linking these experiences to his current situation. By consistently providing therapeutic encounters that were supportive and safe, the therapist allowed Mr. Jones to disclose his fears about the other inmates, his lack of trust in the custody staff and other clinicians, and his sense of helplessness and despair that led him to attempt suicide. Yet this did not ensure that Mr. Jones would continue to make progress in his treatment. Without fundamental changes in the level of safety afforded by this prison environment, he remained at risk for incapacitating mental illness and further attempts at suicide.

Toch & Adams, 2002; Zamble & Porporino, 1990). Although the published literature on this topic is limited, there have been suggestions that prison drug or gambling debts can lead to violence from other prisoners as a means of enforcement (Stringer, 2000), and sexual exploitation and gang politics (e.g. power struggles both between and within gangs, pressure to join gangs, drug trafficking and orders to carry out violence) have also been documented. Threats to specific prisoner subgroups, including sex offenders, those from cultural or racial minority groups, informants and those from law enforcement backgrounds, are also common (e.g. Åkerström, 1986; Gaes, Wallace, Gilman, Klein-Saffran & Suppa, 2002; Skarbek, 2014; Struckman-Johnson & Struckman-Johnson, 2006). In addition, and more generally, forceful and aggressive behaviour has been noted to be heavily entrenched in prison cultures (see Hepburn, Griffin & Petrocelli, 1997; Marquart, 1986) reflecting a high degree of objective threat for all prisoners.

Liebling and Arnold (2004) have discussed safety as a fundamental quality of the prison environment, referring to it as a determinant of the 'moral performance' of an institution. It is also likely to be strongly associated with the quality of care that is offered. We know, for example, from studies conducted in forensic mental health settings that perceptions of the social environment have an impact upon levels of care (Clarke, Rockett, Sloane & Aiken, 2002; Griffin, Hogan, Lambert, Tucker-Gail & Baker, 2010; Kangis, Gordon & Williams, 2000; Langdon, Cosgrave & Tranah, 2004; Langdon, Swift & Budd, 2006), with some evidence also suggesting that fear of violence is negatively and significantly related to patient-reported quality of care (Arnetz & Arnetz, 2001). Long et al. (2011) have also reported that perceptions of safety are also correlated with a range of factors that potentially impact therapeutic outcome in these settings, including internal motivation, lack of confidence, treatment session attendance, ratings of the psychotherapy alliance, risk behaviours and the number of management of aggression incidents, including seclusions.

The prison environment can exacerbate threats to personal safety through its influence on social behaviour, as illustrated in the findings of a landmark study in the early 1970s that came to be widely known as the Stanford Prison Experiment (Zimbardo, 1972, 1973). In this study a group of male university students who had been assessed as psychologically healthy were randomly assigned to roles as either 'guards' or 'prisoners' in a mock prison environment set up in a university building. The experiment was designed to run for two weeks, but had to be terminated after only six days because of the escalating levels of harassment and abuse that the 'guards' were inflicting on the 'prisoners'. Because the participants had been assessed as psychologically normal and were randomly assigned to the different roles, Zimbardo concluded that it was situational factors rather than personality factors that had created the negative and damaging dynamic that resulted in an institutional climate that was overtly dangerous.

Similar issues were considered in the more recent investigation into abuses of detainees by US armed forces in Iraq (see Schlesinger, Brown, Fowler & Horner, 2004). Zimbardo, and other experts who gave evidence at the inquiry, argued that environmental conditions in the now infamous Abu Ghraib prison facility in Iraq were primarily responsible for creating a social climate in which some shocking abuses of prisoners occurred. Factors such as poor training, high levels of environmental stress, insufficient staffing, inadequate oversight, confused lines of authority, evolving and unclear policy and a generally poor quality of prison life were all identified as key features of the Abu Ghraib prison environment. While the Department of Defense personnel responsible argued that it was a 'few bad apples' which led to the abuse, social science experts insisted that environmental factors played a much bigger role than the personality characteristics of a few individual soldiers (Zimbardo, 2007).

These analyses are useful insofar as they can help us to understand more about how threats to personal safety in institutional settings can have systematic causes (and require systemic responses, see below). It is also true, of course, that prisons typically house those with long histories of violence (as victims and perpetrators) which not only serve to increase the level of threat that is present, but also heighten personal vulnerability, especially in certain groups such as female prisoners or those who are either young or old or physically infirm (see Aday, 2006; Miller & Najavits, 2012). In addition, there is some evidence to suggest that certain groups of offender, such as child sex offenders, will present with particular psychological profiles that increase their sensitivity to threats in the prison environment (see Marsa et al., 2004) in much the same way as Mr. Jones' personal history provided the context for much of what transpired after his imprisonment.

## Safety and psychotherapy

The importance of feeling safe is widely considered to be key to therapeutic change across most psychotherapeutic approaches (see Bachelor, Meunier, Laverdiére & Gamache, 2010). An initial goal of therapy is typically to provide a safe environment in which clients can examine threatening aspects of their experience. There are a number of important consequences of feeling safe in therapy, one of the most significant of which, according to Watson, Goldman and Vanaerschot (1998), is the ability to self-disclose. For Watson and colleagues, it is only through self-disclosure that clients are able to engage in the "self-examination, deconstruction and reorganisation of their experience" (p. 64) that is required for personal change; this also mitigates against the effects of the power imbalance that exists between client and therapist. In their words it helps clients to "replace their introjected value systems with their own organismic valuing process, which is open to information from a variety of sources and leaves individuals free to behave and experience in more open and comprehensive ways" (p. 63). It has similarly been argued that therapists who act as 'attachment figures' (Bowlby, 1988) provide a physical and emotional safe haven and a "secure base from which clients can explore and reflect on painful memories and experiences" (Mikulincer, Shaver & Berant, 2013, p. 607). According to both Kohut (1977) and Linehan (1997) empathic responding is the most effective way to make clients feel safe.

In the group treatment room, a lack of (perceived) safety may lead prisoners to withhold personal information that could be of substantial benefit. A study by Renwick, Black, Ramm and Novaco (1997), for example, noted the resentful, distrustful and even combative style of some participants in therapeutic groups. Kozar and Day (2009) also encountered reports of situations in which therapists who deliver violent and sexual offender rehabilitation programmes described thinking that they were going to be attacked. Others had threats made against them, either direct or indirect. For example, one prisoner attending a group therapy session asked a therapist if she was worried that someone might hit her, while another therapist described how she sat "with her heart pounding" when a prisoner was expressing his hostility. Another described being told that a prisoner was having someone follow them home. It would be unrealistic to expect other prisoners listening to these interactions to perceive the treatment room as a safe place for full and frank self-disclosure.

The term 'safety' is sometimes used in therapy to refer to the affective component of the relationship or bond that is formed with the therapist. This is an area of rehabilitative practice in which different perspectives exist when working with prisoners. While some believe that therapists need to remain detached in order to maintain their objectivity, others feel that they need to develop a strong bond to ensure that their relationship can withstand challenges (see Kozar & Day, 2009). Related to this is the advice offered by Marshall, Marshall, Serran and O'Brien (2011) that therapeutic interactions should be characterised by two key elements: relationship and structure. Relationship refers to a therapist showing warmth, respect, interest and enthusiasm while engaging in non-blaming communication, whereas structuring involves the effective reinforcement and appropriate modelling of pro-social attitudes and behaviour. We suspect that the presence of both is likely to improve prisoner perceptions of personal safety when participating in treatment.

## Treatment readiness and the sense of self

Another perspective on the relationship between safety and therapeutic outcomes is offered by the concept of treatment readiness. It has been proposed that readiness encompasses both the internal components of treatment responsivity (e.g. offender motivation, problem awareness, emotional capacity to engage with psychological treatment, goals and personal identity), as well as external components that are specific to the environment in which treatment is offered (Day, Casey, Ward, Howells & Vess, 2010). A general model of readiness has been elaborated, referred to as the Multifactor Offender Readiness Model, or MORM (Ward, Day, Howells & Birgden, 2004). This model defines treatment readiness as the presence of characteristics (states or dispositions) within either the client or the therapeutic situation which are likely to enhance therapeutic change.

Within this framework for treatment readiness, two factors that are relevant to our current focus are likely to interact in ways that bear upon therapeutic outcomes. One is the internal readiness factor of personal identity or sense of self. The other is the environmental factor of safety, especially threats to safety stemming from the constant risk of physical confrontation. When confronted with experiences of powerlessness that are endemic to imprisonment, individuals may seek to regain a sense of power and control to the self. Prisoners often behave aggressively in response to perceived disrespect and challenges to their status and masculinity. This may be especially true for male inmate populations whose definitions of masculinity are based on toughness, aggression and the capacity for violence. For those whose identities were not defined by aggressive masculinity prior to imprisonment, the prison environment may lead them to present such a persona in order to deter victimisation (Edgar, O'Donnell & Martin, 2003). Many male prisoners may therefore engage in aggressive or violent confrontations in order to ensure their personal safety and retain their possessions, as well as to re-affirm their masculine identity (Butler, 2008). This self-perpetuating interaction between environmental pressures and the inmates' sense of self is likely to be pervasively counter-therapeutic.

Considering again the example of Mr. Jones, we can envision the pressures he would face to project a tough and aggressive persona. Failing to do so would subject him to further victimisation, especially if he believed that the prison authorities and clinical staff could not adequately protect him. If he feels compelled to conform to the environmental pressures and norms of violent masculinity, even if these are not consistent with his underlying sense of self, this will likely raise barriers to meaningful therapeutic engagement and positive therapeutic change. On a more pragmatic level, the necessity to be willing to engage in violence in response to confrontations is likely to lead to institutional rule violations and subsequent sanctions. These sanctions can include placement in higher security prison units and restriction or loss of programming opportunities. Effective treatment can be facilitated by recognising the underlying threats to safety caused by prisoner confrontations and the search for respect. Helping inmates create a more secure sense of self, one that is not as vulnerable to perceived challenges to their masculine identity, may buffer the effects of the typical prison environment.

## Making prisons safer

So far in this chapter we have sought to explore the idea that safe prisoners are those in which successful treatment or rehabilitation is at least possible. In a context in which prison administrations around the western world have dedicated significant resources to the development and delivery of rehabilitation programmes that aim to reduce the risk of re-offending, there is an obvious logic underpinning efforts to understand the impact of any factor that hinders therapeutic progress. This helps to explain why treatment provided in the community accounts for much larger reductions in recidivism than when it is offered in prison (see Andrews, 2006; Andrews & Bonta, 2010).

A focus on prison safety is, we suggest, also helpful insofar as it raises some important questions about how matters of prison security should be positioned in relation to efforts to provide therapeutic intervention (Parker, 2006). This is clearly illustrated in the writings of Brookes and Mandikate (2010), who were therapeutic prison managers at Grendon Underwood in the UK at a time when the therapeutic services of the prison were subject to a high level of scrutiny following the escape of three prisoners. Their observations, and subsequent attempts to develop an organisational culture in which security and therapy were seen by all staff as compatible, are summarised in the following quote:

> Sometimes it is convenient to divide operational and non-operational staff
> into separate camps. And sometimes, certain individuals in each of those camps

may seek to keep that division alive and active, perhaps to meet their own purposes and needs. The reality is, however, that good security at Grendon needs good therapy and good therapy needs good security, especially with the demographic characteristics and offence histories of Grendon's population. (p. 244)

It is this context that Camp's (1999) observation that prison staff and administrators sometimes regard the opinions of inmates as "little more than individual and collective whining" (p. 252) becomes of real practical significance. Homel and Thomson's (2005) simple comment that prisons are "designed to be places of punishment" (p. 101) highlights how we should not expect prisons to be safe. Threats to personal safety will not always be taken seriously, and may be regarded by some as deserved and legitimate in light of the actions that led to imprisonment.

So how might prisons be made safer and, in theory, more conducive to rehabilitation? For Brookes and Mandikate (2010) this involves a whole-of-organisation commitment to maintaining a safe and supportive environment. There are clearly things that can be learned in this respect from the extensive literature on the causes of prison riots, disturbances and general disorder. For example, Struckman-Johnson and Struckman-Johnson (2000) reported that certain structural features of prisons, such as large population size, racial conflict, barracks housing, inadequate security, and a high percentage of inmates incarcerated for a crime against persons, are significantly related to an increase in sexual coercion rates. Cooke (1992) further identifies the importance of staff–inmate communication, staff training and experience, and staff morale on prison disorder. One of the most comprehensive pieces of work on this topic, a systematic review by Gadon, Johnston and Cooke (2006), concluded that prison structure (supervision and security level, population mix and prison size), staff features (length of employment and number of years of experience), temporal aspects of the prison (how a person's time and space are organised), location (recreational areas, dorms, cell) and prison management all predicted prison violence. They also found a lower rate of prisoner–staff assaults in institutions in which a greater percentage of prisoners were involved in programmes relating to education, vocational and industry. In addition, prison overcrowding has been consistently identified as a particular issue that "intensifies all forms of discontent and germinates new frustrations" (Crewe, 2009, p.453).

Another promising area of development involves peer support groups. Although various groups have been described in the professional literature, empirical studies of their effectiveness remains limited (Perrin & Blagden, 2014). It is easy to envision, however, how such groups may contribute to improved safety in the prison environment and support therapeutic effectiveness. Inmates may have a level of accessibility and credibility with fellow prisoners that prison staff do not provide. A peer support volunteer may be easier for many inmates to identify with; inmates may see such an individual as someone who has similar experiences, and often a more similar background. This contrasts with custody and clinical professionals, who are seen as being less like them, and less able to relate to their personal issues. When provided with relevant training and support by prison officials or external agencies, peer support inmates can contribute to reducing conflict and de-escalating situations that might otherwise lead to violence or self-harm.

Being an inmate volunteer in a peer support role can also have positive therapeutic benefits to the individuals who fulfil these roles. This may relate back to the concepts addressed above regarding treatment readiness and the sense of identity. Perrin and Blagden (2014) describe a process of reconstructing the self, slowly but steadily replacing the 'old me' through enacting roles consistent with a good and more moral identity. Other researchers have reported that self-identification and a positive self-image were significant predictors of positive post-prison outcomes (LeBel, Burnett, Maruna & Bushway, 2008). Peer support programmes may therefore contribute both to a better prison environment which broadly supports the therapeutic process, and to positive individual changes in those who volunteer, facilitating the transformation of the self in therapeutic ways.

Recent years have also seen growing interest in the idea of trauma-informed correctional practice which places personal safety at the very heart of the correctional enterprise and identifies a number of different ways in which safety might be promoted (see Burrell, 2013; Miller & Najavits, 2012). These include reception screening and orientation processes, the development of institutional values, staff training, prisoner housing policies, behavioural interventions and the use of force, as well as the provision of therapy (see Table 6.1).

Specialist rehabilitation and treatment prisons provide examples of how thinking in this way might inform the process of rehabilitation. Kennard (2004), for example, describes the prison therapeutic community as "a 'living learning situation' where everything that happens between members (staff and patients) in the course of living and working together, in particular when a crisis occurs, is used as a learning opportunity" (p. 296). The prison 'community' is thus used to provide a range of life situations in which members can re-enact and re-experience their relationships in the outside world, with opportunities provided through a group and individual therapy process to examine and learn from any difficulties that are experienced. Threats to personal safety, and the ways in which these are managed, are thus identified as central to therapeutic change in all prison therapeutic community models of practice (Greenall, 2004), whether these are behavioural or psychotherapeutic in focus (see Day & Doyle, 2010).

Of course not all prisons are the same, and whilst therapeutic community prisons or those prisons that seek to implement the principles of trauma-informed care will dedicate considerable resources into promoting prisoner personal safety, others are not in a position to implement similar approaches. As Ross, Diamond, Liebling and Saylor (2008) note, actual prison conditions can vary considerably in terms of the physical fabric of the institution, the harshness of the regime and social organisation. There may also be important cultural and jurisdictional differences that influence the types of managerial and therapeutic responses that are required. For example,

**TABLE 6.1** Trauma-informed approaches to improving the safety of prisons

| Area of practice | Example |
| --- | --- |
| Organisational commitment | A statement about shared responsibility for maintaining a safe and supportive environment; a process for informing staff and prisoners of these principles; and for addressing violations of the principles. A values statement specifying that all individuals must be treated with respect; that no harassment or abuse of any kind will be tolerated; and that prisoners will not be subjected to categorical treatment based on actual or perceived race, ethnic group identification, national origin, religion, gender, sexual orientation, gender identity, mental or physical disability, or HIV status. |
| Human resources | Having adequate staff (including mental health or other specialty care) to engage prisoners, head off violence or other abuse, and provide support for both prisoners and staff in relation to traumatic events. Staff should be trained on what trauma is; how it is exacerbated by immaturity and disabilities; what kinds of things may cause re-traumatisation; how to recognise and respond to trauma-related behaviour in the institutional setting; and how staff deal with their own experiences of trauma. |
| Structure | Environments that are highly structured, with predictable and consistent limits, incentives and boundaries, as well as swift and certain consequences such that inmates are treated fairly and equally are thought to be safer than those which are not. |
| Conflict resolution skills | One of the most overt threats to safety is the use of force in managing problematic behaviour. Staff should be trained to provide positive role models, and manage confrontation and conflict so as to minimise it. Correctional practices, such as pat downs and strip searches, frequent discipline from authority figures, and restricted movement, may re-enact trauma dynamics. Where the prison is seen as unjust or arbitrary, resentment occurs and has the effect of being counterproductive. |
| Provide effective treatment for trauma | Those with traumatic histories may experience a range of factors that heighten their sense of threat (e.g. affect dysregulation, numbing, callousness, avoidance, sensitivity to negative emotion) and influence their interpersonal engagements (e.g. attribution bias, moral disengagement, alienation, rejection sensitivity). The treatment of these symptoms can therefore have an important role to play in ensuring the safety of prison environments. |

*Source*: adapted from Burrell (2013).

gangs are a powerful and pervasive force in the prisons of some countries (e.g. USA, New Zealand) and are implicated in much of the institutional violence that happens. Specialist responses are clearly required are manage the threats to safety that arise as a result of gang behaviour (see our case example, above).

## Conclusions

In this chapter we have suggested that prisoner perceptions of personal safety are likely to significantly impact their ability or willingness to engage in meaningful rehabilitation. It follows that those prisons which seek to provide effective treatment and rehabilitation should consider how they might best adopt an explicit focus on the implementation of measures to protect personal safety and promote well-being at the level of both organisational policy and therapeutic practice. It is not our intention, however, to stereotype or mischaracterise the typical prison experience or to exaggerate the threats that are present in many prisons. And so to conclude on what is a more positive note, we cite Shefer (2010), who reflects on the observation that prisons (in England and Wales) have "undergone important humanising processes in the last two decades, especially with regard to staff culture, physical facilities and prisoner entitlements" (p. 3). For Shefer this does not necessarily mean that imprisonment is any less painful than it has been in the past, but rather that threats are now likely to be more psychological in nature rather than simply a consequence of authoritarian regimes. We argue that a greater appreciation of the nature and impact of these threats will, inevitably, facilitate the delivery of more engaging and ultimately more effective rehabilitation.

## References

Aday, R. H. (2006). Managing aging prisoners in the United States. In A. Wahidin & M. Cain (Eds.), *Aging, Crime and Society* (pp. 210–229). Cullompton, UK: Willan Publishing.

Åkerström, M. (1986). Outcasts in prison: The cases of informers and sex offenders. *Deviant Behavior*, 7, 1–12.

Andrews, D. A. (2006). Enhancing adherence to risk-need-responsivity: Making equality a matter of policy. *Criminology and Public Policy*, 5, 595–602.

Andrews, D. A. & Bonta, J. (2010). Rehabilitating criminal justice policy and practice. *Psychology, Public Policy, and Law*, 16, 39–55.

Arnetz, J. E. & Arnetz, B. B. (2001). Violence towards health care staff and possible effects on the quality of patient care. *Social Science and Medicine*, 52, 417–427.

Bachelor, A., Meunier, G., Laverdiére, O. & Gamache, D. (2010). Client attachment to therapist: Relation to client personality and symptomatology, and their contributions to the therapeutic alliance. *Psychotherapy: Theory, Research, Practice, Training*, 47, 454–468.

Bowlby, J. (1988). *A Secure Base: Clinical Applications of Attachment Theory*. London: Routledge.

Brookes, M. & Mandikate, P. (2010). Managing and adapting to increased security and audit requirements within a prison-based therapeutic community: The recent experience of HMP Grendon. *Therapeutic Communities*, 31(3), 239–252.

Burrell, S. (2013). *Trauma and the Environment of Care in Juvenile Institutions*. Los Angeles, CA & Durham, NC: National Center for Child Traumatic Stress.

Butler, M. (2008). What are you looking at? Prisoner confrontations and the search for respect. *British Journal of Criminology*, 48, 856–873.

Camp, S. D. (1999). Do inmate survey data reflect prison conditions? Using surveys to assess prison conditions of confinement. *The Prison Journal*, 79, 250–268.

Clarke, S. P., Rockett, J. L., Sloane, D. M. & Aiken, L. H. (2002). Organizational climate, staffing, and safety equipment as predictors of needlestick injuries and near-misses in hospital nurses. *American Journal of Infection Control*, 30, 207–216.

Cooke, D. J. (1992).Violence in prisons: A Scottish perspective. *Forum on Correctional Research*, 4, 23–30.

Crewe, B. (2009). *The Prisoner Society: Power, Adaptation and Social Life in an English Prison*. Oxford, UK: Oxford University Press.

Davies, S. (2004).Toxic institutions. In P. Campling, S. Davies & G. Farquharson (Eds.), *From Toxic Institutions to Therapeutic Environments: Residential Settings in Mental Health Services* (pp. 20–31). London: Gaskell.

Day, A., Casey, S., Ward, T., Howells, K. & Vess, J. (2010). *Transitions to Better Lives: Offender Readiness and Rehabilitation*. Devon, UK: Willan Publishing.

Day, A. & Doyle, P. (2010).Violent offender rehabilitation and the therapeutic community model of treatment: Towards integrated service provision? *Aggression and Violent Behavior*, 15, 380–386.

Edgar, K., O'Donnell, I. & Martin, C. (2003) *Prison Violence: The Dynamics of Conflict, Fear and Power*. Devon: Willan Publishing

Gadon, L., Johnston, L. & Cooke, D. (2006). Situational variables and institutional violence: A systematic review of the literature. *Clinical Psychology Review*, 26, 515–534.

Gaes, G. G., Wallace, S., Gilman, E., Klein-Saffran, J. & Suppa, S. (2002). The influence of prison gang affiliation on violence and other prison misconduct. *The Prison Journal*, 82, 359–385.

Gordon, A. & Wong, S. (2002). *The Violence Reduction Program: Facilitator's Manual*. Unpublished manuscript. Canada: Regional Psychiatric Centre and the University of Saskatchewan, Saskatoon, Saskatchewan.

Greenall, P.V. (2004). Life in a prison based therapeutic community: One man's experience. *British Journal of Forensic Practice*, 6, 33–38.

Griffin, M. L., Hogan, N. L., Lambert, E. G., Tucker-Gail, K. A. & Baker, D. N. (2010). Job involvement, job stress, job satisfaction, and organizational commitment and the burnout of correctional staff. *Criminal Justice and Behavior*, 37, 239–255.

Harding, R. (2014). Rehabilitation and prison social climate: Do 'What Works' rehabilitation programs work better in prisons that have a positive social climate? *Australian & New Zealand Journal of Criminology*, 47, 163–175. doi: 10.1177/0004865813518543.

Hepburn, J. R., Griffin, M. L. & Petrocelli, M. (1997). *Safety and Control in a County Jail: Nonlethal Weapons and the Use of Force*. Arizona State University website. www.ncjrs.gov/pdffiles1/nij/grants/180316.pdf.

Homel, R. & Thomson, C. (2005). Causes and prevention of violence in prisons. In S. O'Toole & S. Eyland (Eds.), *Corrections Criminology* (pp. 101–108). Sydney: Hawkins Press.

Kangis, P., Gordon, D. & Williams, S. (2000). Organisational climate and corporate performance: An empirical investigation. *Management Decision*, 38, 531–540.

Kennard, D. (2004). The therapeutic community as an adaptable treatment modality across different settings. *Psychiatric Quarterly*, 75, 295–307.

Kohut, H. (1977). *The Restoration of the Self*. New York: International Universities Press.

Kozar, C. & Day, A. (2009). Developing the therapeutic alliance in offending behaviour programs: A qualitative study of its perceived impact on treatment outcomes. *APS College of Forensic Psychologists Conference*, Melbourne, February 27–March 2.

Langdon, P. E., Cosgrave, N. & Tranah, T. (2004). Social climate within an adolescent medium-secure facility. *International Journal of Offender Therapy and Comparative Criminology*, 48, 504–515.

Langdon, P. E., Swift, A. & Budd, R. (2006). Social climate within secure inpatient services for people with intellectual disabilities. *Journal of Intellectual Disability Research*, 50, 828–836.

LeBel, T. P., Burnett, R., Maruna, S. & Bushway, S. (2008). The 'chicken and egg' of subjective and social factors in desistance from crime. *European Journal of Criminology*, 5, 131–159.

Liebling, A. & Arnold, H. (2004). *Prisons and Their Moral Performance: A Study of Values, Quality, and Prison Life*. Oxford, UK: Oxford University Press.

Liebling, A., Crewe, B. & Hulley, S. (2011). Conceptualising and measuring the quality of prison life. In D. Gadd, S. Karstedt & S. F. Messner (Eds.), *The Sage Handbook of Criminological Research Methods* (pp. 358–372). London: Sage Publishing.

Linehan, M. M. (1997). Validation and psychotherapy. In A. Bohurt & L. Greenberg (Eds.), *Empathy Reconsidered: New Directions in Psychotherapy* (pp. 353–392). Washington, DC: APA.

Long, C. G., Anagnostakis, K., Fox, E., Silaule, P, Somers, J., West, R. & Webster, A. (2011). Social climate along the pathway of care in women's secure mental health service: Variation with level of security, patient motivation, therapeutic alliance and level of disturbance. *Criminal Behaviour and Mental Health*, 21, 202–214.

Marquart, J. W. (1986). Prison guards and the use of physical coercion as a mechanism of prisoner control. *Criminology*, 24, 347–366.

Marsa, F., O'Reilly, G., Carr, A., Murphy, P., O'Sullivan, M., Cotter, A. & Hevey, D. (2004). Attachment styles and psychological profiles of child sex offenders in Ireland. *Journal of Interpersonal Violence*, 19, 228–251.

Marshall, W. L., Marshall, L. E., Serran, G. A. & O'Brien, M. D. (2011). *Rehabilitating Sexual Offenders: A Strength-Based Approach*. Washington, DC: American Psychological Association.

Mikulincer, M., Shaver, P. R. & Berant, E. (2013). An attachment perspective on therapeutic processes and outcomes. *Journal of Personality*, 81, 606–616.

Miller, N. A. & Najavits, L. M. (2012). Creating trauma-informed correctional care: A balance of goals and environment. *European Journal of Psychotraumatology*, 3, 17246. doi: 10.3402/ejpt.v3i0.17246.

Parker, M. (Ed.) (2006). *Dynamic Security: The Democratic Therapeutic Community in Prison*. London: Jessica Kingsley Publishers.

Perrin, C. & Blagden, N. (2014). Accumulating meaning, purpose and opportunities to change 'drip by drip': The impact of being a listener in prison. *Psychology, Crime & Law*, 20, 902–920.

Renwick, S. J., Black, L., Ramm, M. & Novaco, R. W. (1997). Anger treatment with forensic hospital patients. *Legal and Criminological Psychology*, 2, 103–116.

Ross, M. W., Diamond, P. M., Liebling, A. & Saylor, W. G. (2008). Measurement of prison social climate. *Punishment & Society*, 10, 447–474.

Schlesinger, J. R., Brown, H., Fowler, T. K. & Horner, C. A. (2004). *Final Report of the Independent Panel to Review DoD Detention Operations*. Retrieved 10 June 2015 from www.prisonexp.org/pdf/SchlesingerReport.pdf.

Shefer, G. (2010). *Doing Rehabilitation in the Contemporary Prison – The Case of One-Wing Therapeutic Communities*. Unpublished PhD thesis, Cambridge University.

Skarbek, D. (2014). *The Social Order of the Underworld: How Prison Gangs Govern the American Penal System*. Oxford, UK: Oxford University Press.

Stringer, A. (2000). *Women Inside in Debt: The Prison and Debt Project*. Paper presented at the Women in Corrections: Staff and Clients Conference convened by the Australian Institute of Criminology in conjunction with the Department for Correctional Services SA and held in Adelaide, 31 October–1 November 2000.

Struckman-Johnson, C. & Struckman-Johnson, D. (2000). Sexual coercion rates in seven midwestern prison facilities for men. *The Prison Journal*, 80, 379–390.

Struckman-Johnson, C. & Struckman-Johnson, D. (2006). A comparison of sexual coercion experiences reported by men and women in prison. *Journal of Interpersonal Violence*, 21, 1591–1615.

Toch, H. & Adams, K. (2002). *Acting Out: Maladaptive Behavior in Confinement*. Washington, DC: American Psychological Association.

Ward, T., Day, A., Howells, K. & Birgden, A. (2004). The multifactor offender readiness model. *Aggression and Violent Behavior*, 9, 645–673.

Watson, J. C., Goldman, R. & Vanaerschot, G. (1998). Empathic: A post-modern way of being. In L. S. Greenberg, J. Watson, and G. Lietaer (Eds.), *Handbook of Experiential Psychotherapy* (pp. 61–81). New York: Guilford Press.

Zamble, E. & Porporino, F. (1990). Coping, imprisonment, and rehabilitation: Some data and their implications. *Criminal Justice and Behavior*, 17, 53–70.

Zimbardo, P. G. (1972). Pathology of imprisonment. *Society*, 9, 4–8.

Zimbardo, P. G. (1973). On the ethics of intervention in human psychological research: With special reference to the Stanford prison experiment. *Cognition*, 2, 243–256.

Zimbardo, P. G. (2007). *The Lucifer Effect: Understanding How Good People Turn Evil*. New York: Random House.

# 7

# REHABILITATING OFFENDERS

## The enabling environment of forensic therapeutic communities

*Michael Brookes*

> *A calm and dispassionate recognition of the rights of the accused against the State, and even of convicted criminals against the State, a constant heart-searching by all charged with the duty of punishment, a desire and eagerness to rehabilitate in the world of industry all those who have paid their dues in the hard coinage of punishment, tireless efforts towards the discovery of curative and regenerating processes, and an unfaltering faith that there is a treasure, if you can only find it, in the heart of every man – these are the symbols which in the treatment of crime and criminals mark and measure the stored-up strength of a nation, and are the sign and proof of the living virtue in it.*
>
> – Churchill, 1910

## Rehabilitation and HM Prison Service

The importance attached to rehabilitation within the English and Welsh criminal justice system can be found in the opening words of the National Offender Management Service Business Plan 2014–2015 (NOMS, 2014) where, directly above the Statement of Purpose, is the strapline 'Preventing victims by changing lives'. Furthermore, within that Statement of Purpose is the commitment to reduce reoffending and to support rehabilitation by helping offenders to reform their lives. This reflects the significance that the 2010–2015 UK Coalition Government placed on their being effective national rehabilitation systems and procedures. Initial proposals were set out in the green paper 'Breaking the Cycle' (Ministry of Justice, 2010) and developed further in their strategy document 'Transforming Rehabilitation' (Ministry of Justice, 2013).

To facilitate this focus on rehabilitation, a Service Specification for Rehabilitation Services – In Custody (NOMS, 2015) has been developed.

A fundamental requirement is for staff to motivate prisoners to access and participate fully in the most appropriate rehabilitation services for their needs. Additionally, staff are to encourage prisoners to understand and accept their responsibilities to engage with appropriate rehabilitation services. This includes staff addressing prisoners' anti-social attitudes, thinking and behaviours through pro-social interaction and engagement, and supporting prisoners to access services to manage employment, housing, finance, family relationship and welfare needs. Education, mental health care and drug reduction services are to be provided along with accredited offending behaviour programmes and therapeutic communities.

These requirements have to be delivered within the context of each establishment being a safe, secure and decent facility, where there are appropriate levels of physical, procedural and dynamic security, matched to the risks presented by prisoners detained in each particular establishment. Additionally, the rehabilitation services and activities provided cannot exist in isolation to the regime that is operating within each prison and to the prison climate which has developed. However, for the rehabilitative process to be effective, there needs to be a regulated, boundaried, enabling environment with rules fairly and consistently enforced by staff who are authoritative yet with a positive attitude towards prisoners with a rehabilitative disposition (Crewe, Liebling & Hulley, 2011, 2014). What though are the features of an enabling environment which would assist custodial-based rehabilitative activities and processes?

## Enabling environments

Identifying salient features of an enabling environment was the challenge set for the Royal College of Psychiatrists College Centre for Quality Improvement (CCQI) and their Enabling Environments Awards project. The Enabling Environments initiative arose out an awareness of the positive impact some companies and organisations had on both staff and those they were providing a service to. It was observed that in these organisations managers tended to be concerned with the well-being of their staff. This created a sense of shared responsibility for one another. Through day-to-day interactions and the sensitive delivery of management processes, personal growth, social learning and change were evident. Organisations noted for displaying these characteristics included those working in child care, with the homeless, in school settings and in prison 'departments' or 'units' (Johnson & Haigh, 2011; Haigh, Harrison, Johnson, Paget & Williams, 2012).

The task for the Enabling Environments Development Group was to identify the crucial elements of these organisations to provide a mechanism by which their work could be understood. This could then form a basis of assessment for the determination of an Enabling Environments award. It could also create a framework and platform for undertaking a self-review of management functioning leading to an internal dialogue and team discussions to improve, where necessary, performance and relationships with one another. This is in line with all CCQI projects as they seek to audit or review services against established guidelines and standards with the aim of supporting services to improve the quality of care they offer (Royal College of Psychiatrists, 2015a).

The Enabling Environment Development Group determined that a positively enabling environment would be one:

- In which the nature and the quality of relationships between participants or members would be recognised and highly valued.
- Where the participants share some measure of responsibility for the environment as a whole, and especially for their own part in it.
- Where all participants – staff, volunteers and 'service users' alike – are equally valued and supported in their particular contribution.
- Where engagement and purposeful activity is encouraged.
- Where there are opportunities for creativity and initiative, whether spontaneous or shared and planned.
- Where decision-making is transparent, and both formal and informal leadership roles are acknowledged.
- Where power or authority is clearly accountable and open to discussion.
- Where any formal rules or informal expectations of behaviour are clear; or if unclear, there is good reason for it.
- Where behaviour, even when potentially disruptive, is seen as meaningful, as a communication to be understood (Haigh et al., 2012, p. 37).

In explaining the Enabling Environments Award the Royal College of Psychiatrists (2015b) state that while good relationships promote well-being, many organisations and groups fail to address this aspect of people's lives. Consequently, enabling environments are:

- Places where positive relationships promote well-being for all participants.
- Places where people experience a sense of belonging.
- Places where all people involved contribute to the growth and well-being of others.
- Places where people can learn new ways of relating.
- Places that recognise and respect the contributions of all parties in helping relationships (Royal College of Psychiatrists, 2012).

The Enabling Environments Award is then a quality mark given to those who can demonstrate they are achieving an outstanding level of best practice in creating and sustaining a positive and effective social environment (Royal College of Psychiatrists, 2015c).

## Enabling environments standards

Ten enabling environment standards were developed by the Enabling Environments Advisory Group with the objective of being able to be applied across a variety of settings. These are:

- Belonging – The nature and quality of relationships are of primary importance.
- Boundaries – There are expectations of behaviour and processes to maintain and review them.
- Communication – It is recognised that people communicate in different ways.
- Development – There are opportunities to be spontaneous and try new things.
- Involvement – Everyone shares responsibility for the environment.
- Safety – Support is available for everyone.
- Structure – Engagement and purposeful activity is actively encouraged.
- Empowerment – Power and authority are open to discussion.
- Leadership – Leadership takes responsibility for the environment being enabling.
- Openness – External relationships are sought and valued (Royal College of Psychiatrists, 2015c).

When these standards are met the Enabling Environment Award can be approved by the Royal College of Psychiatrists College Centre for Quality Improvement (CCQI), and the Therapeutic Community Accreditation Panel, the body which, in addition to recommending the accreditation of NHS and voluntary sector democratic therapeutic communities, now undertakes a similar function in respect of the Enabling Environment award.

## Enabling environments and prisons

A pivotal feature of enabling environments is then the quality of relationships between those in positions of power and authority and others who either have different roles and responsibilities within that organisation or who are the recipients of services provided. This is particularly important in a prison environment, especially on the quality of life prisoners experience. This has been recognised in the 2014–2015 NOMS Business Plan, where one of the priorities for meeting the NOMS decency commitment is the promotion of effective staff–prisoner relations where 'Every Contact Matters' (NOMS, 2014). Acknowledged is that what makes the difference is the preparedness of staff to be active, present, caring and engaged (Gooch, Treadwell & Trent, 2015). While these occur in many prisons they are essential elements of prison therapeutic communities where prison officers have a key role in the therapeutic process (see Clements, 2009).

## The development of therapeutic communities

The creation of a positive 'atmosphere' and the beneficial effect this can have on treatment efficacy was recognised by the World Health Organization (1953, p. 17).

Although it was recognised that this was an intangible concept, the World Health Organization report from their Expert Committee on Mental Health considered that psychiatric hospitals were neither a general hospital nor a prison, but a therapeutic community with a key component being relationships between those living and working in that hospital – staff:staff, staff:patients and patients:patients (p. 18). Important elements in the creation of a constructive atmosphere were considered to be the preservation of the patient's individuality, the encouragement of good behaviour and the assumption that patients are trustworthy, combined with the presumption that they retain the capacity for a considerable degree of responsibility and initiative.

This report built upon the experiences of those who had developed a therapeutic community approach (a term first described by Main, 1946) to the treatment of soldiers returning to the UK during the Second World War at Northfield, the large military psychiatric hospital in Birmingham and to Mill Hill, London (see Whiteley, 2004). The defining features of these 'therapeutic communities' were that hospital treatment was no longer confined to a therapeutic hour but became a continuous process operating throughout the waking life of the patient, with the traditional hierarchical pyramid of authority flattened to promote more interaction between patients, nurses and doctors, and the concept of community promoted with daily life and activities reflecting better 'real life' and relevance to patient needs and aspirations.

In seeking to identify principles which were unique to therapeutic communities Rapoport (1960) identified four key factors: 'communalism', 'democratisation', 'permissiveness' and 'reality confrontation'. 'Communalism' was the creation of an environment where personal communication was encouraged so that all residents were able to share and experience a sense of belonging; 'democratisation' was the process by which all residents and staff have an equal opportunity to participate in the life and organisation of the therapeutic community; 'permissiveness' involved the empowering of residents to express their thoughts, feelings and emotions without sanctions being imposed; and 'reality confrontation' was the opportunity to inform residents how their behaviour was impacting on others – both fellow residents and staff. This is described further in Akerman and Mandikate in this volume.

Consequently, therapeutic communities enable residents to have significant involvement in the practicalities of how that community operates and the decision-making responsibility that is associated with this. Dependency on professionals was discouraged with active leadership by residents vital to a community's safe and effective functioning (Campling, 2001). This was assisted by seven interrelating features: 'care', 'creation of a communal atmosphere', 'collaboration and participation', the 'valuing and respecting of each individual', 'being safe and having clear boundaries', 'the enabling of emotional and personal development' and 'having a multidisciplinary approach' (Brookes, 2009).

With each person, staff and resident knowing that they are important to each other it became possible to give accurate, often challenging, feedback. This assisted in the development of increased awareness and new skills. Interpersonal and emotional issues could be openly discussed and trusting relationships formed. This 'living-learning' experience also resulted in difficult behavior being tolerated and talked through. Social learning arising from interpersonal interactions was therefore facilitated, enabling previous patterns of behaviour to be replaced with new more acceptable ways of living and acting.

## HMP Grendon: a therapeutic community prison

HMP Grendon came into being following the publication of the 1939 East–Hubert report which had recommended that a special institution should be built in which prisoners could be treated by psychotherapy (1939 East-Hubert report). This followed their conclusion that psychotherapy, as an adjunct to an ordinary prison sentence, appeared to be effective in preventing or reducing the chance of future anti-social behaviour, provided the cases to which treatment is applied are carefully selected.

That Grendon was to be a different type of prison establishment was emphasised by the Rt. Hon R.A. Butler, Home Secretary when he commented, on the laying of Grendon's foundation stone on 1 July 1960, that "the regime must be flexible with the accent on treatment; and success will depend above all on an enlightened staff-inmate relationship, together with close co-operation at all levels between the different members of the staff" (Snell, 1963).

Given the success that operating a therapeutic community had with assisting returning prisoners of war and then with those considered unsuitable for either psychotherapy or other forms of psychiatric intervention, who displayed anti-social actions, harmful sexual conduct, addictive behaviours and mental health difficulties, the first senior management team at HMP Grendon decided to adopt this therapeutic model when the prison opened in 1962. This was to be based on the UK democratic therapeutic community approach, rather than the US hierarchical therapeutic community concept for substance abusers.

Since its opening Grendon has received many commendations. Within the mental health profession Grendon was regarded as a notable practice site in the seminal publication *Personality Disorder: No Longer a Diagnosis of Exclusion – Policy Implementation Guidance for the Development of Services for People with Personality Disorder* (NIMHE, 2003). In this best practice document Grendon was described as a specialist centre for the treatment of personality disorder particularly as it gives rise to serious offending. The five therapeutic communities within the prison were described as offering intensive group psychotherapy, social therapy, art therapy and psychodrama, with a strong emphasis on multidisciplinary working and each team consisting of a forensic psychologist, prison officers, probation officer and psychodynamic psychotherapist. The focus of much of the work was considered to be on disordered relationships, which often arise from intolerable and uncontainable feelings, and the outcome of violence or other offending. Through exploring the past and present residents can begin to make sense of their cycles of being abused and abusing and through forming reparative relationships with staff over a period of years, the energy for violence can be ameliorated.

Using rather different language HMP Grendon has been positively evaluated by HM Chief Inspector of Prisons in the reports produced by numerous Chief Inspectors since Grendon opened. For example, in the introduction to the latest Grendon report (HM Chief Inspector of Prisons, 2014), based on an unannounced inspection in August 2013, the Chief Inspector commented that:

> [C]ommunities are central to the way every part of the prison operates. Prisoners are given a real say in the day-to-day running of the establishment and therefore have far more influence over their experience of prison life than at normal prisons. This all happens within the context of the usual security imperatives of a category B prison holding men who have been sentenced to indeterminate or long determinate sentences.... Perhaps counter-intuitively, Grendon was a more demanding environment than many more conventional prisons; the process of facing up to and being challenged about past and current behaviour and attitudes was, rightly, very tough.... There was very little need for formal disciplinary processes and substance misuse was well controlled.... At the core of the prison were excellent staff-prisoner relationships, which had maturity and depth.... Strategic management of resettlement was good. The prison's therapeutic approach provided prisoners with substantial benefits, helping them to address risk factors and difficulties in coping with institutional life.... Support to help prisoners maintain contact with their children and families was impressive. (p. 5)

That Grendon has survived for over 50 years and is still being positively appraised is in many ways quite remarkable. Many other attempts within the Prison Service to work with difficult populations in specialised facilities have not survived. The Special Units established after the Control Review Committee (CRC) report (Home Office, 1984) at HMPs Hull, Lincoln and Parkhurst were closed in 1995. This had been the first attempt to develop a more strategic and systematic way of managing prisoners with very serious behaviour problems (HM Chief Inspector of Prisons, 2015). Similarly, a number of other democratic therapeutic communities opened after HMP Gredon have not survived including The Max Glatt Centre at HMP Wormwood Scrubs (previously known as the Annexe), the Albatross Unit at HMYOI Feltham, the Chiltern Unit at HMYOI Aylesbury and the therapeutic community at HMYOI Glen Parva which operated for 17 years before closing in 1996 (Rawlings, 1998). In Scotland, the Barlinnie Special Unit was closed in 1994, despite successes with some of the country's most hardened criminals (Wilson, 2014). Recently opened facilities have reassuringly survived for longer including therapeutic communities at HMPs Dovegate, Gartree, Send and Warren Hill (previously located at HMP Blundeston) and the Close Supervision Centres (CRCs) at HMPs Wakefield, Woodhill, Full Sutton, Manchester and Whitemoor.

The work of Grendon was also acknowledged in the Bradley Report (Bradley, 2009) following his review of people with mental health problems or learning disabilities in the criminal justice system. This report recognised that HMP Grendon had created a setting where prisoners, through exploring the past and present, can start to make sense of the cycle of abuse, begin to form reparative relationships with staff and, over a period of years, turn away from violence. This led Lord Bradley to recommend that in conjunction with other government departments, the Department of Health, the National Offender Management Service and the NHS should develop an inter-departmental strategy for the management of all levels of personality disorder within both the health service and the criminal justice system, covering the management of individuals with personality disorder into and through custody, and also their management in the community (p. 109). The resulting Offender Personality Strategy (Benefield et al., 2015; Joseph & Benefield, 2012) led the Chief Inspector of Prisons to comment that while Grendon used to be an anomaly in the prison system and that its future always felt insecure, the new national offender personality disorder pathway identified a clear role for Grendon and other therapeutic prisons and that there was now the real prospect that Grendon's value as an important national resource, working successfully with some of the system's most serious offenders, will be fully realised (HM Chief Inspector of Prisons, 2014, p. 6).

## Therapeutic communities as enabling environment

Rarely when therapeutic communities and the effectiveness of the therapeutic community model are considered is the impact of the environment in which these changes take place discussed. Alongside books describing individual therapeutic community prisons (Genders & Player, 1995; Morris, 2004; Parker, 1970 on HMP Grendon and Cullen & MacKenzie, 2011; Brown, Miller, Northey & O'Neill, 2014 on HMP Dovegate), what has been documented and evaluated is the population profile and personality changes of men engaging with the therapeutic process (Duggan & Shine, 2001; Newberry & Shuker, 2012), institutional behaviour changes (Shine & Hobson, 2000; Newton, 2010), the governing of a therapeutic community prison (Bennett, 2006, 2007a), security/therapy dynamics (Brookes & Mandikate, 2010; Leggett & Hirons, 2007), the cultural sensitivity of therapeutic communities (Bennett, 2007b; Jones, Brookes & Shuker, 2013), offender rehabilitation (Stevens, 2013) and issues of race and power within a therapeutic community prison (Bennett, 2013). Prisoner perspectives of Grendon have been documented by Brookes (2010a) and the experiences of BME men by Brookes, Glynn and Wilson (2012) and Newberry (2010a). Work with veterans have been described by Bonnett, Akerman and M.T. (2014) and by Brookes, Ashton and Holliss (2010).

The difficulties of working with a population as complex as those in Grendon has been set out by Shuker (2004) where he states that "criminal behaviour, which is maintained by a diverse spectrum of cognitive, attitudinal, social and interpersonal factors, requires an intervention structure which is highly conscious of the difficulties in achieving and maintaining change" (p. 66). Recognising that offence-paralleling behaviour can assist in this process (Dowdswell, Akerman & Lawrence, 2010) is important as is the relationship between therapeutic community (TC) core principles, social climate and treatment structures (Shuker, 2013), and drawing upon the good lives (Akerman, 2011; Brookes, 2010b) and recovery (Brookes, 2012) models. Regime activities can also assist the treatment process, including the annual debate between Grendon residents and Birmingham City University students (Brookes, 2014), 'good vibrations' music events (Wilson, Caulfield & Atherton, 2009) and having an artist in residence (Caulfield, 2014).

In summarising treatment outcome (Birtchnell, Shuker, Newberry & Duggan, 2009; Shuker & Newton, 2008) and reconviction studies (Cullen, 1994; Marshall, 1997; Taylor, 2000), Newberry (2010b) comments that research evaluating changes in the psychological well-being and attitudes of prisoners has found Grendon residents:

> [E]xperience less anxiety and depression, are less hostile, tough-minded and impulsive, and have fewer negative relating tendencies. Furthermore, Grendon residents are less likely to be reconvicted than prisoners selected for Grendon but who do not come to Grendon, and those who remain in treatment for at least 18 months demonstrate a reduction in reconviction rate of between one-fifth and one-quarter (Newberry, 2010b, p. 357).

What though are the environmental factors which contribute to this treatment success? In developing the 'Multifactor Offender Readiness Model', Ward, Day, Howells & Birdgen (2004) considered that treatment readiness is a combination of both internal and external factors. In addition to offenders being cognitively, emotional and volitionally ready to change, they needed to be in an environment where interventions are possible and supported, where treatment gains are sustained and generalised, and where self-disclosure and openness is encouraged. This should not only be from clinicians but also from front-line prison officers and their managers.

Such environments are an integral aspect of effective custodial therapeutic communities and in attaining core therapeutic community standards. Since 2002, the Royal College of Psychiatrists 'Community of Communities' quality network has developed and then periodically revised an agreed set of standards by which therapeutic communities operate so as to set a professionally agreed specification of what constitutes TC practice, underpinned by ten core standards (Royal College of Psychiatrists, 2015d). Those standards having an environmental component are:

- Community Members are encouraged to form a relationship with the Community and with each other as a significant part of Community life (Core Standard 3).
- Community Members work together to review, set and maintain Community rules and boundaries (Core Standard 4).
- All behaviour and emotional expression is open to discussion within the Community (Core Standard 6).
- Community Members take part in the day to day running of the community (Core Standard 7).

Such settings where prisoners are accountable to each other and where a culture of collaboration, openness and learning is present contain the 'quintessence of a therapeutic environment' (Haigh, 1999, 2013), enabling attachment (a culture of belonging), containment (a culture of safety), communication (a culture of openness), involvement or inclusion (a culture of participation and citizenship) and agency (a culture of empowerment). This is facilitated, as Shuker (2013) explains, by the interrelationship between core TC principles (decision making and responsibility, therapeutic boundaries, involvement and participation, accountability), social climate (safety, therapeutic alliances, culture of debate and exploration, learning opportunities, shared treatment goals) and treatment structures (small group work, prisoner-led community meetings, community roles and responsibilities, offence paralleling framework).

## Measuring the impact of the TC environment

In recent years there has been a growing recognition of the importance of social climate, which can be considered to be a multidimensional, multifactorial construct (Tonkin, 2016), with those institutions that create a healthy social climate experienced by staff and residents as safe and supportive. Conversely, in institutions considered unsafe where staff are unsupported, there are greater levels of verbal and physical aggression and more frequent episodes of seclusion (Long et al., 2011; Ros, van der Helm, Wissink, Stams & Schaftenaar, 2013; van der Helm, Stams, van Genabeek & van der Laan, 2012). Furthermore, positive social climates lead to more satisfying staff–resident interactions, increased resident internal readiness and motivation to engage with the treatment programme and other rehabilitation activities, stronger resident–therapist relationships and greater pre-to-post-treatment change (Beazley & Gudjonsson, 2011; Bressington, Stewart, Beer & MacInnes, 2011; Day, Casey, Vess, & Huisy, 2011; van der Helm, Beunk, Stams, & van der Laan, 2014).

While the first and most commonly used measure of social climate was the Ward Atmosphere Scale (Moos, 1974, 1989) and its forensic version, the Correctional Institutions Environment Scale (Moos, 1987), a more recent questionnaire which is easier and quicker to administer is the Essen Climate Evaluation Schema (Schalast, Redies, Collins, Stacey & Howells, 2008). This explores therapeutic hold (support therapy and therapeutic change), residents' cohesion and mutual support and safety (experience of aggression and violence). In assessing the impact of the social climate at HMP Grendon (Tonkin & Howells, 2009; Tonkin et al., 2012) both prisoners and staff reported that they generally felt safe and supported in their physical and emotional needs. Indeed they evaluated the social climate at HMP Grendon more favourably than staff and patients within high secure hospitals and in other European mental health settings.

In the United Kingdom, Her Majesty's Prison Service monitors the social climate in all prisons across England and Wales every two years using the 'Measuring the Quality of Prison Life' (MQPL) questionnaire developed by Liebling and Arnold (2002). This is based on known factors impacting on the quality of life experienced by prisoners. What has been found is that therapeutic communities have the highest quality of life when compared with other secure prisons (Ministry of Justice, 2009; Shefer, 2010).

MQPL surveys were undertaken at HMP Grendon in April, 2004, February 2007, June 2009, November 2011 and October 2014 with the mean scores from these surveys being 7.65 (April 2004), 6.98 (February 2007), 6.53 (June 2009), 7.08 (November 2011) and 7.32 (March 2014). Even in 2007, the year of the lowest score, when communities at Grendon were preparing for the closure on one wing and the merging of the induction unit with another community as part of the heating refurbishment project, Grendon was still positivity appraised. Prisoners commented that the therapy was really useful, that 'special things' happen at Grendon, and that the treatment helped them get to the core of their problems, enabled them to see other points of view and provided them with alternative ways of solving problems. Prisoners in the various groups the MQPL team organised also said they felt that the therapy at Grendon was much more useful than other programmes, such as CALM or ETS, which they felt did not take long enough to uncover their real issues.

## Conclusion

A critical component of prison therapeutic communities is the enabling environment in which treatment takes place. This is both a function of a prison establishment or unit operating as a therapeutic community but also a consequence of senior management decisions to initiate and then support a regime based on therapeutic community principles. It involves senior managers adapting prison service rules and orders to accommodate therapeutic community standards. In doing this they are though applying management practices and values that are key components of any enabling environment and which could be applied in other prison settings (see Bennett & Shuker, 2010).

The key enabling environment features which contribute to the operational and therapeutic effectiveness of prison therapeutic communities include maintaining good quality relationships between staff and residents with staff and residents being equally valued; encouraging residents to take responsibility for their environment; and for residents to be purposefully engaged in the life of their community. This includes participating in work and community tasks assigned to them, and making constructive use of their leisure time and any opportunities available for being creative and innovative, whether these are spontaneous, shared or planned. Additional factors comprise transparent decision-making, acknowledgment of formal and informal leadership roles, the exercise of power and authority being clearly accountable and open to discussion, and clarity of formal rules and informal expectations of behaviour, with all behaviour, even when potentially disruptive, being seen as meaningful, as a method of communication to be understood.

Empowering therapeutic communities to practice as an enabling environment in order to provide a place of belonging where the nature and quality of relationships are of primary importance is essential. This involves the setting of clear boundaries and expectations of behaviour with effective communication channels and arrangements in place. The physical and psychological safety of residents and staff is recognised with support available for everyone; consequently, all behaviour and emotional expression is able to be explored and appraised. Additionally, managers take responsibility for the environment being an enabling one with external relationships sought and valued. This provides an effective counterbalance to the tendency of therapeutic environments to become too insular and inward looking and, thereby, failing to broaden the experience and outlook of community members. This outward-looking focus helps the community to maintain a balanced perspective.

In such a setting the therapeutic process can become rooted in standard practice enabling residents to feel safe enough to explore their deep-rooted psychological needs, patterns of behaviour and thought patterns which cause them concern, knowing that they will be valued and appreciated and not rejected.

## References

Akerman, G. (2011). Offence paralleling behaviour and the custodial good life at HMP Grendon. *Forensic Update*, 104, 20–25.

Beazley, P. & Gudjonsson, G. (2011). Motivating inpatients to engage with treatment: The role of depression and ward atmosphere. *Nordic Journal of Psychiatry*, 65, 95–100. doi:10.3109/08039488.2010.502244.

Benefield, N., Joesph, N., Skett, S., Bridgland, S., d'Cruz, L. & Turner, T. (2015). The offender personality disorder strategy jointly delivered by NOMS and NHS England. *Prison Service Journal*, 218, 4–9.

Bennett, J. (2013). Race and power: The potential and limitations of prison-based democratic therapeutic communities. *Race and Justice*, 3(2), 130–143. doi:10.1177/2153368713483323.

Bennett, P. (2006). Governing a humane prison. In D. Jones (Ed.), *Humane Prisons* (pp. 129–140). Oxford: Radcliffe.

Bennett, P. (2007a). Governing Grendon prison's therapeutic communities: The big spin. In M. Parker (Ed.), *Dynamic Security: The Democratic Therapeutic Community in Prison* (pp. 203–212). London: Jessica Kingsley.

Bennett, P. (2007b). Why do relatively few BME residents choose to come to Grendon? Introduction to the third Grendon Winter Seminar, 23 January 2007. *Prison Service Journal*, 173, 5–8.

Bennett, P. & Shuker, R. (2010). Improving prisoner-staff relationships: Exporting Grendon's good practice. *The Howard Journal*, 49(5), 491–502.

Birtchnell, J., Shuker, R., Newberry, M., & Duggan, C. (2009). An assessment of change in negative relating in two male forensic therapy samples using the Person's Relating to Others Questionnaire (PROQ). *Journal of Forensic Psychiatry and Psychology*, 20(3), 387–407.

Bonnett, S., Akerman, G. & M.T. (2014). One intervention for ex-service personnel in custody: The veterans group at HMP Grendon. *Forensic Update*, 115, 34–39.

Bradley, K. (2009). *The Bradley Report*. London: Department of Health.

Bressington, D., Stewart, B., Beer, D. & MacInnes, D. (2011). Levels of service user satisfaction in secure settings – A survey of the association between perceived social climate, perceived therapeutic relationship and satisfaction with forensic services. *International Journal of Nursing Studies*, 48, 1349–1356. doi:10.1016/j.ijnurstu.2011.05.011.

Brookes, M. (2009). Directing therapy at HMP Grendon: Learning by experience. *Therapeutic Communities*, 30, 292–299.

Brookes, M. (2010a). The impact of Grendon on changing lives: Prisoner perspectives. *The Howard Journal*, 49, 478–490.

Brookes, M. (2010b). Putting principles into practice: The therapeutic community regime at HMP Grendon and its relationship with the 'Good Lives' model. In R. Shuker & E. Sullivan (Eds.), *Grendon and the Emergence of Forensic Therapeutic Communities: Developments in Research and Practice* (pp. 99–113). Chichester: Wiley-Blackwell.

Brookes, M. (2012). Recovery within a prison therapeutic community: Setting the scene. In D. Alred & G. Drennan (Eds.), *Secure Recovery: Approaches to Recovery in Forensic Mental Health Settings* (pp. 156–171). London: Routledge.

Brookes, M. (2014). The annual BCU/HMP Grendon debate: What are the benefits? *Prison Service Journal*, 216(November), 50–57.

Brookes, M., Ashton, C. & Holliss, A. (2010). Assisting veterans at HMPs Grendon and Springhill. *Prison Service Journal*, 190, 3–9.

Brookes, M., Glynn, M. & Wilson, D. (2012). Black men, therapeutic communities and HMP Grendon. *Therapeutic Communities: The International Journal of Therapeutic Communities*, 33(1), 16–27.

Brookes, M. & Mandikate, P. (2010). Managing and adapting to increased security and audit requirements within a prison based therapeutic community – the recent experience at HMP Grendon. *Therapeutic Communities*, 31, 239–252.

Brown, J., Miller, S., Northey, S. & O'Neill, D. (2014). *What Works in Therapeutic Prisons*. Basingstoke: Palgrave Macmillan.

Campling, P. (2001). Therapeutic communities. *Advances in Psychiatric Treatment*, 7, 365–372.

Caulfield, L. (2014). *Final Evaluation of the Artist in Residence at HMP Grendon*. Retrieved from http://artsevidence.org.uk/media/uploads/finalartistinresidencereportaugust2014.pdf.

Churchill, W. (1910). *House of Commons Debates*, 5th series, vol. 19, col. 1354, 20 July. Retrieved from http://hansard.millbanksystems.com/commons/1910/jul/20/class-iii.

Clements, J. (2009, October). The therapeutic role: The importance of prison officers. *Gatelodge*.

Crewe, B., Liebling, A. & Hulley, S. (2011). Staff culture, use of authority and prisoner quality of life in public and private sector prisons. *Australian and New Zealand Journal of Criminology*, 44, 94–115.

Crewe, B., Liebling, A. & Hulley, S. (2014). Heavy-light, absent-present: Re-thinking the 'weight' of imprisonment. *British Journal of Sociology*, 65(3), 387–410. doi:10.1111/1468-4446.12084.

Cullen, E. (1994). Grendon: The therapeutic community that works. *Therapeutic Communities*, 15(4), 301–311.

Cullen, E. & MacKenzie, J. (2011). *Dovegate: A Therapeutic Community in a Private Prison and Developments in Therapeutic Work with Personality Disordered Offenders*. Hook: Waterside Press.

Day, A., Casey, S., Vess, J. & Huisy, G. (2011). *Assessing the Social Climate of Prisons*. Retrieved from www.criminologyresearchcouncil.gov.au/reports/02-0910.pdf.

Dowdswell, H., Akerman, G. & Lawrence (2010). Unlocking offence paralleling behaviour in a custodial setting – A personal perspective from members of staff and a resident in a forensic therapeutic community. In M. Daffern, L. Jones & J. Shine (Eds.), *Offence Paralleling Behaviour* (pp. 231–243). UK: Wiley.

Duggan, L. & Shine, J. (2001). An investigation of the relationship between arson, personality disorder, hostility, neuroticism and self-esteem amongst incarcerated fire-setters. *Prison Service Journal*, 133, 18–21.

East, W.N., & Hubert, W.H. de B. (1939). *Report on the Psychological Treatment of Crime*. London: HMSO.

Genders, E. & Player, E. (1995). *Grendon: A Study of a Therapeutic Prison*. Oxford: University Press.

Gooch, K., Treadwell, J. & Trent, R. (2015). Preventing and reducing prison bullying. *Prison Service Journal*, 221, 25–29.

Haigh, R. (1999). The quintessence of a therapeutic environment. In R. Haigh & P. Campling (Eds.), *Therapeutic Communities: Past, Present and Future* (pp. 246–257). London: Jessica Kingsley.

Haigh, R. (2013). The quintessence of a therapeutic environment. *Therapeutic Communities: The International Journal of Therapeutic Communities*, 34(1), 6–15. doi:10.1108/09641861311330464.

Haigh, R., Harrison, T., Johnson, R., Paget, S. & Williams, S. (2012). Psychologically informed environments and the "Enabling Environments" initiative. *Housing, Care and Support*, 15, 34–42. doi:10.1108/14608791211238412.

HM Chief Inspector of Prisons (2014). *Report on an Unannounced Inspection of HMP Grendon 5–16 March 2013*. London: HM Inspectorate of Prisons.

HM Chief Inspector of Prisons (2015). *Report on an Announced Thematic Inspection of the Close Supervision Centre System*. London: HM Inspectorate of Prisons.

Home Office (1984). *Managing the Long-Term Prison System: The Report of the Control Review Committee*. London: HMSO.

Johnson, R. & Haigh, R. (2011). Social psychiatry and social policy for the 21st century: New concepts for new needs. Part two – the "Enabling Environments" initiative. *Mental Health and Social Inclusion*, 15(1), 17–23. doi:10.5042/mhsi.2011.0054.

Jones, L., Brookes, M. & Shuker, R. (2013). An exploration of cultural sensitivity: The experiences of offenders within a therapeutic community prison. *Race and Justice*, 3(2), 144–158. doi:10.1177/2153368713483324.

Joseph, N. & Benefield, N. (2012). A joint offender personality disorder pathway strategy: An outline summary. *Criminal Behaviour and Mental Health*, 22, 210–217. doi:10.1002/cbm.1835.

Leggett, K. & Hirons, B. (2007). Security and dynamic security in a therapeutic community prison. In M. Parker (Ed.), *Dynamic Security: The Democratic Therapeutic Community in Prison*. London: Jessica Kingsley Publications.

Liebling, A. & Arnold, H. (2002). Measuring the quality of prison life. *Home Office Research Findings 174*. London: Home Office Research, Development and Statistics Directorate.

Long, C. G., Anagnostakis, K., Fox, E., Silaule, P., Somers, J., West, R. & Webster, A. (2011). Social climate along the pathway of care in women's secure mental health service: Variation with level of security, patient motivation, therapeutic alliance and level of disturbance. *Criminal Behaviour and Mental Health*, 21, 202–214. doi:10.1002/cbm.791.

Main, T. (1946). The hospital as a therapeutic institution. *Bulletin of the Menninger Clinic*, 10, 66–70. Reprinted (1996) in *Therapeutic Communities*, 17(2), 77–80.

Marshall, P. (1997). *A Reconviction Study of HMP Grendon Therapeutic Community*, Home Office Research and Statistics Directorate, Research Findings No. 53.

Ministry of Justice. (2009). *MQPL Survey Carried out at HMP Grendon, June 2009: Supplementary Report Illustrating a Comparison of Dimension Scores to Those from 15 Other Training Prisons*. London: Ministry of Justice.

Ministry of Justice. (2010). *Breaking the Cycle: Effective Punishment, Rehabilitation and Sentencing of Offenders*. London: The Stationery Office.

Ministry of Justice. (2013). *Transforming Rehabilitation: A Strategy for Reform*. London: The Stationery Office.

Moos, R.H. (1974). *Ward Atmosphere Scale Manual*. Palo Alto, CA: Consulting Psychologists Press.

Moos, R.H. (1987). *Correctional Institutions Environment Scale.* Palo Alto, CA: Consulting Psychologists Press.

Moos, R.H. (1989). *Ward Atmosphere Scale Manual* (2nd ed.). Palo Alto, CA: Consulting Psychologists Press.

Morris, M. (2004) *Dangerous and Severe: Process, Programme and Person: Grendon's Work.* London: Jessica Kingsley.

National Institute for Mental Health for England (NIMHE). (2003). *Personality Disorder: No Longer a Diagnosis of Exclusion.* Leeds: Department of Health.

Newberry, M. (2010a). The experiences of Black and Minority Ethnic (BME) prisoners in a therapeutic community prison. In R. Shuker & E. Sullivan (Eds.), *Grendon and the Emergence of Forensic Therapeutic Communities: Developments in Research and Practice.* London: Wiley-Blackwell.

Newberry, M. (2010b). A synthesis of outcome research at HMP Grendon therapeutic community prison. *Therapeutic Communities,* 31(4), 356–371.

Newberry, M. & Shuker, R. (2012). Personality assessment inventory (PAI) profiles of offenders and their relationship to institutional misconduct and risk of reconviction. *Journal of Personality Assessment,* 94(6), 586–592.

Newton, M. (2010). Changes in prison offending amongst residents in a prison-based therapeutic community. In R. Shuker & E. Sullivan (Eds.), *Grendon and the Emergence of Forensic Therapeutic Communities: Developments in Research and Practice.* London: Wiley-Blackwell.

NOMS. (2014). *National Offender Management Service Business Plan 2014–2015.* Retrieved from www.gov.uk/government/publications/noms-business-plan-2014-to-2015.

NOMS. (2015). *Service Specification for Rehabilitation Services – In Custody.* Retrieved from www .gov.uk/government/uploads/system/uploads/attachment_data/file/427957/2015-05-18_Rehab_Service_CU_Spec_P3.0.pdf.

Parker, T. (1970). *The Frying Pan.* London: Hutchinson.

Rapoport, R. (1960). *Community as Doctor: New Perspectives on a Therapeutic Community.* London: Tavistock.

Rawlings, B. (1998). *Research on Therapeutic Communities in Prisons: A Review of the Literature.* Retrieved from www.dldocs.stir.ac.uk/documents/rawlings.pdf.

Ros, N., van der Helm, P., Wissink, P., Stams, G., & Schaftenaar, P. (2013). Institutional climate and aggression in a secure psychiatric setting. *The Journal of Forensic Psychiatry & Psychology,* 24, 713–727. doi:10.1080/14789949.2013.848460.

Royal College of Psychiatrists. (2012). *Enabling Environment Leaflet.* Retrieved from www .icha.org.uk/uploads/files/enabling_environments_leaflet_2012.pdf.

Royal College of Psychiatrists. (2015a). *CCQI National Clinical Audits, Service Quality and Accreditation Projects.* Retrieved from www.rcpsych.ac.uk/workinpsychiatry/qualityimprovement/ccqiprojects.aspx.

Royal College of Psychiatrists. (2015b). *What Is the Enabling Environments Award?* Retrieved from www.enablingenvironments.com.

Royal College of Psychiatrists. (2015c). *Enabling Environments Standards.* Retrieved from www.rcpsych.ac.uk/pdf/EE%20LS%20Standards%20Document%202015%202.pdf.

Royal College of Psychiatrists. (2015d). *Service Standards for Therapeutic Communities,* 9th Edition. Retrieved from www.rcpsych.ac.uk/pdf/Service%20Standards%20for%20Therapeutic%20 Communities%209th%20Ed%20FINAL%20-%20For%20%20Website%20-%20Copy.pdf.

Schalast, N., Redies, M., Collins, M., Stacey, J. & Howells, K. (2008). EssenCES, a short questionnaire for assessing the social climate of forensic psychiatric wards. *Criminal Behaviour and Mental Health,* 18, 49–58. doi:10.1002/cbm.677.

Schubert, C.A., Mulvey, E.P., Loughran, T.A. & Loyosa, S.H. (2012). Perceptions of institutional experience and community outcomes for serious adolescent offenders. *Criminal Justice and Behavior*, 39, 71–93. doi:10.1177/0093854811426710.

Shefer, G. (2010). The quality of life of prisoners and staff at HMP Grendon. In R. Shuker & E. Sullivan (Eds.), *Grendon and the Emergence of Forensic Therapeutic Communities: Developments in Research and Practice* (pp. 247–263). Chichester: Wiley-Blackwell.

Shine, J. & Hobson, J. (2000). Institutional behaviour and time in treatment among psychopaths admitted to a prison-based therapeutic community. *Medical Science Law*, 40(4), 327–335.

Shuker, R. (2004). Changing people with programmes. In D. Jones (Ed.), *Working with Dangerous People: The Psychotherapy of Violence* (pp. 55–68). Oxford: Radcliffe Medical Press.

Shuker, R. (2013). Treating offenders in a therapeutic community. In L. Craig, L. Dixon & T.A. Gannon (Eds.), *What Works in Offender Rehabilitation: An Evidence Based Approach to Assessment and Treatment* (pp. 340–358). Chichester: Wiley-Blackwell.

Shuker, R. & Newton, M. (2008). Treatment outcome following treatment in a prison-based therapeutic community: A study of the relationship between reduction in criminogenic risk and improved psychological well-being. *British Journal of Forensic Practice*, 10(3), 33–44.

Snell, H. K. (1963). The new prison at Grendon Underwood. *The Medico-Legal Journal*, 31, 175–188.

Stevens, A. (2013). *Offender Rehabilitation and Therapeutic Communities: Enabling Change the TC Way*. Oxford: Routledge.

Taylor, R. (2000). *A Seven Year Reconviction Study of HMP Grendon Therapeutic Community*. Research findings no. 115. Home Office Research Development and Statistics Directorate.

Tonkin, M. (2016). A review of questionnaire measures for assessing the social climate in prisons and forensic psychiatric hospitals. *International Journal of Offender Therapy and Comparative Criminology*, 60, 1376–1405. doi: 10.1177/0306624X15578834.

Tonkin, M. & Howells, K. (2009). *Social Climate in Secure Settings: A Report for HMP Grendon*. Peaks Academic and Research Unit, Rampton Hospital: Institute of Mental Health.

Tonkin, M., Howells, K., Ferguson, E., Clark, A., Newberry, M. & Schalast, N. (2012). Lost in translation? Psychometric properties and construct validity of the English Essen Climate Evaluation Schema (EssenCES) social climate questionnaire. *Psychological Assessment*, 24, 573–580. doi:10.1037/a0026267.

van der Helm, P., Beunk, L., Stams, G. J. & van der Laan, P. (2014). The relationship between detention length, living group climate, coping and treatment motivation among juvenile delinquents in a youth correctional facility. *The Prison Journal*, 94, 260–275. doi:10.1177/0032885514524884.

van der Helm, P., Stams, G. J., van Genabeek, M. & van der Laan, P. (2012). Group climate, personality, and self-reported aggression in incarcerated male youth. *The Journal of Forensic Psychiatry & Psychology*, 23, 23–39. doi:10.1080/14789949.2011.633615.

Ward, T., Day, A., Howells, K. & Birgden, A. (2004). The multifactor offender readiness model. *Aggression and Violent Behavior*, 9, 645–673.

Whiteley, S. (2004). The evolution of the therapeutic community. *Psychiatric Quarterly*, 75(3), 233–248.

Wilson, D. (2014). *Pain and Retribution. A Short History of British Prisons, 1066 to the Present*. London: Reaktion.

Wilson, D., Caulfield, L. S. & Atherton, S. (2009). Good vibrations: The long-term impact of a prison-based music project. *Prison Service Journal*, 182, 27–32.

World Health Organization. (1953). *The Community Mental Hospital: 3rd Report of the Expert Committee on Mental Health*. Retrieved from http://apps.who.int/iris/bitstream/10665/37984/1/WHO_TRS_73.pdf.

# 8

# CREATING A THERAPEUTIC COMMUNITY FROM SCRATCH

## Where do we start?

*Geraldine Akerman and Patrick Mandikate*

This chapter describes the opening and early months of a new community within a world-renowned prison, Her Majesty's Prison Grendon. HMP Grendon opened as a prison-based therapeutic community in 1962, and runs with five democratic therapeutic communities (DTCs) and an assessment unit. The 'living-learning' experience offered within a DTC has been found to be effective in treating men with complex emotional and interpersonal needs (Marshall, 1997; Shuker & Newton, 2008; Taylor, 2000; Warren et al., 2003). Warren et al. (2003) described a DTC as offering the most promising evidence for effectiveness in producing long-term symptomatic and behavioural improvements in both personality disordered clients and in general offender populations. DTCs provide a supportive environment to effect change for those with complex emotional and interpersonal needs. This chapter will describe the difficulties inherent in the development of a pro-social culture in a prison setting and the way the environment was used to enable the evolution of a therapeutic community. Lessons learned are discussed with a view to helping others in similar endeavours.

## The democratic therapeutic community model

The premise of a democratic therapeutic community (DTC) was developed over many years and in various settings. Maxwell Jones (1946, 1952, 1968), along with others, developed the DTC philosophy and explained the research he was undertaking into the symptoms the patients who were presenting with 'battle fatigue' (breathlessness, chest pains, giddiness and persistent fatigue) and found that the men he was treating responded well to group discussion. His patients were largely men returning from war, with symptoms akin to what would now be described as post-traumatic stress disorder and exhibiting problematic behaviour. Jones noticed that the men were benefitting from discussing their experiences with others who had suffered similar problems and that they also benefited from a more egalitarian environment rather than a traditional psychiatric hospital in which the doctor is the expert and patients were grateful and compliant. Social learning evolved, whereby residents communicate how they feel, listen to feedback from others and practice new ways of solving problems and relate to others, i.e. learning from their society (see Akerman, in press; Shine & Morris, 1999; Shuker & Sullivan, 2010; Stevens, 2010; Whiteley, 2004) whereby it was found that the environment in which treatment took place could be construed as the agent of change. Rapoport (1960) described his view of the 'Community as doctor' emphasising the importance of the environment and not just the expertise of the staff. Rapoport highlighted the need for democratisation in decision-making, achieved through regular community meetings in which the activities of daily living in the community are discussed and debated. This can seem a very alien concept to a resident (the DTC term for prisoners) who has just transferred from a prison setting in which they are forced to obey orders and have no say in the decisions made by staff. Roberts (1997) described a DTC as a collective and collaborative entity; this is the primary therapeutic instrument, which also encompasses psychodynamic therapy, in which personal development can be encouraged. The therapy enables exploration and working through of motivation and largely unconscious drives and maladaptive responses to a traumatic and abusive childhood.

## HMP Grendon

From its opening in September 1962 as an experimental psychiatric prison, the Grendon programme underwent many changes and evolved into a treatment programme which was described and accredited in 2000 (HMPS/NOMS, 2003; Shine & Morris, 1999). Initially it housed young offenders and adult males who were deemed to need psychiatric intervention but who were not psychotic. The first governors were medical superintendents and it was many years before a traditional operational manager was appointed governor in 1993. Genders and Player (1995) describe how initially the purpose was to ease the personal distress the residents were suffering; preventing re-offending was secondary. However, over time it had to prove its efficacy in reducing re-offending and the Home Office made recommendations as to how this could proceed, including the need to take more serious violent and sexual offenders, and housing what Shine and Newton (2000) described as damaged, disturbed and dangerous residents.

The model developed further using the core principles of a DTC, these being:

- **Democratisation:** This involves shared responsibility and decision-making with transparency in decision-making and channels of communication throughout each individual community and the wider prison establishment.
- **Communalism:** This principle requires that domestic tasks are shared and distributed throughout all members. It helps residents to make links with others as they disclose their struggles and share their experience of similar issues; it also provides coping strategies and instils hope that things will improve.

- **Permissiveness:** This involves the ability to tolerate behaviour and communication that would generally be sanctioned. This enables such behaviour, thoughts or attitudes (conscious and unconscious) to be discussed and their functions to be understood, resulting in the development of more pro-social alternatives. Permissiveness encourages the resident to express their characteristic patterns of behaviour, in order to receive feedback as to how this behaviour is experienced by others and to resolve interpersonal difficulties. The environment should help the resident to demonstrate previous patterns of behaviour thus enabling this to be understood and open to modification when required.
- **Reality confrontation:** This is being able to explain to others (and importantly being able to hear) how a resident's behaviour, views and management of emotions impacts on others. For instance, if a resident is irresponsible or not taking responsibility for their actions, this is open for analysis by the group and community and how it impacts on others is discussed. Many residents will state that such feedback has not been given to them in the past, or if it has it has not been heeded. Yalom (1980) spoke of the mirror being held up to the resident, and describes how residents find it difficult to see themselves as others do.
- **Living-learning environment:** Whereby all interactions are seen as a learning opportunity. All aspects of the community are fed back to the wider community and exclusive relationships are discouraged to avoid secrecy and collusion.
- **Culture of enquiry:** Allowing all aspects of the community to be questioned and explored. Residents often comment that trivial interactions are analysed, and can find the need for this level of enquiry perplexing. However, as a pattern of behaviour develops they can recognise the underlying meaning and purpose to their often automatic responses.

Akerman (2010), Genders and Player (1995), Haigh (1999) and Sullivan (2010) spoke of the need for attachment to the community and the importance of joining and leaving the community appropriately, which would not be the general experience for those in the community and their past relationships. Therefore, the environment needs to be nurturing and supportive. McNeill (2006) highlights the importance of community, personal and social contexts in promoting desistance from offending, which is helped by the individual being a member of society in which they have rights and responsibilities. McNeill (2014) also describes how important it is for an individual to belong to and be accepted by a non-offending community to aid desistance from offending. HMP Grendon prides itself on its collaboration with external agencies, and hosts regular conferences, seminars, open days, and events which enables residents to socialise with relevant professional staff.

Maruna and Farrall (2004) discuss the need for primary desistance (a change in behaviour) and secondary desistance (a shift in self-identity), and the DTC provides the opportunity to develop and practise these aspects of self. Attachment theory (Bowlby, 1979; Rich, 2006) indicates that having an insecure attachment style is likely to lead to an individual thinking that others cannot be relied on to provide comfort and support. Those who have an anxious attachment style tend to fear rejection from others and those who have an avoidant style can mistrust others and so avoid making emotional connections with others. Those who have developed a secure attachment style are more likely to be able to think they can rely on others and that their opinion would be valued. Those with a secure attachment style are more likely to be able to consider others' point of view and trust them, and make more considered decisions, whereas those with anxious or avoidant attachment would be more inclined to impulsive actions, with less thought for the impact this would have on others. These styles may well be reflected in therapeutic relationships with staff and other residents. Therefore, over time patterns of behaviour and thinking help residents identify how they relate to others and what impact this has on relationships. Rich (2006, p. 302) emphasises that the environment in which treatment is provided is paramount, such that it provides attunement, empathy, meta-cognition, self-regulation and self-responsibility. Furthermore, the environment enhances the sense of security and trust in others, by their actions, not just words, providing a sense of security and trust in relationships with others. Within an established community this culture is inherent (although it can be affected by day-to day events) but in this instance the staff were aware of needing to develop this in the new wing.

Throughout the journey of therapy the resident will know that they will leave as some point, they will hear stories of others who have done so successfully (as well as those who have struggled), and can make plans as to how they will cope in the various situations they are likely to encounter. Importantly, they will be able to detach in a planned manner and with a sense of themselves as an autonomous individual.

## The opening of a new wing

Due to a need for refurbishment of the fabric of HMP Grendon one wing was emptied, and each community rotated to that wing whilst work was completed on the resulting empty wing. As the refurbishment of the establishment progressed the assessment unit was housed temporarily on the empty wing, and during that time sadly a resident committed suicide. This naturally led to a sense of shared trauma within the residents and staff team. This had been the first time for many years that a resident had taken their own life and so impacted on Grendon as a whole, which takes pride in caring for those in emotional distress.

While the work was completed there was discussion and consultation throughout the establishment led by the Therapy Policy Committee as to the identity of the new community. Options considered included young offenders, female offenders or those with a particular need (for instance ex-service personnel) or particular offences. It was decided that it should be a community of men who have committed a range of offences and should be developed with men from the waiting list rather than a mixture of residents from other established wings, in order to prevent disruption to therapeutic work already underway. The staff team, who all volunteered to join the new community, consisted of a lead therapist (second author), forensic psychologist (first author), a group analyst, two senior officers and eight prison officers. Most of these members of staff had experience of working on other wings (therapeutic communities) at HMP Grendon and so were keenly aware of the challenge this would provide. Two officers were newly recruited from another establishment and so like the new residents were learning about DTC principles. Due to pressure of being short-staffed there was limited time available for staff to get to know each other during the time leading up to the opening of the wing along with pressure of recruiting new residents for the community. This involved visiting other establishments and explaining how Grendon functioned. In addition, staff could be required elsewhere in the establishment to cover other duties. The staff group was, however, able to discuss a cascading supervision structure where the senior clinical staff would be supervised by the lead therapist and in turn they would supervise a group of officers each.

Once the refurbishment was completed the wing opened on 9 November 2009 with six residents who had been assessed as suitable for therapy on the assessment unit. These men became the backbone of the wing and although they were new to therapy themselves, they gradually became culture carriers for the wing. Tasks were allocated to enable the wing to function. Some of the first jobs allocated were chair and vice chair, the two residents who would manage the business of the wing. On an established community this role would generally be held by a resident who had been in therapy for nine months or more. The two men were voted by the other community members as those who understood therapy and how it works. Thus the first chair and vice chair were placed in a challenging role for men who themselves were so new to therapy. They rose to this challenge admirably, learning as they went along how to take on this role. They spoke to staff and community regularly and decisions were discussed and made on a democratic basis. The early community meetings were attended by the six residents and often equal numbers of staff. They continued to discuss the impact the recent suicide had on them; early community meetings included discussion of the loss of life and thought was given about allocating the cell in which it took place. All such discussion happened with the residents, many of whom had experiences of suicide in their past both inside of and outside custody, and discussions highlighted that some still appeared desensitised to the impact. As is the case in such events the effects are drawn out by the processes involved in custody, for instance the police investigating the death and the inquest, held some months later.

Despite this, the residents were encouraged to take up their role as culture carriers (discussed further in Akerman, 2010; Genders & Player, 1995, Shine & Morris, 1999), members of the community (staff or residents) who have experience of therapy and can model it for other less experienced members. It is generally acknowledged that newer residents place more faith in what is said by their peers than by staff. Therefore, it was important for the pro-social minority to find their voice in shaping the culture. Residents and staff worked hard together to prepare the physical environment, decorating, furnishing, growing plants, putting up paintings and so forth, with a great sense of satisfaction as each task was completed. These tasks helped to develop a joint culture between staff and residents rather than them and us. Each person had their place in the evolving community with the emphasis on developing a culture that is lived rather than a group which is attended (Morris, 2004). In line with the Good Lives Model (Ward & Gannon, 2006; Ward & Stewart, 2003) much thought was given to what goals had been sought through offending and how this can be achieved in another way (see Frost and Ware in this volume for further discussion of the GLM in DTCs). Consideration was given to the residents and their previous experiences of trauma and how these may manifest in this therapeutic environment. Every effort was made to equip residents with the necessary skills to satisfy their life values in a way which does not have a negative impact on others (Akerman, 2011). Rogers (1993) encouraged the development of an environment in which the client can reach their optimal potential. In line with humanistic person-centered psychology, this would include collaborative, genuine relationships and the willingness to remove the hierarchy traditionally present between a therapist and client. Likewise, ongoing consideration is given to previous experiences of care, which may have been neglectful, and damaged. Rogers also spoke of the importance of the 'good life' as early as 1969 and the need to relate on a person-to-person level with unconditional positive regard. These beliefs underpin the DTC. Brookes (2010) described how a prison-based DTC could provide the environment in which good lives goals could be achieved. As community members became more known to staff and residents, the strengths-based approach was utilised to help them practice skills in a pro-social manner.

Residents worked together to complete everyday tasks: cooking, cleaning and decorating and furnishing the wing. For those who found this difficult (for instance a resident refusing to clean the staff toilets) the underlying issues were explored and understood. Anti-authority attitudes were highly prevalent, as would be expected in a group of residents so new to the process of a DTC. When processes were questioned in community meetings (for instance why a resident should clean or cook, water plants or feed fish), it proved an opportunity to explain the therapeutic programme. A further reason emphasis is placed on developing individual strengths and abilities is that it is acknowledged that intense exploration of past misdemeanors can feel persecutory and demoralising, whilst positive reinforcement is used to help develop self-esteem and recognise self-worth. Tilley (2000) emphasises the importance of the context in which actions happen as much as what actually happens.

The DTC programme manual (NOMS, 2013) describes how the accredited model is intended to run including ten core components:

- Community living
- Community meetings
- Small therapy groups
- The opportunity to hold emergency meetings if required
- Integration of core creative psychotherapies
- Work, education, supportive interventions, recreation, taking positions of responsibility

- A multidisciplinary staff team
- Staff working practices being in keeping with the DTC model
- Individual therapy plans and regular reviews
- Links to the community outside of the DTC setting and support during and after transfer

## A community is born

Each community has its own set of rules known as the constitution. The first constitution was written during the early series of community meetings involving less than ten residents and staff. It was therefore heavily influenced by other constitutions from more established wings and from the models of the staff group who were experienced DTC practitioners. While the numbers built up on the wing community meetings were held every day to discuss the day-to-day living and to allocate required tasks and work through interpersonal difficulties. If a resident had done something to cause difficulty for others, a minute was placed in the community meeting book; the resident affected would describe how he felt and the other resident involved could explain their actions. At the start of each community meeting the residents introduced themselves when a new member had joined. Initially they introduced themselves by name and offence. This was discussed with the community and the importance of other ways of being known was considered. Residents were encouraged to talk about what they enjoyed to do, what they were good at, their hopes for the future, etc. It was thought to be important for residents to describe other aspects of their life and to highlight why they had decided to engage in treatment, as this would remind them why they were making this journey. It was also thought that by introducing themselves by their offence the residents were developing a hierarchy of offending, which is not deemed to be conducive with a DTC. Furthermore, it failed to highlight positive aspects of the individual. The resident is then acknowledged by the community (including staff) in a more holistic manner with his aspirations for change highlighted. Maruna (2001) spoke of the importance of residents voicing their aspirations and how this narrative helped reinforce their intentions to change and so this was encouraged.

The therapy at HMP Grendon aims to challenge anti-social behaviour through helping the residents recognise and express their emotions in a pro-social manner. This involves exploration of past thoughts, feelings and behaviour, some of which can be manifested in the present. This is known as offence paralleling behaviour, (OPB) (Akerman, 2011, 2012; Dowdswell, Akerman & 'Lawrence', 2010; Jones, 2004). Jones (2004) suggested that OPB might be represented by thoughts, feelings or actions that may or may not have obvious similarities to the offence. Jones explains that the DTC allows exploration of which behaviour, displayed in which situations, encountered in which emotional states may be relevant to offending. The residents are encouraged to tolerate emotions rather than use previous avoidant strategies (such as not thinking about the issue, moving away from it, or self-soothing using alcohol, drugs, or offending) and understand their function. Many residents have experienced emotions linked to separation (for example grief, being placed in care of local authorities and so forth) and these are discussed and understood, with new emotional management skills being developed. In parallel, members of staff are also able to develop emotional management skills from supervision, where their own losses and countertransference arising from work with residents can be discussed and understood and new skill sets gained.

## The developing community

As the community evolved it became a safer environment in which OPB could be tolerated. Initially, in the new community, anxiety was evoked when voices were raised, as memories of previous experiences of resulting violence were induced. However, over time it was recognised that conflict could be resolved without resorting to violence. Residents recognised their ability to voice their feelings without the need to act on them; the requirement was that they remain in their seat. Residents will explore relationship dynamics throughout their life and how these had failed and could be improved. Members of staff model the use of compassion (Gilbert, 2010) in order to facilitate the understanding of how emotions can be expressed appropriately. Gilbert explains that criticism is internalised during developmental stages, which in turn feeds the threat system. When this is evoked feelings of shame are experienced and this can elicit the freeze, fight or flight response. Therefore, it is important for treatment to be effective that the environment strives not to evoke these emotions, but if it they are aroused they are recognised and managed. Gilbert suggests the use of 'compassionate self-correction', identifying when the critical voice is aroused, taking the time to calm emotions and create a kind compassionate response, as one would with a good friend. The principle of the Good Life Model that offenders are human beings with essentially similar needs and aspirations to non-offenders is used to help residents become part of the community and so recognising how we may feel in their position is paramount.

Over the following weeks more residents joined the community as recruitment increased, some coming from the assessment unit and others direct from other prisons. The gradual buildup of membership meant that there was constant revisiting of the principles of a DTC and explanation of the reasons for the structure of the day. It was vital that a community was developed with a shared vision and joint responsibility, rather than being staff-driven or having unexplained rules imposed. Opportunities were given to learn from mistakes and develop a pro-social culture. Applying democracy in prison was not without its challenges, as some new residents viewed it as an opportunity to do what they wanted rather than what was needed for the greater good of the community. Staff found themselves representing positive and negative authority figures and role models as to what would be expected in therapy. Many of the residents held strong offence-supportive attitudes and found it particularly difficult to be challenged by their peers. It took many months (March 2010) until there were enough residents to form small groups and so during that time there were daily community meetings, which evolved into a safe place to explore interpersonal difficulties and challenge offence-supportive beliefs.

Topics for discussion included their offences, their reasons for engaging in therapy, the extent to which they were integrated within the wider establishment, when they could start to go onto the main exercise yard with other wings and so forth. The decision was taken by the lead therapist (in line with his Institute of Group Analysis training) not to commence small groups until the resident numbers increased sufficiently to introduce five groups with a minimum of five residents each. This model creates a buffer zone for potential loss of membership in the early development of a group. Once there were enough residents to form five groups there would be one group per week and four community meetings, following the pattern on the assessment unit, in order to help the residents to get acclimatised to therapy. This early structure also enabled staff to mirror the assessment unit's initial psychometric assessment of new recruits who had come directly onto the wing, bypassing the assessment unit.

As numbers increased there were three therapy groups per week and two community meetings, as is the pattern in the other communities at HMP Grendon. During the early groups it took time for residents to feel safe to discuss their childhood and offending history, and to tolerate this being feedback to the community. In a DTC it is essential that all aspects of therapy are kept in the open and all groups are feedback to the wider community. Following a therapy group the community meets and hears a summary of the content and dynamics of each group in order to ensure that all are aware of current issues and who may need additional support. This process also helps in the gradual dismantling of criminal values (developing a fundamental sense of belonging and connectedness with others; see Needs, this volume) that extends to beginning to identify with one who informs. It took some time to develop the culture in which it was recognised that by feeding back more detail from the small therapy groups those in other groups would be in a better position to offer support to each other and make decisions when voting for job applications, jobs as representatives and so forth.

Later, when a Fantasy Modification Programme (Akerman, 2008) was ran on another wing, involving a resident from G wing, they found it difficult to understand why this was fed back, as at that stage they had not yet been involved with other core creative psychotherapies, such as psychodrama or art therapy, groups which would have been fed back to the wider community. However, it evoked useful discussion about why groups are fed back; each question raised enabled the reasoning behind all aspects of the DTC model to be explained and emerging situations were used to learn from. The feedback allowed the discussion of sexual thoughts and fantasies, a topic which had been difficult to raise in a new community. It also led to discussion about the importance of recognising the similarities in different offences, rather than marginalising sexual offending and fantasy.

## Developing the enabling environment

In his seminal paper, Haigh (2013) comments on the requirements of a healthy environment in which a healthy personality can develop; such an environment includes:

- Healthy attachment and sense of belonging
- Containment and feeling safe
- Communication and a sense of openness
- Involvement and inclusion/citizenship
- Agency and being empowered

Haigh highlights how an enabling environment seeks to redress the balance of previous loss, neglect and deprivation and thus the DTC aims to help residents to understand the impact these experiences have had on them and to be a reparative experience. He highlights the importance of the first contact with potential residents and staff, as this can have a major impact on the subsequent relationship.

One particularly poignant memory from the emerging new community was when a new resident moved to the wing, having transferred directly from a dispersal (i.e. high security) prison. He came into the wing with all his belongings in clear bags, and was taken to a group room, where the officers checked through the bags to ensure that they contained no prohibited items. The resident stood to attention in the middle of the room, having just stepped off the prison transport (fondly referred to as a 'sweat box') with his arms folded. On entering the room the first author introduced herself, welcomed the resident to the wing and suggested he sit down and have a cup of tea while this process was completed. He looked distinctly alarmed by this. On reflection, he could have been uncomfortable at being watched by a stranger while his personal belongings were being searched, and how shaming this process may seem. However, the new community member seemed to take it in his stride. As new residents joined the community their suspicion and mistrust was often apparent. Many Grendon residents speak of their confusion when they are met by uniformed staff when they arrive in reception, and introduced by their first names, as in another prison setting this would not happen. This can evoke suspicion and lead them to feel unsafe rather than what is intended.

## Essential components of a DTC

The need for containment and tolerance for the expression of primitive emotions (such as rage, infantile pain, despair) characterises the DTC. In other settings within the prison system such emotions would meet with censure and punishment, whereas in a DTC such emotions are processed and validated, such that they no longer become overwhelming and in need of enactment. Residents are encouraged to describe their negative thoughts, not put them into action. In addition the DTC provides the play space (Winnicott, 1965) in which new ways of being and relating can be explored and mistakes can be made and learned from. It is important that this happens within a structure with clear rules for the resident to rile against and feel contained by. Having open communication helps residents challenge states of paranoia and persecution, enabling them to see reality rather than their anxious perceptions. Importantly, it also allows them to learn tolerance for not knowing and surviving in a grey area, which can be terrifying at times (Akerman & Geraghty, 2015).

The all-encompassing nature of the DTC provides a rich environment in which to learn how residents live with others (the living-learning experience) (Cullen, 1994, p. 239) and provides many opportunities to explore how they communicate with others. It is also important for residents to overcome their resistance to examining their thoughts, feelings, and behaviour in such minute detailed issues which they often view as unimportant and transitory. The need for agency and empowerment is also paramount. If the residents take shared responsibility for decisions they feel more of a sense of ownership for how their life in the DTC progresses. In addition desistance theory (e.g. Maruna, 2001) highlights the importance of developing an image of self with a crime-free future, "the need to develop a pro-social identity for themselves ... understand and account for their past and understand why they are 'not like that anymore'" (p. 7). Later, Maruna and Mann (2006) emphasised the importance of an individual taking responsibility for their own behaviour and making good, through instilling optimism and hope; cornerstones of a DTC.

## Psychological characteristics of prisoners on G wing

As part of the process of assessment men complete a battery of psychological tests to assess their characteristics, suitability for treatment and so forth. As stated previously some residents went directly to the new wing, whereas others transferred from the assessment unit. As is the case on the assessment unit a number of men who transfer to Grendon would be unsuitable for therapy for a number of reasons. They may want to return to where they came from, finding that it is not what they expected. Alternatively, they could be found not suitable for a number of reasons (lack of motivation, not being willing to explore their behaviour, etc.) and so be returned to their sending establishment. It was noted that the residents who went directly to G wing had a higher mean score than the other groups on the Personality Assessment Inventory (PAI) (Morey, 1991). The PAI is a self-administered, objective inventory of adult personality designed to provide information on critical clinical variables. The responses on the RXR scale indicated that they were the least motivated to engage in treatment.[1] Another important finding was that residents who went directly to G wing had higher scores on the PAI Antisocial Features and PAI Aggression scales compared to residents who spent time on the assessment unit first (prisoners who went directly to G wing had similar scores to those who were transferred/or returned to their sending establishment (especially on the Antisocial Features scale).

Unfortunately, these results were not available at the time of allocation as they were completed on G wing. Finally, those who were transferred or returned to their sending establishment (returned to unit, RTU) were more tough-minded and less likely to portray themselves in an unrealistically favourable light compared to those who stayed.

## Trauma within the community

The wing was rocked on 1 August 2010 when one resident murdered another. This was the first time such an incident had happened since Grendon opened in 1962. The subsequent police investigation resulted in the conviction of the perpetrator and was followed by a Public Inquiry and the inquest into the death (Prisons and Probation Ombudsman for England and Wales, PPO, 2013), a process which took a further three years. In the immediate aftermath of the murder, as the community was still in its infancy, there were residents who found it difficult to maintain their change and would not comply with police enquiries and so they were transferred back to their sending establishment. Other than these seven men, three other men were returned to their sending unit for being deemed unsuitable (which is in line with the assessment unit at HMP Grendon) and three were transferred for other reasons. Three residents were temporarily transferred to the assessment unit for their own safety as they had agreed to give evidence to the police. One of these three would later decide it was unsafe for him to return to therapy and therefore he was transferred to a prison of his choice. The other two returned to the wing and continued with their therapy.

In the immediate aftermath of the murder, community meetings were held with the express aim to engage the community in mourning the death of one of its members and the loss of others through the described transfers. Other residents and staff spent many years working through the trauma this event had on them. It provided an opportunity for some residents to experience the aftermath of such an event, which they may have not experienced. Some had given evidence against the assailant, again evoking powerful emotions and helping them develop empathy for those who had been in a similar position in relation to their offences. The murder had a profound and long-term effect on residents and staff throughout the establishment and was the subject of sensitivity meetings and supervision for many years afterwards. Much thought was given to how and if it could have been prevented. Recommendations made by the PPO, which are on public record, were incorporated into practice throughout the establishment.

Following the murder it took a while for processes on the new community to return to their familiar pattern. The loss of residents was felt and dynamics changed initially, with fear and mistrust felt by staff and residents. Much thought was given as to how to work through the tension between residents, staff and the two groups (see Lewis, this volume, for further discussion on managing ruptures in relationships). The resonance of not knowing why the murder had happened and what had been missed was ever-present and caused a deep wound in the community and establishment. Residents began to speak of how they were affected by the murder in their community as well as the possible effects on the local communities of those they had offended against – something most residents had 'not given thought to before'; this proved cathartic. As each issue was processed (for instance by those who had witnessed the murder, those who had tried to prevent the incident and death, those who had been close to the assailant, or those concerned about others having murderous fantasies) and discussed, tension reduced gradually. Some months later, there was collaborative work with some of the 'first to arrive on scene' residents and staff using the Mental Health in-reach service within the prison for the residents and external CBT services for staff. Services were held to commemorate the life of the victim, and events such as the trial and inquest reminded the community of the tragedy and were discussed as and when they occurred, and the resulting emotions processed.

Unsurprisingly the early months following the murder evoked difficult emotions for those most traumatised by the murder, namely extreme fear, distress, anguish, anger, rage and shame (Rosenbaum & Varvin 2007). There were limits as to how much DTC treatment could help in some cases, where the episode was seen as linked inextricably to the setting that was intended to foster change. Some of the requests from residents for transfer were through lack of trust of the therapists on the wing. Such emotions, though usually experienced by residents in treatment in Grendon, were intensified by the traumatising experience of the murder. Despite this the community continued to develop, albeit scarred by the experience. A further milestone was one of the first men leaving, having completed 18 months of therapy. Much of the literature relating to Grendon highlights the need for a minimum of 18 months as a requirement of joining. Whereas on other established communities it is clear to see that few residents have achieved their treatment goals by that time, in a community where no such role models were present this was not evident. The resident concerned applied to leave, as is the process, and though he was given feedback by other residents that there was further work that he needed to undertake he remained adamant that he was leaving, which he did. This process helped others who had thought they would be ready to leave at the 18-month stage to see that this may not be plausible and most others remained longer than that.

## Conclusion

It is very difficult to know where to end a chapter describing an entity which is still developing and evolving. The full documentation of the experiences of trauma in the aftermath of the murder cannot be made here and are perhaps for another chapter, but needless to say the resonance remains with the residents and staff. There were many notable landmarks in the developing of the new therapeutic community, for instance, the open disclosure of offences and seeing this being supported and empathised with, the writing of the first wing constitution, the commencement of small groups, the murder and response to it, the first DTC Prison Service and TCTC Audits and Peer Reviews in early 2011 (which had been postponed from December 2010), the first resident leaving having 'completed' therapy and so forth. Since its inception the wing has undergone a great deal of change but continues to work effectively, with all of its original members having left HMP Grendon at the time of writing. The core creative psychotherapies of art therapy and psychodrama are now firmly established. Some residents have gone on to less secure conditions and are working towards their release, others have been released and continue to thrive in the outside community and one has become the father of twins, while sadly others have breached license conditions and so returned to custody. As would be expected with men with such profound complex needs, there is no guarantee that time spent in a DTC would have long-lasting effects. Therefore, there is continued need for exploration of the impact of the context of treatment in addition to the ongoing support they receive as they progress further, as discussed elsewhere in this volume. That said many ex-residents remain in contact with Grendon, informing of their progress and maintaining their attachment to the establishment. The chapter was written in order to help others beginning such an endeavour see some potential highs and lows, and to share what we have learned.

## Note

1  However, the Treatment Rejection scores are low for all three groups; a score of below 43 suggests that the individual acknowledges major difficulties in their functioning and perceives the need for help in dealing with these problems.

## References

Akerman, G. (2008). The development of a fantasy modification programme for a prison-based therapeutic community. *International Journal of Therapeutic Communities*, *29*, 180–188.

Akerman, G. (2010). Undertaking therapy at HMP Grendon with men who have committed sexual offences. In E. Sullivan & R. Shuker (eds.), *Grendon and the Emergence of Forensic Therapeutic Communities: Developments in Research and Practice* (pp. 171-182). Oxford, UK: Wiley.

Akerman, G. (2011). Offence paralleling behaviour and the custodial good life at HMP Grendon. *Forensic Update*, 104, 20–25.

Akerman, G. (2012). Sexual offenders, offence paralleling behaviour and how it relates to risk. *Forensic Update*, 105, 17–24.

Akerman, G. (in press). Communal living as the agent of change. In D. Polaschek, A. Day & C. Hollin (eds.), *The Wiley International Handbook of Psychology and Corrections*. London; New York: Wiley.

Akerman, G., & Geraghty, K. (2015). *Tolerating the Intolerable: Working with Transference and Counter Transference to Toxic Material in a Prison-Based Therapeutic Community*. Paper presented at the Division of Forensic Psychology annual conference. Manchester Metropolitan University, 1-3 July.

Bowlby, J. (1979). *The Making and Breaking of Affectional Bonds*. London, UK: Routledge.

Brookes, M. (2010). Putting principles into practice: The therapeutic community regime at HMP Grendon and its relationship with the 'Good Lives' model. In E. Sullivan & R. Shuker (eds.), *Grendon and the Emergence of Forensic Therapeutic Communities: Developments in Research and Practice* (pp. 99–114). UK: Wiley.

Cullen, E. (1994). Grendon: The therapeutic community that works. *Therapeutic Communities*, 15, 301–311.

Dowdswell, H., Akerman, G. & Lawrence (2010). Unlocking offence paralleling behaviour in a custodial setting - a personal perspective from members of staff and a resident in a forensic therapeutic community. In M. Daffern, L. Jones & J. Shine (eds.), *Offence Paralleling Behaviour* (pp. 231–243). UK: Wiley.

Genders, F. & Player, E. (1995). *Grendon: A Study of a Therapeutic Prison*. Oxford, UK: Oxford University Press.

Gilbert, P. (2010). *The Compassionate Mind. A New Approach to Life's Challenges*. London, UK: Constable.

Haigh, R. (1999). The quintessence of a therapeutic community: Five universal qualities. In P. Campling & R. Haigh (Eds.), *Therapeutic Communities: Past, Present and Future*. London, UK: Jessica Kingsley.

Haigh, R. (2013). The quintessence of a therapeutic community. *Therapeutic Communities: The International Journal of Therapeutic Communities*, 34, 6–16.

HM Prison Service (HMPS) (2003). *Democratic Therapeutic Communities: Core Model Theory Manual*. London, UK: HM Prison Service.

Jones, L.F. (2004). Offence paralleling behaviour. In A. Towl & G. Towl (Eds.), *Needs: Applying Psychology to Forensic Practice*. BPS. Oxford, UK: Blackwell.

Jones, M. (1946). Rehabilitation of forces neurosis patients to civilian life. *British Medical Journal*, 1, 533-535

Jones, M. (1952). *Social Psychiatry: A Study of Therapeutic Communities: A New Treatment Method in Psychiatry*. New York, NY: Basic Books.

Jones, M. (1968). *Social Psychiatry in Practice: The Idea of the Therapeutic Community*. Harmondsworth, UK: Penguin.

Marshall, P. (1997). A Reconviction Study of HMP Grendon Therapeutic Community, Home Office Research Findings No. 53. London, UK: Home Office Research and Statistics Directorate.

Maruna, S. (2001). *Making Good: How Ex-Convicts Reform and Rebuild Their Lives*. Washington, DC: American Psychological Association.

Maruna, S. & Farrall, S. (2004). Desistance from crime: A theoretical reformulation. *Kolner Zeitschrift f ur Soziologie und Sozialpyschologie*, 43, 171–194.

Maruna, S. & Mann, R.E. (2006). A fundamental attribution error? Rethinking cognitive distortions. *Legal and Criminal Psychology*, 11, 155–177.

McNeill, F. (2006). A desistance paradigm for offender management. *Criminology and Criminal Justice*, 6, 39-62.

McNeill, F. (2014, May 23). Three aspects of desistance? [Web log post]. Retrieved from http://blogs.iriss.org.uk/discoveringdesistance/2014/05/23/three-aspects-of-desistance/.

Morey, L.C. (1991). *Personality Assessment Inventory – Professional Manual*. Lutz, FL: Psychological Assessment Resources, Inc.

Morris, M. (2004). *Dangerous and Severe: Process, Programme and Person: Grendon's Work*. London, UK: Jessica Kingsley Publications.

National Offender Management Service (NOMS) (2013). Democratic therapeutic communities in prisons. Accredited Core Model Theory manual.

Newcomen, N. (2013). Prisons and Probation Ombudsman for England and Wales, PPO (2013). *A Report by the Prisons and Probation Ombudsman Nigel Newcomen CBE, Investigation into the death of Mr. Robert Coello at Stoke Mandeville Hospital on 1 August 2010, while a prisoner at HMP Grendon.* Unknown location: Author.

Rapoport, R. (1960). *Community as Doctor: New Perspectives on a Therapeutic Community.* London, UK: Tavistock.

Rich, P. (2006). *Attachment and Sexual Offending: Understanding and Applying Attachment Theory to the Treatment of Juvenile Sexual Offenders.* Chichester, UK: John Wiley & Sons Ltd.

Roberts, J. (1997). How to recognise a therapeutic community. *Prison Service Journal,* 111, 4–7.

Rogers, C. (1993). *A Therapist's View of Psychotherapy: On Becoming a Person.* UK: London. Redwood Books.

Rosenbaum, B. & Varvin, S. (2007). The effects of extreme traumatization on the body, mind and social relation. *International Journal of Psychoanalysis,* 6, 6–17.

Shine, J. & Morris, M. (1999). *Regulating Anarchy: The Grendon Programme.* England, UK: Springhill Press.

Shine, J., & Newton, M. (2000). Damaged, disturbed and dangerous: A profile of receptions to Grendon Therapeutic Prison 1995–2000. In J. Shine (ed.), *A Compilation of Grendon Research* (pp. 23–35). Leyhill Press. Available HMP Grendon. Grendon Underwood, Aylesbury, Bucks HP18OTL.

Shuker, R. & Newton, M. (2008). Treatment outcome following intervention in a prison-based therapeutic community: A study of the relationship between reduction in criminogenic risk and improved psychological well-being. *The British Journal of Forensic Practice,* 10, 330.

Shuker, R. & Sullivan, E. (Eds.) (2010). *Grendon and the Emergence of Forensic Therapeutic Communities in Research and Practice* (pp. 186–201). Chichester, UK: Wiley-Blackwell.

Stevens, A. (2010). Introducing forensic democratic therapeutic communities. In R. Shuker & E. Sullivan (Eds.), *Grendon and the Emergence of Forensic Therapeutic Communities in Research and Practice* (pp. 7–24). Chichester, UK: Wiley-Blackwell.

Sullivan, E. (2010). Reflections on Grendon: Interviews with men who are about to leave. In R. Shuker & E. Sullivan (Eds.), *Grendon and the Emergence of Forensic Therapeutic Communities in Research and Practice* (pp. 186-201). Chichester, UK: Wiley-Blackwell.

Taylor, R. (2000). *A Seven Year Reconviction Study of HMP Grendon Therapeutic Community, Home Office Research Findings No. 115.* London, UK: Home Office Research, Development and Statistics Directorate.

Tilley, N. (2000). Realistic evaluation: An overview. Paper presented at the Founding Conference of the Danish Evaluation Society, September.

Ward, T. & Gannon, T. (2006), Rehabilitation, etiology, and self-regulation. The good lives model of rehabilitation for sexual offenders. *Aggression and Violent Behaviour,* 11, 77–94.

Ward, T. & Stewart, C.A. (2003). Criminogenic needs and human needs: A theoretical model. *Psychology Crime and Law,* 9, 125–143.

Warren, F., Preedy-Fayers, K., McGauley, G., Pickering, A., Norton, K., Geddes, J.R. & Dolan, B. (2003). Review of treatments for severe personality disorder. Home Office Online Report 30/03. Retrieved from https://bulger.co.uk/prison/reviewtreatsseverePD.pdf.

Whiteley, S. (2004). The evolution of the therapeutic community. *Psychiatric Quarterly,* 75(3), 233-248.

Winnicott, D.W. (1965). *The Maturational Process and Symbolic Play.* London, UK: Hogarth Press.

Yalom, I. (1980). *Existential Psychotherapy.* New York, NY: Basic Books.

# 9

# PSYCHOLOGICALLY INFORMED PLANNED ENVIRONMENTS

## A new optimism for criminal justice provision?

*Nick Benefield, Kirk Turner, Lucinda Bolger and Claire Bainbridge*

Optimism for the rehabilitation of serious offenders and those individuals who have complex psychosocial problems is generally in short supply, not only in Britain but across the world. The administration of justice, and the relationship between it and the psychosocial status of those in need of change, is a real tension. Two key factors need to be brought together: firstly the essential nature of a collaborative strategy between professionals in the health and justice services, and secondly, the recognition that people are deeply affected, both positively and negatively by the conditions and environments in which they live their lives.

In the case of the criminal justice system in England and Wales, this requires both the health and the justice system to recognise the value of trained and managed environments in which offenders are living. The implementation of the Joint NHS and NOMS (National Offender Management Service) Offender Personality Disorder Strategy (NHSE, 2015) is providing a programme to meet the first of these needs. The development of models for providing improved psychologically informed living is, as part of this strategy, being developed through the implementation of a specified design for Psychologically Informed Planned Environments (PIPEs) in prison and Approved Premises (AP) (probation hostel) settings. If we are to have a new optimism about improvements to the rehabilitation of those at greatest risk of serious offending, then this strategy and the roll out of a network of PIPEs offers hope for change that can be evaluated.

This chapter is intended to open the discussion on the conceptual understanding of the roots of this work, and how PIPEs are being developed and tested. It also represents the beginning of a longer and wider debate about effectiveness in response to an individual's personality, character or psychological make-up as they challenge societal expectations.

## Context and the psychosocial background

The ideas and theories that underpin the concept of a PIPE are not new. Rather, these developments are a reformulation and restatement of previous work, which focused on trying to understand more about our internal life and its relationship to our thinking and behaviours. The emotional, psychological and developmental nature of who we are, based on the development of psychological, social and psychoanalytical research into human development, is the foundation of the theory base for the development a PIPE model to be tested in the field. In research terms these conceptual frameworks remain hypothetical but will continue to be tested, through the development of practice models and their evaluation.

The PIPE model continues to evolve, for example by being introduced at different stages of the pathway, and therefore is subject to review and adaptation based on the experience of implementing a new model of practice. The design, development and early field-testing of this model formed a core part of the NHS/NOMS Offender Personality Disorder (OPD) Pathway programme. The core aim of this joint strategy was to design and implement a system for addressing the needs of offenders who posed a high risk of harm to others, who were likely to have a personality disorder and where there was a clinically justifiable link between their personality difficulties and their offending.

At the time of the development of the new OPD strategy, a number of offenders were nearing the end of their treatment within the Dangerous and Severe Personality Disorder (DSPD) services, and it was clear that a progression pathway was required. Some of the offenders in these intensive treatment services had been resident for five years or more, and over that time many had made use of what was on offer to them, taking the risk of engaging in treatment, and importantly, in establishing relationships with others. Moving from such contained and psychologically informed environments back to an ordinary prison wing often presented a hugely challenging experience, and for many of these offenders, progress they made in DSPD services was at risk of being lost, or undermined, when placed back in an environment where staff were not trained to understand their difficulties from a psychological perspective. Designing a progression service where staff were trained and supported to understand the offender's complex needs, and therefore better able to support them in maintaining and implementing what they had learned, became paramount.

The PIPE model, as it is now understood, was deemed to 'bridge the gap' in service provision, and go some way towards supporting the development of a 'pathway' of interventions for offenders likely to have personality disorder (Benefield et al., 2015). It was considered to be a service that could provide key support for offenders between other significant elements of their rehabilitative journey such as treatment, or release to less secure environments including the community. With time however, it is a model of working that has the potential to be developed in a broad range of both residential and community settings, in order to facilitate and manage the psychosocial development of children and adults in public, private and third sector services.

The reduction of risk and anti-social behaviour rightly remains one of the primary outcomes of the collaborative initiative between the NHS and NOMS, via the OPD Programme. As part of the response to this, the PIPE model is predicated on the belief that psychosocial stability, and the development of a more mature, personal and social life, are essential elements to affect the long-term outcome of the treatment and rehabilitation of offenders. This requires exposure to better relational experience on which to model future lifestyles and identities.

## Attention to a continuous relational environment

The outcome of individual psychosocial development in humans is undoubtedly facilitated or inhibited by the conditions the environment provides, irrespective of culture, psychological or social context. The environment in this context is considered to include physical, emotional and social provision from the earliest stages of life, even pre-natal, and involves both the genetic and psychosocial legacy of parents. At the heart of this environmental provision is the qualities and failures in the primary attachment between the person and important others (Bowlby, 1965).

The chronic deprivation of good enough conditions, where there is exposure to persistent and high levels of stress, uncertainty and anxiety, and a failure to be protected from serious or repeated trauma, is a significant factor in adults who present as persistently asocial. Relational experience, in particular the availability of consistent, boundaried and non-judgemental, age-appropriate support is essential. The impact of a stable period of pro-social living and social experience is thought to support longer term psychosocial stability. Much of human development can be seen in the context of environmental settings in which the interaction between the individual and their external world finds optimal conditions for attachment, growth in learning, emotional literacy, adult psychological capability and pro-social interdependent living (Winnicott, 1965a).

## Environments: establishing enabling and facilitating conditions

To go some way in meeting this need within institutional settings, the provision of a developed, psychosocially informed environment requires that the training, skills, experience and supervision of staff groups is more focused. Thinking in a psychodynamic way about the meaning of behaviour and how a relationship is best managed is vital if the value of daily relational work is to be maximised. It acknowledges a complex interaction, both internally in ourselves and in our relationships with others and is focused on understanding of the interactive nature of emotional and psychological life in which we, and the other person, play a part. Attention to all relational exchange and group dynamics, and their potential to both support and undermine psychosocial growth, is essential.

For every individual, the boundary between the internal and the external world is a continuous interaction between ourselves and others at both conscious and less conscious levels of thinking and feeling. This exchange never stops, but we can manage the interface to protect and support our internal emotional stability, personal psychological safety and sense of ourselves as a separate but secure person.

The outcome of these exchanges will either support or undermine well-being and stability, dependent on the degree of emotional vulnerability or resilience of the individual. To achieve the best of relational life we need the support of a facilitating and enabling environment in which the conditions for satisfactory emotional development are met to a 'good enough' level (Winnicott, 1965a).

This theoretical stance is drawn from a long history of environmental approaches, spanning almost a century. Key contributions from the work of William Tuke, Homer-Lane and others (Kennard, 1983) explored and tested in practice the use of the environment for the treatment of those with complex needs, difficulties and mental illnesses echoed by the social psychiatry approaches of Maxwell Jones (Jones, 1962) and Robert Rapport (Rapport, 1960). These novel approaches sought to treat and care for a wide range of complexities in society, working with post-revolution orphans, maladjusted children, those with learning difficulties and mental illness, and more recently those with personality disorders and those who have committed criminal offences.

For many offenders the nature of their life course means significant periods of poor quality emotional life or living experience, often involving failed or destructive relationships, in particular the absence of a sufficiently continuous and consistent period of primary attachment. This need for a sufficient period of secure attachment to another person is crucial; it provides conditions in which the capacity to think, rather than react, and the resultant ability to reflect thoughtfully on events and provide extended periods of internal stability are made possible.

The degree to which individuals are able to tolerate and process the intimacy and vulnerability of such an attachment relationship can be limited by a fragmented or damaging experience of development. In this sense, any managed environment needs to provide an experience of daily living that models and supports better quality, secure relating (Winnicott, 1965a). Through effective communication and negotiation, the needs of the individual and their conscious and unconscious reality can be more closely understood and attended to.

Within a criminal justice setting, offenders and staff can be affected by the environment in a way that is either a satisfactory psychological experience or can re-enforce asocial modes of relating. The management of the day-to-day, 24/7 nature of life in this setting, including its culture, customs and operational arrangements, can therefore either support or undermine the capacity for thought or reflection. How a prisoner is locked into or let out of a cell, how they are fed, how daily minute-by-minute interactions are managed and how communications are understood can offer the opportunity for positive relational experience. Administering the necessary constraints of security without dismissal or 'disrespect' offers the core challenge in creating and managing the environmental experience and providing opportunity for positive rather than negative learning. At its heart this approach requires a level of awareness, understanding and thoughtful response to the psychological and emotional state of the other person.

In the context of a pathway of treatment and rehabilitation, the provision of environments that provide conditions to counter a risk of deterioration and instead support progression are essential. It is important therefore that we understand what is meant by the concept of a good relational environment. By this we mean a setting that can provide:

- Relationships that are consistent and reliable, to support the principle of secure attachment where this capacity is otherwise fragile (Dethiville, 2014).
- Support for the appropriate stages of psychosocial skills and capability in the individuals and social groups involved (Erikson, 1950).
- Interpersonal interactions and responses that support the emotional and psychological processing of experience (Winnicott, 1965b).
- Protection from unreasonable levels of impingement that will cause prolonged or high levels of anxiety beyond the capacity of the individual to manage (Winnicott, 1965b).
- Facilitation of the capacity for thinking, reflection and action as opposed to feeling and reaction.
- Living arrangements and activities that are supportive of individual well-being and pro-social relating (Makarenko, 1951).
- Organisational structures and expectations that support thinking and emotional management in patients/offenders and the staff groups (Menzies-Lyth, 1970).
- A setting in which actions are informed by conscious psychological thought in planning and acting in the environment thereby establishing 'smoother' management of psychological/emotional life (Winnicott, 1965b).
- Support to acknowledge the failure or lack of 'fit' between environmental realities and individual need (Winnicott, 1975).
- A setting where leadership consciously, actively and authoritatively protects the boundary from the disruptive impingement of the conditions for psychological thinking (Kennard, 1983).

Whilst these environmental conditions are comprehensive, many of them can be particularly challenging to implement and maintain in the criminal justice setting. In seeking to achieve better conditions for relationship work to flourish, the aim is to provide a 'good enough' rather than ideal situation (Winnicott, 1975). A 'good enough environment' is where efforts to model and communicate are sufficient to create the experience that the environment is facilitative and enabling to the individual, rather than lacking in emotional and psychological understanding. In effect, what is sought is a sense of the appropriate 'good enough fit' between the person and their world. In such a 'fit' the total environment facilitates the individual to go on 'being' without recourse to earlier, more primitive defences against anxiety and threat.

## Creation of a 'good enough' framework

The task at the heart of the PIPE development required the design of a well-informed, psychosocial environment, which focused on the overall provision of living or relating experience.

Designing a specification to promote the creation of a 'good enough' environment led to the development of a set of principles that informed the PIPE design:

1.  The PIPE maintains its intention to support personal and relational experience.
2.  Staff are always involved in making meaning from everyday interaction.
3.  The PIPE actively supports communication, exchange and dialogue.
4.  The importance of relationships is recognised and acknowledged.
5.  PIPEs support thoughtfulness and thinking.
6.  The PIPE encourages choice, appropriate to the person's capacity.
7.  The PIPE recognises the importance of interdependence.

Translating these conditions into operational practice requires a model that offers a framework for service providers that is not too restrictive, whereby the spirit of the PIPE approach is not lost within existing organisational cultures and practices. It became apparent that specific core components, consistent to all PIPE services, were needed to provide structure and guidance to the pilot sites, and to promote a system level of understanding of the PIPE approach.

Six sites were identified to undertake the original pilot of the model, two prison wings for adult men, two for women and two services in Approved Premises. At a later stage a seventh service became operational, testing the model in the high secure prison estate. Each of these contrasting settings had to be borne in mind when developing the overall service model, with sites following an outline specification for the pilot phase.

The ingredients of the PIPE model needed to present opportunities to support staff to grow in competence and confidence as well as make meaning of their experiences, supporting them to understand the context of the relationships they were creating and managing. It was also important to take into account how it would best support those offenders making a transition after a long period of treatment without destabilising them, but rather supporting the consolidation and generalisation of their work so far. This application of the model, now referred to as 'Progression PIPEs', provided the first opportunity for an evaluation of the model in practice.

Periods of transition are often regarded as difficult for those living with personality disorder, with NICE guidelines for borderline personality disorder (NICE Guidance, 2009) making specific references to managing endings and periods of transition. As discussed earlier, in their early lives offenders were often not provided with a safe enough environment to attach securely to another person. In these situations, attachments to others can grow slowly and with a great deal of wariness. They can relatively easily suffer a relational rupture, and therefore attention to the process of joining and leaving was particularly important to keep in mind.

It was clear that some of the relational opportunities the model needed to offer would not necessarily occur naturally in the given contexts, which tended to operate on rigour and rules. It was important therefore that any artificially created relational opportunities felt safe and contained and would not contradict the host organisation's rules and protocols, enabling the services to approach these opportunities with confidence.

As designed and designated environments, PIPEs are required to operate on the basis of being a 24/7 environment in which all activities are opportunities for growth and individual learning. A PIPE therefore operates in the context of maximising the ordinariness and relational richness of institutional life. They do not intend to remove all unhelpful experience that human beings come into contact with on a day-to-day basis and those living in a PIPE are required to go out into activities or employments where, as with the outside world, no special support is provided. The PIPE conditions only exist in the PIPE setting itself, the wing or hostel, and not in other environments in the institution or community. The service therefore needs to support any capacity within individuals to operate in different environments by using the supporting experience of PIPE life as a more reliable emotional foundation for the experiences of the wider world.

A PIPE is not a defined treatment intervention but rather a stage in a treatment pathway that supports specific treatment interventions. It aims to create a consistently 'pro' rather than 'anti' social relational world where positive verbal exchange and negotiation can be modelled. Additionally, parallel behaviours can be observed and explored. It is important that the staff group seek to develop conditions that balance environmental demands with a realistic assessment of the emotional capacity of their population.

## The primary task of a PIPE

All of the components that constitute a PIPE need to work together to consider the holistic needs of both the individual and the environment, and work collectively towards the primary task of the environment itself. Rice (in Miller & Rice, 1967) defined the primary task as "that task that the organisation must provide for the organisation to survive" (p. 62). In the case of a PIPE, in order to survive it must provide a stable residential setting in which the focus on individual and group interaction aims to establish conditions that facilitate pro-social relating. It is essentially a change of attitude and culture in staff and residents which creates a sustainable, therapeutic, social setting. Delivery of these elements, through the core components, requires a critical set of conditions and operational requirements:

- A distinct physical setting protected from boundary incursion and organised to discourage (unhelpful) institutional behaviour and expectations.
- A consistent staff group, psychosocially trained and supervised, the baseline requirement being KUF (Knowledge and Understanding Framework) awareness level training, enabling environment training (see below) and ideally basic group work skills.
- Enhanced staff numbers dependent on offender numbers aimed at providing time and availability for more attentive relating and individual time between staff and residents.

- Clinical and operational leadership, directly on the frontline, carrying joint responsibility for the delivery and maintenance of the PIPE regime.
- Provision that is based on a 24/7 design.
- Organisational buy-in to the development of a culture which challenges institutional and subcultural behaviour.

## The PIPE core components

### 1.   An enabling environment culture

One component of an enabling environment (EE) is the requirement for the residents and staff to come together to facilitate discussion and decision-making, so it was considered important that all sites introduced this as a central aspect of PIPE life. This required a consistent and reliable relational foundation with a clear rationale that could be easily understood by those living and working in the PIPE, and those in the wider organisation.

**The enabling environment** – the enabling environment (EE) process, developed by the Royal College of Psychiatrists, focuses on the social and relational aspects of the environment embodied in ten service standards, described by Haigh, Harrison, Johnson, Paget & Williams (2012) as follows:

1. Belonging
2. Boundaries
3. Communication
4. Development
5. Empowerment
6. Involvement
7. Leadership
8. Openness
9. Structure
10. Safety

The EE standards seemed to capture the essence of what it was hoped to achieve with the PIPE 'milieu', and were established as a core component within the PIPE model. They support PIPE services to think about the whole environment, how staff and residents come together to talk and think about their experience and their environment, promoting a collaborative approach to decision-making. However, in order for the PIPE to be truly psychologically informed, the model needed to incorporate planned intentional ways of naming unconscious processes. Staff training and supervision go some way to help with this, as well as the extra frontline staffing resource allocated to PIPEs. In addition to this however, it was considered important to have staff available to 'be' around offenders; the PIPE is a relational model, and by definition this requires an opportunity to relate.

In the context of institutional life it is possible to plan, consciously think about and determine how the environment operates so that it facilitates learning and growth rather than reinforces asocial and emotionally destructive behaviours.

Offenders who have lived on a PIPE have talked about what they have learnt from watching a member of staff model an appropriate way of dealing with a difficult situation: "I didn't realise until that point that there was an alternative way to react to someone shouting at you; I thought you either walked away and let them win, or got aggressive back. But he (officer) didn't do that; he talked to him calmly, and listened to what he had to say, and they talked it over and it was sorted".

## 2. Workforce development & training

It was clear from the beginning that the model would require a significant workforce development component, in particular focusing on psychological awareness, and this would only be effective if supported by consistent and regularly delivered clinical supervision.

The overall approach to training needed to flexible and responsive to each PIPE setting, but contain some core elements relating to the understanding of personality disorder and the expected elements of a good quality relational environment. The Knowledge and Understanding Framework (KUF) provides a consistent level of awareness training for PIPE staff to improve their understanding of personality disorder and therefore work more effectively with their offender population. In addition, training from the Royal College of Psychiatrists as part of their enabling environments process, as described above, was also delivered as an essential requirement for PIPE staff. Training and development remains a focus for all new and established PIPEs, with Clinical Leads devising bespoke local packages to facilitate on-going staff development, as well as accessing other nationally available training.

## 3. Supervision

The development and containment of the staff group is a core task for any PIPE service, not only promoting psychologically informed practice but providing vehicles for making sense of the interactions, experiences and relationships they encounter. A group analytic supervisory model was incorporated into the PIPE specification to promote and facilitate the staff team's thinking about the PIPE as a whole, dynamic environment. This is enhanced by regular one-to-one supervision of staff by the local Clinical Lead. Brown (2014) explains the supervision process within PIPEs as follows.

> The emphasis of the supervision is on the relational level from both a conscious and unconscious perspective, on what happens as people come together, on what is happening in the individual key worker sessions, in the groups and in the whole group; the PIPE itself. External influences are also considered from a systemic and group process perspective. (p. 346)

Clinical observation indicates that those offenders who have successfully completed PIPEs appear more able to retain their capacity to insert thinking between impulse and action; to sustain positive and helpful relationships, to talk about their feelings, address conflict and more appropriately seek help. (p. 350)

Once staff members have a mechanism for making sense of their experiences, through training and supervision, the next focus for PIPE services is the consideration of the wider environment and the development of a planned and structured milieu.

## 4.   A 'socially creative' approach

As part of the provision of opportunities for relating on the PIPE, 'socially creative sessions', initially referred to as the 'creative' sessions, were incorporated into the model to offer increased opportunities for residents to come together and work on a group task.

This coming together as a group can be challenging for people who have a diagnosis of personality disorder as "being with others feels habitually so overwhelming that they avoid social contact" (Turner, Lovell & Brooker, 2011, p. 342). This research suggests that "participating in creative and arts-based social activities offers a level of stimulation that distracts people from the pain of 'being together'" (p. 342).

The groups commonly focus on life and social skills and can also offer support to applications such as the Good Lives Model (Ward & Brown, 2004). For an observer, it may seem that each participant is creating their own piece of work (e.g. a personal greetings card for a family member) but they are doing it alongside their peers and importantly alongside staff. Thwarted and deprived experiences (both in childhood and as an adult) have meant that many PIPE residents have reduced competencies in many areas that most would take for granted. Enhancing life skills (such as cooking, gardening, sewing, hygiene) and social skills (coming together to engage in activities such as team sports, debates, music) allow all members of the community, staff and residents, a sense of achievement through shared activities. These sessions orchestrate a shared sense of belonging through coming together to participate in *ordinary* pursuits that otherwise may lie outside of the experience in a custodial setting.

The focus on 'creativity' can provide offenders with an avenue for self-reflection, which can be less threatening than traditional therapy and treatment. Turner et al. (2011) suggest that:

Understanding how 'artworks' relate to one's own and others' lives uncovers hidden layers of meaning which add a richer dimension to these exchanges. Being able to acknowledge the thoughts and feelings arising in a space that does not feel alienating reinforces this sense of connection and well-being, promoting the acceptance and mutual support which lay the foundations for a 'relationship' to grow – with both the self and with the 'outside' world. (p. 342)

The opportunity to be together as a community is an important aspect of the PIPE model. An explicit intention of the model is to maximise ordinary experience, and 'bring the outside in', for life inside prison to replicate life outside as much as is possible. This is important for a number of reasons: for the initial progression PIPE pilots, offenders needed to 'test' their new skills in an environment that was supportive, but also provided challenges. For this reason competition is often an element of the socially creative sessions. In addition to this, offenders and staff have to tolerate activities alongside people they would not ordinarily choose to mix with, and this may challenge them to manage their reaction in a pro-social way. Anecdotally, both prisoners and staff had told one of the authors (LB) that this has enabled them to see people in a new light, and to address their misconceptions.

Other activities can be whole PIPE events, for example the women in one prison PIPE organised events to raise money for ovarian cancer, and allowed for group members to be involved at all stages of the event, from planning and organising, advertisement, baking cakes and participation in a sponsored walk.

The social-creative sessions are arguably the most challenging of all the components, particularly with regards to engaging, stimulating and offering 'experiences' to diverse groups of men and women, a significant amount of whom present with complex needs. Supporting staff to manage the tension between 'wearing two caps' (that of custodian and 'carer') is a key challenge in delivery of the shared task. Equally there is a tension between the objectives of creating and providing new, relationally sound experiences for the residents in PIPEs, whilst also considering the levels of acceptability for activities that are present in the criminal justice system. Supporting the components to work together, by ensuring the experiences of staff in these activities are made sense of through supervision, is essential for this kind of activity to be effective.

## 5. Developing a key worker relationship

Tolerating frustration and difference of others, as well as learning that many of the people around you will step in to support you if you learn how to ask for help, are valuable lessons for life outside of the prison or AP. Regular key worker, or personal officer, sessions within the PIPE provide an opportunity for staff to explore in more detail some of the behaviour they have witnessed on the PIPE, and are another a core component of the model. They help offenders manage issues related to transition, fitting in, addressing unmet treatment needs, and achieving personal goals in a pro-social way. This relationship is an important one as it provides an opportunity for the offender to connect more closely with another person. This has been described by Wilmot and McMurran (2013), whose research into the treatment for offenders with personality disorder noted that "the majority of change processes described by participants were behaviours of other people outside formal therapy sessions" (p. 604).

In order to help offenders aim for appropriate, positive and pro-social goals, the PIPE model incorporates the Good Lives Model (GLM) and the key worker sessions are often the vehicle for this. Purvis, Ward and Willis (2011) described the GLM as a "strength-based rehabilitation framework that is responsive to offenders' particular interests, abilities and aspirations" (p. 6) Personal officer/key worker sessions further promote the relational emphasis of the PIPE model. They provide an opportunity to connect with another in a genuine relationship that can have relevance to both parties, as one PIPE prisoner summarised, "we worked well together, and developed a good and trusting relationship, even when I didn't like what he was saying".

Personal officers/key workers help offenders identify a few key goals and enable them to work towards them, for example participation in educational activities, personal hygiene, planning progression and engineering a sense of agency and independence during custody. Essentially these sessions can provide the conditions for relational security to thrive and on some level begin to allow reparation for attachment pathology within the 'good enough' facilitating environment.

The key worker session is an integral component of the model, drawing together the other strands of thinking and experience and bringing it to the present context, the here and now. This could include an officer or hostel supervisor working with the resident over a long period of time, building confidence to take part in some of the socially creative activities being delivered, jointly, collaboratively making sense of the PIPE experience together, a form of co-production.

## 6. Structured provision

Paying attention to the relationship between the individual and their treatment pathway also requires particular attention in a PIPE. Delivery of 'structured sessions' provides one of the more formal aspects of relational exchange within the PIPE setting, and can be tailored to respond to the needs of the resident population and the group as a whole.

The core aim of these sessions is to provide a planned and structured opportunity to consider current issues that relate to the offender's pathway and criminogenic need, and their life experiences to date, for example disruption, loss and separation. The sessions aim to promote talking and thinking together and to develop emotional and psychosocial confidence and competence. Structured sessions provide an opportunity to address thematic issues arising in the group, allowing residents to share their experiences with peers in a formal, structured and contained setting.

As mentioned earlier, it is known that the type of offenders coming to the PIPE may have difficulty with change, in particular with transitions. In addition to this many will not have been in any kind of employment for some years, including prison industries. Structured sessions often include a focus on 'transition' to enable offenders to cope with change, for example their change in role from long-term group participant to prisoner at an ordinary location or from being in custody to living in the community.

The group also offers an opportunity to develop some identification with the purpose of the PIPE. This is particularly important for those individuals who have chosen to opt out of other opportunities for social interaction on the PIPE. For those arriving from an environment where they have been accustomed to intensive group support, the group can aid transition by providing a consistent group setting, yet without the therapeutic dynamic they may be familiar with.

## *Summary of PIPE components*

Providing the overall framework for delivery of a 'good enough' psychosocial environment, all of the core components of the PIPE model, described above, need to be present within the setting, ensuring that they are suitably planned, psychologically informed and considered holistically as an approach, each one complementing the delivery of another. The six core delivery components of a PIPE are summarised as follows:

- An enabling environment foundation
- Training and workforce development
- Supervision
- Socially creative sessions
- Key worker sessions
- Structured sessions

## Putting the requirements into operation

It is probably fair to say that the development of the initial PIPE services was 'organic', in that PIPEs evolved over their first few years of operation – and continue to do so. Whilst the early specification work had formed the essential frame of the core components, this had sufficient flexibility to be introduced in a way that was meaningful for that particular PIPE, the local circumstances, the population and cultures.

One advantage of this approach was that the PIPE did not have to manage an unsuitable framework imposed upon them, and the principles of involvement and participation could be reflected in the creation of the services itself. What was experienced as a disadvantage at the time was that there was not always an immediately answer to exactly how sessions should run, or how experiences would be offered. Decisions and dilemmas had to be talked over, worked through and learnt from and fed into the growth of the service and its developing milieu.

In time, as patterns emerged, it was possible to develop a consistent implementation plan to support new PIPEs, which highlighted the stages each PIPE had to go through in order to be 'fully operational'. This plan introduces the structures and critical ingredients that need to be established, introducing the components in a considered manner to best support the cultural growth of the service, one which is focused on the process, as opposed to the content.

Establishing and protecting the physical location of the environment is one of the first requirements, and has the greatest impact on the viability of the developing PIPE. In order to meet this need and to mitigate against boundary incursion, the PIPE should be housed on a discreet unit or, in the case of a hostel, encompass the entire facility (Turley, Payne & Webster, 2013).

Whilst the actual physical layout and construct of the PIPE is arguably less important than the relational aspects, it was considered that a protected boundary facilitates safe relating. Examples of this include the offenders feeling safe enough to eat together, something that some residents had never experienced. PIPEs should also aim to develop spaces for staff and offenders to sit comfortably and have conversations with each other, and spaces that support group processes and interactions.

In all cases to date, PIPE services have integrated into existing physical environments in hostels and prison wings. These vary in size, with the largest being 60, and the smallest 14. The size of the PIPE at each level will be a balance between the organisational and physical operation of the institution and the optimum numbers to allow for personal relational exchange. In therapeutic settings, although 100 participants can be considered, daily interpersonal relating and community management indicates optimally around a maximum of 20 to 30 participants will encourage engagement (Jones, 1962). This requirement will be a challenge in current prison settings, particularly with wings up to 60 in size. Group size matters in terms of complexity of group dynamics and the sheer availability of time and staff for relational working and this will need to be understood where group sizes are larger. The larger services need to pay particular attention to this dynamic, considering how voices can be heard and needs met with a larger group.

In addition to the physical conditions, a further essential early task is to assign the right people to the job. The PIPE needs to be 'held' by a committed leadership team who can develop a shared view in what needs to be delivered, and who are prepared to challenge existing ways of working, and manage the risks of trying new ones. It was clear from the beginning, and has been borne out over time, that the leads for PIPE services (Implementation Lead, Strategic Lead, Operational Lead and Clinical Lead) to a large extent make it what it is. In order to offer continuity and containment to the service, a two-year commitment was required from those involved, noting the challenges in the frequency of moves within senior staff in the host organisations. The principle of creation of authentic joint leadership however, between clinical and operational leaders, is one of the most critical factors in successful implementation of a PIPE. The promotion of joined up thinking, in this case between two different professional disciplines, supports the implementation of the principles of delivery for the OPD Pathway. It also provides the containment and reassurance to both staff and offenders in adopting a different way of thinking and operating together.

Linking the organisational pieces together, the Clinical Lead role required a blend of strategic thinking, clinical expertise and personal authority. As the role began to develop it was apparent that some of those external to the PIPE struggled to identify this role as anything other than 'wing psychologist' or 'consultant' to the team. In contrast, the role of the Clinical Lead is to manage and lead the environment/milieu. A number of experienced disciplines are potentially suited to the post of Clinical Lead in a PIPE, not limited to psychologists. In all cases however, a developed clinical skill set, established over a number of years post-qualification, experience of working with offenders and significant personal authority have shown to be essential. In the creation of the environment, considering this as a whole system, the Clinical Lead needs to operate at a macro level, with the service as its 'client', in contrast to working individually with offenders. This requires always holding in mind the core relational task of the PIPE, and promoting this in others through training, supervision, full integration into the service as a member of the frontline team, and active consideration of the psychosocial aspects of its delivery on a day-to-day basis.

Identifying and establishing the PIPE staff team had its challenges. Whilst some services, particularly the prisons, were in a position to identify and assess the staff most appropriate for adopting this way of working, this was not always possible in the Approved Premises. Often entire existing staff teams had to be brought into the idea of adopting a new way of working. In all cases working to establish relationships within newly formed multi-disciplinary teams, and providing opportunities for staff to make sense of their experience of this change was important.

There have been a striking number of occasions where staff have shared their astonishment at how being given time to get to know offenders, including increased time to read case notes, deliver activities and share experiences, can throw new light on why an offender may behave in a particular way. This awareness can enable staff to better understand what drives and motivates the offender, and consequently enable the member of staff to facilitate change. An important part of this process is often the development of empathy and compassion as staff begin to understand in more detail why an offender 'chooses' to react in a certain way. It is not however a job that all staff feel is suited to them, and through the pilot phase it was acknowledged that the PIPEs need to consider how to support staff who felt unable to work in this way. This support might include additional training and additional supervision, but it might be that in time the conclusion is reached that their working style or personality is not suited to working in a PIPE setting.

In response to leading, modelling and supervising all PIPE experiences, it was clear that those in the Clinical Lead role needed an appropriate space themselves to understand the psychological and group processes that were present. A national clinical governance structure was therefore developed, including a regular 'business' meeting where PIPE Clinical Leads from across the country meet to discuss current issues. In addition, a group analyst consultant was provided to deliver a regular and parallel process of supervision with clinical leads. This process has been critical to the development of PIPE cultures and is described in detail by Brown (2014). As the number of PIPE sites has increased these processes have been protected and maintained, having been identified as a mandatory part of the delivery of any PIPE.

National and regional forums and networks for operational and strategic leads have also been established as part of the Offender Personality Disorder Pathway programme.

## PIPEs in practice in the Offender PD Pathway

The initial specification for the piloting of PIPEs in prisons and Approved Premises focused on testing a 'Progression' application PIPE model in two very different settings: a closed institution and an open community setting of a hostel. Early research findings into the enabling features of PIPEs (Turley et al., 2013) highlighted that a key enabling factor within a PIPE was the establishment and maintenance of safe and supportive relationships between staff and residents, taking into account the availability of staff and the role of mutual respect. The research study, which looked into the early phase of PIPE developments, also reported the positive and enabling impact of taking a collaborative approach and the central role of formal and informal activities within the model. It concluded that the approach needed to be supported by a consistent, committed and well-informed staff team, highlighting the key role of the PIPE Clinical Lead in supporting and developing staff.

With both research and anecdotal evidence supporting the application of the PIPE model, the refinement and development of the model continued, with all sites operating to one core consistent model of delivery, applied in different settings. More recently work has begun to consider the application of the model at the 'Preparation' phase of an offender's pathway, prior to treatment activity, but also the residential 'Provision' application supporting offenders who are undertaking treatment.

### Preparation PIPE

The 'Preparation' application of the PIPE model is aimed at preparing offenders for treatment, and the management of the transition to a treatment setting. This is to provide a living experience which offers exposure to, and expectation of, pro-social relating, where talking is encouraged and acting out discouraged. It is an introduction to the language, thinking and likely psychological demands of a psychosocial treatment service. Its objective is to help residents achieve treatment readiness. Whilst we expect that demand from within the prisons will be high, selection to a Preparation PIPE requires careful consideration to ensure that the mix of offenders remains stable and safe enough. It will at times need higher levels of management intervention for the group to maintain the ethos of the PIPE against lower levels of identification with a psychosocial environment.

### Provision PIPE

Provision PIPEs are run alongside treatment programmes and are designed to support and enhance treatment goals. As with all models, the Provision PIPE provides a 24-hour-a-day lived experience, although offenders often undertake their treatment elsewhere in the establishment, coming back to the PIPE at the end of the day.

## Progression PIPE

Admission to Progression PIPEs is only on the basis of the completion of an intensive treatment programme, or significant development within a sentence plan. The progression experience seeks to encourage more active and independent participation in the organising of PIPE life, with the objective of testing and consolidating acquired psychosocial relationship skills acquired in treatment.

## Premises (community rehabilitation) PIPE

In the OPD Pathway, Approved Premises provide the essential step-down residential facilities from custody to community. However, the nature of their intake can challenge their capacity to meet the core criteria for becoming a PIPE. The key difference is the control on admissions being tied to post-intensive intervention. In addition, not all residents will fit the OPD Pathway criteria of high risk of offending, although currently some AP PIPEs are working with the NPS senior managers to help them prioritise men and women on the OPD Pathway. Within this context, the integrity of the environment requires a high level of skill and commitment from the staff group who, more than in other settings, will need to actively create and protect the PIPE conditions.

## The development of PIPEs

With the interest and number of PIPEs continuing to grow, working to protect the fidelity and the essence of the PIPE model now becomes the new focus. Working with challenging populations, particularly in the preparation phase, will test all aspects of the model, including the resolve and resilience of staff groups as well as of the offenders themselves. Being exposed to new, and in turn challenging, experiences will require considerable containment and support. The same can be said of the PIPE services as they are being rolled out, with central leads needing to ensure that services continue to share experiences and make meaning out of these to inform planned responses and approaches. The development of service standards for PIPEs is the logical next step within the PIPE journey, translating the critical elements, described above, into measurable standards that can be applied in all settings.

Capturing the spirit and essence of a PIPE in practice is no easy task, however it remains critical for the future and success of the services. Five years into service delivery, a range of experiences to date have been captured and reported on, with the national evaluation of the services due to report in 2017. Following the initial evaluation of the PIPE pilot (Turley et al., 2013) described above, further detailed studies and papers have emerged. These include consideration of PIPEs in the high secure prison estate (Preston, 2015), resident expectations (Bennett, 2014), PIPEs in Approved Premises (Castledine, 2015) and the experience of officers working in a PIPE in a lifer prison establishment (Bond & Gemmell, 2014). Complementing these papers is a growing suite of local, at present unpublished, studies that consider the changing social climate, staff knowledge, and understanding offender transition. These studies can only ever go part of the way in describing the changes to the lived experience of the men and women engaged in PIPE services.

In the delivery and development of the appropriate conditions for supporting growth and development of a complex offender population, PIPEs are moving one step closer to the provision of a 'good enough' experience, for those living and working within them, and offer some optimism to the rehabilitation of offenders, their reduction in risk of reoffending and the improvement of their psychological health and well-being.

## References

Benefield, N., Joseph, N., Skett, S., Bridgland, S., d'Cruz, L., Goode, I. & Turner, K. (2015). The Offender Personality Disorder Strategy jointly delivered by NOMS and NHS England. *Prison Service Journal*, 218, 4–9.

Bennett, A. (2014). Service users' initial hopes, expectations and experiences of a high security psychologically informed planned environment (PIPE). *Journal of Forensic Practice*, 16, 216–227.

Bond, N. & Gemmell, L. (2014). Experiences of prison officers on a lifer Psychologically Informed Planned Environment. *The International Journal of Therapeutic Communities*, 35, 84–94.

Bowlby, J. (1965). *Attachment and Loss*. New York: Basic Books.

Brown, M. (2014). Psychologically informed planned environment (PIPE): A group analytic perspective. *Psychoanalytic Psychotherapy*, 28, 345–354.

Castledine, S. (2015). Psychologically informed and planned environments – A community perspective. *Probation Journal*, 62, 273–280.

Dethiville, L. (2014). *Donald W. Winnicott: A New Approach*. London: Karnac Books.

Erikson, E.H. (1950). *Childhood and Society*. New York: Norton.

Haigh, R., Harrison, T., Johnson, R., Paget, S. & Williams, S. (2012). Psychologically informed environments and the 'enabling environments' initiative. *Housing Care and Support*, 15(1), 34–42.

Jones, M. (1962). *Social Psychiatry in the Community, in Hospitals and in Prisons*. Springfield, IL: Charles Thomas Springfield.

Kennard, D. (1983). *An Introduction to Therapeutic Communities*. London: Jessica Kingsley.

Makarenko, A.S. (1951). *The Road to Life*. Moscow: Progress Publishers.

Menzies-Lyth, L. (1970). *The Functioning of Social Systems as a Defence against Anxiety, Tavistock Institute of Human Relations Pamphlet No. 3*. London: Tavistock Institute of Human Relations.

Miller, E.E. & Rice, A.K. (1967). *Systems of Organisation: The Control of Task and Sentient Boundaries*. London: Tavistock Publications.

NHSE (2015). The Offender Personality Disorder Pathway Strategy 2015. www.england.nhs .uk/commissioning/wp-content/uploads/sites/12/2016/02/opd-strategy-nov-15.pdf.

NICE Guidance (2009). *Borderline Personality Disorder Guideline, No. 78*. National Collaborating Centre for Mental Health. London: British Psychological Society.

Preston, N. (2015). Psychologically Informed Planned Environments (PIPEs): Empowering the institutionalized prisoner. *Forensic Update*, 117, 7–14.

Purvis, M., Ward, T. & Willis, G.M. (2011). The Good Lives Model in practice: offence pathways and case management. *European Journal of Probation*, 3(2), 4–28.

Rapport, R. (1960). *Community as Doctor*. London: Tavistock Publications.

Turley, C., Payne, C. & Webster, S. (2013). Enabling features of Psychologically Informed Planned Environments. *Ministry of Justice Analytical Series, NOMS*, 1–47.

Turner, K., Lovell, K. & Brooker, A. (2011). '… and they lived happily ever after': 'Recovery' or discovery of the self in personality disorder? *Psychodynamic Practice*, 17(3), 314–346.

Ward, T. & Brown, M. (2004). The good lives model and conceptual issues in offender rehabilitation. *Psychology, Crime & Law*, 10, 243–257.

Wilmot, P. & McMurran, M. (2013). The views of male forensic inpatients on how treatment for personality disorder works. *Journal of Forensic Psychiatry and Psychology*, 24(5), 594–609.

Winnicott, D.W. (1965a). *The Family and Individual Development*. London: Tavistock Publications.

Winnicott, D.W. (1965b). *The Maturational Processes and the Facilitating Environment*. London: The Hogarth Press.

Winnicott, D.W. (1975). *Through Paediatrics to Psychoanalysis*. London: The Hogarth Press.

# 10

# DEMOCRATISATION, DISABILITY AND DEFENCE MECHANISMS

## Reality confrontation in Rampton

*Jon Taylor*

## Introduction

In his powerful book, *The Lucifer Effect* (2007), Philip Zimbardo describes the complex array of psychological, situational and social factors that can influence individual behaviour. Drawing on his work in the Stanford Prison Experiment and his subsequent investigation into the abuse of prisoners at the Abu Ghraib prison in Iraq, Zimbardo provides compelling evidence for the potential influence of the social context. Although it is not unique to highlight the role of environmental factors in determining individual behaviour (stimulus–response psychology is based directly on the relationship between external factors and individual responses), Zimbardo offers a unique insight into the subtle interaction of the social setting, the group dynamic and the individual, suggesting in his conclusion that individual responsibility may be mitigated by the culture of their setting.

Secure psychiatric hospitals offer a fertile base for the Lucifer Effect. As total institutions (Goffman, 1961), the bulk of the patient experience takes place within the secure perimeter. The experience of dining takes place alongside the same group who share employment, sleeping and *medication time*. Neighbours in a psychiatric ward have the same doctor and the same psychotherapist, the same personal trainer, the same banker and the same teachers. The residents of a psychiatric community don't choose their menu, nor do they have the opportunity to switch their bank account. Their experience of the Internet is often closely supervised, while the smart watch remains a distant fantasy.

In short, the life of a secure psychiatric patient bears little resemblance to a *community* life. Yet hospitals claim to offer recovery, a range of experiences that support the individual to return to a non-psychiatric group. And recovery is supported by a plethora of structures that pretend to operate outside of the psychiatric system to defend the patient from Lucifer's grasp. Advocacy has become an industry that offers sanctuary for patients but can also inhibit open dialogue, foster dependence, facilitate splitting and undermine patient assertiveness. Simultaneously, the emergence of safeguarding and complaints systems, whilst intended to offer protection for the vulnerable, can inadvertently promote bullying and intimidation, of both staff and patients, as a side effect of this protection and support of the vulnerable (Taylor, 2012). Neither advocates nor safeguarding officials intend harm; yet the systems allow for harm. And while recovery is evident and researchers strive to demonstrate their evidence, the Lucifer Effect remains a consistent and persistent bedfellow.

This chapter describes an attempt to introduce difference into an institutional culture. In this instance this involved the development of a democratic therapeutic community (DTC) within a high secure learning disability setting. The chapter outlines the background to this development before describing the inception of the model. The clinical characteristics of the men who went to live on the TC are described along with some early outcome data. The chapter concludes with a reflective and personal account of the challenges and dynamics that developed around the TC.

## Background

Rampton Hospital is one of three high secure psychiatric hospitals in the UK, the trinity being completed by Ashworth and Broadmoor. The hospital provides a national resource for men with a learning disability who require care and treatment in high security. All admissions to the hospital have to meet specified criteria: an individual must present a grave and immediate danger and suffer from a mental disorder as defined by the Mental Health Act. For men with a learning disability, there is no other secure hospital provision in England and Wales that is able to accommodate this level of risk. As a consequence, the National High Secure Learning Disability Service (NHSLDS) caters for men with a diverse range of clinical needs.

As part of the relocation of the service to a purpose-built 48-bed (four wards) facility in June 2010, a comprehensive review of the clinical service model was undertaken. A treatment model for the service was developed on the basis of the clinical characteristics of patients and, with the exception of a generic assessment ward, the remaining three wards were designed to provide clinically sensitive inpatient settings. All men admitted to the hospital would first reside on the assessment ward for a period of six months or more with their subsequent transition to a treatment ward being decided by the multi-disciplinary formulation developed during this assessment phase. One of these treatment wards, Cheltenham, was identified to provide a treatment milieu for men with mild learning disability and severe personality difficulties. The treatment milieu was based on the DTC model developed at HMP Grendon and was simultaneously a precursor to the development of prison-based TCs for prisoners with a learning disability.

Men who were referred to Cheltenham had the opportunity to test out the model prior to transfer. A liaison nurse and a liaison patient would provide anyone referred to the ward with relevant information, answer questions and attempt to manage pre-transfer anxiety. The testing would then involve attendance at community meetings for a period of at least four weeks along with opportunities to join in with social activities taking place on the TC. Although this referral process was developed prior to the opening of the TC it was nevertheless reviewed by community members on a number of occasions and revised in light of experiences for both the community and newly admitted men.

In order to support the referral process a number of key admission criteria were also established. Again drawing on the model operating within the prison service, men referred to the TC were generally likely to have prominent personality difficulties (defensive reactions to trauma), needed to be able to participate in group work (as seen in the testing-out period), be relatively free from active psychotic symptoms (or managed effectively by medication) and show some degree of emotional and behavioural stability. In reality, these criteria were guidance rather than absolute, and pragmatic decisions about bed occupancy often had to be prioritised over clinical criteria. Nevertheless, the process of referral and admission was respected, allowing for a welcoming arrival based on the formation of relationships rather than a simple transition.

## Introduction of the TC

The decision to open a TC was taken in January 2010, with the opening due six months later in June of the same year. As has been mentioned, an assessment service and two other treatment functions were to be opened alongside the TC and a new model for multi-disciplinary working was being introduced alongside these developments. The service was undertaking a considerable metamorphosis, not just in terms of the fabric of the buildings but also in respect to the ambition for treatment delivery and patient care.

The ambition to develop and deliver a high-quality service for offenders with complex mental health difficulties and a learning disability had been planned for many years prior to the move to the new buildings. As the final hurdle was cleared, however, a new challenge was presented alongside what was already a considerable ambition: financial cutbacks (misleadingly and euphemistically labelled as cost improvements). The solution to financial pressures was envisaged to be the merger of directorates within the hospital, with the learning disability service being joined to the mental health service. The irony of this merger would not be lost on anyone who was familiar with the work of Wolfensberger (1984) or O'Brien (1981), both of whom had been highly influential in shaping learning disability service before the millennium. However, the impact of such a merger was clearly unknown at this stage and whether it would prove to be complimentary or complicating (or cost improving) would only become clear in time. What was clear, however, was that the merger created a pairing in which *mental health* outnumbered *learning disability* at a ratio of about 3:1. The voice of the learning disability service was therefore both diluted and marginalised and any democratisation of decision making within the new service was prejudiced in favour of *mental health*.

Discussions about the treatment model for the new service were undertaken by senior clinicians over an extended period of time. To the authors' knowledge, the final decision about the treatment model was taken by a senior clinical group and was shared with staff at an unveiling in January 2010. A this point the opening of a TC was made public, though at this stage neither the staff team nor the patient group had been identified for any of the wards.

When the ward opened six months later, the staff team had all *volunteered* to work on a TC. The voluntary nature of staff selection was pragmatic; all members of the nursing staff identified two clinical areas that they would like to work in and each was allocated to one of these. The patients were allocated according to clinical presentation. The men who were identified to live on the TC were those who presented with dominant personality disorder traits, had demonstrated some degree of treatment resistance and had gained little from the range of treatments that had been traditionally available. Allocation to the TC was therefore also pragmatic for the patients; to some degree the men who moved to live on there had exhausted other options.

The January meeting stimulated a plethora of activity in the service. For the TC there were a number of agreements designed to support the ward staff, including recurring half-day awareness sessions, visits to prison TCs and training in group work skills. Approximately half of the nursing team were supported to visit prison TCs and five staff were released from duties to attend a half-day awareness raising session. Unfortunately, no other training took place prior to the TC opening. It is therefore perhaps reasonable, if not more than reasonable, to say that there were no culture carriers within the residential staff team and very few within the wider professional groups when the TC opened. There was enthusiasm in abundance and a healthy slice of cynicism, but the ability to model, demonstrate and carry the culture and core principles was significantly compromised.

Patients and staff were instead socialised into the model over a 6- to 12-month period. A range of typical TC practices were introduced over time, with two community meetings and two small therapy groups, reflective staff groups and whole community activities taking place each week about a year after the ward opened.

In order to support the development of a therapeutic culture and support nursing staff to deliver the therapy groups, four psychologists were directly involved in the running of the TC. Furthermore, due to the care model developed across the new service, three consultant psychiatrists and three distinct clinical teams were involved with the patients who lived on the ward. In other words, with the exception of the nursing team, there was little continuity in relation to the patient–professional relationships across the TC. The sense of communalism was perhaps more akin to a foster home than a family home.

## Working and living on the ward: the community

Thirteen men went to live on the ward at the beginning of June 2010. Approximately 35 members of a nursing team joined them, along with three clinical teams. Although there was a wealth of experience of working in forensic LD settings, there was almost no experience of working in TCs. Indeed, there was greater experience with TCs amongst the patient group than the staff group with some of the men having experienced prison TCs prior to transfer to hospital.

The men who moved on to the TC had a range of difficulties and presented a number of challenges to the embryonic culture. The clinical characteristics of the men have been described previously in some detail (Taylor, Morrissey, Trout & Bennett, 2012) and are therefore not repeated here. However, in the context of forensic TCs it is pertinent to note a number of characteristics. First, the men were all sectioned under the Mental Health Act (1983) and were therefore detained in order to receive treatment. Their active consent, and indeed voluntary participation in a milieu treatment, was not required and indeed had not be obtained prior to the opening of the unit. Second, a significant proportion of them men had never engaged in group-based treatments and most were highly ambivalent about all treatment. Early engagement on the various groups that took place on the community was poor and only half of the men attended groups in the weeks and months after the TC opened. Third, by definition all of the men residing on the TC suffered from a mental disorder as defined by the Mental Health Act and their mental disorder was of sufficient severity to warrant detention in order to receive *medical* treatments. Many of the men had been diagnosed with serious mental illness, including both psychotic conditions and major mood disorders. Similarly, many of the men presented with personality traits of such magnitude that they would traditionally have attracted a diagnosis as psychopathic.

Nevertheless, despite the challenges inherent in the difficulties experienced by the men, and despite the challenges experienced in the preparation of the TC, the formal structures were introduced over time and the men and the staff team gradually became increasingly involved in their community. The TC opened with two community meetings taking place at each end of the week with all members of the multi-disciplinary staff team present. The only exception to this was for the Responsible Clinicians who, for pragmatic reasons around timetabling, did not take part in any community groups.

Small therapy groups were introduced approximately four months after the community meetings had started. Psychologists were allocated to each small group in order to support ward-based staff in group facilitation, with the intention being to reduce the level of psychology input as the TC developed. The original model allowed for the men on the TC to continue to access a range of therapeutic programmes that took place outside of the community group (for example sex offender treatment). Over time the plan was to increase the number of small groups running on the TC, thus removing the need for men to engage in treatments outside of their peer group.

Reflective meetings for the staff group took place after each of the community groups. As well as allowing time for the staff team to process the group sessions, this time became critical in the development of culture carriers within the staff group. These meetings enabled staff members to question the methodologies of the TC, express anxieties and begin to understand the practical implementation of Rapoport's (1960) four core principles. It could be argued that these meetings were the single most important aspect of the TC in the early days and it is perhaps unlikely that the TC would have developed into such a strong community without them.

Alongside the more formal therapeutic practices, the growth of a sense of belonging and communalism were fostered with whole community activities and shared mealtimes. Although there were challenges to both of these (see later), such shared experiences were considered crucial in the formation of respectful and containing therapeutic alliances.

## Living on the ward: early data and lived experiences

A central component of the plan that was developed to support the opening and implementation of a TC was a formal and rigorous evaluation of the impact of the model. Research funding was obtained and an independent psychology assistant was involved in all of the data collection and analysis. From the outset, the evaluation was designed as a mixed-methods project aiming to capture treatment effects alongside the more phenomenological experiences of the patients. Experiences of the staff team were similarly included in the evaluation, though the wider multidisciplinary team were not included.

In terms of the men who were resident on the TC, changes were apparent in three areas: engagement and readiness, sense of belonging and therapeutic alliances and clinical presentation. As mentioned previously, when the TC first opened attendance at the large group meetings was poor. It was not uncommon for a significant proportion of the men to refuse to join the meetings and a number of those who did join the meeting would nevertheless refuse to take part or leave early. To describe attendance as poor is, however, perhaps unfair and fails to respect the significant challenges inherent in group therapy for the first group of men living in a new and uncertain treatment model. The fact that attendance increased dramatically over the first six months offers some insight into the courage of the resident group and the ability of the nursing team to manage and contain anxiety. Within six months attendance was almost 100 per cent at both large and small group meetings. Furthermore, special meetings were called regularly at the behest of the men and a second small group per week was being planned. By the end of 2014 only two men had been moved off the TC as a consequence of their unsuitability (or the unsuitability of the treatment model).

The increased engagement with the formal therapeutic activity is perhaps best understood in terms of the men's changed perceptions of the ward culture. The men's perception of the ward culture was formally measured at six monthly intervals using the Essen Climate Evaluation Schema (Schalast, Redies, Collins, Stacey &

Howells, 2008). The EssenCES is a 17-item questionnaire designed to assess the social and therapeutic climate of forensic psychiatric wards. The scale was developed from research across 17 hospitals in Germany and identified a three-factor structure: Patients' Cohesion (PC), Experienced Safety (ES) and Therapeutic Hold (TH). Patients' Cohesion is the sub-scale that measures the overall attitude to the level of support and care they receive from peers and staff, as well as their ability to receive these. Experience Safety measures patients and staff's belief of how dangerous, aggressive or intimidating the ward can be, while Therapeutic Hold relates to the staff on the ward and their dedication and input into the care patients receive. A survey on 46 wards in UK High Secure Hospitals confirmed the original three-factor structure among both staff and patients (Howells et al., 2009; Tonkin et al., 2012). Repeated administration of the EssenCES (Bennett & Morrissey, 2013) indicated that the men gradually increased their sense of both experienced safety and patient cohesion, a change that is not insignificant given the complex clinical presentation of a number of the men living on the ward. Similarly, the perceived therapeutic hold of the TC improved over time and became increasingly aligned to the perception held by the staff team. Indeed, the findings from repeated administration of the EssenCES suggested that the culture of the ward was rated more favourably by the men living in the TC than had been found in both the Howells and Tonkin studies.

Notwithstanding these improvements in the *lived experience* of the patients, the modern NHS demands evidence of change in clinical presentation and psychopathology. The men who moved to live on the TC all presented (on average that is) with severe and enduring personality and psychiatric phenomena. Furthermore, they presented with significant criminogenic need and risk (Bennett & Morrissey, 2013). The men had all experienced serious trauma in their lives and had come to manage their trauma in ways that were damaging and harmful to others. In short, they presented with a complex and enduring array of clinical difficulties. In terms of the research hypothesis underlying the development of the TC and the evaluation of the clinical effectiveness of the TC, clinical changes were predicted in relation to risk, personality presentation and psychiatric difficulties. The evaluation of the TC indicated that clinical changes in the predicted direction were evident (Morrissey, Taylor & Bennett, 2012; Morrissey & Taylor, 2014), with the men showing comparatively less pathology both over time and in relation to a comparison group. However, change was more likely for internalising problems such as self-esteem, anxiety and depression, than for externalising problems such as violence and hostility. The mean number of violent incidents did not reduce over time, though there was nevertheless a strong trend towards a reduction in seclusion hours, with an increase in seclusion being observed in a comparison ward during the same time period. In a study investigating the effectiveness of the approach developed at HMP Grendon, Shuker and Newton (2008) found clinical and statistically significant change on a range of measures targeting offence-related risk and psychological health. Furthermore, for those men who remained in therapy for some time (i.e. over 18 months) the changes in psychological health proceeded change in offence-related risk. The authors argue that the two domains of treatment augment and support each other and lends support to the notion that psychological well-being may be viewed as a readiness or responsivity variable. The improvements in attendance at groups on the TC, alongside the improved experiences found in the EssenCES data, would seem to support Shuker and Newton's theory and suggests that the men who were living on the ward responded to the treatment milieu, at least in the early days, by developing more robust self-esteem.

In a follow-up study (Morrissey & Taylor, 2014), further clinical changes were evident amongst those men who had remained in treatment. After two years, nine patients continued to live in the TC (three had progressed to less secure conditions and one had moved within the service). Self-rated personality disorder traits, maladaptive schema relating to personality disorder, and clinician rated psychopathy (using the PCL-SV) were measured at the start of treatment, and after two years. There were significant reductions found in anti-social, schizoid and paranoid traits, and in schemas relating to entitlement, defectiveness, emotional inhibition and vulnerability. Clinician ratings of psychopathy did not change over time, though changes in the items rated using the PCL-SV were not anticipated.

Shifts in the perception of the ward culture were also observed within the staff team. Staff members were asked to complete the EssenCES within the first two weeks after opening and at six-month intervals up to and including 18 months after the opening of the unit, thus capturing data at four distinct points in time. Alongside the EssenCES, staff took part in focus groups and from the two data collection methods a number of themes emerged (Taylor & Trout, 2013). When the TC first opened the staff team expressed a certain amount of anxiety about the men due to the high levels of psychopathic traits, general levels of personality disorder and previous treatment failures. Furthermore, staff expressed concerns about their own ability to operate a TC. During focus groups staff spoke about the need to develop their own working practices (many of whom hadn't worked together before), and described concerns about their ability to contain large group meetings and anxiety in relation to the consequences of offence disclosures within the community. It was therefore notable that the repeated administration of the EssenCES showed a noticeable increase in the staff perception of patient cohesion.

A similar increase was found in the staff teams' perspective of Experienced Safety. Staff members identified key changes in their practice as critical to these improvements and cited positive ways of working, increased understanding of patient risk and having a more tolerant approach to patient behaviours (permissiveness). Staff members who contributed to the focus groups suggested that the increase in awareness of the men's risk, and particularly the ability of the men to self-regulate and discuss their risk, added to the sense of safety on the ward, and the use of the agenda to explore behaviour within a large group supported a move from managing risk-related behaviours to an exploration of risk-related behaviours.

Perhaps somewhat curiously, these positive developments amongst the staff team were not reproduced in relation to their perception of their care and treatment of community members. Taylor and Trout (2013) have suggested that staff perception of therapeutic hold may have reduced as a result of the willingness of the team to listen to feedback from patients rather than a real deterioration in nursing practice. Equally, of course, the more negative perception of self may have reflected an internalisation of the critical feedback directed towards the ward staff from hospital managers. Certainly a number of the EssenCES questionnaires were completed whilst the TC toiled under the threat of closure and repeated complaints about poor security-related practices, including allowing patients to express high levels of emotion (permissiveness).

The opening of a TC within the National High Secure Learning Disability Service was a substantial challenge for the staff group, the patient group and for the wider system. Concerns about balancing the need for security with the needs of therapy, and diverse and multiple demands at a time of significant change, formed a fragile foundation for a TC. However, both staff and patients described an increased sense of purpose, greater understanding and insight into risk, increased tolerance of more challenging and risk-related behaviour and improved relationships. Objective measures of internalising phenomena revealed overall improvements for the men living on the TC and the ward became a more peaceful and less violent living environment. As a context for the delivery, and indeed the receipt of treatment, such experiences provided a sense of optimism and encouragement for change and development. Nevertheless, despite these encouraging developments, there were a similar number of ongoing challenges experiences by the TC. The remainder of this chapter describes some of these challenges and attempts to offer some tentative hypotheses about their genesis.

## Phenomenology: bringing the individual experience to the group data

The (brief) summary of the data emerging from a two-year evaluation of the TC provided encouraging results and laid the foundation for similar services to be developed. A TC informed service was developed at Calderstones NHS trust for men with LD and PD and a medium secure service mirroring the treatment model on Cheltenham was opened by St. Andrews Healthcare in 2012. In parallel, a TC for prisoners with LD was opened at HMP Dovegate in January 2013 with a similar provision open at HMP Gartree a few months later. HMP Grendon, a unique prison in the UK custodial system, followed suit in January 2014. Nottinghamshire Healthcare Trust, the NHS organisation responsible for the delivery of services at Rampton Hospital, also won the contract to deliver the health components to two of the prisons operating TCs for prisoners with a learning disability.

In truth, however, albeit the kind of truth that emerges from an individual experience, the optimistic data concealed the challenges that faced the embryonic TC and disguised the courage and downright tenacity of the team who worked on the ward to cultivate a therapeutic community. A number of challenges had been predicted from the start: how the patient group would respond to a new treatment model, how the nursing team would respond to the more open reality confrontation that would be encouraged and how we could coordinate and integrate three

Responsible Clinicians and three clinical teams. There were other challenges that had been less anticipated, these being the responses that came from outside of the community rather than from within. Concerns about security were articulated from the outset. Reduction in seclusion rates was interpreted as a liberal and unsafe ward culture, while the processes that promote democratisation were seen as evidence that 'the lunatics had taken over the asylum'. When staff began to order bread so that patients and staff could eat toast together, concerns that hooch brewing was endemic were quickly used to halt any possibility of shared mealtimes.

Those challenges were certainly evident as the TC structures were slowly implemented. However, what wasn't anticipated was the political and/or organisational response that was directed towards the ward and the staff team working to implement the TC practices and philosophical principles.

Within the original proposal for a TC there was a clear intention to develop a high quality and empowering residential setting. To facilitate this proposal the standards developed by the Community of Communities, a quality assurance component of the Royal College of Psychiatrists, were used to guide the project and establish an objective quality measure. Membership of the Community of Communities was formally included in the proposal and active participation in the peer review cycle had been agreed. However, access to the Community of Communities was prohibited by senior managers during the first three years of the TC's development. In a meeting between the new nurse management team across the service and a selection of staff from the TC, one manager made his/her reservations about external scrutiny clear with the proverbial 'over my dead body' declaration. When it was finally agreed that the standards could be used to guide future development of the TC, the author was then instructed not to involve any of the patients. It is perhaps fair to say that the *Secret Hospital* felt prominent and dominant during this time.

However, despite the challenges involved in the various conversations concerning audit standards and peer reviews, perhaps the single biggest challenge to the ongoing growth of the community came from an internal investigation into the sustainability of the treatment model. On the back of the security concerns cited above and alongside a perception that there was a limited need for such a treatment (an insufficient number of patients with personality disorder), the new management team requisitioned a review of the TC. From the outset it was made clear to staff working on the community that there were three potential outcomes from the review. First, the TC could continue to operate in the manner outlined in the original proposal. In other words, the ward would remain a 13-bed DTC. Alternatively, the ward would be reduced in size and would function as a six-bed TC. The implication of this outcome would be that the nursing team would have been expected to run a TC on one side of a ward building and operate a different model on the other side of the building. The final possibility would see the TC closed.

If the irony of the review was not seen alongside the data that was being published (Morrissey et al., 2012), it was certainly evident as Rampton Hospital (in the form of Nottinghamshire Healthcare NHS trust) won the contract to provide the health component to two newly commission TCs for prisoners with a learning disability. A number of the posts included in the staffing complement for the prison TCs were filled by the trust through recruitment or by seconding staff who were already employed at Rampton. For many working on the TC at Rampton the trust's active promotion of its involvement in the prison TCs was hard to reconcile alongside the direct threat of closure for its own TC. To suggest that the two positions were uncomfortable bedfellows is a striking understatement.

## Disabling discourses

The experience of being involved in the opening of a TC in the National High Secure Learning Disability Service was multi-faceted. It was an invigorating and energising time. Both the staff and patients showed remarkable courage while many members of the wider professional group were both patient and encouraging. The evaluation of the service model and the positive findings emerging from the first two years was reward for the hard work and endeavour shown. The spirit of TCs, perhaps best captured in the concepts of empowerment, compassion and mutual respect, were strikingly evident.

It was perhaps these experiences, or rather the incongruence of these experiences with the reaction of the wider organisation, that formed the foundation for a sense of confusion, despondency and *madness* that accompanied the excitement and energy. And a certain amount of this energy was expended in the staff reflection and process meetings in an attempt to make sense of these incongruent experiences. The remainder of this section provides an overview of these reflections and offers some tentative hypotheses to make sense of the *madness*.

One concept that resembles the relationship that developed between the TC and the wider hospital is the process of malignant alienation described by Watts and Morgan (1994). In an analysis of risks facing patients who staff find difficult to like, Watts and Morgan highlight how the deterioration in relationships between and patient and others includes a loss of sympathy and support from staff. This separation of the patient from those around him or her is thought to be generated by a combination of patient characteristics and poor staff support. Whittle (1997) suggests that this process is particularly poignant in forensic psychiatric services as service users in these settings evoke particularly strong counter-transferential feelings as a consequence of both their psychiatric condition and their offending behaviour. Whittle goes on to argue that staff can struggle with their own feeling of disgust, shame and fear, but also with feelings of excitement. This struggle can then get cut off from the staff consciousness and projected into the patient who subsequently becomes increasingly marginalised. However, if we consider the process of malignant alienation at the level of the institution rather than at the level of the individual then perhaps the institution can separate itself from one if its constituent parts, particularly if the characteristics of that part are unpalatable to the institution. The practice of democratisation and tolerance were certainly described as unpalatable at times and the experiences of the TC in the wider service felt similarly alienating. The inquiry into the value and viability of the TC, followed by an inquiry into the findings of the inquiry, was unique to Cheltenham. The remaining wards in the learning disability service (and indeed in the wider learning disability/mental health service), faced no such inquisition and no other ward was repeatedly asked to justify its practices. In the context of understanding a process of malignant alienation, perhaps the TC was behaving in ways that the wider system could not tolerate and therefore the TC invited and evoked a hostile reaction. The TC narrative then became trauma focused and the more the trauma was told the more the wider system acted out the traumatising narrative.

If malignant alienation can take place within large systems and allow the dominant system to marginalise a sub-section or part of itself, then it seems equally plausible that other group dynamics could be acted out within the system or between different parts of the system. Another group process that has been widely described is mirroring. As far back as the 1960s group analysts recognised the mirroring that can happen between people in a therapeutic setting. Foulkes (1964) described the way in which group members can unconsciously act out the behaviour of central characters being described by other group members. If we move from analytic theory to systems theory we may begin to understand how the mirroring that Foulkes described could be manifest between levels within a system. Cronen, Pearce and Harris (1982) and Pearce (2005) propose a model for understanding how meaning may be constructed and communicated between different parts of a system, organisation or group. In their description of the coordinated management of meaning, Cronen et al. offer some insight into the way that a system or group may understand behaviour and communicate in a particular manner, while another group or part of a system may ascribe an alternative meaning. Appreciating that there are influencing factors between the different levels, Cronen et al. and Pearce identify the conflict or miscommunication that can arise from the different levels (one man's meat, as the saying goes).

So perhaps one man's success is therefore another man's failure. The data emerging from the NICE-funded evaluation of the TC was positive: reduced rates of seclusion (Taylor et al., 2012), reduced internalising problems (Morrissey et al., 2012) and reduced personality pathology (Morrissey & Taylor, 2014). Cheltenham's meat had a sour taste outside of the TC, however, and the wider system called for a review to consider the viability of the TC in a high secure setting. From the outset, three options were announced for the future of Cheltenham: to remain, to be reduced to a six-bed facility and operate on one half of a ward or to be closed down. The review, which took two years to complete, concurred with the empirical data and recommended that the TC should be actively supported by the senior managers. The wider system then reviewed the review. And cashed the cheques that paid for TCs for prisoners with a learning disability.

The wider system could be understood in many ways. It would be easy, though lazy, to just pathologise the wider system and view the actions of senior staff as bad, ill-considered or damaging. However, an understanding analysis offers the potential of a more useful insight into the difficulties encountered around the developing

TC on Cheltenham. Hinshelwood (2002) has suggested that a key task facing staff working in psychiatric settings is to contain anxiety. He further suggests that staff are faced with an unenviable task of supporting patients to face their 'unbearable suffering'. Staff, by proxy, must therefore do the same and tolerate the suffering of patients whilst simultaneously acknowledge their own vulnerability to such suffering. Building on these ideas, Campling (2004) argues that whole institutions face a similar task and, as with individual staff members, the institution may resort to defence mechanisms in order to tolerate this unbearable suffering. There are a number of defences available to both individuals and organisations to tolerate the intolerable. A common defence in psychiatric settings is to split the staff and patient groups and amplify the differences between the two. Staff become healthy care givers while patients become damaged, dangerous or sick. Healthy carers, of course, will require sick patients in order to be proficient at their jobs, while patients will require caring staff if they are to believe in the possibility of recovery. In order for the process to be sustained both groups will need to exchange projections and invest their goodness or badness in the other group, the side effect of which is to deny common humanity.

As with the process of malignant alienation and the mirroring process observed in groups, these projections and splits can equally occur at the level of the organisation. Cheltenham was doing things differently to the traditional hospital practices at Rampton and it was clear, from the hooch suggestions to the security concerns, that these differences were difficult for some to assimilate. For the hospital to remain well, and support its habitual practices, Cheltenham needed to be seen as problematic. At some level the organisation projected its own badness into the TC and resisted the narrative emerging from the formal evaluation. Isolating the TC from the Community of Communities and initiating and sustaining the review allowed the organisation to split away from one of its constituent parts and *punish* the bad part. At least it was able to do so until the organisation was able to create 'thinking space' around Cheltenham and begin to explore and understand the reactions that the TC had stimulated.

An awareness and insight into the concepts of malignant alienation, mirroring and the (mis)communication of meaning between different levels of a complex and convoluted system may allow organisations to begin to understand and explore their own dynamics. Creating a reflective space for managers and allowing an open and honest dialogue between senior members of an organisation and those who deliver the service at the coal face may reduce the toxic exchange of projections, minimise splitting and subsequently promote a more compassionate culture.

Despite the more difficult experiences that arose around the opening of the first TC in the National High Secure Learning Disability Service, Cheltenham continues to operate as a therapeutic community. The wider system, in spite of the early reaction to the ward milieu, has supported its continued growth and has ensured its survival. The success of Cheltenham and indeed the eventual ability of the wider system to enjoy this success, has stimulated the opening of a TC in a medium secure service (with remarkably similar outcome data) and has laid the foundation for the development of a TC in a low-security setting. The development of therapeutic communities at different levels of security allows offenders with a learning disability to progress along their treatment pathway whilst engaging in the same style of treatment, thus offering a greater prospect of recovery and rehabilitation. The development of care and treatment based on a pathway model *between* levels of security is a fairly new approach to forensic mental health care and its value remains to be seen. However, regardless of the clinical benefits to patients, the data that emerged from Cheltenham indicates the positive culture that is engendered by the core principles of a DTC. The mutual respect and compassion, described by both staff and patients, offers a design for residential learning disability services in the post-Winterbourne climate.

## References

Bennett, C. & Morrissey, C. (2013). *Cheltenham Therapeutic Community: A Service Evaluation.* Retford, UK: Nottinghamshire Healthcare NHS Trust.

Campling, P. (2004). A psychoanalytical understanding of what goes wrong: The importance of projection. In P. Campling, S. Davies & G. Farquharson (Eds.), *From Toxic Institutions to Therapeutic Environments: Residential Settings in Mental Health Services* (pp. 32–44) London: Springer Science and Business.

Cronen, V.E., Pearce, W.B. & Harris, L.M. (1982). The coordinated management of meaning: A theory of communication. *Human Communication Theory*, 61, 89.

Foulkes, S.H. (1964). *Therapeutic Group Analysis.* London: Allen and Unwin.

Goffman, E. (1961). On the characteristics of total institutions. In R.K. Cannan & J.O. Cole (Eds.), *Symposium on Preventive and Social Psychiatry* (pp. 43–84) Washington, DC: Walter Reed Army Medical Centre.

Hinshelwood, R.D. (2002). Abusive help–helping abuse: The psychodynamic impact of severe personality disorder on caring institutions. *Criminal Behaviour and Mental Health*, 12, (Suppl S2), S20–S30.

Howells, K., Tonkin, M., Milburn, C., Lewis, J., Draycot, S., Cordwell, J., … & Schalast, N. (2009). The EssenCES measure of social climate: A preliminary validation and normative data in UK high secure hospital settings. *Criminal Behaviour and Mental Health*, 19(5), 308–320.

Mental Health Act (1983). Code of Practice. Department of Health.

Morrissey, C. & Taylor, J. (2014). Changes in personality disorder traits following 2 years of treatment in a secure therapeutic community milieu. *Journal of Mental Health Research in Intellectual Disabilities*, 7(4), 323–336.

Morrissey, C., Taylor, J. & Bennett, C. (2012). Evaluation of a therapeutic community intervention for men with intellectual disability and personality disorder. *Journal of Learning Disabilities and Offending Behaviour*, 3(1), 52–60.

O'Brien, J. (1981). *The Principle of Normalisation: A Foundation for the Effective Services.* London: Campaign for Mentally Handicapped People.

Pearce, W.B. (2005). The coordinated management of meaning (CMM). In *Theorizing Communication and Culture* (pp. 35–54) Beverly Hills, CA: Sage.

Rapoport, R.N. (1960). *Community as Doctor.* London: Tavistock.

Schalast, N., Redies, M., Collins, M., Stacey, J. & Howells, K. (2008). EssenCES, a short questionnaire for assessing the social climate of forensic psychiatric wards. *Criminal Behaviour and Mental Health*, 18(1), 49–58.

Shuker, R. & Newton, M. (2008). Treatment outcome following intervention in a prison-based therapeutic community: A study of the relationship between reduction in criminogenic risk and improved psychological well-being. *The British Journal of Forensic Practice*, 10(3), 33–44.

Taylor, C. (2012). Complaints as a tool for bullying. In J. Adlam, A. Aiyegbusi, P. Kleinot, A. Motz & C. Scanlon (Eds.), *The Therapeutic Milieu under Fire: Security and Insecurity in Forensic Mental Health* (34, p. 63) London: Jessica Kingsley Publishers.

Taylor, J., Morrissey, C., Trout, S. & Bennett, C. (2012). The evolution of a therapeutic community for offenders with intellectual disability and personality disorder: Part one – clinical characteristics. *Therapeutic Communities: The International Journal of Therapeutic Communities*, 33(4), 144–154.

Taylor, J. & Trout, S. (2013). Lessons from the front line: Working with offenders with learning disability and personality disorder in a high secure therapeutic community. *Mental Health Review Journal*, 18(1), 44–52.

Tonkin, M., Howells, K., Ferguson, E., Clark, A., Newberry, M. & Schalast, N. (2012). Lost in translation? Psychometric properties and construct validity of the English Essen Climate Evaluation Schema (EssenCES) social climate questionnaire. *Psychological Assessment*, 24(3), 573.

Watts, D. & Morgan, G. (1994). Malignant alienation: Dangers for patients who are hard to like. In G. Adshead & C. Jacob (Eds.), *Personality Disorder: The Definitive Reader* (pp. 89–97) London: Jessica Kingsley Publishers.

Whittle, M. (1997). Malignant alienation. *Journal of Forensic Psychiatry*, 8(1), 5–10.

Wolfensberger, W. (1984). A reconceptualization of normalization as social role valorization. *Mental Retardation*, 34(2), 22–26.

Zimbardo, P.G. (2007). *Lucifer Effect*. London: Blackwell Publishing Ltd.

# 11

# RELATIONSHIPS, SOCIAL CONTEXT AND PERSONAL CHANGE

## The role of therapeutic communities

*Richard Shuker*

*The essence of man is no abstraction inherent in each single individual. In its reality it is the ensemble of social relations.*

— Karl Marx (Marx & Engels, 1845)

## Introduction

Therapeutic communities provide an intervention for offenders which emphasises principles of respect, decency and humanity as important ends in themselves. These values have been central to their work well before they became widely acknowledged as being essential in attempts to 'rehabilitate' (Tew, Vince & Luther 2015) and integrated into practice within UK penal establishments. Prison-based therapeutic communities pre-date the development and implementation of the offending behaviour programmes which are now delivered on a large scale in the majority of prisons, and have provided a therapeutic intervention in UK prisons for over half a century.

One of the most important contributions which therapeutic communities have made to forensic interventions has been the priority placed on providing a social and organisational structure which promotes the conditions for change, and an environment where healthy relationships and social participation can flourish. This chapter will describe how the values and principles of therapeutic communities are relevant when building healthy psychosocial environments within penal settings. It will discuss how the clinical framework and social arrangements within therapeutic communities can lead to productive and safe relationships where shared values provide the conditions for personal and social change. The chapter will explore the significance of social climate and its role in creating the conditions for healthy relationships. It will discuss how power and authority are exercised and how within this environment power comes to be accepted as legitimate and how decision-making is driven by consensus. The chapter will provide an analysis of how the social and structural factors within therapeutic communities create conditions for cooperative, supportive and productive relationships and how these factors interact to provide a social climate enabling change. It will conclude by discussing how the rich social context of therapeutic communities can assert a profound effect on behaviour and consider the implications for how healthy collaborative relationships can be established within other forensic settings.

## Therapeutic communities: origins and background

Therapeutic communities provide a social environment which use social and group processes to bring about change (Lees, Manning & Rawlings, 1999, see also Akerman & Mandikate and Brookes, this volume). They emphasise the importance of collaborative therapeutic relationships in a context which enables full social participation and responsibility. 'Therapy' constitutes the learning which occurs in all group, social and community activities.

Therapeutic communities have questioned the assumption that effective treatment will only be provided by searching for the 'right' type of programme delivered by the most knowledgeable and skilled clinicians. Instead, they have focussed on the idea that unless the *conditions* for treatment are right, people are unlikely to be helped. They make an assumption that unless the treatment setting fosters relationships where ownership, safety and collaboration are valued, unless open communication is routed within the social system, and unless responsibility for personal recovery is given to the individual and the community in which treatment occurs, outcomes are likely to be limited, short-lived and ineffectual. Social expectation and social responsibility are central to this; those taking part in treatment must also be allowed and enabled to participate fully in the choices and decisions which affect their day-to-day living. Above all, relationships characterised by trust, respect and accountability are emphasised as central in creating the conditions essential for personal change.

## Behaviour and social context

Attempting to understand human relationships by reducing them to individual factors without a consideration of the social context in which they occur fails to recognise that people are at their core social beings. Without studying the structure and functioning of societal, situational or contextual factors the study of behaviour and interpersonal relationships becomes to a large degree pointless. Likewise, attempting to understand how people relate without also looking at how they are placed in relation to each other within the wider social context misses something crucial. The work of Sherif and Sherif (1969) and their studies of intergroup conflict demonstrated that relationships depend on the nature of the interdependencies between groups within the wider social systems. In different circumstances group processes can either provide a moderating influence promoting social good or act as a force for collective harm. Sherif and Sherif (1969) observed that the impact of the social context was such that those who were regarded as the 'cream of the crop' in one community could, in other contexts, display anti-social and radically altered patterns of behaviour.

This work powerfully demonstrated how social processes such as conflict develop over time, and how "changes in structural context wrought psychological changes in perceptions, feelings, and actions" (Reicher and Haslam, 2014, p. 826). It also demonstrated that changes in social context have a powerful influence on individual and group behaviour. Where the social situations in which people live become defined by competition and rivalry and groups become positioned against each other, relationships adopt a mistrustful, hostile and suspicious quality. One of the most revealing features of Sherif's work was showing the interdependent nature of the social world and individual psychologies. What also becomes apparent is the primacy of the social context in relationships, and whether these are characterised by prejudice and hostility or harmony and cooperation; what is also clear is that social context is a key factor in intergroup cohesion and reconciliation. This work suggests that violence is not part of any 'human essence' but is derived from the character of our social relationships, and as Reicher and Haslam (2014) suggest, it is at the "group level at which we must operate to bring about social change – enjoining us to transform the social relationships of competition between groups" (p. 828).

A wealth of studies exploring the nature of social relationships, behaviour and context (Asch, 1955; Milgram, 1974; Haney, 1973) have demonstrated the power of the group in influencing interpersonal behaviour. Group processes have the capacity to determine the nature of those interpersonal relationships which form the social norm and those which come to be defined as socially deviant. Platow and Hunter (2014) emphasise this point, suggesting that "group processes and inter-group relationships should be studied at the group level, not the interpersonal level [and] individual behaviour, made possible only through individual minds, cannot be understood through an analysis of those minds removed from the social context" (p. 840). Looking at this body of work, what emerges is that patterns of behaviour are so heavily dependent upon the social world that attempts to understand or improve interpersonal relationships by separating them from the social context may be of limited value.

## Penal settings and social relationships

Prisoners are impelled to establish social relationships and alliances; relationships are formed in order to provide safety, protection and status, fill social and physical voids, and alleviate collective deprivation (Crewe, 2009). Social structures determine social outcomes and have the capacity to either constrain or enable the formation of social relationships. These structures are particularly apparent within institutions. Goffman (1961) observed the ritual quality to social exchanges within 'total institutions', which he argues ultimately served to remove inhabitants' identities and reproduce and maintain social order. Roles were adopted which allowed inhabitants to deal with the pressures of their confinement and deprivation. Sykes (1995) also recognised that social relationships within prisons were largely determined by the roles inmates assumed. He suggested that social positions adopted were determined solely by social structures, rather than the individual attributes. Whilst this may underplay the relevance of individual factors in understanding how relationships develop, what is apparent is that the penal context has the capacity to powerfully influence behaviour. It can have the capacity to create the conditions for violence and conflict or the potential to act as a catalyst for change (Crewe, 2009); it can also at its best have the capacity to enable individual and groups to work together collaboratively (Cullen, 1997). What is evident is that the social context within institutions matters and it has the capacity to shape radically different patterns of social relationships.

Context determines the nature of relationships, how power is exercised and the extent to which a violent subculture is able to form the dominant norm. Scott (2015) argues that "although prisoner violence is relational and dependent upon a number of contingencies, it is embedded in and socially produced by the situational contexts of daily prison regimes" (p. 60). He argues that in prison culture, violence is often considered legitimate and "institutionally structured" in settings more likely to dehumanise than rehabilitate. Hierarchies between prisoners are accepted and physical violence an inevitable consequence of hierarchies where some prisoners are deliberately placed into social categories perpetuating stigmatisation. He also argues that "institutionally structured situational contexts" (p. 60) such as overcrowding, restriction of movement (for example to educational and religious events), lack of privacy and competition for limited resources create a culture where relationships will inevitably be unhealthy.

## Social context, prisons and power

In order to make sense of the context in which relationships are shaped within prisons, another important feature of prison life must be understood: how power is exercised and the factors determine how power is received. Crewe and Liebling (2015) observe that difficulties in establishing the right balance between security and harmony is evident in the history of the Prison Service. They argue that whilst a form of safety can be achieved by minimising prisoner contact, this clearly comes at the expense of decency and well-being. On the other hand, providing prisoners with autonomy and responsibility can present certain risks to order and security. Crewe (2009) summarises the types of power exercised in prisons which can range from overt cohesion to more subtle forms of manipulation and inducement where, for example basic possession can become levers to control and manipulate behaviour. The habits and rituals which individuals or groups become tied to can also serve to maintain social order (Goffman 1961).

However, social and political trends can also exert a profound influence on behaviour and the quality of human relationships. This can be seen in something as fundamental as that experienced in the relationship for instance between a psychologist and a prisoner, where interventions based on a theoretical assumption that personal deficits are the primary cause of offending can bring an impersonal and punitive dimension to the therapeutic relationship (Needs, 2016; see also Shingler & Needs, this volume). Crewe (2009) comments on the significance of a number of important political and social trends affecting this relationship; these include the emphasis on public protection, a less forgiving attitude towards prisoners and risk reduction being regarded as largely synonymous with rectifying cognitive and interpersonal deficits. What has occurred, he argues, is a movement away from psychologists practising their traditional professional role in developing therapeutic alliances aimed at reducing distress and promoting psychological well-being. The changing quality of this relationship not only reflects the explicit imbalance of power but in its most extreme form has the capacity, he argues, to subordinate the complexity of personality and identity in a similar way to that observed by Goffman (1961) within asylums. Relationships typified by authenticity and concern have the potential to become negated by social and structural changes.

Whilst this may be a generalisation which many forensic psychologists may not recognise in their practice, a system in which profound imbalances of power exist or where power lacks legitimacy has significant implications for the quality of the prison regime. Prisoners lack agency and the risks of a strong prison subculture become heightened. As more power is removed, the temptation for prisoners to find other ways of exhibiting agency increases. Grievances can become unheard or unexposed with prisoners either too afraid or cynical to raise concerns.

In their analysis of the different ways in which power is exercised in private and public sector prisons, Crewe and Liebling (2015) identify 'heavy' and 'light' prison cultures with 'heavy' cultures more oppressive than those seen as 'light'. They also identify 'absent' or 'present' cultures ('present' staff were more involved and their authority more embedded in daily culture than staff who were considered 'absent'). Getting the balance right becomes crucial in creating a safe regime. Where authority is under- or overused, or used carelessly or sporadically, this has the potential to establish a culture where violence has the potential to flourish. Where authority is absent but heavy, staff are relatively withdrawn and the formation of good relationships becomes difficult and low priority. A shift towards absent cultures has "seen a more distant and mistrusting relationship between prisoners and prison officers and the delegation of power by staff to certain prisoners" (Crewe & Liebling, 2015, p. 14). Such developments can provide a fertile environment for violence.

When exploring how power is received in prisons, a further consideration is why in some circumstances power can be exercised by consensus where in others it is rejected or undermined. Beetham (1991) reasons that power needs to be regarded as legitimate if those who have power exercised over them are to consent and that legitimacy can only be derived where power "is acquired and exercised in accordance with established rules" (supra note 50). Procedures and outcomes need to considered as fair for power to be construed as legitimate (Bottoms & Tankebe, 2013) and where this occurs prisoners are more likely to work within rather than subvert, present with a veneer of compliance, or rebel against the system of power. The presence of shared values can create and sustain legitimacy; in other words, where shared values exist, so do the conditions for power to be seen as legitimate.

The contribution therapeutic communities make to establishing social arrangements within organisations so that power and authority are experienced as legitimate and trust is established will be considered later on in this chapter.

## Context, behaviour and therapeutic community structures

Attempting to change behaviour without considering the role and power of the social context in shaping, modifying and reinforcing behaviour is likely to lead to change that is only short-lived. One of the criticisms of offending behaviour programmes is that the disproportionate amount of effort placed into bringing about individual change neglects to sufficiently acknowledge that patterns of behaviour are contextually driven and reinforced (Augimeri, 2001).

The way in which groups are organised in relation to each other has a profound impact on interpersonal relationships. Any social or organisational structure which sees groups positioned against each other, vying for power, influence, status and limited resources is likely to elicit prejudice, hostility and violence. Where there are social structures which promote communication, shared goals and cooperation, the opposite is likely to occur. In order to understand how therapeutic communities improve relationships, safety and interpersonal cooperation (Newton, 1998; Gunn & Robertson, 1982; Shuker & Newberry, 2010; Rivelin, 2010; Tonkin et al., 2012) it is necessary to understand their social structures and their underlying value and principles. These will be briefly described below:

- *Open communication*: Structures which allow open discussion and communication are central to a therapeutic community. Therapy groups, open feedback sessions and community debriefs occur on a daily basis. Community meetings and staff/resident forums which allow an interface with the wider organisation provide opportunities for influence, discussion and feedback.
- *Agency and empowerment*: All within the community, including staff, negotiate the nature of power and how this is exercised. All prisoners become responsible for decisions affecting individuals, groups and the community as a whole. Decisions are made by consensus and voting mechanisms (where staff have a seldom used but acknowledged veto) provide genuine responsibility to residents. Resident-elected prisoners chair community meetings; prisoners vote on all decisions made whether these concern what jobs fellow residents should have, decisions about de-selection or sanctions for rule breaking, or whether members have made sufficient progress to be supported in their plans to leave the community.

- *Involvement*: A 'living-learning' culture (Main, 1983) provides the context for residents to have genuine opportunities for involvement, decision-making and ownership. Residents have responsibility for organising community events, recreational and social activities, and deciding who has positions of community influence. The community and wider context within which it is placed value its role in providing opportunities for learning and personal change.
- *Accountability*: Residents are accountable to each other for their actions. There is a powerful and dynamic process of social feedback. Community meetings, groups and feedback sessions promote an exploration of residents' behaviour (known as a 'culture of enquiry') and its impact on other group members and the wider community. Genders and Player (1995) refer to this as a process of social analysis where actions are explored in a rigorous process akin to 'microscopic precision'.
- *Shared goals and rule-setting*: Members of a therapeutic community establish a written constitution governing behaviour which is reviewed and revised. The rules governing non-violence and abstinence from drugs are widely shared and enforced. Creating safety becomes a central goal for all. The community is affected by breaches of this constitution; for example where serious breaches of trust occur, the community will decide, along with the staff team, whether effective sanctions should be imposed which could have a wider impact on its members.

An apparent contradiction can be observed when considering the therapeutic community structures and their capacity to promote personal change. What occurred in the total institutions described by Goffman (1961) is in some ways mirrored within therapeutic communities. Rhodes (2010) considers total institutions as being "understood as unusually bounded and constrained assemblages organised to produce habits of docility through specific practices of authority" (p. 205). Rituals abound and this destabilises residents' previous identities. Rhodes asserts that therapeutic communities are founded as a retention of the 'total apparatus' where rules, scrutiny, intimate personal disclosures becoming public knowledge and elaborate disciplinary expectations form the basis of its social structures. However, the social arrangements of therapeutic communities deliberately provide an alternative to institutions designed to alienate and disempower and instead provide the social climate most likely to lead to personal change.

## Conditions for change

How does the social context described above form the right conditions for people to build healthy relationships? How is it that instead of an atmosphere of violence, competition and hostility the conditions for cooperation exist? A number of relevant social and organisational factors within therapeutic communities need to be considered when exploring how they provide those conditions necessary for change to occur. These will now be discussed further.

## Safety and belonging

The structures described create the conditions for safe and predictable relation-ships and alliances. The secure base required for healthy development recognised in attachment theory (Ainsworth, 1991) is found within therapeutic communities. The environment is psychologically and physically secure and provides the basis for exploration and change. Structures deliberately engender a culture of belonging such as those marking the referral, joining and leaving of residents (Haigh, 2015), and the culture of responsibility allows residents to invest socially and emotionally in the life of the community to which they can become strongly attached.

## Social interaction and feedback

Community living and the social participation and ties within therapeutic com-munities reduce isolation. Prisoners learn much about the background, histories and experiences of those they live with; emotional expression is encouraged and authentic relationships emerge in a therapeutic climate which values personal dis-closure and trust.

People in therapeutic communities are able to learn about themselves in relation to others and the social feedback they receive. The community essentially provides the 'looking glass' by which individuals come to understand themselves, how they are experienced by those around them and how their behaviour affects the lives of others.

## Expectations and affirmation

The expectations and norms present in other prisons mean that prisoners often have to live up to and conform to a moral code which promotes violence as a means of social problem solving. There can be strong negative repercussions for those who wish to live outside of this value system and this limits the extent to which considering and embarking upon a process of personal change is possible. The social context of the therapeutic community provides structures and practices which allows people to 'behave well' (Cullen, 1997). These social and moral codes within the community (such as respect, non-violence and collective accountability) are explicitly defined in a written constitution. Therapeutic communities have an implicit set of values which affirm and validate the intrinsic good in people and their capacity to change. Personal change is collectively valued as an important end and a journey which can only be embarked upon when others are actively involved in this process.

## Hope, meaning and identity

The values and principles of therapeutic communities are linked into their approach to how personal change is achieved. These values emphasise personal empowerment, collective responsibility and a culture of purpose. Residents take ownership, and in doing so are free to determine their own futures. A sense of meaning and purpose become established in a culture which allows prisoners to form identifies likely to facilitate change.

Therapeutic communities see 'therapy' and 'community' as inextricably linked where the social context shapes personal narratives and prisoners learn to define themselves as being worthy of trust, respect and having the capacity to 'do good'. Their explicit cultural message allows a self-narrative to be inculcated where prisoners' core self becomes defined as that which has the capacity to do good, and lead a productive and valuable life. Through their focus on autonomy, valued identities and shared human goals, therapeutic communities are able to provide the conditions for change which can be understood from both the desistance perspective (Maruna, 2011) or good lives ideas (Ward, 2002).

Psychotherapy and community living have the capacity to instil hope and optimism whether about personal and social change or future possibilities. Many prisoners seeking treatment already believe that change is possible and realistic. Therapeutic communities harness this hope by recognising that given the innate capacity of people to find meaning and fulfilment in their lives, personal change is achievable.

### Cooperation and collaboration

The balance between 'present/absent' and 'light/heavy' authority becomes negotiated with therapeutic communities, providing an example of a penal culture where authority is both present and light. What prevents the misuse of responsibility can be understood in a number of different ways. The community is collectively affected by individual members' rule-breaking. There are routine opportunities for scrutiny and reflection on members' behaviour and close working alliances between residents and staff form a platform for trust which residents can be unwilling to betray.

The structural factors of a therapeutic community promote cooperation. Defining, agreeing and working towards shared goals creates conditions for collaboration. Therapeutic communities thrive on a strong sense of interdependency within the community where members are reliant on each other to create safety. Power is construed as fair and it is this sense of legitimacy which promotes a culture of cooperation rather than antagonism.

The final sections of this chapter will look at how and why power in a therapeutic community comes to be regarded as legitimate and how the social structures within therapeutic communities can create the conditions for trusting relationships to develop.

## Relationships, power and authority in therapeutic communities

How does the social climate of therapeutic communities allow legitimate power to develop and be sustained and how is this relevant when creating collaborative relationships? Something which becomes clear is that the presence of shared goals works for the benefit of staff and prisoners, and cooperation exists where systems of joint working are regarded as being for the common good. This is further established where decision-making is transparent and fair, those making decisions are accountable and boundaries and expectations are clear. Power is negotiated through the structures which allow rules for daily living to be established, discussed and if necessary reviewed and modified. What is apparent is the importance of a system of shared goals and concerns where "power is legitimate to the extent that the rules of power can be justified in terms of beliefs shared by both dominant and subordinate" (Beetham, 1991, supra note 50). It is these shared goals which foster a culture of cooperation.

The most important shared goal within therapeutic communities is that of establishing safety. For most, goals also include the desire for personal change, the need to find resolution to personal distress, and to establish a sense of belonging in a relationship of trust. The climate of safety and cooperation enables alliances and carefully boundaried, supportive relationships to be established with staff. To make sense of why power is regarded as having a high level of authenticity, and why relationships between those in power and those being governed are driven by consensus, a further part of therapeutic community culture needs to be examined, that of the culture of trust.

## The role of trust

Prisons where fairness and safety are experienced provide the basis for a rehabilitative social climate to develop. The social climate becomes potent where the environment is able to develop and affirm an identity beyond that of an 'offender' and where people can find a sense of meaning and purpose. Where relationships are experienced as trusting, the conditions for a climate enabling personal change become strengthened (Maruna, 2011). Trust, and its absence, plays a powerful part in determining psychological well-being of prisoners and staff. Liebling (in press) describes the concept of the 'failed state' prison and the social and political context present in some prisons, which can lead to radicalisation. Prisons characterised by mistrust and high levels of distance and fear can lead to inmate disenfranchisement and resentment. Relationships play a central role here; where there are perceptions of powerlessness and discrimination, a sense of exclusion and disadvantage and a lack of safety, fairness and purpose, anger and alienation grow. A 'politically charged' climate emerges, legitimacy of power can diminish and the conditions for radicalisation can become established; religious identities can have an appeal in their capacity to provide power, meaning, recognition and autonomy in climates with a heightened sense of fear and disorder. Differences in levels of political charge, tension and fear were, she found, explained by differences in the nature and quality of staff/prisoner relationships within that prison. Crucial to this were levels of well-judged and 'intelligent' trust and the perceived legitimacy of the regime. Where prisoners were given respect and recognition and where staff worked alongside prisoners who were given appropriate levels of autonomy, the regime was seen as more legitimate and radicalisation less likely. Whilst wider social and economic factors influence prison culture, prisons where safety, trust and decency are embedded within the relationships consistently experience more effective outcomes. Ballatt and Campling (2011), in their analysis of the how culture is interlinked with an organisation's values, assert that environments where relationships are characterised by interest, kindness and attunement to the needs of those being cared for lead to mutual trust. Where trust is present, they argue, this promotes effective working alliances, and it is these which lie at the heart of effective clinical and organisational outcomes.

## Therapeutic communities and the conditions for trust

Therapeutic communities prioritise activities and structures which enable supportive and trusting relationships to emerge. Trust can inevitably develop between those disclosing intimate personal details about their past and their offences, and therapy groups enable residents to explore aspects of their lives to which they often feel a profound sense of shame, sadness and regret. However, other factors which are often absent in penal contexts and limit the potential for trusting relationships to develop are also acutely embedded within therapeutic community culture.

Firstly, physical safety allows relationships to develop and a culture of openness instils a degree of confidence that the relationships being invested in are genuine. Secondly, structures encouraging and enabling communication and openness allow residents to assess the sincerity and genuineness of others. Behaviour is often regarded as authentic where prisoners are able to show vulnerabilities and emotions other than anger. Thirdly, whilst the forced interaction necessitated in other prisons can create a climate of suspicion, scepticism and mutual mistrust, therapeutic communities present conditions which allow mutually supportive, sincere and trusting relationships to grow. Fourthly, although prisons can contain "structural impediments" (Crewe, 2009, p. 306) which can limit the extent to which relationships can be authentic and genuine (Sykes, 1958; Jewkes, 2005), the social structures within TCs provide the conditions which enable strong relationships to be built. Fifthly, obstacles to trust which make prisoners reluctant to risk forming strong bonds such as fear of emotional vulnerability and disappointment (Cohen & Taylor, 1972) are also more easily overcome in therapeutic communities.

A social context with allows openness, involvement, accountability and communication has the capacity to create a climate of trust; where the interlinked structures within a TC generate a culture of belonging and safety, the conditions for trust are strengthened. Empowerment, inclusion and respect, often missing in penal settings where there are high levels of mistrust and alienation (Liebling, in press), are embedded in the structures which underpin the daily practice of therapeutic communities.

## Conclusion

Therapeutic communities recognise the power of social context in individual change. They have recognised that the nature of social relationships profoundly influences the effectiveness of treatment. In addition, they acknowledge that social structures have the capacity to cause people to behave in radically different ways, whether decent and humane, or callous and uncaring. Rather than providing individualising and pathologising accounts of behaviour and social processes, therapeutic communities recognise the overwhelming importance of context; their practice is based on a system of values and social structures which provide the conditions for people to establish positive and respectful relationships.

Therapeutic communities also bring an optimistic message that people can get on with each other and work for the common good if the conditions are right; violence is by no means inevitable and cooperation and collaboration can occur where individuals, instead of being in competition against each other, can identify and work towards a system of shared goals. Interlinked social structures create conditions for individuals to develop relationships which are respectful and trusting, and social participation and involvement engender a sense of belonging, purpose and ownership; processes which allow openness and collective problem solving promote trust, empowerment and well-being.

In one sense, instead of creating the hostility and competition often found in prisons, the collectivistic nature of therapeutic communities enables reconciliation and harmony to emerge. Positive relationships emerge where structures allow trust to be built, where people feel safe and that they belong and where they are actively involved in and participate in the physical and social environment for which they are held accountable.

What do therapeutic communities bring, and how relevant are they, to discussions about how prison environments can be 'rehabilitative'? Social structures such as joint decision-making and shared working enable power and authority to be experienced as legitimate; and defining and working towards shared goals which are in everyone's best interests allow staff and prisoners to respect and value one another. The emphasis on structures allowing communication between staff and prisoners is central to how trust is established, how power is seen as legitimate and how differences are negotiated. A social context which enables cooperation through having a clear identity, common purpose and the explicit message that prisoners are responsible for their own lives and capable of doing good can exert a potent impact on expectations and the self-efficacy of the individual and the organisation; and a value system which is translated into an explicit set of rules dictating non-violence and social participation, and which is reinforced by a strong cultural message that all are expected to participate and to work closely alongside each other can create cooperation.

The experiences of therapeutic communities lend much to discussions of how positive relationships can be established elsewhere. Trust and cooperation will emerge where the conditions created do not entail individuals and groups being positioned against each other but rather encourage shared goals to be pursued. A social context which allows pro-social roles and identities to be adopted and internalised, and where power is exercised in a way which is seen as legitimate, has a powerful impact on the relationships which exist within it. Perhaps the most significant contribution of therapeutic communities to the development of therapeutic environments in forensic settings is in their capacity to foster a culture of hope, positive expectations and trust. In doing so they are able bring out the best in those who reside in them and demonstrate that prisons can be places where trust, decency and safety are a reality.

## References

Ainsworth, M. (1991). Attachments and other affectional bonds across the life cycle. In C. M. Parkes, J. Stevenson-Hindle & P. Marris (eds.), *Attachment Across the Life Cycle* (pp. 33–51). London: Routledge.

Asch, S. E. (1955). Opinions and social pressure. *Scientific American*, 193, 31–35.

Augimeri, L. K. (2001). Providing effective supports. In K. Douglas, D. Webster, S. Hart, D. Eaves & J. Ogloff (eds.), *HCR-20 Violence Risk Management Companion Guide* (pp. 135–146). Burnaby, BC: Mental Health, Law and Policy Institute, Simon Fraser University.

Ballatt, J. & Campling, P. (2011). *Intelligent Kindness: Reforming the Culture of Healthcare.* London: Royal College of Psychiatry Publications.

Beetham, D. (1991). *The Legitimation of Power.* Basingstoke, UK: Palgrave Macmillan.

Bottoms, A. & Tankebe, J. (2013). Beyond procedural justice: A dialogic approach to legitimacy in criminal justice. *Journal of Criminal Law and Criminology*, 102(1), 119.

Cohen, S. & Taylor, L. (1972). *Psychological Survival: The Experience of Long-Term Imprisonment.* Harmondsworth, UK: Penguin.

Crewe, B. (2009). *The Prisoner Society: Power, Adaptation, and Social Life in an English Prison.* Oxford: Oxford University Press.

Crewe, B. & Liebling, A. (2015). Staff culture, authority and prison violence. *Prison Service Journal*, 221, 9–14.

Cullen, E. (1997). Can a prison be a therapeutic community? The Grendon template. In E. Cullen, L. Jones & R. Woodward (eds.), *Therapeutic Communities for Offenders.* London: Wiley.

Genders, E. & Player, E. (1995). *Grendon: A Study of a Therapeutic Prison.* Oxford: Oxford University Press.

Goffman, E. (1961). *Asylums: Essays on the Social Situation of Mental Patients and Other Inmates.* Harmondsworth, UK: Penguin.

Gunn, J. & Robertson, G. (1982). An evaluation of Grendon prison. In J. Gunn & D. Farrington (eds.), *Abnormal Offenders, Delinquency and the Criminal Justice System* (pp. 285–305). Chichester, UK: Wiley.

Haigh, R. (2015). The quintessence of a therapeutic environment: The foundations of the Windsor Conference 2014. *The International Journal of Therapeutic Communities*, 36(1), 2–11.

Haney, C., Banks, W. & Zimbardo, P. (1973). Interpersonal dynamics in a simulated prison. *International journal of Criminology and Penology*, 1, 69–97.

Jewkes, Y. (2005). Loss, liminality and the life sentence: Managing identity through a disruptive lifecourse. In A. Liebling & S. Maruna (eds.), *The Effects of Imprisonment* (pp. 366–388). Cullompton, UK: Willan.

Lees, J., Manning, N. & Rawlings, B. (1999). *Therapeutic Community Effectiveness: A Systematic International Review of Therapeutic Community Treatment for People with Personality Disorders and Mentally Disordered Offenders.* York, UK: University of York, NHS Centre for Reviews and Dissemination.

Liebling, A. (in press). *Towards a 'Failed State' Theory of Prison Effects.*

Main, T. (1983). The concept of the therapeutic community: Variations and vicissitudes. In M. Pines (ed.), *The Evolution of Group Analysis*. London: Routledge & Kegan Paul.

Maruna, S. (2011). Why do they hate us? Making peace between prisoners and psychology. *International Journal of Offender Therapy and Comparative Criminology*, 55, 671–675.

Marx, K. & Engels, F. (1845). *The German Ideology, Including Theses on Feuerbach*. Amehurst, NY: Prometheus Books.

Milgram, S. (1974). *Obedience to Authority: An Experimental View*. New York: Harper & Row.

Needs, A. (2016). Rehabilitation – writing a new story. *The Psychologist*, 29(3), 192–195.

Newton, M. (1998). Changes in measures of personality, hostility and locus of control during residence in a prison therapeutic community. *Legal and Criminological Psychology*, 3, 209–223.

Platow, M. J. & Hunter, J. A. (2014). Necessarily collectivistic. *The Psychologist*, 27, 838–841.

Reicher, S. and Haslam, S. A. (2014). Camps, conflict and collectivism. *The Psychologist*, 27, 826–828.

Rhodes, L. A. (2010). 'This can't be real': Continuity at HMP Grendon. In R. Shuker & E. Sullivan (eds.), *Grendon and the Emergence of Forensic Therapeutic Communities* (pp. 203–206). Chichester: John Wiley & Sons.

Rivelin, A. (2010). Suicide and self-injurious behaviours at HMP Grendon. In R. Shuker & E. Sullivan (Eds.), *Grendon and the Emergence of Forensic Therapeutic Communities* (pp. 265–280). Chichester: John Wiley & Sons.

Scott, D. (2015). Eating your insides out: Cultural, physical and institutionally-structured violence in the prison place. *Prison Service Journal*, 221, 55–62.

Sherif, M. & Sherif, C. W. (1969). *Social Psychology*. New York: Harper & Row.

Shuker, R. & Newberry, M. (2010). Changes in interpersonal relating following therapeutic community treatment at HMP Grendon. In R. Shuker & E. Sullivan (Eds.), *Grendon and the Emergence of Forensic Therapeutic Communities* (pp. 293–304). Chichester: John Wiley & Sons.

Sykes, G. (1958). *The Society of Captives: A Study of Maximum Security Prison*. Princeton, NJ: Princeton University Press.

Sykes, G. (1995). The structural-functional perspective on imprisonment. In T. Blomberg & S. Cohen (Eds.), *Punishment and Social Control: Essays in Honor of Sheldon L. Messenger*. New York: Aldine de Gruyter.

Tew, J., Vince, R. & Luther, J. (2015). Prison culture and prison violence. *Prison Service Journal Issue*, 221, 15–19.

Tonkin, M., Howells, K., Ferguson, E., Clark, A., Newberry, M. & Schalast, N. (2012). Lost in translation? Psychometric properties and construct validity of the English Essen Climate Evaluation Schema (EssenCES) social climate questionnaire. *Psychological Assessment*, 24, 573–580. doi:10.1037/a0026267.

Ward, T. (2002). Good lives and the rehabilitation of offenders: Promises and problems. *Aggression and Violent Behaviour*, 7(5), 513–528.

# 12

# WEARING TWO HATS

## Working therapeutically as a discipline prison officer

*Emma Guthrie, Laura Smillie, Annette McKeown and Claire Bainbridge*

> *Relations between staff and prisoners are at the heart of the whole prison system....*
> —Home Office, 1984, Paragraph 16

There are numerous studies indicating 'therapeutic alliance' as a key factor that encourages meaningful change with individuals in prison (e.g. Ross, Polaschek & Ward, 2008). Bordin (1994) usefully describes three specific aspects of a therapeutic alliance: (a) the alliance needs to be collaborative in nature, (b) demonstrate an affective bond between the client and staff member, and (c) importantly identify an agreement between these two individuals regarding goals and plans for the future. It has been argued that it may be the *quality* of the relationship between the therapist or staff member and the individual as opposed to the *type* of treatment which impacts most upon outcomes (Bedics, Atkins, Harned & Linehan, 2015). In prison environments, psychological treatment interventions are introduced frequently with well-informed aims of reducing the risk of re-offending. Often, heavily guided psychological treatment interventions note strong emphasis on adherence to a particular treatment manual. Although following such stringent treatment guidelines can help guide practitioners, over-reliance on these can at times distract from the crucial importance of the therapeutic relationship between the staff member and the prisoner (Gannon & Ward, 2014; Marshall, 2009). Respectfulness, confidence, flexibility and genuineness can all influence an individual's response to treatment (Norcross & Wampold, 2011). As key qualities which underpin the therapeutic alliance, these further highlight the importance of therapeutic relationships in working towards therapeutic change (Horvath, 2001).

This chapter will focus on prison officers' experience of balancing therapy and discipline roles within the prison environment. Two of the authors are discipline officers working within the Offender Personality Disorder (OPD) Pathway, and have worked with female offenders in the Primrose Service and Psychologically Informed Planned Environment (PIPE) for a number of years. The chapter will firstly examine historical and theoretical considerations to guide understanding of the balance between therapeutic and discipline roles for prison officers, before considering the role of officers who work particularly with females with personality disorders. In order to consider the challenges presented when working with complex individuals, a number of case studies will be described. Finally, the chapter will conclude with consideration of how these reflections can be put into practice.

## Historical considerations

In the past in Britain, there was very little need or political movement for the establishment of prisons. With a dichotomy approach, those found guilty of a crime were sentenced to death, whilst those found innocent were set free. Under King Henry II's rule in the 12th century, courts began to be established and the first prison (Newgate) was built in London. As imprisonment as a means for punishment began to gain momentum during the latter half of the last millennium, thought needed to be given to how assailants would be incarcerated, who was needed to manage their stay (and importantly prevent their escape), and the conditions in which people would be housed. It was not however until the late 18th century that John Howard, the High Sherriff of Bedfordshire at the time, began to call for wideranging reforms to be initiated, including the need for paid staff within the institutions (Howard, 2013).

Throughout the last 30–40 years or so, the role of the prison officer has developed from the perception of being merely a 'turnkey' or disciplinarian to one that recognises the significance of staff–prisoner relationships to the effective running and management of establishments (Home Office, 1984). However, the concept of the therapeutic relationships and their importance is not a new one. Broadmoor Hospital was the setting for a radical change in process and attitude towards the treatment of those in confinement. In 1870, Dr William Orange introduced the concept that individuals with personality disorder or mental illness should be treated with decency and be given empowerment over their own recovery. He created a moral treatment ethos within a high secure environment that we may now refer to as sociotherapy (Wilkins, 2012). Individuals were given paid job roles and staff members and patients were encouraged to interact in social activities together. Although this may not have been widely researched or reported upon in its infancy, it certainly reflected a positive step forward. Individuals felt considered and that staff held a genuine concern for their well-being, and they were encouraged and supported to be involved in their journey of recovery. As a result many thrived. However, this did not come without political complications. Dr Orange's innovative changes raised controversy and resistance by many, including staff members as well as the public.

This ambivalence continues to be reflected in more current opposing views held by many within a custodial setting. Some staff have confidence that positive therapeutic relationships can reduce the likelihood that offenders will commit further crime, however others believe that punishment and restriction of choice contributes positively to reform. Considering the benefits of offender involvement and the formation of appropriate relationships between staff and offenders in more modern times, Buonifino and Mulgan (2006) identified links between increasing unhappiness of individuals when there is a decline in mutual support. This in turn results in increased isolation and mental illness. We know from exploring the desistance literature that among the criminogenic needs of female offenders (with personality disorder particularly), poverty, isolation, emotional instability and a lack of personal agency and are all contributory factors to further criminal activity (Huebner, DeJong & Cobbina, 2009; Maruna, 2001).

## Recent initiatives

In prison settings, the Every Contact Matters initiative reflected existing literature on the crucial nature of therapeutic alliance (National Offender Management Service, 2014). Every Contact Matters presented the concept of the importance of each and every communication between staff and prisoners. The initiative highlighted the positive impact these interactions could have upon the offender and their view of themselves, staff and their environment. The initiative also echoed notions Ian Dunbar introduced over twenty-five years before which outlined the "dynamic of security" (Dunbar, 1985, p. 43). Dynamic security reflected that prison security was more than simply locking doors and following procedures. It identified that security is enhanced by engaging with offenders in a humane and empathic manner and this can then in turn improve security (Dunbar & Langdon, 1998). The foundation of Every Contact Matters and improving 'dynamic security' emphasises the development of meaningful relationships with uniformed and non-uniformed staff and offenders. These concepts also reflected the translation of therapeutic alliance theoretical constructs into practical strategies implemented in prison settings.

Empirical research which has examined prison officers' perceptions of therapeutic alliance has emphasised the importance that daily interactions hold for both prison officers and prisoners (e.g. Crawley, 2004; McManus, 2010; Taylor & Trout, 2013). In additional research, some prison officers described daily interactions as a "series of informal interventions" (Braggins & Talbot, 2006, p. 23). The latter research simultaneously highlighted challenges that prison officers encountered through balancing roles where they often described their primary function as related to security, discipline and operational roles. This was described in conflict to another role of being "all things to all people". In relation to the latter point, comments from prison officers included "To some of them we're mother, father, brother, sister. We're all they've got" (p. 23).

For prison officers working on a Psychologically Informed Planned Environment (PIPE), using an Interpretative Phenomenological Analysis (IPA) study, Bond and Gemmell (2014) highlighted main themes identified by prison officers which included 'role conflict', 'relationships', 'growth' and 'impact'. This research emphasised the contrast between positive aspects and more challenging aspects of working as a prison officer within this environment. Again, it was noteworthy that the role of 'relationships' was identified as a key theme when working with this population. Taken as a whole, research emphasises the multi-faceted relational role prison officers are presented with. Gilbert (1997) distinguishes between four different typologies of prison officers and presents distinctions between (a) the professional, (b) reciprocator, (c) enforcer and (d) avoider. Using Gilbert's (1997) typology, the professional refers to a prison officer who is open-minded, insightful and considered in their responses. The professional prison officer is described as a prison officer whom resorts to restraint as a last resort. The reciprocator refers to a prison officer who wishes to help others, tends to adopt clinical strategies and tends not to use restraint or physical strategies even when such strategies may be warranted. The enforcer refers to the prison officer who is rigid with rules, seeks out infractions of rules and can present as aggressive in their approach. The avoider refers to the officer who avoids contact with those detained in prison, does not consider their offence and avoids conflict (Liebling, Price & Shefer, 2012). Although Gilbert's (1997) work is based on prison officers in the United States (US), it serves to highlight the multiple roles prison officers can adopt (Liebling et al., 2015).

## Theoretical considerations

Drawing from attachment literature (e.g. Bowlby, 1980), findings indicate relational aspects are fundamental when working with offenders (Ireland & Power, 2004) and especially female offenders (Covington, 2008). Given the high incidence of trauma in female offenders (Bloom, Owen & Covington, 2004; Palmer & Hollin, 2006; Corston, 2007) the need to create secure attachments becomes extremely important (Moloney, van den Bergh & Moller, 2009). Therapeutic interactions present the opportunity to provide offenders with new experiences which can influence their understanding and expectations of relationships. For women, this is particularly important given that many women in prison will have expectations that interpersonal relationships are defined by abusive, unpredictable, distressing and pathological characteristics (Belknap, 2014). Building relationships also has particular relevance in custody when considering the importance to women of the need to belong and build self-identity (Corston, 2007). The relevance of these issues is also paramount with male offenders with recent research identifying an increase in identification with Islamic culture which was hypothesised to be linked to a variety of reasons including the search for 'identity' (Liebling, Arnold & Straub, 2011). Overall, these considerations have key roles when planning and developing environments and for staff development and recruitment for services working with complex offenders. New attachment experiences in custody with multi-disciplinary and therapeutic staff have the potential to help offenders re-formulate their understanding and expectations of relationships in a very powerful way (e.g. Mikulincer & Shaver, 2010).

Psychodynamic concepts such as 'holding' (Winnicott, 1953, 1971) and 'containment' (Bion, 1959, 1962) are useful frameworks to understand the containing aspects of both the prison environment and therapeutic relationships offenders can build with staff. The term 'holding' refers to the supportive environment that a therapist is able to create for a client and mirrors the nurturing and caring behaviour a mother will display to her child, thus resulting in a sense of trust and safety. Containment (Bion, 1959, 1962) was originally described as the process where a mother receives intense projection from the child and she helps the infant process these experiences in less painful manner. In a therapeutic context, containment refers to the process whereby therapists/establishments can act as a 'container' of painful thoughts and feelings and help individuals process and understand them in a more adaptive and meaningful way.

Research has indicated small prisons are generally experienced as more positive than larger prisons. In smaller prisons, the quality of staff–prisoner relationships was described in a more positive manner than larger prisons (Johnsen, Granheim & Helgesen, 2011). Physically smaller environments may be experienced as more 'holding' and safer to prisoners. Smaller prisons may also have higher staff–prisoner ratios, which can provide greater opportunity to increase the time spent on building relationships. This is consistent with the Every Contact Matters initiative, which may result in a more containing experience for prisoners. More broadly, the constructs of holding and containment are also consistent with the Royal College of Psychiatrists (2010) Enabling Environment initiative, which emphasises connectedness and belonging (Johnson & Haigh, 2011). Consistency in forensic environments is also a key consideration when examining contextual factors conducive to therapeutic alliance. The importance of providing a stable and consistent workforce with appropriate skills and confidence, as well as trust in leadership has been highlighted (Liebling et al., 2015).

In 2011, the Department of Health and Ministry of Justice devised a new Offender Personality Disorder (OPD) Pathway directed at men and women with severe personality disorder. Treatment directions are premised on existing findings on the importance of therapeutic relationships (Joseph & Benefield, 2012). Services are generally for a small number of prisoners and include preparation, treatment and progression services. These services exist for young offenders (e.g. Aylesbury Pathways Service), male offenders (e.g. Westgate) and female offenders (e.g. Primrose Service). Within each site, therapeutic relationships are a key underpinning strategy to treatment directions. Psychological Informed Planned Environments (PIPEs) offer preparation, provision and progression pathways for offenders on the OPD pathway. PIPE settings provide offenders with a supportive environment to practice and consolidate skills they have developed. Emphasis has been placed on consideration on relational consideration for both staff and prisoners throughout the OPD Pathway (Brown, 2014). Existing documentation linked to the OPD Pathway includes *Working with Personality Disorder: A Practitioner's Guide* (Department of Health, 2011). This key document emphasises the importance of therapeutic relationships and of maintaining consistent longer term relationships with the offender. The importance of understanding that offenders may re-enact unhelpful relationship dynamics is a further aspect which is emphasised within this guide.

Using formulation strategies to help prisoners and staff teams to understand these parallels and repeating patterns can help increase their insight into their difficulties and increase therapeutic alliance (Motz, 2001).

## The role of the prison officer

Traditionally prison officers have been viewed solely as having a disciplinary role which may have encouraged us to view prisoners almost exclusively as perpetrators. When we explore the Prison Service Statement of Purpose however, a prison officer's role has always been defined as much more than that:

> Her Majesty's Prison Service serves to protect the public by keeping in custody those committed by the courts. Our duty is to look after them with humanity and help them lead law abiding and useful lives in custody and after release.

Liebling, Price and Shefer (2012) advocate that in recent years, prison work has become varied, testing and specialised, despite the role of the officer being seen, even with the prison, as "low visibility work" (p. 2). However, is it possible to balance the discipline role with a more therapeutic approach? As Devine, Greener, Laws and Phillippo (2014) note, "balancing the therapy role with the discipline role is both challenging and rewarding" (p. 30–31). Often expectations of prisoners regarding their interactions with prison staff is one of an austere approach and therefore adjustment to a more therapeutic way of working can be difficult and often confusing for both parties. Over forty years ago, Thomas (1972) recognised the confusion that many prison officers felt regarding what he saw as the major conflict of their role – security versus rehabilitation. It may be widely recognised, theoretically at least, that interpersonal effectiveness plays a core role within practice as prison officers. However this quality therapeutic relationship requires skill and is not always easy to form and may be due to personal values and beliefs let alone maintain. Modelling pro-social behaviours is integral to this therapeutic role. Devine et al. (2014) suggest that this is best achieved when staff increase their own awareness and insight, consequently allowing for a reduction in inappropriate or less helpful interactions to occur.

Two of the authors of this chapter jointly have 30 years' experience as prison officers working within high secure settings, and have worked with a large number of women with an array of complex problems. On a daily basis an eclectic mix of situations and behaviours is encountered that highlights not only the challenges associated with maintaining an empathic yet boundaried relationship with the women we work with, but also the importance of a therapeutic dynamic within this environment.

In order to illustrate a small number of these situations, a number of personal encounters that highlight the relevance and challenges of interpersonal relations between staff members and women with personality difficulties are presented.

The following are fictional examples that are an amalgamation of experiences encountered over the last few years.

## Leigh

Leigh is a 42-year-old woman who received a ten-year sentence for a violent offence against a minor. She has experienced a protracted history of physical, sexual and emotional abuse from her mother, grandmother and other members of her family. Listening to her talk about her childhood and reading her social services records was considered to be very challenging. Leigh presented a lot of the time in a very childlike manner. She would frequently suck her thumb, she frequently sought out staff time and she wore clothing and displayed body language that was more fitting of a young child than a grown woman. She would often wear t-shirts depicting cartoon characters and wear ribbons in her hair, and when she talked about something she particularly gained joy from, she would giggle and excitedly wave her hands in the air. It was not unusual for staff members to communicate with her in a way that reinforced this immaturity; for example, the simplest of tasks, like cleaning her floor or making phone calls on her behalf, would be completed for her as opposed to encouraging autonomy. Leigh appeared capable of completing tasks on her own yet seemed to willingly accept 'help' from others. Prior to incarceration, she reported being an ardent traveller, usually taking trips without additional support, and portrayed a life of independence and skill.

In the most straightforward sense, her behaviour in custody could of course be thought about in terms of her receiving little care or support from those charged with her care as a child. Despite formulating and understanding this difficulty, consistent management was not always maintained. This was especially true for staff members dealing with her habitual self-harming behaviours. Although she was viewed as having severe vulnerabilities at times when she presented as 'childlike' in manner, when she self-harmed she was often thought about or referred to as manipulative. This view may have been derived from the times these incidents occurred, for example, as staff were finishing their detailed shift or when there was an incident being dealt with involving another female on the same wing. It became almost impossible for staff to view her actions with an empathic lens when they felt her behaviour was orchestrated to 'seek attention' and prevent them from going home.

As a discipline member of staff working with Leigh on a regular basis in a therapeutic way, it was possible to explore this behaviour with her and highlight the link between specific times of day and her thinking, feelings and self-harm behaviour (Marzano, Ciclitira & Adler, 2012). Without the opportunity to do this, a non-empathic stance of her behaviour may have been maintained and it may have been more likely to respond to her in a less than sympathetic manner (as previously observed). Although incredibly frustrating at times, it was important to take the time to consider the function of Leigh's behaviour so as not to contribute to further dysfunctional interactions. This would have undoubtedly affected the relationship between her and staff in a negative way and affected her ability to gain insight and progress with her recovery.

## Anna

Anna is convicted of arson and serving an indeterminate sentence (IPP) and has a substantial history of substance misuse and aggressive behaviour. For a number of months, Anna resided on the PIPE wing in the prison and her engagement with the unit and staff was generally considered to be positive. She was very creative and enjoyed taking part in group sessions. She could also be very supportive of her peers and staff. In discussion with staff she presented as very open and honest.

Throughout her time on the unit Anna was frequently found to be using illicit substances. Her substance misuse included illegal drugs and consuming alcohol hand wash mixed with fruit juice. After every incident she would discuss her reasons with staff and vacillate between taking responsibility for her actions and expressing remorse, and blaming 'the system' for her issues. When she was remorseful she could eloquently explain everything that she had learned from engaging in psychological interventions. She was able to quote the information very positively, which in turn gave hope for her to move forward. However, her abstinence would be brief and then she would slip again and so the cycle continued. Anna could become very aggressive when she was in the cycle of drug misuse, partly due to increasing debt and feeling pressure from her peers but also because her withdrawal created feelings of stress and anxiety.

On a particular occasion, Anna was in a group session with other prisoners and staff when she became embroiled in an altercation with another resident. Staff intervened but despite attempts to de-escalate the situation Anna was required to be restrained as she could not calm down and withdraw from the altercation. Unfortunately, the incident continued and she had to be returned to her cell by staff where it took some time for her to eventually calm down and speak about the incident. The following day Anna was once again very remorseful about her behaviour and also apologised to staff for 'forcing them' to be involved in a violent situation with her. She discussed how she could have managed the situation differently at length and was able to verbalise exactly how she should have reacted but had been unable to do so during the event.

Having knowledge of Anna's history prior to incarceration and an understanding of subsequent formulations regarding her difficult and problematic behaviour meant that being part of the team of staff that were involved in the restraint of Anna would be very challenging. Consequently, it is no surprise that staff became concerned about the effect that such incidents may have on the therapeutic relationship between themselves and the prisoner concerned.

## Ruth

Ruth is a 19-year-old woman serving a life sentence for the murder of her friend. She witnessed the murder of her brother at a young age and during her teenage years her behaviour, including drug and alcohol misuse and some obsessional behaviours, became increasingly challenging for her family to cope with and as a result she spent some time moving between local authority care placements. Ruth is an individual who presents with high levels of anger and paranoia. This paranoia impacted enormously on her ability to engage in treatment designed to address thinking styles, and her interpersonal style would be considered as challenging by professionals. It was difficult to maintain a balance between the discipline and therapeutic relationship with Ruth, with the latter the most challenging to maintain. Her presentation was constantly (with fleeting exceptions) aggressive and intimidating and often left staff feeling highly aroused with both anxiety and anger at being treated so appallingly when simply trying to help her. She would often take a dislike to staff (often for no obvious or understood reason), and would subsequently become aggressive and accuse the staff member of trying to 'wind her up'. Her behaviour would become increasingly hostile, and she would be noticed to spit as she shouted. Staff would notice that she became tense and would clench her fists as she would shout at them. Despite attempts to de-escalate the situation or to reassure Ruth that she was being listened to, her aggressive behaviour would increase. It made no difference if staff spoke to her calmly; if anything this seemed to antagonise the situation. As a result staff would report feeling intimidated by Ruth and how they were hesitant to engage with her.

It would be tempting for discipline staff to use their authority and instantly escort Ruth to her cell or safer place and place her on the Governor's Report whenever she presented in such a way. However, it is recognised that by doing so, negative repercussions for an already fractured therapeutic relationship would be likely to occur. However, it is also recognised that it is also not helpful for staff not to be able to tolerate any level of disrespect either. Through consistent and mindful management of her behaviour, Ruth would stop shouting and calm down. Staff were then able to discuss the incidents with her and why this needed to be communicated to her wider multi-disciplinary team via her prison record. In order to reduce levels of paranoia, it was considered to be appropriate to discuss the repercussions of her behaviour whilst this information would be shared with other professionals.

### Chelsea

Chelsea is sentenced to life for a serious violent offence which she committed as a teenager. She had a very difficult childhood characterised by insecure and broken attachments, parental alcohol misuse and domestic violence as well as a long history of substance misuse and aggression. She was initially introduced to the wing as a 'problem child' due to having a lengthy discipline record of assaults on staff and damage to property. After a period of good behaviour on the wing she was encouraged to engage with the therapeutic processes of the unit. She was very keen to be involved as she had been previously very curious about the various activities available and she engaged very well. She enjoyed being part of the group sessions and also was very open in one-on-one key worker sessions.

Chelsea constantly sought time with staff and her peers and it seemed very obvious that she craved affection both physically and emotionally. On a regular basis she would try to obtain this by either acting out, crying or being overly friendly. Maintaining boundaries with Chelsea was challenging as she would often seek affection, make inappropriate declarations and attempt to receive physical contact such as hugs from staff. When this behaviour was challenged it often resulted in a 'temper tantrum' possibly due to feelings of rejection or abandonment, most likely a legacy of her childhood experiences. During these outbursts she would need constant reassurance that staff's reaction was nothing personal and purely a professional issue that would be raised with any other prisoner, but she would normally respond with uncontrollable crying claiming 'nobody likes me'.

Chelsea tended to receive negative attention from many of her peers for various reasons and was viewed as an 'informant' because she spent a lot of her time talking to staff. She was referred to by other residents as the staff members' 'favourite prisoner' because of her over-friendly attitude towards them and she was also classed as a general irritation due to her loud behaviour and what could be perceived as constant attention seeking. It was a continuous battle to balance managing her behaviours and the pull of wanting to parent her as well as dividing attention amongst the other prisoners who also needed support.

## Reflections

These case studies identify the complexity and diversity of issues working therapeutically as a prison officer. Within a prison environment, at times the presenting behaviour (e.g. violence, self-harm, substance use, boundary breaking) can be so extreme and challenging that the behaviour itself can become the focus as opposed to consideration of the function of the behaviour. When the presenting behaviour includes negative attitudes and targeting behaviour towards prison officers the challenges of working therapeutically can be further intensified. Understanding the function of the presenting behaviour (Johnstone & Dallos, 2014) and building and maintaining a therapeutic alliance can help in understanding and addressing these challenges (Bond & Gemmell, 2014; Gilbert & Leahy, 2007).

It may be challenging for some to see how being a prison officer working therapeutically with residents on the OPD units can enhance the job role and increase job satisfaction. There are rewards for doing a good job in the Prison Service which include the feeling that you might have made a difference in a person's life, helping someone to make progress in their sentence or witnessing positive behaviour change in an offender. Offering an empathic response to challenging behaviours helps this hugely. As Liebling (2006) has observed, fairness, trust and safety are among the few essential core values that are required in custodial settings, not least as a way to promote and instil relational security. It is important for staff to recognise each small feeling of 'victory' in order to maintain motivation to work in such a complex area. Prison officers should feel empowered to take each and every one of these 'victories', however small, and use them to spur them forward. This concept is perhaps considered within the Self-Determination Theory (Ryan & Deci, 2000) and focuses primarily on internal sources of motivation including a need to gain knowledge or independence.

Self-Determination Theory suggests that people need to feel three things in order to achieve psychological growth: competence, connection or relatedness and autonomy. Competence can be described as learning new and different skills and being able to master tasks. Prison officers working within the Offender Personality Disorder Pathway are given extra training to work therapeutically with residents on the units. This often encourages many to continue to improve their education by completing academic courses including diplomas or degrees. As highlighted in the case studies, prison officers working in therapeutic roles will find that every day is an education and some occasions can be more educating than others. Connection or relatedness is achieved by feeling a sense of belonging and attachment to others, and is particularly pertinent to the recovery process (Clarke, Lumbard, Sambrook & Kerr, 2015). If a prison officer has the skills to develop a therapeutic alliance with the individuals they work with, this working relationship will be considered helpful and will be able to assist both parties with the work they are trying to do. Autonomy is attained when people feel in control of their behaviours and goals, and prison officers who work therapeutically are more likely to achieve this as they have the opportunity to work as an individual, showing more of their own personality. As mentioned previously, when working within the Offender Personality Disorder Pathway, staff receive opportunities for training in a number of areas, including case formulation and understanding personality disorder, to assist them with this.

In conclusion, being able balance the culture of dynamic and relational security with a more therapeutic approach can be a difficult skill to master and takes empathy, patience, positivity, a desire to want to help people achieve their potential and most importantly, a sense of humour. Demonstrating an effective use of authority whilst at the same time modelling appropriate and desired behaviours is essential when attempting to instil change or teach problem-solving skills with individuals who previously have engaged in disruptive and maladaptive behaviours. As Devine et al. (2014) advocate, engagement in regular supervision, training and when necessary, de-briefs, is crucial for developing therapeutic skills. When a prison officer manages to achieve this it can help towards gaining a feeling of satisfaction and fulfilment and can be uplifting and make for an enjoyable career.

## References

Bedics, J.D., Atkins, D.C., Harned, M.S. & Linehan, M.M. (2015). The therapeutic alliance as a predictor of outcome in dialectical behavior therapy versus nonbehavioral psychotherapy by experts for borderline personality disorder. *Psychotherapy, 52*, 67.

Belknap, J. (2014). *The Invisible Woman: Gender, Crime, and Justice*. Boston: Cengage Learning.

Bion, W.R. (1959). Attacks on linking. *International Journal of Psycho-Analysis, 40*, 308–316.

Bion, W.R. (1962). The psycho-analytic study of thinking. *International Journal of Psycho-Analysis, 43*, 306–310.

Bloom, B., Owen, B., & Covington, S. (2004). Women offenders and the gendered effects of public policy. *Review of Policy Research, 21*(1), 31–48.

Bond, N. & Gemmell, L. (2014). Experiences of prison officers on a lifer psychologically informed planned environment. *Therapeutic Communities: The International Journal of Therapeutic Communities, 35*, 84–94.

Bordin, E. (1994). Theory and research on the therapeutic alliance: New directions. In A.O. Horvath & L.S. Greenberg (Eds.), *The Working Alliance: Theory, Research and Practice*. Chichester, UK: John Wiley & Sons.

Bowlby, J. (1980). *Attachment and Loss* (Vol. 3). New York: Basic Books.

Braggins, J. & Talbot, J. (2006). Wings of learning: The role of the prison officer in supporting prison education. *Prison Service Journal, 168*, 1–70.

Brown, M. (2014). Psychologically Informed Planned Environment (PIPE): A group analytic perspective. *Psychoanalytic Psychotherapy, 28*, 345–354.

Buonifino, A. & Mulgan, G. (2006). *Goodbye to All That*. Retrieved from www.guardian .co.uk/society/2006/jan/18/communities.guardiansocietysupplement.

Clarke, C., Lumbard, D., Sambrook, S. & Kerr, K. (2015). What does recovery mean to a forensic mental health patient? A systematic review and narrative synthesis of the qualitative literature. *The Journal of Forensic Psychiatry & Psychology*, 1–17, online first.

Corston, J. (2007). *A Review of Women with Particular Vulnerabilities in the Criminal Justice System*. London, UK: Home Office.

Covington, S. (2008). The relational theory of women's psychological development: Implications for the criminal justice system. In R. T. Zaplin (Ed.), *Female Offenders: Critical Perspectives and Effective Interventions* (2nd ed., pp. 135–164). Sudbury, MA: Jones & Bartlett Publishers.

Crawley, E. (2004). *Doing prison work: the public and private lives of prison officers*. Devon: Willan Publishing.

Department of Health (2011). Working with personality disordered offenders: A practitioners guide. Retrieved from www.justice.gov.uk/downloads/offenders/mentally-disordered-offenders/working-with-personality-disordered-offenders.pdf

Devine, S., Greener, G., Laws, K. & Phillippo, B. (2014). Balancing the therapy role with the prison officer role, *Forensic Update, 114*, 29–33.

Dunbar, I. (1985) *A Sense of Direction*. London: Home Office.

Dunbar, I. & Langdon, A. (1998). *Tough Justice: Sentencing and Penal Policies in the 1990s*. Oxford: Oxford University Press.

Gannon, T.A. & Ward, T. (2014). Where has all the psychology gone? A critical review of evidence-based psychological practice in correctional settings. *Aggression and Violent Behavior, 19*, 435–446.

Gilbert, M. (1997). The illusion of structure: a critique of the classical model of organisation and the discretionary power of correctional officers. *Criminal Justice Review, 22*(1), 49–64.

Gilbert, P. & Leahy, R.L. (Eds.). (2007). *The Therapeutic Relationship in the Cognitive Behavioral Psychotherapies*. East Sussex, UK: Routledge.

Home Office (1984). *Managing the Long-term Prison System: The Report of the Control Review Committee*, London: Home Office.

Horvath, A.O. (2001). The alliance. *Psychotherapy, 38*, 365–372.

Howard, J. (2013). *The State of the Prisons in England and Wales*. New York, NY: Cambridge University Press.

Ireland, J.L. & Power, C.L. (2004). Attachment, emotional loneliness, and bullying behaviour: A study of adult and young offenders. *Aggressive Behavior, 30*, 298–312.

Johnsen, B., Granheim, P.K. & Helgesen, J. (2011). Exceptional prison conditions and the quality of prison life: Prison size and prison culture in Norwegian closed prisons. *European Journal of Criminology, 8*, 515–529.

Johnson, R. & Haigh, R. (2011). Social psychiatry and social policy for the 21st century: New concepts for new needs - the 'Enabling Environments' initiative. *Mental Health and Social Inclusion, 15*, 17–23.

Johnstone, L. & Dallos, R. (2014) *Formulation in psychology and psychotherapy: Making sense of people's problems*. Hove: Routledge.

Joseph, N. & Benefield, N. (2012). A joint offender personality disorder pathway strategy: An outline summary. *Criminal Behaviour and Mental Health, 22*, 210–217.

Liebling, A. (2006). Prisons in transition. *International Journal of Law and Psychiatry, 29*, 422–430.

Liebling, A., Arnold, H. & Straub, C. (2011). An exploration of staff–prisoner relationships at HMP Whitemoor: 12 years on. Revised Final Report, Ministry of Justice, National Offender Management Service. Cambridge Institute of Criminology Prisons Research Centre. London: National Offender Management Service.

Liebling, A., Price, D. & Shefer, G. (2012). *The Prison Officer*. 2nd Edition. London, UK: Routledge.

Liebling, A., Schmidt, B., Crewe, B., Auty, K., Armstrong, R., Akoensi, T., Kant, D., Ludlow, A. & Levins, A. (2015). *Birmingham Prison: The Transition from Public to Private Sector and Its Impact on Staff and Prisoner Quality of Life – a Three-Year Study*. London, UK: Ministry of Justice.

Marshall, W.L. (2009). Manualization: A blessing or a curse? *Journal of Sexual Aggression, 15*, 109–120.

Maruna, S. (2001). *Making Good*. Washington, DC: APA Press.

Marzano, L., Ciclitira, K. & Adler, J. (2012). The impact of prison staff responses on self-harming behaviours: Prisoners' perspectives. *British Journal of Clinical Psychology, 51*, 4–18.

McManus, J. (2010). The experience of officers in a therapeutic prison: an interpretative phenomenological analysis. In Shuker, R. & Sullivan, E. (Eds), *Grendon and the Emergence of Forensic Therapeutic Communities: Developments in Research and Practice*. Chichester, UK: John Wiley & Sons, Ltd.

Mikulincer, M. & Shaver, P. R. (2010). *Attachment in Adulthood: Structure, Dynamics, and Change*. New York: Guilford Press.

Moloney, K.P., van den Bergh, B.J. & Moller, L.F. (2009). Women in prison: The central issues of gender characteristics and trauma history. *Public Health, 123*, 426–430.

Motz, A. (2001). *The Psychology of Female Violence: Crimes against the Body*. East Sussex, UK: Brunner-Routledge.

National Offender Management Service. (2014). *Business Plan 2014–2015*. London: National Offender Management Service.

Norcross, J.C. & Wampold, B.E. (2011). Evidence-based therapy relationships: Research conclusions and clinical practices. *Psychotherapy, 48*, 98–102.

Orange, W. (1870). Inside Broadmoor Episode 1 (2013). Retrieved 3 October 2014 from www.channel5.com/shows/inside-broadmoor-2013/episodes-1-560.

Palmer, E.J. & Hollin, C.R. (2006). Criminogenic need and women offenders: A critique of the literature. *Legal and Criminological Psychology, 11*, 179–195.

Ross, E.C., Polaschek, D.L. & Ward, T. (2008). The therapeutic alliance: A theoretical revision for offender rehabilitation. *Aggression and Violent Behavior, 13*, 462–480.

Royal College of Psychiatrists. (2010). *Standards for Enabling Environments*. London, UK: Royal College of Psychiatrists.

Ryan, R.M., & Deci, E.L. (2000). Self-determination theory and the facilitation of intrinsic motivation, social development, and well-being. *American Psychologist, 55*, 68–78.

Taylor, J. & Trout, S. (2013). Lessons from the front line: Working with offenders with learning disability and personality disorder in a high secure therapeutic community. *Mental Health Review Journal, 18*, 44–52.

Thomas, J.E. (1972). *The English Prison Officer since 1850*. London, UK: Routledge & Kegan Paul.

Wilkins, P. (2012). Person-centred sociotherapy: Applying person centred attitudes, principles and practices to social situations, group and society as a whole. *Hellenic Journal of Psychology, 9*, 240–254.

Winnicott, D.W. (1953). Transitional objects and transitional phenomena: a study of the first not-me possession. *International Journal of Psycho-Analysis, 34*, 89–97.

Winnicott, D.W. (1971). *Playing and Reality*. London: Psychology Press.

# 13

# THE ENABLING ENVIRONMENTS AWARD AS A TRANSFORMATIVE PROCESS

*Sarah Paget and Roland Woodward*

## Enabling Environments: how they came about

The most complete description of the process of bringing the Enabling Environment (EE) concept into being is in the paper 'Psychologically informed environments and the "Enabling Environments" initiative' by Haigh, Harrison, Johnson, Paget and Williams (2012). The paper describes the way in which the idea for EE and the EE Award was created by the EE Development Group functioning under the auspices of the Royal College of Psychiatrists' Centre for Quality Improvement (CCQI).

The EE project built upon the work done by the Community of Communities, a quality improvement and accreditation network for therapeutic communities (TCs). It developed in response to expressed need from services who wished to demonstrate the therapeutic qualities of their service. Having come across the Service Standards for Therapeutic Communities (Paget, Thorne & Das 2015) they identified with the underlying principles and values of TCs, but were less sure about the model as a whole in their settings or sector. TCs utilise a psychosocial approach to the treatment of individuals with a range of disorders that lead to difficulties engaging with self and others. The context and the environment where treatment or therapy takes place is the central tool. In other settings there is acknowledgement that the psychosocial environment contributes positively to treatment efficacy and the EE Award was an attempt to identify what factors need to be in place in order for an environment to have a positive therapeutic effect.

Haigh et al. (2012) describe the way in which the concept of EE and EE Award developed. The Core Values of Therapeutic Communities (Community of Communities, 2008), which underpin the TC standards and anchor them in a distinctly value-based approach, were a useful starting point. They helped the group to centre on the value of relationships and engagement with self, others and the environmental context. The term 'Enabling Environment' was useful as a generic term

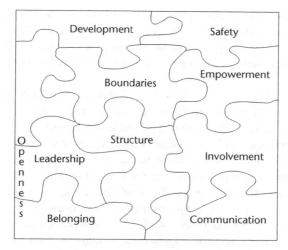

**FIGURE 13.1**  The Enabling Environment Matrix.

to describe good practice across a wide range of sectors of contemporary social life and was "an attempt to find or create a much broader vision of constructive relationship-forming to aid and inform service developments that did not rely primarily on themes and theories of treatment or care" (Haigh et al., 2012, pp. 35–36).

The team worked to maintain a common sense approach to factors that increase a feeling of safety and of being supported, to foster growth and well-being and have an enabling effect on staff and residents. Using the TC standards, feedback from services and the professional expertise of the group and others, the group distilled ten underpinning principles that together would lead to an environment being enabling. These were further explored within the context of the 'grey literature' of policy statements from government departments, statutory regulatory bodies and professional associations as well as a broad literature review. Each principle is an essential element in creating an environment that promotes growth and development for service users and staff.

Collectively, they provide an integrated and sustainable Enabling Environment matrix that promotes belonging and inclusivity, safety and containment which in turn supports a positive approach to risk, necessary for personal growth and interpersonal learning (Figure 13.1).

The principles and the standards and processes that operationalise them fit together like a jigsaw and are mutually dependant on each other to create a fully functional whole organisational system. Individually they will improve the quality of service provision but it is their collective presence that is the embodiment of an Enabling Environment.

## The relationship between the core principles

The core principles exist in some settings more naturally than others. Schools, for example, tend toward a more reflective and open space that supports their primary task where the culture or atmosphere of the environment is viewed as critical for the development of the children and young people. Even in schools however, the same approach is not always evident in relation to staff even though there is often a clear correlation between demoralised and burnt-out staff and children's learning outcomes.

The EE Award was set up to allow services that achieved high levels of psycho-social awareness and practice to be recognised and to highlight these qualities in other settings such as children's homes, mental health facilities, prisons and so forth.

Once the principles and the standards had been agreed it was necessary to establish a way of recognising these in action in the environment. What would we see in an environment that put relationships at the heart of their service?

It was proposed that these principles should be able to be expressed as "generic standards for practice, and then operationalised, and customised with more sector specific operational criteria where needed, yet always with an explicit recognition of the need to evidence the application of values as the central aim" (Haigh et al., 2012, p. 136). The group found that "some identifiable principles or standards seemed to consistently underlie and articulate what were seen to be the main issues in positive practice" (p. 37).

The EE principles and standards elucidated by the group are as follows:

- **Belonging:** The nature and quality of relationships are of primary importance.
- **Boundaries:** There are expectations of behaviour and processes to maintain them and review them.
- **Communication:** It is recognised that people communicate in different ways.
- **Development:** There are opportunities to be spontaneous and try new things.
- **Involvement:** Everyone shares responsibility for the environment.
- **Safety:** Support is available for everyone.
- **Structure:** Engagement and purposeful activity are actively encouraged.
- **Empowerment:** Power and authority are open to discussion.
- **Leadership:** Leadership takes responsibility for the environment.
- **Openness:** External relationships are sought after and valued.

The process of assessment was not to be prescriptive; each service would do things in their own way reflecting the nature of the service and client group but also the environment in which they functioned. Criteria needed to be indicative of achieving the standard but flexible to allow for differences in delivery. The assessment process needed to reflect the underpinning principles of openness and reflection; it should encourage communication and thinking among members of the service and most of all it should promote learning and development within the service and engagement with others. In short the process should both identify as well as help create EEs.

The portfolio assessment process was developed because it mirrored the National Vocational Qualifications (NVQ) that many potential services would be familiar with but also a model of education that supports a priori learning and development.

This was important as the process should value the work that services were doing rather than just impose new ways of doing things. The approach enables services to demonstrate competencies and provide their own ideas for how they meet the standards, whilst supporting them to recognise the 'enabling' nature of the work they already do. Each standard has accompanying criteria which identify specific activities or behaviour that would demonstrate that the standard is met; however, these are not exclusive and services can put forward other alternatives as long as they can support them with their reasoning and understanding of why it demonstrates that they meet the standard. The whole process, as with NVQs, encourages reflection, development of knowledge and a more in-depth understanding of what they do and why. The process enables services to make links between processes and procedures and the experience of implementation, for example linking a buddy policy with creating a sense of belonging thereby facilitating a relationship between self and others.

The portfolio was intended as the vehicle for reflection and change. Services would be required to work together, involving both staff and service users, to compile evidence for the standards; this both enables opportunities for services to begin to develop working with service users (involvement and empowerment) and contributes to the process of gaining the Award. This was emphasised by the experience of a member of the Award programme who commented that engaging residents in the process had led to the service becoming an Enabling Environment:

> [F]inding out what (they) thought they meant, not just what we as staff thought ... we became an enabled environment – they knew the process, why we were doing it, could see it wasn't a box ticking exercise, but it was evidently in their benefit. Honest discussion about their views on what could be improved. We noticed a real improvement in the mood and behaviour of the resident group [and it] did seem to impact on the mood of the hostel which highlighted early on how important this could be. (Guassardo, 2016)

## Enabling Environment: an adjective or a noun?

Central to the understanding of what the EE Award represents is the appreciation that the EE Award is not given to a service for being a 'thing' but for demonstrating that it is engaged in an active process of quality improvement in the delivery of its service. It is an adjective that describes a dynamic, reflective and learning service that is continually trying to provide the best possible environment for everyone involved with it to develop, grow and flourish. This adjectival element to the Award is often the most misunderstood element of the EE initiative. Services often ask for examples of EEs, so that they can go and 'see' one; an EE is as much an experienced emotional state as is it is a set of observable procedures, protocols or standards. An EE can be highly individual for any given service and almost any service can be an EE in its own unique way. Every service interprets and applies the ten principles and standards in their own way. The best example of this distinction is in relation to trees. For something to be defined as a tree it must have a trunk and branches, roots and leaves. On the whole we expect trees to be green but few would argue that the beautiful copper beech was not a tree because it had different coloured leaves. Similarly the oak and the Christmas tree could not be more different but they are both trees. Comparison can be helpful in some cases but on the whole, the tree, like EEs, have taken a broad understanding of some basic 'tree standards' and developed a range of ways to achieve them.

Of course where this becomes further complicated is whether a service is an enabling environment or an Enabling Environment. An EE is a noun, in that it describes somewhere that has achieved the EE Award. It has been recognised as meeting the standards and has completed a process to achieve this recognition. There will be many services functioning as enabling environments, who either have no knowledge of the principles and standards, have no desire for the Award or will be in the process of achieving it. Equally there are many who might describe themselves as enabling environments but are far from being enabling. Developing a process of this type necessarily means naming it, and this has implications. The EE project has developed a term that describes services that have the ability to demonstrate the 10 core standards, and that they operate as an integrated whole. Services wanting to be recognised as an 'Enabling Environment' will need to participate in the process. In addition, the fact that the EE Award is a process makes it unusual and not something that can be attained and then forgotten about as if it is was a one off examination or qualification. The EE Award brings with it expectations for the future and raises questions about the 'here and now' practice and delivery of the service. Being an 'Enabling Environment' necessitates a culture of reflective practice, participant involvement, increased interpersonal interaction and meaningful activity in an ongoing way.

## Therapeutic environments and the Criminal Justice System

Clearly the nature of personal relationships is at the heart of the standards and echoes what many people have said about the work of the Criminal Justice System (CJS) for many years. There are many specialist services in the prison and probation services that are obviously highly dependent on interpersonal relationships and are deliberately designed on a psychosocial basis. The therapeutic communities of Grendon (Genders & Player 1995; Shuker & Sullivan 2010) and Dovegate (Brown, Miller, Northey & O'Neill 2014; Cullen & Mackenzie 2011) are obvious examples, however there are an increasing number of Psychologically Informed Planned Environments (PIPEs) and assessment and treatment units which rely heavily for their theoretical and evidence based practice on the therapeutic community research and theory bases. These specialised services have mainly been introduced to service the Offender Personality Disorder Pathway that has replaced the Dangerous and Severe Personality Disorder (DSPD) services.

EEs are different in that they are neither clinical interventions nor incubators for people to consolidate and internalise the work they have undertaken via a range of interventions offered. EEs are conceived as identifiable spaces in which service providers (staff) and their recipients (service users, offenders etc.) are able to thrive because of the naturally occurring interpersonal and reflective factors within their living/working environment. It is a culture based on values that has relationships at its centre.

This conceptualisation makes assumptions about what is 'enabling' based on clinical interventions that are intentional. Therapeutic communities have been described as "search engines for meaning" (Woodward, 2011, p. 127), where participants actively seek change through exploration of meaning, and PIPEs by definition are planned and informed by psychology. Can an EE occur spontaneously or develop through a collaborative exploration of the standards that seem to underpin a healthy and salugenic environment without the intention of personal change? We suggest it can.

## EEs and the criminal justice sector

In his Perrier Lecture of 2013, 'Contraction in an Age of Expansion: An Operational Perspective', Ian Mulholland, the Deputy Director of Public Sector Prisons, noted that it was Ian Dunbar in 1985 who had highlighted the crucial role that the relationships between staff and offenders played in maintaining and providing 'dynamic security', a sentiment that was reiterated by Jo Pilling in 1992 and Martin Narey in 1999, the latter in his speech 'Taking the Prison Service into the 21st Century', given at the 10th Annual Eve Saville Memorial Lecture in May of that year. Mulholland not only echoed the view that personal relationships were crucial but discussed the adoption of 'Every Contact Matters':

> We used the term 'Every Contact Matters' because it neatly encapsulated the idea that however small or fleeting, experience and the desistance research shows that even the most common day-to-day interactions between everyone who works in a prison and the prisoners can and do make a difference. (Mulholland 2013)

Both Martin Narey and Ian Mulholland make reference to the research work of Alison Liebling, and Ian Mulholland noted that:

> The difference now is that due in no small part to the illuminating research Alison Liebling, Ben Crewe and Susan Hulley at Cambridge have conducted over several years, we have a better grasp of how to make provision of a sort which can enable the best sort of staff-prisoner relationship to flourish. (Mulholland 2013)

The advance in prison research over the years has been increasingly useful and informative as the cultural paranoia and distrust in prisons of almost anyone who came into the prison with a research brief has decreased. This, it is suggested, has diminished over the years due the influence of modernising the prison service and the changing cultural and legal environment that has evolved from the mid 1970s. Reading various publications such as Cohen and Taylor (1976), Fitzgerald and Sim

(1979), Liebling and Price (2001) and Crawley (2004) it is clear that prison work has become more accessible over this time and more carefully thought about. This is especially true of the emotional components of prison life for both staff and residents as more emphasis is placed on the nature of the containment relationship than punishment and the maintenance of power.

Alison Liebling and David Price's book *The Prison Officer* (2001) very clearly demonstrates that it is not only the nature and quality of the relationships that make all the difference to the living and working experience of staff and offenders but also crucially the way in which staff employ their discretion. The elements that enable that discretion to be wisely and compassionately used, we would argue, is greatly enhanced by an enabling environment.

What is clear is that for a long time now it has been acknowledged that interpersonal relationships are crucial to the functioning of the prison system and associated services. Generation after generation of senior managers and leaders of the services have consistently placed this crucial factor at the heart of the daily functioning of the work and living experience of both prisons and probation premises. This view is now being added to consistently by the research which focuses on this area and is ongoing. Alison Liebling and her team continue to work in the field and have recently collected data from several prisons which begin to look at those units that are adopting the EE standards. We wait with anticipation for the results to be published. Alongside this source of research there continues to be research of the specialist services from which the original thinking about EEs stemmed, namely the therapeutic communities. Brown et al. (2014) published the results of over seven years of research at the Dovegate therapeutic community. Notably one of the key findings was the centrality of being able to 'talk' and that the loss of the environment that enabled that to happen was a major issue of those returning to the normal landing locations. Once again the importance of interpersonal relationships that enable a level of meaningful communication and continued exploration of how the individuals make meaning of their world is plain to see.

## The National EEs in Prisons and Probation Programme (NEEPPP)

In 2013 the Offender Personality Disorder Programme, as part of the National Offender Management Service, contracted the Royal College of Psychiatrists Centre for Quality Improvement (CCQI) to support services along the pathway, in prisons and probation, to achieve the EE Award. The funding allowed for three Regional EE Leads to develop and deliver training specific to these services and support their development as EEs. This involves training, mentoring and supervising the process from adoption to completion.

## Explaining to people what EE means

In these current times of organisational change within the CJS with such processes as 'benchmarking, 'fair and sustainable work roles' and chronic staff recruitment issues taking place, it can be difficult to persuade people that EEs are not cromulent and are worth bothering with, that there are possible positive outcomes for everyone. Understandably some staff perceive EE and the EE Award as yet another initiative which will die out after two years and will be replaced by the latest fad in psychosocial management. Managers and staff have compared EE to Investors in People and other quality improvement systems, however it appears that because of the fundamental factors in EE and the way it can induce cultural creep into areas of an organisation that were not the original service involved, EE is producing a generalised momentum of change. Where staff are experiencing more relaxed and less anxiety-provoking atmospheres in the work place, colleagues are naturally asking how they are achieving it and want it for themselves in their own areas of work.

By creating an EE, especially with a population where there are high levels of personality disorder (PD), we are able to mobilise factors that meliorate the destructive elements of PD behaviour. In Haigh (2013) five experiences are judged necessary for healthy primary emotional development: attachment, containment, communication, inclusion and agency. These can be deliberately re-created in therapeutic environments to form a structure for secondary emotional development. In the CJS PD pathway we are working with a client group who are often fragmented, excluded, disempowered, un-boundaried and disconnected. An EE offers the opportunity for the five experiences necessary for emotional development and creates the opportunity to encourage happier, healthier people and improved outcomes.

## EEs as safe spaces?

What appears to be happening in the EE is that 'safe spaces' are being created in which people who have experienced difficulty in the childhood attachment process are responding to the interpersonal environment and, in some cases, forming attachments to others for the first time. In Bowlby's (1980) original conception of attachment he describes a process whereby a child finds a space in which it feels safe from which it can move off into the world and return to if overtaken by anxiety. In much of the literature the focus has been on the relationship between mother and child and the issue of a safe space that can be returned to has been subject to less scrutiny. It is possible that in creating EEs we are replicating the basic conditions for attachment to take place. One service in the community that had worked hard with a resident reported that he had moved off into the general community to his own lodgings and work environment. On the Christmas Eve after his move out into the community the staff of the service saw him sitting on their garden wall. Staff invited him in for a drink and something to eat but he declined saying, "I just needed to know you were still here" and went on his way. In a similar vein there are lessons to be learnt from the therapeutic community at HMP Gartree. When it was set up it had a policy of not allowing ex-members to return and visit. Many of the residents returned to the main prison and would be found talking to old group members through the dividing gate between the therapeutic community wing and the general prison location. As time progressed this behaviour seemed to have passed but the team found that most of those that had left the TC had managed to get themselves onto the same wing and on the same landing. They were meeting regularly in a cell and continuing what they had done in the community. In essence they had tried to make for themselves the safe space that they had become attached to in the therapeutic community. At that point the mistake was realised and the TC welcomed back previous residents. After all when children return from university they are not turned away on the basis that the parents have done the 'attachment thing'. They come home to their safe space in the world, not necessarily their parents per se.

With personality disorder being related to attachment disorder in the literature it seems both appropriate and timely that we are realising that providing EEs as part of the personality disorder pathway is beneficial, if a little serendipitous. It remains a challenge to us to test our observations and the hypotheses that we are generating on the basis of these.

## How to get the EE Award

The attainment of the EE Award is via a portfolio of evidence submitted to the EE Award team at the CCQI. The portfolio in essence is the evidence for the reflective process of the service and the activity which arises from that process. Invariably the process produces three major things in services:

1. Increased interaction between staff and offenders
2. An increase in activity that meets the needs of the offenders
3. An increase in the focus on the staff experience

The experience of the EE Award team is that if a service is enabling and has a reflective practice in place then the evidence falls out of the day-to-day work of the service. Those services that create the opportunities for staff and offenders to meet, communicate and share ideas as well as creating opportunities for participants to test these ideas and try new things, within the limits of their environment, will have an abundance of examples to demonstrate the enabling nature of their service.

Evidence is gathered for each of the standards by gathering together materials that answer the questions posed by the defining criteria of the standards. For example the first defining criteria of Standard 1, "the nature and quality of relationships are of primary importance", is evidence that offenders, when entering a service, are encouraged to interact with other offenders and staff. Services with a well-defined referral, reception and induction process will be able to demonstrate how well they encourage interpersonal interaction by a number of processes: the way they include other offenders to be part of the welcoming process for new people, how much of the initial process is contributed to by the resident group and the range of activities that are immediately available to the new person. In some services the prospective resident is written to by an existing resident to introduce himself or herself and maintain a pen pal relationship with the person until the new resident arrives and they can meet, the pen pal often becoming the mentor/buddy for the new person.

There is a wide range of criteria across the ten standards for the service to consider. This in itself often prompts the staff team to begin a dialogue between themselves and with the resident group that they would not have otherwise had. Once this process starts it tends to lay down new cultural norms or expectations, which propels the EE process forward. An example of this was an Approved Premises that originally signed up for the award and had completed half a portfolio when they met with one of the EE Leads. When asked how the input from the residents had been captured in the portfolio the response was that it had not because they had not been involved. After some discussion about the nature of EEs the process was reviewed and the resident staff team adopted a new consultative approach. The outcome has been that the service now holds house meetings and regularly creates activities in partnership with its resident group.

Of course the evidence is not taken on face value; questionnaires are sent to all service users and staff to gain their views and experience of the service. For staff the issue of them being enabled by the organisation in which their service is embedded is important as there is equal emphasis on a service being enabling for both staff and offenders. What people report as being experienced is matched up to the evidence in the portfolio and if it appears to the independent assessor that there is sufficient congruity they will visit the service in person to verify their view. Only then will a service be recommended to the awarding panel at the Royal College of Psychiatrists, who, if they agree with the assessor's recommendation, will confer the award.

## Lessons learned about starting out

In the process of supporting a service starting out on the EE Award process it has become apparent that there are a number of factors to take into account. Every service is at a unique position in relation to the award when it starts out. The experience of the EE Leads is that some services are already very enabling and can easily point to examples of practice that will provide obvious evidence whilst other services are operating on a different model or are clearly less functional in the areas of the standards.

Services that are delivering within a small well-defined space are likely to be more enabling than others simply because the physical environment creates higher opportunities or interpersonal interaction. As the physical size of the service increases this decreases as people can avoid or miss each other. It is also a general principle that as the space increases so does the capacity of the space, but the offender/staff ratio tends to decrease so that there is less staff to go around. This naturally reduces the level of interaction, even when the programme is group based.

Many of the services in the CJS have a historical cultural problem at an organisational level with inclusion of its resident group. Where the health services have recently been focussed on including experts by experience and patients at all levels of the organisation and in planning new services, the CJS finds this difficult. The underlying culture of management by control and command has traditionally excluded inclusion of offenders, the exceptions being the therapeutic communities. With the introduction of the PIPEs and treatment and assessment services related to personality disorder a new culture is evolving to include the offender population into the daily organisation and management of the service environment both physical and psychological. Where any service is in this development can vary widely.

The leadership of the organisation from which the applying service comes is also a strong factor in how well a service is supported in its effort to be enabling. The culture setting that is a product of leadership in a service can have a profound effect on how a participating service is viewed by the host organisation. Where new services that are attempting to be more enabling are viewed as being at odds to the received culture of the organisation, resistance is high. If a senior leadership team is openly encouraging and demonstrates involvement with the service, making it clear that this is where the values of the organisation lie, then the service tends to thrive. This is a crucial factor for staff, who in a friendly culture find greater acceptance for their work amongst peers, whereas if they are viewed as being out of the mainstream culture of the organisation they experience mistrust and resistance to their work.

The maturity of the service is also an issue. Many of the teams that have embarked on the EE Award are starting up new services and have either had to draw new teams together from existing resources or have been resourced through a contracting out process. In both cases the recruitment of staff has often created issues that have meant that staff have worked below their optimum strength, with all the attendant problems that this brings. In some cases the introduction of contracted services has brought together professions that have not previously been used to working together. A good example of this is the introduction of occupational therapists into teams, something that is new to the prison service. Bringing teams together in new services is a difficult art and combining the EE standards adds a framework that can either be useful or be perceived as a hurdle to be surmounted. How a team views this is often an indicator of where the team is in its development.

A major factor in this equation is the turnover of the client group. Some of the Approved Premises have an expectation that their residents will stay no longer than three months and that to move someone through transition quickly to a community-based placement is a success. This is not a bar to being enabling but it does mean that staff have to be vigilant in maintaining the culture. In other services the time residents are in the service is expected to be anything up to three years or longer in the case of high-risk populations. In this situation roles can be developed and culture carriers nurtured so that there is a shift of cultural maintenance toward the resident group. This frees the staff to do other things including the enhancement of their reflective practice.

So the appreciation of where a service is in its development in relation to the EE standards is an important element of the EE process. It is an element that has become more important as time has progressed and we have learnt more about the processes of EEs. It is why an increasing emphasis has been placed on the initial self-assessment that services are asked to undertake prior to setting out on the journey.

## What next for EEs?

Currently there is considerable appetite in the criminal justice sector for EE principles and process. The Award, whilst central to demonstrating that services meet the standards, takes second place to the developmental aspects of the process. Even at these early stages there are considerable challenges for the process, one of which is being able to establish 'whole prison' EEs. The NEEPPP initiative allows us to explore the potential for these options in a number of settings and to learn from their experience. A range of services already hold the Award, from Approved Premises and prison wings funded as PIPEs, to a gym and mainstream prison wings. Many of the services are in the newly developing OPD Pathway, but some are not and it cannot be emphasised enough that EEs may be found in a wide range of work and service environments. At the moment areas of specific need are being supported and focussed on but the development of the whole process continues. The development of an EE pathway is being piloted in Wales, regional groups of Approved Premises are being developed across the south of the country, and work is ongoing to develop models of EE support and development based on clusters of similar services, for example in the Closed Supervision Centres. This work develops the EE principles to a wider environment than the service itself, so that the wider structures echo the principles which is then reflected in individual services. This is proving a fruitful and productive process; it enables shared learning and collaborative working between services, but also engages senior managers in the EE process of quality improvement, and challenges them to embrace the standards in how they manage the services.

The EE team aim to provide services with in-house trainers so that the EE skill and intellectual capital of the services are maintained. EE champions are being trained to act as reference points and resources to their establishments and services and increasing numbers of team members are being trained in portfolio-building skills. It is hoped that the current programme of work will build and support a strong network of self-supporting EEs with supportive links to the EE central team.

Key to much of this work is support from the management of establishments and services and work has begun on developing an EE competency framework for staff and in particular for leadership. Being able to contain and provide the opportunity to establish and maintain an EE with all its attendant advantages demands high levels of trust and confidence from managers, which sometimes feels countercultural or in conflict with the security constraints of the normal management role. However having said this, there is great potential in EE being able to support senior management teams to deliver regimes that are in line with the stated aim and values of the National Offender Management Service (NOMS). The clearly stated vision of NOMS can be supported by EE, especially the underpinning values, of which "empower and support staff, and work collaboratively with others" and "treat offenders with decency and respect" are clearly relevant.

There are therefore significant debates and explorations to be had which will hopefully usher in a new phase where the EE approach is one vehicle for transformation across the CJS. At the very least, it is clear there is an appetite and opportunities for the EE principles and standards to be integrated into the culture of all CJS settings, leading to staff that are meaningfully engaged and invested in their work and offenders that experience and test new ways of relating to others, their environments and ultimately themselves. In the words of one member of staff in an Approved Premises:

> I think it's improved the well-being of both staff and resident group. It's had a huge impact on addressing the passivity of ex-prisoners and people in the prison system ... [a] huge benefit of EE is to empower people to think for themselves, be responsible for themselves, all in a very humane way. There's a prison system where they're 'done' to, and they come here and in the EE system they're 'done with'. It is a tool for building self-esteem. (Guassardo, 2016)

## References

Bowlby, E.J.M. (1980). *Attachment and Loss* (Vol 3 Sadness and Depression). London, UK: Pimlico.

Brown, J., Miller, S., Northey, S. & O'Neill, D. (2014). *What Works in Therapeutic Prisons*. London: Palgrave Macmillan.

Cohen, S., & Taylor, L. (1976). *Prison Secrets*. London, UK: Pluto Press.

Community of Communities. (2008). Retrieved from www.rcpsych.ac.uk/PDF/CSCV%20 Final%20Briefing%20Paper.pdf.

Crawley, E. (2004). *Doing Prison Work: The Public and Private Lives of Prison Officers*. Cullompton, UK: Willan Publishing.

Cullen, E. & Mackenzie, J. (2011). *Dovegate: A Therapeutic Community in a Private Prison and Developments in Therapeutic Work with Personality Disordered Offenders*. Hampshire, UK: Waterside Press.

Fitzgerald, M. & Sim, J. (1979). *British Prisons*. Oxford, UK: Blackwell.

Genders, E. & Player, E. (1995). *Grendon: A Study of a Therapeutic Prison*. Oxford, UK: Clarendon Press.

Guassardo, J. (2016). EE AWARD; Telephone Interview Report. Royal College of Psychiatry, College Centre for Quality Improvement. Unpublished.

Haigh, R. (2013). The quintessence of a therapeutic community. *Therapeutic Communities: The International Journal of Therapeutic Communities*, 33(1), 6–15.

Haigh, R., Harrison, T., Johnson, R., Paget, S. & Williams, S. (2012). Psychologically informed environments and the "Enabling Environments" initiative. *Housing, Care and Support*, 15(1), 34–42.

Liebling, A. & Price, D. (2001). *The Prison Officer*. Abingdon, UK: Willan Publishing.

Mulholland, I. (2013). Perrie Lectures: Contraction in an age of expansion: an operational perspective. *Prison Service Journal*, 211, 14–18.

Narey, M. (1999). *Taking the Prison Service into the 21st Century*. 10th Annual Eve Saville Memorial Lecture. Retrieved from www.crimeandjustice.org.uk/resources/taking-prison-service-21st-century.

Paget, S., Thorne, J., & Das, A. (2015). *Service Standards for Therapeutic Communities, 9th Edition*. Retrieved from www.rcpsych.ac.uk/pdf/Service%20Standards%20for%20Therapeutic%20Communities%209th%20Ed%20FINAL%20-%20For%20%20Website.pdf.

Shuker, R. & Sullivan, E. (Eds.). (2010). *Grendon and the Emergence of Forensic Therapeutic Communities: Developments in Research and Practice*. Chichester, UK: John Wiley & Sons Ltd.

Woodward, R. (2011). *The Director's Tale: A Search Engine for Meaning*. In Cullen, E. & Mackenzie, J. (Eds.), *Dovegate: A Therapeutic Community in a Private Prison and Developments in Therapeutic Work with Personality Disordered Offenders*. Hampshire, UK: Waterside Press.

# 14

# CREATING AN ENABLING ENVIRONMENT IN HIGH SECURITY PRISON CONDITIONS

## An impossible task or the start of a revolution?

*Alice. L. Bennett and Jenny Tew*

## Introduction

An effective 'Enabling Environment' achieves a set of standards that focus on effective working relationships to create a sense of belonging. Achieving an Enabling Environment within a prison setting may be considered unfeasible, particularly with high-risk and/or personality disordered prisoners and the necessary security requirements for this population. However, serious consideration of this aim is warranted given the needs of these individuals and the introduction of the Offender Personality Disorder Pathway, bringing an increase in service provision for those likely to have a personality disorder diagnosis. Services are further enhancing their provisions in order to provide Enabling Environments for the high-risk prisoner population. The Westgate Unit, a high security personality disorder treatment service, applies Enabling Environment principles within its working. Its psychological underpinnings, staffing models, regimes and physical environment complement this approach and lessons learnt from this have increased ways of working therapeutically with this specific client group. This has resulted in the Westgate Unit achieving the Royal College of Psychiatrists' Enabling Environment Award. The Westgate Unit's work, along with its ongoing evaluation, has also prompted a surge of motivation and action towards applying several of the core principles from the Westgate Unit to other High Security Prison settings, creating further Enabling Environments and developing the culture of the whole of the High Security Estate to become more rehabilitative.

The concept of an Enabling Environment comprises key features that establish and maintain a sense of belonging through a focus on relationships (Johnson & Haigh, 2011). Enabling Environments can be created in a broad range of settings, including secure forensic ones such as prisons. It can be challenging to establish an Enabling Environment within the secure and punitive environment of a prison but notwithstanding this, connectedness and positive working relationships can still be achieved in these settings. High security prisons house some of the most disruptive and complex individuals within the prison system. These establishments necessarily employ strict levels of security procedures to ensure that prisoners cannot escape and that their behaviour is safely managed while they are in custody. On the face of it, it would seem that high security prisons and Enabling Environments are completely incompatible with each other. Surely ideas such as power and authority being open to discussion and spontaneity being encouraged would undermine the order and control needed to safely operate such establishments? However, one unit within a high security establishment has found that, not only is an Enabling Environment possible, it actually assists in achieving the Prison Service aims, including the maintenance of security levels. The Westgate Unit within HMP Frankland opened in 2004 and now has the Enabling Environment Award. The work of Westgate is contributing to a review of the culture across the whole of the High Security Prison Estate and the translation of a number of the principles to other prisons and units.

This chapter briefly outlines the context for the Westgate Unit and the nature of its population. It then describes how the Enabling Environment principles are being applied in this setting, the learning over the last ten years related to creating an Enabling Environment for this population and how this is starting to be used across the High Security Prison Estate.

## The prison context

Her Majesty's Prison Service (HMPS) is part of the National Offender Management Service (NOMS). Its aim is to protect the public by keeping in custody those committed by the courts, helping them to lead law abiding lives both while they are in prison and after release. Despite the aims of the Prison Service, including the rehabilitation of individuals, it has been noted that prisons have a number of features that are detrimental to therapy and therefore to rehabilitation (Day & Doyle, 2010).

Following some high profile security breaches Lord Mountbatten conducted an inquiry into prison security in 1966. A notable recommendation from his report was the introduction of a system of security classification for prisoners (Home Office, 1966). Rather than having one maximum security prison, as Mountbatten proposed, a number of dispersal prisons were created that would house the most dangerous and highest security risk prisoners. As such the High Security Estate (HSE) was formed.

The Prison Service HSE is made up of eight establishments across the country. Its population includes Category A prisoners, whose escape would be highly dangerous to the public, the police or the security of the state and for whom the aim must be to make escape impossible (NOMS, 2013). The HSE also incorporates five Close Supervision Centres (CSCs) within its establishments. These are small, highly restrictive, self-contained units that manage those whose behaviour poses a significant risk to others or the good order of the establishment; these may or may not be Category A prisoners. Additionally, the Department of Health and Ministry of Justice recognise research suggesting that approximately two-thirds of those who have committed offences meet the criteria for at least one personality disorder (Department of Health & NOMS, 2011), warranting specialist services for this client group within the HSE.

## The Offender Personality Disorder Pathway

The Dangerous and Severe Personality Disorder (DSPD) programme was launched in 2001. Its background has been well documented (for example, Howells, Krishnan & Daffern, 2007). This initiative delivered services for individuals who presented a high risk of re-offending linked to severe forms of personality disorder. The under-pinning philosophy of the DSPD programme was that public protection would be best served by addressing the mental health needs of a previously neglected group. Part of this service was a purpose-built unit (The Westgate Unit) within HMP Frankland, an HSE prison in the north-east of England.

In 2011, the Department of Health and Ministry of Justice started a new approach to working with individuals with severe personality disorders, moving away from the previous DSPD programme (see www.personalitydisorder.org.uk/criminal-justice/about-dspd-programme/ and www.dh.gov.uk/health/2011/10/offender-personality-disorder-consultation-response/ for more details). This new strategy is co-commissioned by the Commissioning and Commercial Directorate in NOMS and NHS Specialised Commissioners and is known as the Offender Personality Disorder Pathway (Joseph & Benefield, 2012). The new pathway recognises the various stages of an individual's journey, from conviction and sentence to community supervision and resettlement, and ensures that treatment focuses on relationships and the social context in which people live. Within the reconfiguration from DSPD to the pathway model, Westgate continues to deliver the same service but with slightly amended suitability criteria.

## The Westgate Unit population

The Westgate Unit is a 65-bed purpose-built standalone unit offering a personality disorder treatment service for high-risk, male prisoners. The unit is separated into three discrete units. The suitability criteria for the Westgate Unit have slightly changed since it originally opened in line with the Offender Personality Disorder Pathway model (Joseph & Benefield, 2012). The current suitability criteria comprises three factors: being at high or very high risk of violent and/or sexual reoffending; having a severe and complex personality disorder as measured by the International Personality Disorder Examination (IPDE) (Loranger, 1999) and the Psychopathy Checklist – Revised (PCL-R) (Hare, 2003); and a functional link between personality pathology and offending behaviour. This final factor is assessed by the development of a case formulation. Previously, the suitability criteria specified a minimum number of personality disorder diagnoses on the IPDE along with a minimum score on the PCL-R. The new focus on *complexity* of personality disorder means that the service is better able to meet the needs of the intended population within the pathway model.

At the time of writing, 265 men have been admitted to the Westgate Unit for assessment. Eighty-two per cent of this group have been serving a life or indeterminate sentence, higher than the level of indeterminate prisoners in the wider DSPD population (Kirkpatrick et al., 2010). Prisoners accepted for the Westgate Unit have an average PCL-R score of 29.76, indicating a level of psychopathic traits higher than the general UK prison population (Cooke, Michie, Hart & Clark, 2005). They also have an average of three personality disorder diagnoses according to the IPDE.

This is clearly a high risk and complex population. Research suggests that levels of psychopathic traits relate to compliance with institutional rules and regimes (Leistico, Salekin, DeCoster & Rogers, 2008), and response to treatment (Tew, Harkins & Dixon, 2013). It is also the case that those with personality disorders have been found to struggle to engage in and complete treatment programmes (Howells & Tennant, 2010). Individuals with high levels of psychopathic traits have been found to be less likely to generalise and maintain skills learnt in treatment than those with lower levels of these traits (Blud, Thornton & Ramsey-Heimmermann, 2003).

All these issues make the environment of treatment for the Westgate Unit particularly significant. Establishing effective working relationships with this client group, as well as repairing them when they inevitably encounter problems, is challenging. In the treatment setting these difficulties have been linked to fear of trusting staff and showing vulnerability within treatment (Timmerman & Emmelkamp, 2006). This highlights the importance of incorporating standards into the environment in order to maximise opportunities for a sense of connected belonging to be promoted and developed.

## Enabling Environments

The idea of Enabling Environments comes from the recognised need to have an increased psychological awareness within health and social environments (Johnson & Haigh, 2011). Enabling Environments are designed to promote a sense of belonging and opportunities to develop and learn new skills through establishing positive and supportive relationships (NOMS & NHS England, 2015). The Royal College of Psychiatrists introduced the Enabling Environment Award as a mark of an organisation that is particularly successful in this aim. The award is made up of a set of ten standards that they identify as necessary for a nurturing social environment, namely Belonging, Boundaries, Communication, Development, Involvement, Safety, Structure, Empowerment, Leadership and Openness. These standards are each made up of a number of criteria that outline how the standard can be achieved for 'recipients' and 'providers'. Organisations submit a portfolio of evidence of how these standards are met in order to achieve the award. When compiling their portfolio, the Westgate Unit found that a number of Enabling Environment standards could be achieved, despite the high secure setting, and they gained the Enabling Environments Award in 2016.

## The Westgate Unit as an Enabling Environment

The Westgate Unit offers a range of structured interventions including the Chromis suite of programmes (Tew & Atkinson, 2013) and treatment components that have been specifically developed by Westgate Unit staff (Bennett, 2015). In order to manage responsivity issues and treatment interfering behaviours presented by this population, there is also an Imminent Needs Service and Supporting Services (Wood, 2015; Bennett, 2015). While this formal work is essential, it was recognised from the start that successful rehabilitation of this challenging population requires a broader approach than this. Offending behaviour programmes are only as good as the environment they are delivered in (Blagden & Thorne, 2013; Woessner & Schwelder, 2014) with an institution's culture being found to impact on both programme engagement and effectiveness (Lipsey & Cullen, 2007). As already highlighted, the nature of the Westgate population brings added reasons as to why the environment is a significant issue. This broader focus makes the unit a therapeutic environment as opposed to a programmes unit.

The unit incorporates physical features, psychological theory and a structured regime which supports the balance required to achieve an Enabling Environment within this high security prison context.

### Physical features

Firstly, the physical environment is an intentionally built, standalone unit that provides a spacious environment with a great deal of natural light relative to older, mainstream wings. This helps to facilitate elements of the structure and boundaries standards for everyone on the unit. The layout provides good visibility around the unit which can contribute to a feeling of safety for all. The unit is separated into three discrete units, creating smaller 'communities' for both staff and prisoners to operate in. This facilitates the development of relationships and helps individuals have more involvement in how their unit looks and runs.

### Psychological theory

The core principles of treatment on Westgate are embedded across the whole unit. They provide consistency across the whole regime and offer opportunities for skills generalisation. This contributes to the core principles of ensuring control and choice; understanding complex needs and personal relevance; being future focused; working collaboratively and transparently; providing novelty and stimulation; and recognising the need for status and credibility (Tew, Bennett & Atkinson, 2014).

As part of operationalising these principles, everyone on the unit is asked to abide by the Conditions of Success. These are three simple conditions that aim to help break down barriers and promote collaborative working. The conditions are: keep an open channel of communication; be respectful at all times, no matter what; and participate constructively. Everyone is required to comply with these, staff, prisoners and visitors, and everyone has the right, and responsibility, to appropriately challenge those who do not. This means that prisoners can question staff if they feel they have not been respectful to them or if they have not communicated what is happening.

Responsibility and active engagement are encouraged through the Strategy of Choices (Bush, 1995). This is a communication strategy that combines exercising authority with respect for someone's right to make their own decisions. It was developed to set boundaries and promote self-responsibility in group work with anti-social, anti-authority people in prison and is employed across Westgate. The strategy requires staff to define someone's options and the consequences of those options followed by asking the individual to choose what they are going to do. This encourages individuals to take responsibility for their own decisions without giving them permission to break the rules. The use of choice has been identified as an effective way of supporting the engagement and risk management of individuals with high levels of psychopathic traits (Harris, Attrill & Bush, 2005).

The Empowerment standard of the Enabling Environments Award encompasses the idea that power and authority need to be open to discussion. This is understandably problematic in a high security prison setting where staff are responsible for maintaining security and safety. While the Conditions of Success allow prisoners to challenge staff who they feel do not keep an open channel of communication or who do not speak to them respectfully, this did not initially sit well with some prison officers in the service who believe that prisoners should be told what to do and be made to do it, without question. While it is challenging for some staff to accept being questioned by prisoners, over time officers on the Westgate Unit who have adopted this approach have found that it can be helpful. One member of staff has reflected, "it makes you think as you forget how you come across sometimes. We sometimes expect them to do things we don't always do ourselves". It also helps the conditions have more genuine meaning; if staff did not have to treat prisoners in the same way then it would undermine the conditions and simply reinforce any negative views and resistance that prisoners may have towards authority. Staff sharing this learning has helped to bring others on board.

Staff have also highlighted that this approach has enabled them to see what prisoners really want and what they are capable of. In addition, the Conditions of Success, managed through the Strategy of Choices, actually help to provide the balance that is needed between control and flexibility required for an enabling and rehabilitative environment. This balance is a critical part of what makes a prison effective. As one officer reflected:

> If you give people a choice they think about things more. When prisoners have a choice they're more considered, there's less conflict, less damage and vandalism and less adjudications. You don't come to work expecting fights or trouble all day.

This was a view supported by prisoners; as one commented, "there's a lot more trust here and it makes you want to not mess up". Despite the restrictive nature of prisons and the need for staff to retain overall control, prisoners can be asked to make genuine choices in most situations, for example, whether or not to agree to rules as a condition of taking part in a particular activity, or whether or not to follow a simple request. Choosing not to comply leads to less attractive consequences than choosing to comply. It is likely that choosing not to comply will lead to increased external management by the prison and therefore reduced control and choice for the individual.

Westgate officers are still prison staff first and foremost and so are still required to ensure the good order and discipline of the unit. As such they may have, for example, to physically restrain prisoners at times, something that may seem at odds with the Enabling Environment approach. However, they have found that going back and discussing situations with prisoners after the event, explaining why things happened and helping the individual to consider what they could do differently next time does help to maintain open and supportive relationships within clearly defined boundaries. These relationships help to manage incidents and individuals and make a better atmosphere for everyone.

While prisoners questioning staff brings some challenges, staff questioning each other is also not an easy process. To operate effectively and for staff to challenge each other in a meaningful way, forums needed to be provided for this to be done in a safe and contained manner. This allows for relationships among the staff team to be maintained and even strengthened through this process. It has also been noted that there needs to be relevant consequences for staff, just as there are for prisoners, for those who choose not to work in this way. Prisoners observe how members of staff treat each other and are sensitive to any apparent inequalities in how the conditions are applied.

The Westgate Unit and the treatment within it incorporate the Good Lives Model (Ward & Brown, 2004). This is a strengths-based approach to rehabilitation. The Good Lives Model says that we all try and achieve certain things in our lives and people offend as they do not know how to achieve these things in a more positive way. Staff and prisoners work collaboratively to identify personally meaningful goals that prisoners can work towards and progress is reviewed against these. This approach helps staff to get to know what prisoners really want, helps to engage prisoners with something that really matters to them, and empowers them to develop the positive aspects of their lives.

## The regime

The Westgate Unit's regime is responsive to its specific population and, as far as the high security setting will allow, is highly compatible with the Enabling Environment standards. For example, prior to engaging in the assessment process, prisoners spend a period of time in a 'living phase'. This allows new prisoners time to get to know staff and each other, encouraging the development of working relationships (Wood, 2015) and encouraging involvement in the unit's structured and varied regime. This time helps some prisoners feel safe to discuss their treatment needs and have opportunities to practise skills from treatment in the wider environment when the time comes. This initial phase of the regime involves non-treatment aspects such as physical education, horticulture and education (Bennett, 2015). In addition to this complementary regime, prisoners in this living phase are encouraged to gain experience in group work through Active Learning sessions. These are informally delivered, psychologically underpinned, group sessions that constitute part of the clinical framework. The aim of Active Learning is to prepare prisoners for engagement with group-based treatment components. Within Active Learning, prisoners have the opportunity to explore and practice skills related to communication, trust, planning, personal disclosure and teamwork in an informal, practical environment such as the unit's sports hall. These sessions are delivered by a combination of clinical and physical education staff (Bennett, 2015; Wood, 2015).

## Staffing

Staff selection, training and knowledge have been critical to the success of this way of working with this population (Atkinson & Tew, 2012). Maintaining boundaries, safety and structure while still supporting empowerment, belonging and involvement for this population requires skill and resilience. Everyone needs to understand and agree with the unit's ways of working, meaning that there is a significant investment in selecting, training and supporting appropriate staff.

The importance of relationships and clear and consistent leadership on Westgate is also applied to the unit's staffing model. Each unit within Westgate has a dedicated operational staffing team. A relatively recent change within the staffing model has been for a chartered psychologist to be allocated responsibility to each unit. This has helped to have a consistent clinical lead alongside operational staff during forums such as individual unit briefings. These psychologists also coordinate a rota of weekly prisoner case formulations. These sessions ensure that each unit's staff team are psychologically informed and attuned to individuals' relevant behaviours that may be manifestations of their personality traits. More widely, a multidisciplinary staffing group is employed throughout all aspects of the clinical work conducted on the Westgate Unit. This means that teams responsible for referrals, assessments and treatment delivery are staffed by multidisciplinary teams which aid decision-making and information-sharing (Bennett, 2015). It has been found that officers can experience conflict in balancing their therapy and security roles (McManus, 2010; Polen, 2010), an issue also reported by Westgate staff. This ongoing tension requires training and support that is sensitive to both elements, something that the multidisciplinary approach across all levels of staff helps to support.

In order to structure expectations appropriately, this model of working is introduced to Westgate prisoners during the induction process where multidisciplinary staff introduce themselves as relevant to the prisoner. Each prisoner is allocated a 'key worker cluster' of prison officers (as opposed to one personal officer being allocated which is practice within mainstream establishments). Accounting for shifts and annual leave this helps to maximise the chance that there is a key worker officer on duty daily for each prisoner. Additionally, all prisoners are allocated a clinical case manager (either a trainee psychologist or a therapist), an offender supervisor (responsible for organising sentence planning and associated risk reports) and a clinical nurse specialist (responsible for mental health assessment and support). This staffing model ensures consistent staff are involved with each prisoner and encourages the development of a therapeutic alliance (Ross, Polaschek & Ward, 2008) between prisoners and relevant staff.

## Learning from the Enabling Environments Award process

The Westgate Unit's approach to treating its client group provides ways of achieving Enabling Environments standards within high security conditions. However, compiling this evidence highlighted areas for further learning and development which triggered some changes. For example, the therapeutic aspect of the Westgate Unit has increased with the introduction of creative sessions in June 2015. This complements Enabling Environments standards of Belonging, Development and Involvement. While this occurred as a result of a prison-wide requirement to increase the level of prisoners' meaningful activity within establishments, senior management chose to fill this additional regime time with more therapeutic activity (as opposed to clinical or generic work activity) in the form of creative sessions.

Creative sessions are underpinned by the development of strengths (or protective factors), in line with the Good Lives Model, complementing the risk-reducing aims of treatment. It is not just the content of these sessions that is compatible with the Enabling Environments ethos but also the process of their development as these sessions were planned and implemented by a staff/prisoner team in consultation with the senior management team. This was the first time a staff/prisoner steering group had been employed on the unit and it was found that this approach greatly helped to effectively introduce the sessions. Sessions needed to be linked to the 'Good Lives' goals and/or the Enabling Environments standards and in light of government budget cuts, needed to require little or no cost to the organisation. The joint approach to planning and development helped to ensure they were both relevant and realistic. Currently the creative sessions include album review club, mobile team challenge, comic book club, and classical music club. Additionally, craft sessions such as making cards and Christmas decorations accrue funding which is invested back into these projects.

After being accustomed to their prison officer roles within a structured prison regime, it took time for staff to adjust to the freedom of being creative and autonomous within these new sessions. This was shown through staff's preference for a small number of sessions with the intention of expanding more widely over time. This was in contrast to senior management who wanted as many options as possible in order to provide prisoners with a range of choice. Some creative sessions have been less popular due to them competing against established sessions within the regime such as gym sessions. At the time of writing, this difficulty is being explored, with options of having dedicated time within the core day for creative sessions or more choices available over time. As a result of being in a high security environment, barriers needed to be addressed for the successful implementation of these creative sessions. For example, security and health and safety requirements meant that all ideas had to be risk assessed prior to being implemented. This required a significant amount of planning and multidisciplinary work but, perhaps surprisingly, there have been no insurmountable concerns raised to date.

At the time of writing, key worker sessions are also being piloted on the Westgate Unit. These form part of the Supporting Services offered by the unit. These sessions occur every 4–6 weeks, attended by the prisoner, an officer from their key worker cluster and the prisoner's clinical case manager. Additionally (when relevant), offender supervisors and clinical nurse specialists also attend. Key worker sessions have the following aims:

- To establish and maintain effective staff–prisoner relationships
- To maximise effective multidisciplinary teamwork in relation to prisoners
- Preparing prisoners for clinical milestones (assessment, treatment and progression planning)
- Highlighting areas of progress (for example skills generalisation).
- Identifying ongoing areas of need, resulting in goal setting

These therefore also contribute to the Enabling Environments standards of Belonging, Development and Involvement. Staff running these sessions have autonomy over which of the key worker session aims are prioritised, informed by their current knowledge and contact with the prisoner. Goals are set collaboratively and reviewed in subsequent sessions. The role of a key worker officer also allows for check-in contact to take place between sessions if necessary. Once the pilot is complete it will be evaluated, considering the perspectives of staff and prisoners and the aims of the sessions. This will allow any necessary amendments to be made.

A further development informed by collating evidence for the Enabling Environments Award has been that each of the three units now holds community meetings. These are weekly and are co-run between staff and prisoners. These meetings provide a further forum for prisoners to raise ideas about how to improve the environment and regime, staff to pass on information about any developments, events or changes and anyone to question things that may have happened. Contrary to the fear that these meetings may generate security and disciplinary problems for staff to deal with they have actually helped the units to feel safer and more stable.

Awareness of the Enabling Environment standards has also helped to increase the input that prisoners have over their physical environment. In prison the environment is tightly controlled as part of maintaining security, particularly within high security establishments. Prisoners on one unit asked to personalise their communal space, a request initially seen as problematic by staff. However, after asking prisoners to show how this would link to the Good Lives goals, ways were found to manage the security issue associated with the materials required to do this. It was agreed to focus on the appearance of the pillars in the central area of the unit. The prisoners themselves decided how these should be decorated and took responsibility for the highly detailed murals that have been painted on each pillar.

While there are many ways in which Westgate achieves the Enabling Environment standards, there are notable limitations within a high secure forensic setting that should be acknowledged. The requirement of security restrictions, boundaries and a structured regime limit opportunities to offer spontaneity to staff and prisoners, part of the Development standard of the award. One timetabled creative session is based on the prisoners' own units, where prisoners and staff are responsible for identifying how to spend this session. This and other similar opportunities allow for some spontaneity within the structured regime. Whilst this difficulty with spontaneity within High Security Estate processes is acknowledged, prisoners are encouraged to try new activities and are certainly supported to understand their risk and risky behaviour, also elements of the Development standard.

## Is it successful?

There is a programme of research being completed to consider the impact of the Westgate Unit regime as a whole and elements within it (Tew et al., 2014). While the impact of this approach with this population in this setting is still being formally evaluated there are encouraging findings emerging, findings that further highlight the importance of the environment.

Considering the difficulties this population have engaging in treatment it is encouraging to note that the components of a core treatment programme on Westgate, the Chromis programme, have a completion rate of between 82 per cent and 98 per cent (Tew et al., 2014) suggesting that individuals are supported within sessions and on the unit to complete the treatment that they start. It is also encouraging that the regime monitoring recording the number of activity hours delivered each week show that prisoners are also engaging in the wider regime (Tew et al., 2014).

While engagement is encouraging, this is only part of the picture in terms of establishing whether an environment is enabling for individuals. Considering the lived experience is also important and research on the Westgate Unit has been exploring this area. For example, Tew, Bennett, Dixon & Harkins (2015) examined Chromis participants' experience of treatment and their time on Westgate. The individuals all found treatment challenging but worthwhile and all felt they had made changes as a result of this experience. Notably they highlighted that while it was down to their own determination why they completed treatment, the staff, other participants and the environment were seen as 'make or break' factors that impacted on their ability to achieve this. This further highlights the importance of relationships and the wider environment for engagement and progress in treatment.

Research specifically looking at the lived experience of Category A prisoners at Westgate found themes that were congruent with core elements of an Enabling Environment (Preston, 2012). This study identified three relevant, super-ordinate themes: 'Identity within a social world', 'Embracing change' and 'Maintaining stability throughout change'. Preston considered these to encapsulate the nine core elements of an Enabling Environment that existed at the time. This suggests that Westgate is successful at providing this type of environment for these individuals.

Looking specifically at one element of the Westgate Unit regime a thematic review of the art classes offered found themes that related to cooperating with others, staff and the regime, working within set boundaries and getting acknowledgement for their work (Bilby, Caulfield & Ridley, 2013). These are all areas relevant to Enabling Environments (Johnson & Haigh, 2011) and desistance from offending (McNeill, Farrall, Lightowler & Maruna, 2012). At the time of writing, a research study exploring the lived experience of Westgate's first staff/prisoner steering group is also in progress. It is hoped that this will further inform our understanding of the impact of service-user involvement on the unit and guide decision-making about how best to continue with this.

Alongside this work it is important that evidence is gathered regarding generalisation of treatment gains across the whole regime as part of assessing progress in treatment and the effectiveness of the environment. Considering the nature of the population this helps to ensure individuals can 'walk the walk and not just talk the talk'. There are a number of studies highlighting the positive impact of treatment for individuals (for example Tew, Bennett & Dixon, 2015; Tew, Dixon, Harkins & Bennett, 2012 but work is still ongoing and research to date has not included comparison groups.

## Taking the learning out to the wider High Security Estate

While it is acknowledged that the evaluation of the Westgate Unit remains ongoing, the benefits, at least in the short term, of this approach for staff, prisoners and the service as a whole cannot be ignored. As a result, some of the underpinning principles of the Westgate Unit have already been taken and successfully applied to the regime of a Close Supervision Centre (CSC). The CSC at HMP Full Sutton, a high security prison in Yorkshire, opened in January 2014 and offers a management and progression function. In contrast to the Westgate Unit, CSCs house prisoners who do not necessarily agree to be there. Despite this, prisoners engage in a regime with the aim of lowering their risk and progressing out of the CSC system. For many, this progressive step involves the Offender Personality Disorder Pathway. Full Sutton's CSC unit now successfully employs the Conditions of Success and Strategy of Choices within its regime alongside working as collaboratively as possible with prisoners and involving them in their own care and the running of the unit. This includes prisoners having an element of choice in how they spend some of their time, within specified boundaries, and them having forums to contribute ideas for further improving the regime and environment. The development of this unit shows that even in the most restrictive of environments prisoners can be communicated with openly, empowered to take active responsibility for themselves and their environment and engage in as much purposeful activity as security will allow.

A clinical review of the CSC provision made recommendations for elements of this approach to be applied across all CSCs, with the regimes of these units all encouraging as much social interaction and active engagement as operational requirements will permit. Units are creative in how communication can be encouraged even when prisoners cannot physically be together, for example through how they work with staff, the use of message boards and having situations where prisoners can see and talk to each other while still being physically separated. The CSC service is currently in the process of applying for Enabling Environment status, with each site applying individually but the service as a whole working together to achieve this.

The HSE is not aiming to re-create Westgate across its establishments; this would neither be helpful or appropriate. However, elements of this approach do form part of the wider work across HSE to develop a more rehabilitative culture. This work builds on the work of Alison Liebling and colleagues, particularly their work within the HSE (for example Liebling & Arnold, 2012).

NOMS first commissioning intention is to 'Enhance public protection and ensure a safe, decent environment and rehabilitative culture' (NOMS, 2014). There is a significant overlap in the essential core elements of what makes a culture rehabilitative and what makes an environment enabling. An Enabling Environment and a rehabilitative culture both require clear boundaries and a sense of safety, everyone getting involved to make things better, hope in the possibility for change, and the development of personal responsibility alongside collaborative working. The quality of our relationships is critical to both. Several prisons are now working towards having particular wings or units recognised as Enabling Environments.

The HSE is working with staff and prisoners to raise awareness of the importance of our culture, including elements of the existing culture that are rehabilitative and should be expanded and those that hinder rehabilitation. This is with the aim of engaging everyone in the process of change. While active engagement is part of an Enabling Environment and is necessary for cultural change, involving a wide range of staff and prisoners in this work helps to ensure that it is more successfully embedded into the establishment, rather than being a cause championed by few that quickly gets forgotten. Trying to change the culture and ethos of a place takes time. Given the elements that make up culture it also does not lend itself well to being created and maintained through structured systems of targets and audits. The prison service culturally recognises and rewards concrete tasks and outcomes and so there has been work done at a senior manager level to raise awareness of why a 'one size fits all' approach is not helpful to achieving meaningful change and why a careful balance is needed between providing guidance while still allowing individuals in each prison, who know the establishments best, to determine how to practically interpret and implement this and at what pace to do it at.

Work is underway to embed the Conditions of Success and Strategy of Choice across all eight prisons. As is the case on Westgate, this will help the principles from treatment become embedded across the prison, which supports a number of the Enabling Environment standards. HSE prisons are also reviewing the extent to which prisoners can be actively engaged in their own sentence and the prison environment. Rehabilitative culture committees, with prisoner representatives, are leading on the implementation of these strategies. Despite the high levels of security, HSE sites are involving prisoners in a number of ways, identifying how the regime and environment could be improved and delivering initiatives such as peer worker schemes and interventions awareness sessions to staff and prisoners. Significant processes such as the Category A review process have also been reviewed to make them more empowering and supportive. Increasing engagement, individual responsibility and a sense of hope all help make the process more enabling. It can also improve the stability of institutions as frustrations over long-term imprisonment and complex routes for progression impact on prisoner violence (Liebling & Arnold, 2012). This work is also requiring the HSE sites to work together to share their experiences and learning, to help generate hope for change and to sell the benefits of this work for everyone in this setting.

There are challenges to applying the principles of a discrete enabling and rehabilitative environment such as Westgate to a whole prison. To a certain extent staff and prisoners on Westgate choose to be there and accept it is a treatment unit aimed at helping prisoners address their offending behaviour. Many staff and prisoners across high security are more sceptical or even suspicious of such a focus. Prisons have found that careful selection of key people to lead this work is critical. As suggested in the literature (Tait, 2011), where there are resilient people who explicitly promote the attitudes, beliefs and behaviours associated with this approach in their day-to-day interactions and are able to inspire this in others, there seems to be more genuine acceptance from others. To help initiate this significant shift in the prisons at a time of financial uncertainly and political change, there has also been a focus on generating hope for change. As part of this staff from Westgate and Full Sutton CSC have visited other prisons and shared their experiences of working in this way. Sharing their initial concerns and how they adapted to this from their previous officer role has helped to allay some people's fears and sell the very real benefits, particularly for staff, of going through this change.

This sharing of experience has in itself contributed to the development of the Openness standard for Westgate and the Full Sutton CSC. This process has included the need for evaluation of their work as well as staff and prisoners sharing their experiences and learning, with staff visiting other units, discussing how they have managed the difficulties they faced in developing this type of environment within a high secure setting. The units have also welcomed a wide range of visitors to show how they put the theory into practice and to allow prisoners to voice their experiences of what is important in establishing and maintaining an effective rehabilitative environment.

## Conclusion

The Westgate Unit's development has led to the Enabling Environment Award being achieved within a personality disorder unit in a high security prison. Whilst implementing some of the areas discussed here can be challenging, particularly for whole HSE establishments, they actually work to support the aims of the HSE rather than compromise them. They are compatible with improving institutional behaviour, supporting the progression of prisoners and helping to reduce long-term segregation, all key aims of the prison service. They promote an ethos that encourages this population to meaningfully take personal responsibility and engage in assessment and treatment processes as well as the wider regime. They also encourage relationships that are critical for reducing risk and in the effective day-to-day management of a prison.

While this work, particularly the expansion to the wider HSE, is clearly ongoing, the very fact that this work has been considered and is starting to be implemented represents a significant shift in how the service works with these populations, for the benefit of staff and prisoners. If HSE prisons can develop more rehabilitative cultures and specific units can effectively work towards being Enabling Environments, then this approach is possible in any setting.

## References

Atkinson, R. & Tew, J. (2012). Working with psychopathic offenders: Lessons from the Chromis program. *International Journal of Forensic Mental Health*, 11, 299–311.

Bennett, A.L. (2015). The Westgate service and related referral, assessment, and treatment processes. *International Journal of Offender Therapy and Comparative Criminology*, 59, 1580–1604.

Bilby, C., Caulfield, L. & Ridley, L. (2013). *Re-imagining Futures: Exploring Arts Interventions and the Process of Desistance*. London, UK: Arts Alliance.

Blagden, N. & Thorne, K. (2013). HMP Whatton – A prison of change. *Prison Service Journal*, 208, 3–9.

Blud, L.M., Thornton, D. & Ramsey-Heimmermann, D. (2003). *Psychopathy and Response to Cognitive Skills Programmes: Analysis of OBPU Research Data*. Unpublished report for Her Majesty's Prison Service.

Bush, J. (1995). Teaching self-risk management to violent offenders. In J. McGuire (Ed.), *What Works: Reducing Reoffending*. Chichester, UK: John Wiley & Sons.

Cooke, D. J., Michie, C., Hart, S. D. & Clark, D. (2005). Assessing psychopathy in the UK: Concerns about cross-cultural generalisability. *British Journal of Psychiatry*, 186, 335–341. doi: 10.1192/bjp.186.4.335.

Day, A. & Doyle, P. (2010). Violent offender rehabilitation and the therapeutic community model of treatment: Towards integrated service provision? *Aggression and Violent Behavior*, 15, 380–386.

Department of Health & National Offender Management Service Offender Personality Disorder Team. (2011). *Response to the Offender Personality Disorder Consultation*. London, UK: Department of Health.

Department of Health/Ministry of Justice. (2011). *The Offender Personality Disorder Strategy*. London, UK: Department of Health.

Hare, R. D. (2003). *Hare Psychopathy Checklist-Revised (PCL-R)*: 2nd Edition. Toronto, CA: Multi-Health Systems.

Harris, D., Attrill, G. & Bush, J. (2005). Using choice as an aid to engagement and risk management with violent psychopathic offenders. *Issues in Forensic Psychology*, 5, 144–151.

Home Office. (1966). *Report of the Inquiry into Prison Escapes and Security (The Mountbatten Report)*. London, UK: HMSO.

Howells, K., Krishnan, G. & Daffern, M. (2007). Challenges in the treatment of dangerous and severe personality disorder. *Advances in Psychiatric Treatment*, 13, 325–332.

Howells, K. & Tennant, A. (2010). Ready or not, they are coming: Dangerous and severe personality disorder and treatment engagement. In A. Tennant & K. Howells (Eds.), *Using Time, Not Doing Time: Practitioner Perspectives on Personality Disorder and Risk* (pp. 33–44). Chichester, UK: Wiley.

Johnson, R. & Haigh, R. (2011). Social psychiatry and social policy for the 21st century: New concepts for new needs – the 'Enabling Environments' initiative. *Mental Health and Social Inclusion*, 15, 17–23.

Joseph, N. & Benefield, N. (2012). A joint offender personality disorder pathway strategy: An outline summary. *Criminal Behaviour and Mental Health*, 22, 210–217.

Kirkpatrick, T., Draycott, S., Freestone, M., Cooper, S., Twiselton, K., Watson, N. & Maden, T. (2010). A descriptive evaluation of patients and prisoners assessed for dangerous and severe personality disorder. *The Journal of Forensic Psychiatry & Psychology*, 21, 264–282.

Leistico, A.R., Salekin, R.T., DeCoster, D. & Rogers, R. (2008). A large-scale meta-analysis relating the hare measures of psychopathy to antisocial conduct. *Law & Human Behaviour*, 32, 28–45.

Liebling, A. & Arnold, H. (2012). Social relationships between prisoners in a maximum security prison: Violence, faith and the declining nature of trust. *Journal of Criminal Justice*, 40, 413–424.

Lipsey, M.W. & Cullen, F.T. (2007). The effectiveness of correctional rehabilitation: A review of systematic reviews. *Annual Review of Law and Social Science*, 3, 297–320.

Loranger, A.W. (1999). *International Personality Disorder Examination Manual: DSM-IV Module*. Washington, DC: American Psychiatric Press.

McManus, J. (2010). The experience of officers in a therapeutic prison: An interpretative phenomenological analysis. In R. Shuker & E. Sullivan (Eds.), *Grendon and the Emergence of Forensic Therapeutic Communities: Development in Research and Practice* (pp. 217–232). Chichester, UK: Wiley-Blackwell.

McNeill, F., Farrall, S., Lightowler, C. & Maruna, S. (2012). How and why people stop offending: Discovering desistance. *IRISS Insights*, 15. Retrieved 15 January 2014 from: www.iriss .org.uk/resources/how-and-why-people-stop-offending-discovering-desistance.

NOMS. (2013). Category A function: The review of security category – Category A / Restricted status prisoners. *Prison Service Instruction 08/2013*.

NOMS. (2014). *NOMS Commissioning Intentions from 2014*. London, UK: NOMS.

NOMS & NHS England. (2015). *Working with Personality Disorder: A Practitioners Guide*. (2nd Ed.). NHS England Publications Gateway Reference 04004.

Polen, J. (2010). Behind locked doors: An exploration of therapeutic processes within a prison therapeutic community. *British Journal of Psychotherapy*, 26(4), 502–521.

Preston, N. (2012). 'Enabling environments': The lived experience of category a prisoners on a dangerous and severe personality disorder unit. *Forensic Update*, 108, 32–38.

Ross, E.C., Polaschek, D.L., & Ward, T. (2008). The therapeutic alliance: A theoretical revision for offender rehabilitation. *Aggression and violent behavior*, 13(6), 462–480.

Tait, S. (2011). A typology of prison officer approaches to care. *European Journal of Criminology*, 8, 440–454.

Tew, J. & Atkinson, R. (2013). The Chromis programme: From conception to evaluation. *Psychology, Crime & Law*, 19, 415–431.

Tew, J., Bennett, A.L. & Atkinson, R. (2014). The treatment of offenders with high levels of psychopathy through Chromis and the Westgate Service: What have we learnt from the last 8 years? In M. Fitzgerald (Ed.), *Psychopathy: Risk Factors, Behavioral Symptoms and Treatment Options* (pp. 1–29). New York, NY: Nova Publishers.

Tew, J., Bennett, A.L. & Dixon, L. (2015). *A Multiple Case Study Investigation into the Chromis Programme*. Manuscript in preparation.

Tew, J., Bennett, A.L., Dixon, L. & Harkins, L. (2015). The Chromis experience: An interpretive phenomenological analysis of participants experience of the Chromis programme. *International Journal of Offender Therapy and Comparative Criminology*. Advanced online publication. doi: 10.1177/0306624X15586037.

Tew, J., Dixon, L., Harkins, L., & Bennett, A.L. (2012). Investigating changes in anger and aggression in offenders with high levels of psychopathic traits attending the Chromis violence reduction programme. *Criminal Behaviour and Mental Health, 22*, 101–201. doi: 10.1002/cbm.1832.

Tew, J., Harkins, L. & Dixon, L. (2013). What works in reducing violent reoffending in psychopathic offenders. In L.A. Craig, L. Dixon & T.A. Gannon (Eds.), *What Works in Offender Rehabilitation: An Evidenced Based Approach to Assessment and Treatment* (pp. 129–141). Chichester, UK: Wiley-Blackwell.

Timmerman, I.G. & Emmelkamp, P.M. (2006). The relationship between attachment styles and Cluster B personality disorders in prisoners and forensic inpatients. *International Journal of Law and Psychiatry, 29*(1), 48–56.

Ward, T. & Brown, M. (2004). The good lives model and conceptual issues in offender rehabilitation. *Psychology, Crime & Law, 10*(3), 243–257.

Woessner, G., & Schwedler, A. (2014). Correctional treatment of sexual and violent offenders: Therapeutic change, prison climate, and recidivism. *Criminal Justice and Behavior, 41*(7), 862–879.

Wood, F. (2015). Working with personality disordered offenders: Responsivity issues and management strategies. *Prison Service Journal, 218*, 24–30.

# 15

# ESTABLISHING ENABLING ENVIRONMENT PRINCIPLES WITH YOUNG ADULT MALES IN A CUSTODIAL SETTING

*Rachel O'Rourke, Annie Taylor and Kevin Leggett*

As part of the commissioned Offender Personality Disorder (OPD) service (Department of Health and Ministry of Justice, 2012) at HM Young Offender's Institution (HMYOI) Aylesbury, Enabling Environments (EEs) (Royal College of Psychiatrists Centre for Quality Improvement, 2013) were agreed for two residential wings. These wings are physically separate from the OPD service and the EEs have been developed, maintained and 'owned' by the establishment.

To provide context and to illustrate the rationale for developing an OPD service and the EEs, it is helpful to understand that the establishment has a reputation for holding a particularly challenging and high-risk young adult population. A recent inspection report by Her Majesty's Inspectorate of Prisons (HMIP) observed the following about the establishment: "[I]t holds the longest sentenced young male offenders in the prison system, including a large number of young adults serving life sentences and indeterminate sentences for public protection and the behaviour of some of these young adults is very challenging, others are very vulnerable and plenty are both" (HMIP, 2013, p. 5). Furthermore, a recent needs analysis of the population at the establishment identified that 32 per cent of the population met the OASys (Offender Assessment System) criteria for possible personality disorder (PD), 37 per cent were identified as high risk on static risk measures for future violent and general offending and 17 per cent met both the PD and high-risk criteria (McMurran, Beeley & Kane, 2013).

The EE standards are intended to provide an environment where a focus on psychological treatment for individuals is possible and in doing this, they are designed to capture the essence of social and relational engagement. The HMYOI Aylesbury OPD service plan particularly recognises this in terms of using the EE structure and ethos to aid the establishment in its provision of "care and management based on firm and safe boundaries" (London Pathways Partnership & Prison Design Phase Team, 2014; p. 34). This chapter is intended to explore and explain the experiences associated with the introduction of an EE into one of the residential wings at the establishment. The first part of the chapter examines in more detail the theory that underpins and guides the rationale for utilising EEs with young adults. There is then a description of the operational application of the EE standards and theory to one of the residential wings at the establishment. Finally the establishment's Governing Governor provides his perspective and describes some of the experiences, challenges and benefits associated with introducing EEs to young adults and the staff that work with them.

## The rationale for establishing EE principles with young adult prisoners

As part of the new OPD strategy, HMYOI Aylesbury was offered the opportunity to set up a new service for the young adult male prisoners in its custody (aged 18 years to 21 years). The aims of the OPD strategy, e.g. a reduction in repeat serious sexual and/or violent offending, improved psychological health and an improvement in the competence, confidence and attitudes of staff working with complex cases, overlapped with the need to improve relational outcomes, particularly on the establishment's wings. This suggested that the work to develop an emerging personality disorder service at the establishment should include working towards the EE award. It was an opportunity to put the emphasis back on relationships in the prison as being the central vehicle for change.

Consistent with the idea of an EE as a therapeutic environment that supports change, it was envisaged that a standards-based EE award could lead to enhancing supportive, positive relationships between staff and young prisoners. However, despite such work being of intuitive relevance, there was still a need to ensure that working towards an EE approach and award fitted with what we know works well with the needs of adolescents and young adults.

### What is known about the theoretical basis for such work with young adult males?

Research over the last twenty years in neuroscience and psychology has agreed that there are clear biological consequences to the 'tasks' of adolescence (Spear, 2000; Steinberg & Cauffman, 1996). Teenagers have to become independent from family and parent figures and to affiliate to their peer group and so may worry more than other age groups about being excluded (see Rose, 2004). The teenage brain undergoes substantial development at a time of life when brain plasticity is heightened and susceptible to incorporating a large volume of information from the environment. The environment moulds and shapes the way the brain develops during childhood, but now we know that this continues during adolescence and onwards to the mid-twenties. The social environment presents as an opportunity to address and progress the maturity, thinking and behaviour of all those in the care of HMYOI Aylesbury. Therefore a prison wing presents an ideal opportunity to influence the development of the personality at a time when there is also a need to rehabilitate. The window of opportunity for maximising the effect of positive peer influence and social interaction on emotional and social maturation is large.

It is known that young people in custody have a greater prevalence of poor mental health, with 95% of 16–20 year olds having at least one mental health problem and 80% having more than one (Bradley, 2009). Emerging personality difficulties also play a role; PD is generally considered to be a result of disrupted and distorted development and often arises out of the impact of trauma, which is compounded and consolidated by subsequent transactions within the interpersonal environment. A large body of empirical research shows that people with PD diagnoses report an unusually high number of traumatic events during their childhood. In particular, young offenders have been shown to have experienced adverse and traumatic life events, at home, in the community and in custody (Paton, Crouch & Camic, 2009). The possible consequences of this are evidenced by authors such as Rose, Freeman and Proudlock (2012), who showed that exposure to traumatic events can be an important antecedent to a range of serious and chronic mental health problems such as PD (see also Ozer, Best, Lipsey & Weiss, 2003; Stouthamer-Loeber, Wei, Loeber & Masten, 2004). It is important though that it is not assumed that the presence of trauma in someone's background always leads to psychological sequela as it is also established that there are other mediating factors and multiple pathways to PD, e.g. the quality of the attachment experience can moderate the effect of the trauma (Paris, 2009). All such previous experiences are part of the tapestry of maladaptive attitudes and behaviours that we hoped the EE work would help to address.

The HMYOI Aylesbury OPD service development team had a clear understanding of the need to respect the adversity and trauma that many of the young prisoners in custody have experienced, the developmental consequences of which are still alive in their daily functioning. If trauma can affect individuals on a biological level, including their emotional processing and interpersonal functioning, then service development needs to be alert to how bringing staff and prisoners closer together to work on relational issues might have unexpected consequences, e.g. triggering hyper-sensitive responses to relational problems, increasing impulsivity and hyperactivity, outbursts of anger and other regressive behaviours. EE development has to take account somehow of the need for management and containment of the service users, yet be brave in focusing on the relationship as the vehicle for change. The principles underpinning the EE idea present an opportunity to address the needs of the young adults in a holistic way via a skilled and supportive circle of people (prisoners and staff). A noteworthy innovation is that young adults with difficulties coping with boundaries, discipline or authority find they are being invited to work alongside or even take a lead in such areas themselves. However, all of these considerations point to the need to not simply transplant EE principles into a prison wing with an expectation that they will operationalise easily and quickly. Specialised YOIs are skilled in taking ideas and initiatives and adapting them for their population, by planning and preparing in more depth with regard to those issues that are likely to be especially challenging due to the age and background of the young adults held there.

## How EE principles are helpful in creating a supportive but boundaried environment

A process orientation places a priority on 'how' things are done. It is a willingness to remain open, and follow new directions by trusting that the appropriate outcome will emerge from a shared journey. However, this is not always how the work of a prison takes place. More usually it is characterised by a series of opposing tasks, usually done by separate staff and teams, such as security versus rehabilitation, and authoritative decision-making versus collaborative ventures. However, what other rehabilitative task could be more important than helping the young prisoner find a new way of being with others that allowed for mistakes within a context of containment, for involvement with responsibility and acknowledged uncertainty whilst holding a solid hope for change?

So, the role an EE plays in offender treatment is the underpinning need to provide a secure base: structure, routine and the opportunity to address the ability to relate (Adshead, 2004; Lorenzini & Fonagy, 2013). If that work is not done first, then the young adult can present still as challenging, unstable and chaotic and lacking the necessary skills to be able to process past (let alone future) issues. When the young man has developed functional but inappropriate ways to cope, such as denial of previous trauma, an expectation of hostility in the world and from others and a set and limited idea of what is possible, then that experience has to be fully taken account of in service development and therapeutic work (Janoff-Bulman 1989; Cason, Resick & Weaver, 2002). The hope is to bring about a focus on developing their present and future selves, to develop an optimistic future orientation and to develop trust with others by offering attachment security to young adults who often had not just insecure childhood attachments, but sometimes traumatic or terrifying ones. Research has shown how a lack of support and optimism in one's socioeconomic background affects aspects of future orientation as well as showing how patterns of possible selves are sometimes sensitive to context and culture (Clinkinbeard & Murray 2012).

There is little published however, to guide the implementation of whole group living approaches solely with young adults, whilst much is known about the difference between young adults and mature adults in terms of immature behaviours, such as immaturity of moral judgement and egocentric bias, social information processing deficits and social skill deficiencies (Gibbs, Potter, Barriga & Liau, 1996). Young adults can present with a wide variety of behavioural, emotional and cognitive disorders, including mental illness, and often with co-morbid substance abuse. They tend to come from social backgrounds that are marked by disrupted early attachments and socio-economic deprivation (Broidy et al., 2003), multiple losses and traumas, adverse life events, physical or sexual abuse (Vizard, French, Hickey & Bladon, 2004), family discord, poor academic achievements, learning difficulties, substance misuse and criminality (McCrory, De Brito & Viding, 2011). Life experience is likely to reflect a deficit in consistent and reliable relational support. Therefore taking on a holistic approach with such a client group was always going to be brave and ambitious.

Generally though, there is a body of work and commentary on the possibility of such holistic approaches. When institutions adopt the therapeutic community model (see Howard, 2004; Johnson & Haigh, 2011) or take a whole prison approach to tackling bullying (see Ireland, Jarvis, Beck & Osiwoy, 1999; Liebling & Price, 1999; Liebling, 2002), then lessons are learned about how service development needs to pay attention to issues such as fairness, safety and the distribution of power for success (Liebling, 2004). Such research suggests the need to bridge the gap between interventions delivered in silo departments in prisons and the life of the prisoner on the wing to bring about a psychologically informed environment. Such approaches can be more effective in improving behavioural and emotional control and social functioning and reducing aggressive and violent behaviour as they are consistent with and supportive of the treatment process and objectives.

The development of an EE on a prison wing was going to play a core role in the life of every prisoner who lived on it, as well as being a part of the specific treatment pathway for those young adults who were suitable for the new emerging personality difficulties service. These are young adults with insecure attachment experiences, often presenting as socially avoidant, extremely sensitive to social rejection and with a difficulty in the necessary reciprocity of healthy group living. The development of an EE was adding to the suggestion that the wing on which they lived could be a secure base for them, yet it was going to be overlaid on the existing context of power and control in the prison; the principles of the EEs were likely to bring challenges for power sharing relationships between prisoners and staff.

The establishment's Governor discusses this later in this chapter, but it is important to acknowledge that whilst there is a growing acceptance in the National Health Service that involving service users in the delivery and planning of interventions is an effective model for change, Her Majesty's Prison Service (HMPS) is only recently beginning to recognise and value the importance for its population, with, for example, the setting up of prison councils and greater prisoner involvement in their environment and regime. It is worth bearing in mind, particularly in large organisations with political agendas thrust on them, that involvement work can sometimes be vague activities that have little meaning at all (see Stickley, 2006). However the Prison Reform Trust report 'Barred Citizens' (Levenson & Farrant, 2001) described how more than half of UK prisons offer some sort of council and an evaluation of the pilots in 2004 showed that complaints in one prison had reduced by 37 per cent since the council become active. The survey findings showed that councils brought more benefits than drawbacks including helping to manage conflicts, providing a space for tensions to be discussed, contributing to the smoother running of prisons and improving relationships between staff and prisoners.

As well as being new and important ground for prisons and prison staff to cover, this has a special resonance in a YOI. To offer agency, trust and participation in a democratic decision-making process could be seen to be demanding for those young adults struggling to be independent in a healthy way. Such individuals can misuse trust given to them and may have limited experience of responsibility and cooperation with others. It asks that young prisoners with adverse life experiences, who test boundaries often in risky and inappropriate ways, who are likely to have trauma and emotional problems and who present a danger to others (and sometimes themselves) take up the offer to participate and get involved in how their environment is run. It offers the chance to address the often hostile dependency prisoners have on prison staff, which at this age has the extra layer of challenge when few in the population had independence prior to custody anyway. Yet the young adults were being invited to find their place between, for example, boredom and purposefulness, trust versus suspiciousness, and lack of control versus stability and routine.

## Operational application of the EE principles: translating theory into practice

Developing an EE within a custodial setting is challenging and may feel counterintuitive to the 'top-down' and authoritarian way prisons have historically operated (e.g. Fisher & Staples, 1994; Ireland, 2002). This has the potential to elicit resistance, which needs to be acknowledged and managed early on to reduce the adverse impact on the implementation process. Developing the understanding that an EE can bring about relational enrichment, improve the way the environment feels for everyone and promote and support a more inclusive and collaborative way of operating is helpful here (Department of Health & Ministry of Justice, 2013; RCP, 2013). More specifically, where EE conditions are established, fostered and nurtured, they allow a greater emphasis on psychological treatment (Tyrer et al., 2010; Turley, Payne & Webster, 2013). Indeed, the attraction of the EE to the criminal justice setting and the OPD Pathway (Department of Health & Ministry of Justice, 2012) is that it places an emphasis on the holistic approach outlined in the Bradley Report as vital in aiding the treatment and support of those with mental health difficulties (Bradley, 2009).

What follows is a broad description of the process undertaken when introducing an EE into a residential wing at HMYOI Aylesbury. It is recognised that the experiences at this establishment may not be fully applicable to other establishments undertaking similar work, but may provide some indications about how to approach the process.

### Planning an EE

An initial step is to identify an EE project manager to oversee implementation and maintenance of the EE. They do not need to be a manager, but should be confident and comfortable in their relationships with managers, have knowledge about operational policy and requirements as well as be able to challenge, question and query existing processes that do not align with the EE ethos. At HMYOI Aylesbury, this person had autonomy and devolved decision-making power that was clarified early on with the Governing Governor. There were occasions when it was necessary to discuss and resolve issues with senior management and having a project manager with the skills to know how and when to act upon something was important.

The EE ethos promotes a focus on collaboration, designed to improve relationships and encourage shared responsibility for the environment (Haigh, Harrison, Johnson, Paget & Williams, 2012). This is pertinent to the criminal justice setting, given the positive impact that relationships can have on recidivism (Hasselrot & Fielding, 2010). Collaboration between staff and offenders might seem unusual to some who have worked for a long time in the secure custodial estate, but worked well at Aylesbury. Introducing this early on might be challenging, however perseverance is important and those with concerns need to be heard in order to help encourage the early discussion of solutions to help empower and engage people. It was effective at Aylesbury for the project manager to facilitate early meetings for staff, where the rationale for the EE was discussed and where staff could ask questions and voice concerns. These were then used to shape the approach taken to engage as many as possible in the implementation process. A separate meeting for offenders was also facilitated to explain the EE, why it was being introduced and the importance of their involvement.

These early meetings are likely to fuel discussions between staff and offenders and the momentum this creates can be harnessed to start the implementation process. One of the first areas of focus should be on a review of existing provision against the ten EE standards. These standards (RCP, 2013) are:

1. Belonging: The nature and quality of relationships are of primary importance.
2. Boundaries: There are expectations of behaviour and processes to maintain and review them.
3. Communication: It is recognised that people communicate in different ways.
4. Development: There are opportunities to be spontaneous and try new things.
5. Involvement: Everyone shares responsibility for the environment.
6. Safety: Support is available for everyone.
7. Structure: Engagement and purposeful activity is actively encouraged.
8. Empowerment: Power and authority are open to discussion.
9. Leadership: Leadership takes responsibility for the environment being enabling.
10. Openness: External relationships are sought and valued.

The RCP provides a self-assessment tool (SAT) which encourages thinking about how the standards relate to existing work at the establishment, where there are areas of achievement as well as areas that require work. The SAT is worth doing in detail as it forms the basis for the action plan that moves an establishment towards operating as an EE. At HMYOI Aylesbury, the young adults and staff completed the SAT separately with the intention of providing an understanding of different perspectives on the standards. These were collated into one SAT, identifying areas of strength (i.e. where criteria were being met) and those requiring improvement or which might be challenging to achieve. The EE project manager had overall responsibility for ensuring this took place.

During the action planning process, the ability to think creatively and interpret the standards to fit the needs of the environment is vital. For Aylesbury, it was beneficial to include people with specialist expertise knowledge at this stage, such as regional psychology team members, occupational therapists, prison officers and prison service managers, to pool knowledge to translate the EE theory into practice and to help the EE fit the establishment while simultaneously challenging the establishment to fit the EE. It was at this point we were able to explore concerns about the application of specific criteria. For example, 'spontaneity' is a difficult concept to consider within the confines of a secure custodial environment. However, by involving people with a broad range of expertise, we were able to unpick this and contextualise it. Being spontaneous in prison could then be thought of as being responsive, such as facilitating a different activity at the last minute (puzzle sheets or a quiz) instead of outdoor exercise when there is wet weather. As noted, the EE ethos represents a new way of thinking and working for prison establishments and it is important that elements of the standards are not dismissed simply because they seem unmanageable to achieve at first glance.

## Implementing an EE

The action plan generated from the SAT forms the basis for the EE implementation process and should be regularly reviewed. While the EE project manager retains overall strategic and operational responsibility for the implementation process, day-to-day oversight of the action plan can be delegated to the EE committee. This can help promote collaboration and a sense of ownership and empowerment over the changes (e.g. Turley, Payne & Webster, 2013).

In Aylesbury, offender EE committee roles were advertised and an application process was used to elevate and promote the importance of the work and build a sense of community using a bottom-up process where responsibility for successful EE implementation is shared. This approach is contrary to traditional top-down decision-making in prisons but chimes with the EE ethos. There is also a close association between the emphasis of the EE award on a service's commitment to putting relationships at the heart of their work and the factors known to improve and increase employee engagement with their workplace. These include processes such as having greater involvement in decision-making, being able to have a voice, accessing opportunities for development and supporting individual health and well-being (Dale, 2010). Increased engagement in the working environment benefits employees and leads to greater job performance and satisfaction (MacLeod & Clarke, 2009). While the top-down 'just do it' approach is likely to work in the short term, increasing engagement by providing the conditions under which people work more effectively helps the working environment to thrive (Dale, 2010). These values are mirrored via the EE standards and support a true bottom-up approach to enhancing the living and working environment.

Once the EE committee has been formed, the action plan from the SAT process can be implemented. The committee takes delegated responsibility for the operational strand of the implementation process with the project manager overseeing the strategic approach. The committee is also a useful place to start evidencing adherence to the EE ethos. For example, Aylesbury EE committee rotated the role of committee chairperson to involve staff and offenders. Actions such as this are very much in line with the EE standards, particularly belonging, empowerment, leadership and development. Furthermore, where there is a mix of EE committee membership (staff and offenders), there is opportunity for joint working and actions can be allocated in such a way to encourage people to work together with others they might not usually collaborate with.

During implementation, taking a rounded, holistic approach will help to ensure standards are not treated as 'stand-alone' ideals to work towards and are thought of in conjunction with the other standards. Each standard has its merit, but it is the way they interact that makes the EE effective in the promotion of psychological well-being (Johnson & Haigh, 2011). Shared interest groups (music, reading, gardening, poetry, yoga, relaxation, team games and sports tournaments) provide structure, a desire for involvement in the environment and opportunities to support personal development and well-being. They can be led by staff and/or offenders, which promotes joint working, and rotating the person leading the group can provide opportunities for leadership. Be mindful during this implementation stage of cultural or religious differences, disability or any other aspect of diversity that might make engagement with activities or aspects of the environment more difficult or challenging. Taking a responsive approach to this and engaging with all should provide ideas for alternatives and alterations that can ensure inclusivity for all.

Creative thinking can also be helpful when managing the operational challenges associated with implementing an EE at a time when resourcing within HMPS is limited. During EE implementation at Aylesbury, the establishment experienced unprecedented staffing level challenges, which often meant prioritisation of 'core' functions (security, residence and regime) over other areas of the prison. These constraints can make change seem unmanageable and it is important to remember the EE standards are adaptable to the existing environment and should not require wholesale change in all areas. Where resourcing may discount something, part of what makes the environment enabling is the way these challenges are managed. For example, formal staff supervision may be difficult to achieve, so a drop-in surgery for those wishing to access supervision or advice can be considered. Staffing regular activities for groups of offenders might be difficult due to staffing levels and so can be undertaken on a rotational basis.

## Evidencing an EE

Evidencing progress via the EE portfolio is important and worth considering early on during the action planning process. Copies of new initiatives or processes can be included, such as a welcome pack, induction process, wing/EE timetables, EE newsletter, 'you said, we did' process and mentor/buddy scheme for new staff and offenders. Photocopies of redacted meetings minutes, records of staff awareness training worksheets/manuals, printouts of activity registers and feedback sheets, staff professional development records or printouts of emails where problems have been resolved without lengthy bureaucratic processes can all be helpful evidence. Some of the most powerful evidence can come from photographs of people taking part in activities or from individuals writing down their thoughts or observations about something that has happened.

The project manager should take overall responsibility for drawing together the evidence into a portfolio and cross-referencing it, as much will be applicable to more than one standard or criterion. The work should be evidenced in an accessible way to demonstrate progress made and the way the establishment is embracing the EE ethos. The portfolio is a holistic representation of the approach taken to running that part of the establishment and an opportunity to demonstrate the hard work that went into making the changes. A mock assessment via the RCP can be helpful to provide feedback on areas to further address. Once the portfolio is complete and submitted and accreditation awarded, work will need to continue to maintain the changes in order to retain accreditation, which was achieved in March 2016. While the establishment will need to keep a focus on the EE, it is unlikely that the level of required work for implementation will be required to maintain it. Much of the ongoing maintenance work can be undertaken by an EE committee of staff and offenders overseen by a nominated manager.

## How to manage the introduction of EE principles: the Governor's perspective

HMYOI Aylesbury can look after up to 444 prisoners and has a reputation for managing the most disruptive and dangerous long sentenced young prisoners as well as those with significant learning difficulties and offending behaviour needs. With effective staff and prisoner relationships being a key requirement in developing and maintaining a safe and decent prison, it is easy to see why an EE might be regarded as a promising development within a custodial setting. High-quality relationships are prioritised within an EE; positive relationships promote well-being, people experience a sense of belonging, everyone involved contributes to the growth and well-being of others, people can learn new ways of relating and contributions from all parties are recognised and respected.

The culture of an organisation can be complex and difficult, and the implementation of any form of change can be a significant challenge. HMPS is no exception. Furthermore, the job of a prison officer is a rewarding but demanding vocation; prisoners are normally compliant and accept the circumstances in which they find themselves, but some are vulnerable, needy, angry, desperate, non-compliant or violent. At a time when there are staffing shortfalls due to vacancies, the pressures of the job become more acute. Staff need to believe that any change is going to be of benefit, that it can work and will be worth the effort.

For a number of years the senior management team at Aylesbury had sought to develop meaningful engagement with prisoners, to seek their views on the implementation of future developments or policy changes. With the help of User Voice, an organisation led by ex-offenders, this was taken further to build structures that enable productive collaboration between service users and providers, the Governor set up and chaired a prison council made up of elected representatives of prisoners who meet regularly to discuss the way in which the prison is run. These initiatives helped to develop a culture within the prison where staff and prisoners believed and felt that their views were valued and that they could have a real say in how the environment in which they lived and worked could be developed.

Over the year that the new OPD Pathway service has been in operation, the staff that work within it have helped to promote not only the work of the service but the principles under which it operates. Members of staff volunteered and were selected to work within it. Some difficult prisoners have engaged with the service and staff across the prison have noted significant positive changes in behaviour. This has helped to provide some hard credibility not only to the therapeutic work undertaken but to the idea that a place can be developed where staff and prisoners work together in a safe and decent way, with much reduced stress and anxiety.

The senior management team decided that the best residential area to pilot an EE would be F wing, which can look after up to 53 residents. The majority of the prisoners on this wing are about to, are or have participated in one of the two sex offender treatment programmes run at the establishment. It also looks after those considered vulnerable or who might cope poorly in the mainstream prison environment and who tend to lack the social and interpersonal skills that would normally be associated with this age group. Instances of self-harm are higher on this wing, but recorded instances of violence against others are considerably lower than elsewhere in the prison and relationships between staff and prisoners are recognised to be of a high standard. In general the anti-authority views of prisoners tend to be lower on this wing compared to others, as are anti-therapeutic views amongst staff.

It was important to ensure that the staff on F wing were committed to developing the residential area as an EE, and that the right first-line managers were selected to take the work forward on a day-to-day basis. Many methods were discussed to decide how best to select people to work on the unit. In the end each existing member of F wing staff was told what the EE was about, how we were going to get there and what the outcomes were going to be. They then had a choice as to either stay on F wing or request a move to another unit. All staff elected to remain on the unit and engage with the work. F wing was registered with the RCP as part of the EE programme in September 2014.

Prior to any changes taking place on the wing a series of forums and focus groups took place. On one occasion all 53 residents attended a single meeting where the project and the general principles of EE were discussed. Smaller groups of staff and prisoners subsequently met to ascertain where they felt they were in terms of meeting the standards and to agree what changes and improvements would be needed. As a direct result of these meetings a detailed action plan was drawn up.

Staff also had the opportunity to visit established EEs as well as attend presentations and meetings at the RCP in London.

For staff, working in prison can be all about the authority and influence they have over others but especially about which one to use, when and to what degree. Using their authority is about utilising the moral legitimacy that prisoners believe them to have to instruct them to do something whereas using influence is about persuasion (Liebling & Tait, 2006). Good prison officers effectively do this dynamically on a daily basis and the best do it without even thinking about it (Hay & Sparks, 1991). Even those officers can be sceptical or wary of giving any of this control, actual or perceived, to prisoners. This is why it is so key to ensure that time is taken to introduce the idea of creating an EE in a structured way that allays any fears and clearly spells out the outcomes and benefits for all. Light touch monitoring of order and control indicators such as the number of violent and other incidents, or number of adjudications or other disciplinary measures, might be expected to demonstrate the benefits of improved staff/prisoner relationships and of working towards and achieving an EE as well as a safe, decent and secure prison.

It was important to ensure that any of the changes being made to the unit were done so in a measured way and not rushed. Time had to be allowed for changes to be embedded, both procedurally and culturally, before they could move onto the next step. Staff and prisoner relationships that were already good became better and prisoners became more confident in their interactions with each other and staff. They also became more knowledgeable about their wing but also of the establishment as a whole. After approximately three months of working towards the standards, a piece of research was conducted by a member of the regional psychology team. The results showed a higher level of adherence to the ten standards on F wing compared with the other two wings and on three of the standards in particular (with a 98 per cent return rate from F wing). Follow-up surveys are planned to take place to further measure progress. It is also worth noting that since the EE project started on F wing there has been a 120 per cent increase in the number of prisoners on the higher level of regime due to their consistent positive behaviour whilst those on the basic regime have dropped to nil. These figures help to reflect how behaviour and cooperation have improved on F wing and the progress that has been made in relation to the standards.

When the EE was first implemented on F wing, three prisoners (one from each landing) were elected onto a committee to guide the work forward. This committee also included the wing manager, Pathway staff and wing officers. From these meetings a set of wing rules emerged. The role of committee chair is rotated between the three prisoner members after each meeting. This role is simply to manage the meeting and to gain some additional experience of doing so. Staff and prisoners are also encouraged to submit suggestions, which are discussed at committee meetings. Responses are then recorded and displayed for everyone to see on the 'you said, we did' notice board. Forums are also regularly facilitated for staff, prisoners and both groups combined. Prison managers regard these meetings as important and ensure that members of staff are freed up to attend even when there are shortfalls to be managed. A wing subcommittee has also been formed of staff and prisoners to focus on how the physical environment can be improved on F wing. This is a significant development as it shows that those who work and live on F wing are taking a real ownership of the physical environment. The subcommittee has received support from senior managers who attend meetings when requested and action agreed recommendations.

One of the main benefits of living on F wing as an EE is the access to additional activities which is very much appreciated by staff and prisoners. For staff it creates greater diversity in their role and for prisoners it creates a more varied regime for them to participate in. It is important that there is a psychologically informed benefit to these activities and that they are not just a different form of association or time out of cell. It has been noted how the engagement with some of these activities has presented staff and prisoners with the opportunity to reassess how they interact and there have been instances of marked positive changes. Some issues still exist, but on the whole the relationship between staff and prisoners is very good. Some of the extra activities on offer included a gym club solely for more vulnerable prisoners, a domestic skills group where other prisoners on the unit help with cell cleaning, showering, washing and ironing, a walking club, quiz nights organised by prisoners, a book club, a reading aloud group and a relaxation group where prisoners are taught relaxation and stress coping techniques.

One issue identified early on was the desire by those who self-harmed to address their behaviours. A self-harm group was set up exclusively for F wing prisoners, and run in conjunction with the OPD Pathway service and Aylesbury's safer custody team. This group is regularly attended by eight prisoners who seek support and no longer wish to self-harm. Early feedback is positive.

The following are comments from residents and staff about living and working on the EE:

> I help shy people talk to others to make friends and I can see them become relaxed and happy. I see them go from being too scared to leave their cell or have a shower to signing up for quizzes and other activities, making new friends on the wing.
>
> Daryl, prisoner and welcome rep

> Firstly I would like to say a big thank you to all the F wing staff for all the support and effort that they have put into my sentence, I don't think I would have got through it without them. Being part of the Enabling Environment has built my confidence and relationships with staff and prisoners. I'm going to be sad to leave everybody, but also very happy to! Thank you!
>
> Jack, prisoner, entry in leavers' book

> When I first went in I felt nervous, frustrated. But when I first started to read the first two lines it was all right. I felt fine after that, but everyone was

supportive and when I finished they gave me praise, which gave me goose bumps.

Darryn, prisoner talking about the reading aloud group

I would like to thank you for giving us the opportunity to create a better environment our wing [sic]. I was asked to be a guitar teacher by staff, and this activity benefits many. The sound of music greatly reduces the stress levels with huge benefits to us prisoners. Thank you again for this opportunity.

Eduard, prisoner who mentors others in music

Having worked on F wing as the EE was being implemented I can say how enthused I am by the project. What can be perceived as subtle changes in attitude can make the world of difference to staff and prisoners alike.

Colin, former Senior Officer on F wing

G wing has also started the process of working towards becoming an EE. The lessons learned from these two projects will help inform the establishment wide rollout on the remainder of the residential and activity areas. The Governor is also working closely with the RCP to develop a set of measures that will help underpin the standards that will help segregation units in prisons and other separation areas in Immigration Removal Centres achieve the EE accreditation. The biggest challenges will always be engaging the staff and prioritisation of resources to undertake the associated work in an environment where all prisons in England and Wales have been benchmarked against strict criteria which has reduced any spare staff flexible working time to a minimum. The time taken to complete the action plans and collate the portfolio of evidence should not be underestimated.

It is hoped that by using the EE principles, we at Aylesbury will achieve a healthy environment that supports the development of best practice, promotes standards and monitoring of methods and identifies learning and training needs, one that also helps in the development and maintenance of a safe, decent and secure place for staff to work and prisoners to live in and improve themselves. It is hoped that improved relationships will help prisoners to more effectively manage distress and anxiety, thereby reducing acts of self-harm and reducing the risk of suicide. Staff will be able to access training that will increase their psychological understanding, which will also assist with this. In our work it is vital that prisoners are made to feel like a person and not an 'it', that they are listened to, cared for, supported, acknowledged and trusted. EEs go a long way to achieving this.

## Conclusions

The process of working towards achieving the EE certificate is what brings about healthy and sustainable group living. No one at Aylesbury was naive about the difficulties of changing and maintaining a therapeutic culture inside a prison and allowing shared ownership of a custodial environment. However if culture is the shared personality and climate of a place, (Deal & Kennedy, 1982), then the findings so far are that it can be used to facilitate change by bringing people together to develop good ideas and best practice. The recognition in EE development is that the quality of daily interactions is as important as big initiatives. EEs offer a model of the social and relational environment in which change and development can best be facilitated. This also requires that the leadership can make a difference by instilling belief and providing a safe structure for change to take place as well as ongoing support and supervision of the work.

As this chapter discusses, the journey to develop any EE is likely a difficult one as it requires multiple viewpoints brought together into a consensus, and probably a more difficult one in a prison wing holding young adults in custody. What certainly cannot happen now is that the work stops and the wings that have started the EE work and have made previously unthinkable changes somehow lose that impetus and culture. The next important phase of the work now that one wing is settled into the EE framework and another is nearing that point is to manage the transition of the young adults onto other wings or other prisons. We know that most young people need extra support to transition into other settings, especially adult services, but the task may now be greater if the EE development has brought about stronger and more meaningful relationships with peers and staff in the YOI (see Campling, Davies & Farquharson, 2004; Haigh, 2013). Leaving a therapeutic environment could now represent the loss of a significant attachment and maybe the most difficult part of the EE work is the negotiation of the leaving of anyone from the place (see Humphreys & Bree, 2004).

## References

Adshead, G. (2004). A matter of security. The application of attachment theory to forensic psychiatry and psychotherapy. In F. Pfäfflin & G. Adshead (Eds.), *Forensic Focus*. London & New York: Jessica Kingsley Publishers.

Bradley, K. (2009). *The Bradley report: Lord Bradley's review of people with mental health problems or learning disabilities in the criminal justice system*. Retrieved from www.centreformentalhealth .org.uk/pdfs/Bradley_report_2009.pdf.

Broidy, L., Nagin, D., Tremblay, R., Bates, J., Brame, B., Dodge, K., Fergusson, D., Horwood, J., Loeber, R., Laird, R., Lynam, D., Moffitt, T., Pettit, G. & Vitaro, F. (2003). Developmental trajectories of childhood disruptive behaviours and adolescent delinquency: A six-site, cross-national study. *Developmental Psychology*, 39(2), 222–245.

Campling, P., Davies, S. & Farquharson, G. (2004). *From Toxic Institutions to Therapeutic Environments: Residential Settings in Mental Health Institutions*. London, UK: Gaskell.

Cason, D., Resick, P. & Weaver, T. (2002). Schematic integration of traumatic events. *Clinical Psychology Review*, 22, 131–153.

Clinkinbeard, S. & Murray, C. (2012). Perceived support, belonging, and possible selves' strategies among incarcerated juvenile offenders. *Journal of Applied Social Psychology*, 42(5), 1218–1240.

Dale, S. (2010). Examining the link between performance and employee engagement in a forensic setting: Care enough to perform well? In C. Ireland & M. Fisher (Eds.),

*Consultancy and Advising in Forensic Practice: Empirical and Practical Guidelines* (pp. 143–162). Chichester, UK: John Wiley & Sons Ltd.

Deal, T. & Kennedy, A. (1982). *Corporate Cultures: The Rites and Rituals of Corporate Life.* Harmondsworth, UK: Penguin Books.

Department of Health and Ministry of Justice (2012). *The offender personality disorder strategy and commissioning intentions – version 1.* Retrieved from http://home.hmps.noms.root/ Intranet/ShowBinary?nodeId=/Repo/HQ/internal_communications/presentations/ PD_strategy_summary_-_handout_v4_October_2012.pdf.

Department of Health and Ministry of Justice (2013). *A guide to psychologically informed planned environments (PIPEs).* Retrieved from http://home.hmps.noms.root/Intranet/ ShowBinary?nodeId=/Repo/HQ/internal_communications/guide_handbook_ manual/PIPEGuide_JUL2013.pdf.

Fisher, J. & Staples, J. (1994). Involvement commitment: The staff consultation process at HMP Full Sutton. *Prison Service Journal*, 92, 10–12.

Gibbs, J., Potter, G., Barriga, A. & Liau, A. (1996). Developing helping skills and prosocial motivation of aggressive adolescents in group programs. *Aggression and Violent Behaviour*, 1(3), 283–305.

Haigh, R. (2013). The quintessence of a therapeutic environment. *Therapeutic Communities: The International Journal of Therapeutic Communities*, 34(1), 6–15.

Haigh, R., Harrison, T., Johnson, R., Paget, S. & Williams, S. (2012). Psychologically informed environments and the 'Enabling Environments' initiative. *Housing, Care and Support*, 15(1), 34–42. doi: 10.1108/14608791211238412.

Hasselrot, B. & Fielding, C. (2010). Enabling environments for sexual offenders in Swedish prisons. *Sexual Offender Treatment*, 5(2). Online publication. Retrieved from www.sexual-offender-treatment.org/88.html.

Hay, W. & Sparks, R. (1991). What is a prison officer? *Prison Service Journal*, 83, 2–7.

Her Majesty's Chief Inspector of Prisons (HMIP) (2013). *Report on an unannounced inspection of HMYOI Aylesbury by HM Chief Inspector of Prisons.* Retrieved from www.justiceinspectorates.gov.uk/hmiprisons/inspections/hmyoi-aylesbury/.

Howard, T. (2004). The physical environment and use of space. In P. Campling, S. Davies, & G. Farquharson (Eds.), *From Toxic Institutions to Therapeutic Environments: Residential Settings in Mental Health Services* (pp. 69–78). London, UK: Gaskell.

Humphreys, N. & Bree, A. (2004). Difficulties with attachment and separation: Joining and leaving a therapeutic community. In P. Campling, S. Davies, & G. Farquharson (Eds.), *From Toxic Institutions to Therapeutic Environments: Residential Settings in Mental Health Services* (pp. 55–66). London, UK: Gaskell.

Ireland, J. (2002). Bullying in prisons. *The Psychologist*, 15, 130–133.

Ireland, J., Jarvis, S., Beck, G. & Osiwoy, S. (1999). Recent research into bullying in prison. *Forensic Update*, 56, 4–10.

Janoff-Bulman, R. (1989). Assumptive worlds and the stress of traumatic events: Applications of the schema construct. *Social Cognition*, 7, 113–136.

Johnson, R. & Haigh, R. (2011). Social psychiatry and social policy for the 21st century: New concepts for new needs – the 'Enabling Environments' initiative. *Journal of Mental Health and Social Inclusion*, 15(1), 17–23. Retrieved from http://biblioteca.esec.pt/cdi/ ebooks/docs/Johnson_Social_psychiatry.pdf.

Levenson, J. & Farrant, F. (2001). *Barred Citizens: Volunteering and Active Partnership by Prisons.* London: Prison Reform Trust.

Liebling, A. (2002). Measuring the quality of prison life. *Research Findings, No. 174.* London, UK: Home Office.

Liebling, A. (2004). *Prisons and Their Moral Performance: A Study of Values, Quality, and Prison Life.* Oxford, UK: Oxford University Press.

Liebling, A. & Price, D. (1999). An exploration of staff-prisoner relationship at HMP Whitemoor. *Prison Service Research Report*, p. 6. London, UK: Home Office.

Liebling, A. & Tait, S. (2006). Improving staff-prisoner relationships. In G.E. Dear (Ed.), *Preventing Suicide and Other Self-Harm in Prison* (pp. 103–117). London, UK: Palgrave MacMillan.

London Pathways Partnership & Prison Design Phase Team (2014). *HMYOI Aylesbury complex needs service: Implementation and operational service plan (version 9.0).* Internal report.

Lorenzini, N. & Fonagy, P. (2013). Attachment and personality disorders: A short review. *FOCUS: The Journal of Lifelong Learning in Psychiatry*, 11(2), 155–166.

MacLeod, D. & Clarke, N. (2009). *Engaging for success: Enhancing performance through employee engagement. A report to government.* Retrieved from http://dera.ioe.ac.uk/1810/1/file52215.pdf.

McCrory, E., De Brito, S. & Viding, E. (2011). The impact of childhood maltreatment: A review of neurobiological and genetic factors. *Frontiers in Psychiatry*, 2, 48. doi: 10.3389/fpsyt.2011.00048.

McMurran, M., Beeley, C. & Kane, E. (2013). *HMYOI Aylesbury: Emerging personality difficulties needs assessment.* Unpublished manuscript. England, UK: Nottingham Institute of Mental Health, Nottinghamshire NHS Trust and the University of Nottingham.

Ozer, E., Best, S., Lipsey, T. & Weiss, D. (2003). Predictors of posttraumatic stress disorder and symptoms in adults: A meta-analysis. *Psychological Bulletin*, 129, 52–71.

Paris, J. (2009). A prospective investigation of borderline personality disorder in abused and neglected children followed up into adulthood. *Journal of Personality Disorders*, 23(5), 433.

Paton, J., Crouch, W., & Camic, P. (2009). Young offenders' experiences of traumatic life events: A qualitative investigation. *Clinical Child Psychology and Psychiatry*, 14(1), 43–62.

Rose, J. (2004). The residential care and treatment of adolescents. In P. Campling, S. Davies, & G. Farquharson (Eds.), *From Toxic Institutions to Therapeutic Environments: Residential Settings in Mental Health Services* (pp. 219–226). London, UK: Gaskell.

Rose, S., Freeman, C. & Proudlock, S. (2012). Despite the evidence – why are we still not creating more trauma informed mental health services? *Journal of Public Mental Health*, 11(1), 5–9.

Royal College of Psychiatrists College Centre for Quality Improvement (2013). *Enabling environments standards.* Retrieved from www.rcpsych.ac.uk/PDF/EE%20Standards%20-%202013.pdf.

Spear, P. (2000). The adolescent brain and age-related behavioral manifestations. *Neuroscience and Biobehavioral Reviews*, 24, 417–463.

Steinberg, L. & Cauffman, E. (1996). Maturity of judgment in adolescence: Psychosocial factors in adolescent decision making. *Law and Human Behavior*, 20, 249–272.

Stickley, T. (2006). Should service user involvement be consigned to history? A critical realist perspective. *Journal of Psychiatric and Mental Health Nursing*, 13, 570–577.

Stouthamer-Loeber, M., Wei, E., Loeber, R. & Masten, A. (2004). Desistance from persistent serious delinquency in the transition to adulthood. *Development and Psychopathology*, 16(4), 897–918.

Turley, C., Payne, C. & Webster, S. (2013). *Enabling Features of Psychologically Informed Planned Environments.* Retrieved from www.gov.uk/government/publications/enabling-features-of-psychologically-informed-planned-environments.

Tyrer, P., Duggan, C., Cooper, S., Crawford, M., Seivewright, H., Rutter, D., Maden, T., Byford, S., & Barrett, B. (2010). The successes and failures of the DSPD experiment: Assessment and management of severe personality disorder. *Medicine, Science and the Law*, 50, 95–99. doi: 10.1258/msl.2010.010001.

Vizard, E., French, L., Hickey, N. & Bladon, E. (2004). Severe personality disorder emerging in childhood: A proposal for a new developmental disorder. *Criminal Behaviour and Mental Health*, 14, 17–28.

# 16

# THE HEART AND SOUL OF THE TRANSFORMING ENVIRONMENT

## How a values-driven ethos sustains a therapeutic community for sexual offenders

*Andrew Frost and Jayson Ware*

*Hate the sin, love the sinner ...*

— St Augustine, Letter 211, c. 424

## Introduction

Therapeutic communities (TCs) rely on the activation of energies latent within, but common to, any human group. The intervention involves harnessing these energies in collaborative efforts to promote rehabilitative intentions. This chapter is about our experiences of working with prison-based therapeutic communities for men who have offended sexually. More specifically, it focuses on efforts to evoke the underlying values critical to such communities, to incorporate them in the therapeutic method, and to give expression to them in promoting rehabilitative ends. We argue that in the absence of such intervention, alternative values inimical to the therapeutic community are likely to take hold.

Forensic TCs consider the contribution of interpersonal dynamics within the facility in terms of a systemic whole. This includes and incorporates the empowered agency of its residents (inmates). A range of forums, systems and practices are established to provide the contexts, settings and opportunities for these dynamics to emerge, and thus to support the rehabilitative endeavour. So, for example, a twice-weekly community meeting might be convened, organised and chaired by a revolving committee of residents. The therapeutic community treats every encounter afforded by these arrangements as an opportunity for therapeutic change – a step toward transformation.

Even so, such arrangements cannot operate in an ethical vacuum. The culture of prison-based programmes tends to be influenced significantly by institutional phenomena, such as the 'inmate code' (see Ricciardelli, 2014). Such traditions are largely implicit and are founded on rigid power relations. They tend to be proscriptive of openness and of democratic agency, and are therefore inimical to the pro-social spirit of therapeutic change. In the TC, these rigid, narrow and hierarchical structures continually vie for ascendancy with therapeutic discourse. In our initial experiences working in prison-based TCs, while regular and frequent community meetings were held to consider impediments to the sustenance of the therapeutic community, and while staff of the institution convened to consider the progress of residents toward individually negotiated goals, little consideration was given to how residents might resist the insidious invitations of the mainstream prison ethos.

Indeed, the published work on TC refers, for the most part, to its function as a "living-learning situation" (Cullen, 1994, p. 239), as a "social learning laboratory" (Yalom & Leszcz, 2005), or a "culture of enquiry" (Lees, Manning & Rawlings, 1999). There is little explicit reference, however, as to the identity or moral philosophy of the TC – its substance (although, see Fortune, Ward & Polaschek, 2014). What should 'pro-social' conduct (Trotter, 1999) look like in the sex offender TC? What does the sex offender TC stand for? To be fit for purpose, therapeutic community arrangements must be established and maintained in the context of values, standards and principles, such as the value placed on relationships that are based on mutual respect rather than exploitation and abuse. It is therefore insufficient to merely provide therapeutic conduits without attention to their ethics.

In this chapter we present the contention that the values context is a critical but generally overlooked component of TC-grounded intervention. It is the missing link that sits between offender treatment principles and TC practice – the heart and soul.

We begin by briefly reviewing pertinent developments in the field of sex offender rehabilitation and the rise of context-focused treatment, with illustrative examples from prison-based sex offender treatment programmes. In applying learning from our research, practice and management experiences in establishing and maintaining successful prison-based therapeutic communities, we propose a basis for establishing an ethics-based set of principles to which all TC members can be expected to actively support. Finally we demonstrate how these factors have been woven into TC-based treatment regimes.

## Current frameworks for sex offender treatment

Offender rehabilitation has evolved significantly over the last forty years. Treatment programmes were initially derived from theoretical propositions about the origin and maintenance of the behaviour and clinically-derived notions about what targets needed to be addressed. Such programmes are now largely based on the outcome of extensive empirical tests of these clinical ideas (Marshall & Laws, 2003). Currently, two frameworks dominate the thinking in sex offender rehabilitation efforts: the Risk-Need-Responsivity (RNR) model (Andrews & Bonta, 2010) and the Good Lives model (GLM) (Ward & Stewart, 2003b).

The most extensively researched model of offender rehabilitation is the Risk-Need-Responsivity model. This model provides the structure under which correctional interventions should be organised. According to it, service provision and intensity should be focused on higher risk offenders (risk). Treatment should target those characteristics of offenders that are both functionally related to offending and amenable to change (criminogenic need). These first two principles can be said to represent the content of and eligibility for treatment – 'what' and 'who'. The third principle is concerned with tailoring and providing services in ways that are most likely to promote engagement, uptake and transformation (responsivity). Whilst the least considered and developed of the three principles, responsivity has central relevance to the topic of this chapter, as it pertains to the 'how' of treatment. Extensive research has shown that the proper application of these principles results in the reduction in recidivism among various types of offenders. Hanson, Bourgon, Helmus and Hodgson (2009) demonstrated that the same is true for the treatment of sexual offenders. Notwithstanding these results, the RNR model has been critiqued by those who, whilst not denying the necessity of targeting risk and needs, believe that the RNR model is insufficient as a comprehensive rehabilitation framework (e.g. Ward, Yates, & Willis, 2012). Such criticisms largely point to the (over-)emphasis on risk management and individual deficits, and the under-emphasis on contextual, processual or ecological factors relating to the individual offender (Frost, 2011; Frost & Connolly, 2004; Ware, 2011; Ward & Maruna, 2007).

Developed as an alternative to RNR, the GLM is a framework for offender rehabilitation based on the premise that a reduction in risk of reoffending is generated when offender capabilities and strengths are enhanced.

According to the GLM, individuals commit criminal acts because they lack opportunity or capability to achieve valued goals by appropriate means. Proponents suggest that the RNR paradigm's narrowly-focused and avoidance-driven targets of change should be, as much as possible, complemented by approach-focused and positively-directed efforts to assist those who have offended to lead more fulfilling lives. The fulcrum of this argument is that offenders, in resorting to criminal acts, are essentially striving to achieve universally-sought human goods that otherwise appear to them unattainable. The nature and direction of change in rehabilitative efforts should therefore assist clients in identifying the goods they have sought to achieve through anti-social means and in supporting their efforts in attaining them by alternative, pro-social means and through empathic considerations. This can be addressed, then, by lessening the appeal of exploitive strategies, in part by enhancing skills and motivation in attaining goals by way of pro-social means. Ward, Vess, Collie and Gannon (2006) hypothesise that, because a range of primary human goods – such as competency, intimacy, mastery – can be attained by sexual means, resorting to sexual abuse can be considered a predictable response to a range of personal and interpersonal difficulties (potential criminogenic needs). Sexual offenders – those who use sexual means abusively in attempting to meet their needs – may have learned to respond habitually in this way.

Whilst intuitively appealing to treatment providers, there is as yet little research demonstrating GLM's effectiveness relative to the RNR model (Gannon, King, Miles, Lockerbie & Willis, 2011; Whitehead, Ward & Collie, 2007; Netto, Carter & Bonell, 2014).

At the same time, studies indicate that a good number of existing programmes have been revised or developed to include or reflect both RNR and, increasingly, GLM or strength-based principles (e.g. McGrath, Cumming, Burchard, Zeoli & Ellerby, 2010; Ware & Bright, 2008; O'Sullivan, 2014). Marshall and others (Marshall et al., 2005; Ware & Marshall, 2007; Marshall, Marshall, Serran & O'Brien, 2011) have continued to champion approaches to treatment that are broader in concept, more sensitive to human condition, and 'positive' or strengths-based. They have advocated for more active attention to context and process features of treatment (see also Ware, 2011). There has been a further push for greater attention to the humanistic and relational functions of therapy (e.g. Frost, Ware & Boer, 2009). This has highlighted the appeal of relationally-based practice methods such as group therapy, and therapeutic communities, which we have organised under the banner 'social therapy' (Frost, 2011).

## Social therapy arrangements in sex offender treatment

Social therapy, in our view, reflects a broader concern with systemic and dynamic aspects of therapeutic relationships. We argue that potential effective therapeutic relationships exist beyond those established between a therapist and the offender. We are interested in the therapeutic benefits proceeding from a matrix of relationships among those involved in therapeutic systems: relationships between therapist and offenders (therapeutic alliance), relationships offenders have with each other (group climate) and the relationships between offenders and all other staff, *as well as* the relationships that all parties have with the group or the community as a whole (group climate and therapeutic community). We will address qualities of each of these in turn.

Despite considerable evidence of the relative importance of relational factors in general therapeutic change (see our references below to Duncan, Miller, Wampold & Hubble, 2010), this aspect of sex offender treatment remains under-developed. Marshall and Burton (2010) reviewed the literature arguing that group process factors are critically important to treatment effectiveness. They examined four process features: (1) therapist characteristics, (2) client perceptions of the therapist, (3) the therapeutic alliance and (4) the treatment group climate. The first three factors all relate, at least in part, to relationships between offenders and therapists. This has been shown to be critically important. Marshall, Serran, Fernandez, Mulloy, Mann and Thornton (2003) reported that the therapist features of warmth, empathy, rewardingness and directivenss accounted for between 30% and 60% of the variance of indices of behaviour change. Confrontation by therapists was negatively correlated with treatment changes. Both Hudson (2005) and Williams (2004) have also shown that confrontational or coercive approaches to treatment reduced the engagement of participants.

A range of group process opportunities are potentially available to enhance treatment effectiveness (Ware, Mann & Wakeling, 2009). This matter also remains under-researched. Beech and Fordham (1997) and Beech and Hamilton-Giachritsis (2005) found that within groups of sex offenders, emotional expressiveness and the presence of group cohesiveness were positively related to treatment change. Pfäfflin, Bohmer, Cornehl and Mergenthaler (2005) also found that emotional expressiveness, particularly when accompanied by an intellectual understanding, was a significant predictor of treatment changes. Elsewhere, we (Frost, Ware & Boer, 2009; Ware, Frost and Boer, 2015) have drawn attention to the need for sex offender therapists to have a greater appreciation of these relationally-based groupwork methods. In our view, groupwork represents much more than a practitioner conducting therapy with a collection of individual offenders simultaneously; the group is a therapeutic instrument in itself. Examples of relevant groupwork-specific concepts and their related skills include immediacy (working with the 'here-and-now'); use of self; focal conflict theory (e.g. Kline, 2003); stages of group developmental (e.g. Tuckman, 1965); and corrective interpersonal feedback (Cohen, 2000; Leszcz, 1992). In the absence of attention to these (and other) groupwork-specific techniques, countless opportunities to assist change are lost. Furthermore, neglecting group dynamics might be decidedly counterproductive by allowing the emergence of unhelpful dynamics to emerge (Frost et al., 2009). With specific regard to the sex offender treatment frameworks, groupwork provides both an opportunity to directly target criminogenic needs (RNR) and to enhance offender capabilities and strengths (GLM). An informed and supportive group therapist will work with the group in providing an environment conducive to mutual self-disclosure and interpersonal feedback. In such an environment group members are more likely to articulate and clarify their life aspirations, goals, intentions and commitments, and to form strategies that represent safe, respectful and gainful (i.e. 'good') lives (see Frost, 2011).

Whilst there has been recent momentum in correctional work towards appreciating the importance of the network of relationships between therapist and group members, comparatively little attention has been directed to the broader relational importance of the therapeutic environment. This is particularly so in instances where treatment is delivered in institutional facilities, such as prisons or secure hospitals. Although these environments are beset with natural, yet unhelpful, components – such as anti-social norms (as represented by inmate codes), lack of autonomy and isolation from family, social networks, and even fellow inmates – they potentially provide therapeutic opportunities otherwise unavailable in other contexts (Frost, 2011; Ware, Frost & Hoy, 2010). In effect, they provide for an extension of the group therapy process. As noted by Frost and Connolly (2004), protracted incarceration may offer opportunity for therapeutic immersion, singleness of purpose and freedom from distraction. The concept of the therapeutic community (TC) has emerged from the recognition of these opportunities (Baker & Price, 1995). As a "living-learning situation" (Cullen, 1994, p. 239), every event and any relationship within the environment is considered a learning opportunity, with the potential to enhance therapeutic gain. There is increasing empirical evidence in support of this assumption (see, for example, Brown, Miller, Northey & O'Neill, 2014; Shuker & Newberry, 2010). Supplementing this, qualitative studies report that TC residents consider the support of other residents and staff, a safe and friendly environment (Boswell & Wedge, 2003), and the 'out-of-group' environment (Frost & Connolly, 2004) to be important to their treatment success.

In this way, all relationships within TCs are considered potentially therapeutic and the attention of residents is continually directed towards therapeutic goals. TCs are built around the development and maintenance of a social environment in which residents' experiences occur against a background of consistent and predictable principles designed to facilitate comprehensive re-socialisation. In essence, the TC is an immersive context: therapeutic opportunities exist 24 hours a day, seven days a week. The common element is the provision of a communal living experience, encouraging open communication and promoting psychological and social adjustment.

## Ethically-derived principles in social therapy

It is apparent from the foregoing review that social therapeutic arrangements, such as group therapy and TC processes, represent a promising and significant role in sex offender treatment programmes. Nevertheless, we perceive a common oversight in integrating TC principles and sex offender programme requirements. This concerns the conscious activation and promotion of an ethically-derived TC value base: a values charter. Our position is that a values charter sits between TC principles and rehabilitative treatment principles, and that it has the potential to purposefully connect them to the enhancement of both. We proceed by presenting a rationale for our approach. We argue here that this is a necessary step in the authentic and active engagement of programme clients as a community of concern around sexual abuse.

Reasoning in support of this contention and describing its application in the field is our chief purpose here, and we devote the remainder of this chapter to this. We proceed by drawing on current research and theory about transformative personal and interpersonal change and then relate this knowledge to the 'active ingredients' of social therapy. We then apply tenets of strategic thinking in terms of mission, vision and values alongside current models of offender rehabilitation. Finally, we present a TC practice example from our experience as practitioners, managers, and supervisors.

## Rationale for considering ethical principles

Typically, TC principles and resources support the goals of forensic programmes by promoting pro-social conduct. At the level of the individual offender, treatment typically targets highly specific offending-related dynamic factors associated with a range of functional domains, such as social competence and emotional regulation.

While the usefulness of redirecting the individual residents toward discrete aspects of change at this level can be readily appreciated, in the absence of commitment to an underlying and community-wide philosophy, the process is at risk of failing to engage the internal motivation of clients (see McMurran, 2009; Miller & Rollnick, 2013); without a shared allegiance to a set of guiding values, the TC's "culture of empowerment" (Veale, Gilbert, Wheatley & Naismith, 2015, p. 289) requires the constant direction, exhortation and prompting of programme staff. Moreover, it is at risk of capture from adverse influences, such as the inmate code, rather than the sustenance of meaningful client accountability.

## Values and offender rehabilitation

Day and Ward (2010) present the argument that offender rehabilitation is a value-laden process. In following Kekes (1993), they define values as "important features of individuals' lives and experiences, based on human needs and shared living conditions, that reliably meet their core interests and promote individual and community well-being" (Day & Ward, 2010, p. 290). As such, they conclude that values "reflect individuals' judgements about what kind of activities and experiences are worth pursuing in their lives and likely to meet their core and related interests" (p. 290). In terms of rehabilitative enterprises then, values are reflected in offenders' and clinicians' underlying beliefs about the rehabilitative process and as such underlie their various actions in moving away from abusive practices and toward a fulfilling, 'good' life. Fortune et al. (2014), in linking key themes from GLM and TC, contribute to this thinking in concluding that the shared value placed on the quality of therapeutic relationships indicates promise in the use of TC as a platform for contributing to improving outcomes for offenders.

## How people change: the 'common factors' approach

In the second edition of their volume, *The Heart and Soul of Change* (Duncan et al., 2010), the editors (Hubble, Duncan, Miller & Wampold, 2010), drawing together the body of research amassed over 40 years, point to convincing evidence from transtheoretical research that factors predicting successful outcome in psychotherapy are *common* across models and techniques. That is to say, success factors are shared "ingredients or elements" (Hubble et al., 2010, p. 28) that exist in all forms of psychotherapy. These factors are summarised here as client-related factors, positive expectation, strength of therapeutic relationships/alliance strength and therapist characteristics. The authors stress, however, that the key to the success of these factors lies in their interactive *combination*, rather than as discrete additive components. This aspect of their findings is especially significant for social forms of therapy, such as TC, because here the residents can be considered to have both client *and* therapist roles ("community as doctor"; see Rapoport, 1960). In short, the community as a whole, with its complexity and dynamics, combine to represent a change modality in its own right. Alongside the contributions of institutional staff, residents share in the therapy of each another in a systemic whole: a milieu. The meaning of 'therapeutic alliance', in this setting, is not restricted to a therapist–client dyad (see Frost, 2011), but is a more inclusive and extensive construct that involves the active engagement all members of the TC.

With these considerations in mind, it is clearly important to the efficacy and integrity of the TC that it takes on a distinct 'corporate identity': not in the vernacular manner associated with large-scale, opulent commercial branding, but in the sense of a felt sense of shared mission. In our experience, this identity should be explicitly elicited and developed, embraced and promoted. Even where the (therapeutic) community might be otherwise punctilious in, for instance, conducting regular, frequent meetings and forums, without self-possessed collective purpose, charged with vigour in pursuing clear intentions and commitments, proceedings are likely to become vapid and mechanical. To extend the organic metaphor employed by Duncan et al. (2010), we argue that a purposefully-driven TC requires not just a central nervous system – insentiently stimulating dependent limbs – but a vital *heart and soul* to inspire and invite more autonomous and accountable expression of 'good lives'. Moreover, in any human system, be it group, community or institution, there will be a predominating ethos. In the real-world network of prison relations, in the absence of an explicitly identified core set of values, it is the inimical properties of the inmate code that are likely to hold sway.

## Community values mission and vision

In applying these important ideas to TCs, it is informative to consider the approach of other, 'outside' community organisations. It is evident that most organisations, including non-profit entities, develop mission and vision statements framed to articulate, distinctively and precisely, their particular purpose. Such statements are typically built around a set of values. The intention of these entities is to focus and concentrate the energies of the organisation as a whole onto a distinctively defined purpose on the basis of commonly held principles. The TC, we suggest, might usefully be seen in terms of a community voluntary organisation; that is, as a deliberately constituted, internally-motivated non-profit entity established for the fulfilment of social or community good (see Schwabenland, 2006). In this sense it goes beyond an individual focus; it is a communal endeavour, in which value is co-created. And, in terms of TC principles, it is in the act of this co-creation where much of the therapeutic 'profit' lies. If it is accepted that the TC sets out to actualise moral agency and client empowerment on a democratic foundation, then it makes sense to identify and establish a context-specific agenda for change that is embraced by all community members: a 'shared vision' of its aims and objectives. There are questions fundamental to the heart and soul of the community organisation: What do we do? Why do we do it? What do we stand for? Should these questions be openly deliberated upon by the TC, community members are less likely to habitually and slavishly follow a set of rules and regulations to which few might be heartily committed, or even properly conscious of. A well-conceived and shared value agenda, and the opportunities to reflect on the intentions and commitments of its members, contribute to qualities such as community cohesiveness, social capital and resource-related qualities that might well have been be lacking in the lives of residents outside of the TC.

## An approach-oriented and strengths-driven direction

While there are certainly areas of disagreement between the two predominant rehabilitation frameworks, there is a general consensus that rehabilitative transformation requires the replacement of one set of life strategies with another (Andrews, Bonta & Wormith, 2011; Ward, Yates & Willis, 2012). Using the TC method as a way of responding to the tenets of both RNR and GLM models in a forensic context, we propose that a set of value principles can be deduced from the anti-social strategies commonly employed by offenders in their maleficent attempts to attain human goods. Our chapter proceeds now with a proposal for determining such a set of principles derived in this way. Using the obverse logic of GLM and principles of successful desistance (Maruna, 2001), we consider how those strategies might be 'turned around' to reveal what a values charter might look like in this case.

Our approach in seeking to replace anti-social/abusive strategies to attain human goods then is to prescribe their *opposites*, that is, to promote pro-social/respectful strategies. This, we argue, not only promotes more appropriate strategies, but encourages a direction that is approach-oriented, strengths-driven, and integrative.

## Toward value-based principles for a sex offender TC

As we have outlined above, a tendency toward criminal forms of conduct can be understood in terms of the perceived unavailability, for one reason or another, of pro-social means of attaining human goods (Ward & Stewart, 2003a). Because sexual behaviours can offer a reliable pathway to meeting a range of primary human goods, it is hypothesised that resorting to sexual exploitation is a predictable response to a range of difficulties (Ward, Vess, Collie & Gannon, 2006). We agree with the human rights–based model of rehabilitation of Ward and others (Ward & Birgden, 2007; Ward & Connolly, 2008) predicating offender responsibility on access to human goods that are necessary for an offence-free life (such as a sense of personal competence, personal meaning and relatedness) rather than merely the avoidance of risk.

We consider then that the solution to meetings one's needs appropriately (pro-socially) lies in identifying life practices that are likely to result in the attainment of human goods, but which take into proper account the rights, needs and feelings of others in doing so.

## Generating a set of ethical principles for a sex offender TC

In our experience, the core objective of the sex offender TC is often articulated in practice in terms of simple argots, such as 'no more offending', or 'no more victims'.

However, this simplistic mantra-style approach generates avoidance-oriented injunctions which, as objectives, tend to fix attention on what is unwanted rather what is morally desired (Ward et al., 2006). In order for a community ethos to be successful there should be agreement on positively-framed, shared objectives: in other words, 'approach goals'.

Previously, in an article on therapeutic communities for sexual offenders, we (Ware, Frost & Hoy, 2010) proposed a set of five general interpersonal domains for rehabilitative attention. These are derived from our analysis of contextual and behavioural factors across sexual offence cases. As such they represent the range of themes common to most such cases, namely: exploitation, sexual grooming, secrecy and concealment, collusion and blame-shifting. We will now briefly review these themes in turn. Alongside each, we generate an interpersonal behavioural axiom that represents the *opposite* of that offending-related factor. We will then go on to consider implications for the treatment context in terms of behavioural principles. In this way, we intend to propose a set of value-based principles for sex offender TCs.

**From relationships based on exploitation to relationships based on mutual respect.**   Sexual abuse, like other form of violence, generally involves the misuse of power in some form. Functionally, this results in the subjugation and control that makes interpersonal exploitation possible. Such power can take a variety of forms, including physical, psychological, socio-political and economic. In cases of the sexual abuse of children, the mandate of adult authority is typically misappropriated by the offender. It is this fear-based or manipulative dominance that the offender uses in an attempt to attain the human goods that he has not attained for want of considerate and empathic accommodation.

The antithesis of abuse can plausibly be defined as *respect*. In the context of the prison-based sex offender TC, respect should be transacted mutually as evident in, for instance, custodial officers' communication with offenders and in therapy team members' relations with custodial staff (see Butler & Drake, 2007, for a view on the consideration of respectful relationships in a prison setting). Acknowledgement and honouring of the contribution, worth and dignity of one another through one's everyday conduct should be an expression – indeed an expectation – of the sex offender TC culture.

**From sexual 'grooming' to genuine interpersonal support.**   Sexual grooming (see Preble & Groth, 2002) involves the pre-abusive attempts of perpetrators to lessen resistance to sexual intrusion. It establishes a bridge to the abusive nature of the relationship by way of desired resources, such as 'affectionate' individual attention.

As habitual practice associated with abuse, grooming is likely to be observed in forensic TC settings in the form of manipulative and disingenuous use of human relationships. Its antithesis is expressed through a communally-displayed attitude of care and concern for other community members and in attachment to the institutional community as a whole. In their mutual form these attitudes represent the benefits of altruism described by Yalom and Lescz (2005). In behavioural terms, this extends to residents' commitment to inviting others to take on the ethical principles of the TC by way of principled living with others.

**From secrecy and concealment to openness, directness and honesty.** The theme of secrecy is inseparably related to child sexual abuse. This is instantiated in intra-familial offending, where the perpetrator typically recruits victims into supporting secrecy by presenting the abuse as a benign facet of the relationship. Alternatively (or additionally), the abuser suggests that intolerable consequences will result from its disclosure. In these ways, secrecy functions to conceal abusive events, their antecedents and their consequences. Once the fact of the abuse is revealed outside of the abusive system, even an enduring pattern of sexual abuse will almost certainly end. Secrecy is, therefore, a critical factor in forms of abuse that are perpetuated partly through factors that prevent the abuse coming to the attention of those in a position to address it.

In any context the qualities of transparency, openness and directness (assertiveness) and honesty are antithetical to abuse; in the sex offender TC they would ideally be inherent. However, being typically absent from the offender's interpersonal repertoire, and certainly alien to most facets of the institutional life of the prison, confronting established silence and concealment carries risk, and therefore requires the commitment of a critical mass within the community. In our experience TC residents acknowledge that deafness and blindness to abusive behaviour contributes to the misery of most inmates and there is in fact widespread appetite for resisting it.

**From collusion to collaboration and co-operation.** Collusion as a factor in sexual abuse takes the form of an attachment to, or tolerance of, conduct, attitudes and beliefs that support sexually abusive behaviour. Culturally supported definitions of 'respect' based on masculine notions of hierarchy and male privilege represent an example here. The expression of such collusive sentiment supports abuse by contributing to the acceptability of abuse-related justification. In clinical work, terms such as 'offence-process thinking' refer to factors that promote and perpetuate abuse.

Where there is sub-cultural tolerance of such thinking, such as the hypermasculine contexts of mainstream prison environments, abuse is more likely to thrive. A commitment to identifying and challenging such instances contributes to a sense of connectedness and attachment in collective opposition to abuse. In an example from practice, one resident's attempt to win favour by joking at the expense of women was received by the group not with mirth, but with questions about the usefulness of the misogynistic thinking underlying such a gambit. The men asked, how did this fit with a felt commitment to forming functional intimate relationships? Moreover, the emergence of such collective opposition also plays a part in overcoming the alienation and isolation that are often the forerunner to sexually offensive conduct.

**From blame-shifting to personal responsibility.** When confronted with their abusive behaviour, perpetrators typically seek to attribute responsibility to other persons or influences. The offender will blame a 'nagging' partner, a 'willing' victim, or the direct impact of drink or drugs. Blame-shifting is an attempt to evade responsibility.

This habit is often observed in institutional setting as a means of abrogating personal responsibility. Alternatively it is a means of declining invitations to engage with the therapeutic milieu in the communal effort to maintain the health and well-being of the community. Secure institutions, by their nature, sometimes inadvertently contribute to the habit of irresponsibility by imposing highly disciplined regimes, observed in narrow and rigid routines and rosters around daily living.

Responsibility and accountability are also considered important factors in sex offender treatment. Personal responsibility is a hallmark of democratic TCs. In accepting there is no one and nothing else to blame, one rids oneself of a justification for offending and is simultaneously invited to consider how one allowed such self-defeating thinking to take hold. Related to responsibility and accountability is the construct of personal agency. Personal agency, in turn, marries the construct of 'readiness' for treatment (Ward, Day, Howells & Birdgen, 2004) to the energies that are put into active participation to achieve treatment outcomes (see Melnick, De Leon, Thomas, Kressel & Wexler, 2001). We therefore take the view that opportunities in the TC to promote and enhance a sense of personal agency within an anti-abusive, pro-social milieu should be a central theme in this work. In terms of transferring this notion into the prison yard and other custodial settings, this requires that the individual takes on, as far as is practicable, personal responsibility for his daily life including inputs and outcomes. Building a sense of personal empowerment, we contend, engenders a sense of personal efficacy often missing from the perspectives of those who sexually offend.

It is perhaps worth stating here that the habits and practices that this context seeks to invite and to invoke are important not simply in terms of countering, in a subtractive sense, the components of a lifestyle that is functionally related to the commission of abuse. Typically the history of abusers includes early adverse experiences, disruption to attachment, and even complex trauma. A history of dysfunctional adaptation to these experiences might help explain predisposition to sexual offending. Through intensive and protracted exposure of residents to the environment we have described it is intended that an alternative, more positive, experience of social response becomes available. The goal is a more satisfying lifestyle – a better life, one in which the relative attractiveness of abuse is lessened. General implications for management of sex offender TCs.

Attitudes conducive to transformational change must be supported with the active generation and promotion of a sub-culture that supports such change and that refuses to collude with the practices that support abusive conduct. In the prison environment abusive practices typically include scapegoating, silencing and bullying tactics, as well as more direct forms of intimidation. Such regimes are resistant to therapeutic intervention and contribute to the oppression of the great majority of inmates. There is clearly an ironic and parallel process occurring in the mainstream prison hierarchy that the ethical principles outlined might both illuminate and counter.

In general terms, this sub-culture is supported by policies involving:

- Devolving responsibility to residents as work groups who organise and impart their own discipline
- Questioning the organisational assumption that 'A good prison unit is a quiet prison unit'
- Maximising fairness and transparency across all TC dealings

Our managerial experience suggests that where management pursues these policies, mainstream inmate codes begin to unravel, as offenders refuse to remain silent about evidence of, for example, a physical or sexual assault. In turn, institutional rigidity begins to loosen.

We have also found that it is important that all groups across the TC take up these principles and that management does not just become part of an authoritarian discourse that parallels and mirrors abuse. This requires that staff members, in responsible demonstrations of power through authority, demonstrate respect for residents as persons, and appreciation of their attempts to trial new ways of behaving; they should neither collude with nor tolerate sentiments that support exploitation. This is a tricky path and requires dexterity in handling interpersonal relationships.

We have sought to institute conditions where this is more likely to succeed through the concerted expression of anti-abusive sentiment in community meetings and other forums. It is in these forums where the 'public' witnessing of abusive practices is identified and their contribution to well-being challenged. Respectful practices, on the other hand, are highlighted and celebrated. Community meetings, because they are attended by all community members, and are seen to have the active support and positive sanction by all components of the community, are perhaps the principal setting for this. With these institutional habits in place, less formal encounters and interactions within the community are more likely to become the conduits for the expression of the community's principles.

## Conclusion

We set out in this chapter to advocate the purposeful management of value-driven factors as active ingredients in sex offender TCs. In making this case we drew on current thinking around sex offender treatment in general, and then wove in both up-to-date knowledge about processes of personal change alongside the learning from our own experience in working at clinical directorship and management roles in prison-based sex offender units. We examined the notion of a therapeutic system that relies on integrity and synergy for success, highlighting the central role of values. Value principles based on ethical ways of being provide the driving force in bringing to life the properties of the TC, and therefore the goals of rehabilitative treatment. We conclude that authentic engagement in a rigorous and exacting programme of change requires the establishment of a milieu in which client agency and participation have a central role in upholding highly explicit principles that are at once supportive of human rights and contrary to abusive conditions.

## References

Andrews, D.A. & Bonta, J. (2010). *The psychology of criminal conduct* (5th ed.). Newark, NJ: Matthew Bender.

Andrews, D.A., Bonta, J. & Wormith, J.S. (2011). The Risk-Need-Responsivity (RNR) model: Does adding the Good Lives Model contribute to effective crime prevention? *Criminal Justice and Behavior*, 38(7), 735–755.

Baker, D. & Price, S. (1995). Developing therapeutic communities for sex offenders. In B.K. Schwartz & R. Cellini (Eds.), *The Sex Offender: Corrections, Treatment and Legal Practice* (Vol. 1, pp. 19.11–19.14). Kingston, NJ: Civic Research Institute.

Beech, A. & Fordham, A.S. (1997). Therapeutic climate of sexual offender treatment programmes. *Sexual Abuse: A Journal of Research and Treatment*, 9, 219–223.

Beech, A.R. & Hamilton-Giachritsis, C.E. (2005). Relationship between therapeutic climate and treatment outcome in group-based sexual offender treatment programs. *Sexual Abuse: A Journal of Research and Treatment*, 17, 127–139.

Boswell, G. & Wedge, P. (2003). A pilot evaluation of therapeutic community for adolescent male sexual abusers. *Therapeutic Communities*, 24(4), 259–276.

Brown, J., Miller, S., Northey, S. & O'Neill, D. (2014). *What Works in Therapeutic Prisons: Evaluating Psychological Change in Dovegate Therapeutic Community*. Basingstoke, UK: Palgrave Macmillan.

Butler, M. & Drake, D.H. (2007). Reconsidering respect: Its role in Her Majesty's Prison Service. *The Howard Journal of Criminal Justice*, 46(2), 115–127.

Cohen, B.D. (2000). Intersubjectivity and narcissism in group psychotherapy: How feedback works. *International Journal of Group Psychotherapy*, 50(2), 163–179.

Cullen, E. (1994). Grendon: The therapeutic community that works. *Therapeutic Communities*, 15, 301–311.

Day, A. & Ward, T. (2010). Offender rehabilitation as a value-laden process. *International Journal of Offender Therapy and Comparative Criminology*, 54(3), 289–306.

Duncan, B.L., Miller, S.D., Wampold, B.E., & Hubble, M.A. (Eds.). (2010). *The Heart and Soul of Change: Delivering What Works in Therapy* (2nd ed.). Washington, DC: American Psychological Association.

Fortune, C., Ward, T. & Polaschek, D.L.L. (2014). The good lives model and therapeutic environments in forensic settings. *Therapeutic Communities*, 35(3), 95–104. doi:10.1108/TC-02-2014-0006

Frost, A. (2011). Bringing good lives to life: Applying social therapy to work with sex offenders. In D.P. Boer, R. Eher, L.A. Craig, M.H. Milner, & F. Pfäfflin (Eds.), *International Perspectives on the Assessment and Treatment of Sexual Offenders: Theory, Practice and Research* (pp. 433–447). Chichester, UK: John Wiley.

Frost, A. & Connolly, M. (2004). Reflexivity, reflection, and the change process in offender work. *Sexual Abuse: A Journal of Research and Treatment*, 16(4), 365–380.

Frost, A., Ware, J. & Boer, D.P. (2009). An integrated groupwork methodology for working with sex offenders. *Journal of Sexual Aggression*, 15(1), 21–38.

Gannon, T.A., King, T., Miles, H., Lockerbie, L. & Willis, G.M. (2011). Good lives sexual offender treatment for mentally disordered offenders. *British Journal of Forensic Practice*, 13(3), 153–168.

Hanson, R.K., Bourgon, G., Helmus, L. & Hodgson, S. (2009). The principles of effective correctional treatment also apply to sexual offenders: A meta-analysis. *Criminal Justice and Behavior*, 36, 865–891.

Hubble, M.A., Duncan, B.L., Miller, S.D. & Wampold, B.E. (2010). Introduction. In B.L. Duncan, S.D. Miller, B.E. Wampold, & M.A. Hubble (Eds.), *The Heart and Soul of Change: Delivering What Works in Therapy* (2nd ed., pp. 23–46). Washington, DC: American Psychological Association.

Hudson, K. (2005). *Offending Identities: Sex Offenders' Perspectives of Their Treatment and Management*. Portland, OR: Willan.

Kekes, J. (1993). *The Morality of Pluralism*. Princeton, NJ: Princeton University Press.

Kline, W.B. (2003). *Interactive Group Counseling and Therapy*. Upper Saddle River, NJ: Prentice-Hall.

Lees, J., Manning, N. & Rawlings, B. (1999). *Therapeutic Community Effectiveness: A Systematic International Review of Therapeutic Community Treatment for People with Personality Disorders and Mentally Disordered Offenders*. York, UK: York Publishing Services.

Leszcz, M. (1992). The interpersonal approach to group psychotherapy. *International Journal of Group Psychotherapy*, 42(1), 37–61.

Marshall, W.L. & Burton, D.L. (2010). The importance of group process in offender treatment. *Aggression and Violent Behavior*, 15, 141–149.

Marshall, W.L. & Laws, D.R. (2003). A brief history of behavioral and cognitive behavioral approaches to sexual offender treatment: Part 2. The modern era. *Sexual Abuse: A Journal of Research and Treatment*, 15(2), 93–120. doi:10.1177/107906320301500202

Marshall, W.L., Marshall, L.E., Serran, G.A., & O'Brien, M.D. (2011). *Rehabilitating Sexual Offenders: A Strength-Based Approach*. Washington, DC: American Psychological Association.

Marshall, W.L., Serran, G.A., Fernandez, Y.M., Mulloy, R., Mann, R.E. & Thornton, D. (2003). Therapist characteristics in the treatment of sexual offenders: Tentative data on their relationship with indices of behavior change. *Journal of Sexual Aggression*, 9, 25–30.

Marshall, W.L., Ward, T., Mann, R.E., Moulden, H., Fernandez, Y.M., Serran, G.A. & Marshall, L.E. (2005). Working positively with sexual offenders: Maximizing the effectiveness of treatment. *Journal of Interpersonal Violence*, 20(9), 1096–1114.

Maruna, S. (2001). *Making Good: How Ex-Convicts Reform and Rebuild Their Lives*. Washington, DC: American Psychological Association.

McGrath, R.J., Cumming, G.F., Burchard, B.L., Zeoli, S. & Ellerby, L. (2010). *Current Practices and Emerging Trends in Sexual Abuser Management: The Safer Society 2009 North American Survey*. Brandon, MA: The Safer Society Press.

McMurran, M. (2009). Motivational interviewing with offenders: A systematic review. *Legal and Criminological Psychology*, 14(1), 83.

Melnick, G., De Leon, G., Thomas, G., Kressel, D. & Wexler, H.K. (2001). Treatment process in prison therapeutic communities: Motivation, participation, and outcome. *American Journal of Drug and Alcohol Abuse*, 27(4), 633–650.

Miller, W.R. & Rollnick, S. (2013). *Motivational Interviewing: Helping People Change* (Vol. 3). New York, NY: Guilford Press.

Netto, N.R., Carter, J.M. & Bonell, C. (2014). A systematic review of interventions that adopt the "good lives" approach to offender rehabilitation. *Journal of Offender Rehabilitation*, 53(6), 403–432.

O'Sullivan, K. (2014). Paradigms for rehabilitation in Australia and the Sydney Desistance Project. *British Journal of Community Justice*, 12(2), 81.

Pfäfflin, F., Böhmer, M., Cornehl, S. & Mergenthaler, E. (2005). What happens in therapy with sexual offenders? A model of process research. *Sexual Abuse: A Journal of Research and Treatment*, 17(2), 141–151.

Preble, J.M. & Groth, A.N. (2002). *Male Victims of Same-Sex Abuse: Addressing Their Sexual Response*. Baltimore, MD: Sidran Press.

Rapoport, R. (1960). *Community as Doctor*. London: Tavistock.

Ricciardelli, R. (2014). An examination of the inmate code in Canadian penitentiaries. *Journal of Crime and Justice*, 37(2), 234–255. doi:10.1080/0735648X.2012.746012

Schwabenland, C. (2006). *Stories, Visions and Values in Voluntary Organisations*. Aldershot, UK: Ashgate.

Shuker, R. & Newberry, M. (2010). Changes in interpersonal relating following therapeutic community treatment at HMP Grendon. In R. Shuker & E. Sullivan (Eds.), *Grendon and the Emergence of Forensic Therapeutic Communities: Developments in Research and Practice* (pp. 293–304). Chichester, UK: Wiley Blackwell.

Trotter, C. (1999). *Working with Involuntary Clients: A Guide to Practice*. New South Wales, Australia: Allen & Unwin.

Tuckman, B.W. (1965). Developmental sequences in small groups. *Psychological Bulletin*, 63(6), 384–399.

Veale, D., Gilbert, P., Wheatley, J. & Naismith, I. (2015). A new therapeutic community: Development of a compassion-focussed and contextual behavioural environment. *Clinical Psychology & Psychotherapy*, 22(4), 285–303. doi:10.1002/cpp.1897

Ward, T. & Birgden, A. (2007). Human rights and correctional clinical practice. *Aggression and Violent Behavior*, 12, 628–643.

Ward, T. & Connolly, M. (2008). A human rights-based practice framework for sexual offenders. *Journal of Sexual Aggression*, 14(2), 87–98.

Ward, T., Day, A., Howells, K. & Birgden, A. (2004). The multifactor offender readiness model. *Aggression and Violent Behavior*, 9, 645–673.

Ward, T. & Marshall, W. L. (2007). Narrative identity and offender rehabilitation. *International Journal of Offender Therapy and Comparative Criminology*, 51(3), 279–297.

Ward, T. & Maruna, S. (2007). *Rehabilitation: Beyond the Risk Paradigm*. London, UK: Routledge.

Ward, T. & Stewart, C. (2003a). The relationship between human needs and criminogenic needs. *Psychology Crime & Law*, 9(3), 219–224. doi:10.1080/106316031000112557

Ward, T. & Stewart, C.A. (2003b). The treatment of sex offenders: Risk assessment and the good lives model. *Professional Psychology, Research and Practice*, 34, 353–360.

Ward, T., Vess, J., Collie, R.M. & Gannon, T.A. (2006). Risk management or goods promotion: The relationship between approach and avoidance goals in treatment for sex offenders. *Aggression and Violent Behavior*, 11(4), 378–393.

Ward, T., Yates, P., & Willis, G. M. (2012). The Good Lives model and the Risk Need Responsivity model: A critical response. *Criminal Justice and Behavior*, 39, 94–1190.

Ware, J. (2011). The importance of contextual issues within sexual offender treatment. In D. P. Boer, R. Eher, L.A. Craig, M.H. Milner & F. Pfäfflin (Eds.), *International Perspectives on the Assessment and Treatment of Sexual Offenders: Theory, Practice and Research* (pp. 299–312). Chichester, UK: Wiley.

Ware, J., & Bright, D. A. (2008). Evolution of a treatment programme for sex offenders: Changes to the NSW Custody-Based Intensive Treatment (CUBIT). *Psychiatry, Psychology and Law*, 15(2), 340–349.

Ware, J., Frost, A. & Boer, D. (2015). Working with sex offenders. In K. Sullivan, A. King, & T. Nove (Eds.), *Group Work in Australia* (pp. 252–267). Sydney, Australia: Institute of Group Leaders.

Ware, J., Frost, A. & Hoy, A. (2010). A review of the use of therapeutic communities with sexual offenders. *International Journal of Offender Therapy and Comparative Criminology*, 54(5), 721–742.

Ware, J., Mann, R.E., & Wakeling, H. (2009). Group versus individual treatment: What is the best bodality for treating sexual offenders?. *Sexual Abuse in Australia and New Zealand*, 2(1), 2–13.

Whitehead, P.R., Ward, T. & Collie, R.M. (2007). Time for a change: Applying the Good Lives Model of rehabilitation to a high-risk violent offender. *International Journal of Offender Therapy and Comparative Criminology*, 51(5), 578–598.

Williams, D.J. (2004). Sexual offenders' perceptions of correctional therapy: What can we learn? *Sexual Addictions & Compulsivity*, 11, 145–162.

Yalom, I.D. & Leszcz, M. (2005). *The Theory and Practice of Group Psychotherapy* (5th ed.). New York: NY: Basic Books.

# 17

# THE ROLE OF ENVIRONMENTAL FACTORS IN EFFECTIVE GENDER-RESPONSIVE PROGRAMMING FOR WOMEN IN THE UNITED STATES

## Current status and future directions

*Dana J. Hubbard and Betsy Matthews*

According to the Bureau of Justice Statistics (2014) there were 215,332 women incarcerated in state and federal prisons or local jails at year-end 2013. These numbers reflect a 50 per cent increase in female imprisonment since 1980. Despite this unprecedented growth, progress has been slow in the area of effective rehabilitation of women and providing an environment in which these programmes can be effective. Prisons steeped in androcentric policies and practices, the environments of prisons and jails, and social and economic barriers to reentry create environments that are ill-suited to the special needs of women.

There is growing awareness that women follow a different pathway into crime and the criminal justice system. For example, male offending is more often associated with aggression, risk-taking and economic independence, all positively valued features of masculinity (Messerschmidt, 1993), while female offending is more often associated with responses to life problems and relationships (Belknap, 2007; Owen, 1998). Indeed, much of the literature reports on women's pathways to crime as being ridden with relational problems, sexual abuse, mental illness and economic marginalisation (Belknap, 2007; Bloom, Owen & Covington, 2003; Chesney-Lind & Pasko, 2013; Daly, 1992; Reisig, Holtfreter & Morash, 2006).

While some attention in the last decade has been given to the unique needs of women, and even the idea that women need to be in a safe, therapeutic environment, little attention has been paid to the impact that prison and community environments have on women as they try to transition out of the criminal lifestyle. In this chapter, we discuss the history of women's imprisonment and introduce readers to the tenets of effective rehabilitation for women. We then explore environmental factors within prisons that undermine women's rehabilitation and discuss strategies for counteracting these factors. Finally, we review desistance research that highlights the importance of social and environmental factors in promoting positive change, and explore strategies for increasing women's likelihood of successful re-entry and desistance from crime.

## Brief history of women's imprisonment

In the early nineteenth century, women were imprisoned with men as part of the general population. The amount of segregation increased as decades passed with women first being housed in separate areas within male institutions, then to separate buildings on the same grounds, and finally to separate institutions (Chesney-Lind, 2003). The Indiana Reformatory for Women, built in 1873, was the first adult female only correctional facility.

Although segregation addressed issues of privacy and sexual assault from male inmates, these separate women's prisons were still steeped in patriarchal ideals (Stohr, Lero Johnson & Lux, 2015). Women received training for domestic positions and services were aimed at moulding women into proper ladies. Some believe that segregation led to the neglect of women prisoners, with small numbers of female inmates translating into few resources being allocated for programmes and services designed to address their needs (Belknap, 2007; Chesney-Lind, 2003).

The neglect of women prisoners continued well into the 1970s. The lack of resources and services for women led to calls for equal treatment. Supreme Court Justice Ruth Bader Ginsburg even called for a return to co-ed prisons as a way to address the disparate treatment of male and female inmates (Marcus, 2005). Then came the famous War on Drugs. The War on Drugs became a 'War on Women', with the rise in the rate of imprisonment for women outpacing that of men by 195 percent (Chesney-Lind, 2003).

This trend has persisted even as the rate of incarceration for men has declined. In 2014 there were over 215,000 women in our jails and prisons (Bureau of Justice Statistics, 2013). This translates into a national incarceration rate of about 58 per every 100,000 women in the general population. Consistent with the tough-on-crime approach, male-oriented practices like chain gangs and strip searches seeped into women's prisons, leading feminists to abandon the idea of prison parity and call for an end to gender blind approaches to jailing women (Chesney-Lind & Pasko, 2013). The call has shifted to one of 'different but equal treatment' that avails women of quality programmes and services that address their unique needs (van Wormer & Bartollas, 2013).

## Effective rehabilitation for women

There is an on-going debate about the extent to which specialised programmes are needed for women (Hubbard & Matthews, 2008). Scholars who have studied 'what works' to reduce recidivism assert that the same general principles of correctional intervention apply to both males and females (Andrews et al., 1990; Cullen & Gendreau, 2000; Gendreau, 1996; Latessa, Cullen, & Gendreau, 2002).

In contrast, feminist scholars assert that specialised, gender-responsive practices are needed that recognise key psychological and social differences between males and females (Belknap, 2007; Belknap & Holsinger, 1998; Bloom, 2000; Chesney-Lind, 2003). The key tenets from each body of literature are summarised below.

## 'What works' literature

Evidence-based practices, or those propagated by the 'what works' literature, are those that, through repeated studies, are shown to be associated with reductions in recidivism. According to these researchers (see Andrews, 2006; Andrews et al., 1990; Lowenkamp & Latessa, 2005) the effectiveness of treatment programmes varies significantly depending on the extent to which they adhere to four key principles.

According to the risk principle, programmes that match offenders to a level of treatment and control that is commensurate with their risk of recidivism will be more effective. That is, those who are more likely to recidivate should receive more intensive treatment and monitoring. Empirical studies of the risk principle's applicability to women offenders address two key research questions. The first pertains to whether or not generic risk assessment instruments are predictive of women's recidivism. Studies of the Level of Service Inventory-Revised (LSI-R), a popular risk assessment instrument adopted by numerous states, found it to be predictive of female recidivism (Lowenkamp, Holsinger & Latessa, 2001; Smith, Cullen & Latessa, 2009). The second question pertains to whether or not matching women to a level of control based on their predicted risk of recidivism actually yields lower rates of recidivism. Lovins, Lowenkamp, Latessa and Smith (2007) found support for the risk principle with women in residential treatment programmes; higher risk women in residential treatment had a lower probability of recidivism as compared to lower risk women in the same treatment.

The need principle directs programmes to target criminogenic needs for change. Criminogenic needs are those that are associated with the offender's criminality. If we address those needs, we have a better chance of reducing the likelihood of recidivism. Several studies of criminogenic needs have revealed similarities between males and females with the strongest needs being anti-social peer associations, anti-social beliefs and values, anti-social personality (e.g. lack of empathy, impulsiveness) and family relationships (Farrington & Painter, 2004; Hubbard & Pratt, 2004; Simourd & Andrews, 1994). Other research, however, has revealed a set of criminogenic needs (e.g. parenting stress, economic marginalisation, mental health, substance abuse) that are more prevalent among women and/or that affect women in more detrimental ways (Blanchette & Brown, 2006; Hannah-Moffat & Shaw, 2003; Reisig et al., 2006; Van Voorhis, Salisbury, Wright & Bauman, 2010).

The responsivity principle includes two components. First is general responsivity, which suggests that programmes should utilise cognitive-behavioural models of treatment that have been found to be most effective among offender populations. Hubbard and Matthews (2008) asserted that, despite a lack of research on cognitive-behavioural programming for female offenders, there are reasons to believe they would be effective. For example, there is sufficient research suggesting that cognitive distortions and processing deficits contribute to arrange of maladaptive behaviours among females (see Bennett, Farrington & Huesmann et al., 2005; Owens & Chard, 2001; Simourd & Andrews, 1994; Young, Martin, Young & Ting, 2001). Additionally, there is research demonstrating that these approaches are effective in treating depression and eating disorders among females (Schapman-Williams, Lock & Couturier, 2006; Wood, Harrington & Moore, 1996). Most relevant, perhaps, is the study of *Moving On*, a cognitive-behavioural programme for women on probation, which resulted in lower rates of recidivism for participants as compared to a matched sample of non-participants (Gehring, Van Voorhis & Bell, 2010).

Second is specific responsivity, which suggests that individualised programmes and services are needed to promote the likelihood of success in treatment. For example, treatment that is culturally specific contributes to better treatment retention and, ultimately, better results. Likewise, women's programming that addresses the aforementioned factors that are more prevalent among women (i.e. responsivity factors) are likely to be more effective. For example, programmes designed to address substance abuse and trauma (an important responsivity factor for women in particular) simultaneously have produced favourable outcomes including improvements in drug and alcohol use and mental health disorders (Covington, Burke, Keaton & Norcott, 2008; Najavits, Gallop & Weiss, 2006).

It is the specific responsivity component that begins to overlap with gender-responsive programming. Feminist scholars, however, assert that programmes must be developed through a gender lens rather than merely tweaking male-oriented principles to accommodate females (Belknap, 2007; Bloom et al., 2003; Chesney-Lind & Pasko, 2013). That is, they argue that 'what works' principles were, primarily, derived from studies of programmes for males and question their applicability to females. Their chief complaint is that these gender-neutral principles ignore the unique needs of women and the contextual nuances of the treatment environment that might hinder positive transformation.

## Gender-responsive literature

The gender-specific literature focuses on four guiding principles. The first principle instructs agencies to recognise the characteristics of the women in prison and how they are different for men. Following are sample statistics that demonstrate these differences:

- According the Bureau of Justice Statistics' *Mental Health Problems of Prison and Jail Inmates* (2006), 73 per cent of women of women in prison suffered from mental health issues compared to 55 per cent of men.
- Nearly 6 in 10 women in state prisons reported that they had been sexually abused before the age of 18 (Bureau of Justice Statistics, 2013). Some estimates in other studies put the percentages of sexual abuse at up to 95 per cent (Belknap, 2007).

- Approximately 70 per cent of women under correctional supervision have dependent children compared to 32 per cent for men (Bureau of Justice Statistics, 1999).
- There has been much research and acknowledgement of the drug use of women offenders. Women offenders serving time for drug offences make up about 30 per cent of the state prison populations yet the number who report using drugs at the time of the offence is much higher (Bureau of Justice Statistics, 2014).

The second principle calls for programmes for women that are based in specific theories of women's offending and development including the pathways model, relational theory and trauma theory (Covington & Bloom, 2006). The pathways model suggests that many women offenders follow similar pathways to offending behaviours. It points to research that reveals that the lives of women are often shaped by sexual abuse during early childhood, and that this experience produces and sustains a criminal lifestyle characterised by drug use, mental health issues and prostitution.

Another theory that explains women's criminality is relational theory. This theory suggests that women and girls get their identity through relationships with others (Covington & Bloom, 2006; Gilligan, 1982; Miller, 1976). In terms of criminality, women cite broken relationships and attempts to keep relationships as contributing to their crimes. This is especially relevant in the drug and alcohol addiction literature whereby women cite their reasons for using as self-medicating as a means of coping with broken relationships and/or attempting to keep a relationship (Covington & Bloom, 2006; Miller, 1976).

Finally, trauma theory acknowledges the high rate of victimisation among justice-involved females. This recommendation has to do with creating a positive and safe context for interventions to take place. Creating a trauma-sensitive culture requires all persons within that environment to be trained on the effects of trauma and how they can avoid reenactment for girls and women (Farragher & Yanosy, 2005; Wright, Van Voorhis, Salisbury & Bauman, 2012). Agencies who have implemented trauma-sensitive therapy with girls have reduced the number of critical incidents and many have eliminated the need for physical restraint (Farragher & Yanosy, 2005). Programmes for women that address co-occurring substance abuse and post-traumatic stress disorders have also produced positive results (Messina, Grella, Cartier & Torres, 2010; Najavits et al., 2006).

The third principle advocates for rehabilitation efforts that focus on addiction, mental health and trauma through an individualised approach. According to Covington and Bloom (2006) services should be comprehensive and focus on what we know about women offenders and the theories that guide their criminal development. Programmes such as family therapy, group therapy, expressive therapy and cognitive behaviour treatment should be utilised. In addition, while substance abuse treatment is essential, the treatment should focus on women who are dually diagnosed (mental health and substance abuse).

The fourth and final principle instructs agencies to build therapeutic environments that are based on "safety, respect, and dignity" (Covington & Bloom, 2006, p.13). Gender-specific advocates admonish the harsh nature of the prison environment. Covington and Bloom (2006) suggest that the environment needs to be inviting, non-institutional, homelike, and welcoming. They suggest that women's treatment centres need to be like a sanctuary for women where they can heal and recover. Prison environments are often responsible for re-traumatisation of women and often re-create the abusive environment these women are accustomed to (Covington & Bloom, 2006).

## *Integration of gender-neutral and gender-responsive principles*

Research reveals that programmes that adhere to the risk, need and responsivity principles, are implemented as designed, and are subjected to quality assurance measures do contribute to greater reductions in recidivism (Andrews, 2006; Andrews et al., 1990; Lowenkamp & Latessa, 2005). An early meta-analysis by Dowden and Andrews (1999) of 26 studies supported the application of these gender-neutral principles to women. Moreover, in a recent meta-analysis of 37 studies published between 2000 and 2013, Gobeil, Blanchette, and Stewart (2016) found that gender-neutral and gender-responsive programmes were equally effective for female offenders. Further analysis by Gobeil et al. (2016), however, revealed that when only the 18 studies with the highest methodological quality were included, gender-responsive interventions were significantly more likely to be associated with a reduction in recidivism than were gender-neutral interventions, particularly for those women who "followed gendered pathways into the criminal justice system" (p. 317).

Given mixed results, and the nascent research on programmes for female offenders, Hubbard and Matthews (2008) have argued for an integration of both literatures, asserting that each contribute relevant guidance to programmes for female offenders. When looking at the programmes that are offered in current prison programmes for women, it appears as if both bodies of literature are gaining acceptance. For example, in the Northeast Ohio Reintegration Center, a prison for women in Ohio, their programmes range from Thinking for a Change and Cage your Rage (cognitive behavioural programmes based in the 'what works' literature) to programmes such as Healthy Boundaries, Moms in Touch, Boundaries with Kids, and Life Skills (programmes more in tune with gender-responsive principles).

Although some progress has been made, a lot of work remains before we can adequately address the needs of women in our criminal justice systems. The next section of this chapter discusses the environment of prisons and how detrimental they are for women.

## Women and the prison environment

Incarcerated women have higher rates of mental health and substance abuse problems than their male counterparts. They have also experienced high rates of trauma and homelessness prior to their incarceration. For many women, this trauma continues behind prison walls. The incidence of sexual abuse of women in prison is difficult to measure due to varying opinions about what constitutes sexual abuse, different methods of data collection and underreporting. Two national studies suggest that 13–17 per cent of inmates report sexual victimisation that involves another inmate or staff (VanNatta, 2010). Neither report, however, separated the data by gender or by whether the abuse was perpetrated by staff or other inmates. For reasons cited above, as well as the patriarchal prison environment, it is likely that sexual abuse in women's prison is more widespread than these statistics suggest.

Michelle VanNatta, in a 2010 article, explores multiple forms of sexual abuse within women's prisons. Four of these occur at the hands of rogue employees. The first, and probably the rarest, form of sexual abuse is physical force, or rape. Second, prisoners are coerced into sexual contact through threats of harm or deprivation of basic resources. Third, inducements, or the promise of goods or special treatment, are offered in exchange for sex acts. Fourth is the sexual contact that occurs within the context of an on-going romantic relationship.

According to a 2007 national study by Beck and Harrison, over 22,000 women reported experiencing physical force, pressure or offers of special favours or privileges. Another 22,000 reported consensual sexual contact with staff. VanNatta (2010) challenges the extent to which sexual acts are consensual given the power differentials between staff and inmates, and, to their credit, most states recognise this and consider even consensual sexual acts with inmates to be a crime. However, the extent to which prison administrations actively try to put an end to these types of relationships or pursue charges is questionable.

According to VanNatta (2010), the other forms of sexual abuse in women's prisons are sanctioned by institutional policies and practices and are more common. Strip searches, for example, are required upon a woman's entry into the institution. They can also be conducted after visitation and in the case of a suspected security breach. Most states consider them to be a legitimate part of security and control within a prison. Most prisons prohibit males from strip-searching females except for in the case of an emergency. But, as VanNatta (2010) points out, what constitutes an emergency is not always clear, and even when conducted by women, strip searches are humiliating and degrading.

Lastly, VanNatta (2010) reports that women inmates report that sexual harassment and sexual surveillance occur regularly. Seventy per cent of survey respondents in Illinois reported that staff called them offensive names and berated them in front of others. And, over half the prisoners reported that male correctional officers watched them while they used the toilet, showered or dressed. VanNatta (2010) suggests that males within women prisons are viewed by some as 'super authorities' with gender-based power differentials and control over even the most private moments of women's lives.

VanNatta (2010) acknowledges that it may seem extreme to consider strip-searches and surveillance as sexually abusive. But, she argues, it seems as if they would be traumatic for anyone, and especially for those with a history of sexual victimisation. And clearly these practices contain elements of abuse – they are forced upon women by people in positions of power and create extreme vulnerability and discomfort for women.

As previously indicated, it is likely that staff sexual abuse is grossly underreported. VanNatta (2010) states that many women refuse to report abuse for fear that they won't be believed or that they somehow invited the abuse. Even when they want to report the abuse, they are dissuaded by the limited access to a telephone, medical personnel or legal or emotional support. Moreover, VanNatta (2010) asserts that women who do get the courage to report are routinely placed in administrative segregation for their protection while the allegation is being investigated. With segregation comes isolation and even more limited access to goods and services. Then, if the allegation is determined to be false, a sanction may be imposed that extends the women's prison sentence or her time in segregation.

The environment of most women's prisons supports all forms of sexual abuse. The only sure way to lessen the incidence of staff sexual abuse for women is to reduce their rate of incarceration. Short of that, attention to staff selection and training on trauma-informed services are likely to reduce women's victimisation (Wright et al., 2012) as are whistleblowing programmes akin to those that have been implemented in other organisational environments (see Francis & Armstrong, 2011; Yeoh, 2014).

Women's needs cannot be adequately addressed in traditional patriarchal institutions. Although there is a movement toward gender-sensitive practices in prison, change has been slow. It seems as if women must continue to fight for equal rights in prison just as they do in the free world.

## Women's reentry/desistance literature

An important body of research focuses on how one 'desists' from crime, or transitions from criminal to non-criminal conduct (see Giordano, Cernkovich & Rudolph, 2002; Maruna, 2001; Sampson & Laub, 1993; Warr, 1998). We have drawn five major conclusions from a growing body of literature on women and crime desistance that help us understand the importance of social and environmental factors in promoting positive change.

First, it is clear that motherhood plays a significant role in the lives of women following conviction and/or imprisonment in terms of both the meaning of the role and its accompanying obligations. The maternal role can serve as both a catalyst and impediment to women's desistance from crime. Some research identifies wanting to provide and care for children as a pro-social force in women's lives (Byrne & Trew, 2008; Cobbina, 2009; Cobbina & Bender, 2012; Giordano et al., 2002; Huebner, Dejong, & Cobbina, 2010; McIvor, Jamieson & Murray, 2000). For example, Giordano et al. (2002) found that for many women in their sample, being a mother was a source of positive identity formation; the desire to be a 'good mother' didn't support drug use and other anti-social behaviours. Additionally, half of the women in Cobbina's (2009) sample spoke about the separation from their children as costs of crime that they wanted to avoid. Other research, however, suggests that the obligations and strains that come with the maternal role contributes to anti-social behaviours (Brown & Bloom, 2009; Ferraro & Moe, 2006; Richie, 2001). Brown and Bloom, for example, found that women returning from prison struggled to provide for their children's basic needs and to regain their parental authority. This, paired with hostility from their children's caretakers during their incarceration, challenged their reintegration and desistance efforts.

Second, supportive relationships with family and friends are prominent themes in women's desistance narratives (Bui & Morash, 2010; Cobbina, 2009; Dowden & Andrews, 1999; Giordano et al., 2002; Herrschaft, Veysey, Tubman-Carbone & Christian, 2009; Leverantz, 2011, 2014; O'Brien, 2001; Sommers, Baskin & Fagan, 1994). According to Herrschaft et al. (2009), most (73.9 per cent) females in their sample of formerly incarcerated persons identified relationship-related factors (e.g. support of family, friends or caring professional) as being the most salient factors in their transformation process. In contrast, all of the men mentioned status-relationship factors (e.g. employment, education) as being the most important. Leverantz (2011), in her study of 43 African-American women, found that support from family of origin was important to successful transitions. Being a good daughter or sister was a critical component of their identity, and despite tensions related to past abuse and negative childhood events, women in their study were reportedly grateful for the advice and emotional support their families provided. Giordano et al. (2002) found that women were more likely than men to view marriage as a catalyst for change regardless of their level of marital attachment. That is, rather than love or happiness experienced within the marital relationship, women implicated their 'role as wife' in the change process because of the stable and conventional lifestyle it provided. Giordano et al. (2002) concluded that, for women in particular, it was not the mere presence or quality of social bonds, but the cognitive transformations made within the context of these relationships that promoted positive change.

Third, desistance research has shown that, not only are informal relationships such as family, significant others and friends important for a successful reentry, but there is evidence that formal relationships can serve as an element of support for women (Cobbina, 2009; Leverantz, 2014). Cobbina's (2009) interviews with 50 current and formerly incarcerated women revealed that many women attributed their success to a positive, supportive parole officer who would listen and provide encouragement. Similarly, Leverantz's (2014) research on residents of the Mercy Home, a Chicago halfway house for women released from prison, suggests that the camaraderie and support of programme staff was important to women's success. The Mercy Home employed ex-offenders as mentors and programme monitors. These staff members provided residents with role models whose backgrounds mirrored theirs and helped them to envision their future selves.

Fourth, in contrast to males who identify status related factors (e.g. employment, education) as being the most important to their desistance (Herrschaft et al., 2009), women seldom identify employment as a prominent factor in their desistance. As noted by Giordano et al. (2002), these findings may reflect the limited opportunities for stable and meaningful employment for women. Giordano et al. (2002) and Leverentz (2014) reported that many of the women in their research who were able to attain employment faced daily struggles to keep their jobs because of child care, health and transportation problems. These struggles, coupled with few perceived rewards from low paying jobs in non-rewarding work environments, impeded their desistance.

Fifth, the desistance research emphasises the role of personal agency in women's pathways out of crime. For example, during in-depth interviews conducted by Cobbina (2009) and Sommers et al. (1994), women cited their personal resolve and choices as that which helped them avoid the criminal lifestyle. Moreover, both Cobbina (2009) and Leverentz (2014) noted that although desistors and persistors faced similar adverse social circumstances, desistors were better able to navigate these circumstances. Relatedly, desistance research highlights the role that perceptions of self and cognitive transformations play in women's desistance. Desistance was associated with pride in accomplishments (Giordano et al., 2002), a newfound stake in conventional identities (Giordano et al., 2002; Sommers et al., 1994) and increases in self-confidence and self-efficacy (Leverentz, 2014).

The desistance research represented here affirms much of what we know from studies of the precursors to the criminal behaviour and recidivism of women. Both bodies of research point to the greater significance of relationship factors for women, affirm the role of cognitive factors in criminal behaviour and suggest that children play significant roles in the lives of women as both catalysts and impediments to positive change.

The findings from research on crime desistance provide new knowledge and insights about individual and social factors associated with women's criminality. At this juncture, we have identified five specific and interrelated implications for correctional practice and one daunting philosophical challenge to current correctional practice in the United States.

The first implication for correctional practice involves a shift to a strengths-based approach to intervention. Desistance research shifts the discourse from a focus on deficiencies and risk factors to a focus on personal agency and transformative factors (McNeill, Farrall, Lightowler & Maruna, 2012). For example, rather than only viewing women's existing relationships as detrimental to desistance, it recognises women's sense of responsibility to the family and community as positive characteristics reflective of an ethics of care (see Leverentz, 2011). This shift in discourse and approach takes advantage of protective factors and other characteristics of women that have long explained their lower rates of crime than males (e.g. greater empathy, stronger moral inhibitions) and reflects a more gender-responsive model of intervention (van Wormer and Bartollas, 2013). It will be no easy task, however, for agencies invested in the current risk, or deficit-based, models of intervention.

Second, the desistance research provides support for the use of cognitive-behavioural interventions (CBIs) with women. Feminist criminologists (see Covington & Bloom, 1999; Kendall and Pollack, 2003; Wald, Harvey & Hibbard,

1995) have argued that CBIs are not an appropriate model of intervention for women who are less likely than men to exhibit the type of anti-social attitudes and values that many of these programmes are designed to address (Covington & Bloom, 1999). They also have asserted that CBIs pathologise women's criminal behaviour rather than recognise it as a natural response to the victimisation and other forms of oppression they experience (Kendall & Pollock, 2003). Although there is some validity to these arguments, CBIs can be strength-based and address the cognitive factors that research suggests are associated with women's desistance from crime. That is, they can target self-efficacy and teach coping and interpersonal skills needed to manage troubled relationships. Conducted within the context of a strong working alliance and a safe therapeutic environment, CBIs are likely to promote positive behavioural change (Hubbard and Matthews, 2008; Wright et al., 2012). A recent study of Van Dieten's (2010) *Moving On* programme found initial support for the use of gender-responsive CBIs to address female criminality in general, and self-efficacy in particular (Gehring et al., 2010). Certainly, more research is needed to attest to the merits of gender-responsive CBIs, but it would seem that a sufficient body of literature has been amassed to support their implementation.

Third, agencies should provide mothers with the support and services needed to be successful in their maternal role. The research previously reviewed suggests that self-identity is central to the desistance process, and for women, primacy is often given to their identity as mother. When this identity is undermined by conviction and/or incarceration, women must work through relationships with caretakers, financial problems and housing restrictions to restore parental authority in their children's lives (Brown & Bloom, 2009). The extent to which they are successful impacts their self-perceptions, stake in conformity and, ultimately, their success on parole. For this reason, Brown and Bloom (2009) assert that a women's identity as a mother should be placed at the forefront of the re-entry process, and that priority should be given to support and services designed to help them renegotiate their mother–child relationships.

Fourth, services should be provided that help women navigate difficult familial relationships. Through theorising and empiricism, we have long understood that the nature of family relationships (e.g. anti-social, strained or conflict-ridden, weak attachments) has a strong impact on women's criminality. The solution has usually involved trying to isolate women from anti-social others through conditions of community supervision that prohibit these affiliations. Although some desistance research supports this approach (see Cobbina, 2009; Sommers et al., 1994), it can be logistically challenging given the anti-social behaviour of family members and the financial and housing constraints that limit women's ability to move out of their current home or neighbourhood. Moreover, the desistance research demonstrates that relationship issues are far more complex than this solution would suggest. It's not the mere presence or absence of a relationship that determines whether a woman engages in subsequent crime; it's the meaning of the relationship in her life that matters (Giordano et al., 2002). Women's identities are rooted in their roles as wife, daughter and mother (Leverantz, 2011). As noted by Leverentz (2011) and Maruna & Roy (2007), the 'knifing off' of these relationships is likely to leave a void that contributes to other types of emotional strains that are equally culpable in the return to crime.

Finally, agencies should provide opportunities to connect with pro-social others through mentoring, education, self-help groups and faith-based programming (Matthews & Hubbard, 2008). These connections provide a source of instrumental and expressive social support that women need to buffer themselves from adverse circumstances they might face. They also provide women with the opportunity to create new roles for themselves and the beginning of a new life narrative (Giordano et al., 2002; Maruna, 2001) that is more conducive to desistance.

In the United Kingdom, where desistance research is more prevalent, a new model of correctional intervention has emerged called 'desistance-focused practice' (McNeill & Weaver, 2010). This model shifts the goals of correctional intervention from rehabilitation and deterrence, which require changes in the individual, to reintegration, which requires changes in the individual *and* acceptance by the community. In the United States, the 'what works' or 'evidence-based' model focuses, primarily, on changing the individual, or building human capital, through the provision of programmes and services that address important criminogenic needs. Farrall (2002) asserts that the current challenge for corrections is to find ways to build social capital, or the type of social networks that generate opportunities and resources needed for more pro-social endeavours. This is particularly important for women ex-offenders who, according to Cobbina (2009), have limited access to social networks needed to gain legitimate employment and participate in other pro-social alternatives.

According to Leverentz (2014, loc. 3997), the current rehabilitation and deterrence-based models of correctional intervention reflect an "illusion of returning prisoners' unilateral control over their own reentry", and keep us from confronting the social and legal inequalities that impede women's desistance from crime. The desistance-focused model, however, calls for corrections professionals to extend their role beyond the provision of programming and supervision, and become advocates in the courts and community. We can, and should, continue to expend resources on helping women develop the skills and attitudes needed to find and maintain legitimate employment, to become a good parent or to escape their addictions, but without the social support and social capital necessary for success, desistance will be difficult to achieve.

## Conclusion

The past few decades have seen a change in the treatment for women in correctional settings. The gender responsive advocates have long been champions of the need to delve deeply into the lives of women and recognise that 'gender matters'. Clinicians have worked tirelessly to promote rehabilitation that reflects women's experiences. One factor of upmost importance is creating a healing environment for the women in corrections. It is true that the prison environment has not produced many positive rehabilitative outcomes for men, but it is especially problematic for women. Women offenders tend to be victims of childhood physical and sexual abuse and domestic violence. Bad relationships with others is often what brought them to prison and good relationships are essential to keep them out of trouble. The prison and post-prison environments must support women offenders' healing if we hope to reduce recidivism and, ultimately, help woman desist from crime.

## References

Andrews, D. A. (2006). Enhancing adherence to risk-need-responsivity: Making quality a matter of policy. *Criminology and Public Policy*, 5, 595–602.

Andrews, D. A., Zinger, I., Hoge, R. D., Bonta, J., Gendreau, P. & Cullen, F. T. (1990). Does correctional treatment work? A clinically relevant and psychologically informed meta-analysis. *Criminology*, 28, 369–404.

Beck, A. & Harrison, P. (2007). *Sexual Victimization in State and Federal Prisons Reported by Inmates, 2007. Bureau of Justice Statistics.* Washington, DC: U.S. Department of Justice.

Belknap, J. (2007). *The Invisible Woman: Gender, Crime, and Justice.* Belmont, CA: Wadsworth.

Belknap, J. & Holsinger, K. (1998). An overview of delinquent girls: How theory and practice have failed and the need for innovative changes. In R. Zaplin (Ed.), *Female Offenders: Critical Perspectives and Effective Intervention* (pp. 31–59). Gaithersburg, MD: Aspen.

Bennett, S., Farrington, D. P. & Huesmann, L. R. (2005). Explaining gender differences in crime and violence: The importance of social cognitive skills. *Aggression and Violent Behavior*, 10, 263–288.

Blanchette, K. & Brown, S. (2006). *The Assessment and Treatment of Women Offenders: An Integrative Perspective.* West Sussex, UK: John Wiley and Sons.

Bloom, B. (2000). Beyond recidivism: Perspectives on evaluation of programs for female offenders in community corrections. In M. McMahon (Ed.), *Assessment to Assistance: Programs for Women in Community Corrections* (pp. 107–138). Lanham, MD: American Correctional Association.

Bloom, B., Owen, B. & Covington, S. (2003). *Gender-Responsive Strategies: Research, Practice, and Guiding Principles for Women Offenders* (NIC Publication No. 018017). Washington, DC: National Institute of Corrections.

Brown, M. & Bloom, B. (2009). Reentry and renegotiating motherhood: Maternal identity and success on parole. *Crime & Delinquency*, 55, 313–336.

Bui, H. N. & Morash, M. (2010). The impact of network relationships, prison experiences, and internal transformation on women's success after prison release. *Journal of Offender Rehabilitation*, 49(1), 1–22. doi:10.1080/10509670903435381.

Bureau of Justice Statistics (1999). *Special Report: Women Offenders.* Washington, DC: U.S. Department of Justice.

Bureau of Justice Statistics (2006). *Mental Health Problems of Prison and Jail Inmates.* Washington, DC: U.S. Department of Justice.

Bureau of Justice Statistics (2013). *Prisoners in 2013.* Washington, DC: U.S. Department of Justice.

Bureau of Justice Statistics (2014). *Correctional Populations in the United States.* Washington, DC: U.S. Department of Justice.

Byrne, C. & Trew, K. J. (2008). Pathways through crime: The development of crime and desistance in the accounts of men and women offenders. *Howard Journal of Criminal Justice*, 47, 238–258.

Chesney-Lind, M. (2003). Reinventing women's corrections: Challenges for contemporary feminist criminologists and practitioners. In S. Sharp (Ed.), *The Incarcerated Woman: Rehabilitative Programming in Women's Prisons* (pp. 3–14). Upper Saddle River, NJ: Pearson Education.

Chesney-Lind, M. & Pasko, L. (2013). *The Female Offender: Girls, Women, and Crime.* Thousand Oaks, CA: Sage.

Cobbina, J. (2009). *From Prison to Home: Women's Pathways in and out of Crime.* Washington, DC: National Institute of Justice (Document No. 226812).

Cobbina, J. E. & Bender, K. A. (2012). Predicting the future: Incarcerated women's views of reentry success. *Journal of Offender Rehabilitation*, 5, 275–294.

Covington, S. & Bloom, B. (1999). Gender-responsive programming and evaluation for females in the criminal justice system: A shift from what works? To what is the work? Paper presented at the fifty-first annual meeting of the American Society of Criminology, Toronto, Ontario, Canada.

Covington, S. & Bloom, B (2006). Gender-responsive treatment and services in corrections settings. *Women and Therapy*, 29, 9–33.

Covington, S. Burke, C., Keaton, S. and Norcott, C. (2008). Evaluation of a trauma-informed and gender-responsive intervention for women in drug treatment. *Journal of Psychoactive Drugs*, Suppl. 5, 387–398.

Cullen, F.T. & Gendreau, P. (2000). Assessing correctional rehabilitation: Policy, practice, and prospects. In J. Horney (Ed.), *Policies, Processes, and Decisions of the Criminal Justice System; Criminal Justice 2000* (Vol. 3, pp. 109–175). Washington, DC: National Institute of Justice/ NCJRS.

Daly, K. (1992). Women's pathways to felony court: Feminist theories of lawbreaking and problems of representation. *Southern California Review of Law and Women's Studies*, 2, 11–52.

Dowden, C. & Andrews, D. (1999). What works for female offenders: A meta-analytic review. *Forum on Corrections Research*, 11, 18–21.

Farragher, B. & Yanosy, S. (2005). Creating a trauma-sensitive culture in residential treatment. *Therapeutic Community: The International Journal for Therapeutic and Supportive Organizations*, 26, 97–113.

Farrall, S. (2002). *Rethinking What Works with Offenders: Probation, Social Context, and Desistance from Crime.* Cullompton, Devon: Willan Publishing.

Farrington, D. & Painter, K. (2004). *Gender differences in risk factors for offending.* Research, Development and Statistics Directorate, UK. Retrieved 11 May 2005 from www .homeoffice.gov.uk/rds.

Ferraro, K. J. & Moe, A. M. (2006). The impact of mothering on criminal offending. In L. Alarid & P. Cromwell (Eds.), *In Her Own Words: Women Offenders' Views on Crime and Victimization.* New York: Oxford University Press.

Francis, R. D. & Armstrong, A. (2011). Corruption and whistleblowing in international humanitarian aid agencies. *Journal of Financial Crime*, 18, 319–335.

Gehring, K., Van Voorhis, P. & Bell, V. (2010). "What works" for female probationers? An evaluation of the Moving On program. *Women, Girls, and Criminal Justice*, 11, 6–10.

Gendreau, P. (1996). The principles of effective intervention with offenders. In A. Harland (Ed.), *Choosing Correctional Options That Work: Defining the Demand and Evaluating the Supply* (pp. 117–130). Thousand Oaks, CA: Sage.

Gilligan, C. (1982). *In a Different Voice: Psychological Theory and Women's Development.* Cambridge, MA: Harvard University Press.

Giordano, P. C., Cernkovich, S. A. & Rudolph, J. L. (2002). Gender, crime, and desistance: Toward a theory of cognitive transformation. *American Journal of Sociology*, 107(4), 990–1064.

Gobeil, R., Blanchette, K. & Stewart, L. (2016). A meta-analytic review of correctional interventions for women offenders: Gender neutral versus gender-informed approaches. *Criminal Justice and Behavior*, 43, 301–322.

Hannah-Moffat, K. & Shaw, M. (2003). The meaning of "risk" in women's prisons: A critique. In B. Bloom (Ed.), *Gendered Justice: Addressing Female Offenders* (pp. 69–96). Durham, NC: Carolina Academic Press.

Herrschaft, B. A., Veysey, B. M., Tubman-Carbone, H. R. & Christian, J. (2009). Gender differences in the transformation narrative: Implications for revised reentry strategies for female offenders. *Journal of Offender Rehabilitation*, 48(6), 463–482. doi:10.1080/10509670903081250.

Hubbard, D. J. & Matthews, B. (2008). Reconciling the differences between the "gender-responsive" and the "what works" literatures to improve services for girls. *Crime & Delinquency*, 54, 225–258.

Hubbard, D. J. & Pratt, T. C. (2004). A meta-analysis of the predictors of delinquency among girls. *Journal of Offender Rehabilitation*, 34, 1–13.

Huebner, B. M., DeJong, C. & Cobbina, J. (2010). Women coming home: Long-term patterns of recidivism. *Justice Quarterly*, 27, 225–254. doi:10.1080/07418820902870486.

Kendall, K. & Pollack, S. (2003). Cognitive behavioralism in women's prisons: A critical analysis of therapeutic assumptions and practices. In B. Bloom (Ed.), *Gendered Justice: Addressing Female Offenders*. Durham, NC: Carolina Academic Press.

Latessa, E., Cullen, F. & Gendreau, P. (2002). Beyond correctional quackery: Professionalism and the possibility of effective treatment. *Federal Probation*, 66, 43–49.

Leverentz, A. (2011). Being a good daughter and sister: Families of origin in the reentry of African American female ex-prisoners. *Feminist Criminology*, 6, 239–267.

Leverentz, A. (2014). *The Ex-Prisoner's Dilemma: How Women Negotiate Competing Narratives of Reentry and Desistance* (Kindle DX version). Retrieved from Amazon.com.

Lovins, L. B., Lowenkamp, C., Latessa, E. & Smith, P. (2007). Application of the risk principle to female offenders. *Journal of Contemporary Criminal Justice*, 23, 383–398.

Lowenkamp, C., Holsinger, A. & Latessa, E. (2001). Risk/need assessment, offender classification, and the role of childhood abuse. *Criminal Justice and Behavior*, 2, 543–563.

Lowenkamp, C. T. & Latessa, E. J. (2005). Increasing the effectiveness of correctional programming through the risk principle: Identifying offenders for residential placement. *Criminology and Public Policy*, 4, 263–290.

Marcus, R. (November 15, 2005). The Ginsburg fallacy. *The Washington Post*. Retrieved from www.washingtonpost.com/wp-dyn/content/article/2005/11/14/AR2005111401021.html.

Maruna, S. (2001). *Making Good*. Washington, DC: APA Press.

Maruna, S. & Roy, K. (2007). Amputation or reconstruction? *Journal of Contemporary Criminal Justice*, 23, 104–124.

Matthews, B. & Hubbard, D. J. (2008). Moving ahead: Five essential elements for working effectively with girls. *Journal of Criminal Justice*, 36, 494–502.

McIvor, G., Jamieson, J. & Murray, C. (2000). Study examines gender differences in desistance from crime. *Offender Programs Report*, 4, 5–9.

McNeill, F., Farrall, S., Lightowler, C. & Maruna, S. (Fall 2012). How and why people stop offending: Discovering desistance. *Journal of Community Corrections*, 7–8, 15–17.

McNeill, F. & Weaver, B. (2010). *Changing Lives: Desistance Research and Offender Management*. Glasgow: Scottish Centre for Crime and Justice Research. Retrieved from www.sccjr.ac.uk/documents/Report%202010%2003%20-%20Changing%20Lives.pdf.

Messerschmidt, J. W. (1993). *Masculinities and Crime: Critique and Reconceptualization of Theory.* Lanham, MD: Rowman and Littlefield.

Messina, N., Grella, C. E., Cartier, J. & Torres, S. (2010). A randomized experimental study of gender-responsive substance abuse treatment for women in prison. *Journal of Substance Abuse Treatment*, 38, 97–107.

Miller, J. B. (1976). *Toward a New Psychology of Women.* Boston, MA: Beacon Press.

Najavits, L. M., Gallop, R. J. & Weiss, R. D. (2006). Seeking safety therapy for adolescent girls with PTSD and substance use disorder: A randomized controlled trial. *Journal of Behavioral Health Services & Research*, 33, 453–463.

O'Brien, P. (2001). *Making it in the "Free World": Women in Transition from Prison.* Albany, NY: State University of New York Press.

Owen, B. (1998). *In the Mix: Struggle and Survival in a Women's Prison.* Albany, NY: State University of New York Press.

Owens, G. & Chard, K. (2001). Cognitive distortions among women reporting childhood sexual abuse. *Journal of Interpersonal Violence*, 16, 178–191.

Reisig, M. D., Holtfreter, K. & Morash, M. (2006). Assessing recidivism risk across female pathways to crime. *Justice Quarterly*, 23, 384–405.

Richie, B. E. (2001). Challenges incarcerated women face as they return to their communities: Findings from life history interviews. *Crime and Delinquency*, 47, 368–389.

Sampson, R. J. & Laub, J. H. (1993). *Crime in the Making: Pathways and Turning Points.* Cambridge, MA: Harvard University Press.

Schapman-Williams, A. M., Lock, J. & Couturier, J. (2006). Cognitive-behavioral therapy for adolescents with binge eating syndromes: A case series. *International Journal of Eating Disorders*, 39, 252–255.

Simourd, L. & Andrews, D. (1994). *Correlates of Delinquency: A Look at Gender Differences.* Ottawa, Canada: Department of Psychology, Carleton University.

Smith, P., Cullen, F. & Latessa, E. (2009). Can 14,737 women be wrong? A meta-analysis of the LSI-R and recidivism for female offenders. *Criminology and Public Policy*, 8, 183–208.

Sommers, I., Baskin, D. R. & Fagan, J. (1994). Getting out of the life: Crime desistance by female street offenders. *Deviant Behavior*, 15, 125–149.

Stohr, M. K., Lero Johnson, C. & Lux, J. (2015). Understanding the female prison experience. In F. T. Cullen & P. Wilcox (Eds.), *Sisters in Crime Revisited: Bringing Gender into Criminology* (pp. 351–370). New York: Oxford University Press.

Van Dieten, M. (2010). *Moving On: A Program for At-Risk Women.* Center City, MN: Hazelden Publishing.

VanNatta, M (2010). Conceptualizing and stopping state sexual violence against incarcerated women. *Social Justice*, 1, 27–52.

Van Voorhis, P., Salisbury, E. J., Wright, E. M., & Bauman, A. (2010). Women's risk factors and their contributions to existing risk/needs assessment: The current status of a gender-responsive supplement. *Criminal Justice and Behavior*, 37, 261–288.

van Wormer, K. & Bartollas, C. (2013). *Women and the Criminal Justice System*, 4th ed. New York: Pearson.

Wald, R., Harvey, S. M. & Hibbard, J. (1995). A treatment model for women substance users. *International Journal of the Addictions*, 30, 881–888.

Warr, M. (1998). Life-course transitions and desistance from crime. *Criminology*, 36(2), 183–216.

Wood, A., Harrington, R. & Moore, A. (1996). Controlled trial of a brief cognitive behavioral intervention in adolescent patients with depressive disorders. *Journal of Child Psychology and Psychiatry*, 87, 737–746.

Wright, E. M., Van Voorhis, P., Salisbury, E. J. & Bauman, A. (2012). Gender responsive lessons learned and policy implications for women in prison: A review. *Criminal Justice and Behavior*, 39, 1612–1632.

Yeoh, P. (2014). Enhancing effectiveness of anti-money laundering laws through whistleblowing. *Journal of Money Laundering Control*, 17, 327–342.

Young, T. M., Martin, S. S., Young, M. E. & Ting, L. (2001). Internal poverty and teen pregnancy. *Adolescence*, 36, 289–305.

# 18

# CONTEXTUAL INFLUENCES IN PRISON-BASED PSYCHOLOGICAL RISK ASSESSMENT

## Problems and solutions

*Jo Shingler and Adrian Needs*

Many forensic psychologists spend an increasing amount of their time conducting, reporting and defending risk assessments on prisoners. Both the futures of prisoners and the safety of the general public are potentially at stake with every risk assessment conducted. The technology of risk assessment (centred upon protocols derived largely from empirical studies of group differences) has become increasingly refined. Yet people and outcomes can be subject to processes beyond those envisaged or intended by developers or policy-makers. Indeed the worlds of both practitioners and their clients can be seen from the perspective of multiple interacting, even competing systems spanning areas such as affiliations, ideologies, accountabilities and resources (McDermott, 2014).

A great deal has been written about the dynamics, experiences and consequences of life in custodial settings for prisoners (see Ross, Polaschek & Ward, 2008). There is evidence that the prison environment impacts substantially and differentially on staff and prisoners (Haney, Banks & Zimbardo, 1973; Zimbardo, 2007) whilst contingencies and other aspects of the 'human performance system' (Rummler & Brache, 1995) influence how personnel conduct tasks in any setting. Despite this knowledge, the implications of contextual factors for the practice and outcomes of risk assessment remain largely unexplored (Elbogen, 2002). Little is known about how the assessor and the 'assessed' approach the interview, their priorities and strategies, what they bring to the interview, what they generate between them and how the process impacts on the outcome of the risk assessment. The aims of this chapter are to consider potential contextual influences and processes from our own perspectives, as psychologists conducting risk assessment, and from the perspectives of prisoners. We will reflect on the ways in which they may impact upon practice as well as offering suggestions for ways forward.

## The prison

### The impact of imprisonment on prisoners

The concept of 'pains of imprisonment' (Sykes, 1958) drew attention to the significant deprivation of freedoms, activities and choices experienced by prisoners. Similarly, the concept of 'prisonisation' encapsulated the process of adaptation to prison rules, regime, routines and subculture in which prisoners' skills and capabilities are undermined, they become dependent on others for progress and take on the 'prisoner' role in order to cope (see Irwin & Owen, 2005). In a similar vein, Goffman (1961) described prison as a 'total institution' that demands control over all spheres of the prisoner's life including the setting aside of the 'non-prisoner' identity and the taking on of the prisoner role. In these terms, prison is seen as a dehumanising and stigmatising environment (Wyner, 2003; Crewe, 2009) that poses "profound threats to the inmate's personality or sense of personal worth" (Sykes, 1958, p. 64) and erodes prisoners' sense of personal identity, leaving them with impersonal and pejorative labels (Crawley, 2004; Cullen & Newell, 1999). It has also been argued that imprisonment is criminogenic, resulting in higher levels of recidivism than alternatives, with the higher the level of security and the harsher the prison regime, the greater the negative impact on recidivism (Listwan, Sullivan, Agnew, Cullen & Colvin, 2013).

There have been dissenting voices to the view that prison inevitably has profound, detrimental and irreversible effects on prisoners. Issues of individual differences in response and methodological shortcomings in much of the relevant research have been raised (Bonta & Gendreau, 1990; Porporino & Zamble, 1984). How personal vulnerabilities interact with particular stressors remains underexplored since the need for research in this area was highlighted over a quarter of a century ago (Zamble & Porporino, 1990). Furthermore, whilst the exclusion of phenomenological studies in Bonta and Gendreau's (1990) meta-analysis avoided conflation of *fears* of psychological deterioration and *actual* deterioration, it did little to capture experiences of imprisonment. Insights can be gained from qualitative research (e.g. Brown & Toyoki, 2013; Harvey, 2007; Toch, 1975) and accounts of ex-prisoners who have written about their experiences (James, 2003; Warr, 2008; Wyner, 2003). It is through a combination of qualitative and quantitative research that important and influential concepts such as 'legitimacy', the fundamental concern of prisoners with appropriateness, fairness, efficiency and decency and the 'moral performance' of prisons have emerged (Liebling, 2004). Furthermore, Liebling (1999, p. 341) concluded that: "The effects literature is without a sufficient affective dimension. Fear, anxiety, loneliness, trauma, depression, injustice, powerlessness, violence rejection and uncertainty are all part of the experience of prison".

The limited available literature suggests that prison-based risk assessment may reinforce many of these 'pains of imprisonment', in that it has been described as callous and lacking in individuality of approach (Warr, 2008; Crewe, 2009). Crewe (2011) described psychological assessment as a form of purgatory, particularly for indeterminate sentenced prisoners, who felt unsure of how to navigate the opaque environment of assessment. Attrill and Liell (2007), in a rare survey of prisoners' views, found that risk assessment was perceived as one of the most stressful aspects of the life sentence and a process that was seen by some as unfair due to its focus on past behaviour and neglect of change, progress and strengths. Similarly, Liebling (2011) commented on the ever-present threat of risk assessment for prisoners, and how it affected their ability to trust, minimised their sense of self-efficacy and left them feeling trapped, vulnerable and hopeless. In particular, prisoners reported not feeling able to challenge aspects they disagreed with in case it went against them. Liebling commented: "In this unsafe environment, the experience of being scrutinised and assessed was life-sapping" (p. 542).

## The impact of the prison environment on psychologists

In an ethnographic study of prison officers lasting several years, Crawley (2004) noted how some prison officers saw themselves becoming more suspicious, cynical and insensitive to prisoners' distress as a result of prison work, with the prevailing cultural norms of many prisons maintaining and cementing this view as well as pessimistic views about rehabilitation. This increase in cynicism and de-individualising of prisoners was also commented upon by Warr (2008). Crawley (2004) suggested that cultural pressure not to show compassion, sensitivity and concern seemed to result in prison officers learning not to feel them: this was consistent with prison officers' own views of how they had been changed by their work. Other commentators have highlighted the need to take a more nuanced view (e.g. Hay & Sparks, 1991; Liebling & Tait, 2006), though feeling blamed, abused and powerless can be a source of distancing and resentment (Jones, 1997) and tensions between demands such as security and rehabilitation, flexibility and enforcement within the prison officer role can be difficult to reconcile (Steiner & Wooldredge, 2015).

The likelihood that such pressures are not confined to prison officers is illustrated by research into stress and 'burnout'. Gallavan and Newman (2013) echoed earlier research with prison officers (e.g. Schaufeli & Peeters, 2000) in drawing attention to the prevalence in correctional mental health professionals of emotional exhaustion, depersonalisation (cynicism towards or lack of concern for clients) and a decrease in perceptions of personal accomplishment and effectiveness. Aspects such as working within highly bureaucratic institutions and with clients who exhibit negative behaviours were also identified as salient sources of stress and burnout. Secondary exposure to traumatic stress from listening to clients' accounts of traumatic childhoods and listening to or reading detailed accounts of serious and sometimes lethal violent and/or sexual offences was noted. Such exposure appeared to be associated with risk of a range of negative outcomes, including "depression, posttraumatic stress and poor professional judgement" (p. 116). Additional sources of stress on forensic mental health practitioners noted by Elliott and Daley (2013) encompassed conflicts between work life and home life, low job status and lack of support within the workplace. The above themes have emerged with some consistency in studies of other professionals in the criminal justice system including police and probation officers (Brown, 2004). One of the few published investigations found that correctional psychologists seemed to be particularly vulnerable to occupational stress and burnout when compared to psychologists working in other settings (Senter, Morgan, Serna-McDonald & Bewley, 2010). These authors found that correctional psychologists experienced greater degrees of burnout and reported lower levels of job satisfaction and a significantly lower sense of competence and personal production at work relative to psychologists employed to work with veterans or in counselling centres. Certainly they can be faced with complex demands and responsibilities even at an early stage of their careers (Brown & Blount, 1999; McDougall, 1996; Needs & Capelin, 2004).

As mentioned briefly in the opening paragraph, prisoners and professionals alike can be seen as engaged in multiple systems. From the perspective of complexity theory (Guastello, Koopmans & Pincus, 2009; Pycroft & Bartollas, 2014) these include a staff member's relationships with managers, bureaucracy, prisoners, family and other staff members (both in general and with specific individuals or groups of individuals). A similar analysis can be applied to prisoners. The impact and interaction of these systems can mean that guidelines and procedures are not always applied as intended (Pycroft & Bartollas, 2014). A greater awareness of the systems and contexts surrounding, in this case, risk assessment could help to explain and understand unexpected effects and outcomes.

To summarise, within the context of risk assessment it is understandable that aspects such as organisational culture, stress or concerns about the implications of risk assessment decisions could affect the approach of the psychologist and prisoner to the assessment, as well as potentially impacting judgment and decision making (Crawley, 2004; Needs, 2010; Warr, 2008; Adshead, 2014). It might be argued that 'evidence- based' protocols help provide a focus and degree of standardisation that guards against such extraneous influences; but do they rule them out? As noted by Elbogen (2002), there is a separation in the risk assessment literature between *prescriptive* research (*what* clinicians should do) and *descriptive* research (*how* they actually do it). This gap in the 'how' of risk assessment urgently needs to be bridged if the experience and outcome of risk assessment is to be improved for both assessors and the assessed.

## The interview: background influences

There is an emphasis on objectivity in risk assessment and the preponderance of structured risk assessment tools has tended to reinforce this pseudo-scientific image (see Campbell, 2007). However, the interview as an interaction between two people with different priorities, expectations, beliefs and experiences remains central to the process. Both prisoner and psychologist are part of an array of systems and contexts which will arguably impact on how they approach the interview. We will discuss these themes in more detail.

## The prisoner in the interview

When a prisoner is informed that he is due to be interviewed for a risk assessment (psychological or otherwise), this is likely to trigger a range of reactions. The prisoner's past experience of risk assessment (such as being turned down for parole on the basis of a risk assessment, feeling humiliated and judged, or alternatively feeling valued and heard) might be expected to influence his attitudes and beliefs about assessment and assessors and consequently affect his presentation in the current interview. Even if this is a first risk assessment, prisoners are not immune to rumour and gossip from peers or other sources.[1] When adding to this the high stakes nature of risk assessment, particularly from the perspective of prisoners serving indeterminate sentences, it is understandable that prisoners report risk assessment as being a particularly stressful part of their sentence (Attrill & Liell, 2007); this in itself is likely to impact on the nature and extent of the information shared by the prisoner in the interview.

Indeterminate sentenced prisoners are dependent on favourable risk assessment reports being submitted to a panel of the Parole Board in order to secure release or progression to lower security prison conditions.[2] This process is not always straightforward or transparent, and there is arguably a political dimension. Attrill and Liell's (2007) survey noted that prisoners viewed risk assessment as being too heavily influenced by the media. Jacobson and Hough (2010) described the indeterminate sentence for Public Protection[3] (IPP) as unfair, unmanageable and 'Kafkaesque' (p. 51), highlighting the complex, disorientating and frightening nature of associated procedures. An inspection of the management of life-sentenced prisoners (HMCIP & HMIP, 2013) found that in many cases, uncertainty, inconsistency and confusion characterised the management of lifers throughout their sentences, with prison staff at times not knowing how to best advise life-sentenced prisoners (Crewe, 2011).

At a more personal level, Jewkes (2005) described the life sentence as a form of bereavement, resulting in loss of social identity. She commented how being sentenced to life in prison results in significant life course disruption – typical milestones of life and roles such as parenthood and employment are denied or significantly disrupted. Men serving life sentences may consequently experience loss of a sense of control and purpose. Jewkes compared the impact of being given a life sentence with being diagnosed with a terminal illness – the person has to cope with an enduring sense of uncertainty, of not knowing when, if ever, this sentence will come to an end. This sense of uncertainty and powerlessness is also reflected by Crewe (2011) and Warr (2008). Additionally, many prisoners serving indeterminate sentences, especially those who have killed or committed other serious violent or sexual offences, have to cope with the psychological consequences of what they have done and the impact on a range of other people (Adshead, Ferrito & Bose, 2015). Against a background of exclusion from society and disruption or threat to existing social bonds, 'lifers' have to adjust to prison life at the same time as not knowing when they will return to their 'normal life'. Resources and opportunities to achieve a satisfactory reconciliation of issues related to identity, meaning, control and belonging necessary for successful transitions and a sense of stability (Ashforth, 2001; Needs, this volume) are profoundly limited.

With prisons housing some of the most socially excluded and damaged individuals in society (McNeill, 2012), past contexts can also exert a powerful influence on what prisoners bring to the interview. Some prisoners have a pervasive and long-standing tendency to perceive the world and interpersonal situations in adversarial terms (Logan, 2013; see Chapter 2). Dissimulation, manipulation or self-aggrandisement can be seen as justified or adaptive and may resonate with earlier experiences (Bernstein, Arntz & de Vos, 2007). There is scope for 'transference' of thinking, feelings and behaviour patterns that originated in the often distant past that in turn may elicit a negative response or 'counter-transference' from the interviewer (Barros, Rosa & Eizirik, 2014; Logan, 2013). Insecure attachment strategies may be manifested through mistrust and a limited capacity to reflect upon and articulate feelings; they may also be associated with tendencies to limited exercise of empathy, psychological exploration, problem-solving or self-regulation (Ansbro, 2008; Fonagy & Target, 1997; Ward, 2002). As discussed elsewhere in this volume, some individuals may be sensitised to shame by their offending, past trauma or limited opportunities for acknowledgement of self-worth. Indeed shame may have been an important aspect in the genesis of their offending (Gilligan, 2003; Velotti, Elison & Garofalo, 2014). Some prisoners or patients may nonetheless be well-practised in avoiding censure or reprisals by leading 'double lives' that are sustained by inhibiting disclosure (Lord & Willmot, 2004; Rogers & Dickey, 1991).

In summary, when considering the broad contextual and personal impact of the life sentence, as well as prisoners' existing psychological dysfunction and distress, there are ample reasons for suggesting that an indeterminate sentenced prisoner's response to a risk assessment interview will be multiply influenced.

## The assessor in the interview

Even with our professional training and experience, as psychologists we remain first and foremost human beings, and like prisoners, influenced by our own backgrounds and life histories. We are also part of the prison system, and, again as described earlier, likely to be affected by this context. More specifically related to the risk assessment task, previous assessment reports or accounts of colleagues' previous encounters with the prisoner may well impact on us even before any meeting with the prisoner. There is evidence that assessors are influenced by their colleagues' opinions when making decisions about risk (Carroll & Burke, 1990). Professionals can also be vulnerable to the 'adjustment and anchoring' heuristic (Tversky & Kahneman, 1974). This refers to the tendency to be swayed in our decisions by the initial value with which we start, and to not adjust sufficiently from the original starting point. So if we start a risk assessment by reading an opinion that a prisoner is 'high risk', our opinion may be biased towards this anchor, with the likelihood that we will not adjust it sufficiently as a result of subsequent information. As Ireland (2004) noted,

"This heuristic relates specifically to the tendency to determine your assessment of risk by comparing it to a previous assessment, when in reality your assessment should be independent" (p. 18).

Other potential influences on our approach to risk assessment include professional background, identity and training. Awareness of the possibility and potential consequences of under-estimating risk is also relevant, with any examples from our own experience likely to be particularly salient. Consistent with the 'availability' heuristic (Tversky & Kahneman, 1974), which describes how our assessment of the probability of an event is influenced by the ease with which instances can be brought to mind, many assessors will be mindful that the cases of life-sentenced prisoners who commit serious further offences are usually subject to significant and intense scrutiny and speculation (such as the Anthony Rice enquiry: HMIP, 2006). From a risk assessment perspective, it is easier to retrieve instances of catastrophic failure than it is to retrieve instances of success. We are not generally informed of the latter.

## Psychologists as risk assessors

Toulmin (1982) argued that our approach to any professional task is influenced by our prevailing historical and cultural context and the associated attitudes of our discipline with regard to what is reasonable and acceptable. The discipline of psychology generally aligns itself with the 'scientific method' in which objectivity and neutrality are central (Coyle, 2007; Henwood, 1996; Yen & Tafarodi, 2011). Despite it being a poorly defined term with a rather dubious history, objectivity is seen as morally superior and the hallmark of good science (Daston, 1992) and as such is highly valued by psychologists (Yen & Tafarodi, 2011). This broad professional orientation seems to have contributed to a considerable appetite for structured risk assessment procedures amongst psychologists (Webster & Bailes, 2004)[4] and to a propensity for us to be rather reassured by their apparently scientific nature.[5] By adhering to an empirically derived list of risk factors, organised into a checklist or into domains, we maintain adherence to our ideas of the psychologist as scientist, driven by objective evidence, a member of a community of professionals, unbiased or distracted by personal opinion.

The value of structured risk assessment procedures and their relative superiority in relation to making accurate predictions (see Hanson, Morton & Harris, 2003) is clear.

However, there are limitations to the usefulness of these tools. There is a limit to their accuracy in predicting recidivism, and as they are based on research into large groups, they cannot take into account idiosyncratic factors which may have a strong relationship with offending for a particular client (see below for further discussion of this). Additionally, most structured risk assessment tools require some element of judgement or interpretation – for example, clinical judgement is required to rate the presence, strength and relevance of items on the most recent version of the HCR-20 (Douglas, Hart, Webster & Belfrage, 2013). Toulmin (1982) argued that all types of science require commitment to rationality and objectivity *alongside a degree of context dependent interpretation*. He argued that the presence of judgement does not undermine the value of a discipline, nor does it mean that the discipline is 'less scientific'; judgement is based on the knowledge and experience not just of the individual but of the discipline itself. We encourage psychologists to recognise and embrace this as part of their professional expertise, and reconsider the value of objectivity and the extent to which it is realisable. Our confidence in the objectivity conferred by structured risk assessment tools is potentially misplaced, risks alienating prisoners (who can feel like their individuality is undermined by the application of a 'tool') and constrains professional skills and judgement. We would encourage a more nuanced and flexible understanding of objectivity.

To draw a parallel with professional nursing, Pierson (1999, p. 296) commented on the emergence of an approach designed to ensure consistency and conformity with empirical findings within which individuals are "reduced to measurable, observable commonalities". This was contrasted with a "human science paradigm" in which relationships and "connection between individuals comes forward as a fundamental way of being with, of knowing, and of helping people" (p. 297). Pierson pointed out that the former approach is not necessarily disrespectful or insensitive and the human science paradigm does not necessarily lack direction or become lost in individual subjectivities, and argued that these approaches should be reconcilable. In the context of risk assessment, this might resemble Lilienfeld et al.'s (2013, p. 886) advocacy of "thoughtful integration of the best available scientific evidence … with clinical experience and client preferences/values". Such a standpoint encourages the realistic use of structured risk assessment tools, directs attention towards the relevance of a range of skills in their application and interpretation (see Gannon & Ward, 2014) and displaces emphasis on 'objectivity' as an end in itself. It is argued below that practitioners should be concerned at least as much with 'intersubjectivity' (Pierson, 1999) and the more familiar notion of reflective practice (Schön, 1983).

A concern with objectivity in risk assessment received initial impetus from studies that concluded that the predictive power of unstructured clinical judgements about the likelihood of recidivism is often no better than chance (Grove & Meehl, 1996; Hanson & Morton-Bourgon, 2009). This gathered momentum with a growth in empirical findings identifying factors associated with recidivism that has led to the construction of structured risk assessment tools that reflect them. Much of this has taken place within the rubric of the 'Risk Need Responsivity' framework (RNR: Andrews & Bonta, 2010) and it is generally accepted that the use of a structured tool should form part of every psychological risk assessment. However, RNR-based approaches have been subject to significant criticism, largely from proponents of the 'Good Lives Model' (GLM) of offender rehabilitation (Ward & Stewart, 2003; Ward, Yates & Willis, 2012) and criminologists concerned with desistance from crime (McNeill, 2012). These criticisms are largely centred on the view that RNR takes a reductive and impersonal approach to offenders as "disembodied bearers of risk" (Ward & Stewart, 2003, p. 354; Ward, Mann & Gannon, 2007, p. 88) accompanied by a focus on identifying and removing risk factors, rather than seeing offenders as individuals with strengths, preferences and identities, embedded in social contexts (Ward & Stewart, 2003; Ward & Gannon, 2006). RNR-based risk assessments[6] have been criticised for paying too little attention to prisoners as individuals. RNR is based largely on group differences between those who reoffend and those who do not and between programmes that reduce recidivism and those that do not. This approach is necessary when devising broad guidelines that establish a consistent direction for the design and implementation of defensible approaches to rehabilitation and assessment. However, the emphasis on group level risk factors can limit consideration of possible idiographic risk factors that may be crucial to a specific individual but which have not been encompassed by aggregated data from large-scale research studies. As Polaschek (2012) notes, checking the presence or absence of a list of generic risk factors is no substitute for a full understanding of how an individual came to commit an offence and of processes that are likely to increase risk for a specific individual (Dematteo, Batastini, Foster & Hunt, 2010; Needs, 2015; Ward, 2012). This points us to the value of psychological formulation as a basis for risk assessment (e.g. Sturmey & McMurran, 2011; Douglas et al., 2013), by which we can both take an individually relevant approach as well as being guided by the psychological literature.

It is perhaps unsurprising that an approach founded on generalisation should not give centre stage to the rights and needs of the individual. Within RNR, these are secondary to the right of the public to be protected from offenders (McNeill, 2012; Ward, 2007) and some would say legitimately so (Wormith, Gendreau & Bonta 2012). Yet even the major exponents Andrews, Bonta and Wormith (2011) acknowledged that early versions of the RNR did not do enough to make explicit respect for the personal autonomy and integrity of offenders. This may have been to the detriment of prisoners' motivation to engage in either risk assessment or rehabilitation (Ward, Yates & Willis, 2012). There is evidence to suggest that feeling involved in decisions and feeling like you have been treated with respect by decision makers is related to increased engagement with the decision, regardless of its favourability (Tyler & Huo, 2002). This suggests that taking steps to improve prisoners' experience of risk assessment could result in greater co-operation with assessment and consequent risk management recommendations.

Related to this, some prisoners appear disillusioned and suspicious of the extent to which prison-based psychological practice is dominated by the administration of structured risk assessments to a degree that distrust of psychologists may now be widespread (see Crewe, 2009; Maruna, 2011). Additionally, RNR-based correctional policy and practice has resulted in a reduction in the extent to which many qualified psychologists now engage in direct psychological intervention with prisoners: qualified psychologists have been increasingly directed towards the supervision and oversight of para-professional treatment providers (Gannon & Ward, 2014; Towl & Crighton, 2008). This has led to a further distancing of psychologists from prisoners, a process that risks compounding fears and suspicions about their role, priorities and intentions if not their expertise and experience, as explored further below.

## The prisoner and the psychologist

Research into the nature of professional relationships between prisoners and psychologists is limited, but some investigations have highlighted troubling issues in prisoners' perceptions of correctional psychologists as untrustworthy and hostile (Maruna, 2011). Warr (2008) commented that

> as an inmate, you cannot trust prison staff. This is not because of the individual members of staff or their personal level of trustworthiness. It is a reflection of the power they wield, and the impossibility of trusting someone who holds dominion over you. You are always aware that, at any minute, that power could be brought to bear upon you, with potentially damaging consequences. (p. 23)

Warr related this particularly to psychologists, whom he described as becoming increasingly powerful. Similarly, Sparks (1999) in a survey of life-sentenced prisoners found that lifers experienced significant frustration with psychological assessment: "Prisoners were particularly wary of input from psychologists, whose view they felt was given a disproportionate weight" (p. 22). Additionally, lifers resented brief and infrequent interviews by psychologists who did not know them, yet whose opinion could make a significant difference to their progression. This view was also reflected by Crewe (2011).

Maruna (2011) described his view of the changes in correctional psychological practice, resulting largely from psychologists being increasingly detached from any role in alleviating psychological distress and focusing instead (in a manner described as 'all-consuming') on risk assessment. Crewe (2009) also commented upon this shift in emphasis, presenting the following quote from a prisoner:

> When I first came away, the psychologist was there if you'd got problems, to talk to. She wasn't there to write reports, she wasn't there to judge you, she wasn't there to write reports and manipulate you, she was there to help you if you needed help. Now that attitude's not there. They are there to write reports on you, they are there to judge you, they are there to fucking try and manipulate you. Your interests, your needs are pretty much last on the list. (p. 117)

The perception of power yoked to judging risk could easily inhibit disclosure of problems such as negative thoughts and feelings, even if expressing them might help in present of future coping. Warr (2008) went so far as to say that "the very power that a psychologist wields renders them untrustworthy and therefore makes it impossible for them to make accurate assessments" (p. 25). The generality of such views is unknown and it is far from certain whether Parole Board decisions *are* more influenced by psychologists' reports than by those of other professionals; a recent study (Forde, 2014) suggested that parole decisions were most consistent with recommendations from Offender Managers. Nonetheless the stereotypical view that seems to have gained ground within prisons is that "psychologists … hold the key to release" (Crewe, 2009, p. 121), a belief amongst prisoners that hardly makes risk assessment a neutral process.

It is apparent that prisoners experience the predominant focus on the identification of risk factors as demotivating and stigmatising (Ward & Fisher, 2006; Attrill & Liell, 2007), and complain that their many strengths and achievements are overlooked. Similarly, a focus on offence-paralleling behaviours (Mann, Hanson & Thornton, 2010) increases the opportunities for assessors to identify the manifestation of risk on a daily basis, which prisoners experience as controlling and oppressive (Crewe, 2009), especially if not accompanied by equal attention to daily manifestations of strengths and pro-social alternatives (Jones, Daffern & Shine, 2010). In addition, a perception that RNR addresses psychological distress only as a vehicle for reducing risk, that it is only their capacity for reducing risk that is inherently worthy of attention (Ross et al., 2008), may lead to prisoners viewing psychologists as lacking in compassion and legitimacy. Prisoners tend to see legitimacy as closely tied to opportunities for growth and development (Brown & Toyoki, 2013) and other research suggests that perceived compassion and caring are intrinsic to the reduction of distress (see Miceli, Mancini & Menna, 2009).

As practising psychologists, it is troubling to consider that our profession may be perceived negatively by people we want to help. In an ongoing study of psychologists' experiences of risk assessment (Shingler, Sonnenberg & Needs, submitted), psychologists spontaneously acknowledged the negative attitudes held by prisoners about them, yet were overwhelmingly committed to open, collaborative and respectful relationships with prisoners. This divergence between our motivation and our image needs to be further explored and understood if the process of risk assessment is to be improved. Such exploration would include investigating whether a personal, responsive, strengths-oriented approach might lead to better prisoner engagement, improved collaborative working relationships, greater perceived legitimacy and therefore an enhanced willingness to explore and disclose (Ward, Mann & Gannon, 2007; Liebling, Durie, Stiles & Tait, 2005). It should also include an expanded awareness of the interview process.

## The interview: processes

### Intersubjectivity

An interview is "thoroughly and fundamentally social in its constitution" (Murakami, 2003 p. 238). As with other kinds of social encounter involving dialogue, 'intersubjectivity' – the relationship *between* the subjectivities (including intentions and perspectives) of individual participants – has been seen as a central process (Gillespie &

Cornish, 2010). In this process action is guided by each participant's inferences concerning the intentions and perspectives of the other. Each responds to the other's verbal and nonverbal actions, but what emerges between them is not reducible either to these or to the subjectivity of either participant (Crossley, 1996). To paraphrase Cooper (1967), if we are simultaneously weighing up each other, my weighing up of you includes your weighing up of me (and vice versa). This characteristic makes human beings rather different to the objects of study of, for example, a physicist.

This reciprocal process can bring the intentions and perspectives of each into closer alignment (Boston Change Process Study Group, 2002). For example, conversational sequences tend to become increasingly focused and specific whereas random or completely self-referential utterances would be unlikely to be experienced as communication. The potential power of working to increase alignment of subjectivities is illustrated in research by Paul Taylor and colleagues in the field of crisis negotiation, where increasing synchrony between the concerns and orientations in negotiators' and perpetrators' communications has been associated with successful outcomes (Ormerod, Barrett, & Taylor, 2008; Taylor, 2002). (Conversely, a failure to achieve alignment in this and other contexts appears to have detrimental effects such as conflict, a sense of being misunderstood or unvalued.) As Murakami (2003) notes, in a situation such as an interview, intersubjectivity involves the generation between individuals of a working, shared understanding of what is going on, what is relevant and how what arises should be interpreted. We suggest that an intersubjective perspective can be helpful in enabling assessors to see processes and possibilities in interviews with greater clarity.

Establishing a degree of working agreement, for example, is facilitated by mutual recognition of cultural norms and routines, including that a question will be answered (Athay & Darley, 1981; Norton & Brenders, 1996; Schutz, 1970). Even in seemingly benign contexts such as research interviewing, asymmetry of power is intrinsic; for example, the interviewer is expected to drive the agenda, may use rapport to gain the confidence of and promote disclosure from the interviewee, and reserves the right to focus on contradictions whilst tending to regard any questioning from the interviewee as a challenge to authority (see Kvale, 2006). Interviews in forensic settings take this further by taking place in a wider context of coercion and lack of confidentiality (Meloy, 2005). Despite this, normative expectations will appear to work in favour of a risk assessor and in most cases prisoners comply with the process, at least on the surface. We are reflecting here on the importance of us as practitioners having an awareness of these potential power dynamics in the risk assessment interview, and using this awareness to understand the process and the prisoner in a more nuanced way.

It is possible that elements such as *superficial compliance* may be suspected during the interview. Without reflecting on contextual influences, it is possible that we are more vulnerable to making dispositional attributions and concluding that behaviour observed in the interview context is evidence of persisting anti-social attitudes and tendencies. Adherence to finding evidence for a single (often prematurely formulated) possibility is associated in other investigative settings with lack of experience or expertise (Ormerod et al., 2008). The 'fundamental attribution error' can be taken to a new level when relatively unacknowledged contextual influences include one's own behaviour and how that impacts on the prisoner and consequently his behaviour. As suggested above, what emerges in an encounter such as an interview is the result of a reciprocal process.

Drawing upon the framework proposed by Laing, Phillipson and Lee (1966), Gillespie and Cornish (2010) describe the following. Each member of an interacting dyad responds to his or her own perspectives on a given phenomenon (direct perspectives), his or her perspectives on the other's perspectives (meta-perspectives) and his or her perspectives on the other's perspectives towards his or her perspectives (meta-meta-perspectives). If for example, a prisoner perceives the assessor in essentially mistrustful or adversarial terms this is likely to affect the prisoner's behaviour (for example by increasing guardedness). This in turn influences the behaviour of the assessor (who may see the prisoner as avoiding giving straight answers). The assessor may respond with a more austere or challenging style of 'probing', interpreted by the prisoner as evidence of attempted entrapment and a punitive agenda. Increased guardedness from the prisoner may then be interpreted by the assessor as evidence of lack of cooperation and perhaps the continuation of anti-social attitudes in the manner mentioned above. Negative conclusions about 'attitude' are likely to be drawn by both parties. (Some readers may be familiar with the notion of a 'Betari/Betari's box' or 'Cycle of Conflict' from the field of management, the essential idea of which is that my attitude affects my behaviour which in turn affects your attitude and your behaviour.)

It is not suggested that this illustrative example represents the norm; such processes are often more subtle and a skilled interviewer can change the direction or come to harness a more benign form of reciprocity. However, the example highlights the importance of an awareness of the context of the interview, of the competing priorities and agendas of the prisoner and the assessor, and of one's own interpretations and subsequent behaviour. It also highlights that even adopting, in the interests of 'objectivity', a style that is intended to be neutral may be seen as impersonal and have effects of its own.

Many assessors would concur with recommendations that they adopt a collaborative, respectful, empathic and supportive style in order to elicit the sort of information required during risk assessment (Attrill & Liell, 2007; Marshall, 1994, 2005; Shingler & Mann, 2006; Westwood, Wood & Kemshall, 2011). Something rather similar has been found to be effective in police interviews (Shepherd, 1991; Holmberg & Christianson, 2002). Even though this style is not free from the intrinsic asymmetry of power described by Kvale (2006), it might overcome some of the obvious limitations of an impersonal, pseudo-objective (or confrontational or defensive) style. It is important, though, that communications of warmth and collaboration are maintained throughout the assessment process. It is equally important that people feel they are being listened to and understood (see below). This should not be confused with agreement with what they are saying. Rather it revolves around feeling a sense of acknowledgement and that the psychologist is 'with' them in the situation and responsive, moment by moment; this is a prerequisite of inter-subjectivity (Boston Change Process Study Group, 2002).

If one signals a willingness to engage responsively and with genuine interest in an individual's perspectives, one must deliver. Otherwise, the skills of developing rapport, understandably valued by psychologists, can be experienced as deceptive by prisoners, like a 'Trojan Horse' used as a means of eliciting disclosures that may result in negative outcomes for prisoners, such as the absence of a recommendation for progression (Kvale, 2006; Shingler et al., submitted). Some individuals who have honed a mistrustful view of others are adept at detecting cues of insincerity (La Russo, 1978). In a nutshell, responsiveness and collaboration need to be genuinely and consistently applied throughout the process, not just used as a means of gathering information.

## Reflective practice

To be better attuned to the person one is interviewing it is helpful to be aware of one's own potential positions and perspectives in the interview situation. This is essentially a process of reflection. It may be helpful, for example, for an assessor to differentiate the skills necessary to establishing a working relationship from those concerned with the gathering of information (Logan, 2013). Logan also advises that it is essential for the assessor to be aware of aspects such as his or her own interpersonal style, self-concept and defensive strategies, going so far as to suggest that these can be as important as those of the client. The assessor's flexibility, susceptibility to heuristics and biases, perceived contingencies and understanding of the task, affiliations, beliefs, schemas, attachment styles, professional knowledge and tendencies to counter-transference might be included as part of a process of 'reflection on action' (Schön, 1983) in, for example, supervision and no doubt often are. An important additional process is 'reflection in action', the ongoing thinking by professionals about what they are doing whilst they are doing it (Schön, 1983). An intersubjective approach emphasises the key role of each participant's apprehension of the current states and intentions of the other but also highlights that much of this is non-conscious, with conscious problem-solving mainly occurring when established procedures prove problematic (Boston Change Process Study Group, 2002).

This effective use of largely non-conscious expertise has been noted in other aspects of prison work (Hay & Sparks, 1991).

Keeping what one does in line with one's own intentions moment-by-moment, whilst engaged in a complex task that requires sensitivity and responsiveness to the other person, presents something of a challenge. It can involve, for example, moving psychologically closer or distancing, avoiding something happening or making something happen, regulating the intensity of emotional states, shifting direction, using silence or quieter, less intense moments or enabling transitions to new frames of expectations and norms but as part of a process of engagement with the other rather than as a series of isolated 'moves' or 'skills' (Boston Change Process Study

Group, 2002; Moore, Jasper & Gillespie, 2011; Ormerod et al., 2008). In fact, both reflection 'in' and 'on' action are likely to present the assessor with a balancing task of considerable proportions.

## Balance and engagement

The term 'balancing act' gained currency over a series of interviews concerning psychologists' and prisoners' experiences of risk assessment (Shingler et al., in preparation). Analysis of interviews is still in progress at the time of writing. It is apparent, however, that the metaphor extends from competing concerns such as time constraints and the perspectives of different stakeholders to how far to pursue emergent possibilities such as exploration of a previously undiscussed area or a therapeutic opportunity. There can also be intrinsic tensions such as that within psychologists' 'dual relationship', between concern for public protection and the interests of the individual (Ward, 2013). Some other sources of tension or disequilibrium are fairly easily handled by comparison. For example, making a connection at a human level through empathy and respect does not necessitate setting aside professional boundaries; one would not, for example, expect this of a medical doctor and neither would most prisoners (Allen & Bosta, 1981). However, although we may think in terms of binary oppositions (or pseudo-oppositions) for illustrative purposes, the real challenge is to balance multiple goals, inputs and outputs in a dynamic, embedded system (Marks-Tarlow, 1999). If you prefer, the balancing act has more in common with that of the dancer or fencer than that of the tightrope walker.

The actions and subjectivity of the prisoner must be a constant focus of attention. There must be a willingness to engage actively with the perspectives and intentions of the prisoner in negotiating a shared understanding of the situation and where it is going. Much of this involves the use of skills (and the accompanying orientation) of 'active listening' that are likely to be familiar to most psychologists from the fields of counselling and managing conflict. A prisoner may become entrenched and resist full engagement if he or she does not feel that a genuine effort is being made to at least acknowledge his or her perspectives. Gillespie (2011) describes how under such circumstances people can resort to defending their existing positions through the use of 'semantic barriers'; these might include the invoking of oppositional and dismissive stereotypes concerning 'the system', 'psychologists' or their own vulnerability. The interviews referred to above (Shingler et al., in preparation) were emphatic concerning the importance of openness by the psychologist with regard to aspects such as the aims and process of assessment. This in turn was seen as a prerequisite of trust. Such openness shows consideration of the perspective of the prisoner and openness about one's own. This may in turn encourage openness by the prisoner. Trust facilitates the lowering of semantic barriers (Gillespie, 2011).

Participating in a dialogue in which people relate to each other as subjects rather than objects, that includes understanding *with* others, enables engagement in which each is more likely to be open to new perspectives and information (Cooper, Chak, Cornish & Gillespie, 2013; De Jaegher, Di Paolo & Gallagher, 2010).

Perhaps accompanied by a greater sense of coherence, 'fittedness' with the assessor and validation, this can provide a basis for exploring new vantage points and ways of relating (Boston Change Process Study Group, 2002; Marks-Tarlow, 1999). This might facilitate a greater sense of agency and collaborative engagement that yields a richer range of relevant information, promotes personal insight and complements working towards rehabilitation. Psychologists should not be afraid of subjectivity as an integral part of their field of study (Needs & Towl, 1997); neither should misplaced notions of objectivity based on a limited view of science preclude awareness of intersubjectivity, contextual factors and the operation of dynamic systems. As we have already argued, as psychologists we are understandably drawn to structured risk assessment tools, by virtue of their existing evidence base, their relative ease of application, and their reassuringly scientific appearance. Our position is to apply these tools with a greater degree of contextual awareness, awareness of our own influences and processes, the prisoner's, and of the reciprocal context that we both create in the interview.

## The social and political context

A frequently neglected aspect of the application of psychology in prisons and indeed applied psychology in general is that it takes place in a social, economic and political context. Because psychology is generally portrayed as a 'scientific' endeavour, broader contextual understanding may be neglected or even worse, ignored, often under the guise of misunderstood notions of 'objectivity'.

(Crighton & Towl, 2008, p. 4)

It is clear from a brief exploration of the history of imprisonment in England and Wales (Coyle, 2005) that prisons, prisoners and the management of both are subject to significant political and social influence. Psychologists, prisoners and the process and outcomes of psychological risk assessment are not immune to these pressures (Crighton & Towl, 2008; Ward & Stewart, 2003). Ogloff and Davies (2004) highlighted the reflexive relationship between politics and rehabilitation policy: governmental anxiety about crime leads to harsher sentencing regimes and more people in prison, which in turn leads to economic concerns about the prison budget. This leads to rehabilitation policy that is expected in principle to see an economic return – that is, it must be defensible in the effort to meet governmental needs to drive down correctional spending. This has contributed to a 'managerialist' culture where form-filling, box-ticking, performance targets and audits can eclipse quality, purpose and integrity (Bryans, 2000; Needs, 2010) and where cost-effectiveness is largely a matter of reducing cost.

There is general agreement in the psychological and criminological literature that attitudes towards crime and punishment are becoming increasingly harsh, and criminal justice policy is increasingly prioritising reducing risk over rehabilitation, welfare and improving the lives of 'criminals' (Ward & Birgden, 2007;

Ward & Connolly, 2008). This change is reflected in the change in the statement of purpose of the Probation Service from "advise, assist and befriend" offenders, to "punish, help, change and control" offenders (see HMIP, 2006). Despite this change of direction, Kemshall (2009) commented that there is a general mistrust and lack of confidence amongst the public in professional competence to manage risk. Much of this centres upon high-profile 'failures' of risk assessment, which cause public fear and anxiety and can have a direct impact on correctional risk assessment practice (HMIP, 2006).[7]

There is a wide body of literature that examines the tensions in forensic work between what is good for the offender versus what is good for society. Adshead (2014) argued that modern day correctional practice and focus on the assessment of risk means that the forensic practitioner's duty to the welfare of the client has been 'trumped' by the duty to protect the welfare of others: "it is now not clear if any forensic health care professionals consider themselves to have *primary* duties to promote the welfare of forensic patients" (p. 6). Similarly, Day (2014) commented that for forensic practitioners, the formerly uncontentious goals of promoting the client's welfare, alleviating distress and promoting well-being are frequently challenged by the competing priorities of public protection and risk reduction (see also McNeill, 2012). Despite the seriousness of the crimes that attract mandatory and other life sentences and the level of concern and political involvement in the life sentence, the rate of reoffending of life-sentenced prisoners is low. Once released, the majority of life-sentenced prisoners are successfully resettled into the community, with only 2.2 per cent of those serving a mandatory life sentence and 4.8 per cent of those serving other life sentences reoffending *in any way* – this is compared to 46.9 per cent of the overall prison population (HMCIP & HMIP, 2013). Of course, it could legitimately be argued that the reason for the low reoffending rate amongst lifers is the successful identification of the highest risk prisoners, who remain in custody. It is likely that where there is any shred of doubt about a lifer's risk, that they remain incarcerated. When a person has committed a very serious offence, there is very often an absence of certainty about the extent to which they have changed, especially when the opportunities for demonstrating such change are limited by their ongoing incarceration, and it could be argued, constrained by the custodial environment. Given the low levels of reoffending amongst indeterminate sentence prisoners, sacrificing the liberty of a group of prisoners in order to keep society safer is ethically questionable (Adshead, 2014). More generally, "it is ethically risky to all citizens to allow a few to be sacrificed to benefit the many" (Adshead, 2014, p. 6). It is also unlikely to be effective in promoting desistance from offending (Erooga, 2008).

There have been numerous calls for a more balanced approach to forensic work that fully considers the welfare, rights and needs of both offenders and society (Erooga, 2008; Candilis & Neal, 2014; Taylor, Graf, Schanda & Vollm, 2012; Ward & Birgden, 2007; Ward & Connolly, 2008). Ward (2007) commented that one set of rights should not eclipse another, and that considering the rights of offenders does not automatically mean that public concerns about safety would be overlooked.

Similarly, Adshead (2014) called for a compassionate and therapeutic approach to forensic work. However, there remains a social pressure on correctional psychologists to prioritise public protection. Offender rights are not politically popular, and as psychologists we do not want to find ourselves as the focus of a serious case review, having to justify a recommendation to release someone who went on to commit a serious offence under the "harsh scrutiny of hindsight bias" (Kemshall, 2009, p. 332). It is in this way that societal pressure could begin to exert itself on the risk assessment process. Ward and Birgden (2007) highlighted the potential for intrusion of social and moral values into risk assessment, and warn psychologists of the need to remain mindful of such influences, whilst Adshead (2014) went further, commenting on the advantages to forensic practitioners of taking a cautious, risk averse approach.

It makes for uncomfortable reflection to consider that one of the possible explanations for the low rate of positive recommendations by correctional psychologists for indeterminate sentenced prisoners (Forde, 2014) might be the avoidance of anxiety about potential failure and the professional and personal consequences of such failure. Echoing Clark (1993), there is a significant risk of further devaluing our skills and experience as correctional psychologists if it seems that our opinions are influenced by social and political pressure rather than psychological investigation and formulation. It is imperative that we begin to understand more about the societal influences on us as psychologists, how these might impact upon the process and outcomes of risk assessment and what steps can be taken to ameliorate them.

## Summary and conclusions

We have argued that prison-based psychological risk assessment is influenced by a range of factors, both factors within the assessor and the 'assessed' and wider environmental, social and political factors. Investigations of these areas are lacking, and there is a pressing need to understand the contextual layers and influences in more detail, from the perspectives of psychologist assessors, prisoners and other key stakeholders. There is also a need for more integrated and holistic approaches to risk assessment and for more extensively evidence-based and theoretically informed practice that cultivates and makes best use of the skills, knowledge and experience of prison-based psychologists within an effective, legitimate, humanising and interpersonally sensitive application of structured professional judgement procedures.

## Notes

1 See *Inside Time* – a free magazine available to prisoners and often also available to people visiting a prison (www.insidetime.org).
2 The Parole Board cannot direct the release of an indeterminate sentenced prisoner unless it is "satisfied that it is no longer necessary for the protection of the public that the prisoner be detained" (Parole Board, 2014, Chapter 4, no page number).

3 The IPP sentence was introduced in 2005 as a replacement for the 'Automatic Life Sentence'. As a result of challenges with the administration of the IPP sentence, it was amended in 2008, and eventually abolished in 2012 (see Strickland & Garton Grimwood, 2013). The IPP sentence has been described as one of the "... least carefully planned and implemented pieces of legislation in the history of British sentencing" (Jacobson & Hough, 2010, p. vii).

4 Webster and Bailes (2004) comment on their development of an actuarial scale for predicting violence, and how they were "deluged with requests for the manual on which the scale was based. Practising clinicians seemed undaunted by its lack of demonstrated reliability and validity" (p. 21).

5 The 'pseudo-scientific' nature of structured risk assessment procedures has been subject to criticism, e.g. Campbell (2007).

6 There is some agreement that there is a discrepancy between how RNR principles are actually applied to correctional practice, and how they may have been intended to be applied (for example Polaschek, 2012; McNeill, 2012). For the sake of argument here we will focus on RNR as it is generally applied.

7 In 2005, Anthony Rice murdered Naomi Bryant, nine months after being released from a life sentence for attempted rape. This event was subject to a serious case review by the HMCIP.

## References

Adshead, G. (2014). Three faces of justice: Competing ethical paradigms in forensic psychiatry. *Legal and Criminological Psychology*, 19(1), 1–12.

Adshead, G., Ferrito, M. & Bose, S. (2015). Recovery after homicide narrative shifts in therapy with homicide perpetrators. *Criminal Justice and Behavior*, 42(1), 70–81.

Allen, B, & Bosta, D. (1981). *Games Criminals Play: How You Can Profit by Knowing Them.* Susanville, CA: Rae John Publishers.

Andrews, D.A. & Bonta, J. (2010). *The Psychology of Criminal Conduct* (5th ed.). New Providence, NJ: Andersen Publishing.

Andrews, D. A., Bonta, J., & Wormith, J. S. (2011). The Risk-Need-Responsivity (RNR) model: Does adding the Good Lives Model contribute to effective crime prevention? *Criminal Justice and Behavior*, 38(7), 735–755.

Ansbro, M. (2008). Using attachment theory with offenders. *Probation Journal*, 55(3), 231–244.

Ashforth, B. A. (2001). *Role Transitions in Organisational Life: An Identity-Based Perspective.* Mahwah, NJ: Lawrence Erlbaum Associates.

Athay, M. & Darley, J. M. (1981). Toward an interaction-centered theory of personality. In N. Cantor & J.F. Kihlstrom (Eds.). *Personality, Cognition, and Social Interaction* (pp. 281–308.) Hillsdale, NJ: Lawrence Erlbaum.

Attrill, G. & Liell, G. (2007). Offenders' view on risk assessment. In N. Padfield (Ed.), *Who to Release? Parole, Fairness and Criminal Justice.* Cullompton, Devon, UK: Willan.

Barros, A. J. S., Rosa, R. G. & Eizirik, C. L. (2014). Countertransference reactions aroused by sex crimes in a forensic psychiatric environment. *International Journal of Forensic Mental Health*, 13(4), 363–368.

Bernstein, D. P., Arntz, A. & Vos, M. D. (2007). Schema focused therapy in forensic settings: Theoretical model and recommendations for best clinical practice. *International Journal of Forensic Mental Health*, 6(2), 169–183.

Bonta, J. & Gendreau, P. (1990). Reexamining the cruel and unusual punishment of prison life. *Law and Human Behavior*, 14(4), 347–372.

Boston Change Process Study Group (2002). Explicating the implicit: The local level and the microprocess of change in the analytic situation. *International Journal of Psychoanalysis*, 83, 1051–1062.

Brown, J. (2004). Occupational stress and the criminal justice practitioner. In A. Needs & G.Towl (Eds.) *Applying Psychology to Forensic Practice* (pp. 147–166). Oxford: BPS- Blackwell.

Brown, J. & Blount, C. (1999). Occupational stress among sex offender treatment managers. *Journal of Managerial Psychology*, 14(2), 108–120.

Brown, A. D. & Toyoki, S. (2013). Identity work and legitimacy. *Organization Studies*, 34(7), 875–876.

Bryans, S. (2000). The managerialisation of prisons–efficiency without a purpose? *Criminal Justice Matters*, 40(1), 7–8.

Campbell, T.W. (2007). *Assessing Sex Offenders: Problems and Pitfalls.* Springfield, IL: Charles C. Thomas Publisher.

Candilis P. J. & Neal T. M. S. (2014). Not just welfare over justice: Ethics in forensic consultation. *Legal and Criminological Psychology*, 19(1), 19–29.

Carroll, J. S. & Burke, P. A. (1990). Evaluation and prediction in expert parole decisions. *Criminal Justice and Behavior*, 17, 315–332.

Clark, C. R. (1993). Social responsibility ethics: Doing right, doing good, doing well. *Ethics and Behaviour*, 3(3&4), 303–327.

Cooper, D. (1967). *Psychiatry and Anti-Psychiatry.* London: Tavistock Publications.

Cooper, M., Chak, A., Cornish, F. & Gillespie, A. (2013). Dialogue: Bridging personal, community and social transformation. *Journal of Humanistic Psychology*, 53(1), 70–93.

Coyle, A. (2005). *Understanding Prisons: Key Issues in Policy and Practice.* Maidenhead, Berkshire, UK: Open University Press.

Coyle, A. (2007). Introduction to qualitative psychological research. In E. Lyons & A. Coyle (Eds.), *Analysing Qualitative Data in Psychology* (pp. 9–29). London: Sage Publishing.

Crawley, E. (2004). *Doing Prison Work: The Public and Private Lives of Prison Officers.* Cullumpton, Devon, UK: Willan.

Crewe, B. (2009). *The Prisoner Society: Power, Adaptation and Social Life in an English Prison.* Oxford, UK: Oxford University Press.

Crewe, B. (2011). Depth, weight, tightness: Revisiting the pains of imprisonment. *Punishment and Society*, 13(5), 509–529.

Crighton, D. A. & Towl, G. J. (2008). *Psychology in Prisons* (2nd ed.). Oxford: Blackwell Publishing.

Crossley, N. (1996). *Intersubjectivity: The Fabric of Social Becoming.* London: Sage.

Cullen, E. & Newell, T. (1999). *Murderers and Life Imprisonment: Containment, Treatment, Safety and Risk.* Winchester, UK: Waterside Press.

Daston, L. (1992). Objectivity and the escape from perspective. *Social Studies of Science*, 22(4), 597–618.

Day, A. (2014). Competing ethical paradigms in forensic psychiatry and forensic psychology: Commentary for a special section of legal and criminological psychology. *Legal and Criminological Psychology*, 19(1), 16–18.

De Jaegher, H., Di Paolo, E. & Gallagher, S. (2010). Can social interaction constitute social cognition? *Trends in Cognitive Sciences*, 14(10), 441–447.

Dematteo, D., Batastini, A., Foster, E. & Hunt, E. (2010). Individualising risk assessment: Balancing idiographic and nomothetic data. *Journal of Forensic Psychology Practice*, 10(4), 360–371.

Douglas, K. S., Hart, S. D., Webster, C. D., & Belfrage, H. (2013). *HCR-20V3: Assessing Risk of Violence – User Guide.* Burnaby, Canada: Mental Health, Law, and Policy Institute, Simon Fraser University.

Elbogen, E. B. (2002). The process of violence risk assessment: A review of descriptive research. *Aggression and Violent Behavior*, 7, 591–604.

Elliott, K. A. & Daley, D. (2013). Stress, coping, and psychological well-being among forensic health care professionals. *Legal & Criminological Psychology*, 18(2), 187–204.

Erooga, M. (2008). A human rights-based approach to sex offender management: The key to effective public protection? *Journal of Sexual Aggression*, 14(3), 171–183.

Fonagy, P. & Target, M. (1997). Attachment and reflective function: Their role in self-organization. *Development and Psychopathology*, 9(4), 679–700.

Forde, R. A. (2014). *Risk assessment in parole decisions: A study of life sentence prisoners in England and Wales.* Forensic Psychology Doctorate thesis, University of Birmingham, UK. Available from http://etheses.bham.ac.uk.

Gallavan, D. B. & Newman, J. L. (2013). Predictors of burnout among correctional mental health professionals. *Psychological Services*, 10(1), 115–122.

Gannon, T. A. & Ward, T. (2014). Where has all the psychology gone? A critical review of evidence-based psychological practice in correctional settings. *Aggression and Violent Behavior*, 19, 435–446.

Gillespie, A. (2011). Contact without transformation: The context, process and content of distrust. In I. Marková & A. Gillespie (Eds.), *Trust and Conflict: Representation, Culture and Dialogue.* London: Routledge.

Gillespie, A. & Cornish, F. (2010). Intersubjectivity: Towards a dialogical analysis. *Journal for the Theory of Social Behaviour*, 40(1), 19–46.

Gilligan, J. (2003). Shame, guilt, and violence. *Social Research*, 70, 1149–1180.

Goffman, E. (1961). *Asylums: Essays on the Social Situations of Mental Patients and Other Inmates.* Middlesex, UK: Penguin Books.

Grove, W. M. & Meehl, P. E. (1996). Comparative efficiency of informal (subjective, impressionistic) and formal (mechanical, algorithmic) prediction procedures: The clinical-statistical controversy. *Psychology, Public Policy and Law*, 2, 293–323.

Guastello, S. J., Koopmans, M. & Pincus, D. (2009). *Chaos and Complexity in Psychology.* Cambridge, UK: Cambridge University.

Haney, C., Banks, C. & Zimbardo, P. (1973). Interpersonal dynamics in a simulated prison. *International Journal of Criminology and Penology*, 1, 69–97.

Hanson, R. K. & Morton-Bourgon, K. E. (2009). The accuracy of recidivism risk assessments for sexual offenders: A meta-analysis of 118 prediction studies. *Psychological Assessment*, 21(1), 1–21.

Hanson, R. K., Morton, K. E. & Harris, A. J. (2003). Sexual offender recidivism risk. *Annals of the New York Academy of Sciences*, 989(1), 154–166.

Harvey, J. (2007). *Young Men in Prison: Surviving and Adapting to Life Inside.* Cullompton, Devon, UK: Willan.

Hay, W. & Sparks, R. (1991). What is a prison officer? *Prison Service Journal*, 83, 2–7.

Henwood, K. L. (1996). Qualitative inquiry: Perspectives, methods and psychology. In J. Richardson (Ed.), *Handbook of Qualitative Research Methods for Psychology and the Social Sciences* (pp. 25–40). Leicester, UK: BPS Books.

HMIP (2006). *An independent review of a serious further offence case: Anthony Rice.* Available from www.justice.gov.uk/downloads/publications/inspectorate-reports/hmiprobation/anthonyricereport-rps.pdf.

HMCIP & HMIP (2013). *A joint inspection of life sentence prisoners.* Available from www.justiceinspectorates.gov.uk/hmiprisons/inspections/a-joint-inspection-of-life-sentence-prisoners.

Holmberg, U. & Christianson, S. (2002). Murderers' and sexual offenders experiences of police interviews and their inclination to admit or deny their crimes. *Behavioural Sciences and the Law*, 20, 31–45.

Ireland, J. L. (2004). Compiling forensic risk assessment reports. *Forensic Update*, 77, 15–22.

Irwin, J. & Owen, B. (2005). Harm and the contemporary prison. In A. Liebling & S. Maruna (Eds.), *Effects of Imprisonment* (pp. 94–117). Cullompton, Devon, UK: Willan.

Jacobson, J. & Hough, M. (2010). *Unjust Deserts: Imprisonment for Public Protection*. London: Prison Reform Trust.

James, E. (2003). *A Life Inside: A Prisoner's Notebook*. London: Atlantic Books.

Jewkes, Y. (2005). Loss, liminality and the life sentence: Managing identity through a disrupted lifecourse. In A. Liebling & S. Maruna (Eds.), *Effects of Imprisonment* (pp. 366–388). Cullompton, Devon, UK: Willan.

Jones, L. (1997). Developing models for managing treatment integrity and efficacy in a prison-based TC: The Max Glatt Centre. In E. Cullen, L. Jones & R. Woodward (Eds.), *Therapeutic Communities for Offenders* (pp. 121-157). Chichester, UK: Wiley.

Jones, L., Daffern, M. & Shine, J. (2010). Summary and future directions. In M. Daffern, L. Jones & J. Shine (Eds.), *Offence Paralleling Behaviour: A Case Formulation Approach to Offender Assessment and Intervention* (pp. 315–328). Chichester, UK: Wiley-Blackwell.

Kemshall, H. (2009). Working with sex offenders in a climate of public blame an anxiety: How to make defensible decisions for risk. *Journal of Sexual Aggression*, 15(3), 331–343.

Kvale, S. (2006). Dominance through interviews and dialogues. *Qualitative Inquiry*, 12(3), 480–500.

Laing, R. D., Phillipson, H. & Lee, A. R. (1966). *Interpersonal Perception: A Theory and a Method of Research*. London: Tavistock.

La Russo, L. (1978). Sensitivity of paranoid patients to nonverbal cues. Journal of Abnormal Psychology, 87 (5), 463–471.

Liebling, A. (1999). Doing research in prison: Breaking the silence? *Theoretical Criminology*, 3(2), 147–173.

Liebling, A. (2004). *Prisons and their moral performance: A study of values, quality, and prison life*. Clarendon Studies in Criminology. Oxford, UK: University Press.

Liebling, A. (2011). Moral performance, inhuman and degrading treatment and prison pain. *Punishment and Society*, 13, 530–550.

Liebling, A., Durie, L., Stiles, A. & Tait, S. (2005). Revisiting prison suicide: The role of fairness and distress. In A. Liebling & S. Maruna (Eds.), *Effects of Imprisonment* (pp. 209–231). Cullompton, Devon, UK: Willan.

Liebling, A. & Tait, S. (2006). Improving staff-prisoner relations. In G. E. Dear (Ed.), *Preventing Suicide and Other Self-Harm in Prison* (pp. 103–117). Basingstoke, UK: Palgrave-Macmillan.

Lilienfeld, S. O., Ritschel, L. A., Lynne, S. J., Cautin, R. L. & Latzman, R. D. (2013). Why many clinical psychologists are resistant to evidence-based practice: Root causes and constructive remedies. *Clinical Psychology Review*, 7, 883–900.

Listwan, S. J., Sullivan, C. J., Agnew, R., Cullen, F. T. & Colvin, M. (2013). The pains of imprisonment revisited: The impact of strain on inmate recidivism. *JQ: Justice Quarterly*, 30(1), 144–168.

Logan, C. (2013). Risk assessment: Specialist interviewing skills for forensic practitioners. In C. Logan & L. Johnstone (Eds.), *Managing Clinical Risk: A Guide to Effective Practice*. London: Routledge.

Lord, A. & Willmot, P. (2004). The process of overcoming denial in sexual offenders. *Journal of Sexual Aggression*, 10(1), 51–61.

McDermott, F. (2014). Complexity theory, trans-disciplinary working and reflective practice. In A. Pycroft & C. Bartollas (Eds.), *Applying Complexity Theory: Whole Systems Approaches to Criminal Justice and Social Work*. Bristol, UK: Policy Press.

McDougall, C. (1996) Working in secure institutions. In C. Hollin (Ed.), *Working with Offenders* (pp. 44–60). Chichester, UK: John Wiley & Sons.

McNeill, F. (2012). Four forms of 'offender' rehabilitation: Towards an interdisciplinary perspective. *Legal and Criminological Psychology*, 17, 18–36.

Mann, R. E., Hanson, R. K. & Thornton, D. (2010). Assessing risk for sexual recidivism: Some proposals on the nature of psychologically meaningful risk factors. *Sexual Abuse: A Journal of Research and Treatment*, 22(2), 191–217.

Marks-Tarlow, T. (1999). The self as a dynamical system. *Nonlinear Dynamics, Psychology, and Life Sciences*, 3(4), 311–345.

Marshall, W. L. (1994). Treatment effects on denial and minimisation in incarcerated sex offenders. *Behaviour Research and Therapy*, 32(5), 559–564.

Marshall, W. L. (2005). Therapist style in sexual offender treatment: Influence on indices of change. *Sexual Abuse: A Journal of Research and Treatment*, 17(2), 109–116.

Maruna, S. (2011). Why do they hate us? Making peace between prisoners and psychology. *International Journal of Offender Therapy and Comparative Criminology*, 55(5), 671–675.

Meloy, M. L. (2005). The sex offender next door: An analysis of recidivism, risk factors, and deterrence of sex offenders on probation. *Criminal Justice Policy Review*, 16(2), 211–236.

Miceli, M., Mancini, A. & Menna, P. (2009). The art of comforting. *New Ideas in Psychology*, 27(3), 343–361.

Moore, H., Jasper, C. & Gillespie, A. (2011). Moving between frames: The basis of the stable and dialogical self. *Culture & Psychology*, 17(4), 510–519.

Murakami, K. (2003). Orientation to the setting: Discursively accomplished intersubjectivity. *Culture and Psychology*, 9(3), 233–248.

Needs, A. (2010). Systemic failure and human error. In C. Ireland & M. Fisher (Eds.), *Consultancy and Advising in Forensic Practice: Empirical and Practical Guidelines*. Chichester, UK: Wiley-Blackwell.

Needs, A. (2015). Outrageous fortune: Transitions and related concerns in the genesis of violence. Paper presented at the Conference of the International Academy for Law and Mental Health, Vienna.

Needs, A. & Capelin, J. (2004). Facilitating multi-disciplinary teams. In A. Needs & G. Towl (Eds.), *Applying Psychology to Forensic Practice* (pp. 202–221). Oxford, UK: Blackwell.

Needs, A. & Towl, G. (1997). Reflections on clinical risk assessments with lifers. *Prison Service Journal*, 113, 14–17.

Norton, R. & Brenders, D. A. (1996). *Communication and Consequences: Laws of Interaction*. Hove, UK: Psychology Press.

Ogloff, J. R. P. & Davis, M. R. (2004). Advances in offender assessment and rehabilitation: Contributions of the risk-needs-responsivity approach. *Psychology, Crime and Law*, 10(3), 229–242.

Ormerod, T., Barrett, E. & Taylor, P. J. (2008). Investigative sense-making in criminal contexts. In J. M. Schraggen, L. G. Miltello, T. Ormerod & R. Lipshitz (Eds.), *Naturalistic Decision Making and Macrocognition* (pp. 81–102). Aldershot, UK: Ashgate.

Parole Board (2014). *Parole Board: Oral Hearings Guide*. Available from www.gov.uk/government/organisations/parole-board.

Polaschek, D. L. L. (2012). An appraisal of the risk-need-responsivity (RNR) model of offender rehabilitation and its application in correctional treatment. *Legal and Criminological Psychology*, 17, 1–17.

Pierson, W. (1999). Considering the nature of intersubjectivity within professional nursing. *Journal of Advanced Nursing*, 30(2), 294–302.

Porporino, F. J. & Zamble, E. (1984). Coping with imprisonment. *Canadian Journal of Criminology*, 26, 403.

Pycroft, A. & Bartollas, C. (2014). *Applying Complexity Theory: Whole Systems Approaches to Criminal Justice and Social Work*. Bristol, UK: Policy Press.

Rogers, R. & Dickey, R. (1991). Denial and minimization among sex offenders. *Annals of Sex Research*, 4(1), 49–63.

Ross, E. C., Polaschek, D. L. & Ward, T. (2008). The therapeutic alliance: A theoretical revision for offender rehabilitation. *Aggression and Violent Behavior*, 13(6), 462–480.

Rummler, G. A., & Brache, A. P. (1995). *Improving Performance: How to Manage the White Space on the Organization Chart* (2nd ed.). San Francisco, CA: Jossey-Bass.

Schaufeli, W. B. & Peeters, M. C. W. (2000). Job stress and burnout among correctional officers: A literature review. *International Journal of Stress Management*, 7(1), 19–48.

Schön, D. A. (1983). *The Reflective Practitioner: How Professionals Think in Action* (Vol. 5126). Aldershot, UK: Ashgate Publishing Ltd.

Schutz, A. (1970). *On Phenomenology and Social Relations: Selected Writings*. H. R. Wagner (Ed.). Chicago, IL: University of Chicago Press.

Senter, A., Morgan, R. D., Serna-McDonald, C. & Bewley, M. (2010). Correctional psychologist burnout, job satisfaction, and life satisfaction. *Psychological Services*, 7(3), 190–201.

Shepherd, E. (1991). Ethical interviewing. *Policing*, 7, 42–60.

Shingler, J. & Mann, R. E. (2006). Collaboration in clinical work with sexual offenders: Treatment and risk assessment. In W. L. Marshall, Y. M. L. Fernandez, L. E. Marshall & G. A. Serran, (Eds.), *Sexual Offender Treatment: Controversial Issues* (pp. 225–239). Chichester, UK: Wiley.

Shingler, J., Sonnenberg, S. J. & Needs, A. (submitted). Risk Assessment Interviews: Perspectives of Psychologists and Indeterminate Sentenced Prisoners. Submitted.

Sparks, C. (1999). *Lifers' Views of the Lifer System: Policy Versus Practice*. London: Prison Reform Trust.

Steiner, B., & Wooldredge, J. (2015). Individual and environmental sources of work stress among prison officers. *Criminal Justice and Behavior*, 11, 105–120.

Strickland, P. & Garton Grimwood, G. (2013). *The Abolition of Sentences of Imprisonment for Public Protection*. London: House of Commons Library: Home Affairs Section.

Sturmey, P. & McMurran, M. (Eds.). (2011). *Forensic Case Formulation*. Chichester, UK: John Wiley & Sons.

Sykes, G. M. (1958). *The Society of Captives: A Study of a Maximum Security Prison*. Princeton, NJ: Princeton University Press.

Taylor, P. J. (2002). A cylindrical model of communication behaviour in crisis negotiations. *Human Communication Research*, 28(1), 7–48.

Taylor, P. J., Graf, M., Schanda, H. & Vollm, B. (2012). The treating psychiatrist as expert in the courts: Is it necessary or possible to separate the roles of physician and expert? *Criminal Behaviour and Mental Health*, 22, 271–292.

Toch, H. (1975). *Men in Crises*. Chicago, IL: Aldine.

Toulmin, S. (1982). The construal of reality: Criticism in modern and postmodern science. *Critical Inquiry*, 9(1), 93–111.

Towl, G. & Crighton, D. (2008). Psychologists in prisons. In J. Bennett, B. Crewe & A. Wahidin (Eds.), *Understanding Prison Staff* (pp. 316–329). Cullumpton, Devon, UK: Willan.

Tversky, A. & Kahneman D. (1974). Judgement under uncertainty: Heuristics and biases. *Science*, 185, 1124–1131.

Tyler, T. R. & Huo, Y. J. (2002). *Trust in the Law: Encouraging Public Cooperation with the Police and Courts*. New York: Russell Sage Foundation.

Velotti, P., Elison, J. & Garafalo, C. (2014). Shame and aggression: Different trajectories and implications. *Aggression and Violent Behavior*, 19, 454–461.

Ward, T. (2002). Good lives and the rehabilitation of offenders: Promises and problems. *Aggression and Violent Behavior*, 7(5), 513–528.

Ward, T. (2007). On a clear day you can see forever: Integrating values and skills in sex offender treatment. *Journal of Sexual Aggression*, 13(3), 187–201.

Ward, T. (2012). Moral strangers or fellow travellers? Comtemporary perspectives on offender rehabilitation. *Legal and Criminological Psychology*, 17(1), 37–40.

Ward, T. (2013). Addressing the dual relationship problem in forensic and correctional practice. *Aggression and Violent Behavior*, 18(1), 92–100.

Ward, T. & Birgden, A. (2007). Accountability and dignity: Ethical issues in forensic correctional practice. *Aggression and Violent Behaviour*, 14, 227–231.

Ward, T. & Connolly, M. (2008). A human rights-based practice framework for sexual offenders. *Journal of Sexual Aggression*, 14(2), 87–98.

Ward, T. & Fisher, D. (2006). New ideas in the treatment of sexual offenders. In W. L. Marshall, Y. M. L. Fernandez, L. E. Marshall & G. A. Serran (Eds.), *Sexual Offender Treatment: Controversial Issues*. Chichester, UK: Wiley.

Ward, T. & Gannon, T. A. (2006). Rehabilitation, etiology and self-regulation: The comprehensive good-lives model of treatment for sexual offenders. *Aggression and Violent Behavior*, 11, 77–94.

Ward, T., Mann, R. E. & Gannon, T. A. (2007). The good lives model of offender rehabilitation: Clinical implications. *Aggression and Violent Behavior*, 12, 87–107.

Ward, T. & Stewart, C. A. (2003). The treatment of sex offenders: Risk management and good lives. *Professional Psychology: Research and Practice*, 34(4), 353–360.

Ward, T., Yates, P. M. & Willis, G. M. (2012). The good lives model and the risk need responsivity model: A critical response to Andrews, Bonta and Wormith (2011). *Criminal Justice and Behaviour*, 39(1), 94–110.

Warr, J. (2008). Personal reflections on prison staff. In J. Bennett, B. Crewe & A. Wahidin (Eds.), *Understanding Prison Staff*. Cullumpton, Devon, UK: Willan.

Webster, C. D. & Bailes, G. (2004). Assessing violence risk in mentally and personality disordered individuals. In C. R. Hollin (Ed.), *The Essential Handbook of Offender Assessment and Treatment* (pp. 17–30). Chichester, UK: Wiley.

Westwood, S., Wood, J. & Kemshall, H. (2011). Good practice in eliciting disclosures from sex offenders. *Journal of Sexual Aggression*, 17(2), 215–227.

Wormith, J. S., Gendreau, P. & Bonta, J. (2012). Deferring to clarity, parsimony and evidence in reply to Ward, Yates, and Willis. *Criminal Justice and Behavior*, 39(1), 111–120.

Wyner, R. (2003). *From the Inside*. London: Aurum Press.

Yen, J. & Tafarodi, R. W. (2011). Becoming scientific: Objectivity, identity and relevance as experienced by graduate students in psychology. *Forum: Qualitative Social Research*, 12(2), Art. 26, online first. Retrieved from www.qualitative-research.net/index.php/fqs/article/view/1596.

Zamble, E. & Porporino, F. (1990). Coping, imprisonment, and rehabilitation some data and their implications. *Criminal Justice and Behavior*, 17(1), 53–70.

Zimbardo, P. (2007). *The Lucifer Effect: How Good People Turn Evil*. London: Rider, Ebury Publishing.

# 19

# THE IMPORTANCE OF ORGANISATIONAL FACTORS IN TRANSFERRING THE PRINCIPLES OF EFFECTIVE INTERVENTION TO OFFENDER REHABILITATION IN THE REAL WORLD

*Dominic A. S. Pearson*

A key threat to proponents of rehabilitation in criminal justice is that of disappointing results due to problems in transferring effective practice from research to 'real world' routine delivery. A potential responsivity factor impacting on an offender's readiness to engage with and benefit from treatment is the organisational capacity of an institutional or community forensic service. While internal readiness refers to the offender's mental preparedness, external readiness refers to staff, setting and management characteristics. After reviewing programmatic prerequisites, this chapter reviews evidence on the importance of these external readiness factors as mediators of successful outcome. Their influence is exemplified with discussion of the results of the present author's application, in two different environments, of an evidence-based community supervision programme. The chapter concludes with recommendations for research and practice in rolling out effective interventions in criminal justice environments.

The main aim of agencies responsible for offender management is that of protecting the public by reducing the risk of re-offending. Systematic reviews of the literature have identified that some programmes can reduce risk, while others have no impact or actually increase re-offending. At the same time we have learned that quality of implementation is consistently a significant moderator of treatment effects, where even evidence-based treatment that is poorly implemented can increase re-offending (e.g. Latessa & Lowenkamp, 2006; Lipsey, 2009). Therefore the delivery of effective offender rehabilitation requires that treatment programmes are delivered as intended, being, for example, highly structured with clear aims and tasks for each session; implemented by trained, qualified and appropriately supervised staff; manual based; delivered in the correct treatment style; and located within organisations with personnel committed to the ideals of rehabilitation (Andrews & Bonta, 2010; McGuire, 2002).

Implementation of the 'what works' agenda has been challenging for criminal justice agencies around the world, as seen in the UK with the reported failure of the accredited programmes initiative under the Crime Reduction Programme (see Goggin & Gendreau, 2006; Macguire, Grubin, Lösel & Raynor, 2010). The present chapter focusses on making 'what works' programmes work and supports the importance of providing practitioners with both an experience-based belief in change as well as the competency to support it (Birgden, 2004; Needs & Capelin, 2004). To develop this, the chapter will summarise the relevant principles, identify organisational capacity issues and associated variations in effectiveness, and then illustrate with an example in community supervision.

## Background programmatic conditions: what works in offender rehabilitation

Our understanding of what works in offender rehabilitation has advanced distinctly in the past 35 years, mainly thanks to large-scale reviews of the comparative effectiveness of different programme types and approaches, also known as integrated meta-analyses. The most recent of these, by Lipsey (2009), updated the previous results from the same database, enlarged to 548 study samples, including a range of intervention types and philosophies (Lipsey, 1995; Lipsey & Wilson, 1998). The major findings identified that therapeutic programmes had stronger positive effects than interventions based on discipline or control, and that greater effects were seen among offenders with higher risk levels. These two variables were significant after accounting for methodological variables, and the risk level of young offenders showed the largest and most consistent relationship with reduced recidivism. Among all intervention types cognitive-behavioural and behavioural skill building ranked the highest in recidivism effects, reducing recidivism by 22–26 per cent.

These findings are broadly supportive of those arising from more theoretical broad-based reviews identifying the principles of effective interventions (Andrews & Bonta, 2010; Andrews et al., 1990; Smith, Gendreau & Swartz, 2009). Better effects for therapeutically orientated programmes is consistent with the conclusion that 'human service' is more effective than sole reliance on official punishment. The consistent finding that the intensity of programmes should correspond to participants' re-offending risk is consistent with the empirically derived '*Risk*' principle of effective intervention (Lowenkamp, Latessa & Holsinger, 2006). There was insufficient information in the original research reports for Lipsey (2009) to code the needs that were targeted in treatment and thereby offer support for the second key principle of effective intervention, that criminogenic '*Needs*' should be the predominant focus in efforts to reduce reoffending. However, the general '*Responsivity*' principle was supported by the performance of cognitive-behavioural programmes, because such programmes correspond to offender learning styles due to their action orientation and focus on present, rather than historical, circumstances.

Together the three principles make up the *Risk-Needs-Responsivity* (RNR) model of effective intervention, labelled 'appropriate treatment' (Andrews & Bonta, 2010; Andrews et al., 1990; McGuire, 2002). In the latest review including 374 effect size estimates, there was a small increase in recidivism when none of the principles was adhered to, i.e. the treatment neither targeted higher risk offenders, nor focused on needs associated with re-offending nor used cognitive-behavioural skill building. However adhering to more of the principles had a stepwise positive effect in which the mean reduction was around 2 per cent if one principle was adhered to, 18 per cent with two principles and around 26 per cent with all three (Andrews & Bonta, 2010).

A further key factor in Lipsey's (2009) analysis related to the quality of programme implementation. When analysed within therapeutic philosophy, implementation quality showed the largest and most consistent positive relationship with recidivism – other than that for risk of re-offending. The overriding importance of the quality of implementation led Lipsey to conclude that the average therapeutic programme "can be quite effective if implemented well and targeted on high risk offenders" (p. 145). This is consistent with Andrews and Bonta's fourth principle of effective intervention, that of programme '*Integrity*'. This principle includes not only making sure that the programme is delivered as designed through quality assurance processes, but also ensuring that the programme has well-trained and motivational staff.

## Appropriate treatment with integrity in programme delivery

The principle of programme integrity was originally proposed as a moderator of effectiveness after the extent of the researcher's involvement in programme design and implementation emerged as a factor associated with differential effects (Lipsey, 1995). This was supported by Lipsey's finding that compared to larger scale operations, projects with smaller sample sizes were associated with larger effects (see also Wilson, Bouffard & Mackenzie, 2005). Practical programmes delivered in the real world without the researcher being actively involved were found to have one-half the effectiveness of demonstration programmes, i.e. a 6 per cent decrease as opposed to a 12 per cent decrease (Lipsey, 1999). Demonstration programmes have been characterised as those under greater evaluation scrutiny typically with small samples of under 100, and being under the supervision of an involved evaluator (Andrews & Dowden, 2005). The degree of influence of an evaluator on practice is likely to promote fidelity to programme design (Petrosino & Soydan, 2005).

To test what the key aspects of programme integrity are, Andrews and Dowden (2005) conducted a meta-analysis of its effects on offender recidivism. They identified ten indicators of programme integrity: the programme's basis in theory; the particulars of staff selection, training and supervision; the quality of the programme's manuals and process monitoring; the specifics of sample size and treatment dosage; the degree of adherence to RNR treatment; and the degree of involvement of the programme's evaluator. The inclusion criteria led to the selection of 273 tests. Results revealed that only three indicators showed significant relationships with effect size when controlling for the effects of the others. These were sample size, involved evaluator and selection of staff for relationship skills. The impacts of both 'involved evaluator' and 'small sample size' were however only significant in the presence of the strongest predictor, 'appropriate treatment', denoted by meeting at least two RNR principles. When this was controlled for, no studies were significantly positively correlated with treatment effects under inappropriately designed treatment, even when rated higher on programme integrity ($r = -.03$ to .08). In contrast, under appropriate treatment conditions, significant correlations emerged between programme integrity indicators and outcome ($r = .20$ to .34). Therefore, concerns that the effects could be accounted for by experimenter bias were eased by the fact that small sample size and involved evaluator were only positively related to treatment effects under conditions of appropriate treatment.

The third key indicator of programme integrity in Andrews and Dowden's (2005) meta-analysis was the selection of staff, defined as workers who possess interpersonal influence skills such as enthusiasm, caring, interest and understanding. This calls for the selection of staff with attributes matching the components of effective correctional practice put forward by Andrews and Kiessling (1980) and formalised into the Core Correctional Practices (CCPs: see Box 19.1), including quality relationships and structuring skills. Andrews and Dowden (2005) found that the selection of staff with these skills was only identifiable in 5 per cent of the studies reviewed. The under-emphasis of this component in the primary studies' reports implicates organisational factors. Organisational factors have been added to the principles of effective intervention and make up items 13 to 15 (see Andrews & Bonta, 2010). These include setting, staffing and management features. Since these environmental features outside the design of the programme are under-researched

**BOX 19.1** Core Correctional Practices (Andrews & Carvell, 1998)

1. **Effective use of authority**
   Focussing on the behaviour not the person, and adopting a 'firm but fair' approach in seeking compliance.
2. **Appropriate modelling and reinforcement**
   Acting as an anti-criminal model and consistently showing approval for positive behaviour and disapproval for negative behaviour.
3. **Teaching problem-solving skills**
   Ability to follow a logical sequence of problem-solving steps in identifying and addressing client problems.
4. **Effective use of community resources**
   Making referrals and supporting the client in relation to contact with external agencies.
5. **Quality of interpersonal relationships**
   Working relationships characterised by warmth, openness, empathy and responsiveness. Communication skills include structuring and directiveness.

but can limit programme effectiveness, each is discussed in more detail below. Their impact will also emerge in the evaluations of the illustrative programme, *Citizenship*, discussed towards the end.

## Variations in programme effectiveness by organisational factors

It has been suggested that there can be "a potent interaction between the characteristics of individuals and their settings or situations" (Gendreau, 1996, p. 122), which could be either positive or negative. The concept of responsivity, introduced above, requires the appropriate matching of offenders to programmes and to staff. In recognition that the offender interacts within a treatment environment, the concept can be divided into *internal* and *external* responsivity (Gendreau & Andrews, 1990). Internal responsivity requires therapists to match the modality, content and pace of sessions to specific factors 'internal' to the case including learning style, motivation for change, personality, age, gender, ethnicity and cultural identifications. The impact of internal responsivity is not our present focus. External responsivity, however, is thought to refer to the environmental circumstances under which offenders are motivated and willing to learn (Kennedy, 2001; Serin & Kennedy, 1997), including setting, staff and management characteristics. Having discussed programmatic conditions, we now turn to a discussion of the extent to which these organisational factors influence programme effectiveness in reducing re-offending.

### Impact of setting characteristics on re-offending

Setting of treatment has emerged as a significant moderator of treatment effects in meta-analytic reviews where this has been examined (Andrews & Bonta, 2010; Andrews et al., 1990; Lipsey & Wilson, 1998). A review of these analyses confirmed that community-based treatment yields higher effect sizes than treatment in institutional/residential settings, with an impact of up to 26 per cent in reducing recidivism in the community and of 14 per cent in residential settings (Lipsey & Cullen, 2007). Bonta and Andrews (2007) reported that a community base boosted the effect on recidivism of appropriate treatment to 35 per cent, compared to a limit of 17 per cent for appropriate treatment in residential settings. Enhanced effects of appropriate treatment in the community have led to the inclusion of 'community setting' as a principle of effective intervention, with a recommendation for 'continuity of service' in residential programmes (Andrews, Bonta & Wormith, 2011). Consistent with the need for community reinforcement, 'continuity of programmes and services' in offender management has also been a criterion in the UK Correctional Services Advice and Accreditation Panel's ten accreditation criteria (Macguire et al., 2010).

The underpinnings of the settings effect are still not fully understood. Lipsey (2009) found that the effectiveness of structured counselling was reduced when delivered in custody, and that skill-building programmes were enhanced when delivered in the community to young people not under criminal justice supervision.

These findings hint at a limiting effect of some penal environments. A moderating effect has been recognised, with prisons differing in the extent of control, opportunities for structured learning, and the degree of isolation from external reality. Indeed it is unlikely that interventions that treat the offender in isolation of his/her current life situation should meet with success. Unfortunately these factors have not featured heavily in meta-analyses of offender treatment. The enhanced effects of treatment in the community may indicate that embedding treatment within the offender's natural environment increases the prospect of facilitating real-life learning.

The degree to which the offender perceives treatment as being a personal choice as opposed to coerced may vary depending on the setting. Parhar, Wormith, Derkzen and Beauregard (2008) conducted a meta-analysis of the effect of coercion on offender treatment, including 129 studies of treatment in community and custodial settings. Treatment was generally more effective in terms of reducing re-offending when truly voluntary. Unlike in the community, in custody this was the only circumstance in which treatment was effective: here there was no effect of coerced treatment, including when treatment was offered with the incentive of early release. Thus in a community setting offenders may perceive more personal choice even when treatment participation is a legal requirement (Parhar et al., 2008).

Engagement with offenders in community rehabilitation may actually benefit from the critical problem of attrition and the increasing awareness that the same variables that predict this also predict re-offending (Olver, Stockdale & Wormith, 2011). Olver et al.'s (2011) review of 114 studies found that the best predictors of dropout were not the appealing but offence-unrelated factors such as anxiety or low self-esteem, but rather the proximal treatment responsivity factors (e.g. negative treatment attitude) and the background general criminality factors (e.g. psychopathy). In working with the attrition-related and therefore offence-related issues, treatment providers in the community have a clear need to collaborate with, rather than attempt to compel, offender compliance.[1]

At the same time as working to engage positively with participants, a degree of external pressure in community settings may not be counter-productive and may indeed support internalised motivations to attend. Research in the field most plagued by treatment dropout, domestic violence (DV), supports this idea (Barber & Wright, 2010; Jewell & Wormith, 2010). After analysis of 30 studies of attrition in community treatment for DV offenders, Jewell and Wormith (2010) found that referral source (court ordered or self-referred) was more strongly related to completion than any other violence-related variable, such as criminal history. Court ordered abusers were 16 per cent more likely to complete programmes than were those abusers not required to attend. A later study by Barber and Wright (2010) examined the effect of quality of referral source supervision on programme completion of 481 DV offenders under different levels of judicial monitoring. While controlling for a range of variables including age, criminal history and employment status, they found that increased supervision by the referral source during cognitive-behavioural treatment increased the likelihood of successful completion. They recommended that referring agencies (e.g. courts, police or social services) should inform service users that they will be monitoring and following up on the case and to ensure that this actually happens. This study suggests a benefit for a legitimate threat of enforcement in community treatment for all offenders, but that this works particularly for non-justice diversionary cases.

Andrews and Bonta (2010) examined what variables survived controls for appropriate treatment and thereby enhanced the prediction of effect size in their 374 tests. Controls for methodological considerations such as random assignment, sample size and length of follow-up were included. The factors emerging were consistent with Lipsey (1995): community-based setting; non-justice ownership of the programme; referral to the programme by a criminal justice agency; and an evaluator involved in the design and/or delivery of service. Andrews and Bonta then tested what the effect of appropriate treatment was by allowing adherence to RNR to vary while controlling for these variables. They found that when three or more of the four background conditions were present, appropriate treatment in terms of full RNR adherence was at its strongest (.38) compared to inappropriate treatment (.04). It was clear however that the average effect of appropriate treatment dropped as the number of favourable background conditions dropped: when none or only one background condition was present the mean effect of appropriate treatment was .11 compared to $-.09$ for inappropriate treatment. The importance of an involved evaluator has been discussed above, but the other two variables, i.e. non-justice ownership of the programme and referral by a criminal justice agency, reinforce the importance of a supportive working relationship but with enforceable extrinsic contingencies for non-compliance.

## Impact of staff characteristics on re-offending

There are two dimensions of interpersonal exchange that provide the learning environment for change required by general responsivity (Andrews, 1980). First, offenders generally are more likely to benefit from treatment in the context of a supportive working relationship, or 'working alliance'. Staff skills of interpersonal influence are the second proposed dimension of an environment for behavioural change (Andrews, 1980).

The ability to form and maintain a working alliance is a precursor for interpersonal influence, and so is a key Core Correctional Practice (CCP) under 'Quality of interpersonal relationships' (see Box 19.1). A working alliance is said to comprise three different aspects of the therapeutic relationship: (i) its collaborative nature, (ii) the affective bond between client and worker and (iii) the client and worker's ability to agree on treatment goals and tasks (Bordin, 1994). Dowden and Andrews' (2004) examination of the effect of staff characteristics across 273 recidivism studies indicated a reliable positive effect of 'Quality of interpersonal relationships' ($\Phi = .25$) as measured by defined features of relationships and staff skills. The effect emerged despite a low prevalence of their usage, being codeable in only 5 per cent of studies. 'Appropriate modelling and reinforcement' was only seen in 3 per cent for effective disapproval,[2] and 5 per cent for effective reinforcement. This suggested that the key aspects of a working alliance including relationships and staff skills were at least under-specified and probably under-used. Dowden and Andrews (2004) summarise that the emphasis placed on developing and utilising appropriate staff techniques has been "sorely lacking within correctional treatment programs" (p. 211).

The findings from Dowden and Andrews (2004) are reinforced by studies monitoring traditional probation supervision. A number of studies suggest that without training in CCPs, neither the duration nor the structure of the contact time is focussed on changing criminogenic needs (e.g. Bonta et al., 2011; Bonta, Rugge, Scott, Bourgon & Yessine, 2008; Robinson, VanBenschoten, Alexander & Lowenkamp, 2011; Taxman, 2002). Bonta and colleagues (2008) found that although pro-criminal attitudes and peers were the most frequently identified criminogenic needs in the intake risk assessment, in audiotapes of supervision these needs were also the least frequently discussed. Among 72 adult offenders, attitudes were an identified need in 34 cases but were only discussed in three (8.8 per cent), and officers spent more time discussing enforcement conditions than criminogenic needs. Although officers generally had good relationships skills, they used cognitive-behavioural techniques to influence the offender in less than one in four audiotapes. After the weak 2 per cent impact on re-offending observed across 15 comparative studies of more versus less community supervision (Bonta et al., 2008), these problems suggested the need for training in effective intervention skills.

Despite the low prevalence of CCPs, Dowden and Andrews (2004) found that their presence made an independent contribution to human service programmes. The correlation of effect size and CCP was evident within a variety of settings and case characteristics, including community, institutional, women, men, young offenders and ethnic minorities. However these findings only emerged when the programmes adhered to at least two of the three RNR principles. Therefore work has proceeded to implement and test specially designed RNR training programmes for community supervision officers (e.g. Bonta et al., 2011; Robinson et al., 2011; Smith, Schweitzer, Labrecque & Latessa, 2012; Taxman, 2008).

Staff training within an RNR framework has generally opened with a discussion of the social learning basis for criminal behaviour, and has followed with collaborative exercises to show that thoughts and attitudes influence behaviour in the officers themselves (see e.g. Bourgon, Bonta, Rugge, Scott & Yessine, 2009). The specific intervention skills emphasised have included cognitive techniques such as cognitive restructuring, and behavioural techniques on the effective use of reinforcement and disapproval. Bonta and colleagues found that, despite no pre-training differences, the clients supervised by the officers randomly assigned to training had a two-year re-offending rate (25.3 per cent) that was lower than that of clients of untrained officers (40.2 per cent). In particular, exposure to cognitive techniques was predictive of recidivism, with rates of 19 per cent compared to 37 per cent among clients with no exposure (Bonta et al., 2011). In the second randomised controlled trial, by Robinson et al. (2011), cognitive and behavioural techniques were also used significantly more among trained than usual practice control officers, and there was a concomitant reduction in re-arrests both within and between groups.

These high-quality studies suggest that intervention skills can be improved through training, particularly in regard to the use of cognitive techniques to alter pro-criminal attitudes. This was recently supported in a meta-analytic review of programmes that have trained staff in the principles and practices of effective intervention (Chadwick, DeWolf & Serin, 2015). Chadwick et al. (2015) located ten studies that conformed to the inclusion criterion of training officers in CCPs. Compared to client re-offending of officers not trained in CCPs, training produced a small significant effect on re-offending of trained officers' clients ($d = .22$). The average recidivism rate of the clients of the CCP-trained officers was 36.2 per cent, compared with an average of 49.9 per cent for offenders supervised by officers not trained in CCPs. Although the review's findings should be interpreted with caution due to the small number of studies included, they do suggest a benefit of organisational investment in training officers in effective criminal justice intervention skills using an RNR framework.

## Impact of management characteristics on re-offending

For everyone involved, treatment is implemented amid competing interests, requiring substantial commitment from the organisation as well as from the offender, particularly in the community. In reviewing implementation problems in criminal justice, Goggin and Gendreau (2006) suggested that the field has experienced problems for four overlapping reasons: (i) the trend for 'content free' managers in government, sensitive to political machinations and seduced by buzzwords and quick fixes in the absence of empirical evidence; (ii) ambivalence towards the offender rehabilitation agenda in disciplines such as criminology and indeed among applied psychologists (see Boothby & Clements, 2000); (iii) skills training offered through occasional and discretionary workshops, which is a very poor means of skills transfer (Simpson, 2002); and (iv) programmes implemented without observing effective practice guidelines.

Indeed, emphasising the point that technology transfer requires more than participating in isolated workshops, further follow-up on the Bonta et al. (2011) study reviewed above indicated that skill usage gradually went into remission in subsequent supervision sessions (Bourgon, Bonta, Rugge & Gutierrez, 2012). Bonta and colleagues found that skill dilution over time occurred for officers' relationship skills, behavioural techniques and the global measure of their RNR skills, but not for cognitive techniques. The general weakening of skills occurred despite the rigour of the training process: training lasted for three days and included subsequent monthly small group supervision to discuss use of concepts and skills, the opportunity to submit audiotapes to the trainers for individualised feedback, and an annual refresher workshop. The trainers took measures of each officer's participation in the complete training process, including attendance and participation at monthly meetings, amount of formal feedback requested and received, and on-going supervision participation. High sustained participation was associated with higher skills scores one year later, particularly for the use of cognitive techniques and the discussion of criminogenic needs. Meanwhile the skills scores for the low participation group approached those of the control group officers (Bourgon et al., 2012). The extensive follow-up to the study in officer training highlights the importance of going beyond workshop training and incorporating on-going coaching and support to bring about sustained change in practitioners' behaviour.

Programme integrity can be compromised when offender rehabilitation is superseded by other goals, such as offender work assignments, rather than being at the heart of organisational efforts. This was what Duwe and Clark (2015) described as having happened with their cognitive-behavioural programme for female offenders. To accommodate the institution's other needs the programme was trimmed from twelve weeks' duration to three weeks with the loss of responsivity features including role-playing, skill-building and homework exercises. The adaptation provided an opportunity for comparison of the effects of the programme on participants during the 'high fidelity' period to those on participants during the 'low fidelity' phase. Offenders from the two periods were matched with offenders from the wider population of the institution on variables related to participation, such as level of education at intake, and with each other for 216 participants in total. Across comparisons results suggested that the risk of new arrests and reconvictions post-discharge controlling for length of follow-up was reduced by over 30 per cent in the high fidelity period, while there was a negative effect of participation on re-offending in the low fidelity period. Although the results may relate to offender motivation since the programme was voluntary during the high fidelity period and compulsory later, they are indicative of the negative effects that can result from organisational assaults on programme integrity.

It is likely that adherence to organisational factors may supplement the core evidence-based principles, rather than compensate for them (Andrews & Bonta, 2010). Andrews and Bonta (2010, p. 76) presented a contrast of the effects of integrity to staffing and management characteristics on reduced recidivism. Whereas the 144 studies coded as high in adherence to the organisational principles but as low in adherence to RNR showed a weak non-significant reduction in recidivism ($r = .06$), the 230 tests with high adherence to the organisational principles and RNR showed a significant medium effect ($r = .29$). It is therefore unlikely to be possible to make up for non-adherence to RNR by focussing only on the selection, training and clinical supervision of staff.

## Importance of organisational factors: illustration in probation community supervision

Having outlined the importance of external contingencies on effective practice including an involved evaluator, staff training in CCPs and related organisational commitment, this section gives an account of the development and evaluation of a community rehabilitation programme named *Citizenship*, designed according to the principles of effective intervention.[3] What comes through is the extent to which the programme was operationalised as core business and how this can be compromised when the programme is transported to a different, albeit related, setting.

*Citizenship* was developed in the County Durham area of the National Probation Service in England and Wales with two aims. The first was to fit with the government's strategy on reducing reoffending, but to provide effective services to more offenders than are eligible for accredited offender rehabilitation programmes. The second aim was to focus on re-integrating offenders with their communities, giving the programme its name. *Citizenship* was designed by a steering group of front-line practitioners, led by a local senior manager, under the guidance of a university-based consultant (Professor Clive Hollin). The oversight of a scientist-practitioner forensic psychologist ensured that the programme incorporated the knowledge from the evidence of 'what works' in criminal justice intervention.

A pre-requisite foundation on which to build effective intervention is the existence of a validated risk/needs instrument. This was fulfilled in County Durham because all NPS staff were trained in the Offender Assessment System (OASys: Home Office, 2002). OASys provides officers with a structured framework to record static demographic and criminal background factors as well as current dynamic needs linked to re-offending (listed in Box 19.2 below). Before designing module content, a first step was then to determine the profile of criminogenic needs[4] in the local population ($N = 3,659$), and so OASys profiles were extracted from the system. This showed that the most prevalent need was Employability followed closely by Thinking and Behaviour (see Box 19.2).

**BOX 19.2** OASys criminogenic need profile in County Durham in 2004 (Bruce & Hollin, 2009)

| | |
|---|---|
| Education, Training and Employability | 76.8% |
| Thinking and Behaviour | 75.3% |
| Lifestyle and Associates | 58.3% |
| Relationships | 51.8% |
| Emotional Well-Being | 51.5% |
| Alcohol Misuse | 48.8% |
| Accommodation | 44.7% |
| Attitudes | 43.0% |
| Drug Misuse | 37.4% |
| Financial Management and Income | 31.3% |

Owing to this need profile and an understanding of the benefit of community linkages, the model of change within *Citizenship* was determined to be education, increasing motivation to change and community links. Consistent with the *Responsivity* principle, officers would teach the skill of problem-solving to all offenders in an opening module and would help them apply this approach in each additional module. Some criminogenic needs, such as Thinking and Behaviour, were considered to be within the scope of probation intervention. Other needs, such as Drug Misuse, were considered to be better provided by specialist external input. The decision was taken therefore to focus intervention on Thinking and Behaviour, and make other modules joint pieces of work with external agencies. This meant that the implementation of *Citizenship* required formal links with a number of providers in the local community. This served to embed the programme in the local environment (Bruce & Hollin, 2009).

To provide a necessary breadth of response to the criminogenic needs in Box 19.2, *Citizenship* was designed with a modular structure, as shown in Box 19.3. Induction was a seven-session module, and was compulsory for all offenders as it contained an explanation of the legal requirements of the sentence and reviewed the initial sentence plan arising from OASys. Including these features was a necessary part of making the programme core business, rather than discretionary. After the initial sessions, officers would proceed to facilitate a detailed offence analysis and then a consideration of times when offenders had themselves been victims, as a means of propelling action by generating cognitive dissonance (Draycott & Dabbs, 1998). The problem-solving approach then introduced would be reinforced in the remaining optional modules to address Thinking and Behaviour. The final session of Induction co-produced a 'Theory of Change': a personal *Citizenship* pathway.

Induction therefore culminated in an improved plan for reducing re-offending, meeting the *Needs* and *Responsivity* principles, by finding a match between the participants' self-identified criminogenic problems and the content of the programme. Consistent with the *Risk* principle, the dosage of treatment should correspond to the risk of re-offending. Therefore the number of optional modules selected would correspond to risk, and higher-risk offenders may also participate in an accredited offending behaviour programme. The final 'Next Steps' module provided the opportunity to review and record progress, linking the offender's learning on *Citizenship* with his/her future plans, including what future support is appropriate beyond the end of statutory supervision.

Supported by its in-house psychology team, the organisation decided to do a pilot evaluation in the initial stages of programme implementation (Gray & Pearson, 2006). In addition to impact on reconvictions the pilot sought to measure two service process indicators linked to its model of change: (i) the targeting of offenders' needs to the *Citizenship* modules; and (ii) the extent of referral to external agencies. The sample comprised the first 100 cases supervised by trained staff from the steering group, compared with a matched group of 100 cases supervised by the same staff but terminating before *Citizenship* implementation.[5] Results showed that nearly one-half of offenders had completed the required modules in

**BOX 19.3** Citizenship pathway model

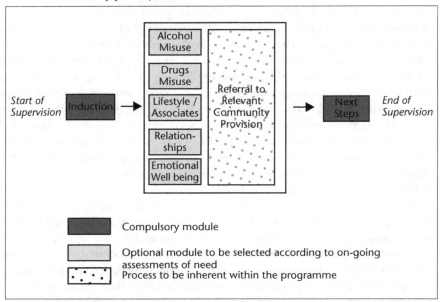

their individual plans, and nearly three-quarters had been referred to external support agencies. Although one-year reconvictions were non-significantly lower in the *Citizenship* group than in the prior practice group, this may have been due to the small sample; the odds ratio suggested that offenders were nearly twice as likely to desist under *Citizenship*. The process of sharing the promising results at team meetings bolstered implementation in the area, and made the case for a wider evaluation.

A full independent evaluation then followed in collaboration with clinical researchers from a local university (Pearson, McDougall, Kanaan, Bowles & Torgerson, 2011). Reconvictions of a total cohort of 3,819 *Citizenship* cases were compared over two years with those of a total cohort of 2,110 usual practice cases from the previous year. Due to differing lengths of time in the community of offenders on the caseload in each cohort, data analysis needed to account for the opportunity to re-offend (time at risk). Controlling for OASys risk score and opportunity to offend, the hazard ratio was 0.71, i.e. the odds of reconviction at any point during the two years were reduced by 29 per cent under *Citizenship*. This effect was achieved with medium- and lower-risk offenders because when levels of risk were examined it showed that high-risk offenders did not show any change. This was not altogether surprising since implementation was compromised with the high-risk offenders due to the greater emphasis on control than on rehabilitation and community reintegration with this sub-group.

The positive impact of *Citizenship* on staff performance and resulting cost savings in County Durham sparked the interest of senior leaders in the neighbouring probation areas. An agreement followed to disseminate the programme materials to the other two areas. Again, due to the presence of an in-house psychology team with links to a consultant forensic psychologist (Professor Cynthia McDougall), it was also agreed to test the effect of the programme on practice in the first of the two new areas, Area B. For financial austerity reasons, Area B probation managers decided to limit implementation to higher risk cases. They saw value, however, in subjecting the programme to the most rigorous level of evaluation scrutiny, a randomised controlled trial (RCT). Since individual randomisation in criminal justice is rarely accepted, the implementation of the RCT would be office-based, comparing cases from offices randomised to the programme with those from waiting list control group offices that would be randomised to the programme after an interval of two months. This plan was attractive to Area B managers because they were attempting to maintain performance standards and the design meant that this effort would not be impaired across the organisation by a wide-scale implementation of *Citizenship*. A phased introduction would be somewhat easier to absorb. Furthermore, there was less need for a separate pilot evaluation because the first offices would provide the required information about logistics needed for wider implementation. The second of the two new areas, Area C, took the view that incremental implementation would be more costly and would bring a weak staff message and so opted to implement area-wide in a 'big bang' approach.

The results of the different implementation strategies on usage of the programme by trained officers in the two new areas have been reported and discussed in full (Pearson, Torgerson, McDougall & Bowles, 2010). Box 19.4 summarises that relative to the area in which *Citizenship* was designed, County Durham, take-up was seriously deflated in the other two areas. The comparison between the two new areas was complicated by the concentration on higher-risk cases in Area B. However, proportionate to the number of cases eligible, the programme was more

**BOX 19.4** Programme implementation in probation areas (from Pearson, Torgerson, McDougall & Bowles, 2010)

| Probation area | Use of programme | Total eligible | Per cent |
| --- | --- | --- | --- |
| Co Durham | 3,072 | 4,078 | 75.3 |
| *Area B | 188 | 426 | 44.1 |
| Area C | 2,325 | 8,439 | 27.6 |
| Total | 5,585 | 12,943 | 43.2 |

*Area B targeted the programme at a more troublesome sub-set of those targeted in the other two areas.

widely adopted in Area B than in Area C. In fact, Area C needed to re-launch the programme: their internal inspections identified that the programme was being applied only sporadically. By contrast Area B was able to implement a schedule of monitoring to correspond to the staggered roll-out of the programme. This allowed the take-up in different delivery units to be compared as practice was gradually mainstreamed. Furthermore the repetition of training in Area B meant that the early offices produced 'champions' that modelled the programme to the later offices, while in Area C there was a low level of confidence and understanding of the programme. The support for the programme overall was not strong in either of the two new areas, however.

The outcome evaluation of *Citizenship* delivery in Area B compared 1,091 medium- and high-risk offenders on supervision randomly allocated to *Citizenship* or usual practice depending on the office to which they reported during a one year period (Pearson, McDougall, Kanaan, Torgerson & Bowles, 2016). Results controlling for OASys risk score and opportunity to offend showed that the odds of reconviction during the year were non-significantly reduced by 21 per cent under *Citizenship* compared to usual practice (hazard ratio = 0.79). However, this was achieved despite only a minority of the *Citizenship* cases receiving the programme. Furthermore, the risk analysis showed that this overall reduction masked a difference by static risk level: the odds of reconviction were reduced by 34 per cent in high-risk offenders, while the larger group of medium-risk cases showed no real change. This was surprising until we saw that more of the higher risk cases were in the group exposed to *Citizenship* sessions. Thus officers appeared to be delivering *Citizenship* sessions more consistently with offenders at high risk of re-offending than with medium-risk offenders, although take-up of the programme overall was low.

Taken together, the experience of transporting *Citizenship* from the area where it was developed to neighbouring areas was contingent on more than having an evidence-based programme. What was noticeable by contrast between the areas was the level of investment in the programme between the originating area and the two new areas. While the originating area's leadership invested in providing a steering group of practitioners who were involved in training, case-file inspections, and subsequent staff briefings to disseminate the findings extracted, the adopting areas wanted to absorb the programme with minimal cost and in the background to other organisational performance agendas. This aggravated the risk of problems with technology transfer caused by isolated workshop training (Bourgon et al., 2012).

## Recommendations for increasing external responsivity in criminal justice environments

In the field of training transfer it is recognised that poor organisational readiness for reforms is often due to the impetus for these only being located in top management who themselves take insufficient involvement in the actual behaviour change process (Broad & Newstrom, 1992). Without essential senior management backing, trainers and interested managers should reconsider whether training should be attempted at all until this improves. Having reviewed a real-world example of transporting evidence-based practice, this final section offers recommendations for promoting and evaluating external responsivity factors in effective offender intervention programmes.

## Measure organisational capacity to deliver effective interventions

One means of assessing how well intervention programmes in a given criminal justice agency are supported by organisational policy and practice is by using the theoretically and empirically grounded Correctional Programme Assessment Inventory (CPAI) (Gendreau, Andrews & Thériault, 2010). The CPAI is a standardised tool including Capacity and Content components, i.e. assessing both the level of organisational capacity for, and the level to which programme content adheres to, effective intervention. Capacity features include organisational factors such as a clear mandate and goals shared at each level of the organisation; programme implementation factors such as selection of evidence-based programmes and empirically documented evidence of the need for them; management/staff characteristics such as a programme director professionally trained in the helping professions who is actively engaged at each level of the organisation;[6] front-line staff that is selected for its personal qualities and skills related to service delivery; interagency communication such as pre-established formal links with other agencies delivering services for offender needs; and evaluation capacity such as monitoring systems for offender treatment progress, fidelity of staff delivery and mechanisms for outcome evaluation. Content components include client risk/need practices; programme characteristics; and staff practitioner skills (CCPs: see Box 19.1).

Lowenkamp, Latessa and Smith (2006) investigated CPAI scores in 38 community residential programmes, and the outcomes of the 3,237 parolee graduates. Unfortunately the majority of programmes failed to reduce re-offending in graduates compared to matched comparison cases. By failing to reduce re-offending community residential programmes could be seen as a programme failure. The results however varied when the CPAI score was accounted for. The overall mean CPAI rating was 'unsatisfactory' at below 50 ($M$ = 45.5 per cent) but the CPAI correlated between $r$ = .26 and $r$ = .44 depending on the component and outcome measure, explaining between 7 per cent and 18 per cent variation in treatment effects. While 24 of the 38 programmes (63 per cent) were in an 'unsatisfactory' score range with only a negligible reduction in recalls to prison, the single programme that was rated in the 'satisfactory' range demonstrated a reduction in recalls of 44 per cent relative to comparison cases. The most predictive components were Pre-Service Client Risk Assessment, and Programme Implementation, suggesting the importance of organisations with evidence-based programmes and staff trained in a validated risk/needs measure. These features were associated with the completion of differential treatment plans followed through in programme implementation (see also Taxman, 2008). Variation in organisational capacity may provide parallel, more nuanced explanations of within-programme variations in effectiveness than differential levels of officer or offender uptake, such as seen in *Citizenship*. Therefore it is recommended that programme evaluations also attempt to measure organisational capacity.

## Provide effective support for the transfer of training

To set the 'transfer climate' for trainees and their managers it is recommended to plan the applicability of training to the work environment before training starts. The primary barriers identified in research by Broad and Newstrom (1992) included 'lack of reinforcement on the job' and 'interference from the immediate environment'. Arguably these are under the responsibility of the team manager and the organisation, not the trainer or the trainee. When the level of effort of role-players was rated by an independent panel of training experts, compared to trainers and trainees, managers were rated as lowest – in particular 'after' training. To have the greatest impact, Broad and Newstom suggest that team managers lay the foundation for transfer before trainees ever even enter training, and then reinforce training on the job in collaboration with the trainer. The range of excellent strategies at each stage of training is listed in Box 19.5.

To avoid the impetus for change residing only/mainly with top management, as seen with *Citizenship* implementation in Area B and Area C, it is recommended that front-line staff is involved and engaged in the change process. Staff understanding, liking, trust and desire for reforms appear to be critical factors for organisational readiness, and time needs to be devoted to securing staff engagement. Inviting staff across grades to participate in the planning of the programme and its training, as in County Durham with *Citizenship*, makes their cooperation in implementing it more likely.

Relatedly, training is rarely designed to facilitate the use of new practices as part of normal routines. In both adopting areas the application to the specifics of the office setting was delegated by the trainers, with training focussing on one-time knowledge-sharing and skill-building. Reforms must occur in the routine environment at the workflow processes level, which varies considerably by organisation. This requires implementation plans that refine work processes in a gradual combination of micro (attitudes and behaviours of individual practitioners) and macro (top-down management systems) strategies. Agency–university partnerships are beneficial in obtaining feedback on how the refinements align with evidence-based practice. Such 'quality improvement' processes (see Rudes, Viglione & Porter, 2013), should allow staff the opportunity to receive adequate time to ask questions and to learn gradually the added value of the reforms for their work. As suggested by Rudes et al. (2013) the impact of such strategies requires controlled evaluation, such as by implementing reforms using a quality improvement process in one area and without one in another, and monitoring the effects on training transfer controlling for baseline differences.

**BOX 19.5** Training transfer strategies for managers (based on Broad & Newstrom, 1992)

## Before Training

1. Identify training needs that are high priority for the organisation
2. Collect baseline data on the trainee's performance
3. Draw up a behaviour contract for training transfer identifying both the trainee's and the manager's responsibilities (e.g. meeting following training to determine highlights and discuss the trainee's action plans)
4. Provide time for trainees to complete pre-training homework
5. Offer an explicit rationale for change (e.g. providing a clear connection between training transfer and promotional opportunities or performance-based rewards)

## During Training

6. Send trainees in pairs from the same unit who are compatible and ready to support each other in transfer post-training
7. Attend training programmes (take a training role) to show public support for the new skills
8. Make trainee attendance at all sessions mandatory, and eliminate interruptions
9. Provide cover for trainees so that they do not return to a backlog that may prevent them even starting to apply their new learning

## After Training

10. Adopt a 're-entry' partnership with the trainee to discuss learning, identify measurable performance standards and foresee barriers to transfer
11. Debrief the trainer to prime follow-up plans
12. Provide opportunities to practice new skills
13. Recognise challenges in follow-up meetings and provide psychological support for transfer
14. Give positive reinforcement (clearly and systematically)
15. Provide positive role models for direct on-the-job guidance
16. Schedule briefings by trainees for their colleagues
17. Provide job aids and support their use in practice (e.g. diagrams, reminder cards)
18. Publicise successes

## *Design training to respond to the organisational context*

A prerequisite of training transfer is skill acquisition, but this needs to be achieved in a way that supports practitioner belief in change. Reviews of evaluations of diverse training strategies indicate that passive dissemination of information is generally ineffective, while interactive approaches such as regular educational workshops involving discussion or practice are more effective (Bero et al., 1998; Gira, Kessler & Poertner, 2004). Johnson and Austin (2006) therefore suggest that problem-based learning is likely to best support the introduction and use of evidence-based practice. Similarly, Needs and Capelin (2004) argue that training should go beyond a narrow focus on tasks, and should contribute to the development of team cohesion and confidence by providing opportunities for the mastery of skills. This recognises the importance of an experienced-based belief in being able to apply the skills on the job. Emphasis on task elements of training can lead to the task being seen as an end in itself, rather than a means to an end. This has been illustrated in the context of misaligned training and practice regarding risk-needs assessment (Viglione, Rudes & Taxman, 2015). One recommendation is for trainers to develop 'application-orientated objectives' with trainees. These are behavioural statements of what the trainees should do once they return to their jobs, cueing them to think beyond the training session.

In cases where the job environment provides little built-in support for the trainee's new skills (support is neutral or negative), a module for 'relapse prevention' is recommended (Broad & Newstrom, 1992). This allows the trainee to take charge of the transfer process. This module should be one of the last sessions in the training programme, where trainees are helped to look for relapse indicators in their own job situations, such as a hostile work schedule or unsupportive co-workers, then analyse coping skills, and then develop and practice (fire drill) a plan to prevent lapses becoming a relapse to old habits. Fire drills should be as realistic as possible to prepare the trainee for real work situations. The final step is 'follow-up on the job' and includes keeping track of accomplishments and determining what reinforcement the trainee will seek. Groups of trainees might get together, or might arrange for the trainer to give a follow-up 'booster' session. Supportive supervisors can provide recognition or other reinforcement, tailored to the individual trainee, for success in transferring new skills. The presence of these features should be specified and their effect on training transfer evaluated.

## Summary

Against a backdrop of 'what works' in offender rehabilitation, this chapter discussed key organisational factors, and reviewed an example of an evidence-based supervision programme that had been implemented, evaluated and transported. Whereas practitioners in the originating area could be said to have had both the experience basis ('the will') and the competency basis ('the way') recommended for cognitive-behavioural culture change to support the 'what works' agenda (Birgden, 2004), by contrast, practitioners in the adopting areas were not involved in developing the programme and so did not benefit from the same experiential background. The culture shift had therefore barely taken hold and was not able to be maintained in the same way, without resourcing of a local steering group and management investment in integrity monitoring and support. The programme was not disseminated as core business. The adopting area was therefore lacking the 'will' to support the culture shift and the 'way' for engaging staff and offenders in the rehabilitation programme. These are elements of external responsivity that can make an important difference to the effectiveness of evidence-based intervention programmes.

## Acknowledgement

Thank you to Russell Bruce, former Chief Executive of Durham Tees Valley probation trust, for his helpful comments on this chapter. His comments were sought because he provided unshakeable leadership in supporting the implementation and evaluation of *Citizenship* as core service delivery in County Durham. I have no doubt that the widespread take-up of the programme in County Durham, as well as its later adoption in Teesside, was strongly related to his commitment to a culture of evidence-based practice.

## Notes

1 From a research perspective it is also advisable to collaborate and thus retain potential non-completers because they must be included in the evaluation's experimental group (to avoid selection bias), and negative effects from these cases risk cancelling out any group-level treatment effect.
2 Effective disapproval was indicated by evidence that the client was told why the staff member disapproved of the behaviour, or evidence that the client was encouraged to consider why the behaviour was undesirable.
3 The original report on the development of Citizenship (Bruce & Hollin, 2009) and those on its evaluation (Pearson, McDougall, Kanaan, Torgerson & Bowles, 2011; Pearson, McDougall, Kanaan, Bowles & Torgerson, 2016) are available elsewhere.
4 Criminogenic needs were those dynamic risk factors with scores over the empirically determined 'threshold of concern' on OASys (Home Office, 2002).
5 Both groups reduced to 85 cases (total sample $N = 170$) after those with accredited programmes or with incomplete supervision were excluded. Accredited programmes cases were excluded to ensure that Citizenship was the subject of the evaluation, rather than accredited programmes.
6 Commitment by management and officers to on-going training and supervision is also included under management/staff characteristics.

## References

Andrews, D. A. (1980). Some experimental investigations of the principles of differential association through deliberate manipulations of the structure of service systems. *American Sociological Review*, 45, 448–462.
Andrews, D. A. & Bonta, J. (2010). *The Psychology of Criminal Conduct* (5th ed.). New Providence, NJ: LexisNexis/Matthew Bender.
Andrews, D. A. & Dowden, C. (2005). Managing correctional treatment for reduced recidivism: A meta-analytic review of programme integrity. *Legal and Criminological Psychology*, 10, 173–187.

Andrews, D. A., Bonta, J. & Wormith, J. S. (2011). The risk-need-responsivity (RNR) model: Does adding the good lives model contribute to effective crime prevention? *Criminal Justice and Behavior*, 38(7), 735–755. doi: 10.1177/0093854811406356.

Andrews, D. A. & Carvell, C. (1998). *Core Correctional Training-Core Correctional Supervision and Counseling: Theory, Research, Assessment and Practice.* Unpublished training manual. Ottawa, Canada: Carleton University.

Andrews, D. A. & Kiessling, J. J. (1980). Program structure and effective correctional practices: A summary of the CaVIC research. In R.R. Ross & P. Gendreau (Eds.), *Effective Correctional Treatment.* Toronto, Canada: Butterworth.

Andrews, D. A., Zinger, I., Hoge, R. D., Bonta, J., Gendreau, P. & Cullen, F. T. (1990). Does correctional treatment work? A clinically relevant and psychologically informed meta-analysis. *Criminology*, 28(3), 369–404.

Barber, S. J. & Wright, E. M. (2010). Predictors of completion in a batterer treatment program: The effects of referral source supervision. *Criminal Justice and Behavior*, 37(8), 847–859.

Bero, L. A., Grilli, R., Grimshaw, J. M., Harvey, E., Oxman, A. D. & Thomson, M. A. (1998). Closing the gap between research and practice: An overview of systematic reviews of interventions to promote the implementation of research findings. *British Medical Journal*, 317, 465–468.

Birgden, A. (2004). Therapeutic jurisprudence and responsivity: Finding the will and the way in offender rehabilitation. *Psychology, Crime & Law*, 10(3), 283–295.

Bonta, J. & Andrews, D. A. (2007). *The Risk-Need-Responsivity model for offender assessment and rehabilitation.* Retrieved from www.publicsafety.gc.ca/cnt/rsrcs/pblctns/rsk-nd-rspnsvty/index-eng.aspx: Public Safety Canada.

Bonta, J., Bourgon, G., Rugge, T., Scott, T. L., Yessine, A. K., Gutierrez, L. & Li, J. (2011). An experimental demonstration of training probation officers in evidence-based community supervision. *Criminal Justice and Behavior*, 38(11), 1127–1148. doi: 10.1177/0093854811420678.

Bonta, J., Rugge, T., Scott, T. L., Bourgon, G. & Yessine, A. K. (2008). Exploring the black box of community supervision. *Journal of Offender Rehabilitation*, 47(3), 248–270.

Boothby, J. L. & Clements, C. B. (2000). A national survey of correctional psychologists. *Criminal Justice and Behavior*, 27(6), 716–732.

Bordin, E. (1994). Theory and research on the therapeutic alliance: New directions. In A.O. Horvarth & L.S. Greenberg (Eds.), *The Working Alliance: Theory, Research, and Practice* (pp. 13–37). Chichester, UK: John Wiley & Sons.

Bourgon, G., Bonta, J., Rugge, T. & Gutierrez, L. (2012). Technology transfer: The importance of on-going clinical supervision in transferring 'What Works' to everyday community supervision. In F. McNeill, P. Raynor & C. Trotter (Eds.), *Offender Supervision: New Directions in Theory, Research, and Practice.* (pp. 91–112). Abingdon, UK: Routledge.

Bourgon, G., Bonta, J., Rugge, T., Scott, T. L. & Yessine, A. K. (2009). *Translating "What Works" into Sustainable Everyday Practice: Program Design, Implementation and Evaluation.* Retrieved from www.publicsafety.gc.ca/cnt/rsrcs/pblctns/2009-05-pd/index-eng.aspx: Public Safety Canada.

Broad, M. L. & Newstrom, J. W. (1992). *Transfer of Training: Action-Packed Strategies to Ensure High Payoff From Training Investments.* Reading, MA: Addison-Wesley.

Bruce, R. & Hollin, C. R. (2009). Developing citizenship. *EuroVista*, 1(1), 24–31.

Chadwick, N., DeWolf, A. & Serin, R. (2015). Effectively training community supervision officers. *Criminal Justice and Behavior*, 42(10), 977–989.

Dowden, C. & Andrews, D. A. (2004). The importance of staff practice in delivering effective correctional treatment: A meta-analytic review. *International Journal of Offender Therapy and Comparative Criminology*, 48, 203–214.

Draycott, S. & Dabbs, A. (1998). Cognitive dissonance 2: A theoretical grounding of motivational interviewing. *British Journal of Clinical Psychology*, 37(3), 355–364.

Duwe, G. & Clark, V. (2015). Importance of programme integrity: Outcome evaluation of a gender-responsive, cognitive-behavioural program for female offenders. *Criminology & Public Policy*, 14(2), 1–28.

Gendreau, P. (1996). The principles of effective intervention with offenders. In A.T. Harland (Ed.), *Choosing Correctional Options That Work: Defining the Demand and Evaluating the Supply* (pp. 117–130). Newbury Park, CA: Sage.

Gendreau, P. & Andrews, D. A. (1990). Tertiary prevention: What the meta-analysis of the offender literature tells us about 'what works'. *Canadian Journal of Criminology*, 32, 173–184.

Gendreau, P., Andrews, D. A. & Thériault, Y. L. (2010). *Correctional Program Assessment Inventory – 2010*. Saint John, New Brunswick, Canada: University of New Brunswick.

Gira, E. C., Kessler, M. L. & Poertner, J. (2004). Influencing social workers to use research evidence in practice: Lessons from medicine and the allied health professions. *Research on Social Work Practice*, 14(2), 68–79.

Goggin, C. & Gendreau, P. (2006). The implementation and maintenance of quality services in offender rehabilitation programmes. In C.R. Hollin & E.J. Palmer (Eds.), *Offender Behaviour Programmes: Development, Application and Controversies*. (pp. 209–246). Chichester, UK: John Wiley & Sons.

Gray, R. & Pearson, D. A. S. (2006). *An interim investigation into the effectiveness of the Citizenship Programme*. Research Study 11. Psychology Unit. County Durham, UK: National Probation Service.

Home Office. (2002). *Offender Assessment System OASys User Manual*. London, UK: Home Office.

Jewell, L. M. & Wormith, J. S. (2010). Variables associated with attrition from domestic violence treatment programs targeting male batterers: A meta-analysis. *Criminal Justice and Behavior*, 37(10), 1086–1113.

Johnson, M. & Austin, M. J. (2006). Evidence-based practice in the social services: Implications for organisational change. *Administration in Social Work*, 30(3), 75–104.

Kennedy, S. M. (2001). Treatment responsivity: Reducing recidivism by enhancing treatment effectiveness. In L. Motiuk & R. C. Serin (Eds.), *Compendium 2000 on Effective Correctional Programming* (Vol. 1). Canada: Ministry of Supply and Services.

Latessa, E. J. & Lowenkamp, C. T. (2006). What works in reducing recidivism? *University of St. Thomas Law Journal*, 3, 521–535.

Lipsey, M.W. (1995). What do we learn from 400 research studies on the effectiveness of treatment with juvenile delinquents? In J. McGuire (Ed.), *What Works: Reducing Reoffending: Guidelines from Research and Practice*. (pp. 63–78). Chichester, UK: Wiley.

Lipsey, M.W. (1999). Can rehabilitative programs reduce the recidivism of juvenile offenders? An inquiry into the effectiveness of practical programs. *Virginia Journal of Social Policy & the Law*, 6, 611–641.

Lipsey, M. W. (2009). The primary factors that characterize effective interventions with juvenile offenders: A meta-analytic overview. *Victims & Offenders*, 4, 124–147.

Lipsey, M. W. & Cullen, F.T. (2007). The effectiveness of correctional rehabilitation: A review of systematic reviews. *Annual Review of Law and Science*, 3, 297–320. doi: 10.1146/annurev.lawsocsci.3.081806.112833.

Lipsey, M. W. & Wilson, D. B. (1998). Effective intervention for serious juvenile offenders. In R. Loeber & D. P. Farrington (Eds.), *Serious and Violent Juvenile Offenders: Risk Factors and Successful Interventions*. (pp. 313–345). Thousand Oaks, CA: Sage.

Lowenkamp, C. T., Latessa, E. J. & Holsinger, A. M. (2006). The risk principle in action: What have we learned from 13,676 offenders and 97 correctional programs? *Crime & Delinquency*, 52, 77–93.

Lowenkamp, C.T., Latessa, E. J., & Smith, P. (2006). Does correctional program quality really matter? The impact of adhering to the principles of effective intervention. *Criminology & Public Policy*, 5(3), 201–220.

Macguire, M., Grubin, D., Lösel, F. & Raynor, P. (2010). 'What works' and the correctional services accreditation panel: Taking stock from an inside perspective. *Criminology & Criminal Justice*, 10(1), 37–58.

McGuire, J. (Ed.). (2002). *Offender Rehabilitation and Treatment: Effective Programmes and Policies to Reduce Re-Offending*. Chichester, UK: John Wiley & Sons.

Needs, A. & Capelin, J. (2004). Facilitating multi-disciplinary teams. In A. Needs & G. Towl (Eds.), *Applying Psychology to Forensic Practice*. (pp. 202–221). Oxford, UK: BPS Blackwell.

Olver, M. E. Stockdale, K. C. & Wormith, S. (2011). A meta-analysis of predictors of offender treatment attrition and its relationship to recidivism. *Journal of Consulting and Clinical Psychology*, 79(1), 6–21. doi: 10.1037/a0022200.

Parhar, K. K., Wormith, J. S., Derkzen, D. M. & Beauregard, A. M. (2008). Offender coercion in treatment: A meta-analysis of effectiveness. *Criminal Justice and Behavior*, 35(9), 1109–1135.

Pearson, D. A. S., McDougall, C., Kanaan, M., Bowles, R. A. & Torgerson, D. J. (2011). Reducing criminal recidivism: Evaluation of citizenship, an evidence-based probation supervision process. *Journal of Experimental Criminology*, 7(1), 73–102.

Pearson, D. A. S., McDougall, C., Kanaan, M., Torgerson, D. J. & Bowles, R. A. (2016). Evaluation of the citizenship evidence-based probation supervision program using a stepped wedge cluster randomized controlled trial. *Crime & Delinquency*, 62(7), 899–924. doi: 10.1177/0011128714530824.

Pearson, D. A. S., Torgerson, D., McDougall, C. & Bowles, R. (2010). Parable of two agencies, one of which randomizes. *The ANNALS of the American Academy of Political and Social Science*, 628(1), 11–29. doi: 10.1177/0002716209351500.

Petrosino, A. & Soydan, H. (2005). The impact of program developers as evaluators on criminal recidivism: Results from meta-analyses of experimental and quasi-experimental research. *Journal of Experimental Criminology*, 1, 435–450.

Robinson, C. R., VanBenschoten, S., Alexander, M. & Lowenkamp, C. T. (2011). A random (almost) study of Staff Trained at Reducing Re-Arrest (STARR): Reducing recidivism through intentional design. *Federal Probation*, 75(2), 57–63.

Rudes, D. S., Viglione, J. & Porter, C. M. (2013). Using quality improvement models in correctional organizations. *Federal Probation*, 77(2), 69–75.

Serin, R. C. & Kennedy, S. M. (1997). *Treatment Readiness and Responsivity: Contributing to Effective Correctional Programming* (R-54). Retrieved from www.csc-scc.gc.ca/research/092/r54_e.pdf.

Simpson, D. D. (2002). A conceptual framework for transferring research to practice. *Journal of Substance Abuse Treatment*, 22, 171–182.

Smith, P., Gendreau, P. & Swartz, K. (2009). Validating the principles of effective intervention: A systematic review of the contributions of meta-analysis in the field of corrections. *Victims & Offenders*, 4, 148–169.

Smith, P., Schweitzer, M., Labrecque, R. M. & Latessa, E. J. (2012). Improving probation officers' supervision skills: An evaluation of the EPICS model. *Journal of Crime and Justice*, 35(2), 189–199.

Taxman, F. S. (2002). Supervision – exploring the dimensions of effectiveness. *Federal Probation*, 66, 14–27.

Taxman, F. S. (2008). No illusions: Offender and organizational change in Maryland's proactive community supervision efforts. *Criminology & Public Policy*, 7, 275–302.

Viglione, J., Rudes, D. S. & Taxman, F. S. (2015). Misalignment in supervision: Implementing risk/needs assessment instruments in probation. *Criminal Justice and Behavior*, 42(3), 263–285. doi: 10.1177/0093854814548447.

Wilson, D. B., Bouffard, L. A. & Mackenzie, D. L. (2005). A quantitative review of structured, group-oriented, cognitive-behavioral programs for offenders. *Criminal Justice and Behavior*, 32(2), 172–204.

# 20

# NIDOTHERAPY

## A systematic environmental therapy

*Peter Tyrer and Helen Tyrer*

## Introduction

Nidotherapy is a collaborative empirical treatment that examines every component of the environment to determine what changes might be made to effect a better fit for a person, be they a psychiatric patient, an offender or just an ordinary citizen. It has been in existence for 20 years and is now beginning to be accepted as much more than a common sense approach to mental illness. In this chapter the essential principles of nidotherapy, its components, and its efficacy, will all be described and illustrated with a detailed single case example demonstrating its differences from other therapies. Finally, efficacy studies are described to show where it is on the evidence-based pathway.

## History

Nidotherapy was first conceived in Paddington, London, in 1996 as a treatment for people with severe mental illness attached to what was then an assertive outreach team. What we recognised fairly early in these teams was the absence of alternatives to existing treatments. Evidence-based psychiatry has made great strides in the last few years but it is powerless to answer the problems of those with severe mental illness who have completely failed to respond to all known effective treatments. As a consequence, the most difficult patients who are attached to assertive outreach teams tend to stay within these teams and make very little progress. Nidotherapy was born from the despair of these people whom I used to describe as being in the Last Chance Saloon. Nidotherapy was their last chance and some aspects of it were introduced into a randomised controlled trial that demonstrated no benefit from assertive outreach therapy (in the form of intensive case management) overall, but did show gains in the hospitals where several of the practitioners had been trained in nidotherapy (Burns et al., 1999).

Since then nidotherapy has gradually disseminated to other parts of the United Kingdom, Sweden, Denmark, Montenegro, India, Iran, Australia and New Zealand. In selecting patients for nidotherapy we think particularly of those who had a wide range of treatments and shown little or no response, and particularly of those who actively dislike or reject treatment in any form. This has been extended to patients with all kinds of personality disorder, but most especially those with treatment resisting (Type R) personality disorder (Tyrer, Sensky & Mitchard, 2003), intellectual disability, chronic anxiety and depressive disorders, health anxiety, dementia and other organic disorders of older age, and eating disorders.

## Why is it novel?

It is reasonable for the readers of this chapter to be a little sceptical at this point. If this treatment covers such a large range of disorders, and is allegedly effective, can we be convinced it really works, as surely no treatment can be so wide-ranging in its effects? It must either be a complex placebo treatment or incorporate much that is already known. Is it merely a fluffy word that creates a new jargon for something we do all the time in treatment? If it really is so effective why has it not been embraced across the NHS and the wider world?

These are natural doubts that need to be answered. The reasons for its novelty are (a) although we think about the environment often in managing patients we do not do this systematically, (b) we fail to engage in a genuinely collaborative treatment effort that allows the patient to be the key driver in the environmental change, and (c) we do not give environmental change the credit it deserves and always tend to make it subservient to other interventions that are more technologically driven. In all these areas attitudes are changing and the environment is being given much more attention now that it has been at any time in the past.

At times in this chapter we will reinforce the points made by giving a case example. Here we start off:

---

### CASE EXAMPLE – INTRODUCTION

*A young man who had a 20-year history of offending, mainly violence towards property and threats of physical violence, was considered incapable of looking after his financial affairs because of drug and alcohol abuse. He used to have major rows with his key worker over his weekly income allowance and made accusations that he was being kept in the dark about his true allowances. He began to make increasingly threatening remarks to all members of the clinical team and a serious discussion took place about his discharge.*

---

## Nidotherapy is a philosophy

In describing nidotherapy we have to admit that it is more than a treatment, it is a philosophy of care with a set of principles to guide. These follow naturally from the simple definition of nidotherapy: the systematic manipulation of the environment to make a better fit for a person with a mental health problem (Tyrer et al., 2003). Elements of the systematic aspect are discussed elsewhere in this book. However, we manipulate the environment all the time in our daily lives to make us feel better, and so if your mood improves when you go to a football match or shop in a department store this in a minor way constitutes nidotherapy, but it would hardly qualify for this conclusion unless it was linked to some more longer lasting improvement than an hour or two.

When we apply for jobs we choose those that fit in with the principle of nidotherapy. We want to be working with people we respect and who respect us, to have tasks that we know we have the ability to perform and to get the self-esteem that always follows from good employment. All these 'make a better fit' for us in society and are generally good for our mental health. The same applies to holidays we take, the friends we choose to meet and the regular leisure activities we undertake. So if this is the case, why do we need to give a formal name to this treatment?

The answer is quite simple. When we function in this way we are practising self-nidotherapy. We do not need any training for this because we are clear in our minds what we want and how to achieve it, and so need no external help. So here you could say common sense is operating. But if you think carefully, there must have been occasions in your lives when you have not been quite your normal self and been mentally troubled, and on these occasions you are not always certain how to react. There are lots of options available, and many, such as taking a holiday, taking time off work due to sickness or changing your work, involve environmental change. And here we are not just referring to a change in the physical environment; the social and personal environments also count in nidotherapy, so there could have been occasions when you have either needed advice from others, or have actually chosen the wrong option – and regretted it.

This is where the philosophy of nidotherapy comes in. If you are fully aware of the pros and cons of the environmental options available you are probably more likely to make a correct decision than a wrong one. You do not have to be clever to learn this; you just have to be aware of the environmental options that may be helpful to you. We live in an age when illness of any sort is expected to have a treatment available for it. Mental illness is now included in this thinking, often quite wrongly, as very frequently there is an environmental solution, not a strictly psychiatric one.

## When do you need nidotherapy from someone else?

The clue to this question is likely to come from our own experience. When everything is going well we usually make the right environmental decisions, but when our mental health is out of kilter we can make mistakes. Now multiply those problems several fold and you can see why so many people with mental illness might need some help in deciding what environmental changes to make.

Even people with very good mental health need nidotherapy from others at times. When faced with important options in life, like coming to a signpost at a crossroads and guessing all the destinations are pretty good, you often choose to take advice from others before making your choice. Of course, you will make the final decision, but the advice you are given adds considerably to the information you receive and often helps in making the final decision. Now some may scoff and say that we are adding jargon to dress up common sense and make it look fancier than it really is. Perhaps this is a fair comment, but what is important is that we recognise the phenomenon; *we use others* to help us to make environmental decisions.

If we go to the opposite pole of poor mental health the need for external nidotherapy is much greater. People with psychotic or neurotic disorders that become chronic are usually stuck in therapy. We mean this in the literal meaning of 'stuck'; they seem to be held in position and cannot move in any direction. Most are subjected to treatments that have been given over many years and which simply have not helped to any significant degree. All therapists seem to be able to do is to give more of the same, which means giving an increase in drug dosage when this form of treatment is given, or 'more intensive' psychological treatment if this is the other chosen way forward. Often if patients decide unilaterally to give up on treatment they go backwards, so most stay stuck in limbo in a state that could be described as 'just tolerable' but no more. Nidotherapy is a way of helping people become unstuck and recharged for life. It is a bold claim but can be supported, and reinforces some of the aspects of what is now called the recovery model (Leamy, Bird, Le Boutillier, Williams & Slade, 2011).

## Reverse Darwinism

We sometimes describe nidotherapy as reverse Darwinism. According to Darwin, the process of competition for any living organism for a place on this planet is determined by natural selection, or in Darwin's original words, 'the survival of the adapted' (most people remember this as the 'survival of the fittest' but this terminology came later). So in Darwinism a large number of individuals are competing for a small number of environments and only the adapted ones succeed. So, according to this doctrine, the chronically mentally ill are clearly not adapted and will fail in competition with their mentally healthy neighbours. Reverse Darwinism describes the opposite. There are more environments than individuals wishing to occupy them so there is a place for everybody. This can only occur by a process of artificial rather than natural selection, but nidotherapy sets itself the task of doing this.

The trick in nidotherapy is to create a set of environments that accommodate the great diversity of people. We are not all fighting for a place in the sun; there are lots of shades that are much preferred and the task of the nidotherapist, in conjunction with the patient, is to find the right degree of shade. Some might argue this is just pie in the sky and everyone really wants the same. This is not true; the social pressures to conform to standard wishes are very strong, but there are many ways of accommodating Thomas Jefferson's aims of 'life, liberty and the pursuit of happiness' without the need to stream along the same route like a crowd to a football stadium.

Darwin himself, in his first book describing the voyage of HMS *Beagle* round the world (Darwin, 1839/2009), marvelled at the diversity of environments in the many countries he visited in his five-year voyage. He anticipated his own theory of natural selection when describing the beak sizes and shapes of different species of finch in the Galápagos Islands in the Pacific Ocean. But in using the words, "seeing this gradation and diversity of structure in one small, intimately related group of birds, one might really fancy that from an original paucity of birds in this archipelago, one species has been taken and modified for different ends" (p. 338), he also marvelled at the range of environments they occupied in islands just a few miles apart.

"But it is the circumstance, that several of these islands possess their own species of tortoise, mocking thrush, finches, and numerous plants, these species having the same general habits, occupying analogous situations, and obviously filling the same place in the natural economy of this archipelago, that strikes me with wonder" (pp. 353–54). It was only one step further to infer that there were differences in the natural environment that had led to this separation of species, hence the 'survival of the adapted'. But these were natural environments unaffected by intruders; nidotherapy plans new, often artificial, environments that are created for the naturally unadapted to allow them a better fit.

"But evolution takes many thousands, if not millions, of years to create new species", so the argument goes, "what has this got to do with changing people's lives during their lifetime?" But in artificial selection, everything is sped up immensely; you only need to look at the different breeds of dogs to appreciate this. And remember the Great Dane is still the same species as the miniature chihuahua. Change can take place even in natural selection over a short time period.

Charles Darwin, ever observant, noted in 1834 in his *Beagle* voyage that there were two forms of cattle, one in the north part of East Falkland, and one in the south, with only a very narrow peninsula connecting the two. The cattle had only been introduced 50 years earlier, but even after this short time Darwin noted of the ones in the north "half were lead coloured" whereas in the south "there were white beasts with black heads and feet" (Darwin, 1839, p. 169). The grassland in the south (Lafonia) covers a flat landscape whereas that in the north is in mountainous terrain. This is another important reminder that environments can alter our dispositions very quickly. And to stress the point, environments in nidotherapy are a complex mix of physical, social and personal ones that together have the capacity to create a unique environment that nobody else wishes to compete for. But it requires a great deal of searching – hence the importance of the joint effort of nidotherapist and patient to find it.

There is also abundant evidence that, when all these elements of the environment are taken into account, people differ greatly in their specific choice of environments, so the idea that there is always competition for them can be challenged. One of our successes in nidotherapy was a patient with great problems in relating to other people. He regarded all of them as 'unreadable' and so tended to get extremely anxious when meeting people and misinterpreting their words and actions. He lived in Central London, not the most suitable place for avoiding social interaction. But with help from colleagues in a local employment office he was able to find work as a night shift attendant in a car park, where the chances of significant social interaction were virtually nil, and prospered in this new setting which most other people would want to avoid. He also wanted to have clear and unambiguous instructions for his work. If he saw something suspicious he reported it to his superior, and if he met someone who should not have been there he had a set of challenging questions prepared in advance. There was little room for doubt or special initiative needed here, and 99 out of 100 people would be bored out of their minds by such a repetitive work existence, but here he thrived, and never lost the vigilance needed for this type of task.

## Skills of the nidotherapist

In our training of nidotherapists we have found, somewhat surprisingly, that the best therapists are ones who have not been formally trained in other mental health technologies. These include clinical psychology, cognitive and behaviour therapy, behavioural activation, specialised mental health nursing and occupational therapy. At the same time the good nidotherapist has to be bright, intuitive, empathic, honest and inventive, and the overused expression, 'thinking outside the box', is a good summary of the skills needed. The main problem created by previous learning is that so many practitioners are too ready to turn from environmental analyses to treating symptoms and behaviour.

The slight disadvantage here is that the best therapists are not always the best informed about other issues such as the evidence-based treatments for the conditions being addressed, and so the best combination is for experienced practitioners to select and monitor the patients for nidotherapy and for the therapists to carry out the main work.

## Stages of nidotherapy

We now have enough introductory information to describe the different phases of nidotherapy and why they are chosen. One of the problems in describing these is that the treatment is a collaborative one with the patient. Although one can have a general notion of how to proceed with therapy, one of the cardinal features of nidotherapy is that it is not only collaborative but requires the patient to fully embrace it. So if a programme, following the rules that we set down in advance, is completely rejected by the patient we have to think again. The different phases described below are therefore not rigid but they illustrate the general principles that tend to apply to all people who receive this form of management.

## Phase 1 – Person–environment understanding (collateral collocation)

Once a patient has been selected for treatment with nidotherapy, a process that involves a full assessment of mental state and functioning (which only proceeds once it has been established that the patient has received all of the effective treatments available), there has to be a genuine understanding of exactly where the patient fits in to his or her environment in all its aspects.

This is easy to say but not easy to achieve in practice for many people. It is not enough to ask people what they want in terms of environmental change without understanding what it is that they really need. In some ways it is the most difficult phase of nidotherapy, because it requires a great deal of empathy to get a proper understanding of the needs of many people who have been ill for a long time. One of the common problems with those who have had chronic mental illness is that they are very happy to complain about all the things that have gone wrong, but when the opportunity comes for a positive change that they have to take responsibility for, they jib and are sometimes genuinely fearful of the things that they have been wanting. Like Tantalus of old, they are constantly trying to reach out to something just out of their grasp but when it comes within their grasp they are not quite sure what to do with it.

---

### CASE HISTORY – PHASE 1

*The nidotherapist sees the patient, not in a clinic or a secure office, but at home in a rather rundown flat. This is frowned upon by the clinical team as it is considered too dangerous (most previous appointments have been made in a police station). The meeting is an informal one but it is clear that there are many problems in the flat that need sorting out. There are also several other practical matters, such as receipt of benefits, washing of clothes and a defective central heating system, that are clearly of environmental concern. The patient is pleased that the nidotherapist has expressed an interest in these matters and they leave on good terms. Two more meetings take place in which the importance of these issues is clarified.*

---

## Phase 2 – Environmental analysis

In this phase every single aspect of the environment is taken into account as part of a systematic assessment of positive and negative aspects. Sometimes this can be done using standard lists (Tyrer, 2009), or it can be done more informally for people who have a clear idea about what their environmental needs are but are unable to achieve them. This exercise is a two-way process. Sometimes the requests are unattainable and facile (e.g. "I want to live in a detached house close by the sea with at least three bedrooms and am expecting the council to pay for this"), and it is a job of the nidotherapist to fashion more realistic goals that can be achieved within a reasonable timeframe. More often, something which appears at first to be a low priority becomes much more important during the course of discussion and is realised as such by the patient.

In this part of the treatment all aspects of the environment are taken into account and this includes what is perhaps the most difficult component of a person's living experience, the personal environment. It is all very well providing a wide range of solutions to environmental problems, but if the person at the end does not feel safe and contented then not much will have been achieved. This perhaps is one of the more challenging aspects of the therapy.

---

### CASE HISTORY – PHASE 2

*Environmental analysis in this case reveals dozens of problems. The patient had been in prison repeatedly for threatening behaviour and damage to property and each time has taken many months to readjust. His home is a shambles: badly heated, with a highly unsanitary kitchen, a non-functioning bath and no bed in the bedroom. He feels rejected by society and his concerns are accentuated by the fact that while he has been in prison everybody else in the block of flats has had their homes redecorated and a new central heating boiler fitted. He reacts inappropriately by getting drunk repeatedly and railing against those more fortunate than himself.*

*In tackling these issues the nidotherapist helps the patient to deal with simple hygiene matters, including how to use launderettes, helps to decorate the kitchen and organises with the local council to have a new boiler fitted and redecoration done as it was unfair that he missed out when all the other flats were decorated in the block where he lives. The nidotherapist also helps the patient to start budgeting more seriously and only to spend money on alcohol and other nonessentials after his basic requirements have been satisfied.*

---

## Phase 3 – Preparing the nidopathway

Once the environmental analysis has been completed it is possible to see the major goals that can be planned. In some cases this is difficult for the nidotherapist to achieve without cooperation from others, and this is especially true when people are detained under compulsory orders and risk management takes priority over everything else (Spencer, Rutter & Tyrer, 2010). It is here that advocacy on behalf of the patient is often needed. Patients with persistent and severe mental illness tend to be very poor advocates for the changes they desire unless they are carefully tutored and others are there to assist them in negotiations.

The nidopathway that is decided may be a major one (e.g. move to a new area with different accommodation) or relatively minor (avoiding seeing a certain relative who undermines the patient) but both could be of major significance. It is this part of the nidotherapy programme that is sometimes mishandled if the therapist takes over and decides, with minimal involvement, what the patient might need. This can happen because of frustration with lack of progress, inability to reach consensus with the patient over environmental change, or simple expediency within a certain time frame.

All these are unwise, as without full cooperation and ownership of the nidopathway, the patient is liable to fail – and then blame the therapist for this. It is therefore essential for both therapist and patient to look at the treatment plan change and sign it off together. Both of them may have reservations about whether it can be achieved but these should be equally shared and ownership clearly placed in the hands of the patient.

---

### CASE HISTORY – PHASE 3

*Solving practical problems in the flat was all very well but not a long-term goal. It took several months before the right way forward could be found and even this was somewhat unsatisfactory. There was increasing conflict between the patient and the mental health services and in the end it was decided to discharge him from care. The nidotherapist felt that further contact was necessary as the patient was so vulnerable and arrangements were made for continuing care to be provided by a specialist general practitioner and by the nidotherapist only. The aim was to find a suitable placement where the patient felt safe and free from harassment from so-called friends who exploited him, and also to make contact with members of his family from whom he had become detached. Both these were achieved in part, with the patient being in semi-supported accommodation and making regular contact with his mother.*

---

## Phase 4 – Monitoring and adjusting the nidopathway

The time period between phases 1 and 4 may be a few weeks or many months and the period of monitoring may show similar variation. The important thing is for the nidotherapist to be on hand when problems arise and not to go back to the beginning. What is often possible during this stage is for the patient to be more accepting, and more responsive, to forms of treatment that had been refused repeatedly in the past. This could apply to medication and other forms of intervention offered by health professionals. For example, by concentrating on the environment only, patients sometimes realise that what they perceive as hostile outside the walls of their home becomes much less hostile when a small dose of medication is taken to relieve paranoid symptoms.

The most interesting aspect of this is that the patient seeks this treatment because of the wish to get better environmental adjustment, whereas if there is persistent direct pressure on the patient to take medication because "otherwise you will relapse" it is much less effective. The breakdown that sometimes occurs between the clinical team and the patient can be repaired during this phase of treatment.

---

### CASE HISTORY – PHASE 4

*In this particular example phase 4 is still continuing. The patient has regular contact with the nidotherapist but at less frequent intervals. He has stopped offending and is now reasonably settled in supported accommodation but still has limited social interactions. He is incredibly grateful that the nidotherapist has stuck by him over a long period and particularly likes reinforcing interviews to keep on track with the original plan.*

---

## Mechanism of change

One of the most important aspects of nidotherapy that goes a long way towards explaining the mechanism of change is the exercise of autonomy. So many of the patients that we treat in nidotherapy have placed themselves, or have been placed, in highly unfavourable environments that, for various reasons, they feel unable to change. A successful nidopathway enhances self-reduction of symptoms.

## Evidence of efficacy

Nidotherapy is a complex intervention and it is often very difficult to disentangle the essential parts that are needed (Craig et al., 2008). In the case of nidotherapy we have moved through the stages of describing individual cases that have benefited (Tyrer, 2002; Tyrer & Bajaj, 2005), through to qualitative analysis of interactions between nidotherapists, patients and clinical services (Spencer et al., 2010), and two randomised controlled trials, one for challenging behaviour in intellectual disability yet to be published (Tyrer et al., 2014), and another in which patients in an assertive community team with multiple pathology were randomised to continue an assertive outreach services alone or to assertive outreach services plus nidotherapy.

This study of 52 patients was too small to yield definitive results but there were benefits in terms of clinical symptoms and social functioning, particularly in those with psychosis and substance misuse (Tyrer et al., 2011). Equally importantly, the cost of care was much less in those treated with nidotherapy as hospital stays were greatly reduced (Ranger et al., 2009).

Nidotherapy is therefore at the stage at which larger definitive trials might be mounted, and in an evidence-based mental health system these are necessary before the treatment could be recommended on a wide scale. Much greater clarity is also needed about the patient groups who will respond best to treatment.

Taken together, the evidence of efficacy of nidotherapy, and its repeated additional benefits beyond those of conventional treatment, make it a subject that is worthy of much greater research. This has been supported by a recent Cochrane review (Chamberlain & Sampson, 2013). However nidotherapy is judged, as a philosophy, complex health technology or necessary standard treatment, it is not going to go away in a hurry.

Currently there is interest and activity in developing nidotherapy in many countries of the world. In Sweden it has proved particularly attractive for graduate workers supporting patients in their own accommodation. In Canada it has helped psychodynamic psychiatrists in dealing with complex patients without the complicating features of transference and countertransference (you do not get these with environmental treatments), and in Iran it is embraced as a treatment that fits in remarkably well with local attitudes and feelings about mental health problems.

## Links to other environmental forms of management

There are several other forms of management in forensic services that to some extent overlap with nidotherapy. For example, the Good Lives Model (GLM) (Ward, Mann & Gannon, 2007) is a framework of offender rehabilitation that has been embraced in sex offender treatment programmes internationally (Willis, Ward & Levenson, 2014) and is now being applied successfully in many other settings with offenders.

The main difference between GLM and nidotherapy is that GLM is primarily involved in building up strengths and capabilities in order to reduce the risk of reoffending. This is not strictly an environmental treatment, although by looking at all aspects of someone's life there are bound to be environmental discussions that could be highly relevant to management.

A more specific environmental strategy adopted by the National Offender Management Service in the UK is Psychologically Informed Planned Environments (PIPEs). These form a key part of the offender personality disorder (PD) strategy (Department of Health [DH] & National Offender Management Service [NOMS], 2011). They are not specifically regarded as treatments, and the idea behind them is that they are specially designed contained environments in which staff and offenders can understand the importance of good relationships and understanding. These environments are not created by discussion with the offenders and to some extent are planned in advance. In nidotherapy the patient is the generator of the environmental change and so in this respect it is very different.

Whether it is necessary for patients and offenders to be the driving force behind environmental change is a matter for discussion and future research. At present we are sticking to this as it appears to be a great motivator of change.

Perhaps the final word should come from a patient who has had this treatment over the longest period, almost 25 years.

> Before I came across nidotherapy I was just regarded as a chronic psychotic patient who would come in and out of hospital like a yo-yo. I would always be filled with awful medication in hospital and stopped it as soon as I had the chance to do so when outside hospital. I was always told these relapses were caused by me not taking these poisonous drugs. Nidotherapy showed the way out of this. I stay out of the way when I have my brief periods of illness and the rest of the time I am well without any form of drug treatment. It is like being released from a prison sentence.

## References

Burns, T., Creed, F., Fahy, T., Thompson, S., Tyrer, P. & White, I. (1999). Intensive versus standard case management for severe psychotic illness: A randomised trial. *Lancet*, 353, 2185–2189.

Chamberlain, I.J. & Sampson, S. (2013). Nidotherapy for schizophrenia. *Schizophrenia Bulletin*, 39, 17–21.

Craig, P., Dieppe, P., Macintyre, S., Michie, S., Nazareth, I. & Petticrew, M. (2008). Developing and evaluating complex interventions: The new Medical Research Council guidance. *BMJ*, 337, a1655.

Darwin, C. (2009). Journal of Researches into the Natural History of the Various Countries visited by HMS Beagle round the world, under the command of Capt. Fitzroy, R.N. 1839. Republished as *Voyage of the Beagle*. Washington, DC: National Geographic Society.

Department of Health & National Offender Management Service. (2011). *Managing the Offender PD Pathway*. London: Department of Health & National Offender Management Service.

Leamy, M., Bird, V., Le Boutillier, C., Williams, J. & Slade, M. (2011). Conceptual framework for personal recovery in mental health: Systematic review and narrative synthesis. *British Journal of Psychiatry*, 199, 455–462.

Ranger, M., Tyrer, P., Milošeska, K., Fourie, H., Khaleel, I., North, B. & Barrett, B. (2009). Cost-effectiveness of nidotherapy for comorbid personality disorder and severe mental illness: Randomized controlled trial. *Epidemiologia e Psichiatria Sociale*, 18, 128–136.

Spencer, S-J., Rutter, D. & Tyrer, P. (2010). Integration of nidotherapy into the management of mental illness and antisocial personality: A qualitative study. *International Journal of Social Psychiatry*, 56, 50–59.

Tyrer, P. (2002). Nidotherapy: A new approach to the treatment of personality disorder. *Acta Psychiatrica Scandinavica*, 105, 469–471.

Tyrer, P. (2009). *Nidotherapy: Harmonising the Environment with the Patient*. London: RCPsych Press.

Tyrer, P., Sensky, T. & Mitchard, S. (2003). The principles of nidotherapy in the treatment of persistent mental and personality disorders. *Psychotherapy and Psychosomatics*, 72, 350–356.

Tyrer, P. & Bajaj, P. (2005). Nidotherapy: Making the environment do the therapeutic work. *Advances in Psychiatric Treatment*, 11, 232–238.

Tyrer, P., Miloseska, K., Whittington, C., Ranger, M., Khaleel, I., Crawford, M., North, B. & Barrett, B. (2011). Nidotherapy in the treatment of substance misuse, psychosis and personality disorder: Secondary analysis of a controlled trial. *The Psychiatrist*, 35, 9–14.

Tyrer P., Tarabi, S.A., Bassett, P., Liedtka, N., Hall, R., Nagar, J., Imrie, A. & Tyrer, H. (2017). Nidotherapy compared with enhanced care programme approach training for adults with aggressive challenging behaviour and intellectual disability (NIDABID): cluster-randomised controlled trial. *Journal of Intellectual Disability Research*, 61, 521–531.

Ward, T., Mann, R. & Gannon, T. A. (2007). The good lives model of offender rehabilitation: Clinical implications. *Aggression and Violent Behaviour*, 12, 87–107.

Willis, G., Ward, T. & Leveson, J. (2014). The Good Lives Model (GLM): An evaluation of GLM operationalization in North American treatment programs. *Sexual Abuse: A Journal of Research and Treatment*, 26, 58–81.

# INDEX